Second Edition

Understanding the Nature of Autism

A Guide to the Autism Spectrum Disorders

Janice E. Jansen, M.S.

With Forewords by
Brenda Smith Myles, Ph.D.,
and June Groden, Ph.D.

Illustrations completed under
contract by Dian Moore

**Therapy
Skill Builders**® ®

from ⓟThe Psychological Corporation
A Harcourt Assessment Company

Reproducing Pages From This Book

As described below, some of the pages in this book may be reproduced for instructional or administrative use (not for resale). To protect your book, make a photocopy of each reproducible page. Then use that copy as a master for photocopying.

Library of Congress Cataloging-in-Publication Data

Janzen, Janice E.
    Understanding the nature of autism : a guide to the autism spectrum
disorders / Janice E. Janzen ; with forewords by June Groden and Brenda
Myles ; illustrations ... by Dian Moore.—2nd ed.
        p. cm.
Includes bibliographical references and index.
    ISBN 0-7616-4126-2 (pbk.)
    1. Autism. I. Title.
    RC553.A88 J36 2002
    616.89'82—dc21

2002152006

Therapy Skill Builders®

from ⑫The Psychological Corporation
A Harcourt Assessment Company

The author gratefully acknowledges permission to reprint the following copyrighted material: "Understand," "Youth So Sober," "Talk," "Happy Feelings," "Lonely Boy," and "In My Mind" by David Eastham, from *UNDERSTAND: Fifty Memowriter Poems*. Copyright © 1985 by Oliver-Pate. Reprinted by permission of the publisher.

"A Lovely Day," "Fiddlesticks," and "Upsets" by David Eastham, from *Silent Words and Forever Friends*. Copyright © 1990 by Oliver-Pate. Reprinted by permission of the publisher.

Excerpts from "Bridging the Gaps: An Inside-out View of Autism (Or, Do You Know What I Don't Know?)" by Jim Sinclair, in *High-Functioning Individuals with Autism,* edited by E. Schopler and G. B. Mesibov. Copyright © 1992 by Plenum Press. Reprinted by permission of the publisher.

Figures 5.1 and 5.2; and Forms 5.5, 5.6, 13.1, 18.1: Developed for Project QUEST, a project funded in part by the U.S. Department of Education, Office of Special Education and Rehabilitation Services, Grant #G00873042688. Adapted with permission from *Project QUEST Inservice Manual* by R. Falco, J. Janzen, J. Arick, K. Wilgus, and M. DeBoer (1990).

Figure 12.1 and Forms 5.4 and 5.8: Adapted with permission from Judevine® Training System by Lois Blackwell (1998).

Forms 5.7, 5.9, 24.1, 24.2, 24.3, 24.4, and 24.5: Adapted with permission from Oregon Regional Autism Services.

0761641262

1 2 3 4 5 6 7 8 9 10 11 12 A B C D E

Printed in the United States of America.

Visit our Web site at www.PsychCorp.com

Published by Therapy Skill Builders, 19500 Bulverde Road, San Antonio, TX 78259, USA, 1-800-872-1726

About the Author

Janice E. Janzen has been involved in the field of autism since 1972, first as an early childhood teacher in a private treatment center and in the public school system in Anchorage, Alaska, and later as an autism specialist for the Oregon Department of Education where she was instrumental in developing services for students with autism across the state. While with the Department, Ms. Janzen was responsible for the support of the regional autism specialists, consulted in difficult situations, developed training materials, and conducted workshops for educators and parents.

Janice Janzen received a B.S. degree in Elementary/Early Childhood Education from the University of Oregon, and a M.S. degree in Special Education/Learning Disabilities from the University of Alaska. While working on her master's degree, Ms. Janzen also received training pertaining to autism at the Judevine Center in St. Louis, Missouri. It was during this period that she began to develop her unique understanding of the learning style of people with autism.

Ms. Janzen has a special interest and concern with the challenges of families of people with autism, and emphasizes the need for families and educators to work collaboratively. She cofounded the Autism Council of Oregon, now the Autism Society of Oregon, an organization for parents and professionals.

She has written numerous technical assistance and special topics papers on autism for distribution by the Oregon Department of Education. Her RAPSOURCE papers on autism, prepared for the Head Start Training Office, Resource Access Project at Portland State University, have been widely distributed.

Since her retirement, Janice Janzen has been traveling the country, consulting, training teachers, and writing. Her second book, *Autism: Facts and Strategies for Parents*, was published in 1999.

Contents

Figures

Reproducible Forms

Foreword by Brenda Smith Myles, Ph.D.

It is difficult to find a book that meaningfully discusses the complex needs of individuals with autism, Asperger syndrome, and related pervasive developmental disorders and the interventions that are considered best practices. One of the most comprehensive books that I have had the great pleasure of using as a textbook in the autism spectrum disorders (ASD) graduate program at the University of Kansas (KU) is Jan Janzen's *Understanding the Nature of Autism: A Practical Guide*. KU offers a series of courses on autism spectrum disorders that includes characteristics, assessment, five courses on methods of teaching students with ASD, and three field-based practices. *Understanding the Nature of Autism* is used throughout these courses because it addresses the aforementioned topics in a user-friendly manner. When Jan told me she was revising the book, my first reaction was that it would be impossible to improve this already amazing book. I was wrong.

The new edition of *Understanding the Nature of Autism: A Guide to the Autism Spectrum Disorders* is a wonderful resource that addresses the characteristics of the autism spectrum disorders and appropriate interventions. Using case studies to effectively illustrate salient points this book provides a comprehensive overview of the characteristics of ASD, individual learning styles, and the impact of ASD on language, communication, and social skills. Topics related to assessment issues are addressed in a practical format that logically leads to developing a balanced program to meet the needs of children and youths with ASD. Interventions in *Understanding the Nature of Autism* are described with clarity and a practical "how-to" stance so that they can be used in individual, small group, large group, and inclusive settings. The end result is a book that is an easy, as well as delightful, read that offers most everything an educator needs to know to effectively teach children and youths with autism spectrum disorders. Educators who teach and/or consult with those providing services to children and youths with ASD will find this a must-have addition to their library. This is a true gift to the educational community.

Brenda Smith Myles, Ph.D.
Associate Professor, University of Kansas

Author of *Asperger Syndrome Diagnostic Scale, Asperger Syndrome: A Guide for Educators and Parents, Asperger Syndrome and Adolescence: Practical Solutions for School Success*, and *Asperger Syndrome and Sensory Issues: Practical Solutions for Making Sense of the World*

Foreword by June Groden, Ph.D.

Janice E. Janzen has undertaken a formidable task in writing this book. She has covered the spectrum of autism by first discussing the definition of autism and then reviewing learning styles, communication, placement and program decisions, the development of programs, management of behavioral problems, and assessment. It can be considered a primer on autism and is an excellent resource for training parents, teachers, and program personnel.

The book is admirable in many respects. It is written so that people of all reading levels can understand and apply the concepts. The strength of the book lies in the many relevant examples that appear throughout the chapters. They show how the principles that are discussed can be applied to actual cases of people with autism, thereby continuously clarifying the information. Although there is a growing body of literature in the field of autism, this book has a number of special features that differentiate it from the others.

The concept of an autism specialist as an interpreter brings new light to the role. Jan Janzen describes the autism specialist as a person who can organize information, give guidance to parents, teachers, and therapists, and design tools to help people with autism function more independently in the community. As an interpreter, the autism specialist has a pervasive role that includes numerous settings—inclusive and special classrooms, private programs, vocational and community settings, and at home—and numerous types of programs—communication, academic, social skills, physical education, and others. The role of the autism specialist as a regular and important member of the support team is also emphasized. I feel this often makes the difference between a successful and unsuccessful program for a person with autism.

Throughout the book there are figures that include descriptions of deficits and strengths of people with autism, and numerous checklists for assessment and evaluation. These figures can be used independently as a helpful resource and a quick reference in all settings. They also can be part of a teacher- or therapist-training packet that can be carried along, left in classrooms, or posted.

The section on the use of visual supports, including the importance of calendars and schedules, is admirable. It underscores the fact that autism still is not understood and that there is a need for these visual systems for both verbal and nonverbal learners.

The case study provided at the end of the book has considerable merit. The study synthesizes all the material and is an excellent summary. It allows the reader to follow one case and shows the sequence from assessment to program design. The steps that lead to goal setting and the description of the actual goals are well done. The information imparted to the reader can make a difference in the daily functioning of the person with autism. The personal accounts from families are very moving and help the reader to gain perspective on how autism affects the lives of parents.

This revised edition covers the full range of ASD including Asperger's syndrome. New and expanded sections, which are welcome additions to the book, include the use of computers and a good description of early intervention. The EI models that are described are both the structured play and floor time approach and the applied behavioral analysis.

The reference list is so extensive and complete that it can be used as a reading list for a course in autism or for further study for those who want to broaden their knowledge in the field. Other helpful resources include lists of organizations, training centers, resource centers, and publications that specialize in autism services.

This book will be appreciated by those who train teachers, parents, and other professionals in the field of autism. The strength of this book is the emphasis on understanding and using many different methods to meet the individual needs of each child. It is a comprehensive and concise book and a welcome addition to the literature in the field. It is apparent from reading this book that Janice E. Janzen has worked "hands on" for many years, and she is able to combine her knowledge of research and theory with applied practices. She is like a master chef who gives all the ingredients to make a recipe successful. Those who read this book will come away with useful information and the ability to put into practice the information they have gleaned.

June Groden, Ph.D.
The Groden Center, Providence, Rhode Island

Preface to the Second Edition

Today in 2002, 6 years after *Understanding the Nature of Autism* was first published, there has been a surge, some would say an epidemic, in the occurance of autism. Further, since 1996, the number of studies of brain development and function in people with autism have also increased. While many of the theories and basic strategies for teaching and supporting these individuals have been sustained, they have been creatively expanded. This revised edition reflects some of the major changes in the field: a) The understanding of autism as a spectrum disorder, b) the recognition of the special challenges of Asperger's syndrome, and c) advances in the use of computer and video technology. Perhaps the most welcome change in the past few years is the dawning acknowledgement that there is no "one right way"—that the "best" programs offer an integrated approach to teaching and intervention that incorporates the best elements of many models to match the very specific needs of each child (Feinberg & Vacca, 2000.)

I want to acknowledge the help and support of many friends and colleagues during this revision process. Valda Fields shared her library of journals, books, and other resources, and saved me a lot of research time. Others who contributed include colleagues from Oregon's Regional Autism Program: Anne Moffett, Barbara Tolbert, Kim Raines-Schmeltzer, Annette Skowron-Gooch, and Marilyn Gense; Valerie Rynne, a mother and editor from Menlo Park, California; Sally Cresswell, director of the Exceptional Child Program in Fort Lauderdale, Florida; June Groden, director of the Groden Center in Providence, Rhode Island; Ruth Falco, Portland State University; Toni Dunbar, the autism specialist for Anchorage Borough School District; and Dawn Stahlberg, director of Autism Training and Support, Inc., Eugene.

As this project comes to a conclusion, I want to take this opportunity to thank the staff of Therapy Skill Builders. Michelle Girard Rolfhus, my editorial project manager, brought together a talented and dedicated team who worked with me to make this revision a reality; I thank her for her encouragement, patience, and flexibility. Editor Tom Myer worked with me early in the process to ensure consistency and clarity of the text. Pam Parmer, project manager, has now supported me through the publishing process three times with skill and composure. Marian Zahora, designer, has again worked with me to create a book design that is accessible and elegant. Production Manager Stephanie Adams kept us on track and moving forward. Editorial Assistant Weslea Miller read the manuscript with care and successfully took on the challenge of indexing this work. And finally, I want to thank my editor, Andrew Joyce, for his attention to detail, dedication, and plain hard work. In the end, that effort has paid off.

Finally, thanks go to my dear husband, Marvin, who took care of everything at home while I prepared this revision.

Preface to the First Edition

Never in my wildest dreams did I ever expect to write a book, but my life has held many surprises and opportunities. I will take this opportunity to acknowledge a few of the many people who have provided insights and support to help me develop the philosophy and strategies presented in this book.

My interest in brain development and the neurology of learning was triggered by my adviser, Mildred Robeck, at the University of Oregon as I was studying for my bachelor's degree in education and early childhood education. When my husband's work took us to Anchorage, Alaska in 1972, my first teaching position was at the Alaska Treatment Center, where I met my first child with autism. Later while studying for my master's degree at the University of Alaska, my graduate supervisor, Marilyn Johnson, added to my understanding of the learning process and helped me compare autism with specific learning disabilities and to articulate the autism learning style.

It was in Anchorage that I saw the strength and power of parents at work; as they helped the Anchorage School district discover the cost effectiveness of developing its own autism services. Margaret Lowe, director of Whaley Center, offered me the opportunity to help develop those autism services.

In 1974, I went as a part of a team to the Judevine Center in St. Louis, Missouri to complete a 3-week Competency Based Training Program. Lois Blackwell, founder and director of the Judevine Center, became my next mentor. From her, I learned the value of the social learning theory and to apply behavioral principles sensitively, respectfully, and effectively. During the next 3 years I taught a demonstration classroom for students with autism and conducted teacher training in Anchorage and surrounding towns. It was during this intense work with children with autism, ages 2 1/2 to 16, that I became fascinated with autism and was convinced that teaching these children was the most creative, challenging, and rewarding job there could be.

The next turn in my education occurred when we returned to Oregon in 1978, at a time when most of those with autism went undiagnosed and unserved. It was while I was employed by the Marion County Education Service District that a colleague, Karen Brazeau, and I collaborated to establish autism services in Oregon. Our first goals were to organize a parent support group and to sponsor a conference. The parent group was established and evolved into the Autism Council of Oregon. This group of parents successfully lobbied the state legislature to fund regional autism services through Oregon's Department of Education.

We received grant funds to replicate the Judevine Teacher Training Model and to cover the costs of basic training in St. Louis for a team from Oregon and advanced training for me. With technical assistance from Judevine, we offered training for teachers and parents around the state. Oregon's first autism conference was a resounding success. Lorna Wing, an international leader in the field from London, was the keynote speaker. The conference attracted major interest from both parents and professionals.

In 1983, when Oregon's Regional Autism Services became a reality, Karen and I were employed by the department to develop the service model that could be implemented in public schools. In this role, we had the unique opportunity to visit some of the major autism centers in the country. Thus began the development of a service model that integrated the work of those at Judevine, Division TEACCH in North Carolina, the Groden Center in Rhode Island, and other nationally recognized centers and leaders in the field of autism.

Until my retirement in 1992, I coordinated the training and support for Oregon's regional autism specialists and provided consultation and training for parents and teachers throughout the state. I particularly want to recognize a few of the first regional specialists who did so much to challenge and expand my understanding of autism: Hedi Bayliss, Judy Fryor, Colleen Nyberg, Annette Skowron-Gooch, and Joyce Stratton. Two of the specialists, Hedi Bayles and Carol Christ, spent many hours helping me organize and clarify the contents of this book. Nancy Marshall, a teacher and school counselor, gave me the perspective of regular classroom teachers.

Many parents shared their stories, anecdotes, and experiences and provided encouragement to write this book. I want to recognize three who allowed me to really understand the parent's perspective and need: Mary Anne Seaton, Diana Lett, and Elaine Piper-Vardas, who became friends as well.

Thanks also go to my editor, Ricky Bourque, who was trained to condense. We had many negotiations and laughs because I was trained to tell the audience what you plan to say, say it, then tell them what you said. I hope our collaboration was successful.

Finally, I must acknowledge the influence of my husband, Marvin, for without his love and encouragement, I would never have become a teacher, nor would I have written this book. He was my first and most honest editor; he read every word, at least twice.

Ultimately, it was the comments of parents and teachers who participated in my classes and workshops that really stimulated this book. One said it best: "I wish you would write it all down so I could review it. . . . Then I could really understand and use it." With the help and support of my friends and my family, this book is a reality. To all of those mentioned and to those unmentioned whose influence and support are remembered and valued, I thank you.

Introduction

UNDERSTAND

I WANT PEOPLE TO UNDERSTAND
I KNOW ITS HARD TO DO
I THINK THEY CAN, IF THEY TRY
UNDERSTAND WON'T YOU?

UNDERSTANDING IS SO HARD
I LONG TO SEE IT REAL
I JUST HOPE, REALLY HOPE
IT'S NOT A LOST IDEAL

—David Eastham:
UNDERSTAND: Fifty Memowriter Poems

In 1985, I read a small book of poems, *UNDERSTAND: Fifty Memowriter Poems*, written by David Eastham. David could not write or speak and was unable to express his thoughts until he learned to communicate on a small computer when he was 19 years old. The eloquence of his poetry (which I quote throughout this book) convinced me that one must be continually aware that there is a sensitive person inside everyone with autism* and that the limit of any person's potential is never certain. David's plea to *UNDERSTAND* represents what I hope to accomplish in this book. (For David's life story and more poetry, read *Silent Words and Forever Friends* by M. W. and David Eastham.)

Understanding the Nature of Autism is a very personal work, written with the encouragement of parents who want others to understand the way their children think and of dedicated teachers who are too busy to search the literature and apply the research—teachers who have said they wish they had known these things sooner.

This book is essentially a reference book that integrates autism research and develops a process for applying this research to meet the very individual learning and behavioral needs of children and young adults with Autism Spectrum Disorders (ASD). Because I am an educator, my primary goal is to insure that children and young adults with autism spectrum disorders receive educational and other services from well-informed parents, professionals and other service providers. Therefore, I may mention but not go into detail about medical, diagnostic, or other treatment issues.

*The terms autism and autism spectrum disorder (ASD) will be used interchangeably throughout this book when the information can be applied to any child along the spectrum, from higher to lower functioning, including those diagnosed with Asperger's syndrome. The term Asperger's syndrome is used when the information applies only to those with high-functioning autism and/or Asperger's syndrome. This issue will be discussed in more detail in Chapter 1.

- In Part 1, the foundation is established for understanding ASD and the impact neurological differences have on the learning and thinking of those represented under this diagnostic label.

- In Part 2, the parent's role and responsibilities are addressed, followed by a review of assessment and evaluation issues. Strategies are provided for solving common assessment problems in order to elicit the best possible information.

- In Part 3, guidelines are provided for making the many decisions that are required for planning effective, individualized educational programs and support.

- In Part 4, a foundation is provided for planning all interventions—the basic processes and strategies to address the deficits and problems most commonly associated with autism (ASD).

- In Part 5, the information from previous chapters is integrated and applied to the process of teaching a broad range of new skills.

- Part 6 serves as a summary of the processes and strategies while addressing some potentially serious problems.

How to Use This Book

Unless you have the time to read this reference book from beginning to end, I suggest that you begin with a review of the Table of Contents to familiarize yourself with the full perspective of the book. Then carefully read Chapters 2, 3, and 8 to understand the nature and effects of autism on learning and behavior. Then read Part 4, where the foundation for intervention is developed. The basic concepts, processes, and strategies presented in these two parts are applied to different situations throughout the rest of the book to address a range of problems. Once you have the foundation, skim the rest of the book and focus on the parts that are of current concern to you. To avoid duplication, references guide the reader between the introduction of a concept to the various applications.

Notes on Style

- There seems to be no agreement about the spelling and labeling of *Asperger's syndrome*. You will also find it referred to as Asperger Syndrome and as Asperger's Disorder. I have arbitrarily chosen to use Asperger's syndrome.

- All information and strategies can be applied to address the individual needs of those of any age or level of ability who have an autism spectrum disorder, including Asperger's syndrome. Examples are provided to show how the strategies have been adapted for individuals in various situations. An example of a situation that occurred at home or at school will also apply to work or community settings.

- The words *unable, inability, do not, or cannot* simply mean that those with autism (ASD) do not automatically understand or learn certain types of information or skills, or they are less able to use them efficiently and effectively. It does not imply that they cannot be taught to compensate for the deficits in some way.

- Terminology used for the various syndromes and disorders are taken from the *Diagnostic and Statistical Manual of Mental Disorders, Fourth Edition* (*DSM–IV*), published in 1994 by the American Psychological Association. Some of the terms may have different meanings in other countries. For example, in the United States, the term *specific learning disorders* or *disabilities* refers to those with average to above average intellectual abilities whose neurological and sensory processes function differently to interfere with specific learning problems such as learning to read (as in dyslexia), to write, to do mathematics, etc. In other countries (i.e., the UK), the term *learning disabilities* refers to mental retardation.

- Most of the behavioral examples were selected from personal experiences; others were shared by parents, service providers, and specialists in autism. Names used in the examples were assigned to represent many different individuals with similar levels of ability. For example, José and others represent many different individuals with severe but classic autism who echo and who are compulsive, literal, and have limited verbal abilities. The examples assigned to José represent situations from early childhood to young adulthood. Jeff, Gabriel, and others represent those individuals with higher functioning autism or a diagnosis of Asperger's syndrome.

- Five mothers contributed some of their personal experiences and thoughts about life with their children in 1995 and updated their stories in 2002. These young men with autism now range in age from 20 to 35—most were in school before we knew what we know now. Their stories are found throughout the book and quotations from their stories appear in the text. These stories provide a way to understand some of the trials and rewards that come as a result of living with autism—a balanced perspective for other parents.

- Ponder the poetry of David Eastham, which is interspersed throughout the book. These particular poems were selected to provide eloquent insights that are intended to keep your attention focused on the reason for this book.

Although the processes and procedures outlined in this book may seem overwhelming at first, with practice they become automatic. These basic strategies can be applied to benefit other students in the classroom as well, especially those with learning disabilities and those who are learning English as a second language. It is my hope that through your understanding of autism and use of these strategies, an increasing number of students and adults will become more independent and lead more interesting and rewarding lives. I also hope that as those who support people with autism spectrum disorders increase their understanding of the nature and perspective of people with autism, they will feel increasingly confident, creative, and rewarded.

The Nature of Autism

A LOVELY DAY

A LOVELY DAY
TO JUMP INTO
THE POOL OF LIFE,
BUT LIFE ILLNESS
IS DAMN SAD

YEARS FALL FROM SKY
TASK WAS HARD
I AGED IN MY MIND QUIETLY
LOVE WAS ALL AROUND
BUT YOUTH* HAD NO
MEANS TO OPEN QUEST
FOR LOVE
IT WAS LIKE A PAIN
FOR SEVENTEEN YEARS

WATCHED PEOPLE
AND LEARNED BEAUTY
OF LIFE
HEART DAMN LONELY
A PERSON SOMEDAY
WOULD SEE FALSE WALL
AND BE A PAL

I HAD A FANTASY
LAST NIGHT AND
I WALKED OUT OF
MYSELF
I WENT SO FAR AWAY
AND SAW MANY THINGS

—David Eastham
In *Silent Words* and *Forever Friends*

*David sometimes called himself Youth.

1

Answers to Commonly Asked Questions

A review of fairy tales, myths, and old medical records indicates that there have been people with autism throughout history. Superstitions were developed to explain the unexpected and the unusual. Individuals with such distinctive features seemed to be "possessed" by devils, or, sometimes, by angels. They were often referred to as idiots, witches, wild people, fools, and sometimes prophets.

The condition received little attention until Leo Kanner, a psychiatrist at Johns Hopkins Medical Center, noted that 11 of his young patients had remarkably similar symptoms. His detailed observations were published in 1943, in a paper that described the symptoms of the condition he labeled early infantile autism (Kanner, 1943). This paper triggered considerable interest and marked the beginning of serious study and research. *Autism* is from the Greek word *autos*, meaning self, implying a narrowing of relationships to people and the outside world.

In 1944, at the University Pediatric Clinic in Vienna, Hans Asperger described a group of older children with disturbed behavior. Asperger described " . . . the subtle, and possibly milder, manifestations of autism in more able children" (Frith, 1991, p. 6). Although the descriptions of Kanner's autism and Asperger's syndrome are very similar and were first published at about the same time, Asperger's work was virtually ignored in the English-speaking countries until 1981, when Lorna Wing published an article describing it. Interestingly, these two men studied at the same university in Austria but did not know each other; and yet both men used the term *autistic psychopathy* in their descriptions (Frith, 1991).

In relation to many other disorders, the study of Autism Spectrum Disorder (ASD) is relatively new. In the intervening years, as we learned more about the condition, controversy has been the order of the day—encompassing everything from definitions to diagnosis, causes, treatments, and interventions. Many of the early theories and associated treatments of autism have been refuted. Much has been learned as research has continued, but there is still much yet to learn—and the controversy continues.

Even though it is now one of the more common disorders many people have had little or no experience with autism. Some people have an impression of autism derived from movies such as *Rain Man*, from news reports, or from psychology classes. But it is not until one is responsible for a child with autism that the complexity of the condition becomes evident.

Some of the most frequently asked questions about autism and the Autism Spectrum Disorders (ASD) are addressed in this overview, but first, let us define some of the terms. Keep in mind that new information continually modifies our understanding, so some of the definitions and some of the answers will undoubtedly change as time passes.

Definitions—A Trip Through the Labeling Maze

Autism

Autism is a neurobiological disorder of development (Pangborn & Baker, 2001; Tsai, 2000) that causes discrepancies or differences in the way information is processed. These information-processing differences affect the ability to:

- Understand and use language to interact and communicate with people
- Understand and relate in typical ways to people, events, and objects in the environment
- Understand and respond to sensory stimuli—pain, hearing, taste, etc.
- Learn and think in the same way as normally developing children

The effects of autism on learning and functioning can range from mild to severe and will depend on the individual's level of intellectual ability, other co-occurring conditions, and experiences. The learning and thinking differences common in autism cause confusion, frustration, and anxiety that is expressed in a variety of unexpected ways, such as withdrawing, engaging in unusual repetitive behaviors, and occasionally, in extreme situations by aggression and/or self-injury.

The learning and thinking style exhibited in autism is unique but predictable, and different from the problems caused by other developmental disabilities.

Asperger's Syndrome

Asperger's syndrome is also a neurodevelopmental disorder that shares many of the same symptoms as autism. The basic differences relate to the fact that Kanner's description of autism was developed from his work with younger children who had more severe delays and discrepancies. Asperger's description was developed while working with older children and adolescents who were quite verbal with intellectual ability within the borderline to gifted range.

Although the verbal abilities of those with Asperger's syndrome initially develop rather normally, the specific problems relate to:

- Understanding and using the language in typical ways (i.e., use is formal and lacks variation in intonation; these individuals often speak in long monologues about their special interests).
- Understanding the perspective of others and managing the give and take of social situations. They are socially awkward with odd body language.
- Intense, overly focused interests and repetitive behavior.

The deficits of those with Asperger's syndrome may be less obvious, but the discrepancies are greater. For example, they are so good at some things that the severity of the language, social naiveté, and perceptual problems are often overlooked.

Before Asperger's syndrome was recognized as a legitimate disorder, many of these individuals were thought to simply have emotional disturbances or to have a specific learning disability. Some of the higher functioning individuals went undiagnosed and were seen as "nerds" or "weirdos" and often harassed by their peers. But many of them would have received a diagnosis of high-functioning autism, more able (Moreno, 1992), near normal (Dewey & Everard, 1974), or mildly autistic (Everard, 1976.) But these terms are misleading for they imply that the problems are minor and that these students will need very little support.

Levy (1988) said that " . . . these high functioning persons usually not only look normal, but may act quite normal much of the time. Yet in spite of this normal appearance on the surface, the effect of autism (Asperger's syndrome) can be every bit as debilitating in any situation which requires social knowledge or skills. The more subtle the skill that is required, the more debilitating the effect."(p. 1)

Individuals with Asperger's and those with high-functioning autism are very vulnerable; they can be set up by their peers, which can result in a variety of difficulties including depression and trouble with the law—incarceration and even suicide sometimes occurs. Yet some are very bright and gifted in some areas—capable of making major contributions to society if they have appropriate support.

There remains a major diagnostic problem; clinicians report that there is as yet no clear way to distinguish between Asperger's syndrome and the higher functioning autism (Attwood, 1998; Eisenmajer et al., 2000; Leekam, Libby, Wing, Gould, & Gillberg, 1996; Mayes & Calhoun, 2001; Schopler, Mesibov, & Kunce, 1998; Wing, 1998). Some question the value of using this new diagnostic label of Asperger's syndrome—should it be eliminated? Others believe that the diagnosis has an important function. The controversy has definitely made an impact on the field. Diagnosticians and service providers are now more fully aware of the continuum of autism. They are not only recognizing this higher functioning group but they have a better understanding of the full continuum and the need for appropriate services.

For an interesting history of Asperger and his syndrome, read the book, *Autism and Asperger syndrome*, edited by Frith (1991).

Pervasive Developmental Disorders (PDD)

In an effort to insure the reliability and validity of research, the American Psychiatric Association (APA) publishes a *Diagnostic and Statistical Manual* (DSM) that spells out the diagnostic features and criteria for the various disorders. Adherence to these criteria ensures that subjects or individuals studied in research projects are as alike as possible.

Pervasive Developmental Disability (PDD) is the term used in this manual to describe a group of severe, early neurodevelopmental disorders characterized by delays and distortions in multiple areas of development, including social and communication skills, and a restricted repertoire of activities and interests. Initially, these disorders were known as Kanner's syndrome or early infantile autism. Now, a diagnosis of PDD indicates the presence of autism or a closely related disorder.

In recognition of the fact that the characteristics of autism can vary considerably in different children, the APA has added several different diagnostic categories under the overall label of PDD. The category of PDD outlined in the fourth revision of the manual (*DSM–IV*) includes Autistic Disorder, Rett's Disorder, Childhood Disintegrative Disorder, Asperger's Disorder, and Pervasive Developmental Disorder Not Otherwise Specified (PDDNOS).

- ■ PDDNOS, or Atypical Autism, is the term used for those who have most of the symptoms of autism but not all, or some of the symptoms are very mild or not clear. PDDNOS is also used for those who once had the complete symptom cluster, but some symptoms are no longer apparent.

- ■ Rett's Disorder and Childhood Disintegrative Disorder are disintegrative disorders that generally begin within the first or second year of life, after a period of normal development. Severe disintegration of skills and abilities follows while the symptoms of autism develop. One of the first symptoms of Rett's syndrome is the loss of purposeful hand movements and the beginning of stereotyped hand-wringing or hand-washing movements. Rett's is most common in girls; Childhood Disintegrative disorder primarily affects boys.

In summary, a diagnosis of PDD implies that the condition has an impact on or pervades all parts of development to some degree. For example:

- Those with mental retardation have a more general developmental disability, with learning and development progressing at a slow but even rate across developmental areas.

- Those with specific learning disabilities (LD) show discrepancies—an uneven pattern of information processing, strengths, and deficits—across developmental areas. Each person with a learning disability has a unique learning style that affects development in one or several specific ways, resulting in learning difficulties, such as learning to read (as in dyslexia), do math, spell, or write.

- Those with PDD have discrepancies and distortions of development. They share a common or predictable pattern of learning strengths and deficits that affects development in a much more pervasive way, with more pervasive social and communication problems that have an impact on the ability to understand and manage themselves in a world of people. Although most individuals with PDD have similar patterns of discrepancies, each has a unique combination and degree of learning strengths and deficits.

Autism Spectrum Disorders (ASD)

In an interesting history of autism, Wing (1991) describes the changes in the understanding of autism over the years. This changing process has involved considerable study and debate, but it is now quite generally accepted worldwide that there is a continuum or spectrum of autism. Wing then quotes Kanner, who once said, "It is well known in medicine that any illness may appear in different degrees of severity . . ." In many countries the term Autism Spectrum Disorders is now used to label this autism continuum.

Note that the term Autism Spectrum Disorders is essentially a synonym for Pervasive Developmental Disorder. Also note that the *Diagnostic and Statistical Manual (DSM)* is revised periodically to reflect new information. Each revision has used different terminology and different criteria to define the various Pervasive Developmental Disorders (Kanner's syndrome, classic autism, early infantile autism, etc.).

The World Health Organization has also published a diagnostic guideline, the International Statistical Classification of Diseases and Related Health Problems, 10th revision (ICD–10), that is used in most other countries.

Commonly Asked Questions

What Causes Autism Spectrum Disorders?

Autism is a syndrome, or condition, with many possible causes. Anything that makes the central nervous system (CNS) develop abnormally can cause autism. The event that initially triggers these developmental differences could occur during fetal development, during birth, or after birth. Although it is not always possible to identify the exact cause of the damage, the following conditions have been implicated (Gillberg, 1990; Gillberg & Coleman, 1992):

- Genetic/Chromosomal factors; autism and other developmental disorders tend to run in some families (Fragile X, Down syndrome, and other genetic disorders commonly co-occur with autism [Rutter, 2000]);

- Pre- or post-natal viral infections, such as encephalitis, congenital rubella, cytomegalovirus, or herpes simplex virus;

- Metabolic imbalances, such as phenylketonuria and thyroid disease;

- Exposure to alcohol and drugs, such as in fetal alcohol syndrome and cocaine-addicted babies;

- Exposure to environmental chemicals, such as lead, mercury, and other toxins;

- Oxygen deprivation or overexposure during or shortly after birth, as in retinopathy of prematurity; and

- Traumatic brain injury from a serious fall or car accident.

Recent autism research is very exciting. With the advances in medical technology and brain-imaging procedures, differences in both brain formation and brain function have been documented. (For further information, read Courchesne et al., 1994; Minshew, 1992; and Peschel, 1994.) In searching for the cause of autism, it is important to know that:

- Autism and other neurodevelopmental disorders are *not* caused by lack of love or inadequate parenting skills;

- Anything that affects the functioning of the CNS can trigger the symptoms of autism; and

- Knowing the cause is important for medical research and to help parents get appropriate genetic and medical information (but parents need to know that early intervention and effective educational programs do not depend on pinpointing the exact cause).

How Many People Have Autism Spectrum Disorders?

ASD has been found throughout the world in families of all racial, ethnic, and social backgrounds. It is four times more common in males. Although autism was once considered a low-incidence condition, it is not as rare as once believed.

Early definitions of "classic" autism, or Kanner's syndrome, led to prevalence projections suggesting that 4 or 5 individuals in 10,000 births would have autism. The current understanding of autism as a spectrum disorder has played some part in the increasing numbers. Baron-Cohen, Saunders, and Chakrabarti (1999) say, "Many clinicians and scientists would nowadays accept that autism, defined by the *DSM–IV*, may be as common as 1 per 1000 children; that Asperger's syndrome may be more common, as high as 3 per 1000 . . . and the Pervasive Developmental Disorder Not Otherwise Specified (PDDNOS) may be even more common." Minshew (2001) found that there were 57 per 10,000 children with autism, Asperger's syndrome, atypical autism and PDDNOS—70% of whom had no retardation. This larger number reflects the understanding that:

- Autism can occur with or without other disabilities—co-occurring conditions can include Down syndrome, tuberous sclerosis, seizure disorders, retinopathy of prematurity (ROP), neurofibromatosis, fetal alcohol syndrome, and cerebral palsy. Some individuals with autism also are blind and/or deaf.

- The symptoms and the effects of autism can range from mild to severe.
- Those affected with an ASD have intellectual abilities ranging from gifted to severely intellectually impaired. The combined effects of autism and other conditions are greater than if any of the conditions occurred independently.

What Are the Symptoms of Autism?

At this time, there are no medical or psychological tests to diagnose autism, so a diagnosis is based on the presence of a cluster of behavioral characteristics or indicators that signal the common developmental discrepancies. Figure 1.1 summarizes the behavioral indicators most commonly found in infants and young children. It is important to understand that:

See Chapter 5 for an explanation of the procedures for determining a diagnosis.

- No single behavior is indicative of autism, nor will a child show all the behaviors listed. The significant factor is a pattern of behaviors from each of the four areas.
- Some of the behavioral indicators may be intense, while others may be relatively mild.
- Some of the behaviors that indicate autism are typically seen at specific stages of normal development. The significant difference in autism is the intensity of the behavior and the persistence of the behavior beyond the normal developmental stage.

Figure 1.1 Behavioral Indicators of Autism in the Young Child

Language/Communication

Has flat or limited facial expressions
Does not use gestures
Rarely initiates communication
Fails to imitate actions or sounds
May have little or no speech, or may be quite verbal
Repeats or echoes words and phrases
Uses unusual vocal intonation/rhythm
Seems not to understand word meanings
Understands and uses words literally

Relating

To people:
Is unresponsive
Has no social smile
Does not communicate with the eyes
Eye contact is limited/fleeting
Seems content when left alone
Seeks social contact in unusual ways
Does not play turn-taking games
Uses adult's hand as a tool

To the environment:
Play is repetitive
Is upset by or resists changes
Develops rigid routines
Drifts aimlessly about
Exhibits strong and inflexible interests

Responses to Sensory Stimuli

Sometimes seems deaf
Exhibits panic related to specific sounds
Is oversensitive to sound
Plays with light and reflections
Flicks fingers before eyes
Pulls away when touched
Strongly avoids certain clothes, foods, etc.
Is attracted to specific patterns/textures/odors
Is very inactive or very active
May whirl, spin, bang head, bite wrist
May jump up and down and/or flap hands
Exhibits unusual or no response to pain

Developmental Discrepancies

Skills are either very good or very delayed
Learns skills out of normal sequence; for example:
    Reads, but does not understand meaning
    Draws detailed pictures, but cannot button coat
    Is very good with puzzles, pegs, etc., but is very poor at following directions
    Walks at normal age, but cannot communicate
    Echoed speech is fluent, while self-generated speech is dysfluent
    Can do things sometimes, but not at other times

Uta Frith, a research scientist at London's Medical Research Council, Cognitive Development Unit, says that in autism, "a disorder that affects all of mental development, symptoms will . . . look very different at different ages. Certain features will not become apparent until later; others disappear with time" (Frith, 1989, p. 1).

At What Age Can Autism Be Identified?

In less than half the cases, the condition that results in autism is likely to be present at birth. Based on their experiences with other children, parents report that their child with autism developed differently from the beginning. But the indicators of autism are generally not obvious until there is a failure to develop some of the early social and communication skills such as eye contact.

- More than half the children appear to develop normally for a period of time, then begin to lose early communication and social skills; or they fail to develop more advanced language and social skills. In these cases, the regressions begin at about 18 months of age (Pangborn & Baker, 2001).

- Pediatricians or language/communication pathologists who see many young children in clinical settings sometimes can detect the indicators as early as 12 to 18 months of age.

- Some more capable and quite verbal young children show few, or only mild, characteristics until they are 8 to 10 years of age, when the demand for higher-level thinking skills, social judgments, and time pressures make the indicators more obvious. Many of these children are likely to receive a diagnosis of Asperger's syndrome.

- Occasionally, the indicators of autism appear later after a severe illness or accident such as encephalitis or traumatic brain injury (Gillberg, 1986).

In a 12-month follow-up study of 2-year-old children referred for possible autism, Lord (1991) reported that more than 80% who received a diagnosis of autism at age 2 continued to receive this diagnosis at age 3. Twenty-eight percent of children who did not receive a diagnosis of autism at age 2 received this diagnosis at age 3.

Why Are These Individuals With ASD All So Different?

All of those with autism share a common symptom cluster, a common learning style, and predictable problems that affect their ability to communicate, socialize, and function in the world. Yet each individual's personality, interests, and responses to problems are conditioned by a variety of factors:

- The interrelationship between the severity of the individual's unique sensory processing disorders and intellectual ability

- The impact of additional disabilities

- Inherited traits, family culture, family interests, family problems and resources, the individual's position in the family (only child, eldest child), and the roles and relationships developed within the family

- Past educational and community experiences

See Chapter 6 for a description of effective educational programs. Also see Janzen (1999), Autism: Facts and Strategies for Parents *for guidelines for evaluating research and selecting treatments.*

All of these factors will influence personality, preferences, interests, and behavior to make each individual unique.

How Is Autism Treated?

"At this time there are no medical or behavioral treatments that cure autism, and it is highly unlikely that anything will be found in the near future that can totally reverse the effects of a developmental process of this magnitude" (Frith, 1989, p. 15). However, a highly structured and specific early intervention and educational program that addresses the predictable deficits of autism remains the most effective treatment to date. The ability to learn new skills to compensate for deficits continues throughout life.

Although no other treatments will benefit every individual with autism, there are a number of treatments that have had very positive effects and have provided relief from some of the symptoms of autism for some individuals. See Figure 1.2 for a list of treatments that are most commonly referred to in the autism literature.

Coordination of educational, medical, and nontraditional treatments is important for optimum outcome.

Figure 1.2 Treatments Most Commonly Mentioned in the Autism Literature

- Structured education and early intervention*
- Communication/language therapy*
- Sensory integraton therapy*
- Occupational therapy*
- Relaxation training
- Medications and drugs to treat symptoms
- Anti-yeast therapy
- Vitamin/dietary approaches
- Auditory integration training
- Music therapy
- Rhythmic entrainment
- Visual training
- Colored lenses
- Osteopathy/craniosacral therapy
- Holding therapy
- Patterning

*See Chapters 11 through 15 for information about integrating these into the educational program.

The following references are excellent resources for more comprehensive information about the various treatments: Gerlach, 2000; Pangborn & Baker, 2001; and Tsai, 2000. Additional resources are listed in Appendix B.

Many individuals with ASD have allergies and digestive problems that exacerbate attention and behavior problems. Many parents and physicians are finding that when these issues are dealt with naturally with special diets and diet supplements, the behavioral symptoms of autism improve as well as their ability to attend and learn.

What Is The Potential for Those With Autism Spectrum Disorders?

It is just as difficult to predict the potential of a child with autism as it is to predict the potential of a normally developing child. Some young children initially may be severely affected by the autism and seem extremely low-functioning, then make amazing gains and learn to cope quite well. Others seen initially as high-functioning or having mild autism can be more seriously affected and more limited in adolescence and adulthood. Some of those with autism live and work independently in the community with some level of support. Most live with their families or in group homes and are supported in regular employment or in sheltered settings (Datlow-Smith, 1990). Many of those with Asperger's will be able to live and work independently—but again they will likely need at least a minimal level of support. Even those with Asperger's who are quite intellectually gifted have difficulty managing some aspects of daily living. Many more individuals with autism spectrum disorders could be much more independent if there were more well-trained personnel in the support service agencies—case managers and staff to support the family, independent and group-home living, and coaches and mentors to support vocational pursuits.

Although there is still no cure for autism, we know that:

- Limited predictions of potential result in lower expectations and fewer opportunities for the child to learn. Expectations that are too high may lead people to minimize the effects of autism and fail to provide the appropriate education and support to help the child reach potential and to live and work independently.

- Adults with ASD are generally very good workers, excelling in jobs that require precision and accuracy rather than speed and judgment. They are employed in offices, hospitals, medical labs, libraries, high-technology sites, universities, food services, retail stores, and other businesses where their special skills and interests are valued and where they have a mentor (Grandin, 1990). Some have completed academic high school programs, and some have acquired advanced degrees with careers in highly specialized fields related to their intense interests. Some with Asperger's syndrome are marrying—with spouses and family providing some support—and a few are having families.

- Most individuals will continue to need some level of support all their lives. This support might range from a mentor to provide periodic assistance to solve social, financial, and practical daily problems to the more intense support of a personal assistant.

- The amount and nature of support must be flexible and continually reevaluated, because illness, family traumas, the loss of a job, or other life problems can raise anxiety levels and decrease the ability to function independently.

- Conventional wisdom indicates that autism is a lifelong disorder. Some individuals may show remarkable improvement, but at least some of the problems of autism are likely to remain. However, there are a few reports of recovery, near recovery, or partial recovery. Although some would say that the initial diagnoses must have been wrong, in at least some cases the diagnosis cannot be faulted (Rimland, 1994).

- Some have learned to communicate by talking, typing, or writing after a lifetime when they were thought to be severely retarded and incapable of communication. There is much about autism that is not clearly understood. For example, there is considerable evidence that internal cognitive processes contrast sharply with overt social and communicative behavior (Quill, 1993). It is totally impossible to determine an individual's abilities and problems or the extent of those problems by outward appearance. This is especially true of those who are higher functioning and those with Asperger's, who may be extremely verbal and obviously intelligent but continue to have serious social and interactive communication problems. For example, one gifted university student almost flunked out of school because none of his professors realized he did not understand how to ask for help or clarification of his assignments. There are also some, perhaps many, who are nonverbal or have very limited verbal abilities, but who nonetheless have outstanding gifts—specific intellectual or vocational abilities, artists and poets, as proven by the poetry of David Eastham.

See Chapter 11: The Gifts of Autism in Autism: Facts and Strategies for Parents *(Janzen, 1999).*

Why Is There So Much Conflicting Information About Autism Spectrum Disorders?

To put this question into perspective, remember that there is little in the world that is certain. Contradictory and conflicting ideas are the rule in education, child rearing, medicine, politics, religion, economics, and almost any other field. Theories are developed to explain complex issues. People become emotionally involved in the support or rejection of one theory or another. Books are written, and the media report bits and pieces of research and opinions. Libraries purchase and keep this material with no system for discarding or labeling material that has been refuted.

Several factors add to the contradictions and conflicting theories in the field. An overview to clarify a few of the factors will give some guidance for evaluating information.

■ Autism is a very complex disorder with a relatively short history of documentation. It takes a long time to research a subject, publish the results, and have it verified or discredited. It takes even longer to put research into practice. Sometimes a child has to grow up before the long-term results can be substantiated or refuted. During this period, teachers, pediatricians, psychologists, and other professionals are trained without knowing those results. Perhaps the most damaging theory that achieved considerable attention and acceptance before 1970 was the idea that autism was caused by parental rejection. One of the most prominent proponents of this theory stated in one of his books that the severity of autism was directly related to the degree that the child was rejected by the parents, even before birth. Those who espoused this theory were prolific writers. This theory, since refuted, continues to have an influence because these books are often the only ones about autism in many libraries and because many professionals were trained during this period.

■ Initially, the low incidence of the disorder limited professional experience. Busy professionals who had never treated or taught a person with autism would have little reason to keep abreast of new information. Therefore, they might not recognize autism in one who does not fit the limited picture presented in their earlier training. This limited experience is likely the reason so many older children and adults were not identified until recently.

■ Diagnostic criteria and labels have changed over the years. Each of the four revisions of the *DSM* reflects the knowledge base at the time of publication and uses different terminology. Some of the labels used in reference to autism over the years include early infantile autism, infantile autism, Kanner's syndrome, classic autism, childhood schizophrenia, symbiotic psychosis, atypical developmental disorder, atypical autism, residual autism, retardation with autistic characteristics, Pervasive Developmental Disorder (PDD), Pervasive Developmental Disorder Not Otherwise Specified (PDDNOS), and autistic disorder. Asperger's disorder or syndrome is the newest label for a subgroup of those with autism.

It is important to be aware of the implications of these different labels when reviewing the records of older individuals who exhibit characteristics of autism but have never received a diagnosis of autism. This is also an important consideration when reading older books on autism.

■ Professional jargon complicates understanding. Although professional jargon helps those within a field to communicate, it impedes the process of communication across fields and with the general public. The language used in the educational field is different than the language in the medical world. Also note that the criteria for receiving autism services in the schools may be somewhat different from that used in the *DSM–IV* or the ICD-10.

Is It Important to Identify Autism Spectrum Disorders? If So, Why? Who Needs to Know?

Yes, it is important to identify or diagnose autism. Diagnostic labels carry information and provide access to information. Think about the person found lying unconscious on the street. The police or medics must consider several options. Is the person drunk? If so, the person is taken either to the hospital or to jail and left to sleep it off. Has the person received a head injury? Does the person have diabetes? If either is true, the person needs immediate medical care. An appropriate decision cannot be made until the reason for the problem is known. If the person has a MedAlert bracelet signifying diabetes, the medic understands the implications of the label and can act quickly. This is the situation for those with autism. Effective decisions can be made only when the proper diagnosis (label) is made and people understand the implications of the label.

There are several very important reasons for identifying autism:

■ The child needs appropriate early intervention. Public Law 101-476 requires the public school system to identify students who have autism and to serve them appropriately. In order for the intervention to be appropriate, it must be based on the realities of autism. Those with autism have a right to services based on an accurate diagnosis.

■ Parents need to have their concerns resolved. Frequently, parents first learn about autism from watching a TV show, from reading about autism, or from talking to another parent who has a child with autism. If their child has attended a program with other children who have developmental delays, it will be obvious that their child is different from the others. Therefore, they are often the first to recognize the symptoms in their child. Until parents get a diagnosis that fits their child's symptoms, they will continue to worry and to search for answers (Akerley, 1984). When the identification is made, they are sad and upset, but usually relieved. One mother said, "Finally, someone else has seen a child like mine. Now I can find out what to do."

Mary Anne Seaton reported, "I remember clearly the day [I first heard that my son had autism]. I even remember what I was wearing, the room that we went to, and my first opportunity to see a child who displayed characteristics similar to my child's. I remember how very kind and gentle [the professionals] were. But most important, I remember [them] saying, 'There is no cure, but if you work very hard, you can make a difference for your child.' Those words and [their] caring attitude toward me were the beginning of turning my life around and setting the direction for [my son] and our family." (See page Chapter 14 for Mary Anne Seaton's story.)

■ The child and the parents need access to appropriate medical services. Parents must be prepared to attend to the symptoms of several medical conditions that are quite common in autism. For example, many children have allergies, metabolic abnormalities, and seizure disorders that affect their ability to function. These children also respond differently to drugs. A standard dose of a drug that is effective for other children may cause a major behavioral outburst, severe lethargy, or extreme activity in a child with autism. Finally, families may have a need for genetic counseling.

- Parents, teachers, and other service providers need access to information and training. Parents need as much information—perhaps more—than teachers and other service providers simply because the child spends more time at home. Also, parents must be lifelong advocates for their child, and they must be prepared to make many complex decisions that will have lifelong effects.

> Parent Christine Marshall said, "Charlie was not diagnosed as autistic until he was 8 years old. I knew he was unique in the first year . . . [Getting the diagnosis of autism] was a very positive step for everyone. Teachers who felt he was weird had more patience, adults around him were more accepting of his odd behavior, and his parents now had articles to read about his uniqueness . . . [The diagnosis helped us get autism services.] . . . In spite of the services available, [we] need to constantly communicate with [the] schools . . . I continue to be Charlie's most reliable advocate." (See Chapter 6 for Christine Marshall's story.)

- Both the parent and service providers need to understand how autism affects learning and behavior. Many treatments and strategies that are generally effective for those without autism can cause major disruptions in behavior and learning in this population. With a common understanding of autism, parents and teachers can work cooperatively to develop appropriate programs and support systems to teach important skills and prevent many of the secondary behavior problems.

- Both the parents and the teacher need emotional support. Parents need the opportunity to meet with other parents and professionals who understand autism and the reality of their lives. The parents' skills and their emotional condition are frequently misunderstood by those who don't understand autism.

> One autism support group, including parents and a few professionals, started their meetings with a family sharing time. At one of the first meetings Mary attended, she said, "I never worry that my child will be kidnapped. They would bring him right back." She quickly covered her mouth and looked around to see how her remark was received. Then she began to cry as she said, "This is the first time I've been able to joke about my child. Other people would think, 'No wonder my child had such terrible problems, with a mother like that.'"

Service providers need support from the child's parents and others who truly understand the complex issues related to autism and the physical and emotional demands that must be faced every day. Well-meaning, sensitive, and highly skilled colleagues are often not able to provide appropriate support or assistance unless they have had specific training or direct experience with autism.

Isn't the Label of Autism Stigmatizing?

A label is stigmatizing only if it is inaccurate and misunderstood or if it is used to isolate a person and limit that person's options. Autism has lost much of its stigma now that more people understand the nature of this severe learning disorder and understand that it is not the result of faulty parenting. The word *autism* should be no more stigmatizing than the words *diabetes, cerebral palsy, arthritis,* or *Down syndrome.*

It is unethical to withhold information or avoid using a label that provides access to important information. A child has a legal right to services based on an accurate diagnosis. Parents can begin to accept and deal more confidently with their child's disability when professionals explain the disorder and use the label in a calm and accepting manner.

What Evaluation Resources Are Available?

When an ASD is suspected, the individual needs two different evaluations. The first evaluation may be provided by a licensed physician (pediatrician, family doctor, or psychiatrist) or psychologist who determines a diagnosis based on the *DSM–IV* criteria. It is important to have a diagnosis by a licensed physician or psychologist at some time because:

- Most medical insurance programs will require this type of diagnosis of autism—in fact, some insurance and some service agencies have yet to acknowledge the diagnosis of Asperger's syndrome or PDD.

- It gives the family assistance in identifying the possible cause of the child's autism and access to appropriate medical and genetic information.

- It provides a base for identifying associated medical problems (seizure disorders, metabolic problems) and general ongoing medical care based on the current autism research (Pangborn & Baker, 2001; Tsai, 2000).

- In some states, this diagnosis may be required as part of the school evaluation; *a diagnosis of autism is necessary for accessing appropriate adult services.*

A family physician who has little or no experience with autism can refer the family to a local child-study center associated with a local university or hospital.

The second evaluation is that offered through the school system to determine whether the child meets the autism eligibility criteria for early intervention and special education services. In the United States, this determination provides the only access to free public educational services.

What Services Are Available Through the Schools?

The mandates of the Individuals with Disabilities Education Act (IDEA), Public Law 101-476, place five basic requirements upon local school districts as they serve those with disabilities from ages 3 through 21.

1. *Free and Appropriate Public Education* (FAPE)

    Each local public school district must provide a free and appropriate public education to all its students, regardless of the nature and severity of any disability. This includes special education and related services (such as speech-language therapy, physical therapy, occupational therapy, psychological services, and transportation), which are provided at no expense to parents.

2. *Assessment*

    Assessment services must be nondiscriminatory; that is, they must be conducted in the child's primary language and have no cultural or racial bias. Educational decisions must be based on a number of assessments and cannot be made on the basis of a single test score.

3. *Individualized Education Plan* (IEP)

An educational program outlined in an IEP must be developed by a team that includes the child's parent(s). The IEP must be reviewed and updated annually.

4. *Due Process*

School districts must follow specific due process procedures to ensure the rights of the child and the parents. These procedures are designed to protect the individual from improper classification, labeling, and placement.

5. *Least Restrictive Environment* (LRE)

Martin (2000) has published an excellent manual to clarify the special education law: Getting Your Child with Autism what They are Entitled to Under Federal Laws.

A continuum of service delivery options must be made available so that students are educated in the least restrictive environment (LRE). The 1997 reauthorization of IDEA states that the general classroom is the presumptive placement *unless it can be explained why* it could not possibly be appropriate if supports are provided. Later amendments to the law also established a framework that made it permissible for states to establish special education services for children from birth through age 2. Infants and toddlers identified as having developmental delays, or who are at risk for such delays, can access services through the use of an Individual Family Service Plan (IFSP) that addresses the family's concerns, priorities, and resources along with the needs of the child. The IFSP can be extended for children ages 3 through 5 years if the family chooses to use a family plan rather than an IEP.

It is important that parents understand the provisions of the federal law known as IDEA. Copies of the federal law and the state's administrative rules are available from the special education department of each local school district or from the state education agency or department.

Summary

Frith (1989) provides a summary of the developmental nature of autism and indicates that all of development from infancy onward will be affected. She says an early-onset developmental difference affects " . . . the very process of building up experiences" (p. 15). She notes that it is unlikely that the impact of any developmental difference can be totally reversed—to leave no trace. We can perhaps say that this is true even today, however, with the advances in medical and educational practice and with intervention beginning at a very young age, we really do not know what the future will hold. We are seeing some children make amazing changes.

In autism it is easy to get caught up or sidetracked by the bizarre, unexpected, and colorful details. Frith urges us to attend to the details only as clues to understanding the whole picture of autism. If we understand the nature of autism, we will be able to provide the support that will help those with ASD have a brighter future.

The Learning Style of Those With Autism Spectrum Disorders

There are no outward physical signs of autism. Unless there are complicating physical disabilities, individuals with autism spectrum disorders not only look like others, they are like their normally developing peers in many ways. For example, they:

- Can do some things better than other things
- Have happy moods and sad moods
- Have unique likes and dislikes
- Have a need for nurturing and support in order to learn

It is the intact and normal appearance of these individuals that is so confusing. When an individual can look and do some things so well, it is assumed that they should be able to do everything just as well. When a child has intense tantrums, withdraws, runs away, or behaves in unexpected ways, people do not understand. When that child cannot explain or defend himself, he is seen as spoiled or deliberately manipulative, disruptive, or non-compliant. Consequently, parents and teachers tend to become frustrated and angry when their efforts to teach and discipline the child are not successful.

The following examples of seemingly disrespectful and disruptive behavior highlight one of the most basic needs of those with ASD: The *reasons* for their actions need to be understood.

> The teacher of the early elementary class gave directions to the children, saying, "Keep your eyes on me." Amy got up and placed her face (eyes) against the teacher's body. Amy's attempt to follow the teacher's directions literally was interpreted as disruptive and inappropriate attention-seeking behavior.
>
> ―――――――
>
> After music class, while children were visiting, putting away the instruments, and moving their chairs, the teacher gave directions for the next activity. Gabriel scrambled up to stand on top of his desk and shouted, "Mrs. Brown, this is no laughing matter!" Gabriel's echoed speech, triggered by sensory overload and confusion, was interpreted as disrespect. Interestingly, the words were those used by his mother when she had reached the end of her patience with him—an example of delayed echolalia.

In an effort to cope with the demands of a very confusing world, those with ASD behave in unexpected and sometimes unacceptable ways. Interventions will be ineffective and often will make matters worse unless others understand why these children learn and behave the way they do.

Lorna Wing, a London psychiatrist and parent of a daughter with autism, is a highly respected pioneer in the field of autism. She has conducted research and written many articles and books. Her conference presentations and her work to further the understanding of autism have had a major worldwide impact. Some years ago, Dr. Wing wrote, "An autistic child can be helped *only* if a serious attempt is made to see the world from his point of view, so that the adaptive function of much of his peculiar behavior can be understood in the context of his handicaps" (Wing, 1980, p. xi).To understand the world from the perspective of individuals with autism, it is necessary to know how they take in and process information, how they think, and how they are likely to respond to certain situations. When one understands the nature of autism, it is possible to identify the cause of many learning and behavior problems. When the cause of the problem is identified, it is possible to respond with more effective strategies.

The Brain as a Computer—An Analogy

The central nervous system (CNS) functions as the computer system for the body. Unlike a personal computer that can do only one thing at a time, the brain is designed with numerous interconnected systems that do many things simultaneously. Messages travel back and forth between the systems to take in, analyze, store, and use myriad pieces of information.

Some things, like breathing and walking, are done automatically without thinking. Other actions require decisions. The CNS automatically triggers the nerves and muscles to act on those decisions. This masterpiece of design and function is ignored and taken for granted until it doesn't work effectively.

To understand the learning and thinking differences in autism, the function of three computer-operated pieces of equipment will expand the analogy of the brain as a computer.

The Input System

We learn about our environment through our sensory system by seeing, hearing, smelling, tasting, touching, and moving (sensory channels.) Think about the sensory input system as a specialized video camera. This camera records everything within the range of its lens (visual channel) and microphone (auditory channel). It also has sensors to record all the odors, the tastes, and the feel of things in the environment. Just as a standard video camera has volume controls and filters to regulate sound, our special camera has automatic filters that modulate the intensity of input from each of its sensors. If the camera is on, everything automatically goes in and is recorded on a tape. If the camera is off, nothing goes in.

Most people have automatic controls on their camera, and it works with few glitches. Most of us can automatically:

■ Scan the environment and direct the camera toward important events

■ Turn the camera on when something important begins and turn it off when those events end

■ Adjust the volume and the filters to screen out background noise or clutter—the unimportant stimulation

But those with autism have little control of the camera, and it has many glitches. These glitches interfere with the smooth and automatic function of the system and make it *difficult or impossible* to instantaneously:

■ Scan the environment and focus the camera on important events:

■ Sometimes the lens is set on wide angle to take in the whole picture. At other times, it is focused on some small detail of particular interest to the individual (e.g., a light bulb, the sound of a fan, the pressure of an elastic waistband, the odors from the kitchen). When the focus is on small details, important events and information occurring in the larger setting may go unrecorded.

- Turn the camera, or the input system, on or off at the correct time:
  - Sometimes a glitch in the camera makes it flutter on and off very quickly, so bits of information may be stored as short units (like a series of snapshots) and there are gaps in the recorded information. Or the camera is not turned on and off at the exact beginning or end of an event, so a tape can contain bits and pieces of unrelated information or events.
  - Think what might happen when the new photographer forgets to turn off the camera and moves about the room during a party. For a period of time the tape would show the targeted scenes, then there might be views of the rug, of people's feet, while all the conversations, the music would be heard in the background. Perhaps this is just a small example of the scrambled messages recorded in the minds of those with autism—it would be difficult to put any important meaning to the input for storage in the memory.

- Adjust the filters to screen out irrelevant background stimulation:
  - Both relevant information and irrelevant clutter are quickly and permanently recorded on the tape and stored as snapshots or sequences (routines). Everything that happens in the environment at any one time is recorded together and is given equal value.

- Adjust or modulate the volume or intensity of the input:
  - The volume or intensity of the input from one or all of the sensors (sensory channels) may be so overwhelming that the camera automatically turns off and stops recording, or it narrows its focus and records only the most familiar and least confusing information while leaving other information unrecorded.

The Information-Processing System

Think about the information-processing system as a computerized videotape editor. This editing device has special features for analyzing and preparing the information for use. It scans the tapes and removes all the background clutter. While it sorts and categorizes the information, it notes relevant information. The editor relates and integrates information from this tape (the new experiences) to information from other edited tapes (past experiences). Finally, the information is labeled for meaning and stored with an efficient cross-referenced system for immediate retrieval and use.

Most people have a wonderfully fast and automatic editing machine to analyze information on their tapes. It allows them to:

- Instantaneously focus on relevant, meaningful information
- Retrieve meaningful information with the clutter removed
- Retrieve information in a sequential order
- Manipulate information to relate and integrate information from one experience to another
- Review information for accuracy, completeness, and clarity

In autism, the tape bypasses the editor, or the editor is defective. Consequently, information is stored by event without analysis for meaning. The tapes are stored with both the important information and the clutter interwoven. The important information, such as an object and its label, would have as much value as the clutter (for example, the holes in the ceiling tile, the reflections in eyes and eyeglasses, or the odor of garlic on a peer's breath). Storage of unedited information without meaning attached makes it *difficult or impossible* to:

- Instantaneously focus on relevant and meaningful events

- Retrieve meaningful information with the clutter removed

- Retrieve information in a sequential order to learn cause/effect relationships, predict future events based on past events, and learn from the consequences of errors

- Manipulate or integrate information from one event or experience to another, to organize information in different ways and to expand and modify information

- Review information for accuracy, completeness, and clarity, to evaluate one's own behavior and to make inferences, judgments, and decisions

The Integration and Output System

Think of the automotive computer as the information integration and output system. The car computer works quietly, quickly, and automatically. The driver is aware of it only when it doesn't work, when the car doesn't move, doesn't stop, or lurches along. This device is preprogrammed with information that causes the car to function in a predictable way. When it works as designed, it anticipates the driver's needs in order to make decisions and sends that information to the gauges and dials on the dash. The computer receives and interprets the driver's commands (decisions) and integrates the command with the relevant information in storage. Finally, it sends messages to the appropriate mechanical system to carry out the command most efficiently.

Most people, like the car with a working computer, can make the decisions that trigger their output system. This allows them to automatically:

- Anticipate and recognize problems and information needs

- Retrieve relevant, clutter-free information voluntarily

- Record decisions that act to trigger motor actions, and then initiate and carry out the actions fluently

Those with autism, like the car with a defective computer, have little control over their integration and output systems. The glitches in their systems make it difficult to *automatically*:

- Anticipate problems and information needs

- Retrieve relevant clutter-free information at will and hold several pieces of information together at one time in order to think about them and mull them over; to generate new ideas and alternatives to make choices, solve problems, and make decisions

- Record decisions in order to initiate and carry out actions fluently

The Analogy Summarized

From this analogy, it is clear that the central nervous system is an amazing system. Although the learning process was explained sequentially, in reality the CNS functions in a continuous, interactive sequence. Information from one system is instantaneously analyzed and edited for meaning, and messages based on that meaning are instantaneously and automatically sent to alter or influence the functioning of other systems. At the same time, the information from a new experience is organized and integrated with relevant information from past experiences until larger, meaningful units or concepts are formed and problems can be solved. For example, normally developing children have many experiences with balls. They see, touch, and hear descriptions of the various kinds of balls—baseballs and beach balls, big and little balls, red and blue balls. At some point, all that information is integrated, it comes together; they see the whole, the *gestalt* of balls, and they think, "Ahh! These are all balls. Even though they are all different, they are all the same in some ways."

Uncluttered information is organized meaningfully and stored for later retrieval and use. Thus, most people automatically learn their language fully; they learn about their culture, and they think and behave in ways that others in their culture can predict and understand.

Children with autism also have many experiences with balls, but the gestalt of each experience will be recorded and stored on separate tapes. That gestalt includes not the meaning, but all the co-occurring relevant and irrelevant sensory elements of the experience. Because they cannot identify the important elements of their experiences with balls, these children might have focused more intently on the stitching of the baseball, the stripes on the beach ball, or the texture of the grass on their bare feet as they played with the tennis ball. The intensity of the wind noise or the airplane overhead may have blocked out verbal descriptions of the events. Thus, children with autism are less likely to automatically or independently learn the complete concept or gestalt of *ball*.

When these processing systems cannot interact and function instantaneously and automatically, as is the situation in autism, the language and the cultural rules are perhaps not even noticed, or they are learned incompletely, out of context, and with distortions. This distorted and incomplete learning results in behavior that is understood only when the information processing style or learning style is understood.

Remember: *Those with autism spectrum disorders are gestalt learners (it all goes in at once in chunks) but they are not gestalt thinkers (the chunks are not automatically analyzed, sequenced, and stored with meaning to be retrieved and analyzed with newer information to form a gestalt, or bigger idea.)*

Effects of the Autism Learning Style

The predictable effects of the information-processing irregularities include both deficits and strengths. The effects are described below under four headings:

1. Reception and processing problems
2. Response problems
3. Attributes
4. Learning strengths

As with all things in autism, there is a wide range of effects; not all individuals will experience the problems to the same degree or in the same way; but the same elements pertain to all to some degree or in a similar way, even for those with Asperger's syndrome. It is also important to remember that this same learning style is also common to those with autism who have co-occurring disorders (i.e., those who are blind, deaf, have cerebral palsy). Therefore, teachers must adapt instruction to accommodate both or all disorders.

The pervasive effect of this learning style on the development of language, communication, and social skills is described in more detail in Chapter 3. The relationship of the learning style to behavior is discussed in Chapter 8.

Reception and Processing Problems

Problem 1: The individual is unable to modulate and process or integrate sensory stimulation.

Some of the most relevant neurobiological research, summarized by Klinger and Dawson (1992), sheds more light on the reception and processing problems seen in autism. First, children with autism fail to orient, process, and respond to new and unpredictable stimuli or events in the same way as their normally developing peers. Klinger and Dawson propose that this "abnormal orienting response may be related to difficulties in arousal regulation" (p. 164). They "hypothesize that children with autism have an unusually narrow range of optimal stimulation," ranging between a lower level that doesn't register with the child at all; to a narrow, slightly higher level that enables the child to orient, attend, and respond adaptively; to an upper level that would cause overarousal, confusion, and aversion or avoidance (p. 165). For more, read Greenspan, Wieder, and Simons (1998).

Assuming that these findings and hypothesis are correct, in the natural course of events those with autism spectrum disorders would likely be in an almost constant state of overarousal, bombarded by the vast array of intense stimulation present in new, changing, and unpredictable situations. Stress from this overwhelming, sometimes painful stimulation leads to defensive actions—the sensory system shuts down, or the individual moves away to avoid the stress or behaves in disorganized and unproductive ways that lead to failure and lowered self-esteem. Learners with autism avoid these intense situations because they are not only confusing and stressful but are likely to be painful and punishing.

To learn to communicate, interact, and function more effectively, one must be in contact with people and must try new things. For this to occur, the stimulation must be regulated to provide just enough (or the right kind of) stimulation to maintain arousal and attention but not so much as to be aversive and avoided. Maintaining a balance between new and unpredictable stimulation and that which is familiar and predictable is a critical part of planning new instruction and for teaching new skills to those with autism.

Temple Grandin, a professional woman with autism, has eloquently described her sensory problems. She notes that her ears were like an open mike or a hearing aid with the volume set on high. She was unable to filter out irrelevant background noise (Grandin & Scariano, 1986).

Others with autism have noted that they knew something was being received but could not tell if it was sound, light, or other stimulation (Cesaroni & Garber, 1991).

Obviously too distracted to work, Gabriel kept looking over his shoulder and saying, "There's a cricket in here." Although the teacher was unable to hear anything, she told him to find the cricket. He went directly to a small bookcase, pulled it out, picked up a cricket, put it outside, then settled to work.

Tony could hear a train coming long before anyone else. He would cover his ears, fuss, and lose focus until well after the train had passed by.

Jason walked at strange angles, back and forth across the hall. One day as his teacher followed him, she noticed that he walked along the edges of the shadows cast by the sun. Jason could not ignore those visual patterns even when he knew he should walk in a straight line.

Matt was very sensitive to the feel of fabrics on his skin; he would strip off his clothes when he could stand it no longer.

Problem 2: The individual has decreased ability to scan an area or environment to identify and focus consistently on the important elements or events.

Research suggests that those with autism have a) an impaired ability to control the direction of attention and b) a striking ability to concentrate attention in one narrow spatial location while being unaware of sensory events at other locations. These differences interfere with learning that depends to a considerable degree on the ability to continuously, selectively, and smoothly shift attention to follow the rapid ebb and flow of objects, actions, sounds, words, gestures, vocal inflexions, facial expressions, internal feelings, memories, and a myriad of other subtle details of the environment. Therefore, "disconnected fragments of information would lack context and temporal continuity" (Courchesne et al., 1994, p. 20).

Those with autism have unexpected information gaps because bits and pieces or whole strings of important information are missed while they focus intently on some irrelevant detail. For example, when looking at a chalkboard, José concentrated on the edges of the board instead of the information on the board. Because his attention was focused on other competing sensory stimulation, he often missed out on directions, rules, and information for lessons.

Problem 3a: Chunks of information that occur simultaneously or very close together in time are quickly associated and remembered.

This has been called gestalt, holistic, or one-trial learning.

Problem 3b: Information is not automatically or independently organized or analyzed to eliminate the clutter, to elicit the meaning, or to determine the relationship of new information to that from past experience.

In essence, they are gestalt learners but they are not gestalt thinkers (Winner, 2000, p. 55). The synergistic effects of these two problems include:

- Unexpected associations or superstitious learning occurs. For example, the light fixture in the classroom dropped to the floor just as one young man bent to take a drink from the water fountain. It was a long time before he would use a drinking fountain again.

- Exploratory or trial-and-error experiences often result in random learning, erroneous associations, and development of nonproductive rituals and routines.

- Repetitious teaching strategies that elicit quick rote responses often lead to meaningless and inflexible learning.

> During free time, José sat in the teacher's chair in the circle area and echoed the total language lesson, including the cues, prompts, correction procedures, and reinforcement. Although he had memorized the total lesson, he could not initiate a request for a drink of water or ask for help.

Tony had been taught to comply with the teacher's requests to stand up, sit down, come here, and other directives. One day he left his desk and walked toward his teacher. As he reached the middle of the room, his teacher said, "Tony, sit down." He immediately sat down on the floor. This very compliant young man did what he was told but had not understood that the teacher meant to sit at his desk.

■ Routines are learned quickly and firmly, but without understanding their total purpose or function. Those with autism are highly motivated to repeat memorized routines even when they are meaningless. It is difficult for them to omit a part of a routine even if it includes random or stereotypic actions that are irrelevant to the purpose of the routine.

Gabriel developed and repeated this recess routine every day until the bell rang throughout the school year: He walked down the path to the curb, down the curb to the steps, and down the steps, where he paused to look at his reflection in the window of the basement door. He walked up a different flight of steps, gave a hop at the top, then returned to the path.

Maria was a capable adolescent who could do many things independently. When she was learning to dress herself, her mother always laid her clothing on the bed in a specific way and prompted her to put them on in a specific order. Now, several years later, despite Mom's many efforts to fade herself out of this task, Maria does not dress herself unless her mother is there to perform her part of the routine. This is an example of an individual who learned quickly that her mother's presence, the cues, and the prompts, all were part of the routine. Maria did not understand that dressing is ultimately an independent task. This kind of prompt dependence is very resistant to change.

To indicate a need to use the toilet, Tim was taught to touch a picture of the bathroom that had been hung on the kitchen door. He learned to do this quickly. When the picture was removed to test his understanding, Tim continued to touch the spot on the door where the picture had been before going to the bathroom. The instructional routine had emphasized touching the card without clarifying the purpose—to communicate with his mother.

José's speech therapist was teaching him to look at people when they called his name. The strategy was to say, "José" as she took his chin and turned his head toward her. José quickly learned to grab his own chin and to turn his head whenever he heard his name. However, he didn't look at the speaker; he simply turned his head. José had learned a motor routine that included the consistently delivered cues and prompts without learning the purpose of the routine.

Because of the inability to automatically or independently analyze and organize information, those with autism will generally be unable to *automatically*:

■ Identify critical elements or meanings, but focus on the details and learn the routine

■ Evaluate information for accuracy or completeness, edit or modify information, or know when more information is needed

■ Retrieve meaningful information at the appropriate time

- Relate information from one experience to another to develop more complex or higher-level meanings, or to generalize information
- Manipulate information flexibly to generate new ideas, or to pretend, imagine, or create
- Apply and adapt rules to fit changing situations or subtle social or cultural norms
- Understand analogies, inferences, and other higher-level thinking skills
- Think about things, solve problems, and make choices and decisions

In summary, the ability to learn quickly and to remember information is a real strength *but only if events and experiences are organized to highlight important elements and relationships*. Without this assistance, the wrong lessons will be learned or the learning will be incomplete but firm and time-consuming to correct.

Problem 4: Information is not retrieved in the correct sequence.

When information is stored without meaning in unrelated fragments or chunks, it is *difficult or impossible to automatically or independently*:

- Learn cause/effect and means/ends relationships
- Learn from experience and from the consequences of one's actions
- Explain or relate events and experiences or answer "Why?"
- Predict and prepare for coming events

Problem 5: Time concepts and the perception of passing time are impaired.

Although the abstract quality of time is difficult for many children to learn, eventually they figure it out. But the problem in autism is more pervasive and may be the cause of confusion and anxiety-based behavior outbursts. Charlie Hart has spent a lifetime trying to understand why his brother and his son, who both have autism, do the things they do. In his book, *Without Reason*, he describes his son's confusion about time. At age 15, his son thought that he would be a child again and be able to do the things he used to do. He could not understand that time flows like a stream, in one direction, irreversibly. If something happens at one moment, it cannot be undone; it will not come back (Hart, 1989).

This impaired sense of time, coupled with the inability to sequence events in the correct order and to predict events, results in the following kinds of problems:

- Random drifting from one thing or place to another with little idea of the beginning or ending of events or the passing of time. For example, one might stand up in the middle of a meal or conversation and simply wander off.
- Compulsive clock watching and/or repetitive questions about time. Those with autism compensate for these problems by remembering the specific times for events and by learning to read time on the clock. But even this does not entirely solve the problem and can cause additional confusion and anxiety. For example, if an event is scheduled to begin at 2:00, one of the following things is likely to occur: The individual may:
  - Refuse to stop looking at the clock until the clock registers 2:00
  - Become very upset if the event does not begin at the exact time
  - Become confused if the exact time occurred while the individual wasn't watching, and may insist on waiting until it occurs again in 12 hours
  - Persist in asking, "When will it be time to . . ." or "Is it time yet?"

- Anxiety related to nonspecific amounts of time and the nebulous language of time. For example, how long is a minute? Five minutes? How long should you wait before asking for help? How can you save or make up time? Words such as *later*, *too late*, *not yet*, *already*, *faster*, *sooner*, *before*, *sometimes*, *pretty soon*, *in a minute*, and *tomorrow* are extremely confusing to those with autism. The one word that Hart's son understood was *never*, because it was specific, clear, and required no qualitative judgment.

Problem 6: Language is understood and used literally.

Even the most capable and verbal children and adults with autism are very concrete and literal in their understanding and use of language. Confusion caused by this literalness is one of the major causes of unexpected learning and behavior problems. Literal interpretation is so common and has such a pervasive effect on the way these individuals function that it is important to periodically review the more complete description of the differences in development of language (see pages 37–39).

When the teacher directed the class to "Turn over your books; it's time for the test," Jeff put his book on the floor and tried to turn his body over the book. This literal interpretation and honest effort to follow the teacher's directions was interpreted as disruptive and attention-seeking behavior.

The PE teacher was trying to teach José to dribble the basketball. She had demonstrated and explained what he was to do. However, José continued to stand still without making any effort to follow her direction. Finally, in exasperation, she said with great emphasis, "José, dribble the ball!" José stood very still as tears rolled down his cheeks and a wet spot appeared on the front of his pants. José's mother had worked hard to teach him not to dribble urine. José had only one very literal meaning for the word *dribble*, and although it was against Mother's rules, he complied with the teacher's request.

Problem 7: Auditory information is not processed efficiently or reliably.

Traditionally, most instruction is provided verbally. Information, directions, rules, correction procedures, prompts, and reinforcement are for the most part verbal. This is not a problem for most people, but those with autism have difficulty processing auditory information reliably. This auditory-processing deficit has such important implications for providing instruction and for interpreting behavior and learning problems that it is important to review the elements of this issue periodically.

One of the common symptoms of autism is the intermittent perception of deafness. In most cases, those with autism can hear. There is evidence that those with autism receive, record, and store verbal information.

- After learning to speak, they repeat or echo the things they hear.

- After learning to communicate, they can talk about information that was not specifically taught.

- They sometimes act on conversations or information directed to others nearby or down the hall.

Other aspects of this auditory processing problem include:

- The overwhelming or painful quality of certain types of auditory stimulation
- The transience of the spoken word; it comes and it is gone, leaving no record for later reference
- Delays and discrepancies in analyzing and retrieving auditory information
  - There is often a significant delay between a verbal request and the generation and production of a meaningful verbal response or motor action. Sometimes this delay is as much as 30 to 45 seconds, sometimes longer.
  - If rushed to respond or if the request is rephrased or changed too soon, confusion and anxiety will increase and result in a behavioral outburst or a lack of response that is often misinterpreted as noncompliance.
- Long chains of auditory information recorded without meaning or without the typical meaning
- A tendency to become dependent on verbal cues and/or prompts
- A tendency for verbal reinforcement, such as "Good working" or "Good talking," to distract the learner from the natural and powerful reinforcing outcome of their actions

In summary, auditory stimulation can be overwhelming, and its transient nature leaves no permanent record for later reference. Because attention is inconsistent and does not always follow the ebb and flow of auditory information, chunks of information can be missed. Parents or teachers are not aware that the information was unrecorded or not understood; and the person with autism does not know that information is missing.

When Kim understood the directions, he carried them out quickly and precisely. But he had many emotional outbursts. An assessment of the problem revealed that he was trying to follow all the directions he heard, even those intended for others in the room. For example, when the teacher directed the students to move their chairs to the group meeting area, Kim was the first student to carry out the direction. As the teacher repeated the direction for some who had not complied, Kim stood up, looked around, frowned, and threw his chair across the room as he dropped to the floor screaming. He was unable to evaluate his own behavior and know that he had done what the teacher said, so the directions must be for someone else. This inability to screen out irrelevant directions is fairly common in autism.

When Tony became upset and began to rock and hyperventilate, four people rushed to him, each talking, soothing, or giving directions. After a few minutes of this, he lunged through the circle of people, knocking a lamp off a nearby table as he ran from the room. The confusion and overwhelming stimulation of people too close and talking excitedly while giving contradictory information led to his behavioral outburst.

Jeff was sitting on the floor pushing a toy truck back and forth. His mother said, "Pick up the toys; it's time for lunch." Jeff continued to push the truck. After about 10 seconds, Mother said, "Come on, put all your toys in the box." He stopped pushing his truck but continued to sit on the floor. Within the next few minutes, his frustrated mother rephrased the direction four more times, each time a bit louder than before. After the third direction, Jeff put his hands over his ears and closed his eyes tightly. Finally, with his eyes shut and his ears still covered, he began to scream and kick. Jeff needed time to process the demand and to switch (transition) from one action to another. The additional requests made with different words increased the confusion.

———————

Robert, a teenager who is also blind, enjoyed working with his tape recorder and listening to music. After learning to play the tapes backward, he began to sing the songs both forward and backward with equal enjoyment. This is an example of the ability to record long chains of auditory information without meaning.

Problem 8: Meaning is not automatically attached to visual information.

For a more complete discussion of strategies for clarifying visual information, see Chapter 14.

Although those with autism have a remarkable ability to remember and manipulate the things they see and an incredible ability to quickly take in chunks of visual information, often the meaning is not attached to the things they see or the words and numbers they can read. There are reports that some individuals have photographic memories—the ability to read a page from a book or memorize the arrangement of objects in a room almost instantaneously. One young man could read just as easily when the page was placed upside down, diagonally, or in the typical position (Hart, 1989). When information is organized and presented in a clear and permanent visual format to highlight the critical elements, sequences, and relationships, most of those with ASD can learn to use it meaningfully.

———————

Jeff began to read the TV Guide over and over again when he was 4 years old. While he could talk about the schedule, he never used the information to select favorite TV shows. Reading without meaning and purpose is common in autism.

———————

José began reading the dictionary when he was 3 years old. When given an IQ test at age 9, he could recite the definition of every word included in the test; but he could not use any of those words in meaningful sentences nor could he use them to communicate or solve problems.

———————

Gabriel watched from the corners of his eyes as the teacher gave him directions. She verbalized the directions while printing the sequence of steps in a checklist format. After she left him, he studied the list briefly, then calmly began to work. Occasionally he referred to the checklist. The teacher sometimes gave him oral directions without the visuals. At those times, Gabriel appeared confused and tense. He would hunch his shoulders and echo part of the directions. When the teacher turned away, he would just sit, doing nothing. If the teacher pressed him verbally to start, he screamed and covered his ears with his hands.

Response Problems

Problem 9: The individual is unable to solve problems and generate new or alternative solutions to fit varied or changing situations.

Problem solving and the ability to generate alternative responses requires the ability to creatively manipulate two or more pieces of meaningful information at one time to reason, evaluate, and make judgments. This is perhaps one of the most difficult issues for those with ASD—especially those with Asperger's syndrome or higher functioning autism.

Temple Grandin has said that she could never think about or relate two things to solve problems unless they were written down. If she could see the two things together, she could visualize their meaning.

The door that Gabriel generally used to enter the school was locked. He struggled briefly to open it but quickly became frustrated and resorted to banging his head on the door until his assistant arrived to stop him. Not only was Gabriel unable to generate a solution to his problem, he was left with a reflexive action of frustration that he was unable to terminate independently.

Problem 10: The individual is unable to totally and automatically control motor (and verbal) responses.

Even though motor skills seemed to be intact and least affected by autism, motor problems were described by Kanner (1943) in his first descriptions of the syndrome and later by Asperger as he described his group of clients. Attwood (1993) summarized some of the early research by saying that those with autism display movements similar to those found in Parkinson's disease. Other movement problems described were poverty of movement, delay in initiation of movement, delay in stopping or changing movements, and rapid fatigue with prolonged tasks.

Some individuals with autism have described the extraordinary concentration and effort it takes to control repetitive and compulsive motor behaviors. "Stereotyped movements aren't things I decide to do for a reason; they're things that happen by themselves when I'm not paying attention to my body . . . As a general rule . . . the more 'normal' [my] behavior appears, the more guarded and anxious [I] am" (Cesaroni & Garber, 1991, p. 309).

Although more research is needed to understand the effects of motor problems on motor responses, many parents and professionals are aware of the following response problems:

- Delays in initiating verbal and motor actions
  - This particularly relates to learning new motor responses. Familiar/meaningful and rote/meaningless responses are more likely to be initiated quickly and fluently.

- Inability to move fluently through an action from beginning to end and to stop one action and switch to another response or action
  - Many responses are repetitive, dysfluent, and/or perseverative. For example, a response or action may be repeated over and over in exactly the same way even when the outcome is painful or unproductive.

    Maria often "got stuck" as she walked through a door. She would step across the threshold, then rock back and forth from one foot to the other until someone interrupted her.

    One day when José asked for a drink, his mother gave him a glass of water. As soon as he finished drinking, he asked for another drink. This time he pushed the glass away. He continued to ask for a drink even though he pushed the glass away each time his frustrated mother handed it to him. After a considerable time, this overwrought child made the sign for music. His mother quickly gave him the audiotapes. He calmed down immediately as he listened to the music. The inability to switch responses or to recall the correct word or appropriate response is a major problem for many.

- Inability to inhibit compulsive thoughts and actions
  - Compulsive actions tend to become more problematic when stress is high and during adolescence. Many compulsions are related to:
    - Intense interests or fears
    - A specific routine or way of doing things
    - Neatness and perfectionist tendencies
    - Time

Maria, whose limited speech was unreliable, had recently learned to communicate by typing with physical support. Each time she walked past the fire alarm, she pulled the handle to trigger the alarm. During the behavioral assessment, the specialist asked Maria, "Why do you pull the fire alarm?" She typed, "It's the only thing in my head when I'm in the hall." Maria was unable to inhibit actions triggered by this compulsive thought even to earn rewards.

José needed to have materials neatly organized and lined up. The hangers on the coat rack were particularly bothersome to him. Whenever a hanger was the least bit out of line, he insisted on straightening and pushing all the hangers to the right side of the rack. It made no difference what he was doing or how intensely he was focused on an activity; when he sensed an errant hanger, he would dash across the room to put it in its proper place.

- Responses and actions that do not match intentions
  - Sometimes individuals with autism have little control over their bodies. This is a fairly new theory that might help to explain some of the unexpected things these individuals do and do not do.

After a period of hard work, Maria, the young woman who had learned to communicate by typing, was restless and fidgety. Her teacher asked, "Do you want a break?" Maria shouted, "No, no, no!" The teacher was surprised by the response because it did not fit the situation, so she repeated her question. As Maria continued to shout, "No, no, no," she took the teacher to the typewriter and typed, "Yes." Later that day, Maria typed, "Listen to what I write, not what I say."

Problem 11: The individual is unable to understand the perspective of others, that people have different perspectives.

Some believe that this "theory of mind" deficit is perhaps the core deficit in autism spectrum disorders (Baron-Cohen, Tager-Flusbert, & Cohen, 1993; Wing, 1992).

This inability to recognize that other people have feelings, thoughts, and beliefs that might be different from their own feelings, thoughts, and beliefs cause major problems during social interactions and conversations. This issue particularly affects those with higher-functioning autism and Asperger's syndrome because they want to be social and have friends but simply do not understand what that means and what they must do to please others or at least to "fit in." They do not understand the hidden messages that people send and receive—that body language, tone of voice, and gestures also send messages.

The terms neurotypical *and* neuronormal *have been used by those with Asperger's syndrome or higher functioning autism to refer to people without autism.*

They refer to themselves as "autists."

For example, it is astounding to us, neurotypicals or neuronormals , that otherwise very capable individuals could be totally unaware of others—that they are themselves astounded to learn that the teacher is talking to everyone in the room, not just to them.

These theory of mind issues must be considered when conducting a functional behavioral assessment and when teaching problem solving skills, conversation skills, and social interaction skills.

Predictable Learning Strengths

Learn more about the gifts of autism in Chapter 11 of Autism: Facts and Strategies for Parents *(Janzen, 1999) and in* Asperger's and Self-Esteem: Insight and Hope Through Famous Role Models *(Ledgen, 2002).*

As we look at the information processing style common to those with ASD, we see that the processing differences cause some severe learning problems, but they also form the basis for learning strengths. Six very important abilities provide direction for structuring interventions and solving problems for those with autism. These are the ability to:

- Take in chunks of information quickly (Gestalt processing);
- Remember information for a long time (excellent long term memory for facts and routines);
- Use visual information meaningfully when taught in meaningful ways;
- Learn long routines quickly and they are highly motivated to repeat familiar routines;
- Understand and use concrete, context-free information and rules; and
- Concentrate on topics of specific interest.

Not only are these characteristics valuable for developing teaching and support strategies, they also provide the basis for unusual talents. There are many talented individuals with autism spectrum disorders who are well-known artists, poets, and scientists as a result of these unusually strong abilities.

Predictable Attributes

It is important to know that those with autism have endearing and positive attributes as well. Generally, those with ASD are:

- Known for their innocence, honesty, and guilelessness—they are not easily socialized to cover their naiveté;
- Not adept at deceiving nor do they try to impress others;
- Not likely to defend or explain themselves even though their actions and their motivation are frequently misunderstood—they rarely complain or whine;
- Compliant—perhaps overly so—when they clearly understand the expectations; and
- Perfectionists who are highly motivated to complete familiar routines perfectly and precisely. This attribute has led to employment in libraries, banks, high-tech companies, and other businesses where accuracy and persistence are valued.

These predictable attributes also provide information that signals a problem and a need for support. For example, whenever a person with autism is thought to be non-compliant, it is most likely that something is misunderstood or interpreted literally or incorrectly, or that some small, seemingly insignificant piece of information is missing. When an individual with ASD appears to be overly sophisticated, it is possible that they are echoing or imitating things they have seen or heard.

Asperger's Syndrome—Special Challenges

Because the effects of the social-cognitive differences in Asperger's syndrome are not obvious to the casual observer—people assume that they understand and can function just like "everyone else." This assumption greatly magnifies their problems.

In general, their learning strengths and deficits and their attributes and gifts are similar to others with autism spectrum disorders but at a higher, or slightly different level. Those with Asperger's syndrome also have the same types of sensory problems—they are often overwhelmed with environmental "noise"—and by the stress that other people provide. Because they are seen as so competent in many ways, they are exposed to more complex social, vocational, and community expectations and situations, often with very little support. They often excel in mathematics, sciences, or the arts, and have an excellent long-term memory for minute details (e.g., schedules, maps, historical facts). With a mentor and appropriate support these strengths and gifts can be expanded and increase the potential for satisfying vocational efforts and friendships.

In general, they do quite well in school during their early years, but after the third or fourth grade, they are often overwhelmed by the greater expectations:

- Homework demands—they are unable to analyze, organize, and integrate information into higher level concepts and ideas, except in some cases when related to intense and obsessive interests. They have difficulty with problem solving and the ability to make decisions. Perhaps even more importantly, most instruction is verbal, when they generally need a more visual, concrete approach. As the complexity of homework increases—with increasing assignments for an increasing number of courses, time constraints, and tests—levels of stress can escalate quickly to crisis level.

- Social situations—As social expectations increase, those with Asperger's syndrome have difficulty understanding the perspective of others—to understand why people do and say the things they do (the "theory of mind" issues, Baron-Cohen et al., 1993). They do not seem able to read facial expressions nor adapt and respond to the nonverbal cues of others. They want to be like everyone else, but seem not to know how. They have difficulty making friends, carrying on a social conversation, and making social decisions; again, their naiveté makes them extremely vulnerable.

- Other factors that intensify the problems as they grow older:

  - Their literal interpretation of information and moral sense of right and wrong makes it difficult for them to accept explanations.

  - They are easily offended by any suggestion of a problem or wrongdoing.

  - They have tunnel vision and such intense interests that they are bored by anything unrelated to those interests.

  - Puberty is very difficult, bringing mood swings and quick reactions to stress; some will require help for depression and other psychiatric disorders.

As with others who have spectrum disorders, those with Asperger's syndrome will need a comprehensive evaluation to determine their unique learning style, the basis for individualizing the strategies outlined in this book. They can be quite independent and make considerable contributions to society if they receive appropriate support from family, teachers, and others—a mentor is especially helpful to support them as they explore and develop their interests. For more information, see Attwood, 1998; Grandin, 1995; Grandin & Scariano, 1986; Ledgen, 2002; Myles,

Cook, Miller, Rinner, & Robbins, 2000; Myles & Southwick, 1999; Newport, 2001; and Williams, 1994.

Issues Related to Co-Occurring Conditions

Although many other conditions or disabilities can co-occur with autism, two have a significant impact that require careful assessment and planning—severe hearing impairments or deafness and severe vision impairments or blindness. Whenever these conditions are present with autism, the intervention planning team must include specialists from both fields. The National Autism Society sponsors the *Autism Network for Hearing and Visually Impaired Persons*.

Autism and Visual Impairments or Blindness

The first and greatest issue in this area is to distinguish the differences between the indicators of autism and the typical behaviors or blindisms that present during certain developmental stages.

Those with both autism and visual impairments require extremely structured environments and structured teaching procedures, yet the usual strategies for both tend to be contradictory. Thus it is essential to have both specialty areas represented during program planning and staff training.

See the following resources for more clarity in identifying and understanding the issues involved in serving these co-occurring impairments: Cass (1998) and Gense and Gense (1994).

Autism With Hearing Impairments/Deafness

Many of those with autism spectrum disorders were at one time thought to be deaf because they often did not respond to their name or other verbal stimuli. But some are also deaf or have mild to severe hearing problems. Although individuals with either disorder typically rely on visual adaptations, those with co-occurring disoders have complicating problems.

For example, if the problems of autism prevent the child from looking at people and understanding gestures and facial expressions, they are unlikely to learn to sign, read lips, or respond to more subtle gestures. Again, it is necessary for specialists from both fields to work together—to assess and interpret the individual child's unique needs, develop appropriate interventions, and deliver appropriate staff and parent training. For additional information see Rosenhall, Nordin, Sandstrom, Ahlsen, and Gillberg, 1999, and Wolf-Schein, 1998. Also check *The Autism Network for Hearing and Visually Impaired Persons*, sponsored by The National Autism Society.

Summary

Parents and teachers are often overwhelmed as they begin to understand the problems faced by those with ASD. It is especially intimidating to realize that these individuals are so dependent upon their caregivers, teachers, and mentors to interpret the world for them. Those with autism are also dependent upon interpreters to help others understand them.

Think how difficult it would be to raise a blind child without knowing he was blind. How confusing it would be to use your best efforts to teach and guide the child who kept bumping into things, spilling things, losing things, and breaking things. Without the information about blindness, how disheartening and frustrating it would be.

Similarly, parents and teachers of those with autism are frustrated and confused when their best efforts never seem good enough, when their child seems so unpredictable. The information on learning style and predictable patterns and problems contained in this and the next chapter provides the foundation for understanding those with autism spectrum disorders. These are two of the most important chapters in this manual. When the individual with autism begins to seem unpredictable, review Chapters 2 and 3 again and again for a new look at the problem. Also study Chapter 8 to understand the affects of autism on behavior.

It is sometimes difficult for parents and teachers to keep a level of perspective as they guide their child toward independence. Be aware that:

1. *The one constant in autism is the inconsistencies.* There seems to be no middle ground. Things are too easy or too hard, thinking and actions are too fast or too slow, there are amazing learning strengths and amazing learning deficits. Those with autism have some unexpectedly advanced information and skills yet have unexpected and surprising knowledge gaps. This is particularly true in Asperger's syndrome. Things that severely affect the rest of us have little impact on those with autism; yet seemingly insignificant, subtle things can disrupt them significantly.

2. *Variable performance is the rule rather than the exception.* What can be done or tolerated at one time may be impossible to do or tolerate at a different time. Expect both progress and regressions. Regressions are often surprising and discouraging, but they are normal in autism. As long as the person's world is structured to clarify information and provide support, skills and abilities will be regained and expanded.

3. *Autism may be a lifelong problem, but learning is also a lifelong process.* Our goal is to capitalize on the information-processing strengths to compensate for the deficits that are to some degree common to those with autism spectrum disorders. It is our role, as their interpreters, to use this information to help them become as independent as possible in the real world.

It is true that those with autism spectrum disorders present major challenges for parents, teachers, and mentors. Yet they also provide major rewards for anyone who takes the opportunity to develop a close relationship with them. The ability to understand and deal effectively with their challenges forces us to be creative and flexible. Those who live with and support children and adults with autism spectrum disorders will never stop learning!

Effects of Autism Spectrum Disorders on Language, Communication, and Social Development

The defining characteristics or symptoms of the autism spectrum disorders are primarily related to the pervasive differences in the development of language, communication, and social skills. This chapter provides an overview, a very brief summary of normal development, and the most typical developmental differences in autism and in Asperger's syndrome. Even though the *DSM–IV* diagnostic criteria says that those with Asperger's have "no clinically significant general delay in language" and even though they are quite often very verbal, they do not master many of the complex and basic concepts that support social and self-management skills. With this information about typical development and the differences in the spectrum disorders, it is easier to interpret the world from the perspective of those with autism. This information provides a foundation for assessing learning and behavior problems and for developing interventions to match their very unique needs.

Typical Development

Early Skills—The First Year

Most babies have an innate drive to learn language and to socialize. This drive is so strong that when the learning systems are intact, children acquire these skills automatically without being taught. Development of these skills begins at or before birth and depends on trial-and-error learning from experiences in the natural environment.

There is evidence that infants begin to listen to voices before birth and that they show a preference for their parents' voices soon after birth. From the moment of birth, infants are bombarded by new stimulation—sights, sounds, the pressure and texture of clothing, temperature changes, and odors. When babies open their eyes, people begin talking to them, labeling and describing the people, objects, and events in their world. They can adjust or modulate the amount of social stimulation they receive by withdrawing their gaze or closing their eyes. When they withdraw or shut their eyes, people pull back and lower their voices. When they open their eyes, people provide more stimulation—an instinctive dance.

Within a very short time, as the sensory system matures, infants learn to shut out extraneous background stimulation, showing a predisposition or preference for social stimuli. They begin to watch people more intently, following their movements and engaging their caregivers with a powerful eye gaze. At a very early age, infants have the ability to continuously and selectively shift attention to follow rapidly changing social scenes and to identify, analyze, and make sense of very subtle expressions, emotions, gestures, and words. This is the foundation for language and social development.

From the beginning, infants turn their heads toward the source of sound. They cry and make random sounds that get attention from others. These reflexive, nonintentional communications take on meaning for both the infants and their caregivers, and the infants' needs are met.

At some time within the first 6 months of life as they develop more control over their facial muscles and their bodies, normally developing infants begin to explore objects and establish two-way social exchanges with their caregivers through imitation of facial expressions and vocalizations. Infants and caregivers expand their mutual interest and pleasure in each other by smiling and vocalizing. No longer are infants simply imitating but actually generating their own responses to keep their caregivers engaged. They begin to signal that they enjoy and want to continue a tickle game by smiling, chuckling, wiggling, and waiting for a response. These actions represent the beginnings of intentional communication.

These simple communicative exchanges are expanded gradually by coordinating attention between the caregiver and an object of mutual interest (joint attention). This mutual sharing of feelings and emotional engagement is a very important step toward feelings of social competence and the ability to communicate. Soon infants begin to point, the first nonverbal gesture to indicate an object of interest. They are persistent in efforts to engage the caregiver to solve a problem.

> After dropping a toy, the infant cries. When mother comes, the baby shifts attention from mother to the toy and back while pointing to the toy on the floor. Mother understands this message quickly and returns the toy. This is an example of a deliberate and intentional behavior used to engage a communication partner and express a need with a conventional signal (looking and pointing) that anyone could understand.

Before the first birthday, infants have developed an awareness that "People (including themselves) have different orientations toward a shared world . . . that people are subjects of experience" (Hobson, 1992, p. 175). Sometime within the first 12 to 15 months of age, infants have learned the value of people and the power of communication. They also have learned the most critical and basic concepts:

- The rules of social exchanges—the basic cause/effect relationship:
  - I do something, you do something. We take turns.
  - I can direct people's attention to my needs and interests.
  - I am competent; people are basically predictable.
- That people and things have names and labels; that they respond to their own names and the names of many familiar objects, people, pets, and actions
- To understand and respond to simple questions and directions
- To make a variety of sounds that increasingly sound like real words

The Second and Third Years

Infants and very young children work intently at play, rehearsing and mastering new skills. The second and third years of life bring an explosion of language learning. By the end of the third year, they have virtually mastered the basics of their native language. They have learned:

- That words have multiple meanings and things have multiple labels
  - Mother has various names: Mom, Mother, Mary, my wife, and others. They have learned that words such as shoe, ball, and animal refer to many different kinds of shoes, balls, and animals. They are not confused between words that sound the same (for example, the color blue and the fact that they blew out their birthday candles).

- That word meanings are dependent upon context, intonation, and inflection:
  - Most 3-year-old children are beginning to use pronouns flexibly. They understand words related to space and time even though the meaning of those words changes depending on who is speaking and the perspective of the speaker (e.g., here, there, behind, up, later, in a minute, soon). At 3 years, children are beginning to tease with words and become aware that words take on different meaning when used in the context of humor, jokes, idioms, and slang.
- To talk in sentences that give information, to ask questions to get information, and to tell others what to do:
  - It is usually safe to assume that normally developing children understand the language they hear at or above the level they can speak; generally they understand the meaning of most words they use to communicate.

Continuing Development

Most children progress naturally, by trial and error, to become competent social members of their culture and their community. The intrinsic interest in people and their actions, coupled with the drive to interact and play, provides many experiences and opportunities to practice communication and social skills. The ability to continuously and selectively shift attention to follow rapidly changing social scenes and to identify, analyze, and make sense of very subtle expressions, gestures, and feelings provides a social perspective that is a foundation for making social judgments.

The intuitive sense of the perspective of others and an awareness of self from that perspective gradually expands to an understanding of perspective that involves knowing:

- What I see; what others see
- What I know; what others know
- What I feel; what others feel
- What I believe; what others believe
- What other people know that other people know
- What the group thinks or feels, based on conventional intuition

This perspective of others, or "theory of mind," shapes behavior and actions (Baron-Cohen et al., 1993). Feelings of embarrassment and the desire to be accepted by the group have a profound effect on social development within a culture. The subtleties of social and cultural rules are fine and require the ability to modify and adapt behavior to match the requirements of different situations. To apply rules flexibly depends on the understanding of perspective, the ability to predict the effects of one's own actions, and the ability to make judgments.

In summary, the innate drive to learn the language and become an interactive member of a culture is supported by an efficient information-processing system and a myriad of positive experiences. Individual differences within the population as a whole depend on inherited tendencies and past experiences. Some people are introverts, and others are extroverts; some are highly sensitive to social blunders, and others are almost oblivious.

Developmental Differences in Autism

Learning the language and learning to socialize typically proceeds so smoothly that the process is rarely thought about unless something goes wrong, as it does in those with autism spectrum disorders. It is important to understand that there is a difference in the early development of those with early-onset autism, whose parents say that their child behaved differently from the beginning, and those with later-onset autism. Those with later-onset autism do initially develop the early skills but for some as yet unconfirmed reason, begin to lose those early social and communication skills and the early learning strategies.

Those with autism have little ability to attend to people and to the rapidly changing action in the natural environment. In fact, each of the requirements for effective trial-and-error learning presents problems for those with autism who are overwhelmed with novel stimulation, who concentrate on very narrow elements of the environment, and who have trouble shifting attention and deriving coherent meaning from sensory input (Courchesne et al., 1994; Hobson, 1992; Klinger & Dawson, 1992).

There are fewer opportunities to hear the language and to practice complex interactive communication skills because interactions and new experiences are often avoided or not taken in and registered. Even play does not seem to be intrinsically motivating for these children. Given the learning style common in autism, it is not surprising that their perspective differs from that of most other people. In fact, it is dangerous to assume that any concept, rule, or skill is clearly or completely understood without instruction.

Jim Sinclair, a young man with autism, has written, "Being autistic does not mean being unable to learn. . . . It does mean there are differences in how learning happens. . . . But what . . . I think is even more basic and [most] frequently overlooked, is that autism involves differences in what is known without learning. . . . [There are] gaps between what is expected to be learned and what is assumed to be already understood" (Sinclair, 1992, p. 295). In the following section, some of those differences are summarized.

Differences in Development and Use of Language

Young children with ASD neither watch people intently nor consistently turn their heads toward sound. It cannot be assumed that all the complexities of the language will be learned automatically, without instruction, because they have difficulty deriving meaning from their experiences automatically or independently. It is not that these children do not learn any language, but the learning is incomplete and specific to their frame of reference, which is different from others'. Major differences are seen in both the meaning of words and the use of language.

Differences in Learning the Meaning of Words

There are differences in the way most children with autism learn the meaning of words. They do not always learn that:

1. *Everything and everybody has a name or label.* When one 11-year-old made this amazing discovery, he walked around the room, pointing to inquire the name of each thing—wall, curtain, window frame, window, table. Once he understood this amazing concept, he was highly motivated to learn other labels.

2. *Things can have multiple labels* (e.g., garbage/trash, bag/sack, woman/girl/ mother).

3. *Words can have multiple meanings.* This causes special problems for those who interpret and use the language literally.

- A single word can label several different things: objects, feelings, ideas, and actions. The word *feel* refers to emotions and sensations as well as the action of touching; *sack* can be a noun (a kind of bag), or it can be a verb (to put things in a sack, or to be relieved of a job.

  As the refrigerator door swung open, the bottle of salad dressing fell to the floor. Tony, 5 years old, said, "Oh, pants down." At school, Tony had learned that dressing means pants up or pants down. A single meaning was associated with a word that had multiple meanings. If Tony had been asked whether he knew the meaning of the word dressing, he likely would have said, "Yes." He did know a single meaning for it; but without instruction, he would not have known that there could be additional meanings.

- Context changes the meaning of many words. The meaning of pronouns and words related to space, location, size, shape, and time depend on nonspecific, subtle relationships and perspective (e.g., here, there, up, behind, later, in a minute, bigger, long, you, I, and so on).

  Jason had lost the privilege of going on the field trip and had to stay at the school. After his class had left, he insisted on standing directly behind Mary, a teacher who remained at the school. Later, as his teacher and Mary were trying to understand this unusual behavior, his teacher remembered that she had said, "You have to stay *behind* with *Mary.*"

- Intonation and inflection change meaning—as in humor and sarcasm. For example, "stop it" and "no" can be said playfully or sharply with serious intent. Word meanings can change when used in the context of idioms and slang expressions.

  Gabriel worried about disasters. One evening he became upset and agitated about the starving children he had just seen on the TV news. When efforts to help him understand the situation had failed, his exasperated sister finally said, with a sarcastic inflection, "You might just as well go bang your head right now," so Gabriel did. Later, as he explained the situation to his mother, he said, "Lisa told me to bang my head, so I did—but I didn't want to." The inability to understand that sarcasm changes meaning, coupled with an overly compliant nature, makes those with autism extremely vulnerable.

  To reinforce Lee's persistence and hard work, the teacher said, "You're really going to town!" Lee looked up soberly and said, "No, I'm sitting right here." On another day when Lee was tired and moving slowly, the teacher said, "Come on, Lee, shake a leg!" He stood up and shook his leg.

4. *Makes incorrect associations and/or interprets words literally.* Those with autism often associate an unusual or erroneous meaning to a word or phrase. The following examples illustrate how this problem affects an overly compliant individual.

At recess time, Amy's teacher said, "It's time for recess; *get on* your coat." Amy quickly threw her coat to the floor and stood on it. This literal interpretation of "get on" and the effort to comply was initially interpreted as disruptive or attention-seeking behavior.

―――――――

José's father said, "Keep your eye on the ball." José picked up the ball and pressed it to his eye.

―――――――

José was learning about the color yellow. His teacher showed him many different yellow objects—a toy truck, block, ball, crayon, pencil—as she said, "This is yellow." Later, she asked José to get the pencil. José made no effort to respond even though he knew what a pencil was and had responded correctly to similar requests before. After repeating the request several times with no response, she said, "Give me the yellow pencil." José handed her the pencil. Because the teacher had just called that specific pencil *yellow*, to José it was no longer simply a pencil.

―――――――

When Tony's family stopped at a motel, his sister opened the sliding door to the balcony just as Tony's brother opened the cat's cage and the cat ran out and jumped off the balcony. Everyone got very excited and someone yelled, "The cat jumped off the balcony!" Now, Tony shouts, "The cat jumped off the balcony" whenever people around him get very excited. This is an example of an association error and delayed echolalia that is often misinterpreted as hallucinations or delusions.

In summary, these language-learning differences have a major impact on life for those with autism spectrum disorders. It is critically important for parents and teachers to understand the effects of the language learning differences in order to: (a) understand why those with autism do some of the things they do, and (b) how to design instruction and support systems to insure that the language is learned more completely.

Differences in Use of Language

Children with autism spectrum disorders do not automatically learn how to put words together to generate or form their own sentences, questions, or directions to clearly express their message. They rarely initiate a question to ask for information or to clarify a situation. Rather, they often *use repetitive or unusual sentence forms that must be interpreted by their listener*. Echolalia, metaphorical language, and repetitive questions and sentence forms are common in autism.

Echolalia

Echolalia is the act of repeating or echoing words or sentences that others have said. These "borrowed" words are generally well articulated and repeated with the same emphasis and vocal quality used by the original speaker.

This ability to echo so precisely is confusing because it makes the individual sound so capable and knowledgeable. However, these echoed words and phrases were recorded and stored "in chunks" without analysis for meaning (Prizant, 1983). *Parents or teachers cannot assume that echoed words carry the typical or expected meaning*. It is more likely that the echoed words are triggered by some element of the current situation that is similar to the situation in which they were first heard. Echolalia is used for a variety of functional reasons (Prizant, 1988). Most likely, when an individual needs to say something and cannot retrieve or generate creative responses, that person uses another person's words from a similar situation—a TV commercial, a rule, a question, a statement, or swear words that were originally made with great emphasis—as in the example of the cat who jumped off the balcony. Some echolalia is not too different from the strategy used by most people when they repeat a word or statement to indicate confusion and a need for clarification.

Just as when learning a foreign language, an individual may be able to echo or repeat chunks of words and sentences fluently, but self-generated words and sentences are often expressed in unusual ways and are delivered slowly, laboriously, and with little expression. So it is in autism, *where words and phrases can be echoed fluently but self-generated words are slow and labored.*

Three types of echolalia are used in autism: immediate echolalia, delayed echolalia, and mitigated echolalia.

1. *Immediate echolalia*

    This classic example of immediate echolalia can go on and on until Mother simply stops the exchange in frustration.

    Mother asks, "Do you want a cookie?"
    The child replies, "Do you want a cookie?"
    Mother says, "No, do you want a cookie?"
    Child responds, "No, do you want a cookie?"

2. *Delayed echolalia*

    The ability to repeat a rule is no guarantee that the rule is understood, that the individual has an appropriate alternative response to the problem, or that behavior will change.

    Whenever Maria had problems with friends, she hit them. Soon the other children began avoiding her. Maria's teacher explained, "The rule is, don't hit; use words. Tell me the rule." Maria responded very precisely, "The rule is, don't hit; use words." A few moments later, as another problem arose, Maria hit the other child as she said, "The rule is, don't hit; use words."

3. *Mitigated echolalia*

    A form of either immediate or delayed echolalia that reflects some change from its original form. Mitigated echoing indicates some basic understanding of the words and/or meanings and attempts to fit it to a specific situation.

    Mother says: "Do you want a cookie?"
    Child says: "Want a cookie?"

Metaphorical language
Metaphorical language involves unusual and sometimes poetic-sounding sentence forms or patterns that do not clearly state the message. The listener is left to interpret the meaning by asking a sequence of questions. Metaphorical language is common in autism spectrum disorder.

    One day Gabriel approached his teacher and said, in a flat, emotionless voice, "Guess what?" He waited for the teacher to say, "What? I can't guess." "There's a wallet on the playground," he said, then waited passively. His teacher paused and thought about Gabriel's style of communication, then asked, "Is the wallet yours?"

Gabriel replied, "Yes." The teacher asked, "Did you lose your wallet?" He replied, "Yes." The teacher asked, "Do you want help to find your wallet?" He answered, "Yes." Gabriel could not deliver a message in a clear and straightforward way. With thoughtful questioning, the teacher was able to elicit his message.

———————

Gabriel opened the refrigerator door and asked his mother, "Is the candy Tom's?" (Tom was his brother.) His mother interpreted his message as she asked, "Do you want the candy?" Gabriel replied, "Yes."

Repetitive questions

Repetitive questions and sentence forms are generally used when information is desperately needed, but an effective question or statement cannot be generated. Therefore, questions or statements that are sometimes unrelated to the real need are repeated in the same way, over and over (as in the example on page 29 of José, who wanted music but kept asking for a drink). The following situation provides another example of repetitive questioning. The anxiety in these situations often erupts in major behavioral outbursts, especially if the questions are ignored.

———————

One young man enjoyed conversations with his family and the school staff. Some-times those conversations were frustrating because seemingly logical or literal answers to his questions failed to satisfy him. One day, he became more and more agitated as he repeated a question over and over, "Is it time to go swimming?" When he didn't get the information he needed, he finally lunged from his chair and raced across the room, bumping people and furniture in his way. He grabbed a magazine, flipped the pages, and pointed to a McDonald's ad as he asked, "Is it time to go to McDonald's?" *This is an example of the inability to retrieve the right words to modify a question without first seeing the word.*

———————

One child who had learned some signs, then became more verbal, cued himself with a sign before he could say the words.

Difficulties in Determining the Level of Understanding

It is difficult to know what individuals with higher functioning autism and with Aperger's disorder truly understand because of their unexpected and surprising gaps and variability. For example, those who are quite verbal often echo words and phrases that are well beyond their comprehension level. To complicate matters, some of their language is understood at a very high level when it is related to an intense interest (such as weather, flags, light bulbs, or architecture). Therefore, the general abilities of these individuals are often overestimated, leading to unrealistically high expectations and less support. These conditions trigger failure, frustration, and severe behavioral outbursts.

It is just as difficult to understand the real ability of those who do not speak. Some parents and teachers who assume that those who do not speak do not or cannot learn to understand language may stop providing verbal information. This under estimation of ability results in under stimulation and fewer opportunities to get information and learn higher-level concepts.

Those with autism become confused when they do not understand the spoken word. When they cannot express themselves freely, they become anxious and frustrated. Nearly every learning and behavior problem is, in some way, related to misunderstanding the language and the inability to express oneself effectively.

Until research shows otherwise, it is assumed that those who cannot speak do learn and respond to language in a way similar to those with autism who learn to speak.

One young man with high-functioning autism or Asperger's syndrome who did not use speech to communicate until he was 12 years old explained, "I simply didn't know that was what talking was for." After he began to talk, expectations were raised significantly. Then, "people [became] impatient when I [didn't] understand things they [thought I was] 'smart enough' to know already or to figure out for myself. . . . [People assumed] that I fail to perform as expected out of deliberate spite or unconscious hostility" (Sinclair, 1992, pp. 295–296).

Differences in Early Interaction and Communication Skills

See Chapter 17 for strategies for teaching early communication and social skills. For a summary of the research in this area, read Facilitating Early Social and Communicative Development in Children with Autism *(Klinger & Dawson, 1992). Also see Greenspan et al.,1998.*

The predisposition and preference for social stimuli that is critical to social learning is lacking or very weak in those with ASD. Social development is not automatic in these young children. "What makes autistic children 'autistic' is the quality of their (relative) engagement with others" (Hobson, 1992, p. 165). Hobson says that even the awareness of others is missing in some of these children.

> During Amy's early years, she showed little or no awareness of others. She paced about the crowded classroom with a small smile as if at some inner amusement, looking into the distance, but never at people. Arms folded across her chest as if to make herself small, she moved among her peers, never ever touching.
>
> ———
>
> After years of being taught social responses, Gabriel is still not particularly interested in people. When he is with his mother, he will greet family friends and respond to interactions that others initiate. Without his mother's presence, he never recognizes those old friends. It is as if he doesn't see them.

The inability to modulate and adapt to the abundance of stimulation provided by people and unstructured social situations is overwhelming, painful, and disorienting to most of these children whose sensory system is disrupted.

> Jeff's mother was very confused by her new baby, who was very fussy. When she picked him up to comfort him, he stiffened his body and screamed. The more she tried to comfort him, the more upset he became. Her inclination was to leave him alone.

Some babies appear to develop normally for 2 or 3 years and then begin to lose their early interactive skills until their social development is similar to those whose autism was obvious at an earlier age. Infants and young children who are later given a diagnosis of autism do not or are unable to automatically:

- Use the normal patterns of eye gaze that are the beginnings of communication—these babies look at others as often, but they do not maintain their eye contact as long as a normally developing child. They do not appear to follow people's movements, nor do they engage people with their eyes in the same way as other infants.

- Become involved in the mutual sharing of feelings and emotional engagement; thus, other people are not reinforced for continuing interactions.

- Engage in the early imitative, turn-taking exchanges; use gaze as a means of sharing attention with others.

- Signal the desire to continue an enjoyable activity or to direct the adults' attention to objects by shifting gaze, pointing, and vocalizing.

- Actively and persistently engage people to provide assistance.
- Convey a clear message.

Some individuals can enlist a communication partner but have difficulty expressing a message clearly, leaving the partner to interpret the message as seen in the previous examples of Gabriel (see page 41).

Children with autism spectrum disorders skip one of the most fundamental stages of social development as they attempt to solve their own problems, seemingly unaware that they could engage someone to help. When efforts to solve the problems are not successful, they may wander aimlessly about or resort to self-abuse or tantrums simply as a reflexive response to frustration.

At 3 years, Amy was emotionally and socially isolated but very observant; she knew that the candy was kept in the cupboard above the refrigerator. When she wanted candy, she would slide a chair to the counter, climb to the top of the refrigerator, try to open the cupboard, then scream and bang her head on the wall when the door didn't open. It never occurred to her that her mother, who was standing nearby, could make it easier.

When Kim had a problem, he would express his need very softly, but people were generally not near enough to hear. He never repeated his need; nor did he move nearer or try to attract the attention of his parents or teacher. Rather, he would pace about and eventually slap his head with his hand. This behavior was often interpreted as unpredictable, unprovoked self-abuse rather than not understanding that he needed to locate a communication partner and persist until the partner attends.

Amy needed a drink. Her teacher was sitting on the floor working with a group of other children. Amy took an empty glass from the counter and wandered about the room. As she approached her teacher, Amy backed up and sat down on her lap as if it were a pillow on the floor—she simply sat passively with no words or sounds. Because the busy teacher didn't notice the glass, she put her arm about Amy and continued to work with the other children. Amy finally got up and wandered away. A less passive child would have had a tantrum.

Tony loved to go to the burger shop down the street. He had learned to order his lunch by pointing to the pictures on the menu, pay for his meal, carry the tray, eat appropriately, and empty the trash into the trash can. However, at that point Tony sat on the floor in front of the trash can and refused to move. He became more agitated as his interpreter and other staff members tried to get him to stand up and leave the shop. Finally they removed him physically. After this happened a few times, staff was ready to terminate community outings. In assessing the situation, the behavior specialist hypothesized that perhaps Tony refused to get up because he didn't know what was to happen next and didn't realize that he could ask for information. After staff prepared and presented Tony with a basic picture sequence of the total event, including what was to happen next, he moved through the sequence with no more problems.

The ability to speak, sign, or label and point to pictures does not ensure that communication, a purposeful interaction between two people, will occur. In general, communication does not develop automatically; it must be taught. Most individuals with autism can learn to communicate spontaneously and intentionally, with varying degrees of proficiency. They can learn:

- To understand and value interactions between people
- That words and signals have power
- A method or system for sending messages, such as gestures, speaking, or pointing to words or symbols

Although these skills can be taught, often they are not used fluently, flexibly, or reliably. Learning to communicate and to interact with others is very difficult for those with autism. It rarely comes naturally or easily.

Differences in Development of Advanced Social and Communication Skills

Many of those with autism spectrum disorders, especially those with Asperger's syndrome, have considerable potential. Most individuals can learn to manage their daily care with varying levels of assistance. They are good workers and can have success in jobs or vocations that match their interests and abilities when mentors and coaches are trained to provide any needed support. However, it is the lack of social judgment and acceptable social skills that most often prevents independent participation in the community.

Not all individuals with autism are withdrawn, lack emotion and empathy, or want to avoid social situations. Many, especially those with Asperger's syndrome feel intense emotions and want to be social, but they do not understand how to express feelings or manage and understand social situations. They especially have difficulty understanding others, what others think and believe—why others do what they do. The current studies of social development in autism provides important information to clarify the nature of these problems. Four very basic skill deficits are closely associated with social deficits, the inability to automatically:

For more information about social development and social perception in autism, read Baron-Cohen, 1988; Dawson & Fernald, 1987; Dewey, 1991, 1992; Dewey & Everard, 1974; Eastham & Eastham, 1990; Frith, 1989, 1991; Hobson, 1992; Kasari, Sigman, Mundy, & Yirmiya, 1990; Sinclair, 1992; Williams, 1992, 1994; Wing, 1992; Yirmiya, Sigman, Kasari, & Mundy, 1992

1. *Understand the perspective of others* and the self from the perspective of others

2. *Identify and make sense of social information* (gestures, facial expressions, nuances of the language, etc.)

3. *Generate or formulate an appropriate response* to match the varied and rapidly changing demands of different situations

4. *Exhibit social judgment*

The effects of these deficits include the following:

- Social rules are learned rigidly and inflexibly, with little understanding that there is a range of acceptable behavior. If told what to do, they will do it exactly, every time, forever. This inflexibility makes it difficult to adapt to changes and to blend smoothly into the social world no matter how hard they try.

> A language test of prepositions required the student to indicate the answer by pointing to the appropriate picture. George was asked, "Show me behind." He responded, "That's not appropriate." To George, "behind" had a single and very literal meaning, and George had learned the rule, "Do not show people your behind; it is not appropriate." In autism, rules are fairly easy to learn, but not easy to modify or apply flexibly.

- Public behavior tends to be the same as private behavior. Without an understanding of the perspective of others in a culture, one would not feel embarrassed or automatically learn social and cultural rules and taboos.

> One young man, who lived with his grandmother, liked to go to the grocery store in the evening to play video games. One evening, his grandmother wanted him to stay home after dinner because she was too tired to go with him to supervise. To solve the problem, she hid his clothes. After his grandmother went to bed, the young man went to the store in his underwear. He had no concept of social conventions.

- Conventional behavior will seem incongruent or startling. Those with autism may see conventional behavior as inappropriate, and unconventional behavior as normal or reasonable, because they do not share a common social perspective or intuitive viewpoint (Dewey, 1991, 1992).

- An inability to organize and manage themselves appropriately in loosely structured situations at parties, during free time, breaks, weekends, and vacations.

> Robert, diagnosed with Asperger's syndrome, lived alone, worked for a major electronics firm, enjoyed his job, and was good at it. His life was fine as long as he maintained his workday routines. However, his supervisor made him take the weekends and holidays off—and worse, he had to take vacations. Robert didn't know what to do with his free time. He became bored and anxious, and the time seemed endless. The inability to manage leisure or unstructured time is a serious but common problem.
>
> ---
>
> One young man paced about the staff room cleaning up the area during breaks. He checked and moved things about in the refrigerator, cupboards, and counter with no regard for ownership. One day, he smelled each lunch bag in the refrigerator and threw away those he didn't like. While he was good at his job, he almost lost it because he was driving the staff crazy. This is an example of the inability to fill unstructured time appropriately and the lack of awareness of the effect of one's behavior on others.

- Have difficulty initiating interactions, entering into ongoing interactions, or negotiating conversations. They cannot read the subtle body language or cues indicating that others are bored or embarrassed and have a desire to change the subject or end an interaction.

> At recess time, Kim would run to the kids swinging on the bars, grab their legs, and pull them down. The children tried to avoid him because they sometimes got hurt. When the children understood that Kim simply wanted to play and when he was taught how to get involved in their play, the children lost their fear of him and helped him out. Although this behavior was initially interpreted as intentional aggression, it illustrates the behavior of a young man who wants to interact but doesn't know how to get involved. This example also highlights the importance of providing information to peers.

- Inability to focus on the relevant information when engaged in a group activity in order to have a common experience to review and share.

> After Jeff returned from his first experience at the races with friends, Jeff's dad asked, "How did you like it?" Jeff replied, "It was amazing! There were 20 sections in the bleachers, with 20 rows of 25 chairs. There were 47 flags around the track—17 were red and white, 15 were blue and yellow, and 15 were green and white." With his attention on the details, he had little ability to share the race experience in a meaningful way with others.

- Friendly social overtures, humor, and jokes are misunderstood.

> In an effort to establish a relationship with Gabriel, a new friend said, "Tell me about your family." Gabriel immediately responded, "What is 81 times 81?" When unable to respond to a broad open-ended question, Gabriel compensated with a question about numbers—a topic he understood.
>
> ────────
>
> As Gabriel was depositing his paycheck, the attractive teller said, "Hi! How are you today?" At home that night, he told his mother that the teller was his girlfriend and that probably he would marry her. The misinterpretation of casual social greetings is a common problem and can have unfortunate consequences. One young man innocently followed a girl to her home after a casual comment.

Even the most capable adults with autism and Asperger's syndrome have difficulty expressing and interpreting the range of emotion and subtle social and cultural rules that others learn automatically. The social and emotional skills they are able to use have been learned from sensitive instruction and long-term intervention. Although those with autism can learn to compensate for some of their social problems, their social interactions are rarely natural and fluent but instead are out-of-step and inappropriate in many ways. They are often dependent on others for organizing and interpreting social situations and for keeping conversations going.

For discussion of intervention and teaching strategies to address the social problems, see Chapters 19, 21, and 22. Also see Greenspan et al., 1998; Baron-Cohen et al., 1993.

Their natural innocence, honesty, guilelessness, and lack of social judgment make them vulnerable to exploitation. They are often misunderstood and easily hurt and they sometimes physically lash out when corrected or teased.

Summary

Wing has suggested that individuals with ASD can be separated into three groups just by the way they handle themselves in social situations (Wing & Attwood, 1987).

1. *Those who appear to be aloof, cut off, and withdrawn.* They are observed on the edges of a social situation, either watching other people socialize or randomly exploring the environment, seemingly oblivious to the interactions going on about them. They are particularly sensitive to the noise, touch, and movement of people. Some of those in this group enjoy a measure of physical contact when they can initiate it themselves and can end it at will. They generally have few reliable communication and social skills, so they are dependent on others to read their limited signals.

2. *Those who are fairly passive.* These individuals also watch interactions and make few social approaches. However, they willingly respond if others initiate an approach, and they are easily led into activities. They often try to fit in by imitating others, but they do not really understand the complexities of the situation. Although they seem to want friends, they misinterpret casual social remarks and are easily hurt by rebuffs and being left out.

3. *Those who are active but odd.* These individuals are actively involved in social situations, blithely unaware of the effect of their behavior on others. These individuals often pursue their intense interests, unaware that their reluctant partners are trying to extricate themselves from one-sided conversations, recitations of facts, or repetitive questions. They appear to know more than they can demonstrate, and their abilities are frequently overestimated because they have some reasonably good social and communication skills. These individuals are easily upset and sometimes aggressive if confused or misunderstood. Many of those with Asperger's syndrome would probably fit into this group (Wing, 1992).

The profound effect of the learning-style differences in autism spectrum disorders cannot be overemphasized. These differences have an incredibly pervasive effect on the ability to interpret the social world and respond to typical situations. Most individuals with autism are unable to tell us when or why they are confused or frustrated. Because they are unable to derive coherent meaning from their experiences and operate from such a different perspective, they are dependent upon us, their parents, teachers, and mentors, to help them make sense of things.

People who are deaf or blind are dependent on others to interpret their world, to organize information, and to give them the tools to function in their world. Although those with autism may be able to see and hear, they have difficulty processing and making sense of the things they see and hear. They, too, need interpreters who can organize information, give them guidance, and design the tools to help them function more independently in the community.

2

Assessment

YOUTH SO SOBER

YOUTH NEED HELP
FROM EVRY SOURCE
HELP US FIND A WAY
SEE OUR NEEDS
HOPE YOU WILL STAY
HELP US FIND A WAY

BE THERE FOR US
FET TO KNOW US
SEE WHO WE ARE

TALK

HOW I ONLY WANT TO TALK
GOD GRANT ME THAT DREAM
YOUTH NEEDS TO WONDER
WHY HIM?
UNUSUAL ROW TO HOE
IT SEEMS

UNDERSTAND THE SILENCE
ROARS IN MY HEAD
TOO ROTTEN YOUTH SAID
PERHAPS IT WILL END

—David Eastham
In UNDERSTAND: Fifty Memowriter Poems

*David sometimes called himself Youth.

4

Parents' Role—Preparing for the Marathon

Once a child is suspected of having an autism spectrum disorder, those suspicions must be confirmed or denied. Parents are understandably anxious and frustrated at this time, not only because they are worried about their child's future, but for a variety of other reasons.

- Parents continue to be worried and fearful. They have probably known or at least suspected for some time that their child was not developing normally. Now, they are relieved yet fearful that they will soon have some answers. If their fears are confirmed, they must deal with an unknown future. If their fears are denied, they must continue to seek answers.

- Parents are tired. In addition to the stress and fears associated with their search for answers, their child has required almost constant supervision. Parents also have other responsibilities that drain their energy—careers and family responsibilities. Many parents have other children or aging parents that require attention.

- Parents are often confused by their many questions and concerns. Where do they go for evaluations and services? What kind of services? Perhaps, they have received conflicting information from various individuals: family, other parents and professionals and from their search of the library and web sites.

- Parents are frustrated. They often do not know how to evaluate the mass of information they encounter. Once they get into a system, there seems to be duplication and delay. This delay is particularly frustrating if parents have been told that their child's best hope is early intervention.

- Parents may also be concerned about who to trust. Parents want to trust the professionals, but some other parents may have told them that professionals cannot be trusted.

These fears and concerns are valid and must be acknowledged by the professionals. In many parts of the world today, it continues to be difficult to find medical and educational professionals who have extensive training and experience with autism. There are at least two reasons for this. First, until quite recently, there were few children with a diagnosis of autism or autism spectrum disorders. So there was never a major demand for specialized training and little opportunity to gain experience.

A second reason for the limited number of experienced professionals is that comprehensive autism training is not easy to obtain. Several major universities, medical schools, public autism service agencies, and a few private autism centers offer excellent training, but it is often expensive and may require considerable travel. Furthermore, the autism training is all too often brief and without the critical follow-up opportunities necessary for real mastery.

The situation has improved in the United States since the enactment of the Individuals with Disabilities Education Act (IDEA). IDEA requires public school systems to identify their students with autism spectrum disorders and to provide a free and appropriate public education for all children, ages 0 to 21. With this mandate, autism resources and services in public schools have expanded. As the numbers of identified students grow, more professionals in many fields receive specialized training and gain experience. However, the need for specialized autism training continues to be a high priority for parents, administrators, teachers, therapists and uncertified aides, and job coaches in the schools and in other community agencies.

The purpose of this chapter is to provide some basic information that will guide and support parents through this most difficult period. If parents and professionals have access to this same information, it can help to establish trusting and cooperative working relationships that can benefit everyone, but especially the children.

The mother of two sons, one with an autism spectrum disorder, Gerlach (1998) adds a touch of perspective by reminding parents that they must play an active role in advocating for their children. They must be involved in dealing with their child's education, and how the school district serves the child's needs; they must persevere with insurance companies to make sure they get all the treatment possible for the child; and they must build a network of cooperative support among family, friends, and service providers. In short, parents must be willing to extend themselves as much and as often as possible on behalf of their child. She reminds parents that "[L]iving with autism is like running a marathon , not a sprint. . . . There is no Magical Mystery Cure, but we must not give up hope for greater understanding of the nature of autism and effective treatments to relieve its symptoms" (Gerlach, 1998, p. 7)

Evaluating the Mass of Information

Evaluating reports of research, family stories, media reports, and the mass of information on the web is complex and exhausting. These five strategies provide a basic screening process.

1. *Any information that proposes the theory that autism is caused by parental rejection* is outdated and unsound. This theory was established before the neurobiological basis of autism was discovered.

2. *Family stories provide valuable and varied perspectives*—however, their child, their family, their perspective, and their resources are not likely to be the same as yours. Consider what they say, but remember that your child's characteristics, your family values, and your resources will be different.

3. *Any material that suggests the use of aversives or punishment* to eliminate inappropriate or "bad" behavior is outdated and of little value for those within the spectrum of autism. This book provides numerous strategies for preventing the "bad" behaviors by teaching more positive ways to communicate and manage frustrations.

4. *Be cautious about the outcomes reported in research papers.* Without more technical information than is possible in this space, it is difficult to determine if those results will have any implications for your specific child. If possible, find knowledgeable people who understand the research and have them explain how or if the outcome of the research would apply.

5. *Any strategy or program that promises or offers a cure*, or suggests that it is the only valid program or strategy, should be rejected. As Gerlach said, there are no "Magical Mystery Cures." The most current reports are that the best approach is one that integrates the best aspects of many different models to match the child's individual needs (Feinberg & Vacca, 2000).

This position is also supported by Rimland (1999, p. 3) who said, "I am dismayed and appalled at the ludicrous position taken by many . . . who claim that Applied Behavior Analysis is the only scientifically validated treatment for autism. Not so! That position is not only false, it is absurd." Simpson (2001) supports Rimland's statement, and expands it by saying, " . . . it is prudent to individualize strategies to fit children and families . . . it is (my) opinion that there is neither a cure for autism nor a single strategy that should exclusively be used to meet the varied needs of those with autism spectrum disorder" (p. 70).

The Parents as Advocates

As noted earlier, one of the primary roles of the parents is advocate. They soon discover that having a child with autism spectrum disorders can become a full-time career that must be balanced with other commitments and duties. Many parents have expanded their advocacy for their own child into careers that improve life for others dealing with autism. The following guidelines can help parents deal with this balancing act.

1. *Educate yourself about autism and special education laws.* This is perhaps the first and most important place to begin. Depending on the parent's preferences, the search may begin at the local library or bookstore, or on the Internet. Begin your search with books that cover the basic issues for understanding the spectrum of autism and information about resources.

   Parents might begin with *Autism: Facts and Strategies for Parents* (Janzen, 1999). This small book would also be an easy-to-read resource for grandparents and other family members and friends to help them understand the problems and issues. This book would also provide quick information for a teacher or administrator who is new to the field.

   The Autism Treatment Guide, Revised (Gerlach, 2000) will save parents a lot of time, for this tiny book provides descriptions and contact information for numerous autism resources, strategies, and programs.

   See Appendix B for web sites, journals, organizations, and other resources.

2. *Seek help from a professional advisor or advocate—one with whom you feel comfortable.* They can provide information that will guide you through the systems. Check first to see if they understand autism and the varied needs of this group of children. This person could be involved in the local early intervention or school program, or associated with an evaluation center. Ask questions and do not be afraid to interrupt a meeting to ask for clarification of terms. Parents have a need and a right to understand all aspects of their child's needs if they are to be effective advocates.

3. *Locate a parent support group* for emotional support and to share information about autism and about services. Be cautious, however; as noted above, no two children will need the exact same intervention strategies or programs. Parents in the United States can locate a local parent group by calling the Autism Society of America (ASA) at 1-800-3AUTISM. ASA has chapters in every state—it sponsors major conferences each summer and publishes a quarterly newsletter, *The Advocate.*

4. *Parents must take care of themselves and their family.* A child's greatest need is to have an emotionally and physically healthy family. Other children and family members will also be concerned, fearful, and even a bit lost because so much parental energy must be focused on the child with autism. Part of this parental energy is naturally expended in the grieving process.

Involve the extended family, grandparents, aunts, and uncles—also friends and neighbors. Give them information about autism and tell them how they can help, for parents do need help. This is particularly true of single parents. Support of family and friends can make it possible for the parents to have some critical relief and time for themselves, with friends, and with their other children.

Leaving their child in the care of another person causes most parents considerable anxiety. Simply remember that safety is the primary concern. Although these children may become upset in a new setting, it is actually important for them to learn that it is okay to be with others and to be in other places.

Finally, take one day at a time. Parents must learn to live with the reality of today, avoid dwelling on the what-ifs and what-thens of the future. Look for and cherish the good things, the small successes, and the humorous events that happen each day.

5. *Organize your child's life.* Those with autism are more relaxed, more purposeful, and happier when their life has order—when they know what is going to happen next, when each day has a fairly dependable structure to it. Parents can work with their child's teacher to develop ways to provide the structure these children need, both at home and school. (See Chapters 8–15 for ways to organize the child's environment, time, and activities, and for ways to give clear directions.)

6. *Set priorities and ask for help.* Most early childhood and public educational programs require a team approach for making decisions and solving the problems that every child encounters. One of your highest priorities is to develop a trusting relationship with this team. When parents trust the team, they can periodically—at least for short periods—focus on other pressing family priorities. Remember that every family must set priorities and give differing amount of energy to the most critical issues at any given time.

7. *Keep track; start a file.* The parent must balance many roles: parent, advocate, interpreter, and manager of information. Parents need to keep records of assessments, anecdotal information about developmental milestones, problems, and service plans. This information must be clear, dated, and above all, kept in some kind of order. This information will be used many times over the years. Perhaps the most important time to have these records is at transition times, when moving to a new school or school system, but especially when moving from educational to adult services.

Keep a notebook available for notes from a teacher, for a record of phone calls if there is a problem. Keeping a record of any changes in the child's behavior can be very helpful when working with the school team to prevent or resolve a learning or behavior problem. This kind of information can be invaluable for a new teacher or respite provider and help them understand the needs of this specific child.

8. *Forgive yourself.* Each family does its best. Stress will likely be a constant companion, and occasionally, parents will make mistakes. They must remember that they are only human, and humans are not perfect. Mistakes here and there are not likely to do permanent damage to a child. Parents must take a deep breath and move on—learning from their mistakes but keeping their perspective. Sometime in the future, most parents find humor in some of these situations.

Finally, the role of advocate is daunting but will be easier with experience. A parent's most important role is to love their child and his or her unique qualities and gifts. Rejoice in small successes. Although it may take time to realize, parents are engaged in perhaps the most creative journey of their life.

Parent/Professional Relationships

Parents and professionals have had many experiences that have affected or shaped their attitudes. When beginning a new relationship to provide the best possible program for a child with an autism spectrum disorder, it is important to enter with an open and accepting attitude. Parents cannot judge a specific professional from their experiences with other professionals nor can they always make judgments about professional competence on the basis of another parent's report. Furthermore, professionals cannot judge a parent by their experiences with any other parent. Each relationship is new and has the potential to be positive.

Because autism is such a complex problem, the ideal situation is for the parents and the professionals to build a sharing and problem-solving relationship or partnership. This type of relationship is supportive and productive for all. Each member of the parent/professional partnership plays a unique role. Both the parents and the professionals have concerns and frustrations:

- Parents have the responsibility to be lifelong advocates for their children. They have a wealth of critical information to share; they have the knowledge of their child's history. Therefore, they must become experts in autism. It is reasonable for parents to check a professional's training and experience; professionals must not feel threatened by parents who have a broad knowledge of autism or who ask about credentials. Rather, parents can be engaged as valuable resources.

- Professionals are skilled and experienced in their own fields and have much to offer both the parents and the child. An effective professional continually seeks information and training about autism issues and strategies, consults with experts, and encourages a cooperative and sharing relationship with parents. An effective professional is never hesitant to say, "I don't know, but let's find out."

- Educators can become defensive because they feel helpless in the face of parents' frustration. Often, professionals are caught in a bind between their concern for the child and family, overwhelming caseloads, and a system that is often short of operating funds and that sometimes seems rigid.

In summary, an open and positive parent/professional relationship is an essential component for any educational program to have positive results. When the home and school can work cooperatively, the child will always benefit.

Accessing Educational Services

Those involved in the educational system do many things because of federal, state, and local laws and administrative requirements. The requirements protect the rights of the child and the family and ensure unbiased and appropriate services. Some requirements also protect the school and school staff. "Paper trails" prove that the correct procedures were followed. Schools are monitored by state and federal education agencies to see that they follow the requirements of the law. If a school system does not comply with the law, it loses federal money and could be open to lawsuits.

The Individuals with Disabilities Education Act (IDEA) specifies that before children can receive special education services, they must be evaluated to determine if they meet the *eligibility criteria outlined in the administrative rules.* Although the process differs somewhat from state to state, the law stipulates that: (a) the evaluation is conducted at no cost to parents, (b) parents must receive written notification of their rights, and (c) they must give their signed consent for the evaluation to occur. To understand your child's rights under the law, see Martin (2000, 2001).

This evaluation process generally includes some or all of the following activities:

- Interviews with parents and a review of the records of past evaluations and diagnoses to document the presence of the indicators of an ASD during earlier development.

- Observations of the child in different settings on different days.

- Interviews with the current or former teacher, or care provider, if any, to identify how the child's behavior differs from the behavior of others of the same age.

- Completion of a speech and language assessment. This assessment generally involves interviews with parents and teachers.

- Completion of a standardized intelligence test and/or developmental rating scale.

- An evaluation of sensory and motor processing skills, and developmental issues.

- Completion of a hearing test.

- Completion of a standardized autism rating scale or checklist. Because autism behavior looks different in different situations, it is critical that this checklist be completed by or with information from one or more people (parents, teachers, and others) who know the child very well and have knowledge of the child's behavior in different situations.

- Receipt of a physician's statement indicating whether any physical factors are contributing to the child's learning problems or need to be addressed by the school.

- Some states may require a physician's diagnosis based on the *DSM–IV* criteria. In other countries, the ICD–10 criteria is used and the process will likely be different.

At the conclusion of this evaluation, the team has information to determine eligibility as well as some of the important information for developing a child's educational plan.

Preparation for the Evaluation and Assessments

Parents who are not already familiar with autism spectrum disorders need some basic information before the evaluation. They must know why autism is suspected and why it is important to recognize the condition if it is present. This basic information is available in Chapters 1–3; other information about the nature of autism would be available from the local school's Special Education Department.

Parents should prepare for the evaluation by making notes of important information. There are a number of reasons for these notes:

- It is often difficult to remember important facts when in a stressful interview.

- Sometimes a child will not show the behaviors of concern during the observation.

- The evaluator's questions may not trigger some of the significant information.

Figure 4.1 Sample: Anecdotal Description of Behaviors

The italicized labels are added to show significance. An actual description would not include these labels.

- Tommy does not seem to hear some loud noises, for example, trucks going by on the street or a door banging, but frantically covers his ears and runs to hide under the table when a specific song is played or when a spoon clinks against a cup (*sensory responses*). He has never answered or come to me when I call his name (*language; lack of meaning*). When he wants something in the cupboard, he gets a chair and climbs up on the counter. If he can't get the door open, he will scream and have a tantrum rather than ask for help (*communication*).

- Whenever he sees a number, he jumps up and down and flaps his hands (*sensory responses*) and begins to count. I have heard him count to 1,000, then quickly count backward to 1. He can label any number he sees (*developmental discrepancy*). The only time we have heard him talk is when he counts or labels numbers (*communication; developmental discrepancy*). The only time he smiles and interacts with us is when we have blocks, cards, or puzzles with numbers on them (*relating to people*).

- When he is alone, he lines up the blocks or cards in a specific order and gets very upset when we stop him (*relating to environment; resisting change*). Frequently he will walk with his head close to walls, fences, or large pieces of furniture so he can "sight" (*sensory responses*). When we have guests who try to hug him, he pushes them away and runs to hide (*relating to people; sensory responses*). . . .

The list can be left with the evaluator at the end of the interview for review while summarizing the evaluation data.

Parents must be prepared to answer questions about:

- Family history. Report any information regarding family members with developmental problems, health of parents, the course of the pregnancy and delivery, and similar questions. Because this information helps to identify factors that may have caused the child's developmental problems, these questions will most likely be asked during the medical evaluation.

- Developmental milestones. At what age did the child first roll over? sit up? walk? smile? say first words? Often it is helpful to have a baby book or medical records available for reference during interviews.

- Information about the child's behavior. See the test forms in Chapter 5 for examples of the questions parents must be prepared to answer—and be prepared with specific examples of the child's behavior—and review Figure 1.1 in Chapter 1. Other evaluators may use different forms and procedures, but the questions will be similar.

Parents also need to be aware of a few other issues related to the evaluations:

- Sometimes the interview questions may seem too personal and perhaps irrelevant to the issue of diagnosing autism or determining eligibility for services. Parents must feel free to ask about the purpose of such questions. They have a right to challenge and refuse to answer any question or statement that suggests they caused their child's autism. The myth that autism is caused by parental rejection or lack of love must not intrude into current practice.

For additional information and strategies for forming more collaborative and effective parent/ professional relationships, see Janzen, 1999; Turnbull & Turnbull, 1990; and Wright & Wright, 2001.

- The diagnostic criteria outlined in the *DSM–IV* is different than the eligibility criteria for special educational services. Also, the eligibility criteria sometimes differs somewhat from state to state. Confusing? This could mean that if a physician or a psychologist determines that a child does not have autism as defined by the *DSM–IV*, the child might still be eligible for autism services through the public school system.

- In some cases, parents or a teacher will identify subtle but very real indicators of autism in a child who is quite verbal and who functions quite well. These signs may not be apparent to the evaluator, or they may seem so mild that they are seen as individual idiosyncrasies not relevant to the child's future development. Consequently, it may be determined that the child does not qualify for autism services. In these cases, the parents and/or the teacher have several options. They can:

    - Ask that the evaluation data be reviewed with the parent so they can provide additional information or correct any information that may have been misinterpreted.

    - Continue to document the subtle signs and when the indicators are more apparent, ask for another evaluation.

    - Ask for an independent evaluation by someone outside the system. The law has provisions for the local school to pay for an independent evaluation in such cases.

Finally, it is important for parents to direct any questions to the appropriate professional. If questions are directed to the wrong person, the answers may be inaccurate, incomplete, and/or misleading. However, when the teacher, physician, and parent share information, the child benefits.

- A teacher is not qualified to discuss the specific causes of autism, related medical problems, or medications.

- A physician is not qualified to suggest educational programs or strategies.

- It is rarely helpful to ask medical or educational professionals to predict a child's potential. There are simply too many variables to make such a prediction with any degree of certainty. The outcome for those with autism is very different today from what it was before appropriate early intervention and special education were available.

Finally, this is the prime time for parents to begin compiling their child's educational and medical records. There will be many times in the future that they will be needed for reference.

See Appendix B for information and resources for advocates.

Summary

The importance of identifying autism spectrum disorders and providing appropriate services cannot be overemphasized. Parents play an important role in an evaluation to determine eligibility for special education services, as well as in the process of developing an appropriate program that addresses the unique needs of their child. Although parents are often highly stressed during this period of uncertainty, the evaluation process provides an opportunity to establish a trusting and cooperative parent/professional relationships that are of major importance for the success of the child. The marathon has truly begun.

Dean's Story

—Written by his mother, Elaine Piper-Vardas

The day had begun sunny and warm. Dean was dressed in his blue pajamas. His hair was long and brown and curled softly around his face. Dean was particularly relaxed and calm as he looked at me from across the room. This morning would mark our final moments as mother and son in a home we had shared together since his birth. Soon Dean's new parents would arrive. His clothes and a few personal possessions were packed into their large, old station wagon. The image of them driving away is burned into my memory forever.

Dean was born March 26, 1970. A year later, he was diagnosed as mentally retarded. A few years later, Dean's father and I divorced. The diagnosis of autism came many years later, when Dean was 9. After many months and long hours of counseling and training, the stark reality set in. As a single working mom, I could not provide the stable home my son needed. The continued turnover of baby-sitters and the inability to find trained, reliable day-care providers made matters worse. Few people wanted to take care of this child with his bizarre behaviors. I felt alone and scared. As the years passed, Dean's behavior worsened from constant screaming into head-banging on the floor and self-abuse. Now I felt afraid. What would his future bring? Who would take care of him as he grew into adulthood? How would I be able to protect him? Who would serve as his advocate in matters of health, education, and family? I realized that I could not care for Dean alone and would need outside help.

I immersed myself into (developmental disabilities) organizations and worked to establish (a 24-hour special needs care facility for developmentally disabled children). I explained to Sister Marian Kathleen the difficulty Dean was having. She told me about a foster family she knew. Within 2 weeks of that conversation, Dean was off to a new life with (his new) family.

Dean was 5 years old. The year was 1975. It was the year we both put our emotional heads through walls. Dean did not understand this change in his life. For the next 3 months, I was not allowed to see Dean. It was a long and tortured time for us. For me, it was a time of agonizing self-punishment. I wanted Dean to have a family—a full-time mother and father with a stable home to support his needs. But I also wanted to be a mother. Then, when I was allowed to visit my son, he ignored me. I remember well that first visit and the sense of devastating rejection. While driving home after that first visit, I cried so hard that I ran into another car. For years, I felt guilt and self-doubt, believing that I had somehow failed. It took Dean many months to accept his new home. It took me many years before I would be able to recognize the wisdom of my decision.

His new foster mother was a great mother. She gave him love, stability, and a family with six children. Their lives were always full of happenings. Dean lived in a real world. He was not protected from chaos. (He went) off to visit (other families), off to Disneyland, off to spend the weekend with Mom. (His new mother) and I became great friends, and I learned to respect her quiet authority and her genuine love for others. The three of us would go on long drives. Dean always loved the open road and a big hamburger at the end of each journey. We spent weekends at the beach several times each year. There were many adventures for Dean, all of which have helped him to develop into the person he is today. He can participate in large groups and go to the mall, out to eat, and to sporting events. He loves a good party. (Just watch out for your wine glass!)

For my part, I had to back away from full-time parenting into the role of advocate. I channeled those parenting energies into organizations and committees that benefit people with disabilities. At one point, I was president of the Autism Council of Oregon.

When Dean was 13 years old, he spent several weeks at the hospital, recovering from spinal rod surgery. Because (his foster mother) was not able to stay with him during this time, I stayed with Dean in the hospital during his recovery. I relished playing the role of caregiver to my son. His foster mother and I grew to respect and love one another—we laughed and cried together. It was during these times that I came to realize that it would take more than one heart, one pair of hands, one person to provide Dean with a good life.

As Dean grew older, it was obvious that his foster family could not continue to care for him. At 21 years old, he was 5'8" and weighed 130 pounds. His outbursts were not as frequent but because of his size, they required more care and physical strength. He required someone to bathe and dress him, brush his teeth, and prepare his meals. He wouldn't be able to get himself out of a house fire. All this and more made caring for Dean a challenge. So we began the search for a new foster home. The agony of wondering whether we would ever find Dean "the right home" took its toll on all of us. It was a difficult and delicate issue because of limited resources, the pressure to make a selection, and the need to respect that gut feeling about which place would be best for my son. Finally (a new family was selected and they agreed) to become Dean's new foster parents.

Just as before, the transition was a nightmare. Difficulty in funding accelerated the transition beyond Dean's ability to accept the changes. He was completely out of control—mad, frustrated, and angry. He seriously abused himself and others. [Note: Dean ultimately spent a week in the psychiatric wing of the local Health Sciences Center for evaluation and to adjust to medication.] Dean showed his strength to survive. His character and life's experiences helped him during a desperate and difficult time.

(At his new home), Dean is respected as an autistic person. (His new mother) keeps herself informed through autism seminars and specialized training which has helped her to create a positive, loving environment. He is always part of the decision-making process and is helped to understand what is expected of him and what will occur. Each stage of change is explained. (His new father's) patience and intuitive skills have helped to accomplish much in Dean's life. (Dean has learned many new skills, he is more social, and is communicating more.) This is a positive and loving family environment. Dean again has a stable, loving home.

An update, 8 years later:

(Dean is now 32 years old.) Most recently, I have had to deal with the physical and emotional realities of a pedophile in close proximity of my son. Though it is believed that Dean was not sexually molested, the experience tore at the fiber of my feelings and sense of motherhood to have him so close to this danger during this time. My son also experienced a severe seizure that has hampered his ability to understand verbal commands and walk. All of this has resulted in the likelihood that we will ultimately have to seek out an alternative residential situation more suitable to my son's changing needs.

I am just thankful that he can walk. I wonder how much longer he can negotiate stairs and lift himself out of a chair. . . . This is my new dilemma. Dean is no longer able to stand up on his own to get out of the bathtub—my husband now must assist him up to his feet and out of the tub. My husband is not going to be able to do this for the long run. We are aging parents and just as Dean's body is degenerating, we are too. It is a frightening time in our lives. My struggle emotionally and physically is to accept these new limitations that Dean's health issues present to us. The struggle is one of expectations. Early on I fought for his every need, defended him at school, at hospitals and in the community. However, I am coming to the realization that I may have to gear expectations differently. . . . Now I struggle for ways to accept his fate and just let him live his journey. . . .

(I) worry over use of and consequences of the many medications he must take . . . it is an ongoing experiment to control behavior, regularity, and seizures . . . and I haven't a clue if we are doing the right thing . . . if his body and mind are further being harmed by all the medications . . . (is there) some other way. . . . (How do we find medical and dental care providers who are) experienced, knowledgeable and willing to take Dean as a client. . . . (Money is a worry) . . . the cost of an aide to help with Dean on weekends would be 4 hours minimum at $18 an hour. What do we do for a trust for Dean that will go for his needs and not affect his Medicare and state benefits? All we come up with is more questions and a feeling of being overwhelmed. Maybe in another 5 years we will have better answers for you. The journey toward my own peace is a bumpy road.

My advice to all parents is to develop for your child a circle of support consisting of professionals and friends who will love and support your child and assist in the decision making for your child's future. After Dean had his severe seizure, we were able to have a meeting at home regarding future planning for Dean that included his doctor, foster home provider, his former teacher, and the staff from his day program. The meeting fostered a better understanding of my son's condition, options for care and a direction for helping Dean. It was also very beneficial for me as a parent to see such devotion to my son.

Over the past 5 years I recognized the heartfelt need to dedicate time and energy for the development of community resources, individualized services and the assurance for a quality of life for those we love . . . (who have) developmental disabilities. During this time I chaired the (State) Commission for Self-Directed Supports comprised of parents, advisors, providers and government representatives charged with the responsibility to establish a broker system for the distribution of dollars to the developmental disabilities community. Out of the experience of dealing with systemic roadblocks and challenges to the commission's intent has come the development of a DD ombudsman model for the resolution of conflicts and difficulties.

Developing working partnerships with providers, governmental agencies and private citizens is still the best bet to attain a true quality of life for the individuals and families in our communities. Question everything! . . . and verify the information you are given. Challenge authority and yourself to find better ways. . . . At the same time, we must learn to trust each other and make each of us accountable for the truth.

Finally, take time to nurture yourself and those you treasure. We as families must have respite so we can continue with renewed vigor to develop ideas and rewarding futures for those we love.

Assessment for Diagnosis and Program Development

A diagnosis of autism spectrum disorders is based on information about a child's development and about how that child moves, thinks, interacts, and communicates in the natural environment. An appropriate program is based on more precise information about the individual's current abilities, the individual's deficits that impact multiple areas of life, and the environmental conditions that impact the individual's ability to focus and learn. To obtain accurate and useful information, an evaluator first must understand the implications of autism on learning and thinking, communication, and behavior (see Chapters 2, 3, and 8). With this understanding, appropriate assessment tools and procedures can be selected and administered; furthermore, behavioral responses can be interpreted more accurately and specifically.

A comprehensive assessment for those with ASD includes both standardized testing and functional assessment procedures. Because the student's educational goals are selected from the following three sources, each area must be assessed:

1. *The goals that address the learning and thinking differences* and deficits that affect the ability to automatically learn critical life skills.

2. *The chronological, age-appropriate developmental skills,* such as language, social, motor, or academic skills.

3. *The functional skills needed for independence* in the home, school, and community.

As noted earlier, parents are the prime source of information about their child's development and functioning. Evaluators enlist the help of both parents and teachers to provide the details of a child's behavior in different situations or conditions that must be considered as a program is developed. This chapter presents information about both the standardized and functional assessment processes and the strategies for obtaining the most useful information.

Standardized Testing

Problems With Standardized Procedures

There are only a few tests standardized for use with those who have autism. The results of many standardized procedures are often of questionable value. The reliability of the scores is affected because those with autism:

■ Display wide discrepancies between visual/motor tasks and those with auditory and verbal demands; between concrete, factual, and rule-based requirements and those that require abstract reasoning and judgment.

■ Display variable ability to perform from day to day or at different times during a day.

■ May not understand the language specified in the standardized procedures, may interpret the language literally, or may be unable to communicate responses effectively.

- May become anxious and unable to perform in situations involving unfamiliar people, settings, materials, and schedule changes.

- May show little motivation to complete tasks and may attempt to avoid the situation or leave the area.

- May become distracted, disorganized, and lose concentration between tasks.

Planning the Assessment

With foresight, a highly skilled examiner can increase the likelihood of obtaining useful results.

1. *Talk with parents and teachers before the testing sessions* to obtain information about reinforcers, the nature of processing delays, the potential triggers for tantrums and out-of-control behavior, and to understand unique language and communication issues. For example, it is important to know:

   - If the individual can reliably use *yes* and *no* to answer questions.

   - If gestures, pictures, or sign language help the individual understand directions.

   - If any words or phrases have unexpected meaning for the individual (for example, "bye" meaning "all done" or "no").

   - How the individual indicates a need for a drink or to go to the bathroom

2. *Arrange for parents or a teacher to observe* the assessment session to verify the results. Otherwise, prepare to videotape the session and review the performance with parents or teachers later. Having parents or a teacher verify the interpretations avoids the possibility that some seemingly irrelevant detail, a subtle sensory problem, or motivation issue does not affect the outcome.

   > While being observed in the play area, Amy was busily engaged at the dollhouse, placing the tiny furniture and talking to the dolls. The play looked creative. However, her mother reported that Amy did and said exactly the same things each time she played with the dollhouse. Without mother's knowledge of Amy's play, the examiner would have interpreted this highly repetitive routine as creative play.

   > ---

   > As Tony watched, the examiner placed a piece of candy under one of three cups on the table, moved the cups about, and directed Tony to "find the candy." Tony continued to rock back and forth in his chair. After several attempts to get a response, Tony's father suggested that the candy be replaced by the strings that Tony flipped repetitively. As this was done, the child immediately became alert, watched the cups intently, and located the cup to find his strings. Like most children with autism, Tony was not motivated by typical reinforcers.

3. *To prevent fatigue and maintain an optimal level of performance,* schedule several short testing sessions rather than one long session.

4. *Develop a relationship with the individual before testing.* Visit the classroom for an introduction, and/or invite the student to the evaluation room before the testing date. Make certain that the teacher prepares the student for this change before test time. Allow some time for exploration of the room before testing begins.

To prepare Jeff for an unexpected testing session, his teacher said, "Jeff, there is a change. At 10:00 you will go to Mr. Brown's office and work with him. When you finish that work, you will come back to class and work with the math flash cards." (Working with the flash cards is a well-liked activity.) As she talked, the teacher printed the new information on a small sticky-note and pasted it on his calendar over the previously planned activities. The note read:

1. Work with Mr. Brown

2. Math flash cards

At 10:00, the teacher gave Jeff the sticky-note and walked with him to Mr. Brown's room. Mr. Brown quickly introduced himself and showed Jeff the things in the room. Jeff watched as Mr. Brown printed out and explained the work schedule, with breaks interspersed between test tasks. The last item on the list was: Math flash cards. As tasks were completed, Jeff crossed them off the list. When all tasks were crossed out, he returned to class with his sticky-note and independently started working with the flash cards.

5. *Select tests that provide separate measures* of language and nonlanguage skills, or use a battery of tests that contains both language- and nonlanguage-based tasks.

6. *Present a broad range of tasks* and begin testing at a point well below the individual's chronological age to ensure success and avoid frustration on initial test items. Continue testing beyond the standardization criteria to identify more advanced skills.

7. *Have note paper or 3" x 5" cards available* for preparing quick visual supports (see Chapter 14).

8. *Place a box or similar container on the floor within reach.* As each task is finished, allow the individual to place the materials in the "Finished" box.

9. *Break from the standardized procedures to probe*, to determine the type or level of support needed for the individual to respond correctly.

10. *End the session while the student is working at an optimal level. Be alert to subtle, nonverbal signs of fatigue, frustration, or confusion.* Respond by altering or adapting the situation in some way to keep the performance at an optimal level and to prevent possible behavioral outbursts. It is better to end the session positively and schedule another session than to create a major behavioral storm that ends with the student wanting to avoid future testing situations.

Strategies to Manage Problems During Testing

Problem: Apparent Lack of Motivation to Complete Tasks

1. *If some parts of the directions are unclear*, the individual often does nothing.

   - Direct the student's attention to the task with nonverbal cues before giving a direction (e.g., shift the material or tap the table near the material).

   - Do not require eye contact, especially if the student is focusing on the materials. The insistence on eye contact can increase stress and distract attention from the materials. Some individuals have difficulty shifting their attention back to the materials.

   - Use gestures to clarify directions.

- Give the directions nonverbally. Model, draw a diagram, or list the sequence or steps required to follow the directions.

- Use only important words when giving directions. Omit unnecessary words and polite forms. Use specific and literal language (e.g., "Put your hands on the table," "Give me the *picture* of the cow").

- Clarify the response mode. Is the student to point, give, draw a circle around, or tell you the answer?

2. *If the individual has a processing delay,* there may be as much as 30 to 60 seconds between a verbal request and a response.

- Pause after giving a request to allow time for processing the request and generating a response.

- Provide a visual reference when restating or rephrasing the directions. Then wait.

3. *If the individual has difficulty initiating and carrying out a motor action* (to point or to give a verbal response), the lack of response may appear to be lack of motivation or noncompliance.

- Provide firm but passive physical support to the hand, wrist, or arm. This type of support can help some individuals focus and initiate a motor response. See page 255 for an illustration of different types of passive support—you are *not* directing the child's hand toward a specific response. This support is different than the more traditional and directive or forceful physical prompting or physical guidance procedures.

4. *If the task is too easy or without meaning* to the individual or the reinforcer is not valued, the lack of response may appear to be laziness or lethargy.

> One test requires the examiner to set out three picture cards and say, "Give me the picture of ____." If there is no response or if there is an error, the examiner makes the task easier (removes one of the cards). When this task was presented, Tony sat quietly and stared out the window. When Mr. Brown removed a card and repeated the request, Tony continued to stare out the window. At this point, Tony's teacher, who was observing the session, suggested that the examiner spread all the cards on the table. As Mr. Brown spread the cards, Tony sat up and scanned them. When the examiner repeated the same request again, Tony quickly picked up the correct card. Tony saw no reason to attend to a boring task with no challenge.

- Acknowledge that some of the tasks may be too easy or seem silly.

- Identify real reinforcers before the session begins. Make sure that these reinforcers can be seen clearly.

- Use contingency statements to direct attention to the expectation (e.g., "Two more, then it's time for a break.").

5. *If the task is too hard,* lack of response may appear to be lack of motivation.

- Ask, "Do you know the answer?" or "Do you know how to do this?" Amazingly, the verbal individual sometimes will simply answer honestly and say, "No."

6. *Some types of seizure activity can result in a lack of response,* giving an appearance of laziness or lack of motivation.

- Before the evaluation, check for the presence of seizures. During the evaluation, make note of subtle behaviors that may be related to seizures.

Problem: Apparent Avoidance; Attempts to End a Task or Leave the Area

1. *Individuals who put hands over their ears*, cover their eyes, put their head down, or try to get under the table may be bothered or fatigued by some subtle sensory element in the room—too much talking, a squeaky fan, flickering fluorescent lights, or the roaring of truck engines across the street.

   - Reflect the individual's need and offer a change or a break by saying something like, "You look tired. Let's go for a walk, and then we'll come back and finish the work." As you talk, mark the task list so the next task is clear.

2. *If several difficult or new tasks are presented in a sequence* and the failure rate is high, frustration and anxiety will build.

   - Adapt the session schedule to alternate difficult with familiar or easy tasks and breaks.

   - Adapt the tasks. Provide a visual reference, decrease the difficulty, or provide assistance until a correct response is achieved. Even this will provide useful information. Teachers need to know what it takes for the student to learn a new task.

3. *If directions are repeated too many times or too loudly* when the individual does not understand what to do, anxiety increases and efforts to escape or stop the situation may lead to out-of-control behavior.

   - Speak softly and avoid repeated demands. If a direction must be repeated, use the strategies described previously for dealing with apparent lack of motivation.

   - Identify and respond quickly to subtle, nonverbal signs of fatigue, frustration, or anxiety (e.g., "You want to stop? Do one more then we will take a break."). Again, it is better to end a session positively than to push the individual into a major behavioral breakdown.

Problem: Distraction, Disorganization, or Disorientation Between Tasks

1. *If unable to track the passage of time* and unsure about the end of the session, the individual may appear distracted and disorganized and may try to leave the area.

   - Develop a task list to clarify the amount of work. The opportunity to cross off the tasks as completed is a concrete way of marking the passage of time. It is highly motivating for most individuals and keeps attention focused in the testing area.

   - Use contingency statements to highlight the relationship of the completed work to the reinforcer (see Chapter 15).

   - Involve the individual in putting materials away. Moving the materials to a Finished box is a concrete way to mark progress and keep the focus in the area.

2. *An inability to scan an area to select and focus on important information,* coupled with anxiety about unfamiliar materials and tasks, can cause disorientation and distraction.

- Quietly describe and label materials as they are placed on the table. This not only keeps the individual focused on the work area but makes the task and the materials more familiar.

- To ease the transition from a table task to a task that requires standing or movement, clarify the directions (with a visual reference) while the individual is still sitting at the table. A marker to indicate where to stand may help the individual become organized in space.

Interpretation of Test Results

It is difficult to determine exactly what individuals with autism really know. Those who have learned to communicate by spelling words are able to read, spell, and communicate at a level much higher than was expected from previous performance on standardized tests. Those with Asperger's syndrome are able to communicate with a large vocabulary. Yet there are times when a bit of probing indicates that a student does not totally understand the full meaning of some of the things he can read, spell, or say. Thus, use caution when interpreting and viewing standardized test results in this population. For example, one young man was able to provide the definitions for every word in the word comprehension test. Yet he was unable to use those words in a sentence. It was later learned that the boy had an intense interest in dictionaries and studied them whenever possible.

As a general rule, those with autism are not deliberately manipulative, negative, or resistant. A clearly understood request will generally receive a correct response if the individual understands any part of request. There are many reasons for no response or an incorrect response. Therefore, when interpreting scores on these standardized tools, keep the following points in mind:

- If testing did not cover a broad enough range of skills, scores may suggest either unrealistically high or unrealistically low expectations.

- Reliance on full-scale or average scores masks the true nature of the individual's abilities. Analysis of performance on each task or subtest and of the overall profile of scores pinpoints learning strengths and difficulties—information that is important when developing instruction and adaptations.

- Modification of standardized procedures will negate the meaning of standardized scores. However, modifications are likely to produce the most valid and useful information for teachers.

Tests Standardized for Those With Autism Spectrum Disorders

Although there are many good standardized tests for a variety of purposes, there are only a handful designed and standardized specifically for those with autism.

- *Psychoeducational Profile—Revised* (PEP–R; Schopler, Reicher, Bashford, Lansing, & Marcus, 1990). This test was developed at Division TEACCH, University of North Carolina School of Medicine, in Chapel Hill, North Carolina. This is a diagnostic and developmental assessment tool for children with autism up to age 12 who are functioning in some areas at a preschool level. It is a useful tool for assessing those thought to be untestable. It employs a flexible administration format, enabling the trained examiner to structure the testing session to the student's needs, and it contains many materials that are interesting to those with autism. Items are organized in seven developmental areas and a separate Pathology Scale. Results provide practical information for educational programming geared to capitalize on the student's strengths to compensate for deficits.

- *Adolescent and Adult Psychoeducational Profile* (AAPEP; Mesibov, Schopler, Schaffer, & Landrus, 1988). Also developed at Division TEACCH, this is a tool for assessing severely disabled adolescents and adults. It is designed to identify levels of functional development and individual instructional needs. It includes three different scales—a Direct Assessment Scale, Home Scale, and School/Work Scale. The AAPEP provides valuable information that identifies functional programming priorities, the impact of various sensory conditions on performance, and the individual's learning style. This tool also requires training for the evaluator.

- *Autism Screening Instrument for Educational Planning* (ASIEP–2; Krug, Arick, & Almond, 1993). This instrument is designed for individuals age 18 months through adulthood. It is more than a test; it is system for intervention planning and measuring progress. It measures the subject's functional level in five critical areas. When the results are plotted according to a standardized procedure, it provides a comprehensive picture of the student's instructional needs.

A number of checklists and rating scales have been developed to use during the diagnostic process or to confirm the presence of the behaviors characteristic of autism as required by IDEA to determine eligibility for special education services. A few of the most commonly used are:

- *The Autism Behavior Checklist* (ABC; Krug, Arick, & Almond, 1993). This is one of the five subtests of the ASIEP–2 described above. The ABC is a 57-item checklist used for initial screening for individuals between the ages of 3 and adulthood who are suspected of having autism.

- *The Autism Diagnostic Observational Schedule–Generic* (ADOS–G; Lord, Rutter, Dilavore, & Risi, 1999). This is a standardized interview and observational assessment. The ADOS offers opportunities for a variety of interactions designed to evaluate communication, reciprocal social interactions, play, stereotypic behavior, restricted interests, and other behaviors that indicate the presence of Pervasive Developmental Disorders. Used with toddlers through adulthood. Specific training is required to administer.

- *The Childhood Autism Rating Scale* (CARS; Schopler, Reichler, & Renner, 1988). This checklist rates the child's behavior and responses in 10 different categories that are strongly related to those with autism spectrum disorders. The total scores are categorized as Non-Autistic, Mildly-Moderately Autistic, or Severely Autistic.

- *Gilliam Autism Rating Scale* (GARS; Gilliam, 1995a). This is a standardized screening and assessment tool for the diagnosis of autism.

- *Gilliam Asperger's Disorder Scale* (GADS; Gilliam, 1995b). This standardized scale is designed to assist in the diagnosis of persons suspected of having Asperger's Disorder.

- *The Australian Scale for Asperger's Syndrome* (Garnett & Attwood, 1995). A questionnaire designed to identify behaviors and abilities indicative of Asperger's syndrome.

- *Asperger Syndrome Diagnostic Scale* (ASDS; Myles, Brock, & Simpson, 2001). A standardized questionnaire designed to aid in identifying the characteristics of Asperger's syndrome in those between the ages of 5 and 18.

Functional Assessment to Determine Goals and Strategies

Most psychologists and therapists who work in the public schools have tools and the training to assess the intellectual, speech and language, motor, and sensory abilities of a child with autism spectrum disorders. To determine developmental goals and intervention strategies, the student's vision and hearing must also be assessed periodically. However, a functional behavior assessment is the most useful tool to select functional goals, those that help the student lead a more independent life.

General Procedures

The purpose of the functional behavioral assessment is to find out how a person actually operates (behaves) in the natural environment (e.g., what does he or she do, and how does he or she do it?) There are two basic procedures for getting this information: interviews and observations.

Interviews

Interviews with parents and teachers provide the information to learn exactly how the individual performs under a broad range of conditions. Information from interviews is more complete and useful when:

- The parents and teachers have an opportunity to review the questions and make notes before the interview. These notes are used to jog memories during the interview. Because the notes may contain important information and examples that were not addressed during the interview, they are left for the evaluator to examine later.

- The evaluator asks open-ended questions to expand and clarify responses (e.g., "Can you tell me more about that?"; "What exactly did Juan do?"; "What did that tantrum look like?"; "What happened first?").

- A group interview can be both productive and efficient. When parents, teachers, and others have an opportunity to share together, one person's example often triggers another person's memory. It is also an excellent way to identify the things the individual does in one setting but not another.

Observations

Observations in various natural settings enable the evaluator to see how the individual functions and the impact of environmental conditions on the ability to function. To see the performance variability from day to day and in various situations, the learner must be observed on at least 2 or 3 different days and in several different settings. *It is as important to observe the individual's performance in settings where problems do not occur* as it is to observe in the settings where problems do occur. With multiple observations, it is possible to establish reasonable expectations, understand what conditions are necessary for optimal performance, and determine the conditions that disrupt effective functioning.

The following procedures elicit the types of details needed to develop an effective instructional and behavioral support plan:

- Identify priority goals and routines

- Assess priority routines and student's current performance

- Assess sensory and instructional demands of routines

- Assess functional communication

- Assess social skills
- Identify preferences and interests
- Assess daily life activities
- Monitor instructional progress and problems

Several of the functional assessment procedures and forms included in this chapter were developed by Falco, Janzen, Arick, Wilgus, and Deboer (1990) for Project QUEST (Quality Educational Services Training Project) at Portland State University in Portland, Oregon. Some forms and procedures were developed and used by the author and other autism specialists in Oregon's Regional Autism Services program. Other forms and procedures were adapted from those developed at the Judevine Center in St. Louis, Missouri.

These are only a sampling of possible forms and procedures for conducting a functional behavioral assessment. Those included in this chapter have some unique features that are especially helpful for eliciting the kinds of detailed information needed to develop effective programs for those with autism spectrum disorders.

Identify Priority Goals and Routines

A student's priorities are identified by a) analyzing the routines that make up a day in the life of the family at home and the peers in the classroom, and b) determining how the individual participates. Target for instruction those routines that would increase the individual's involvement and independence.

Determining Home/School Priorities (Form 5.1)

A completed example of Form 5.1 (page 71) is presented in Figure 5.1 and provides a logical method for identifying and prioritizing functional goals for instruction. This reproducible form can be used to guide an interview with parents as they list their family's daily schedule from the time their child gets out of bed in the morning until bedtime.

The parents identify how the child participates in those activities, the level and type of participation, and how much assistance is provided. Finally, the parents decide which of the routines should be targeted for instruction. (Which would make life more interesting for their child, easier for the family, or would lead to greater independence?). Teachers can complete the form to cover the events and details of the school day.

Once the lists are prioritized, it is relatively easy to identify realistic functional goals that relate directly to specific family and school situations. Parents and teachers have reported that this process is extremely helpful and worth the 1 to 2 hours of interview time. In succeeding years, the time is reduced considerably. When parents become familiar with the process, they can update the forms independently. Once the forms are completed, the meeting to clarify and integrate the information is relatively short.

Other checklists are available for use in situations where parents might feel uncomfortable having school staff review their daily schedules.

Figure 5.1 Sample: Determining Home/School Priorities (Form 5.1)

Adapted with permission from *Project QUEST Inservice Manual* (Falco et al., 1990)

Student: _____ Dean _____ **Age:** ___17___ **Date:** ___5/10___

Completed by: _____

Directions: Ask family members to describe what the student does or is helped to do at home (from getting up, going to school; and from arriving home until going to bed). Teachers can be given a copy of this form to record the childs daily activities from arrival to departure. Identify routines that are age-appropriate and those that are priorities, to be included in the student's IEP. Place a check mark next to the appropriate schedule to the right. Several pages will be required.

Schedule

X Home weekday

— Home weekend

— School weekday

Approximate Time	Routine	Environment/Area	How does this happen now? How much help is needed?	Age Appropriate? Y/N	Priority? Y/N	Comments
6:00 a.m.	Getting up	Dean's bedroom at foster home	Mom goes to his room. He is usually awake and in bed. He is wet (wears diaper at night).	Y (not diaper)	Y	Night toilet training is a priority.
6:05 a.m.	Undressing	Bathroom	Undresses when told to. Takes off pajamas and diaper. Drops them on floor.	Y (not diaper)	N	
6:10 a.m.	Showering/ Bathing	Bathroom	Does not like shower. Requires much physical assistance to use shower. Will sit in bath when it has been prepared. Will rub chest, arms, face with cloth. Will get out of tub when requested.	Y	Y?	Not sure this is a high priority right now.
6:25 a.m.	Drying after shower or bath	Bathroom	Requires physical assistance to dry body.	Y	Y?	
6:30 a.m.	Get dressed	Bedroom	If each item is handed to him with repeated reminders, he can dress; but usually he is assisted with all items. (It takes too long without assistance.)	Y	Y	Mom knows she should work on this, but worries about time.
6:45 a.m.	Free time	Bedroom	Gets out "wrestling" figure and plays with it, or looks at magazine, or watches TV in his room.	N Y Y	N	Mom satisfied with his ability to occupy himself.
7:00 a.m.	Breakfast	Kitchen	Mom gives him prepared food at the table. He eats adequately without assistance. He will carry dishes to sink if reminded and assisted (but usually Mom does it).	Y	Y?	Mom thinks he may be able to prepare a bowl of cereal and put dishes in sink.
7:15 a.m.	Prepare for school bus	Hall closet, bedroom, kitchen	Mom assists him to get his coat and put it on and get his communication notebook. He sits in kitchen and watches for bus.	Y	Y?	Mom is unsure whether he could put on coat and get notebook independently

Assess Priority Routines and Student Skills

The natural components or steps of a routine are identified by observing how peers of the same age do the things they do. Natural cues are discovered by observing how people know when and where to do things. A realistic criterion for mastery is identified by observing how well peers do the routine. Potential problems, natural prompts, and the possible need for adaptations are identified by observing the amount and kinds of help others receive and the type of assistance needed by the individual being assessed.

Functional Routines: Assessment of Student Skills (Form 5.2)

The completed example of Form 5.2, shown in Figure 5.2, illustrates the QUEST format for analyzing the components of priority routines, the student's performance within the routine, and the need for adaptations. Form 5.2 can be found on page 80 and is reproducible.

The importance of identifying the natural components of the routine cannot be overestimated when planning the instruction for those who learn routines exactly as taught. Integrating all of these naturally occurring elements into the instructional plan will help the individual achieve independence at a much faster rate.

Figure 5.2 Sample: Functional Routines: Assessment of Student Skills (Form 5.2) (Page 1 of 2)

Adapted with permission from *Project QUEST Inservice Manual* (Falco et al., 1990)

Student: _____

Routine: Occupy Free Time   **Environment:** Home, school

Component	Natural Cues	Skills	+/o	Quality/Tempo	Need Assist/Errors	What To Do
INITIATE	Time free of tasks/chores/expectations.	Review the list of fee time activities.				
PREPARE	Choices of free time are accessible.	Make a decision, select free time activity.				
PERFORM	Choice made.	Get materials together to do free-time activity.				
	Activity does not require anyone else.	Independently engage in the activity.				
	Activity requires other people to participate.	Find someone to do the activity with.				
	Finished with chosen activity.	Put materials away.				
	More free time left.	Make another choice.				
		(Repeat the steps.)				
TERMINATE	Available free time is gone and materials put away.	Go to next activity/task/scheduled routine.				

Figure 5.2 (*continued*) Form 5.2 (Page 2 of 2)

Adapted with permission from *Project QUEST Inservice Manual* (Falco et al., 1990)

Student: _____

Routine: Occupy Free Time _____ **Environment:** Home, school

Component	Natural Cues	Skills	+/o	Quality/Tempo	Need Assist/Errors	What To Do
PROBLEM SOLVE	Can't think of anything to do. Materials are missing or broken.	Ask parent/teacher for suggestions. Ask someone to help find or repair/replace items.				
ENRICHMENT SOCIAL	Tired of doing same things. Often do solitary activities. Expectations.	Try new activities. Make friends. Do things with others. Use materials correctly. Keep area clean. Maintain acceptable noise levels.				
COMMUNI-CATION	Other persons are available. Can't find or reach materials.	Ask someone to engage in free time with you. Ask someone for help. Get a step stool.				
CHOICE	Variety of free-time choices. Peers/family available.	Choose desired free-time activities. Choose whom you wish to spend free time with.				

Assess Sensory and Instructional Demands of Routines

If the individual with autism is ultimately expected to participate independently in natural activities, it is necessary to identify potential sensory and instructional problems and either adapt the environment, adapt the activity, or develop visual support systems. To determine the potential need for modifications or adaptations, observe:

■ The sensory demands of the environment—the light, noise, crowding, temperature, odors, and other factors

■ The instructional demands—teacher's language level, use of visual supports or requirement for listening, waiting, making judgments, or for cooperative work, etc.

■ The response demands—verbal responses, written work, homework, and others

Checklist for Assessing Environmental Demands (Form 5.3)

This reproducible form (page 82) provides a method for assessing the sensory and instructional demands of the instructional setting. When completing this assessment, the individual's specific abilities, preferences, and sensitivities must be considered.

What Happened (Flow Log) (Form 5.4)

This reproducible form (page 84) is an observation tool adapted from one developed at the Judevine Center (Blackwell, 1998). It provides a simple, objective method of recording the flow of environmental and instructional demands and the type and frequency of a student's response to those demands. It can also record the social exchanges that occur during instruction—the antecedents, the response, and the reciprocation or consequences. This is a useful way to identify instructional and environmental conditions that require modification. Figure 5.3 offers an example of a completed form.

Some of the most valuable information is collected by an observer who becomes open to the gestalt of a setting or situation and records the learner's responses to the flow of simultaneously occurring sensory, instructional, and social events. This flow of events is recorded without evaluation, as quickly as possible. Following the observation, the material is reviewed to decipher abbreviations, fill in missing information, highlight important relationships, and pull out objective frequency and duration data. A bit of practice is required to focus loosely on environmental conditions and the behavior of the learner while writing quickly to record as much as possible.

Additional information and tools

Additional information and tools for assessing sensory issues can be found in *Asperger Syndrome and Sensory Issues* (Myles et al., 2000, pp. 43–63). This book includes a comprehensive but quick reference to a number of assessment tools and procedures.

Figure 5.3 Sample: What Happened (Flow Log) (Form 5.4)

Adapted with permission from *Judevine® Training System* (Blackwell, 1998)

Student: _____Robert — 5 years old_____ **Interpreter:** _____

Setting: _____Classroom — Circle time_____ **Date:** _____ **Consultant:** _____

Directions: Record the flow of events that occur during the observation period. Include sensory conditions, activity demands, and responses. Note the time every few minutes. Also note the type of activity/materials as they change. Record 1:1 interactions in script format. Code to speed recording: T=teacher, S=student, SR=repetitive behavior, etc. When the action is faster than the ability to write, add a dash to note a break in the flow; then simply move on. At end of observation, review the notes and add missed details, clarify abbreviations, highlight critical elements, and pull out specific data.

P=Peers   T=Teacher   R=Robert

Time/Activity/Materials	What Happened
9:30: Singing Time — R. sitting between peers	T. Who wants to pick the next song? P. 3 children raise hands — R — looking out window T. Selects P. — They sing — R. continues staring . . . song ends
9:35: Singing Time — R. sitting between peers	T. "Robert, Come and pick the next song —" R. Looking out window T. Takes his hand to help him up — R. Pulls away
9:40:	T. Turns to peer. Peer picks next song — they sing with motions R. Begins to wiggle fingers and watching his hand and rocks P. Keep singing — at end of song. T. "One more song then time for snack" — She pats R's hand and says, "Robert, you pick the next song" — She pulls him up and assists him to point to song card. R. goes w/only a bit of resistance. R. Back in chair while peers singing — rocking but watching peers
9:45:	Speech Path. comes — stands behind Robert and says, It's time for speech and begins to get him up. R. Screams and holds onto chair . . .

Assess Functional Communication

Although standardized tests can measure many facets of language and communication development, a natural environment is needed for assessing a person's actual communication skills. An examiner can observe the individual in the natural environment or can set up situations that require communication (e.g., putting favorite things in sight but out of reach). However, these procedures are time consuming and limited in scope.

Functional Communication Assessment: Informant Interview (Form 5.5)

This reproducible form (page 84) is used to guide interviews with parents and teachers who know how the individual actually communicates in many situations and under many conditions.

The question, "How do you know when your child . . . ?" is used to discover how the individual requests, rejects, protests, expresses feelings, comments, responds to questions, and acknowledges others. Parents and teachers need time to study the items and make notes about the full range of the child's communicative behavior before the interview. During the interview, the examiner (a special education teacher, a speech-language pathologist, or autism specialist) can help them expand their examples of communicative behavior. The summary sheet, designed as a form and function matrix provides a highly visual summary of the individual's communication skills and major skill deficits.

This tool not only identifies effective communication effort, it also identifies the *accelerating chains of behavior* that occur when communication breaks down and stress increases (refer to Chapter 8). This is a particularly valuable tool for assessing the communication of those with severe behavior problems for those who are highly verbal as well as those who are nonverbal.

Other information and tools for assessing communication:

- *Assessment and Intervention Strategies for Children Who Use Echolalia* (Prizant & Rydell, 1993) and *Communication Intervention Issues for Young Children With Autism Spectrum Disorders* (Prizant, Wetherby, & Rydell, 2000). These references offer a wealth of information about echolalia and strategies for assessing its function as well as intervention strategies.

- *Milieu Communication Project: Pragmatic Protocol* (Pruitting & Kirchner, 1987). This practical and easy-to-use tool for assessing language use is described in a journal article. Thirty aspects of language use are rated as appropriate, inappropriate, or not observed.

- *Communication and Symbolic Behavior Scales* (CSBS; Wetherby & Prizant, 2001). This infant/toddler checklist identifies different aspects of the early development of communication of children with autism ages 6–24 months. With this tool, structured opportunities and unstructured play can be examined within natural contexts while the child is engaged with the caregiver. The CSBS provides information about the child's ability to persist and repair if communicative attempts are not successful. Observed behaviors are rated to elicit seven cluster scores:

  - Communicative Functions;
  - Gestural Communicative Means;
  - Vocal Communicative Means;
  - Verbal Communicative Means;
  - Reciprocity;

- Social/Affective Signaling (use of gaze shifts, etc.); and
- Symbolic Behavior.

Speech-language pathologists who have training and experience to understand issues associated with autism spectrum disorders will know of the many other tools to assess functional communication and the social and pragmatic aspects of language.

Assess Social Skills

Social Skills Assessment: Informant Interview (Form 5.6)

This reproducible form (page 94; created by QUEST) provides an interesting format for assessing 10 functional social skills across eight different situations or contexts.

Social Interaction Checklist (Form 5.7).

This reproducible form (page 98) is an informal tool for assessing and monitoring 15 social interaction behaviors that are important to success in integrated classroom settings. This rating scale was created by Oregon's regional autism specialists. Several times a year, classroom teachers are asked to rate students' interactions, using a 5-point scale. In this way, progress is noted and problems are identified and addressed in a timely manner. Those periodic ratings are recorded on the summary sheet to mark change over time, to see if the student's social behavior is the same across teachers and settings, and *to pinpoint and address subtle signs of potential problems before they escalate.*

Other social-skills information and assessment tools include:

- *I'm Experiencing Technical Difficulties: A Comprehensive Guide to Teaching Social-Cognitive Skills to Students With Asperger's Syndrome* (Schmeltzer, Jordan, & Skowron-Gooch, 2002). This guide contains assessment materials as well as a social skills curriculum and teaching strategies.

- *Developing Leisure Time Skills for Persons With Autism* (Coyne, Nyberg, & Vandenburg, 1999). This is an assessment and instructional guide that teaches independent activities and the essential components of leisure time skills. It includes many games and activities for all ages.

- *The Transdisciplinary Play-Based Assessment: A Functional Approach to Working with Young Children, Revised Edition* (Lindner, 1993). This book can be used to assess the cognitive, social-emotional, communication/language, and sensory motor skills in the context of natural play situations. Designed for use with children functioning between 6-month to 6-year levels, it is useful for developing the child's program plan.

- *The Social Strategy Rating Scale: An Approach to Evaluating Social Competence* (Beckman & Lieber, 1994). This book provides a relatively simple method of measuring social competence in young children with disabilities across multiple contexts.

Identify Preferences and Interests

See Chapter 12 for strategies to develop daily schedules based on the child's preferences.

A necessary element of any intervention plan is to identify those things that will be highly reinforcing and those things that are highly punishing for the student.

Preference Survey (Form 5.8)

This reproducible form (page 99) is adapted from a form created at the Judevine Center (Blackwell, 1998), and is a tool for identifying a student's strong and sometimes unusual likes and dislikes. When completed in detail, this tool identifies people, activities, events, objects, foods, or other factors that trigger positive, negative, or neutral feelings. This survey can be completed by parents, teachers, or others who know the individual well, and it should be reviewed and updated regularly during team meetings.

The information elicited with this form is used to develop very specialized schedules that systematically arrange highly liked activities throughout the day to increase motivation (see Chapter 12). This survey also is used to assess the relationship of activities and activity schedules to problem behaviors.

For completed samples of the Preference Survey, see page 480; and for the Case Study, page 471.

Assess Daily Life Activities

Informant Interview (Form 5.9).

This reproducible form (page 100) is used to identify the relationships of various environmental conditions to a serious behavior problem. It also organizes critical information for modifying an existing program to ensure a balanced and positive daily schedule of events that will support appropriate behavior.

Monitor Instructional Progress and Problems

The reproducible forms for Chapter 5 are found on the pages that follow.

Data must be kept for all instructional activities. Most programs have developed standard data sheets for this purpose. However, monitoring involves more than simply recording errors and correct responses. When teaching those who have autism spectrum disorders, record keeping must be expanded to include the relationship of errors and problem behavior to environmental and instructional conditions. See Chapter 17 for forms and procedures for monitoring instructional progress.

Summary

Both standardized and functional assessment procedures play an important role in developing an appropriate program and selecting appropriate strategies. As noted earlier, there is evidence that "internal cognitive processes contrast sharply with overt social and communicative behaviors" (Quill, 1995, p. 99). Therefore, we cannot let scores on IQ tests limit an individual's educational opportunities. More useful information is gathered when standardized procedures are modified to obtain information about the individual's approach to tasks and the type of assistance needed to accomplish a task. However, while this method may be useful for obtaining information about the person being tested, unless stated otherwise within the test's administration guidelines, modifications to standardized administration procedures invalidates the normed information associated with the score and cannot be reported. Functional assessment procedures are helpful in identifying the types of skills and strategies the individual uses in actual situations as well as those that are not used. These functional procedures answer critical questions to determine how a program should be modified to ensure continuing progress: Why is a skill not used? Is some small piece of information missing that prevents understanding? Could it be that for some reason the individual cannot initiate or perform the motor movements to use the skill? For more examples of Quill's insights, read Granden and Scariano, 1986; Ledgin, 2002; and Mukhopadhyay, 2000.

Determining Home/School Priorities

Adapted with permission from *Project QUEST Inservice Manual* (Falco et al. 1990)

Student: _____   Age: _____   Date: _____

Completed by: _____

Directions: Ask family members to describe what the student does or is helped to do at home (from getting up, going to school; and from arriving home until going to bed). Teachers can be given a copy of this form to record the childs daily activities from arrival to departure. Identify routines that are age-appropriate and those that are family priorities, to be included in the student's IEP. Place a checkmark next to the appropriate schedule to the right. Several pages will be required.

Schedule

— Home weekday

— Home weekend

— School weekday

Approximate Time	Routine	Environment/Area	How does this happen now? How much help is needed?	Age Appropriate? Y/N	Priority? Y/N	Comments

Functional Routines: Assessment of Student Skills

Adapted with permission from *Project QUEST Inservice Manual* (Falco et al., 1990)

Student: _____

Environment: _____

Routine: _____

Component	Natural Cues	Skills	+/o	Quality/Tempo	Need Assist/Errors	What To Do
INITIATE						
PREPARE						
PERFORM						
TERMINATE						

(continued)

Functional Routines: Assessment of Student Skills (*continued*)

Adapted with permission from *Project QUEST Inservice Manual* (Falco et al., 1990)

Student: _____

Routine: _____

Environment: _____

Component	Natural Cues	Skills	+/o	Quality/Tempo	Need Assist/Errors	What To Do
PROBLEM SOLVE						
ENRICHMENT: SOCIAL						
COMMUNI-CATION						
CHOICE						

Student: _____**Environment:** _____**Date:** _____

Use this checklist to identify and determine which adaptations may be necessary. Match the learner's sensitivities and deficits to: (1) the level of environmental stimulation and (2) the demands of the activity. Note examples.

1. **Nature and level of the activity and environmental stimuli**
   (Consider the intensity, frequency, and duration of stimuli.)

   ☐ Noise—Subtle (echoes, fans, lights, halls, street), people (talking, singing, shuffling feet or paper)

   ☐ Noise—Intense (whistles, bells, trains, loudspeakers, machinery)

   ☐ Visual—Objects (pictures, mobiles, lights and shadows, bulletin boards, materials on open shelves), surfaces (wood grain, reflecting, or patterned), people (glasses, jewelry, movement)

   ☐ Odors—People, materials (perfumes, glues, paint, paper), cafeteria, cleaning supplies, nearby businesses (bakery, factory, service station)

   ☐ Touch—People (crowding, touching, holding hands, physical assistance or touch for reinforcement), materials (textures of fabrics, furniture, sticky or rough materials)

   ☐ Movement (Vestibular)—Demand for getting up and down, reaching, stooping, moving about, moving up or down inclines, sitting or standing in one place

   ☐ Taste—Meals and snack foods, exploratory tasting activities for young children

2. **Demands of the event (work or activity)**

   ☐ Complexity of the language used in directions

   ☐ Requirement for written work, oral communication

   ☐ Time pressures

   ☐ Need to keep several thoughts together in a sequence

   ☐ Need for generating new motor and/or verbal responses

   ☐ Requirement for solving problems, using judgment, making decisions

   ☐ Clarity of the beginning and end of the activity or routine

   ☐ Waiting requirements—(for bus, before/after transitions, for help, in line)

   ☐ Participation with others (cooperative teams, assembly lines, competitive activities, partners, large or small groups)

3. **New or unfamiliar elements**

Activity:	☐ New	☐ Familiar
Materials:	☐ New	☐ Familiar
Location:	☐ New	☐ Familiar
Staff members:	☐ New	☐ Familiar
Peers:	☐ New	☐ Familiar

   Other new: _____

Adapted with permission from *Judevine® Training System* (Blackwell, 1998)

Student:_____**Interpreter:**_____

Setting:_____**Date:**_____**Consultant:**_____

Directions: Record the flow of events that occur during the observation period. Include sensory conditions, activity demands, and responses. Note the time every few minutes. Also note the type of activity/materials as they change. Record 1:1 interactions in script format. Code to speed recording: T=teacher, S=student, SR=repetitive behavior, etc. When the action is faster than the ability to write, add a dash to note a break in the flow; then simply move on. At end of observation, review the notes and add missed details, clarify abbreviations, highlight critical elements, and pull out specific data.

Time/Activity/Materials	What Happened

Adapted with permission from *Project QUEST Inservice Manual* (Falco et al., 1990)

Child's name: _____ **Age:** _____

Date: _____ **Interviewer:** _____

Informant: _____ **Relationship:** _____

Directions: The following questions are designed to obtain information about the ways your child communicates. The information will be used to develop the most appropriate communication program for your child.

Please answer each question thoroughly. Add information wherever you want. It is most helpful to get as many examples as possible and to add details, such as, "He is just starting to do this"; "He used to do it"; or, "He does it only when I tell him to do it." Add information to describe how often and how hard your child tries to communicate and how difficult it is to understand. Also note whether your child looks at you when trying to communicate.

EXPRESSING FEELINGS

How do you know when your child:

1. Likes an activity, food, or other? _____

   _____

   _____

2. Does not like an activity, food, or other? _____

   _____

   _____

3. Feels good or happy? _____

   _____

   _____

4. Feels ill or in pain? _____

   _____

   _____

5. Is hungry? _____

   _____

   _____

6. Is uncomfortable? _____

   _____

   _____

(continued)

REQUESTING

What does your child do when he/she:

7. Is anxious or afraid? _____

_____

_____

8. Wants attention? _____

_____

9. Wants more of something? _____

_____

10. Wants you to continue an activity (for example, playing a game or rocking)? _____

_____

11. Wants you to stop an activity? _____

_____

12. Wants you to start a familiar routine (for example, fixing a snack or playing peek-a-boo)? _____

_____

13. Wants help? _____

_____

14a. Wants something to eat? _____

_____

14b. Wants something to drink? _____

_____

15. Wants a certain object? _____

_____

16. Wants to do something? _____

_____

17. Wants to use the bathroom? _____

_____

(continued)

REQUESTING (continued)

18. Wants affection _____

_____

19. Does your child make a choice between several objects when the objects are presented or in view? _____

Describe. _____

_____

20. Does your child make a choice among several activities? _____ Describe. _____

_____

_____

21. Does your child make a choice of an object or activity when the possible selections are not presented or in view?

_____ Describe. _____

_____

22. How do you know when your child does not understand something that someone has said? _____

Does your child ask for clarification by saying, "What?" or "I don't understand" or by doing something like

self-biting? _____ Describe. _____

_____

23a. Does your child ask for information (for example, where someone is, where someone lives, or when a birthday

or holiday will occur)? _____ Describe. _____

_____

23b. Does your child ask the same questions repeatedly? _____

_____

23c. Does your child ask for one thing but appear to want something different? _____ Describe. _____

_____

PROTESTING

What does your child do to let you know that he/she:

24. Does not want to do something or wants to stop doing something? Describe. _____

_____

(continued)

PROTESTING (*continued*)

25. Does not want a specific object or food? Describe. _____

_____

_____

_____

What does your child do when:

26. Not allowed to do or have something desired? Describe. _____

_____

_____

_____

27. A desired object is taken away? Describe. _____

_____

_____

28. The environment or routine is changed? Describe. _____

_____

_____

RESPONDING

Describe your child's response to each of the following:

29. Verbal directions _____

_____

_____

30. Questions that begin with *what, who, where, when, how,* or *why* _____

_____

_____

31. Questions that call for a *yes* or *no* answer _____

_____

_____

(continued)

ACKNOWLEDGING OTHERS (continued)

32. How does your child greet you or others if not prompted? _____

_____

_____

33. How does your child respond when greeted by others? _____

_____

_____

34. Does your child use polite words (such as "Thank you," "Please," and "Excuse me") appropriately? _____

Without prompting? _____

Describe. _____

_____

35. If another child asks for a turn or a toy, will your child acknowledge the request without a prompt? _____

_____

_____

COMMENTING
Does your child:

36. Comment about himself and his own activity? Describe. _____

_____

_____

_____

37. Comment about other people or their actions? Describe. _____

_____

_____

_____

38. Comment about objects or events when the object is present or the event is occurring? Describe. _____

_____

_____

(continued)

COMMENTING (*continued*)

39. Comment about objects or events when the object is not present or the event is not currently occurring?

     Describe. _____

     _____

40. Talk about events that happened in the past or will happen in the future? Describe. _____

     _____

     _____

NONCOMMUNICATIVE LANGUAGE

41. Does your child say the names of objects or people for no apparent reason, without looking at you or relating

     to you? _____ Describe. _____

     _____

42. Does your child talk to himself about what he is doing, is going to do (for example, "Sit down" as he sits down),

     or is not supposed to do (for example, "Don't touch" when beginning to touch something that is off limits), as

     if repeating a rule? Describe. _____

     _____

43. Does your child talk to himself about things that don't appear to be related to the current situation? Describe.

     _____

     _____

VOCABULARY

44. If your child has a limited vocabulary (25 words or so), please list the words and describe any words that are

     used in specific or unusual ways or situations. (Write on the back) _____

     _____

     _____

CURRENT NEEDS

45. What functions, concepts, vocabulary, or forms of communication do you feel are most important for your child

     to learn this year? (Write on the back) _____

(continued)

(continued)

Functional Communication Assessment: Summary

Adapted with permission from *Project QUEST Inservice Manual* (Falco et al., 1990)

Child: _____

Date: _____

Code: / = Uses sometimes
+ = Uses consistently
(Use a different color ink for each informant or setting.)

	Forms of Language and Communication	A. FEELINGS							B. REQUESTING				
		1. Likes	2. Dislikes	3. Feels good	4. Pain	5. Hungry	6. Discomfort	7. Afraid	8. Attention	9. More	10. Continue	11. Stop	12. Start
Speech:	a. One word												
	b. Two or three words												
	c. Complex utterance												
Sign:	d. One word												
	e. Two or three words												
	f. Complex utterance												
Combined forms:	g. One word												
	h. Two or three words												
	i. Complex utterance												
Echolalia:	j. Immediate: Exact												
	k. Immediate: Mitigated												
	l. Delayed												
Nonverbal behavior:	m. Gesture/Pointing												
	n. Manipulation of other												
	o. Vocalizations												
	p. Cries												
	q. Gaze												
	r. Gaze shift												
	s. Proximity: Moves closer												
	t. Proximity: Moves away												
	u. Facial expression												
	v. Head nod												
	w. Bodily contact												
	x. Action (grab, reach, give, other)												
	y. Self-injurious behavior												
	z. Aggressive behavior												
	aa. Tantrum behavior												
	bb. Other:												

(continued)

	B. REQUESTING (continued)											C. PROTESTING					D. RESP.			E. ACKNOW.			
	13. Help	14. Eat/Drink	15. Object	16. To Do Action	17. Bathroom	18. Affection	19. Choose object	20. Choose action	21. Choose without seeing	22. Clarity	23. Information	24. Activity	25. Object/Food	26. Not allowed	27. Taken object	28. Change	29. Directions	30. WH questions	31. Yes/No questions	32. Greeting	33. Response to greeting	34. Polite words	35. Take turns
a.																							
b.																							
c.																							
d.																							
e.																							
f.																							
g.																							
h.																							
i.																							
j.																							
k.																							
l.																							
m.																							
n.																							
o.																							
p.																							
q.																							
r.																							
s.																							
t.																							
u.																							
v.																							
w.																							
x.																							
y.																							
z.																							
aa.																							
bb.																							

(continued)

	F. COMMENT			G. NON-COMPLETED				
	36. On self	37. On others	38. Object/Action	39. Not present	40. Past/Future	41. Say labels	42. Direct self	43. Unrelated
a.								
b.								
c.								
d.								
e.								
f.								
g.								
h.								
i.								
j.								
k.								
l.								
m.								
n.								
o.								
p.								
q.								
r.								
s.								
t.								
u.								
v.								
w.								
x.								
y.								
z.								
aa.								
bb.								

Assessments:

1. Informant: _____

   Date: _____Color code: _____

   Total functions: _____Forms: _____

2. Informant: _____

   Date: _____Color code: _____

   Total functions: _____Forms: _____

3. Informant: _____

   Date: _____Color code: _____

   Total functions: _____Forms: _____

4. Informant: _____

   Date: _____Color code: _____

   Total functions: _____Forms: _____

5. Informant: _____

   Date: _____Color code: _____

   Total functions: _____Forms: _____

6. Informant: _____

   Date: _____Color code: _____

   Total functions: _____Forms: _____

Social Skills Assessment: Informant Interview

Adapted with permission from *Project QUEST Inservice Manual* (Falco et al., 1990)

Student: _____

Date: _____

Informant: _____

Rating code:
- 0 = No opportunity to do it, or never observed
- 2 = Gets it done, but does it inappropriately
- 3 = Does it occasionally or if prompted
- 4 = Does it consistently and appropriately in a variety of situations
- NA = Not applicable

Directions: Read the definitions for Social Skills 1–10 (page 4 of this form). For each situation below, rate your child's performance in each social skill. Give examples of what your child does in each situation.

SITUATIONS	1. Initiate interactions	2. Respond to greetings or initiations	3. Take/ manage/ relinquish turns; share	4. Self-manage	5. Solve problems	6. Provide feedback indicating pleasure or displeasure	7. Offer/ provide/ obtain/ accept assistance	8. Indicate preference/ make choice	9. Follow social rules/ norms/ manners	10. Terminate interaction/ activity
1. Private Independence When alone, how does your child: • Entertain self? (Play video game, listen to music, play cards, . . .)										
• Carry out responsibilities? (Fold clothes, do math, complete a job, . . .)										
2. Friendship Interactions When with a friend, how does your child: • Play or hang out? (Play games, play with toys, listen to music, . . .)										
• Work? (Set table, rake leaves, prepare snack, . . .)										
3. Homogenous Small Group When with 3 or 4 same-age friends, how does your child: • Play? (Structured games, pretend games, other)										

(continued)

Social Skills Assessment: Informant Interview

SITUATIONS	1. Initiate interactions	2. Respond to greetings or initiations	3. Take/ manage/ relinquish turns; share	4. Self-manage	5. Solve problems	6. Provide feedback indicating pleasure or displeasure	7. Offer/ provide/ obtain/ accept assistance	8. Indicate preference/ make choice	9. Follow social rules/ norms/ manners	10. Terminate interaction/ activity
• Socialize? (Hang out, listen to music, go for a snack, . . .)										
• Work? (Plan an outing, cook a meal, . . .)										
4. Heterogeneous Small Group With family or groups of adults and children, how does your child:										
• Play? (Games, . . .)										
• Socialize (Visit, go for a snack, go to a movie, . . .)										
• Work? (Clean up the yard, cook a meal, fix a bike, . . .)										
5. Active, Goal-Oriented Group How does your child participate in a small structured work or play group? (Sports team, job crew, reading group, Scout troop, church group, . . .)										
6. Passive, Goal-Oriented Group How does your child participate as part of an audience with family or friends? (Attending ball game, movie, concert, church, . . .)										

(continued)

Social Skills Assessment: Informant Interview

SITUATIONS	1. Initiate interactions	2. Respond to greetings or initiations	3. Take/ manage/ relinquish turns; share	4. Self-manage	5. Solve problems	6. Provide feedback indicating pleasure or displeasure	7. Offer/ provide/ obtain/ accept assistance	8. Indicate preference/ make choice	9. Follow social rules/ norms/ manners	10. Terminate interaction/ activity
7. Interactions with Stranger in Public Place In a public place (without supervision), how does your child: • Socialize or refrain from socializing with an unfamiliar person? (Help small child or older person, comment to another while waiting in line; avoid making or responding to inappropriate advances, . . .) • Tolerate unexpected behavior of strangers? (Being bumped while in an elevator, ignoring loud shouting from person in the street, . . .) • Engage an appropriate person for help to accomplish a goal? (Asking a clerk for help in locating an item, help in locating a restroom or telephone, . . .)										
8. Public Independence In a public place (without supervision), how does your child: • Engage in a free-time activity? (Jogging on a trail, playing video games in an arcade, . . .) • Accomplish a specific goal? (Buying groceries in a supermarket, riding the school bus, waiting in the airport, . . .)										

(continued)

Social Skills Assessment: Informant Interview

MAJOR SOCIAL SKILLS	DEFINITION
1. Initiate interactions	Gain access to interaction, either to initiate an interaction or enter one already underway; begin an event or exchange
2. Respond to greetings or initiations	Acknowledge others' greetings or initiations and either join an interaction/activity or decline to participate
3. Take/maintain/relinquish turns; share	Engage in reciprocal interaction by filling turns and waiting for responses
4. Self-manage	Follow serial-order routines; respond to expectations in absence of teacher/adult prompts, including the inhibition of responses (self-control) in certain situations
5. Solve problems	Exhibit alternative strategy to complete a task, or seek alternative interaction/activity when previous effort resulted in a negative consequence or difficulty in effecting needs or intent
6. Provide feedback indicating pleasure or displeasure	Provide others with positive feedback rewarding to them; provide others with feedback to indicate that their behavior was inappropriate or unpleasant (with the intent to extinguish or reduce that behavior)
7. Offer/provide/obtain/accept assistance	Is alert to others' need for assistance and spontaneously provides help; recognizes when he needs help and knows who and how to ask; accepts help/information from others when it is offered
8. Indicate preference/make choice	Makes a choice/decision from among alternatives available or presented by others
9. Follow social rules/norms/manners	Adheres to culturally accepted rules and body language, body contact, personal space, and social amenities
10. Terminate interaction/activity	Withdraws from or terminates an interaction, ceasing participation in an activity as desired or appropriate

Adapted with permission from Oregon Regional Autism Services

Student: _____ **Teacher:** _____

Date: _____ **Class:** _____

Directions: Check the column that best describes this student's behavior. Then give examples to describe problems.

Code for rating frequency of each behavior and intensity of the problem:

1 = Consistently uses / No problem
2 = Often uses / Mild problem
3 = Sometimes uses / Moderate problem
4 = Seldom uses / Increasing problem
5 = Never uses / Major problem

BEHAVIOR	Rating 1	2	3	4	5	Describe — give examples
1. Plays with peers during breaks						
2. Responds to questions of peers						
3. Participates in games with other children in the classroom						
4. Participates in games with other children at breaks						
5. Has particular peers with whom this child interacts						
6. Participates in group activities in the classroom						
7. Appears to enjoy time spent in group activities						
8. Responds to teacher questions during whole-group instruction						
9. Talks with other children in the classroom at appropriate times						
10. Helps other children with tasks						
11. Shares materials with other children						
12. Shows concern (verbal or nonverbal) for the problems of other students						
13. Shares feelings at appropriate times						
14. Interactions with adults seem to be of a positive nature						
15. Interactions with children seem to be of a positive nature						

Preference Survey

Adapted with permission from *Judevine® Training System* (Blackwell, 1998)

Student: _____ **Date:** _____

LIKES What people, objects, or activities are liked a lot or selected during free time?	**TOLERATES** What is done when asked, but never done if not asked?	**DISLIKES** What people, objects, or activities are resisted, avoided or rejected?
People	People	People
Activities	Activities	Activities
Sensory	Sensory	Sensory
Foods	Foods	Foods
Other	Other	Other

Assessment of Daily Life Activities: Informant Interview

Adapted with permission from Oregon Regional Autism Services

Student: _____   **Date:** _____

Directions: This form is used to structure an interview to determine the relationship of various conditions to problem behavior. First, parents and/or staff members make notes on a copy of the form prior to the interview. The interviewer then structures questions to clarify the details and to enlarge on the examples. When making comments, give details such as: types of problems, environmental conditions when problems occur, types of assistance, consequences, types of directions, and the possible perspective of the student when problems occur.

Time (from/to)	Activity Location/Supervisor and Group Size	Is this activity:			Does the individual have:		Comments Give details
		Age-appropriate?	Meaningful?	Liked?	Choice? Control?	Problems?	

3

Make Program Decisions

HAPPY FEELINGS

TODAY I FEEL
HAPPY
TEACH ME JOKE
TEACH ME LOVE
AND GREATNESS
TEACH ME FUN
AND TEACH ME
SOME
OF EVERYTHING
YOU
POSSESS

—David Eastham
In *UNDERSTAND: Fifty Memowriter Poems*

Placement and Support Decisions

S*upported education* is a term used to describe a program that provides the positive support necessary to ensure that educational goals are met. The term generally applies to those with disabilities served in integrated or inclusive settings (e.g., a regular classroom in the neighborhood school). The concept of supported education is important to those with autism spectrum disorders, whether they are served in self-contained special classes or are partially or fully integrated into regular classes. To profit from any educational setting or program, students with autism must rely on others to provide support—to organize the environment, design instruction, and interpret the meaning of events. When all elements of a program match individual needs, motivation is high, the learning rate is increased, and behavior is stable.

When critical supports are missing, those with autism become confused and anxious. Increasing anxiety leads to behavior problems that can disrupt learning for everyone in the classroom. Disruptions often result in staff burnout, parent frustration, and transfers to more restrictive settings. Inappropriate settings, programs, and inadequate support are costly. These students acquire a reputation for being noncompliant, disruptive, and destructive when by nature they are generally compliant, naive, and gentle. It is also costly in terms of time wasted—these students have too much to learn and accomplish. They cannot afford to waste time. In one of her early presentations, Ann Donnellan once said that as soon as a child receives a diagnosis of autism, they should be given a T-shirt that shouts out: Don't Waste My Time!

Some of the most successful educational programs for those with autism are implemented in regular, integrated settings. The major issue is not "readiness" for integration in terms of appropriate behavior but how the setting can support learning and productive behavior. The common element in every successful program is an active and committed support team whose members include parents, teachers, and others who are directly involved in providing services.

The Elements of an Effective Program

In a study to determine the elements of effective early intervention programs, Dawson and Osterling (1997) reported that there was "little evidence that the philosophy of a given program is critical for ensuring a positive outcome as long as certain fundamental program features are present" (p. 308). These features include:

1. *The curriculum addresses the deficits of autism.* The curriculum goals for a child with autism are the same as for all other children of the same age plus the six critical goals (see Figure 6.1) that address the common deficits associated with autism.

2. *The environment is organized and highly supportive.* New skills are "first taught in highly structured contexts" that includes "direct interactions with a trained teacher or therapist" (Dawson & Osterling, p. 316). Other elements of a supportive environment include:

- Staff trained specifically to teach children with autism
- Low teacher/child ratio
- Distraction-free organization of space and materials
- Use of visual strategies to highlight relevant information
- Generalization strategies that involve only a few small changes at a time
- Systematic use of prompts and reinforcement

3. *The program addresses the child's need for predictability and routine* to assist and calm children before changes and during transitions. All programs used some form of the following strategies:
   - Visual or concrete cues (schedules, calendars, etc.) with familiar routines during transitions, which gave ample warnings and rehearsal to prepare for new instruction and events.
   - Systematic and frequent, but small, changes in routines.

4. *Problem behaviors are addressed from a functional perspective.* The priority is given to proactive strategies to prevent problem behaviors. They acknowledge that behavior is communication and that behavior problems are a result of lack of skills and an inability to ask for assistance.

   Behavior problems are addressed by trying to discover the message behind the behavior, then altering the environment to avoid the problem or by teaching new skills to solve the problem.

5. *Transitions are structured and supported.* The child needs support for all transitions, from home to school, class to class, or moving from one home to another. This involves training for all involved, transferring information to new staff, preparing the child before transition, and parental involvement.

6. *Parent participation is encouraged and supported.* There is evidence that those with autism spectrum disorders make greater progress when parents and teachers work together and use similar strategies.

7. *Intervention is highly focused and intense.* The child must be highly involved, focused, and alert during instruction. Dawson and Osterling (1997) reported that it is not possible to determine exactly how many hours of focused intervention are required for a positive outcome because every child is unique. Their study and others suggested that the best outcome was achieved when intervention began between 2 to 4 years of age, with at least 20 hours of intervention a week.

8. *Additional features of effective programs include* services of a speech-language/communication specialist and an occupational therapist to address communication and sensory problems, as well as some type of database management system to provide the basis for making program decisions such as to continue or to modify a program.

Perhaps the most critical element of effective programs was the presence of a well-trained staff that understands the learning differences in autism and knows how to incorporate the behavioral and cognitive strategies to address the student's unique needs.

Making Decisions

Basic guidelines for making educational decisions are provided in the federal law. The 1997 reauthorization of the Individuals with Disabilities Education Act (IDEA) specifies that:

- Each eligible individual (ages 0–21) must have an Individual Education Plan (IEP) or an Individual Family Service Plan (IFSP) that includes the related support services necessary to achieve goals.

- A multidisciplinary team must develop the educational plan.

- The general education setting is assumed to be the appropriate placement *unless it can be proven why it could not possibly be appropriate when supports are tailored to the child's needs.*

Also see Martin, 2000, and Wright & Wright, 2001.

There are numerous other regulations and guidelines spelled out in the federal law and the administrative rules of each state. Parents should inform themselves about their child's rights.

Copies of these laws and administrative rules are available from state educational agencies, special education offices of local school districts, and advocacy organizations.

A team approach to the decision-making process brings together those who know the individual best and those with training and experience in educating and supporting others with similar conditions and problems. If this decision-making team operates with a common goal and with common basic principles for selecting alternatives, their decisions are most likely to produce positive outcomes.

Principles for Making Decisions

The *Criterion of the Least Dangerous Assumption*, proposed by Anne Donnellan, Ph.D., suggests the following standard for making educational decisions. "The criterion of the least dangerous assumption holds that in the absence of conclusive evidence, decisions ought to be based on assumptions which, if incorrect, will have the least dangerous effect on the likelihood that students will be able to function independently as adults" (Donnellan, 1984, p. 141). When the common goal of an educational program is to enable students to function independently and productively in the community as adults, then Donnellan's criterion and the following eight principles can guide the team's decisions.

See Chapter 2 for more information about learning style.

1. *The learning style* (strengths and deficits) provides the foundation for understanding problems and selecting program options. *The critical goals that address the deficits of autism provide the basis for setting priorities* (see Figure 6.1).

2. *Teach useful and meaningful skills* in natural, chronological, age-appropriate settings so that students learn when and where to use the skills and the purpose or reason for using them (see Chapters 13 and 17).

3. *Teaching strategies and instructional materials* must be as natural as possible. They must highlight and capitalize on the natural cues, prompts, and reinforcers commonly available in the community so that the student does not become dependent on another person for cues, prompts, and reinforcement (see Chapter 16).

4. *Integrate all therapies and services* to support the total program, to avoid confusion and the learning of unrelated splinter skills.

5. *Adaptations and individualized support systems* must be available and used as needed to support learning and independence in all settings (see Chapters 11–15).

6. *Strengths and interests are developed* and used to compensate for deficits and increase motivation.

7. *A balanced program* that includes a broad range of experiences in many settings and situations is most likely to have a positive and lasting outcome (see Chapter 7).

8. *Expectations and support* must be flexible and at a level to ensure success. Success is an essential ingredient for continuing effort and effective learning (see Chapters 10 and 12).

These eight principles apply to all decision making in autism. However, unique interests, strengths, past experiences, and patterns of development will demand highly individualized options and applications.

> Both Tomas and Leah are 4 years old, and both have autism. They have similar and predictable learning and behavior problems (e.g., they find noise and crowding painful, they show confusion during transitions and in new situations). Tomas is fascinated by numbers and letters. He can count to 1,000 and read words at the fourth grade level but he uses no words for communication. He has advanced visual-motor skills for blocks, pegs, and puzzles, and he can print letters, numbers, and some words. His attention span for most fine motor, reading, or math tasks is almost endless. He is afraid to climb, trips and falls when he runs, has no interest in balls, and cannot put on his coat or carry a chair to the music circle.
>
> Leah communicates and socializes much like a 2-year-old, watching and playing beside the other children. She is agile and can run and climb, throw and catch balls, and she is fascinated with video equipment and computers. Leah's attention span and ability to manipulate this equipment is no less than amazing for a 4-year-old. However, she finds work with puzzles, pegs, blocks, pencils, and crayons extremely frustrating. She does not look at books, numbers, or letters.
>
> Both children need similar adaptations to address the sensory problems, and both need a visual schedule to organize time and help them tolerate transitions and changing activities. However, each program will be designed and implemented very differently.

Critical Goals

The learning style, strengths, and deficits common to most of those with autism spectrum disorders is the foundation for making all decisions, for determining which goals are important as well as for decisions relating to teaching strategies. As noted in Chapter 3, those with autism do not automatically learn some of the most basic and critical skills that other children develop naturally from the day of birth. Priority must be given to these critical goals that address the deficits common to those with autism.

Figure 6.1 Critical Goals That Address the Deficits of Autism

1. **To value people, interact, and communicate intentionally**
   To learn:
   a. That people can provide information, assistance, pleasure, and comfort
   b. To tolerate the closeness of people
   c. To intentionally seek out and spontaneously initiate interactions
   d. To stay in interactions with people; to persist in efforts to communicate
   e. That people have a common but different experience or perspective

2. **To learn the language and to communicate effectively**
   To learn:
   a. That everything has a label (sometimes multiple labels)
   b. That some words have multiple meanings
   c. That words, toys, and pictures are symbols for real things
   d. That words can be spoken and written down
   e. That objects and actions have a purpose that can be labeled
   f. That words can label and define concepts and relationships
   g. To use gestures, objects, and words to communicate meaningfully
   h. To understand the language spoken by others

3. **To tolerate change and accept new experiences; to be more flexible**
   To learn:
   a. That materials, schedules, and settings can be used and arranged flexibly
   b. That there are alternative ways and times to do things
   c. That change is okay and new things can be interesting

4. **To focus on and participate in instruction**
   To learn:
   a. The language of instruction
   b. To watch others for information
   c. To focus on relevant and screen out irrelevant information
   d. To be actively engaged; to try, and to persist
   e. To work independently, in 1:1 situations and in small and large groups

5. **To do things independently, without constant verbal direction**
   To learn:
   a. To follow visual information systems
   b. Effective routines for doing purposeful things

6. **To monitor and manage stress**
   To learn:
   a. To identify stress in self
   b. To ask for and take a break
   c. To relax and then to reengage in the ongoing activity
   d. To accept correction
   e. To solve problems or ask for assistance

To live a productive life as independently as possible, these children must either learn and generalize these skills or have support systems to compensate.

To ensure that these goals will be generalized and applied to the many tasks and problems of life, they must be taught in the context of natural events, in the context of naturally occurring daily activities. It is the naturally scheduled events of a day that form the structure—*the scaffold*—for teaching and generalizing these critical goals while at the same time teaching developmental skills and functional routines.

The Support Team

With some exceptions, the support team members may be the same as those on the assessment and the IEP or IFSP teams. At least four people are needed to make effective educational decisions: parents and/or caregivers, building principal or supervisor, teacher (or teachers), and a specialist in autism. Others who provide related services also participate, either as regular team members or as needed to address specific issues. When appropriate, the individual with ASD would also participate.

1. *Parents must be integrally involved* in the planning and problem solving process because they:

   - Have information from a lifetime with their child in many situations that is essential for understanding the total picture

   - Have responsibility to advocate and provide for their child

   - Must live day-to-day for a lifetime with the results of all decisions

2. *The role of the building principal and/or program supervisor* is to inform the team of school policy and procedures and to make timely decisions about things that might impact those procedures or the budget. When actively involved with the support team, the principal—who is ultimately responsible for everything that happens in the school building—will always be informed and prepared to respond effectively:

   - To participate in and support behavior or disciplinary decisions

   - To answer the questions of other parents, students, and staff members

   - To support the efforts of hard-working school staff

   - To deal with placement, staffing, and staff training issues

3. *The teacher has legal responsibility for the student's total program.* When a student is integrated in a regular class, both the regular classroom teacher and a special education teacher or integration specialist serves on the team.

4. *Specialists in autism contribute training and experiences* with many individuals with autism. Because of that experience, they can interpret the world of autism to the team just as the staff interprets the world to the student. The autism specialist provides balance, perspective, and an objective view to those who are physically and emotionally involved in day-to-day instruction and support. Perhaps their most important role is to help team members adapt strategies and materials to match the common learning style. In addition, the autism specialist provides:

   - Training, feedback, and support to staff

   - Assistance in assessing, predicting, and preventing learning and behavior problems

- Assistance in the ongoing problem-solving process to refine and adapt program components and support systems
- Knowledge of resources for parents and professionals

An autism specialist is most helpful as a regular member of the support team with an opportunity to develop a collaborative, trusting, and supportive relationship with team members, to observe and work with the individual students to understand their unique characteristics, and to provide suggestions to prevent or resolve behavior problems.

The second grade class started each school day by reciting the Pledge of Allegiance. Gabriel did not like to do this activity because it held little meaning for him and he wanted to read the *TV Guide*. As soon as the children began the pledge, he would drop to the floor screaming. The teacher said, "Gabriel, as soon as the pledge is over, you can read your *TV Guide*." Immediately, he stopped screaming, stood up, and finished the pledge with the others. This routine was repeated for several days, until the autism specialist visited and suggested that the teacher reverse the situation: Before Gabriel drops to the floor, let him know that he will get the *TV Guide*. The next morning as class was beginning, the teacher said, "Gabriel, as soon as the pledge is finished, you can have the *TV Guide*." He immediately recited the pledge with the group and got his reward without first doing something inappropriate.

Two 4-year-old boys in the Head Start class were deaf. A teacher for the deaf was assigned to interpret and supplement the regular teaching program. One child was alert and social, continually watching the other children and the regular teacher for information. He also kept his eyes on the interpreter and was rapidly learning to sign. The other child, whose scores on nonverbal tests were in the gifted range, wandered aimlessly about. He did not attend to his peers, the regular teacher, or the teacher who was signing to him. He was not learning to sign. When it was discovered that autism was affecting his ability to learn, an autism consultant was engaged to provide staff training and to work with the team to make program adaptations. This child began to make progress and to attend to peers and staff.

Team Responsibilities

The team has five major responsibilities:

1. *Conduct formal and informal assessments* and incorporate information to develop and implement the educational program

2. *Collaborate to integrate therapies and services* into the total program

3. *Collect important data and keep anecdotal records* to identify and interpret potential problems, and then make program adaptations in a timely manner

4. *Assist in the design, construction, and modification of adaptations*, schedules, and other visual support systems

5. *Support the classroom staff*

Effective team members understand the impact of autism on learning and behavior. They are flexible, nondefensive, and able to brainstorm; they are willing to creatively modify any program or strategy that is not promoting meaningful progress. The Team Planning Checklist (Form 6.1, p. 119) summarizes the team process and the issues that the team must address.

Strategies for Effective Teams

An effective team collaborates and shares information and expertise. For this to occur, members must establish a supportive, non-threatening relationship for open discussion, solving problems, and providing positive feedback. Active involvement with such a team provides many opportunities for personal and professional growth.

Although there are many resources for facilitating the understanding of feelings and roles between parents and professionals, Raaz (1982) and Turnbull and Turnbull (1990) specifically address the issues of autism.

The following strategies can lead to an efficient and effective team that operates proactively:

- Develop a rapport and good working relationship. At the beginning of the school year or whenever a new member joins the team, take the time to establish trust and an open and supportive relationship for discussion and effective decision making.

- Assign an on-site team manager. The manager may or may not be the teacher. The team manager who is easily accessed by regular and support staff calls the team together, keeps it focused on the issues, and monitors communications and follow-through.

- Assign a recorder to keep track of the meeting agenda, major discussion points, and decisions. These notes provide a good history of problems, strategies, adaptations, and progress for future reference.

- Meet regularly and frequently. A team that meets regularly can develop very efficient working relationships and ultimately save time. The members are in a position to review progress, identify and deal with potential problems, and make program revisions *before* problems escalate. It is easier to schedule short, regular meetings early in the year. It is more disruptive and time consuming to pull team members together to deal with emergencies when they already have full schedules, the problems are severe and staff has become fatigued, worried, or defensive. *If things are going well, team members are in a position to reinforce each other and meetings can be brief.*

- Assign one member to bring construction materials to the meeting. The team can construct or refine the student's visual adaptations as quickly as decisions are made. This policy ensures that modifications are made before problems escalate. It also relieves the pressure on the teacher and teaching assistant.

- Take advantage of each member's area of expertise, strengths, and interests.

A good working relationship between team members and frequent but brief regular meetings are the keys to effective decision making.

Staffing

Perhaps the single most important issue is to insure that all school staff is trained to understand the needs of those with autism. Various levels of training should be available; bus drivers, cafeteria workers, the school secretary, school nurses and other school staff need some basic training to know how to manage issues that might arise in the various school settings. The classroom teacher and any teaching assistants who are providing the direct services need in-depth training to understand how to teach and support those with autism spectrum disorders to increase the learning rate and prevent problems.

Teachers in the regular classroom are exceedingly busy meeting the needs of 20 to 30 students, many with special needs. A full classroom includes a lot of action, stimulation, and information. Special classroom teachers are also busy. Although they may have fewer students, each one takes specialized attention. When one of the students in either setting has autism, a teacher will need extra assistance if all students are to have a positive educational experience. The extra assistance is necessary because someone must always be available to:

1. *Keep students with autism alert and actively involved.* Active involvement is perhaps the most critical element of effective early intervention (Dawson & Osterling, 1997).

2. *Identify and respond* quickly to the student's atypical efforts to communicate.

3. *Restructure activities* to capitalize on natural teaching opportunities with peers.

4. *Model and* coach effective communication and social behavior in natural situations.

5. *Monitor and manage problems related to safety issues* (see pages 412–413).

The additional staff assistance can be provided in a variety of ways. The most common ways are to hire, train, and assign an assistant either to the special student or to the classroom teacher. Although the distinctions are fine, there is the potential for several problems when training is provided only to the assistant who is assigned to the student with autism.

- *When assistants are trained and assigned to a specific student*, they are perceived to have the expertise and are often left with full responsibility to make decisions, even though they are not certified. This practice can have legal implications. The teacher, who is legally responsible for the student and the program, is at a disadvantage without the training, information to effectively supervise, provide feedback, and support an assistant.

  - The teacher has little opportunity to establish a relationship with the student, a distinct disadvantage when the assistant is absent or leaves, or when the teacher must represent the child at the team meetings.

  - The student can become isolated from peers and overly dependent on a single adult. A conscientious assistant who focuses all day on a single student becomes highly sensitive to that individual's needs and feelings. Without objective and informed feedback, it is easy to become overly protective, smoothing the way to avoid any stress instead of providing assistance to deal with stress.

- *When the assistant is trained and assigned to the similarly trained teacher*, the staff can work cooperatively, switching roles, solving problems creatively, and structuring opportunities for social interactions. This practice has many advantages; it provides more opportunities for the student to:

  - Become more flexible and able to work with more than one adult

  - Learn to work alone and to share attention as the assistant helps other students

  - Be included in small-group activities

  - Be seen by peers as more capable and independent

  - Become more flexible and able to work with and accept help from more adults in more settings

During free-play periods when peers were busy with toys, Matt routinely gathered all the long, narrow blocks, set them precisely side by side, tensed his shoulders, and grimaced and flapped his hands excitedly as he watched them. When staff, the teacher or the assistant, was available to structure his play and model more creative and interactive play, he learned to interact with more people and played with a larger selection of toys.

Heidi had just moved from the local Head Start class to a self-contained special education classroom in a regular elementary school. Her classmates were children who had various severe physical disabilities. None could speak more than a brief word or phrase and those in wheelchairs had assistants.

Heidi was very alert and active and followed basic classroom directions quickly. Although Heidi was unable to speak, she communicated by shifting her gaze from the teacher to objects and by touching or pointing to things. However, she had not learned to attract the teacher's attention first.

Each day, Heidi's behavior disintegrated. By the end of the first week of school, she screamed, bit her wrist, and banged her head many times a day. Her behavior was so disruptive to peers in adjoining rooms that she was in danger of being moved to an even more restrictive setting.

An autism consultant assessed the situation and found that Heidi's screaming and subsequent self-injury occurred in two specific situations: immediately after an unacknowledged attempt to communicate and after she had complied with a direction but had to wait for peers. For example, when the teacher said, "Line up at the door; it's time for library," Heidi went directly to the door, waited briefly, pointed to the door as she turned toward the teacher, frowned, and eventually screamed and bit her wrist. The teacher, who was trying to get peers to the door, did not see Heidi's compliance and attempts to communicate.

When the principal and staff understood that Heidi needed someone who could attend quickly to her communication and that she needed the stimulation of verbal and social peers, Heidi was integrated into a regular first-grade classroom and a full-time assistant was hired to assist the teacher. Although the plan called for gradual integration, her behavior improved so dramatically that by the end of the second week in the new class, Heidi was functioning successfully.

Staff Support

Teaching and supporting those with autism is demanding. Constant vigilance and quick thinking are required. Although it is a creative challenge, it can be emotionally and often physically draining. For staff to feel competent and be successful—to prevent burnout—they need:

1. *Training* to understand the autism learning style and the strategies to provide positive behavior support. Training is most effective when provided in units over a period of time and when there are opportunities to practice new skills with feedback.

2. *Time to plan.* A consistent, flexible, and productive program is possible only when the teacher and the assistant have time to review the data and make program adaptations together.

3. *Feedback and support.* Just as the staff shapes the student's behavior, the student shapes staff behavior. Without feedback from someone who understands this phenomenon, problems can occur as staff inadvertently become involved in ineffective routines (see the example of Gabriel on page 109).

Related Services

Services provided to compensate for problems and deficits related to or associated with a disability are called related services or related support services. These services ensure that the student benefits from instruction and makes appropriate progress toward goals. Related service needs are determined as the team reviews the assessment information.

Sometimes it is hard for the team to agree on the kinds and the amount of services needed. Although a student might benefit from more intense and comprehensive services, the public school is obligated to provide only *appropriate services—not the most appropriate services* (Board of Education of the Hendrick Hudson Central School District vs Rowley, 1982).

Auditory Integration Training (AIT) is an example of a treatment or therapy that many parents want for their child but that schools often feel is outside their responsibility. AIT is a relatively expensive procedure that requires a 2-week treatment period in special training centers. Because it is not yet clear which individuals may benefit, many school districts refuse to pay.

Commonly Needed Services

The related services most often needed by the student with autism are those that address severe:

- Language and communication problems
- Sensory and motor problems
- Social and behavior problems
- Attention and information-processing problems

Following are the services most commonly needed to address those problems and basic information about the delivery of the service.

- A speech-language pathologist (SLP) is an essential and regular member of the support team. The student needs SLP services in one-on-one sessions, when new skills and concepts are introduced, and/or with a small group of socially competent peers to provide a context for learning interaction skills. Perhaps the most important role of the SLP is to show families and school personnel how to teach and support language and communication all day, every day, and in every situation.

- An augmentative or alternative communication specialist (AAC) who is trained to assess the child's needs and provide technical assistance to augment their current communication and possibly to select and/or adapt electronic communication devices to match a student's specialized need. The AAC also may provide training to parents and staff who support the student's use of the systems or devices. The AAC is a resource to the support team, and generally participates only as needed.

- Specialized equipment. Some students need low-tech communication systems—systems that use concrete objects, picture or word boards, notebooks, and other materials—that are developed and constructed by staff. With advances in technology more communication options are available, such as specialized typewriters, computers, and electronic communication devices with voice output. Voice output devices can support communication for students who have motor problems that make speech and/or handwriting difficult.

■ An occupational therapist (OT). Autism is characterized as a major sensorimotor and sensory-processing problem. An OT understands the neurology of sensory processing and motor functioning. The OT is particularly helpful in assessing and solving problems related to sensory overload, attention, stereotypic behavior, and self-injury. An OT may provide individual therapy and also show parents and teachers how to adapt natural, age-appropriate activities so appropriate sensory stimulation and motor practice are provided throughout the day. An occupational therapist should be a regular member of the support team during early development and when severe and challenging attention or behavior problems occur during later development.

Note: A student benefits if the OT and the SLP work together to coordinate or integrate their services (Twachman-Cullen, 2001).

■ Extra classroom staff is generally needed for at least some part of each day. A younger child most often needs assistance (or an interpreter) full time. The older, more capable student may only need assistance for 15 or 30 minutes at the beginning and end of the day for help in organizing schedules, homework, and materials, or to clarify and resolve interpersonal problems. More assistance is required to allow participation in vocational and community training. Those with Asperger's syndrome often need considerable assistance to understand and manage the regular curriculum (Twachman-Cullen, 2001).

The need for extra classroom assistance varies from time to time. More assistance is needed when there are disruptions at home (e.g., a family illness, a new baby) or at school (e.g., a substitute teacher, preparation for holidays, when the student is learning functional and vocational skills in the community). Medical problems also affect tolerance for confusion, frustration, and ability to function. At certain seasons, allergies may create the need for more assistance.

■ Other related services may be required from time to time. A specialist in learning disabilities, a school counselor, or a school nurse are excellent resources to address specific problems. A special education teacher and an integration specialist can provide important services for students in regular classrooms and to prepare them for transitions to new schools or programs.

Safety Considerations

Safety issues must be addressed in all settings. Those with autism are generally unaware of potentially dangerous situations. At the same time, they have some unique abilities and disabilities that can cause harm to themselves or others. To complicate this situation, they are unable to communicate to seek clarification, ask for help, or report pain or an illnesses. Because parents are aware of their child's specific needs, they must see that specific safety issues are addressed in the student's individual educational program. For more detailed information, see Chapter 23.

Support to Address the Challenges of Asperger's Syndrome

The challenges of those with Asperger's syndrome are similar to the challenges of those at lower levels of the autism spectrum but at a much more complicated level. Wing (1991) quoted Van Krevelen as saying that the low-functioning child with autism "lives in a world of his own," but those who are higher functioning "live in our world but in [their] own way." Although those with Asperger's syndrome generally have average to above average intelligence and have superior rote memory skills, they have special challenges that must be addressed while planning their educational program.

The following description of problems and support needs is adapted from material by K. Williams (1995).

- They are overwhelmed by even minimal changes and become anxious and worry obsessively when unsure of what to expect. Stress, fatigue, and sensory overload can escalate these problems. They often engage in ritualized behavior—sometimes as a calming device. Their stress can rapidly accelerate to a major behavioral episode—sometimes as a response to an offer of assistance.

  - Will require extra support (an interpreter) to prepare and guide them through new tasks, activities, and changes in routines. Extra support is especially important during less structured situations and major transitions. They need a carefully designed schedule that includes time to engage in their special interests and provides consistency while gradually expanding the individual's tolerance for new people, environments, and activities.

- They are overwhelmed by social interactions and social situations but generally want to have friends and be socially involved. However, they do not understand body language and the hidden social rules; nor do they understand the perspective of others. Although they are highly verbal and can make long speeches about special interests, they have difficulty initiating, understanding, and sustaining interactive conversations. Although they look competent, they are naïve and egocentric, thus vulnerable to teasing and being tricked by peers.

  > One young man wanted everyone to follow the rules—for example, if a classmate was talking when he was supposed to be quiet, he would whisper loudly, "Shhh, the rule is—No Talking." He even warned the bullies in the class. They ultimately got him alone and beat him up. He never understood why.

  - Assistance from a speech/language/communication specialist and/or a school counselor will likely be needed to provide individual instruction in social and higher-level language and communication rules and skills—perhaps a social skills group. The presence of a teaching assistant at critical times to protect them from teasing and bullying, and to train and supervise peer buddies to provide support, is also helpful.

- They have limited but intense interests that dominate their minds and conversations. They often lecture and ask repetitive questions about their obsessive interests or hobbies and often refuse to do school work unrelated to special interests.

- Extra assistance or extra teacher attention is generally required to set and maintain specific rules to control and capitalize on these special interests to reinforce participation in other activities. They will need assistance to organize and manage homework. Also, extra support or a mentor can help expand these obsessions and interests to provide recognition for their special knowledge or talents and for future social and vocational opportunities.

- They are easily distracted by both internal and external stimuli. They are disorganized and have difficulty focusing on relevant information and often have difficulty learning in a group situation unless it is relevant to special interests.

  - They require a tremendous amount of structure and an interpreter to clarify rules, procedures, and processes. They need information organized so they see why it is important and how the elements fit together.

- They often have poor large- and fine-motor coordination that affects participation in physical activities and games as well as handwriting. They may have poor, slow, and labored penmanship that makes doing homework difficult. Their clumsiness frequently causes teasing that leads to frustration and increased stress.

  - They may need the assistance of an OT and they may need to be taught to use the computer to complete assignments. They will likely need their schedules, assignments, and testing procedures modified to provide more time to complete written requirements. Their physical education classes may need to be adapted to focus on individual exercise and sports rather than competitive team sports.

- Academic problems often result from their literal and concrete style of thinking. Although they may have average to above average intelligence, they have great difficulty with higher-level and abstract thinking and reasoning that affects comprehension and application skills. They will also likely have poor problem-solving skills.

  - Likely to need services of a speech/language specialist to focus on higher-level language skills. They are also likely to need a learning disabilities specialist to provide adaptations and support for academic work and to teach problem-solving skills to support self-management. They may need to be assigned to work in a learning resource classroom for at least some of their school day.

- Depression, both mild and severe, can be an issue for those in this population. They so want to be "normal" and to do what others are doing, but are so often thwarted by their learning problems. They are often "on the edge" emotionally; without a carefully structured program and sensitive interpreters, frustrations and stress can lead to frequent behavioral eruptions.

Also read the writings of individual who have Asperger's syndrome or those with higher functioning autism: D. Williams, 1994; Grandin, 1992, 1995; Grandin & Scariano, 1986; Newport, 2001; and Ledgin, 2002.

  - They may need the services of a school counselor. Additionally, all school staff need specific training to provide the support needed to prevent escalating stress, and to manage potential out-of-control behavior. Students with Asperger's syndrome need support to broaden their fixations and/or talents to improve self-concept and future options.

For additional resources, see Attwood, 1998; Myles and Southwick, 1999; and Wing, 1998.

Program Decisions

Placement Decisions

The federal law, IDEA, stipulates that placement decisions should be made after all the goals and support needs are identified. The law specifies that a child be placed or served in the most normal environment possible. The most normal setting is assumed to be where the neighborhood children of the same age go to school. If the team determines that adequate support cannot be provided in the setting attended by neighborhood peers, then that decision must be justified.

Setting Requirements

Because those with autism do not automatically transfer learning from one setting or situation to another, it is dangerous to assume that skills learned in isolated settings will transfer to the real world. It is also dangerous to assume that placements in programs outside the local school will result in friendships and supportive relationships with those in the neighborhood. Therefore, the most appropriate settings for most students with autism of any age are generally where neighborhood peers can serve as models and learn to understand and accept the problems of those with autism—and where the necessary support services and systems are in place.

Also consider the following issues as you make the placement decision:

■ Readiness for mainstreaming or inclusion is not dependent on "appropriate" behavior. Inappropriate or problem behaviors are indicators of inadequate or inappropriate support—that some element of the environment, even if in a special class, does not match the individual's need.

> At age 15, Tony was still served in the special class for young elementary and preschool children. This decision was justified because he was unable to speak, had not mastered readiness skills, had periodical violent outbursts, and was socially immature and vulnerable. When observed in that elementary setting during a free-time period, this long adolescent was lying on the rug in the play area randomly manipulating preschool toys. Smaller peers and some staff were afraid of him because occasionally he pushed or hit them when they got too close. Although his teacher was trying to teach him functional skills, he was passive and resisted most instruction. At the end of that school year, it was decided that he must transfer to the special class in the high school.

> After 6 weeks in the new setting, Tony was much more alert and stood tall. He had a job in the library, and he carried books as he walked in the halls, just like his peers. He continued to need a great deal of assistance, but he seemed comfortable in the setting with same-age peers, where there were real and meaningful things to do. His parents reported a much happier son who began to show interest in family activities.

■ Placement in a regular classroom does not ensure success. Without the appropriate staff training, services, and support systems, learning may have little meaning and usefulness. Students with autism can become:

■ Isolated, ignored, and devalued

■ Overstimulated and confused; they can lose control

■ Dependent on others for verbal directions and physical support

- If team members, including the parents, determine the need for a more sheltered or isolated placement, a target date for full inclusion should be set and a plan developed to keep the student in contact with normally developing peers and natural settings, and to transition smoothly between settings.

Summary

The key to a successful placement in any setting is an appropriate system to support effective learning and positive behavior. These services can and are currently provided successfully in a variety of natural settings such as in neighborhood schools and churches, Head Start programs, neighborhood cooperatives, and community colleges.

The strategies to provide an effective program are presented in Part 4, Interventions; Part 5, Teach New Skills; and Part 6, Manage Difficult Problems.

Specifically designed adaptations and instruction are always needed to ensure that instruction is understood and that new skills will be applied and used effectively in a variety of real situations.

In making the final placement decision, consider the criterion of the least dangerous assumption, and ask, which setting is most likely to lead to independence in the community as an adult? Once that question is answered, the appropriate support systems and services can be put into place.

The Support Team Members

1. Parents and/or caregivers   Name_____Phone_____
2. School principal _____Phone_____
3. Teacher(s) _____
4. Autism specialist_____Phone_____
5. Speech-language pathologist_____
6. Occupational therapist _____
7. Other _____

Team Process

1. Plan developed for establishing and maintaining team rapport and process
2. On-site case manager assigned _____Phone_____
3. Recorder assigned _____
4. Regular meeting times established (every 2 or 3 weeks).
5. Plan established for communicating student's priorities to all staff.
6. Plan developed for collecting and reviewing data.
7. Construction materials manager assigned.

The Instructional Setting

1. Is natural and includes age-appropriate peers who are both verbal and social
2. Is organized visually to prevent confusion
3. Has a quiet area for relief from sensory overload
4. Has well-defined work and leisure areas
5. Reflects individual safety considerations

The Instructional Staff

1. Receives ongoing training and support
2. Accommodates student's learning style
3. Identifies and interprets the student's nonconventional communication
4. Gives the student quick and positive feedback
5. Communicates effectively with the student
6. Organizes information visually and concretely to highlight meaning
7. Capitalizes on naturally occurring events and teachable moments
8. Prepares the student for new or changing events
9. Organizes transitions to prevent confusion
10. Predicts and defuses behavioral outbursts
11. Knows how to keep people safe in a crisis

The Program

1. Activities are adapted to address the critical goals for those with autism.
2. The program includes both cognitive/concept development and functional applications.
3. The daily/weekly schedule is balanced to incorporate a broad range of activities.
4. Instruction emphasizes meaning and function vs. rote memorization.
5. Expectations match variations in student's tolerance and functioning level.
6. Strengths and interests are used to compensate for the student's deficits.
7. Teaching strategies include natural cues, prompts, consequences, and reinforcers.
8. Visual strategies are used to clarify meaning and increase student's independence.
9. Related services are integrated into the natural activities and routines of the day.
10. Students are actively involved and alert.

Charlie's Story

—Written by his mother, Christine Marshall

Charlie is a 17-year-old high-functioning young man with autism. Taking time to reflect back over those 17 years helps me recognize how far we have come. I thought that child-rearing would allow me to put into practice all the wonderful knowledge I'd gleaned while getting my master's degree in education and during numerous years of teaching elementary school. I am having a difficult time finding examples of anything in my training or experience that prepared me for coping with a child who did not respond the way those children in the textbooks and classes responded.

Charlie was not diagnosed as autistic until he was 8 years old. I knew he was unique in the first year. Charlie was diagnosed as microcephalic (small head in comparison to the rest of body size) in his early years. This led to testing for mental retardation and other developmental delays, all of which came out negative. Yes, he was slow in some areas but not to a significant degree. What made a difference in these early years was the involvement of patient grandparents and getting him accepted into an exceptional preschool program. Charlie was reading at age 3. I think this was due to grandparents who could sit for hours and play language games and be willing to play these games over and over. (They played "name this object," then talked to Charlie about the object, made words with magnetic letters, and again talked about the words.)

[The question of whether to have Charlie begin] school was one of the few areas where I felt being a teacher made it easier [for me to decide to hold him] back for a year. Although he could read, the social-emotional areas were delayed. I had seen too many parents push children into school because they could read, while not attending to deficits in other areas of development.

During elementary school, getting Charlie labeled was a very positive step for everyone. Teachers who felt he was weird had more patience, adults around him were more accepting of his odd behavior, and his parents now had articles to read about his uniqueness. During this time, the greatest help came from a pediatrician who was able to problem solve and research ways to get Charlie diagnosed; the Cascade Regional Services to help develop ways to work with Charlie in the classroom; and teachers who were willing to work with him.

In spite of services available, parents need to communicate constantly with schools about what is going on with their child's program. An example of miscommunication: At the end of Charlie's elementary career, arrangements were made for a smooth transition to middle school. His schedule was to be hand-selected, and all teachers who would work with him would be given an in-service on autism. At the beginning of the school year, I checked with the school about his schedule and inservice, and discovered that nothing had been done. I continue to be Charlie's most reliable advocate.

Middle school provided the biggest problem, with puberty and homework getting the most attention. Much time was spent helping him so he could work at home and at school on what he thought was too much work. The school was aware of Charlie's autism, and teachers were chosen who could best work with him.

I found I really needed to be aware of his schedule, his classroom expectations, and his homework because he was not going to share that information. Finding one person in the building to coordinate information, meet with the regional people, and keep parents informed is a real must. In both high school and middle school, this role was filled by the resource-room teacher.

High school has presented some of the biggest rewards as well as challenges. Charlie adapted well to the change, thanks in large part to the resource teacher who arranges his schedule and informs Charlie's teachers about his disability and how it may affect his work. Charlie is now seeing himself as being able to succeed in a classroom. The challenge has been dealing with a few problems that developed along with puberty. At 16, everything was moving forward much better than ever expected. Then, a most annoying problem was diagnosed—obsessive-compulsive disorder (OCD). In Charlie's case, the disorder manifested itself with excessive hand washing and the need to straighten things over and over. The last 2 years have been spent trying several different drugs to help alleviate some of the symptoms. Chlomipramine, the first drug, worked wonders. We had a much more social child who said he even felt more social. The drug also helped with the OCD. However, after several months Charles developed a rapid heart rate, and we had to discontinue using Chlomipramine. We tried several other drugs and have chosen to leave him on Prozac until a new drug becomes available. Prozac has helped with Charlie's anxiety and OCD but it hasn't provided all the positive changes of the first drug.

Now we are looking ahead to high school graduation and the future. Fortunately, there are still some services to help with the transition. For me, one day at a time is all I can handle; the future still seems a little overwhelming to ponder for long.

An update, 8 years later:

Charles is almost 26 years old and continues to live at home. Since graduating with honors from high school, his goal has been to attend the University of Oregon and be a Duck. His first stop along the way to the U of O was to spend 6 years taking classes at Lane Community College. Lane has a disabled student services office, which informs teachers that they have a student with a disability and offers to work with accommodations: note taking, testing, etc. Leaving high school has meant leaving the support system that helped educate others about the disability of autism. My husband, Frank, and I soon found out that instructors needed more information about Charles' disability. Frank, who worked at Lane, met with Charles and his instructors about once each term—these meetings seemed to help them better understand Charles' needs. Each term presented new challenges and we had to become adept at asking Charles the correct questions to find out how things were going in class. Problems were as simple as arranging for more time to take a test, or explaining in more detail the characteristics of autism. Most instructors were willing to give Charles a little extra attention, especially as they better understood the disability.

My husband and I retired the summer before Charles transitioned to the U of O with junior status. Although professors are sent a letter from Disability Services at the U of O informing them that Charles is autistic and might need accommodations, most were unfamiliar with how to assist. Having the time to occasionally meet with Charles and his professors has allowed him to avoid serious difficulties. While disability services would like Charles to talk to the professors and/or to an advisor about his need—we have gently persisted that Charles speak for himself; however, he still needs an advocate (in this case his parents) to assist in the communication process.

Autism seems to be a little understood disability. My husband and I need to be vigilant about following Charles' daily life at the U of O and become involved when necessary. We feel fortunate to have the time to support him in reaching his academic goal of a bachelors' degree in general science. Charles seems to love the life of a college student and he also seems to enjoy spending hours doing homework. We've come a long way.

Develop a Balanced Program

There are many considerations for developing an effective IEP or IFSP—a document that lists prioritized goals and objectives and the support required to achieve the goals.

An intervention and support plan is much like a travel plan. It specifies the starting place (current level of functioning); a final destination (goals); and the hotels, restaurants, fuel, and repair services needed along the way (related services, adaptations, and teaching strategies). Travel plans vary from person to person. Some people who are flexible and have few needs require plans with a minimum amount of detail. Others who have many needs and feel insecure in strange places require a highly detailed plan with little left to chance. A skilled travel agent (the support team) carefully assesses the client's needs before developing the travel plan.

Those with autism need travel plans with considerable detail because they are unable to organize information or communicate reliably to cope with unexpected situations. The support team that prepares the plan must know a lot about the individual—the person's moods, abilities, tolerances, and preferences. The team must be prepared to assess and modify the plan regularly to reflect unexpected situations and the changing needs of the client, who is continually learning.

Develop the IEP

Following are some of the issues and considerations for developing an effective and balanced intervention and support plan—one that will cause the least damage if the decisions are wrong or inadequate.

Identify the Destination: Select Goals and Priorities

Teachers and parents sometimes dedicate their efforts to cure their child's autism or at least to make their child look and act "normal." Although parents must continually search for the best treatments and strategies, few children have made the transition from autism to "totally normal." Although such a goal is understandable, it must not be the overall goal. For no matter how hard parents and teachers work, some problems are inevitable and behavior will continue to look somewhat different. One father indicated that life might have been better for his son, now a young adult, if the effort spent on trying to make him look appropriate had been spent in teaching him to be more independent and to have fun.

Types of Goals

Four types of goals are considered in this section: the critical goals, traditional developmental goals, functional goals, and integrated goals.

1. *Critical goals are those based on the deficits of autism* (see Figure 6.1). These goals are given the highest priority and provide the basis for selecting other goals, developing the support system, and adapting activities. The six critical goals have implications throughout the life span for those with autism but the emphasis will be different during different ages and stages of

development, with more emphasis during initial intervention and during periods of high stress. These goals are addressed within the context of ongoing natural activities.

2. *Traditional developmental goals* are based on the orderly, step-by-step sequence of skills learned during the normal development of cognitive, language, social, readiness, and motor skills. The developmental approach is the basis for teaching most academic subjects. Movement to a higher step of the sequence depends on mastery of the previous step, and independence is achieved with mastery of all the steps. Traditional special education was based on this approach—to identify the deficits and remediate until the skills are mastered.

   Because those with autism learn in a holistic rather than a step-by-step sequential mode, rigid adherence to the goals of this traditional approach can lead to:

   - Acquisition of rote, isolated, and inflexible splinter skills that are difficult to generalize or transfer to natural contexts
   - Decreasing motivation to work on skills that have little apparent meaning to them
   - Fewer opportunities to learn how to perform basic life skills, thus limiting options and independence in adulthood

3. *Functional goals* address important life routines and activities that occur in specific natural environments such as home, work, community, and school. The functional curriculum approach teaches students how to participate in meaningful routines that have a highly motivating outcome. Broadly stated, functional goals specify the important life routines the student will learn to perform and the environment where the routine will be taught. An example of an integrated functional goal is: *Given assistance to start the equipment, Amy will play computer games during her leisure time in the classroom and at home.* . . .

   - This functional approach was developed to meet the needs of those with disabilities who are unable to master all the individual developmental steps, and thus as adults never learn to function effectively in the community. The functional approach that teaches skills in the context of meaningful life routines is important for those with autism, who learn routines relatively quickly. Functional programming, if carefully structured, ensures that skills will be generalized and results in greater independence.

4. *Integrated goals* incorporate the critical goals and the developmental goals into the context of the functional goals. Those integrated goals are taught in the context of important life routines such as dressing, preparing meals, and participating in community leisure activities. These integrated goals provide a framework for teaching numerous subskills such as moving, reaching, requesting, and counting. Because important life routines (dressing, shopping, and others) are repeated every day or on a regular basis, there are frequent opportunities to practice, master, generalize, and maintain the skills into adulthood.

Positive Proactive Goals

IEP goals can be negative and focus on eliminating or decreasing inappropriate behaviors. Such goals are limiting and give little direction for positive growth and increasing independence. Although problem behaviors should be addressed in the IEP, goals are most productive when stated positively to specify what the individual will learn. For example: *In stressful situations that occur in the context of natural routines, the student will learn to use a self-control/relaxation response and ask for assistance. . . . One measure of goal achievement could be a decrease in head banging, hitting, or running away.*

Prioritize Important Life Routines

The number of possible functional goals is practically unlimited. Prioritizing to select the most important and timely routines is difficult. Following a comprehensive assessment, the support team members collaborate to make the best decisions. The importance of any potential routine can be determined or weighted by asking four basic questions:

See Chapter 5 for procedures and forms to assess and determine priorities.

1. *Is this goal a family or caregiver priority?* Often, the family's highest priority is to resolve the eating, sleeping, toileting, and behavior problems that dominate family life. Families are also concerned that their children learn to dress and care for themselves, communicate basic needs, participate in family social activities, manage leisure time, help with chores, and manage a job.

2. *Is this goal important and essential?* Will it lead to greater independence and increased self-esteem now and in the future? Does this skill have immediate relevance to solve or prevent recurrence of specific problems at home, school, work, or community environments? Will this skill prevent a serious problem in the future? Will mastery of the goal increase options and increase peer respect and acceptance? For example, the ability to dress independently is important now and in the future. It increases the options to use the community gym and swimming pool and to stay overnight with friends. Learning to dress oneself leads to increased self-esteem and respect from peers.

3. *Is the goal related to the student's special interest or strength?* Has the student expressed interest in this specific job, leisure activity, or course of academic study?

4. *Is it a priority for the support team?* Is it age-appropriate? The different members of the support team see the student in various settings, and they may identify important routines that parents may not have considered. The team must consider the balance of goals and include routines for self-care, leisure, work, home, school, and community.

Special Interests and Academic Studies

Many of those with autism spectrum disorders are highly motivated to learn about areas of special interest. Others are capable of advanced study in highly specialized areas. Development of special interests and aptitudes leads to:

- Increased motivation and self-esteem—feelings of satisfaction and competence
- Increased leisure and vocational options
- Increased respect and peer acceptance
- Opportunities for making friends with similar interests

Academic skills can be taught and strengthened in the context of learning about these special interests and fixations. One young woman with autism was motivated by her high school science teacher to do research and pursue her interest in cattle squeeze chutes. This encouragement and assistance led her to a doctoral degree in animal psychology and an international reputation for excellence in designing cattle-handling equipment for stockyards and major meat-packing firms (Grandin, 1992). Not every student with autism would have such strong abilities, but many are more capable than IQ scores would suggest. In fact, some have said that if we try to cure those with higher-functioning autism or Asperger's syndrome, we will lose our geniuses.

There are several other issues to consider when making decisions about academic goals and curriculum:

- Basic academic instruction begins in early childhood through a language- and print-rich environment. (See Chapters 14, 17, 18, and 19).

- Capitalize on individual interests and fixations. (See Chapter 17).

- Organize and interpret the content meaningfully to ensure functional applications and generalization. (See Chapters 9, 14, 16, 17, and 18).

- Selection of curriculum and strategies is based on learning style. (See Chapters 2, 3, and 9).

Maria was interested in letters. When she and her peers learned letter names and sounds, she memorized them quickly and wanted to "do letters" all day. However, she wanted to use the letters only in a certain order with a certain deck of cards and with people who would repeat the rote scripts. When the teacher tried to move her to the next step, to blend the letter sounds to make words, Maria screamed, kicked, and fell to the floor.

Because she had developed such a rigid routine with the letters, Maria's program was changed in two ways:

1. Her daily schedule provided two times a day to "do letters" as a reinforcing activity following a period of other work.

2. Maria and her assistant developed written labels for the things she did and the objects she used. They planned class activities on charts and made lists for the things Maria needed to remember. As the class reviewed the activities of the day, Maria watched as her assistant wrote out a simple experience story for Maria to take home to show her parents. When Maria discovered that words had meaning and that the spoken word could be written down, she quickly learned to read from this visual, holistic approach. This modified language experience approach was productive in several ways. As she learned new language, it facilitated her recall of events in sequential order; and it prevented behavior problems by preparing her for changes and new activities.

Academic instruction is only one part of a balanced program. Problems are likely to occur when academic goals are overemphasized—when the primary goal is to graduate from high school with peers.

In summary, it is nearly impossible to accurately predict the learning potential of those with autism spectrum disorders, especially during the early years. A rigid adherence to either a developmental or functional curriculum approach can limit opportunities. An integrated approach that enables these students to gain basic information and general knowledge about the world and to engage in advanced study in areas of particular interest and aptitude is particularly needed by those with higher-functioning autism and Asperger's syndrome. Options should remain open, for even some of those apparently lower-functioning students can benefit from the opportunity to learn to read, write, and study other academic subjects.

Without specific instruction, Gabriel had learned to read by the time he was 3 years old. Although he was severely affected by autism, he made good progress in school and was in the regular academic program. He had an assistant who interpreted for him, helped him with his academic studies, and developed a peer network to support him. His parents helped him every night with his homework. With a great deal of effort by all, Gabriel graduated from high school with a regular diploma at age 18.

His friends planned to go on to college, get jobs, and move away from home—Gabriel assumed that he would do these things, too. However, he did not know how to make a phone call, manage money, find his way to the grocery store or the doctor, buy food or clothing, or do laundry. It was hard for him to accept that his high school diploma did not ensure that he had the skills to live away from home. He returned to high school and enrolled in a program for older students with disabilities. He worked hard until he was 21, learning to work, to take care of his basic needs, to manage his anxiety, and to fill his leisure time. At 25, he had a part-time job in an office and lived in an apartment with a friend/mentor. Gabriel has taken some classes at a local community college. His family continues to advocate and provide support whenever needed.

Identify the Starting Place: The Assessment

See Chapter 5 for tools and procedures to conduct a functional assessment.

An IEP, like a travel plan, cannot be developed without understanding the starting place—the current level of functioning in the home and community.

Assessment Goals

An assessment for a person with ASD is similar to that for an individual of the same age who has any other disability; but it is different in that much more emphasis must be given to the details. For example, the basic assessment questions for all individuals with disabilities are:

1. What does this person do now, and what support is currently provided?

2. What do we wish this person could do, and what support will be needed for this person to learn and continue to perform the new skills more independently?

To answer these two questions, an assessment must be conducted to address the individual's ability to function in various environments and their level of development in all the areas affected by their disability. In autism, the assessment must identify very specific details that must be considered when developing the instructional plan:

- Interests, preferences, dislikes
- Sensory problems and tolerance levels
- Reactions to change and new experiences
- Ability to relate and communicate with people
- Level of independence in various situations
- Specific pattern of learning strengths and deficits
- Specific discrepancies in skill development
- Gaps in understanding and use of language
- Gaps in understanding and use of social rules and skills
- Ability to focus on meaningful information in various situations
- Ability to manage anxiety—to relax

The Assessment Process

Because of the nature of the autism spectrum disorders, it is difficult to obtain valid and reliable information from traditional assessment procedures. For this reason, a comprehensive assessment must include two different types of procedures: functional assessment procedures and standardized testing. See Chapter 5 for the tools and strategies to conduct these assessments.

Develop the Daily Plan

Referring again to the analogy of the travel plan: The travel agent develops a daily plan or itinerary after establishing the client's needs and interests, point of departure, and final destination. The itinerary specifies the stops, the points of interest, the information centers, and key services. While the IEP is a guide—an outline of goals and objectives that give direction to the daily instructional program—it does not specify exactly what happens each day.

Teachers are responsible for implementing the IEP, developing the daily activities and schedules that provide the opportunities for achieving the goals. This is a demanding and time-consuming task. Although there are numerous curriculum products and resources on the market to provide ideas and strategies, *virtually all curricular approaches and products need adaptations to match the individual needs of those with autism.*

Essentially, the age-appropriate developmental materials and activities that naturally occur in typical school and community settings and within the ongoing life of the family provide the foundation and structure for achieving the goals. The skillful teacher schedules and structures the natural routines and activities of the day to address the critical, autism-specific goals (see Figure 6.1) and the important developmental and functional goals. *With sufficient planning, many things can be taught in the context of a single situation or activity.*

Amy screams and throws materials when she wants to stop working. She bites her wrist and closes her eyes when peers bump or brush against her. One of her functional goals is to participate in small-group activities that occur in her Head Start class. Two of her critical goals are to increase the amount of time she can tolerate sitting and working beside peers; and to communicate "All done" by pointing to a picture in her communication book.

When her peers work with puzzles, pegs, and other manipulative toys to improve their fine motor skills, Amy works beside them. A teaching assistant working nearby is alert for signs of stress so she can cue Amy to communicate "All done" before she throws materials or bites her wrist. As soon as Amy points to the picture (with some gestural prompting), the assistant acknowledges her message and quickly helps her put the materials away. Other less stressful individual activities that address other goals are prepared for Amy to do while her peers continue with puzzles. In the context of this single activity, Amy is strengthening her fine motor skills, increasing tolerance for working beside peers, and learning to communicate; screaming and throwing behaviors are decreasing.

Matt's functional goals include a job at the library, managing his money, travel in the community, and preparing his meals at home. He is taking science and home economics classes at high school. His critical goals relate to increasing independence, flexibility, and ability to communicate when stressed. To accomplish these goals, he is learning to use a small appointment/reference book (a visual support system) to help him communicate when stressed, manage his flexible schedule, and organize his homework and other chores. As he gains competence in using his support system, he is less dependent on others for verbal directions. Thus Matt is working to accomplish functional, academic, and critical goals each day.

Balanced Daily Plans and Schedules

Just as the most effective IEPs are balanced to address the range of important life routines, the most effective daily plans and schedules are balanced to provide many opportunities. A balanced approach is more likely to lead to success in the community than overemphasizing any one skill, strategy, or approach. A balanced program with a variety of activities, settings, and people leads to greater flexibility and increases options and motivation of students and staff. A balanced plan includes opportunities for:

- Learning developmental, academic, creative, and functional skills
- Work, play, and leisure—seriousness and silliness
- Work and play in various locations and group sizes (alone, in one-to-one sessions, and in small and large groups)
- Student-directed and adult-directed experiences
- Active involvement and quiet recovery time
- Work and leisure that involve movement and quiet sitting
- Helping and receiving help from peers
- New situations balanced with familiar situations
- Difficult and disliked tasks balanced with easier and preferred activities
- Interactions with those of different ages, interests, and abilities
- Instruction and practice in both natural and simulated settings
- Developing special interests and aptitudes

Activities that are scheduled and structured to include this balance are most likely to achieve the IEP goals while also achieving other goals that may have had a lower priority. Learning to play and enjoy leisure activities is as important as learning to work and manage self-care. In the midst of serious work, those with autism and those who support them occasionally need to relax and be a little silly together to relieve the pressure. In other words, those with autism need a broad range of opportunities just as those without disabilities need varied experiences.

Contexts for Instruction

Most new information and skills are introduced and rehearsed in both individual and small-group settings where the learner has the support to think and understand the meaning and purpose. Instruction is transferred almost immediately to natural settings where new skills are practiced within the context of functional routines. Instruction in the natural setting is critical to ensure that the learner attends to the natural cues, is guided by natural prompts, and is motivated by natural reinforcers. Success in natural settings depends to a large extent on the support and instruction that occurs in individual and group instructional contexts.

Individual Instruction

An individual instructional context is important for those with autism of any age because it offers:

1. Reduced stimulation that allows the learner to focus on relevant cues

2. A familiar, stress-free setting and structure for introducing new information and for preparing the learner for changes

3. A supportive and sensitive environment for providing guidance, practical feedback, and an opportunity to practice new skills for coping with everyday problems or personal, confidential issues

One-to-one instruction is especially important for the very young child who is first learning to focus and attend to instruction. These first sessions can be interactive play sessions (see Floortime strategies, Chapter 17), or work sessions at a desk (see strategies for teaching concepts, Chapters 16 and 18).

Other informal one-to-one support and problem-solving sessions occur throughout the day when the learner needs more information, a previously developed skill needs refinement, or when an unexpected problem occurs.

Small-Group Instruction

Many of the critical goals, especially those involving language concepts, social interactions, and cooperative skills, are more naturally introduced and practiced with more competent peers to serve as models. To provide a supportive context and more opportunities to practice these subtle skills, it is generally necessary to bring together a small group of peers on a regular basis. The purpose of these groups is to encourage interaction, group cooperation, and support while involved in natural play, discussion, or work situations. A successful interactive group is structured so that natural interactions are possible and so that everyone enjoys the experience and wants to return. Four types of groups are particularly helpful for learners with autism: play groups, social skill groups, cooperative work groups (such as academic work groups, scout or church groups, and special interest groups), and social support groups for adults.

See Chapter 21, page 372 for more information and strategies for developing and leading successful groups.

Monitor Progress

See Chapter 18 for data forms. Also see Form 5.7, Social Interaction Checklist: Monitoring Tool, in Chapter 5.

Formal data, informal notes, and anecdotal records provide important information for making decisions and for showing progress toward goal achievement. Because initial instruction is designed to prevent errors, the student will nearly always perform a task or a step of the routine correctly. Therefore, progress is measured by changes in the level of assistance required, the level of independence, the frequency and type of reinforcement, and the motivation of the student. Consider the following issues when developing a monitoring plan:

■ Before beginning to teach a new routine or skill it is important to take baseline data to answer the question: How is this student performing this skill or routine now? When the new skill or routine is first introduced, teachers need their hands free to manage materials, prompt and prevent errors, and refine or modify the instruction as soon as a problem is identified. For this reason, delay formal data collection for a day or two. Instead, make notes immediately following instruction. Describe problems, modifications, the level of assistance required, and the student's general attitude.

- Take probe data at least once a week to monitor progress and identify problems on each step of priority routines and the subskills listed on the IEP.

- Keep a notebook for each student for all staff to record anecdotal information each day. Anecdotal information is important for keeping all staff (including therapists and teaching assistants) informed of successes and potential problems. It is important to be aware of potential problems and modify instruction immediately to increase success and prevent critical learning and behavioral problems.

- Present the anecdotal records and formal data to the support team at least once a month for analysis and recommendations. Because minor modifications are made as the need is identified, progress is continuous and the learner maintains a positive attitude and does not practice errors or develop unproductive routines.

Classroom Management

A well-managed classroom is an essential element of a successful program; this is true in all educational programs but critical in programs for those with autism spectrum disorders (ASD). To insure that learning occurs and that behavior problems are prevented the classroom needs to be orderly. Chapters 11 through 14 provide strategies to organize and structure the classroom space as well as the schedules of events to enhance learning and prevent problems. In addition, the following three strategies will insure that staff will know what they are to do and with whom; these systems also keep the teacher informed of the student's performance when working with others.

1. *Develop a staff schedule system that can be easily changed each day*; a pocket chart and 3" x 5" cards works well. This enables the staff to see which child or group they are to work with and what they are to be doing. Mount this in a prominent location where it can be easily checked.

2. *Have a notebook for each student with autism where all staff, including therapists, can access it easily to record data and informal behavioral anecdotes each day.* This information is critical in order to document, understand, and avoid potential problems and to have examples of behavior that show growth and learning. Be certain that these anecdotes are dated.

3. *Have a basic summary or list of the student's priority goals in a place where it can be frequently reviewed by all staff.* This list could be on colored paper or tag board, laminated and placed prominently in the notebook.

Summary

More detailed planning is required to ensure that an intervention program will match the needs of those with autism spectrum disorders.

The time spent in initial planning is time well spent because the learning rate is increased and behavior problems are decreased. Teachers find that *the clarity of instruction required for those with autism also will increase the learning rate of other students in a class*—those with auditory processing difficulties, learning disabilities, attention deficits, other neurological problems, and communication disorders will benefit from this structure. Those who are learning English as a second language and those with stress- and anxiety-related emotional problems also find these strategies beneficial.

Life is a continuing challenge, often overwhelming and frustrating for those with autism spectrum disorders and for those who support them. Parents and teachers feel pressure to accomplish goals quickly. Life then becomes increasingly serious, filled with hard work and effort. Although it is necessary to focus on goals and structure to make life more comfortable and productive, it is also important to have fun. A well-balanced program includes both work and play, seriousness laced with a little silliness.

Humor breaks down barriers and resistance; it reduces stress and makes life worth living. Humor and fun renew the energy for continued effort. David Eastham illustrated the importance of keeping a sense of humor and balance in the following poem. (David sometimes referred to himself as "youth.")

LONELY BOY

JOKES HELP LONELY PEOPLE
THE WORLD DOESN'T SEEM SO BAD
HUMOUR JUST EASES PAIN
YOUTH NEEDS IT TO FORGET THE SAD

KIND PEOPLE GOOD TO KNOW
KILLING BOREDOM OF LIFE
NO ONE UNDERSTANDS
JOKES GOD'S SALVE ON LIFE

NO ONE YOUTH'S LOVER
GOD HAS SEEN TO THAT
JOKES PREVENT CLOSENESS
HOPE TO REMEDY THAT

HOPE GOD HAS A PLAN
HOPE PEOPLE KIND TO KNOW
BOTHERED BY IT GREATLY
LOOKING TO FIND OUT HOW

—David Eastham
In *UNDERSTAND: Fifty Memowriter Poems*

4

Interventions

FIDDLESTICKS

LOONEY EASTHAM
TRYING SO HARD
FIDDLESTICKS
JUMPING OUT IN
THE YARD
FIDDLESTICKS

ROTTEN YOUTH WASTED
ON ME
FIDDLESTICKS
GOD HAS IMITATED A
TREE

I REACH UP,
CANNOT TOUCH
FIDDLESTICKS
WANT TO MOVE AROUND
SO MUCH
FIDDLESTICKS

GUTS ARE NEEDED IN
A TREE
FIDDLESTICKS
HOPELESS TO TRY, ME
AND THE TREE

—David Eastham
In *Silent Words and Forever Friends*

Understanding Stress and Behavior: The Foundation of Intervention

Our understanding of a situation influences or determines our actions. Different perspectives of autism and behavior result in different treatments. When it was discovered that those with autism could learn—that they did respond to instruction based on behavioral principles—behavior modification was the treatment of choice. At that time behavior was defined narrowly, it was seen as purposeful and either appropriate or inappropriate. Strategies for eliminating "inappropriate" behavior involved manipulating the consequences—use of physical restraint, punishment, and sometimes drugs. These strategies, when used with those who had autism, generally resulted in increasingly severe and intense behavior problems.

Now that we understand behavior in a broader and more positive way, and now that we understand the impact of the autism learning style on behavior, we have developed more positive ways to intervene.

Understanding Behavior

This broader understanding of behavior includes the following four concepts:

1. *Behavior is communication*—a logical response to a current situation and an effort to regulate conditions that do not match needs. For example, a hungry infant cries—a reflexive (nonintentional) act. Parents instinctively review a mental checklist to interpret the infant's problem: Is it pain? discomfort? loneliness? hunger? When they identify the purpose or reason for the crying, they can meet their baby's need. In this situation, a reflexive behavior signals a need. The need must be interpreted by others.

> Every so often and for no apparent reason, Jason would hit staff members. An autism consultant who was assessing the problem observed one incident that occurred while several of the residents were boarding the van to go shopping. Just as Jason started to step into the van, he suddenly stopped and turned to leave. A staff member took him firmly by the arm to assist him back onto the van. At that point Jason slugged him in the stomach and ran back to the house. The consultant followed him to his room and observed the following sequence of actions: Jason stood on his bed, removed the ceiling tile, took his belt from the opening, and put it on. Quietly, with no assistance, he returned to the van, got in, sat down, and fastened his seat belt as if nothing had happened. In reviewing this information with parents, the consultant discovered that as a boy, Jason had been taught the rule: You must wear a belt before going outside. In his panic to follow the rule, he had to break away to get his belt. This reflexive (nonintentional) panic response certainly signaled a need, but the unconventional nature of the signal made it difficult for anyone to interpret.

2. *Behavior is a logical response to the environment in which the behavior was first learned.* But in those with autism, the history of the behavior sometimes

gets lost. The intervention is likely to be misdirected without the history that provides clues to the meaning and purpose of the behavior.

> During periods of free time, José ran from wall to wall slamming into the windows with both fists and forearms. After several behavior interventions had failed to eliminate this potentially dangerous behavior, a consultant was called in to conduct a functional assessment. From José's file, it was learned that this behavior began several years earlier when he was living in an institution. During that period, he began to watch ice hockey on TV. When José had nothing else to do, he pretended to play hockey, running from wall to wall and banging on the windows like the professional players bumped or hit the glass walls around the ice rink.
>
> Thus it was discovered that the behavior itself was not inappropriate; the problem was that it occurred in the wrong place. When it was understood that the purpose of the behavior was to fill unstructured leisure time and that there was nothing wrong in pretending to play hockey, staff members capitalized on José's interest. For example, he could be allowed to take free time in the gym, he could watch hockey on TV, and he could be encouraged to save his money to buy videotapes and magazines about hockey or to buy tickets and attend games.
>
> What is most important is that staff used a variety of visual strategies to teach José:
>
> - Why it is dangerous to hit windows
>
> - When and where he could pretend to play hockey, and
>
> - What he could and could not do for free time in various locations.

3. *Behavior is an attempt of the brain to keep itself stimulated or in equilibrium.* Repetitive and stereotypic (R/S) movements are an example of this situation. Behaviors such as rocking, arm and hand flapping, and finger flicking appear to serve as a release of tension and energy. They are more intense versions of our own nervous habits and reflect the individual's emotional state. When asked why they rock, flip their hands, or hop up and down, many individuals with autism say that it makes them feel better or more relaxed. Others indicate that R/S behavior occurs automatically "when (I am) not paying attention to my body" (Cesaroni & Garber, 1991, p. 309).

Repetitive and stereotypic behaviors occur more frequently and intensely during periods of either very high or very low levels of stimulation—when bored, overly excited, frustrated, confused, or very tired. The meaning of these unconventional signals is difficult to interpret without knowing the individual very well.

4. *Behavior is an outward expression of an inward state.* Illness, worries, fears, fatigue, and anxiety have a significant effect on tolerance and control. Initially, the behavioral signals of these internal states are reflexive actions that can be incredibly difficult to interpret.

Medical problems and medications cause a variety of behavior problems, including sudden changes in the pattern of an individual's behavior, self-injury, and behavioral outbursts. There are many examples of problems that did not respond to behavior modification that were corrected when the underlying medical condition was treated (see Figure 23.1).

This broader perspective of behavior removes much of the stigma from those with autism who learn and communicate differently. The person is no longer the problem. Rather, those with autism have problems with logical solutions:

Problem: An environment that does not make sense.

Solution: Environments can be modified to make more sense.

Problem: A lack of skills (social/self-management, communication, and others).

Solution: Skills can be taught.

Problem: A medical problem.

Solution: Medical problems can be treated.

Behavior problems can generally be solved when they are understood as logical and predictable responses to a person's situation.

Stress and Behavior

Stress is a normal part of life. A certain amount of stress provides motivation; but without adequate resources, too much stress is defeating. Studies by Klinger and Dawson (1992) suggested that there appears to be an optimal level of stress required for learning—if we have too little stress, our attention drifts, our sensory system is not engaged. But if we have too much stress our sensory system shuts down and nothing is registered. They indicated that this optimum range is very narrow in those with autism.

The variations in stress depend on such things as physical conditions, competence, feelings of self-esteem, trauma (e.g., losses, grief, worries, excitement), and the level of available support. Most of the time, people function best when the level of stress is balanced by an equal level of competence, confidence, and support.

Daily life is complex for everyone. Many demands and stressors affect a person's ability to be productive and lead a satisfactory life. Life is even more stressful for those with autism spectrum disorders because they cannot always make sense of or adapt to the demands of daily life. Stress, anxiety, and panic are common factors in autism spectrum disorders (Attwood, 1998; Groden, Cautela, Prince, & Berryman, 1994; Groden et al., 2001; Hardy, 1985; Myles et al., 2000).

Analyzing Stress

Suppose that everyone drew a line to reflect the intensity of frustration and anxiety that ebbs and flows throughout a day, a month, a year. Most of the lines—even those of individuals with autism—would be similar, with ups and downs and stretches of calm equilibrium. Some of the lines would show sharper or higher highs and deeper or longer lows. Some lines would have many highs and lows, while others would show long stretches of stable, even temperament and fewer variations.

When a section of each person's line is enlarged to study the sequence and the intensity of stress and behavior that occurs before, during, and after a severe behavioral outburst, a predictable profile is evident (see Figure 8.1). When a problem occurs, stress increases; as stress increases, the intensity of the behavior increases until there is a peak or crisis. Once the crisis is past, the stress drops to a

Figure 8.1 Profile: The Fluctuating Levels of Stress

An illustration of the varying levels of stress that ebb and flow over time. The enlarged area highlights the changing levels of stress that occur before, during, and after a crisis.

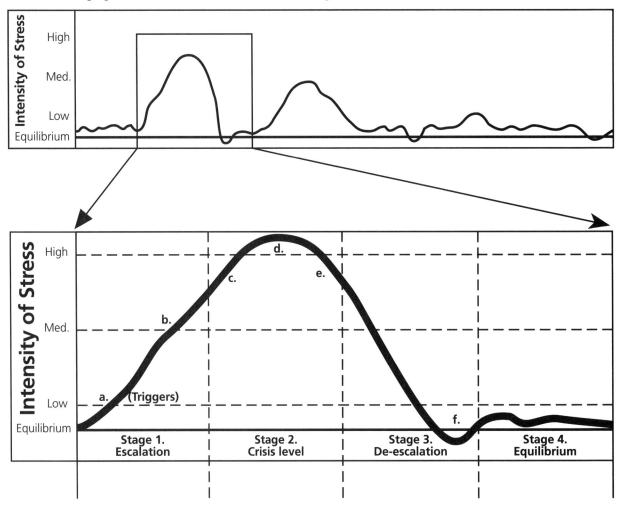

level of equilibrium—the optimum level of stress at which a person can function productively.

Awareness of this ebb and flow of stress is the foundation for intervening positively in the problems of those with autism. The intensity of stress is reflected by the intensity of behavior. Because the individual's need is different at each stage, the intervention goal is different at each stage. Strategies that would be effective at one stage might exacerbate the problem at a different stage. With this understanding, intervention strategies are flexible and designed to match the individual need at any specific point in a given situation.

Interpreting the Behavioral Message

Communication is difficult at best. Even people who are considered to be good communicators can miscommunicate. Body language can alter the conventional meaning of words and much is left to the interpretation of the listener.

The interpretation of messages is easier when people share a common language—signals and signs (body language and words) with culturally determined meanings and rules for use. Then everyone in the culture knows that a smile generally means that a person is friendly and happy or sees some humor in a situation. Everyone would also understand that a smile could have other meanings depending on the situation, the tone of voice, and the facial expression of the speaker.

Because those with autism do not automatically learn the culturally accepted rules and meanings of body language and words, it is difficult—but not impossible—to interpret their behavioral signals. We must look for clues to understand the function or the message behind behavior.

Chains of Behavior

Intense and severe behavior problems generally start with small behavioral signals (see page 159). Most people, including those with autism, begin to show irritation, boredom, fatigue, and confusion in a variety of subtle ways—yawning, stretching, restless movements, frowning, a raised eyebrow, or a questioning facial expression. If the situation does not change or if pressures are added, the feelings are likely to intensify; the individuals may raise their voices, become flushed, breathe harder, or pound on the table.

Most people have learned not to show intense feelings in public. They know how to manage these emotional and stressful situations. They can communicate in an attempt to effect change, they can leave, or they can talk themselves through the situation. Those with autism have little control over their lives and in many cases must depend on others to identify their feelings and needs and make changes in the environment. If the first small signals of a problem are ignored or not interpreted in a way to help resolve the problem, a chain of increasingly intense and severe behaviors is likely to develop. As stress increases, the behavioral signals intensify. This escalating chain of behavioral signals is illustrated in the profile of stress, Figure 8.2.

Figure 8.2 Profile of Stress: The Sequence of an Increasingly Intense Chain of Behavior

Some individuals may show fewer behavioral signals and progress rapidly from the trigger to the highly intense crisis behavior

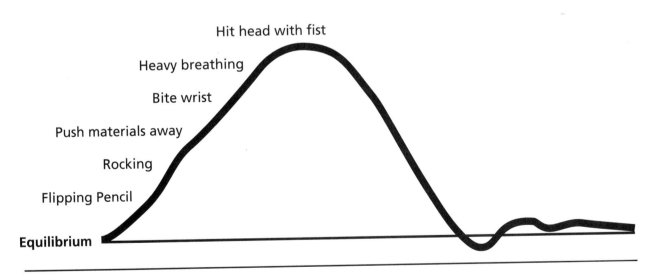

A Single Behavior—Multiple Meanings

Communication serves many functions—to request help, food, a social interaction, or an object; to reject, avoid, or protest a situation; to express feelings; to seek clarification or affection. It is easy to interpret the function of a behavior when a person intentionally uses a conventional signal (for example, stating a message and pointing to a picture or an object to direct the listener's attention to the need). It is more difficult to be certain of a message when the signal is reflexive or non-conventional, when it could have a variety of meanings.

Consider a woman sitting in an audience, tapping and swinging her foot. It would be hard to know why she is making those movements. She might be bored, impatient, or excited. She might also have an itchy foot, a nervous habit, or a need to go to the bathroom. She may be thinking about something that occurred at another time and place. To interpret the exact meaning of that behavior in that specific context, her habits, likes, worries, and past experiences must be known.

Most people can generate a variety of solutions for a single problem (see Figure 8.3a). Those with autism, however, have few alternatives for solving the many problems encountered each day. Therefore, a single behavior may be triggered by many different problems (see Figure 8.3b). For example, a scream could mean, "I need a drink," "Look at me," "I don't want to," "That hurts," "Let's play," "I have to get out of here," or "You haven't heard me, and I don't know what else to do."

Interpreting the meaning of a non-conventional signal at any given time depends on knowledge of the individual and knowledge of the various elements of the situation. Interpreting the meaning or function of a behavior is easier when one knows which situations are often stressful for those with autism.

Figure 8.3 Problems and Solutions

The first circle (a) illustrates that most people can generate a multitude of solutions for a single problem, while (b) illustrates that those with autism have limited solutions or alternatives for dealing with a multitude of problems. If an ineffective (or inappropriate) solution is eliminated (punished) without teaching a new solution, the individual is left with no solutions.

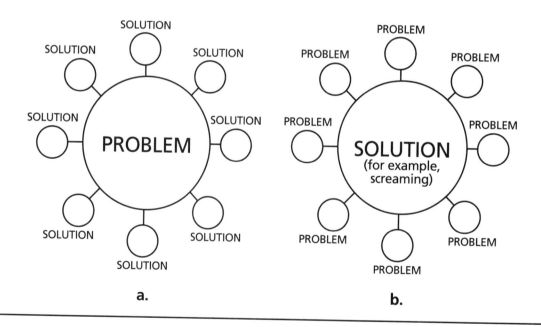

Situations Associated With Problems

Over- or understimulation is at the root of many problems, especially when a person's tolerance is low because of illness, fatigue, worries, or fears. The following situations are frequently associated with increased stress and potential problems:

1. *Situations involving people* are troublesome because of difficulty with or inability to:

   - Ignore or tolerate the abundance of sensory stimulation, such as talking, laughing, touching, odors, patterns of fabrics or jewelry, and changing facial expressions.

   - Understand what other people know, their points of view, their emotions, their social customs, and cultural rules— their communication.

   - Understand and become involved in the quick and ever-changing interactions, games, and activities.

   - Initiate and communicate effectively—especially when under stress.

2. *The inability to ignore, modulate, or organize sensory information.*

   - Noise and confusion of crowded situations, flickering lights, texture of clothing, and other sensory stimulation from outside the immediate area—traffic, talking in the halls, in other rooms or at other tables in restaurants.

   - Physical management—being pulled, pushed, tugged, or physically restrained.

   - Time pressures, too many choices or options, disorganized environments and materials.

   > The calendar, the bulletin board, the pictures, and other writing on the chalkboard distracted José so much that he was unable to copy the spelling words onto his paper. He copied the list quickly after the teacher highlighted his word list with a strip of red crepe paper.
   >
   > ———
   >
   > Matt, who loved to be outside, suddenly refused to go out for recess. After several days, his frustrated teacher discovered that he could not tolerate the odor of blooming sage and never went outside during that period.

   - Worries or fears about health, family matters, or world situations.

   - Boredom or waiting with nothing to do, having to do the same thing over and over, having to do things that are meaningless or too easy, or not knowing when something will end or be over.

3. *Demands* to do difficult, non-preferred activities, having to work on these tasks for too long, being rushed to move faster or to do more, or not knowing when a task will be finished.

   - Repeated demands or repeated directions, especially if they are made in a louder or harsher voice or if the speaker moves closer.

   - Making repeated mistakes, especially when followed by negatively stated corrections made in a loud or harsh voice.

4. *Interruptions and changes*—of schedules, rules, routines, activities, room arrangements, travel routes, or people.

- Someone or something new, or a familiar person or object is missing.

  > When Maria's interpreter left the room without warning, Maria became frantic, visually searching about the room, biting her wrist, and hyperventilating. When the interpreter stepped back inside the door a few moments later, Maria calmly returned to her work as if nothing had happened.

- New, unfamiliar or changed situations, settings, activities, rules, clothing, food, or people.

  > Gabriel frequently went to meetings with his mother. On one occasion the meeting was in an unfamiliar restaurant. He had taken a foreign language workbook and electronic equipment catalogs to work with during the meeting. Shortly after he had spread his work out on the table, the light bulb over his table burned out. It was too dark to read. He began to hyperventilate and rock back and forth. His mother suggested some alternative activities and moved a candle to the table. He stared at the wavering light of the candle and began flicking his fingers close to his eyes. The intensity and noise of his breathing and rocking began to increase. His mother could predict that a major outburst was imminent, and she took him home. The unfamiliar setting, sudden change of plans, and the sensory stimulation of the low, flickering light combined to overwhelm him.

- Transitions from one activity to the next, or from one setting or situation to another.

5. *Lack of information*—not understanding exactly what is to happen now, when or where an event will be, exactly how to do the work, exactly when to start, when work will be over, or what will happen next.

- Misunderstanding or misinterpretation of information, literal interpretations or hearing only a part of the information.

  > Andy, with his interpreter, took the pop cans from the teacher's lounge each day to recycle at a nearby store. The morning after a party in the gym, they were asked to take the cans from the gym also. As Andy started off on his normal route, his interpreter tried to get him to go to the gym, but Andy began to kick, bite his wrist, and hyperventilate. Because Andy had not processed the teacher's verbal directions, he was unprepared for the change.
  >
  > _____
  >
  > Jeff, who loved movie projectors, was quite verbal. He was scheduled to set up the projector so the class could view a movie after the math lesson. While Jeff was sitting across the table from his teacher working on math, another teacher entered the room and asked to use the projector later in the afternoon. When his teacher confirmed the request, Jeff jumped to his feet, leaned across the table, placed his hands around the teacher's throat, and, breathing heavily, brought his face close to hers.

Calmly and without moving, his teacher said, "Jeff, first do your math. Second, set up the projector and see the movie. And third, take the projector to Mrs. Peters' room." Immediately Jeff sat down and continued working as if nothing unusual had occurred.

Jeff's panic and reflexive, unconventional behavior were triggered by his fear that he had lost a favorite activity—a misunderstanding of the discussion and the sequence of events. In his panic, he was unable to use his verbal communication skills to ask for clarification. The situation was saved by an understanding teacher who quickly interpreted the function of the unconventional signal and provided the needed information to defuse the situation and prevent escalation.

Unique Interpretation Problems

Parents and teachers must be prepared to identify, interpret, and respond appropriately to the subtle and not-so-subtle problems and messages of those with autism spectrum disorders. This requires vigilance and extreme sensitivity—the need to be constantly alert is tiring. It can be both confusing and frustrating when the meaning of a behavioral signal is hidden.

Problem 1. We are confused when conventional signals are used unconventionally—when words and gestures that look familiar are used with different, unusual, and unexpected meanings.

This is a frequent problem in autism. Individuals may smile when they are in pain or when sad or confused. They may echo words without understanding the meaning or associate unusual meanings to words. Sometimes these signals seem so appropriate to the situation that their meanings are not questioned. This is particularly true for those with Asperger's syndrome or higher-functioning autism who insert echoed phrases into conversations. At other times, the echoed statement or phrase makes no sense in the specific situation.

Recall the young man who shouted, "The cat jumped off the balcony;" José, who kept repeating, "Drink" when he meant music; and Maria, who said, "No" when she meant "Yes."

Refer to the strategies for dealing with these interpretation problems in Chapters 10 and 20.

Interpretation is dependent upon an understanding of the individual, the common learning style, the various types of communication problems, and awareness of the situations that are likely to trigger confusion and problems.

Problem 2. People get angry when behavior is seen as deliberate and purposeful.

They tend to feel that the individual with autism is deliberately trying to make life miserable, to disrupt, to hurt, or to avoid. When frustration and anger persist, it is natural to want to punish and to avoid. These reactions are likely to make the situation worse. In most cases, individuals with autism are doing the best they can in a very confusing world.

Although the behavior may occasionally be intentional, in most other situations the behavior is reflexive, a quick reaction to confusion, frustration, and anxiety when the individual has no other alternative. There are clues to help determine whether the behavior is intentional or reflexive.

■ Intentional behavior depends on a clear understanding that a specific signal will achieve a specific goal, and a persistent effort is made to engage a listener and to send the specific message.

- Intentional verbal responses are often less fluent, generally delivered more slowly, with a flat vocal quality and little change of expression. Words are often used in unusual combinations, or speech may be excessively formal.

- Unintentional or reflexive behavioral signals are reactive responses to the stimulation and feelings of the moment; they will occur whether or not there is a listener. In some situations, these reactive behaviors are intense versions of primitive and instinctive fight-or-flight responses (such as that shown by Gabriel when he said, "Mrs. Brown, this is no laughing matter" or Jeff, who had his hands about his teacher's throat).

- Reflexive, reactive responses are usually quick, rote, and often smooth and fluent. For example, echolalic verbal messages are delivered quickly; they are well articulated, grammatically correct, and fluent, with expressive vocal quality.

Problem 3. We are confused when someone who can talk or communicate, does not talk or communicate all the time.

Communication is not a natural and automatic process for those with autism. Those who can speak or communicate in other ways under normal and familiar situations forget or are unable to use those skills when they are startled and anxious. As a rule, in stressful situations, communicative behavior is more frequently nonintentional, reflexive, and reactive. But even reactive and nonintentional behavior will have communicative value. It reflects a message about a person's emotional state and about his or her problems. It is up to caregivers and friends to identify, interpret, and help solve the problem.

Problem 4. We get tired of answering the same questions over and over.

See Chapter 20 for strategies to deal with repetitive questions.

Sometimes the signal is a question repeated again and again. Many times these questions are seen as meaningless and are ignored. Sometimes the exact question is answered over and over as the individual gets more and more upset. In these situations, the question is used intentionally and has a legitimate message but the individual is unable to ask the right question so the message must be interpreted by others.

Problem 5. We are confused because the same behavior sometimes is a reflexive response and sometimes is used intentionally.

See Chapters 16 & 19 for strategies to avoid teaching erroneous concepts.

A reflexive, reactive signal can take on meaning if it is consistently and predictably followed by a consistent response. For example, a person who is consistently sent to time-out when head-banging, may bang his head to signal, "I need a break"— especially if the person has no better or more efficient alternative.

In this way, a non-conventional signal, such as repetitive/stereotypic or self-injurious behavior, may be used intentionally to avoid or escape from an unpleasant situation, when initially it was used reflexively in response to a boring, painful, or overwhelming situation. The problem of interpretation is now more complex.

Problem 6. Sometimes the words and the message are understood, but we cannot or do not want to acknowledge the message.

Refer to Chapter 10 for visual and verbal strategies to acknowledge the message when it is not possible to provide what the individual wants.

Parents and teachers often want to ignore a message when it does not fit their agenda. For example, when the individual with autism says, "All done" or "Outside" when the schedule says there is more work to be done, what is a person to do? If the goal is for that person to communicate spontaneously, the person must find out that communication pays off. Therefore, messages must be acknowledged so the power of communication is evident.

Summary

Just as most people have many small and large problems, needs, and wants, those with autism spectrum disorders have many problems, needs, and wants. Although most people have many alternative ways to solve each of their problems, those with autism have limited alternatives and solutions. If information cannot be manipulated to generate and evaluate alternatives and if communication is difficult or unreliable, solutions are likely to be both inappropriate and ineffective. If interventions are simply directed to eliminate the inappropriate behaviors, the individual is left with no solutions (refer again to Figure 8.3). The learning and thinking problems in autism are such that effective support and intervention must be based on accurate interpretations of behavior. The following chapters provide information and guidance to intervene and support those with autism in a positive and productive way to maintain that optimum level of stress.

Intervention Planning—A Proactive Approach

In Charlie's Story, at the end of Chapter 6, his mother Christine Marshall remarked, "I thought that child-rearing would allow me to put into practice all the wonderful knowledge I'd gleaned while getting my master's degree in education and during numerous years of teaching elementary school. I am having a difficult time finding examples of anything in my training or experience that prepared me for coping with a child who did not respond the way those children in the textbooks and classes responded."

The contradictory array of intervention models and strategies reported in the literature of autism is exceedingly confusing (and controversial) for parents and teachers alike. Perhaps the current movement toward integrating the best strategies from all models to match individual needs will help resolve some of those contradictions (Feinberg & Vacca, 2000; Simpson, 2001). Teachers have long known that strategies must be modified for those who learn and see the world differently (see Figure 9.1). But the questions remain, which strategies do we select? And, how do we modify these strategies and apply them appropriately? The following sections should help answer those questions.

Figure 9.1 Typical Teaching Strategies

These strategies are effective for most students, but must be modified for effective use for students with autism spectrum disorders.

- Verbal instruction
- Social rewards
- Role play
- Rigid behavioral programs
- Exploratory and incidental learning
- Logical/natural consequences
- Repetitive practice for retention
- Mastery or criteria skill-based training
- Large-group instruction
- Commercially produced curriculum materials

The Foundation—How Do We Learn?

A brief historical review of the various theories of the learning process will provide the framework for integrating the different models and strategies to meet individual needs. Essentially, it all began with the scientific study of how people learn—producing some basic principles or learning theories. One of the primary principles is that all learning occurs in a specific sequence that includes a cue (or stimuli) that triggers a response (or behavior), which in turn triggers a consequence, either punishing or reinforcing. An extension of this principle is social learning theory—whenever there is an interaction between two or more people, the behavior of one person will affect the behavior of the other.

For a brief and interesting history of learning theories, read Wolery, Bailey, & Sugai, 1988.

The Neurophysiological Approach

Neurophysiologists who study the brain structures and the central nervous system (CNS) have recognized that as learning occurs, neurological pathways are developed that activate ever more complex brain development and higher levels of learning—and that by 5 or 6 years of age, most of the major brain and CNS structures are in place. This study is the foundation of the early intervention movement. As yet, there is no evidence that any one philosophy of treatment builds neural pathways better or more effectively than any other treatment model.

The Information Processing Approach

This approach involved studies of the sensory system (auditory, visual, etc.) and the processes involved in learning—what happens between the input of sensory information and the output, or resulting behavior. Efficient and effective learning depends on the efficiency of these processing systems and the automatic interactions between the systems. The understanding of learning styles is a product of this research. This is critical information as we design interventions to match the unique individual needs of all students. Sensory integration therapy is a product of this approach (Ayres, 1983; King, 1991).

The Cognitive/Developmental Approach

The psychologists developed the theory that an individual's behavior is influenced by environmental conditions and by what a person knows or believes to be true about the environment. The word *cognitive* pertains to the mental processes of knowing—perception, memory, reasoning, and judgment. A child's understanding and beliefs about a situation will depend on the stage of cognitive development that has been mastered. For example, if a child has not yet achieved the stage to understand the perspective of others, he or she will interpret information and behavior from his or her own perspective.

This cognitive/developmental approach is the basis for strategies that call for teachers and parents to arrange the environment so that:

- The child has opportunities to be actively engaged in activities that are interesting, challenging, and at the child's level of understanding while stimulating and supporting the next step of development.

- Growth is promoted through active involvement and interactions with the real environment—so they can learn by doing rather than by being told.

- Feedback is provided as a result of the natural and real consequences of the child's own efforts and actions.

Cognitive teaching strategies provide information in a way to clarify meaning and prevent or correct false beliefs and encourage thinking. When used with students who have autism spectrum disorders, these strategies capitalize on the visual strengths to compensate for the inability to analyze and make accurate sense of environmental events, to analyze and solve problems, and to make judgments.

The developmental, individual difference, relationship-based approach is a product of this approach (Greenspan, Wieder, & Simons, 1998; Peloquin, 2001).

The Behavioral Approach

The behavioral approach is an outgrowth of Skinner's work reported in 1953. The behavioral psychologists who developed these approaches worked under the theory that human/animal behavior can be accurately studied through the analysis of an individual's response to the environment. Learning is defined as an observable change in behavior; behavior is defined as any observable activity that can be measured. Behavioral principles and techniques were developed from this highly systematic study of the effects of various environmental conditions on learning—in essence, behavioral strategies involve varying the types of cues, prompts, and consequences and the way in which they are presented to a learner to achieve a desired effect.

Applied behavior analysis (ABA) is actually a research procedure used to study behavior change, or the effects of different applications of the behavioral principles and strategies to teach important skills and/or to change or eliminate inappropriate behavior. Behavioral principles and techniques are critically important for designing and delivering clear and effective instruction. Although frequently misrepresented, ABA is a useful and flexible method that can be applied in various ways—both structured situations and informal/incidental situations to teach a wide variety of skills, including social, communication, academic, and functional skills. Other commonly used behavioral strategies include: Incidental Teaching, Pivotal Response Training and the Natural Language Paradigm (Koegel & Koegel, 1996).

Lovaas (1987) was one of the earliest to report that these behavioral strategies could be used to teach autistic children (behavior modification). He developed the Intensive Behavioral Intervention program at UCLA and refined the Discrete Trial Training (DTT) model. See Smith (2001) for a brief review and history of DTT.

The Controversy—What Is the Best Approach?

A great deal of time, money, energy, and emotion have been expended in the last several years as the controversy about the "best" treatment for those with autism spectrum disorders has escalated. The most unfortunate aspect of this controversy is that the parents and their children have been caught in the middle—even while there is no conclusive evidence that any one treatment model is best for all children with ASD.

The summer 2001 issue of *Focus on Autism and Other Developmental Disabilities* provided an historical overview of applied behavior analysis in which several authors expressed their concern about ending the controversy. R. L. Simpson indicates his agreement with Rimland (1999), saying, "I am dismayed and appalled at the ludicrous position taken by many other supporters of ABA, who claim that ABA is the *only* scientifically validated treatment for autism. Not so! That position is not only false, it is absurd." Simpson continues, "Exclusive use of any program may be appropriate for some students, families, and professionals, but clearly would not be the preferred intervention under every condition for all." (p. 70).

This statement also expresses the belief of many others (including Brown and Bambara, 1999, and Feinberg and Vacca, 2000) who indicate that there is a growing urgency to end the competition between different camps and to merge the best of each theory. They also suggest the need to integrate the strategies and perspectives as well as staff and parent training—that all need similar training and need to use the same vocabulary. Finally, Feinberg and Vacca (2000, p. 136) suggest that, "Such reframing can defuse tensions among team members and families—(to allow them to) talk about the child as an individual rather than the child as representative of a diagnosis."

An Integrated Approach

The principles and theories developed by these four approaches apply to all people every day. We all (parents, teachers, and students) use and are affected by these principles whether or not we are aware of it—a bit like the laws of gravity. These theories and processes are automatically in force as typically developing children explore and learn from their environment. However, when a child, for any reason, is unable to learn automatically from the environment, teachers and parents must intervene and take a more active role—setting up the environment (the cues), providing assistance (the prompts), and arranging the consequences to ensure that important skills are learned. With autism, the principles must be applied more specifically and more carefully, if we want positive results.

Most well-known programs have integrated the best from various approaches.

An Integrated Intervention Planning Process

As noted above, learning and behavior are influenced not only by the antecedents and the consequences surrounding a situation but also by the interpretations, thoughts, and feelings about the situation. In autism, these interpretations, thoughts, and feelings are influenced by the learning or cognitive processing style. Therefore, this book integrates the principles and strategies from all the above approaches as instructional and support plans are developed. Intervention strategies that are most likely to ensure competence and independence are based on the two basic rules that guide this planning:

1. *Capitalize on learning strengths and individual interests* to compensate for predictable learning problems (see Figure 9.2).

2. *The integration of cognitive, behavioral, and developmental strategies* is guided by the unique learning style of each child with autism spectrum disorders.

    -   An understanding of the learning style gives insight into the perspective of individuals with autism and is essential for predicting potential problems, interpreting assessment results, and developing adaptations and support systems.

    -   An understanding of behavior principles is also important as learning and behavior problems are assessed and instructional sequences are developed and delivered with clarity.

    -   Cognitive strategies provide a broader range of alternatives to ensure that learning is meaningful and more flexible.

Reliance on either rule, to the exclusion of the other, has costly and sometimes paradoxical effects:

-   Important and meaningful skills are not learned or generalized.

-   Unintended and unexpected things are learned.

-   The learner becomes overly dependent on the instructor.

-   The above problems are highly resistant and time consuming to change.

Figure 9.2 Learning Strengths, Personality Traits, and Deficits Common in Autism

The ability to:

- Take in chunks of information quickly—the whole thing
- Remember information for a long time
- Learn to use visual information meaningfully
- Learn and repeat long routines
- Understand and use concrete, context-free information and rules
- Concentrate on narrow topics of specific interest

Predictable Personality Traits

- Perfectionism; honest, naive, and overly compliant

An inability or decreased ability to automatically, consistently, and/or independently:

- Modulate and process or integrate sensory stimulation
- Control attention, scan to identify, and focus on important information (overfocuses on irrelevant details)
- Analyze, organize, and integrate information to derive meaning (memorizes details, rote responses, and rules rather than concepts)
- Retrieve information in sequential order (interferes with learning cause/effect relationships and ability to predict and prepare for future events)
- Perceive and organize events in time and understand language related to time (leads to confusion and time-related anxiety)
- Understand the complex and changing meanings and nuances of the language (understands and uses the language literally)
- Integrate auditory information efficiently (leads to delays in response time and information gaps)
- Generate alternatives or solve problems that involve hypothesis testing and social judgment (often repeats the same responses over and over)
- Modify or generalize information from one situation to another (learns and uses concepts and skills exactly as taught)
- Control thoughts, movements, and responses (perseverates and gets stuck in motor and verbal routines or responses; may seem driven and compulsive)
- Adjust to new or novel information and events (leads to extreme anxiety associated with change and trying new things)
- Initiate communication to ask for assistance or clarification (leads to confusion, frustration, anxiety, and ineffective behavioral responses)
- Perceive social/cultural rules and the perspective of others (leads to confusion, misunderstandings, and unexpected and ineffective responses)

In summary, those with autism are unable to independently integrate bits and pieces of information to make meaning, to expand, or to use information flexibly.

Paradoxical Effects of Learning Strengths

There are both positive and paradoxical effects of the six learning-style strengths that must be considered when planning instruction.

Strength 1. The ability to take in chunks of information quickly—the whole thing.

Gestalt processing, *wholistic learning*, and *one-trial learning* are terms often used to identify this processing style.

Positive effect. With prior organization of the information to highlight relevant details, relationships, and meaning, the learning rate is accelerated.

Paradoxical effect. Without prior organization and editing for relevance and meaning, the chunks of information are cluttered with irrelevant background details and unrelated information. For example, cues, prompts, and reinforcement may be learned and have as much relevance as the critical details.

Strength 2. The ability to remember information for a long time.

Positive effect. When information is organized for clarity of meaning before presentation, information is stored meaningfully, remembered, and available for meaningful use.

Paradoxical effect. Unanalyzed and cluttered information is stored firmly without meaning, and thus is unavailable for integration and effective use.

Strength 3. The ability to use visual information meaningfully.

Positive effect. When information is organized and presented visually, it is available for later reference and compensates for the attention, auditory processing, and sequential memory deficits. The ability to use visual information leads to greater independence from constant verbal directions—cues and prompts.

Paradoxical effect. Irrelevant or background visual details can overwhelm or block attention to relevant information and meaning. For example, the detail of wood grain on a table or reflections in a mirror can override important visual details. Unless the relevant visual details are organized and highlighted, they will not automatically lead to an understanding of the big picture—the major concepts.

Strength 4. The ability to learn and repeat long routines.

Positive effect. When the steps and skills of an important routine are tied together in an integrated sequence with a clear beginning and end and taught fluently without errors, the total routine is recorded together on the same tape. In this way, many functional and meaningful skills are taught and generalized within a fairly short period of time. The opportunity to complete any familiar routine is highly motivating and reduces the need for artificial reinforcers.

Paradoxical effect. Independently developed routines often include extraneous and irrelevant steps that prevent the accomplishment of a meaningful purpose. A familiar routine is likely to be repeated over and over again without modification or useful outcome simply because it provides highly reinforcing predictability and comfort. Severe behavior problems often occur when these rigid routines are interrupted.

Strength 5. The ability to understand and use concrete, context-free information and rules.

(For example, math rules are concrete and never change; social rules change depending on the context.)

Positive effect. Concepts and rules that are clearly defined and presented visually to show the range of applications are learned quickly, and it is more likely that they can be applied to different situations and that they will be applied more flexibly.

Paradoxical effect. Without specifically designed instruction, rules and concepts will not be modified to apply appropriately in different situations but will be used rigidly, exactly as taught and used only in similar situations.

Strength 6. The ability to concentrate on narrow topics of specific interest.

Positive effect. With thoughtful and creative planning and support, topics of specific interest serve as important reinforcers for learning a broad range of concepts and skills, for increasing flexibility, esteem, and peer respect. Special interests are an important vehicle for establishing friendships and they have potential leisure and vocational value. This ability to focus intently on topics of specific interest is the quality that enabled people like Edison and Einstein to contribute so much to the world.

Paradoxical effect. Without concerted effort and organization to broaden the focus and expand the interests, rigidity and inflexibility frequently lead to severe problem behaviors, potential isolation, and limited skills.

When learning style and cognitive/behavioral principles guide interventions, learning rate, flexibility, self-esteem, and independence are increased while learning errors and behavior problems related to confusion, failure and rigidity are decreased.

Three Basic Intervention Processes

To maintain an optimum level of stimulation for effective learning and behavior, intervention involves and revolves around three major processes:

Process 1—Evaluate and Refine

Evaluate and refine the structure of environments, materials, and elements of the teaching/support plan to clarify the situation, maintain focus on learning, and prevent or resolve behavior problems quickly.

Small and seemingly insignificant elements or factors have a profound effect on the ability to focus, learn, and function effectively. Similarly, small and seemingly insignificant adjustments or refinements in the environment or the intervention and instructional plan can make a significant difference. These immediate refinements or modifications prevent anxiety and support an optimal learning environment.

Process 2—Organize and Structure

Organize and structure space, time, and events (including instruction) to compensate for the deficits of autism.

Those who have difficulty processing sensory information must rely on others to provide external structure that reduces distractions, highlights relevant information, clarifies meaning and purpose, and supports independent action.

Process 3—Teach New Skills

Teach new skills to develop and expand competence and independence.

Those whose early learning and development were disrupted by the autism learning style lack many of the subtle but basic understandings and critical skills that peers learn automatically from simply living in the culture. *Many problems of those with autism are related to these concept and skill deficits.*

These three very general processes are dynamic and constantly evolving (see Figure 9.3). Each action, or procedure, is a part of an interrelated, creative problem-solving process that guides and provides a focus for intervention and support efforts. With experience, this process can be applied to match the ever-changing needs of

Figure 9.3 Three Basic Intervention Processes

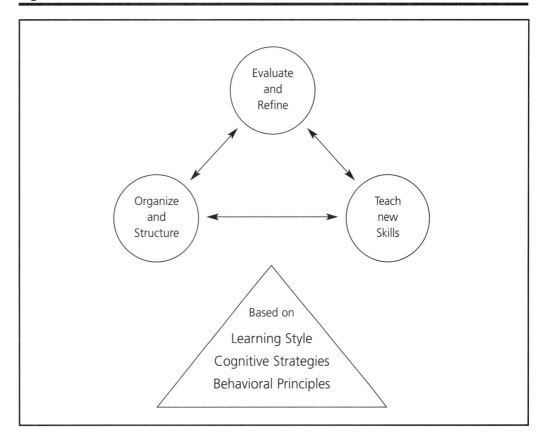

those of any age and ability level who have autism spectrum disorders in varied situations and with varied problems. *The driving force behind these three procedures is the presence of a knowledgeable and sensitive interpreter and guide.*

The Interpreter/Guide

To paraphrase Webster, an interpreter/guide is one who restates in clear language to convey meaning; one who assigns meaning to events, actions, or intentions, and shows the way. An interpreter/guide highlights critical information and directs effort.

Who are the interpreter/guides? Family members; teachers; and educational, vocational, or residential assistants are logical interpreters. Not only do they have the responsibility to provide support, but they are most available. To provide broader experiences and opportunities for their child, families sometimes hire a person to serve as an interpreter (companion) on weekends or evenings. Often peers, family friends, coworkers, or community service providers can be enlisted. For example, when the waitress at a favorite restaurant, a store clerk, an athletic club attendant, or a neighborhood police officer establishes a relationship with the individual, that person generally is more than willing to interpret and provide support if they understand what to expect and how to help. When interpreters have basic training and support, these helping relationships can expand into long-term friendships that provide meaning for both parties.

Qualities of an Effective Interpreter

An effective interpreter must be able *to predict the things that could happen* and know *why they might happen*. This ability to predict potential problems allows the interpreter to be proactive—to intervene in ways to prevent many of the problems.

Without the foundation to predict problems, to understand why they occur, and to act proactively, everyone is left with a feeling of being constantly out of control, constantly reacting to seemingly unpredictable and unexpected situations and problems. Reactive responses tend to make a situation worse; they lead to cycles of out-of-control behavior for the person with autism as well as for those who provide support.

The ability to understand *why* a problem occurs helps the interpreter respond more effectively to those that do occur. The planning and support that are part of this proactive approach help the individual feel and function more competently and comfortably. The interpreter feels more capable and confident as the learner becomes more relaxed and functions more effectively.

The effective interpreter serves as the key that expands the world for those with autism. The interpreter sets the stage for expanding relationships and increasing opportunities. The qualities in the following list are needed for an interpreter to be effective.

1. *The interpreter is alert and sensitive* to the things occurring in the environment; is quick to identify the individual's behavioral signals of confusion and frustration and identify the cause of that confusion and frustration.

2. *The interpreter provides information to clarify* the situation so others in the setting do not become alarmed or negative and so the individual can relax and understand what to do.

3. *The interpreter must have an understanding of:*
   - The learning strengths and deficits common in autism
   - Basic behavioral principles
   - Basic strategies for clarifying information and providing assistance to solve problems

4. *The interpreter must know the individual very well:*
   - What activities are difficult and what are easy?
   - What types of things are confusing or often misunderstood?
   - What things are liked or disliked?
   - What is overstimulating or disorienting?
   - What is calming and comforting?
   - What is boring or frightening?
   - What communication strategies are used under normal conditions?
   - What are the early behavioral signals or signs of stress that highlight a problem?

Develop a Relationship

The following strategies can help an individual with autism spectrum disorders establish a trusting relationship with a new interpreter.

- Prepare the individual with autism before the introduction.
    - Provide the new interpreter's name, hobbies, and interests.
    - Clarify the relationship, describing what this new person will do and where the new interpreter will be involved.
    - Clarify the expectation for the first visit (e.g., when, where, and what will happen).
    - Highlight the critical information with visual references (such as printed words or line drawings).
- Introduce the new interpreter in a familiar setting, with a familiar and liked activity and by a familiar and trusted person. Make the first visit short. For example, the new person may be introduced at a favorite ice-cream store. The visit would end when the dish of ice cream is finished.
- Plan one or two brief visits to simply hang out. The new interpreter could bring some small thing related to a special interest—a magazine, a picture, or a toy. Share a favorite snack, go for a walk, or watch a TV show together. Have fun!
- Do not force conversation or ask too many questions. Be comfortable with quiet sharing. Answer questions.

A new interpreter will be accepted if he or she maintains an open, friendly, and nondemanding attitude; speaks calmly and clearly but not too much; and speaks neither too softly or too loudly during initial visits. With such a beginning, the relationship will generally flourish. If there is not time for this extended lead-in, do as much as is possible.

Summary—An Analogy

If effective intervention and support can be developed from an understanding of the perspective of those with ASD, what might day-to-day life be to one with such a disability? Daily life might be like living in a dream world where people and events fade in and out randomly without any familiar context, where problems have no solutions even when extreme effort is applied. Or, every day might be like the first day in a foreign country. Imagine the overwhelming and disorienting stimulation of the unfamiliar sounds of the language. How confusing and stressful to be unable to find anything familiar in the printed signs or social customs. How frustrating to be unable to ask for assistance. Perhaps life is just as disorienting day after day for those who have difficulty making sense of their social/cultural world, who find it difficult to elicit meaning from their experiences, and who have difficulty understanding and using language to communicate.

Using this analogy, consider having a guest from a very different culture in your home, classroom, or community. This guest uses language with some similar or familiar-sounding words, but the words, gestures, and facial expressions are used in different contexts and with different meanings. This guest expresses emotions in unexpected ways that are difficult to interpret. What would this guest need to feel comfortable and to manage effectively in this new situation?

If no language interpreter is available, the host must serve as both interpreter and guide to devise ways to transmit information from one to the other. It certainly would not be helpful for a host to talk more or to talk louder. To help the guest relax and be comfortable in this new place and to enjoy new experiences, a thoughtful host would most likely:

- Learn as much as possible about the guest's language and cultural background so as to anticipate potentially confusing situations

- Use gestures and draw pictures to convey clear and concise information and to give meaning to the spoken words

- Orient the guest to the physical world—the location of things

- Develop some familiar routines and prepare the guest for changes to those routines with pictures and gestures

- Help the guest communicate needs, questions, thoughts, and feelings—again with the support of gestures and pictures

Above all, the thoughtful host would assume that this guest had feelings, legitimate needs, and the intelligence to learn and solve problems together.

These are the very strategies that are necessary for making those with autism spectrum disorders more comfortable and more able to participate with some degree of confidence in this confusing world.

The principles and processes for making the guest with autism more comfortable, competent, and confident are outlined in the following chapters. An effective intervention plan to address the critical needs and goals of those with autism spectrum disorders is based on cognitive/behavioral strategies and guided by the common learning style. Intervention efforts are based on three strategies:

1. Evaluate and refine (see Chapter 10).

2. Organize and structure events, space, and time (see Chapters 11–16).

3. Teach new skills (see Chapters 17–23).

The presence of an interpreter who has the ability to predict and clarify situations to prevent problems is the first and perhaps the most important element in providing support for the guest from another culture—the individual with autism who has difficulty learning the language and rules of their native culture.

In the remainder of this book, the word *interpreter* is used to refer to a parent, teacher, or other person who is responsible for providing support at the moment. The word *learner* is used to indicate the individual with autism.

CHAPTER 10

Evaluate and Refine to Support Effective Learning and Behavior

The interpreter's primary role is to help the learner with autism spectrum disorders understand and function at an optimal level. To do this successfully, the interpreter must continually evaluate, think quickly, and make immediate decisions in order to resolve problems on the spot.

When stress or behavior problems increase or the learner has difficulty learning a new concept or skill, it usually means that some part of the teaching sequence or some element of the environment is confusing or interfering. At these times, the naive interpreter can step in to a) fix the problem, b) end the activity, or c) ignore the problem and continue to push on in the hope that the emotional/behavioral expressions (and the problem) will go away.

1. *Fixing the problem can lead to dependency* because the learner would never learn how to solve problems or manage stressful situations. Simply fixing the problems will require the presence of an interpreter at all times.

2. *Ending the problem can reinforce inappropriate behavior* as the learner quickly discovers that disliked or hard activities go away whenever they scream or hit themselves.

3. *Ignoring a problem rarely makes it go away*, rather the emotional response is likely to accelerate into a crisis.

   - Repetition of a confusing teaching sequence and repetition of errors is not an effective or efficient teaching strategy, especially for those who take in and remember chunks of information at one time, those who learn quickly when the presentation is clear.

   - When failure and lack of success continues, motivation decreases and the frequency and intensity of behavior problems increase.

   - To push on and ignore the learner's needs is disrespectful and punishing for both the learner and the interpreter, for neither is successful.

Evaluation is an ongoing process, and *refinements must be made as soon as a problem is identified* rather than to wait a week or a month to see what will happen. It is more efficient to maintain an ongoing diagnostic/prescriptive policy. When problems are allowed to continue, it will require major changes and significant time to repair the damage.

Stress Level as a Measure of Effective Programming

Effective intervention that conserves time and energy depends on identifying and analyzing the ebb and flow of stress to find clues for deciding when and how to intervene. The Profile of Stress illustrated in Figure 10.1 is a key for matching intervention efforts to the changing needs of those with autism spectrum disorders.

Variations in the level of stress are identified by subtle and not-so-subtle variations of behavior (e.g., from frowning to screaming). Thus the interpreter constantly evaluates the learner's subtle behavioral signals and the context of those variations for clues to guide intervention decisions; that is, to identify the points or stages of

A more in-depth discussion of stress is found in Chapter 8.

the emotional sequence when specific kinds of intervention are not only critical but most effective.

The primary goal of this ongoing evaluation and refinement process is to defuse stress, avoid the crises, and maintain positive and purposeful efforts directed to learning new skills and increased effectiveness in the community now and in the future.

Figure 10.1 Profile of Stress: Basis for Matching Interventions to Needs

To identify the points or stages of the emotional sequence when specific kinds of interventions are not only critical but most effective

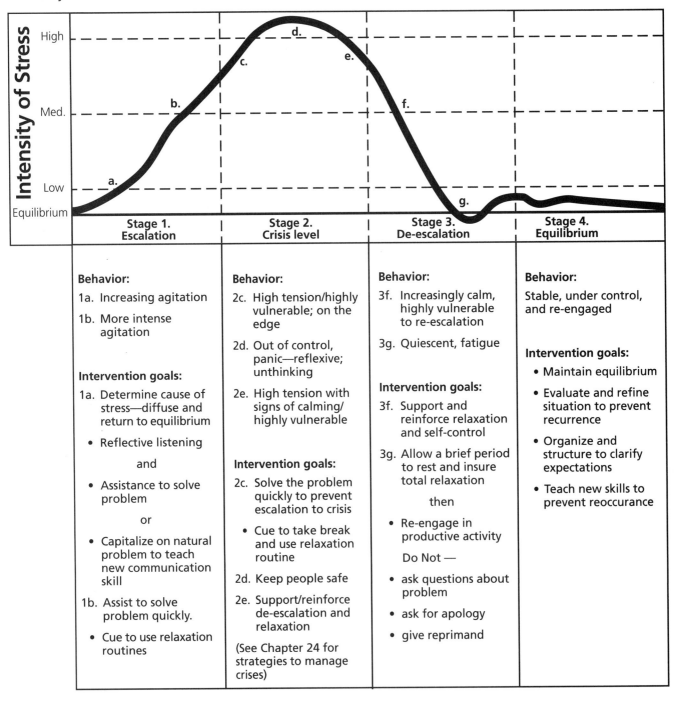

Stage 1. Escalation	Stage 2. Crisis level	Stage 3. De-escalation	Stage 4. Equilibrium
Behavior:	**Behavior:**	**Behavior:**	**Behavior:**
1a. Increasing agitation	2c. High tension/highly vulnerable; on the edge	3f. Increasingly calm, highly vulnerable to re-escalation	Stable, under control, and re-engaged
1b. More intense agitation	2d. Out of control, panic—reflexive; unthinking	3g. Quiescent, fatigue	
Intervention goals:	2e. High tension with signs of calming/ highly vulnerable	**Intervention goals:**	**Intervention goals:**
1a. Determine cause of stress—diffuse and return to equilibrium		3f. Support and reinforce relaxation and self-control	• Maintain equilibrium
• Reflective listening	**Intervention goals:**	3g. Allow a brief period to rest and insure total relaxation	• Evaluate and refine situation to prevent recurrence
and	2c. Solve the problem quickly to prevent escalation to crisis	then	• Organize and structure to clarify expectations
• Assistance to solve problem	• Cue to take break and use relaxation routine	• Re-engage in productive activity	• Teach new skills to prevent reoccurance
or	2d. Keep people safe	Do Not —	
• Capitalize on natural problem to teach new communication skill	2e. Support/reinforce de-escalation and relaxation	• ask questions about problem	
1b. Assist to solve problem quickly.	(See Chapter 24 for strategies to manage crises)	• ask for apology	
• Cue to use relaxation routines		• give reprimand	

Evaluate and Refine: The Process

The evaluation process occurs throughout the day and in every setting. The process includes four steps:

1. Identify the subtle behavior that signals a problem.

2. Analyze to determine the cause or reason for the problem.

3. Determine intervention priority, clarify, and adapt to resolve the problem.

4. Make adaptations and teach new skills to prevent recurring problems.

Step 1. Identify the Behavior that Signals a Problem

A problem is any question or matter involving doubt, uncertainty, or difficulty that causes confusion and frustration—something that will require assistance or a solution. Many things are problematic for those who have difficulty organizing information, generating effective solutions, and asking for clarification or assistance in reliable and understandable ways. There are three important rules for identifying problems:

1. Be familiar with the learner's subtle patterns of behavior.

2. Stay attuned to the subtle variations of attention, emotion, and behavior that highlight increasing levels of stress, frustration, and confusion.

3. Identify small behavioral signals before they reach the crisis stage.

Predictable Warning Signals or Signs of a Problem

Whether able to speak or not, a learner still communicates, but it is left to the interpreter to recognize the message. The following list begins with the earliest and most subtle communication signals.

1. *Physical signs* of confusion, frustration, anxiety, or stress—a flushed face, yawning, stretching, changes in breathing patterns, or hyperventilation.

2. *Repetitive or stereotypic verbal or motor actions*—rocking, pacing, finger flicking, or repetitive questions.

3. *Disorganized behavior* that is random, frantic, or compulsive.

4. *Signs of apathy, lack of motivation, or withdrawal*—covering ears with hands, closing eyes, placing head down on table, limpness or falling limply to the floor, turning away, hiding under a table or behind a couch.

5. *Signs of resistance* (apparent noncompliance)—dropping to the floor, active resistance, pulling away, pushing away or throwing materials, running away.

6. *Emotional outbursts that do not fit the situation*—giggling and laughing when someone is hurt, or standing on the table and shouting.

7. *Self-injury*—biting the wrist, slapping or banging the face or head, poking at the eyes.

8. *Apparent aggression*—pinching, scratching, squeezing the interpreter's hand or arm, biting, kicking, hitting, or threats to pinch, scratch, bite, kick, or hit.

> When confused, Tony simply held his hand over his teacher's hand and waited. If the subtle signal was ignored and demands continued, he pinched the teacher's hand. He had no other way to say, "Wait a minute, what does this mean?" or "Stop, I've about had it."

When confused and in need of assistance, Amy made throaty noises, then began running about the room, kicking at the teacher each time she passed.

These signals may or may not be delivered intentionally or persistently. Some are reflexive reactions or emotional responses to a situation. Even when the behavioral reactions or responses are inappropriate or unacceptable, they do convey a message: "I have a problem."

Step 2. Analyze to Determine the Cause of the Problem

Once a problem is signaled, it is left to the interpreter to identify the cause of the problem. The interpreter must be aware of the situations that cause problems and constantly sensitive to the context of the problem: What is happening near the learner, in other parts of the room, or outside the immediate area that they can hear or see?

Stage 1. Escalation—Identify the cause of the problem

Situations that Typically Cause Problems

The following situations are likely to increase stress and reduce the learner's ability to maintain calm and focus on learning:

1. Situations involving people

2. Over- or understimulation

3. Changes and interruptions

4. Lack of information or misunderstanding information

5. Demands, repeated demands, or making mistakes

6. Physical management

The interpreter who has studied the checklist to identify the cause of a problem, (see Figure 10.2), will always be prepared to analyze and determine the cause of a problem in a timely manner. A more in-depth description of these situations can be found in Chapter 8.

Figure 10.2 Checklist to Identify the Cause of a Problem

The following five questions can be committed to memory and used as a quick mental checklist when a behavior signals a problem.

1. What is new, changed, or missing? (Related to people, time, space, or events)
2. What may have been misinterpreted or misunderstood?
   - The directions? Directions directed to others nearby?
   - A conversation? A conversation between others in another area?
   - Something read in the daily paper or a magazine?
   - Something heard on radio or TV?
   - A word? or concept? a rule?
3. Is some element of the instructional plan or task unclear? For example, does the individual *really understand (is it visually clear):*
   - What to do? Both sides of the picture—what can and cannot be done?
   - Why it is being done (the meaning, outcome, or purpose)?
   - How and where to do it?
   - Where to start? When to start?
   - What materials, people, or equipment are needed?
   - When it is finished?
   - What to do next?
   - When a favorite activity or interaction is scheduled?
   - When help or clarification is needed?
4. Is it a specific communication problem? Does the learner have an effective way to spontaneously:
   - Ask for help or clarification?
   - Get out of a boring or disliked situation?
   - Start or end an interaction?
   - Get a break, relief from overstimulation?
   - Specify choices? Needs?
5. Is some element of the environment confusing, irritating, disrupting or overwhelming (for example, heat, light, noise, textures, crowding, arrangement of materials, work too difficult, a medical problem)?
6. Is boredom and lack of stimulation the issue?

Step 3. Determine Intervention Priority and Resolve the Problem

Whenever there is a problem, the potential for a crisis is present. Thus the interpreter must decide how to direct efforts to resolve the problem to prevent a crisis. Once the cause of a problem is identified, it is time to identify the intervention priority. Figure 10.1 and the flow chart in Figure 10.3 illustrate the thinking process for matching the strategies to the level of stress. An effective interpreter should be trained to automatically use the thinking process described. The decision will depend on the type of problem, the setting of the problem, the individual's emotional state, and the interpreter's priorities:

1. to prevent a behavioral crisis;

2. to maintain the flow of the activity;

3. or to capitalize on the problem situation to teach new skills.

Stage 1. Escalation—Determine the intervention priority, select strategy to defuse.

Figure 10.3 Making Intervention Decisions (Flow Chart)

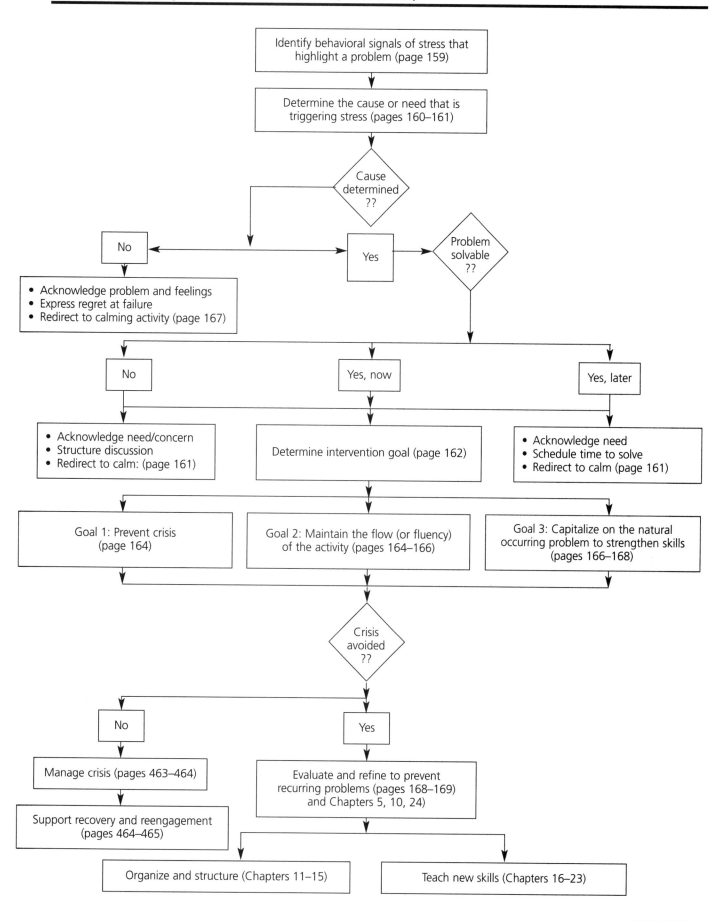

Priority 1. To Prevent a Behavioral Crisis

Criteria: If the emotional state is accelerating rapidly (Figure 10.1—Stage 1b) and/or the individual is too upset to think or to hear and a crisis is imminent, (Stages 2c and d), then the immediate priority is to prevent that crisis and keep people safe.

Interpreter's goal: To defuse the stress, moving directly from Stage 1b or 2c directly to Stages 2e and 3, thus skipping the crisis at Stage 2d.

Strategies for immediate action: (Note that the following strategies are not necessarily sequential. Modifications are made to match the specific individual and the specific situation.)

1. *Maintain a calm, quiet, supportive attitude* that silently communicates acceptance and confidence. ("You are okay. You will be able to handle this, and I will help you if you need it.")

2. *Ignore the behavior but acknowledge the message and tell the learner what to do right now to relax.* If the behavior that signaled the problem was ineffective or inappropriate (such as screaming or hitting), *do not attend to, talk about, or call attention to it.* Attention to an inappropriate behavior can:

   - Serve as a reinforcer and increase the likelihood that it will be strengthened and repeated in other stressful situations or

   - Serve to increase the stress because it gives no direction for immediate action.

3. *Acknowledge the problem and the feeling, and clarify a simple, clear course of action.* ("Did the noise confuse you? Now you can go to your quiet place and relax yourself. Then, I will help you finish your work.")

   In the example on pages 142–143, Jeff thought he was going to miss seeing the movie and had his hands about the teacher's neck. The experienced and very calm teacher ignored his behavior and simply answered his unstated message: "First, do your math. Second, set up the projector and watch the movie. And third, take the projector to Mrs. Peters' room."

4. *Reduce the demands.* When stress and emotions are high, the individual is not in a condition to listen, to learn, to work, or to communicate. The continuation or addition of a stressful requirement will increase the potential for a crisis. Do not require the individual to communicate, to explain, to apologize, or to make choices when stress and emotion are at Stage 2.

5. *Stop talking.* Reduce the amount of auditory stimulation. Use a quiet voice and simple words, and provide printed words or line drawings to clarify the meaning of the words. Often, the very simple act of changing the focus of attention from the individual to the marks on the paper will reduce tension and defuse a crisis.

6. *Reinforce any effort or sign of self-control.* At any slight pause or relaxation of tension, calmly and quietly say, "Good. You can calm yourself," or "Take a deep breath. . . . Good. . . . Now relax your shoulders. . . . Yes, you can relax yourself."

Priority 2. To Maintain the Flow of the Activity

Criteria: When the problem occurs during the initial instruction of a new skill or routine, when an interruption will distract or disrupt others, or when an interruption would call undue attention to the individual, then the priority is to provide only enough assistance to solve the problem immediately and maintain the flow of the routine or activity. This priority is selected only during the Stage 1 levels of stress.

Stage 1. Escalation—Priority: Maintain flow of activity

Interpreter's goal: To repair the situation as fluently and positively as possible.

Strategies for immediate action.

1. *When the problem occurs in a public place:*

    ■ Ignore the behavior and acknowledge the problem.

    ■ Provide calm, clear directions and assistance to solve the problem quickly.

2. *When the problem occurs during the initial presentation of a new skill or routine:*

    ■ Refine the instructional sequence quickly to highlight a natural cue;

    ■ Insert a more effective prompt;

    ■ Alter the arrangement of the space, materials, or information to prevent an error; or

    ■ Stay nearby to prevent a second error.

Maria had quickly mastered all but one step of her new job, which was to fill small plastic containers, firmly press the cap on, then place the containers in order on a tray. While unsuccessfully trying to press the cap down with her fingers and between her palms, she began to lose her focus, move about in her seat, look about, and make whining sounds. As she raised her wrist to her mouth to bite, her interpreter quickly placed a small piece of paper on the work area. In the center of that paper, the interpreter had drawn a circle the size of the container. Without a word, the interpreter demonstrated placing the container on the circle and pressing the cap down, making a snapping sound. When Maria was ready to snap on the next cap, the interpreter touched the circle to direct the placement of the container. With the addition of minimal touch and gestural prompts on the next three containers, Maria had the routine mastered and no more prompting was needed.

Two natural reinforcers provided the incentive to persist in this task: the snapping sound of the cap and seeing the orderly lines of containers filling the tray.

When the organization and structure matched the need, stress was reduced and learning was rapid.

3. *When an error has already occurred*:

- Quickly and quietly refine or add some element to repair or correct the situation so the routine or event can continue.

- After the event, evaluate and refine the instructional plan and/or the environmental situation to prevent recurrence.

- Review and practice the revised routine before encountering the situation again.

> Maria was learning to ride the bus. On her second trip, she got on and moved past the driver without paying. Calmly, her interpreter said, "Oops, Maria, you need to pay. Come, I'll help you." As Maria returned, the interpreter gave her a token so she could pay quickly and not interrupt others. Later, the interpreter prepared a cue card, using simple line drawings to represent each step of the bus-riding sequence. The drawing that represents paying the fare had the money container and token highlighted. They used the card to review each step of the routine once or twice in a simulated setting and just before taking the next bus trip. The interpreter was alert and close by to provide assistance if needed to prevent an error.

Review the situation of Andy (in Chapter 8), who was kicking and hyperventilating in response to a change in his recycling routine. His interpreter quickly prepared a mini-schedule to highlight the changes in the routine, and Andy was able to continue successfully.

Stage 1. Escalation—Priority: Capitalize on the problem to teach new skill.

Priority 3. To Capitalize on the Problem to Practice New Skills

Criteria: When the stress is at a mild or moderate level with no crisis pending (Stages 1a to 1b) and it is not necessary to maintain the flow of the activity, then the priority is to capitalize on the natural and powerful opportunity to practice new communication, social, and problem-solving skills.

Interpreter's goal: To strengthen and generalize new skills.

Strategies for immediate action.

1. *Acknowledge the problem and support active involvement in the solution.*

- Cue to use communication system or self-control and relaxation strategies.

- Provide assistance as needed to ensure that those skills solve the problem quickly and effectively.

- Verbally highlight the solution, the effort, and the accomplishment.

When Amy began to stretch and yawn (*signals of fatigue and a wish to end an activity*), her interpreter acknowledged the message of her behavior by saying, "You look tired [*the problem*] and want to stop working [*the solution and natural reinforcer*]." Then she told her how she could solve the problem: "You can say, 'All done'." Quickly, almost simultaneously, her interpreter provided just enough assistance for Amy to touch the "all done" symbol on her communication board. Then quickly and enthusiastically, the interpreter acknowledged her message. "You are all done. You can stop working and listen to tapes."

Sitting in the language circle, Kim began to scratch and pinch the child beside him. The teacher quickly interpreted, "Bob is too close. Tell him to move over." While speaking, the teacher placed Kim's hands on Bob's arm and gave a gentle push. Bob moved over. The behavior was ignored, the message was acknowledged, and assistance was provided to actively involve Kim in solving his own problem. The teacher's message conveyed both the problem and a solution. Active involvement was reinforced because it ended the unpleasant closeness. At the same time, peers understood that Kim simply had a problem and needed assistance; he was not a bad, mean little boy to avoid.

2. *When the reason for the problem cannot be determined:*

   ▪ Acknowledge that there is a need, and express regret. "I'm sorry, I don't understand." Ask the learner to try another way to clarify the message (for example, "Can you show me with your communication book?").

   ▪ Ask the learner to point to the problem or take you to the problem.

   ▪ List some possible problems on paper with words or line drawings, and say, "Point to the picture of the problem." The learner must have a way to indicate that none of the problems listed is the real problem. Therefore, include symbols to represent yes, no, and none of those.

3. *If the message is still unclear:*

   ▪ Say, "I'm sorry, I don't understand. Let's take a walk and get a drink. Then you can _____"; or, "I'm sorry. We can try to figure it out later. Now you can take a break" (or do some preferred activity).

   ▪ Do not try to distract the learner until he or she knows that the problem was heard and that you regret that you cannot help.

4. *If the problem is something that cannot be resolved immediately:*

   ▪ Acknowledge the message and clarify with a statement, such as:

      ▸ "You want pretzels. They are all gone. Let's put pretzels on the grocery list. Now, do you want a potato chip or a cracker."

      ▸ "You want to see your mother. Remember, you see her on Saturday." Then write See Mother on the calendar and count the days. If the need continues to cause sadness or a problem, continue to refer to the calendar and cross off the days as they go by. In a situation such as this, it may help to suggest making a phone call, writing a letter, or starting a list of things to tell Mother on Saturday. Whatever the situation, clarify the solution visually for later reference. *The critical issue here is that the learner has a legitimate problem and concern and needs respectful assistance to deal with feelings.*

5. *If the problem is related to a worry and concern* about an unsolvable problem (such as famine, war, or the common cold):

- Acknowledge and share the concern, then structure the situation.

> One mother used a journal to resolve recurring and unsolvable problems. When her son was compulsively concerned about crime in the street, the subject was discussed very briefly, and she wrote the following explanation in the journal:
>
> You are really worried about crime in the streets. That worries me, too. Neighborhood groups, legislators, the president, and the police are concerned, too. They are all working to solve crime in the street. Is it your responsibility? No.
>
> Later, whenever the concern was expressed, the young man was referred to the journal. Through this medium, he learned about language, reading, spelling, problem solving, and community and government responsibility.

The opportunities for capitalizing on naturally occurring problems are almost endless, limited only by the creativity and the flexibility of the interpreter and the stress level of the individual. Without the interpreter's assistance, these powerful opportunities would be lost.

Step 4. Make Adaptations and Teach New Skills to Prevent Recurring Problems

The tasks outlined in this step are addressed during the period of equilibrium between problems, when the individual with autism is most relaxed and open to new experiences and learning. This period is illustrated at Stage 4 on the profile (see Figure 10.1). It is the most creative and productive period for interpreters and the total support team. It is at this time when the various elements of the program are refined and new skills are introduced to prevent or to address future problems.

Stage 4. Equilibrium—Evaluate and refine the structure to prevent recurrence.

The four basic tasks to address at this time are:

1. *Evaluate and Refine*

   The support team processes the information and collaborates to apply new insights to both prevent recurrence in the same or similar situations and to intervene more effectively.

   Now that there is evidence that Andy (see pages 142 and 166) does not consistently process or remember verbal information, all his interpreters must remember to support verbal directions with visual reminders in order to prevent similar problems. In addition, Andy's communication system must include a better way to say, "Stop, I don't understand."

   > Tony covered his ears, fussed, and lost his focus for "no apparent reason." It was finally discovered that he could hear the sounds of a train long before others were aware of its coming. He was taught to place plugs in his ears as soon as he heard the noise and to place a sign on an easel that said, "The train is coming." Then he could refocus on the task at hand. (example on page 22)

2. *Restructure or refine elements of the space, time, and events* that are confusing or unclear. Clarify the daily calendar and prepare cue cards, or other visual supports.

3. *Teach new skills or expand and strengthen old skills*—relaxation and self-management procedures, communication skills, problem-solving skills, and others.

4. *Update records*—The interpreter keeps anecdotal records of the problems, the context, and the immediate modifications. These records are shared with the support team. The notes can be brief but with enough detail to highlight the cause of the problems and the issues to address to prevent recurrence.

Summary

This ongoing diagnostic/prescriptive process is the critical element of an effective intervention plan. When solving problems, the interpreter continually evaluates and asks, "Why is the learner doing this in this way?" Once that is decided, the plan and/or the environment can be refined to match the specific needs of the learner at that specific time, and new skills can be taught to prevent recurring problems.

There is an important distinction between supporting to prevent and solve problems and overprotection. Overprotection is unproductive even though it is based on kind and honorable motives, a wish to be helpful, to prevent stress and feelings of rejection and failure. In autism, the individual who is not becoming more independent and capable is regressing, becoming more rigid, more dependent, and more isolated. Overprotection limits and reduces options because the individual never learns how to deal with stress, to solve problems, or to become more competent.

It is productive when learners with autism are provided the support and the skills to actively solve their own problems. Appropriate support and active involvement expands the world and increases options. Competence, confidence, and self-esteem are enhanced. This positive outcome is possible only when the support and teaching strategies are based on the learning strengths and deficits common in autism.

See Chapter 22 for strategies to teach self-control, problem solving, and other self-management strategies.

The strategies suggested in this chapter are expanded in later chapters and applied to many different situations. This evaluation process requires sensitivity, alertness, and quick thinking. It is an essential process that ensures that the critical goals are met: to maintain equilibrium for effective learning and behavior, and to prevent escalating and costly learning and behavior problems.

Organize and Structure Space

Participation in a complex and confusing social and verbal world requires incredible effort—effort that is rarely successful for those with autism spectrum disorders. When effort goes unrewarded or has unpleasant consequences, it is natural to stop trying. Psychologists call this phenomenon *learned helplessness;* it is safer not to try. One parent called it *learned hopelessness.* The conclusion that there is no way to understand and participate effectively in the world leads to defensive actions to avoid failure and punishment. Those who do not understand the world from the perspective or culture of autism often interpret the defensive efforts to avoid failure as laziness, noncompliance, or manipulation.

In Chapters 11 through 16, several systematic processes are outlined for organizing and structuring the environment—the space, the time, and events—to clarify information for those who see this world from a different perspective (Mesibov, Schopler, & Hearsey, 1994). Organization and external structures compensate for the inability to scan an environment, analyze and select the relevant details, ignore the irrelevant details, and elicit meaning and purpose. Organization and structure also reduce anxiety from distractions and overwhelming sensory stimulation while highlighting the critical important information. This systematic process provides a high degree of clarity that:

1. *Increases the ability to focus* on productive and independent activity in the natural community without constant verbal directions.

2. *Provides a familiar, predictable, and comfortable structure* for increasing flexibility and tolerance—adding new experiences and for expanding options.

3. *Increases motivation, success, competence, and confidence.*

4. *Decreases stress and the potential for crises.*

Problems With Space

Homes, classrooms, work, and other community settings are often crowded, sometimes cluttered and noisy. They have an organization that is not readily apparent to one who perceives the world differently, cannot modulate sensory stimuli, and/or make sense of random information. Most people can scan an area and locate the organizational markers, and most people know how to move around in an area to get themselves in the right places. Very young children automatically learn by trial and error that they cannot simply walk directly to their target if other people, toys, or furniture are in their way. Young children also automatically learn to search for things they want and to ask for help in finding them. We know that this automatic learning cannot be assumed in autism. Planning movement through space is often very difficult. Many learners have particular problems organizing, locating, or moving their own bodies in large spaces.

When learners have difficulty scanning, selecting, and making sense of the relevant and important details in the environment, they try to keep the arrangement of details the same. An environment makes sense only if it is familiar. The problem of scanning an area and selecting the relevant information also applies to such problems as locating important information on crowded bulletin boards or chalkboards and deciding where to begin to work on a page, wash a window, or rake leaves.

> The janitor had set up a ladder in the hall to change light bulbs. As José walked to the bathroom, he bumped into the ladder, stopped, and screamed helplessly. He was either unaware that he could move his body around the ladder or he was unable to plan and execute the action.
>
> ———————
>
> Each time Jason entered the classroom, he cruised about straightening the papers on the teacher's desk, the books on the shelf, and the charts and maps on the walls. Even in the middle of other concentrated effort, he would jump up, dash across the room, and adjust a paper, book, or chart that had just gotten out of line.
>
> ———————
>
> Ben could not relax at home until everything had been returned to its exact place. Ben even went from person to person uncrossing their legs and placing their feet side by side on the floor (in response to the rule that shoes are placed side by side in the closet).

The Process for Organizing Space

Like the guide for a person who is blind, the interpreter's role is to organize and structure the objects in space to clarify where things are done, where things are located, and how to move from one place to another. The interpreter also must address the sensory factors that could interfere with optimum functioning.

There are five basic steps for organizing space:

1. Assess to determine unique sensory and spatial problems.
2. Identify the location of activities.
3. Organize and refine the structure of the space.
4. Locate and label materials and supplies.
5. Continue to evaluate and refine.

Step 1. Assess to Determine Unique Sensory and Spatial Problems

Form 5.1, Determining Home/School Priorities (page 79), is one resource for identifying specific problems in an environment. The following behaviors signal problems that might be solved by refining some element of the space:

- Random wandering and searching behavior
- Apparent distraction by details or materials in the space
- Distraction by activity in other areas
- Sudden confusion or disorientation during small or larger transitions
- Leaving an area before the end of an activity
- Moving into off-limit areas
- Distraction or apparent pain from some specific sensory stimulation (for example, covering ears or eyes, running to hide in a dark or quiet area)
- Not beginning a task (for example, the learner just stands or sits as if waiting for something to happen)
- Safety problems

See Myles et al. (2000) for other assessment tools and suggestions.

Step 2. Identify the Location of Activities

What needs to be done? Where is the best place to do it? In general, the answers are the same for those with autism as for others of the same age. For example, homes have places to sleep, cook, eat, and relax. Schools have places for large group, small group, and independent work; eating; playing; or hanging out. The same can be said of most community environments.

The learner with autism spectrum disorders often has a need for two other areas: a quiet *space for relief from stimulation, and an individual work area.*

The Quiet Space

A quiet space is needed at home, school, work, and sometimes in other community settings. This is not the traditional time-out area where a person is placed as a consequence for bad behavior. Rather, it is a positive place where the learner goes to prevent loss of control—a place to find relief from sensory overload and regain composure and control.

The quiet space must be readily accessible and comfortable, in an area somewhat sheltered from the noise and visual stimulation of busy activity. It must be located and arranged for easy supervision—a small area in the classroom or at home, behind a bookcase, divider, or couch. In other settings, a specific spot beside a wall or under a tree in a park, a specific bench in a quiet corner of the mall, or a specific chair or room at a party or at work can be designated to serve as a quiet place.

Areas at school or in the home may need some specific equipment, such as a mat, beanbag chair, mini-trampoline, or rocking chair that contributes a calming effect for the learner. The occupational therapist is an excellent resource for assessing the specific needs of an individual learner.

> While working as a groundskeeper, Gabriel became very agitated as he worried about visits to his mother and the conversations of his coworkers. His interpreter taught him to go to a designated area under a specific tree where he could do his relaxation routine, then return to work.
>
> ———
>
> When 4-year-old Anne begins to get stressed, she runs to a rocking chair, rocks fast for a few minutes, then returns independently to the group. George, 10 years old, crawls under a mat behind a divider where it is quiet and dark. He finds that the pressure of the mat is calming. Brad regains his composure and direction by returning to his special work area where his daily calendar and other visual support systems are located.

The Individual Work Area

The work area for some more capable learners is the same as the work area for peers—a school desk or workstation. However, many learners need a specifically designed work area that combines the functions of a department-store information counter and a workstation in a busy office. This work area serves several purposes:

- It becomes a familiar space where new concepts, skills, jobs, and information can be introduced without conflicting or distracting stimulation.

- It becomes an information focal point where supplies and visual systems (e.g., daily calendar, checklists, cue cards, work files, other visual references) can be arranged to support a variety of independent or cooperative activities in that or other locations. For example, at some times, tutoring can occur in this area or a friend may be invited to work or play cooperatively without interrupting others. In some situations, the learner naturally moves from this area with supplies to work or participate in other locations.

The location and design of this area depends on the age and very specific needs of the learner and the demands of the setting. In general, the area should be located away from major traffic paths and noisy activity. But even when some learners have a visual barrier, they are so distracted by the noise of other activities that they constantly get up and look over or around the barrier. These learners need an area near the back of a room where they can survey the action with a quick glance, then return quickly to work.

A bulletin board or wall for mounting visual references and a shelf or shelves for supplies should be located close by—preferably close enough that it can be reached without moving away from the desk.

Tony wandered randomly about his home, constantly in trouble, becoming more and more frustrated, anxious, and stressed. When his family prepared a personal work station in their home that included his daily calendar, lists of jobs, and leisure options, he finally knew what he could do from moment to moment. When he was taught to follow the visual systems that included directions for his jobs, Tony relaxed and moved with purpose throughout the day. No longer was he unprepared for coming events. No longer did he need someone beside him every minute to tell him what to do or keep him out of trouble. His mother or father organized and explained the schedule to him each day, provided periodic support, and taught him new tasks to add variety and expand his skills.

Step 3. Organize and Refine the Structure of the Space

Homes, schools, and community sites also have special places, or centers, where specific activities occur. Each of these various areas needs clearly defined boundaries to help maintain focus on the specific activity until it ends and to facilitate travel from one area to another.

Boundaries are like frames that separate the material or activity inside the frame from the material or activity outside the frame. Many offices, businesses, and school settings already use rugs, bookcases, and dividers to mark the edge of spaces. For example, at school you can use a rug to define an area for playing with toys, move bookcases and dividers to block out some of the stimulation between areas, and arrange a couch or desks to highlight walkways and control the flow of traffic.

Once the various locations and boundaries are identified, post signs or symbols to designate which events occur in each area—play/leisure, work/vocational, cooking /eating, study, conference or group area, and supplies.

Temporary Markers

Sometimes, temporary markers are needed to define a specific work area or to remind a learner to stay in a specific area. Temporary markers have solved many different kinds of space problems. Amazingly enough, it is often the smallest changes or markers that make tremendous differences. For example:

- A string, yarn, plastic tape, or strip of crepe paper taped across an opening serves as a reminder to stay in or out of an area.

- A small stop sign propped on a chair was all one child needed to stay out of an area.

- Stakes and string can define an area of a garden for planting or weeding.

- A tape line across the middle of a work table can clarify a shared work area.

- A sticky note placed in each corner of a table or at the left top and the right bottom corner of a window identifies starting and ending points for cleaning. The learner is taught to place the notes and to work from top to bottom and from left to right, removing the notes as each area is finished.

- A strip of crepe paper placed around an assignment on a chalkboard defines and isolates it from other material.

- A small piece of tape placed on the gym floor specifies where to stand during calisthenics or where to line up.

- A mark on a specific chair (indoors) or signpost (outdoors) indicates where to stay while waiting for the bus.

These temporary markers are simple to remove when it is time to leave an area or when they are no longer needed. Those who wander or run away are not always aware of natural boundary markers. To prevent harm, it is very important to clarify the boundaries and hazards in every new situation.

The students in the third grade class were asked to copy a favorite poem onto paper and make a decorative frame around it for Mother's Day gifts. As the other children finished, Gabriel was still sitting with a blank piece of paper. His interpreter, who had just returned to the room, said, "Which poem are you going to copy?" Gabriel pointed to the poem. "Which border are you going to draw?" Again, he indicated his choice by pointing. Then the interpreter said, "Where are you going to start?" Gabriel made no response. After a brief pause, the interpreter placed a small x on the paper and said, "Start here." Gabriel immediately sat up and began to work.

Two groups of students were sharing the gym, one on each side of the center line. Matt was riding his tricycle all over the gym, disrupting both groups. To solve the problem, his interpreter, with paper and pencil in hand, knelt down beside Matt and began to draw as he said, "Matt, you can ride your tricycle on this side of the big black line. Can you ride on the other side of the line? No. You can ride on this side of the line." He took Matt to the center line, laid the drawing at the end of the line, and showed him specifically where he could and could not ride. From that time on, Matt rode only in the designated area.

Natural Cues and Markers

To prepare learners for managing themselves in the community, they must be taught to search for markers. They must also be taught the meaning of those natural cues and markers that are there for every one to use. Highlight or point out:

- The light over the checkout stand at the exits in stores.
- The crowd-control ropes in post offices, banks, and airports that signal people to line up in order of arrival.
- The lines painted on streets to define crosswalks.
- The various types of signs.

When learners know exactly what to do, what they cannot do, and where the boundaries are, they are generally cooperative and successful. In the following example, the interpreter was quick to use what was at hand to clarify the situation for Matt.

As the class of 3- and 4-year-old children left the bus for a picnic, the interpreter saw Matt break away and run toward the lake. She quickly followed and caught him at the edge of the lake, got down on her knees, took his hand, and said softly but clearly, "Matt, keep your toes behind this line." (She drew a line in the sand at the edge of the lake.) "You can put your fingers in the water, and you can play with these rocks in the water." (She pointed to rocks and placed one in the water.) "You can play with the sticks in the water." (She pointed to the sticks and placed one in the water.) "Can you put your toes in the water? No. Keep your toes behind this line. You can put your fingers in the water, the rocks in the water, and the sticks in the water, but your toes stay behind this line." (She pointed to and pressed on the toes of his shoes that were behind the line.) "Good! Your toes are behind the line." Then she moved away and watched closely. Two or three times she moved to him and played briefly in the water beside him as she complimented his ability to keep his feet behind the line. Amazingly, Matt enjoyed himself at the water's edge with his feet behind the line for more than 20 minutes until it was time for lunch.

Although this amount of verbal detail might seem excessive for a 4-year-old with limited verbal abilities, learners with autism spectrum disorders *need specific information and all the important and relevant details* in order to *know exactly what they are to do and not to do*. Note that the verbal information was supported with visual references—the line in the sand, the pointing and modeling (placing fingers, rocks, and sticks in the water). Reinforcement was provided in a quiet, natural manner that did not *over-stimulate or distract* Matt from his appropriate play.

Step 4. Locate and Label Materials and Supplies

It is less stressful and easier to participate effectively when materials and supplies are arranged close to the area where they are to be used. Some learners with autism become disoriented and distracted during a search for needed materials. Although there is a great deal of variation from one learner to another, many will not remember where something is stored if it is not in view—they forget to open a closet or cupboard door to look inside. The following suggestions have been helpful for many learners.

- Remove supplies that belong to or are used only by others, or label them clearly (Teacher's things; Dad's things).

- Label storage containers or use clear containers so contents are easy to identify.

- Remove cleaning supplies, medical supplies, and other potentially dangerous materials. Store them in safe and locked areas.

- Label shelves, drawers, and cupboard and closet doors to show where to find and return items.

- Organize a work table by taping three pieces of heavy paper on the table from left to right. Label the piece on the left Supplies, label the one in the middle Work, and label the paper on the right Finished. With these markers, the learner knows where to place a tub or box of supplies, where to do the work, and where to place a tub for the finished work. When the tub of supplies is empty and all the completed work is in the Finished area, it is obvious that the work is completed.

- Develop simple maps to orient a learner to a new setting and as a reference for locating materials or moving from one room or building to another. Many very young children with autism can learn to use maps, a valuable lifelong skill that increases independence. First, teach young learners to use maps of the room, then expand to maps of the building, and community. Some more advanced learners can make their own detailed maps and learn to use commercially prepared maps.

Involve the more competent learner in making future changes in the setting. For example, the learner can help make decisions about a new location for furniture or supplies, help move the furniture and supplies, and help prepare and place signs and labels.

Step 5. Evaluate and Refine

Interpreters continually evaluate the problems and refine the structure to resolve problems as quickly as possible. Once interpreters become aware of the range of problems and the range of simple strategies to clarify and structure space, they become very creative while preventing and resolving a learner's problems.

Summary

As the environment becomes more organized and meaningful, anxiety decreases and independence increases. Many of the problems in space are subtle and have exceedingly simple solutions. A well-organized classroom benefits all the students in a classroom, as many also need visual clarity.

Organize and Structure Events in Time

Most people have considerable control of their lives. To a large degree, people can choose what to do and when to do them. They also can choose not to do many things perceived as unpleasant or disliked. The ability to analyze and make sense of experiences and keep the information in sequential order enables most people to predict future experiences. This ability to predict and prepare for events and to plan and anticipate pleasant events helps them deal with unpleasant or frustrating situations.

Those with autism generally do not have this kind of ability or control. Much that takes place in their lives is planned by others. Often they are coerced or taken into new or unpleasant activities and situations with little or no preparation. When they resist or try to avoid the confusion and stress that is present, their freedom and options are even more limited. These learners become increasingly inflexible. Severe anxiety and behavior problems occur when they must change a routine (e.g., to wear new clothes, see a doctor, move to a new home).

An individually designed calendar, visually representing events in time, compensates for many of these problems. When the calendar is based on a systematically organized schedule, it is perhaps *the most powerful, positive behavioral support system*—a tool that will address the many problems of those who:

- Are fearful and resist changes and new situations;
- Develop rigid, inflexible routines quickly;
- Have difficulty predicting future events; and
- Have a limited number of reinforcing, liked activities.

The calendar, when reviewed each morning, referenced throughout the day, and refined to match expanding skills, provides the natural structure to achieve critical goals (see Figure 6.1, page 107) and supports critical independent behavior. A well-designed calendar system will also:

- Increase flexibility and tolerance for new and changing events;
- Increase active participation, motivation, and persistence;
- Increase language concepts related to time, space, events, and settings;
- Increase ability to communicate preferences;
- Increase ability to work and function independently;
- Increase ability to make choices and decisions for self-management; and
- Decrease the stress from not understanding expectations—one precurser of behavior problems.

This chapter also provides guidelines for systematically organizing events in time—a prerequisite for designing the visual representation of those events, the calendar.

Terminology

The terminology defined below is used in this and the following chapters with very specific meaning:

- Scheduling is a planning process that organizes a sequence of events to achieve a goal.

- A schedule is the product of that planning process. It is a plan or an arrangement of events to accomplish goals.

- A calendar is the visual representation of that plan, always available for frequent reference.

This distinction between a schedule and a calendar is made to emphasize the importance of the planning process involved in ordering the events in time to achieve goals and the importance of the calendar for communicating that sequence of events to the learner.

- A mini-calendar supplements a basic daily calendar and shows the sequence of specific activities scheduled to occur within small blocks of time.

- Transition cues guide the learner from the calendar to the correct location for the activity or from one activity to another—and return to the calendar.

- A calendar system is the combination and integration of all the visual elements to ensure that the learner will know the answers to the questions: What? When? Where? Why? and sometimes How? A calendar system will include a daily calendar, mini-calendar, cue cards, etc.

Scheduling Principles

Unlike most people, those with autism spectrum disorders do not automatically learn to value typical social reinforcers. If they are to become more independent, we must teach them to value the naturally available event of their life; we must increase the number of natural reinforcers. This goal can be met by carefully structuring the schedule of daily events.

The process for developing an effective schedule is based on two generally accepted rules of reinforcement:

1. *If a reinforcing event occurs immediately as a direct result of effort and action* (a response, behavior), it is more likely that the same effort and action will recur and be strengthened.

2. *If a liked activity (a reinforcing event) immediately follows a disliked activity* (a painful or frustrating event), it is likely that the disliked activity will increase its value and become a liked activity—a new reinforcing event (Premack & Collier, 1962).

When these rules are applied as naturally occurring events of the day, sequenced in time, there will be less need to use artificial food and verbal reinforcers. As with other behavioral principles, *alternate or paradoxical effects* can occur unless the principles are applied precisely. For example, if a liked activity is always followed by a disliked activity, the liked activity will become disliked and lose its value as a reinforcer. Therefore, simply alternating liked and disliked activities or randomly interspersing liked and disliked activities will not achieve the desired effect for these learners.

The Process

There are three steps for organizing and structuring events in time to ensure maximum effect:

1. Assess the reinforcing value of activities.
2. Organize the events to develop the schedule.
3. Evaluate and refine the schedule.

Step 1. Assess the Reinforcing Value of Activities

Two procedures are helpful for assessing the reinforcing value of activities and the elements of activities that may trigger problems:

1. *Preference Survey.* This survey provides a format for identifying the activities that the learner likes to do, those that the learner would not choose but would willingly do if asked, and those activities that are resisted or that cause difficulty. The list includes both regularly occurring activities and those that occur periodically, whether optional or required. When completed, this survey provides a great number of activities that can add variety to the schedule.

   See Form 5.6 (page 94) for a reproducible Preference Survey form. See Figure 12.1 (page 181) and the Case Study (page 471) for completed examples of this form.

2. *Assessment of Daily Life Activities.* This assessment pinpoints qualities and sequences of regularly scheduled activities that affect the learner's feelings and behavior. It addresses the importance of the activity as well as whether it is age appropriate, too difficult or too easy; possible choices; and the number and types of problems that occur while participating in the activity. This information is important for modifying a schedule to solve a problem.

   See Form 5.7 (page 98) for a reproducible Assessment of Daily Life Activities Form. See Figure 12.2 (page 182) for a completed example of this form.

Step 2. Organize the Events to Develop the Schedule

To develop an effective schedule, the events are systematically arranged to maximize their reinforcing qualities. The formula in Figure 12.3, which is based on the two principles of reinforcement, guides the sequencing of events to develop the daily schedule and to develop mini-schedules for individual routines or short work sessions.

The major considerations to ensure maximum benefit are:

1. *Begin and end the schedule with familiar and positive activities.* This sets the stage for a pleasant experience and ends on a positive note, and the learner will be eager to return to or repeat the activity at another time.

2. *Follow disliked activities with liked activities* to reinforce hard work and increase tolerance.

3. *Follow liked activities with familiar and tolerated activities* to avoid losing the power of the reinforcing activities and to avoid resistance when ending the liked activity.

4. *Follow familiar or tolerated activities with disliked activities.*

In summary, when disliked activities are scheduled systematically and followed by a highly liked activity, the learner's tolerance and skills will increase. These once disliked activities become tolerated and many will eventually become highly liked, new reinforcing activities.

Caution: If a liked activity is always followed by a disliked activity, it will lose its value as a reinforcer!

The optimum effect of this schedule will be achieved when:

1. The schedule is flexible

2. The schedule includes variety

3. The learner knows what is on the schedule—and the calendar is always available for review of the schedule

4. The schedule is continually evaluated and refined

Figure 12.1 Sample: Preference Survey (Form 5.8)

Adapted from *Judevine® Training System* (Blackwell, 1998)

Student: Becky   **Date:** July 12

LIKES	TOLERATES	DISLIKES
What people, objects, or activities are liked a lot or selected during free time?	What is done when asked, but never done if not asked?	What people, objects, or activities are resisted, avoided or rejected?
Quiet spaces	Reading activities—class	Noise
Animal picture books	Math activities—class	Confusion
Puppets	Spelling and other classes	Cold
Familiar jobs:	Working with flash cards	Lunchroom
• Water plants	Writing activities and worksheets	Gym
• Straighten bookshelves	Language Master/computer	Recess
• Wash sink	Table game with one other person	Unstructured/creative activities
• Feed fish		Putting on outdoor clothing
• Empty waste baskets		Playing active games
Play music tapes		Waiting/sitting and listening
Eat:		Changes
• Crackers with jelly		
• Graham crackers with frosting		
Knead and role clay		
Dress doll		
Stickers		
Puzzles (mazes and jigsaw)		
Drawing lines on paper		
Sitting beside Suzy		
Calendar review process		
Eating lunch/meals		
Walking outside		
Swinging		

Figure 12.2 Sample: Assessment of Daily Life Activities: Informant Interview (Form 5.9)

Adapted with permission from Oregon Regional Autism Services

Student: Becky   **Date:** December 15

Directions: This form is used to structure an interview to determine the relationship of various conditions to problem behavior. First, parents and/or staff members make notes on a copy of the form prior to the interview. The interviewer then structures questions to clarify the details and to enlarge on the examples. When making comments, give details such as: types of problems, environmental conditions when problems occur, types of assistance, consequences, types of directions, and the possible perspective of the student when problems occur.

Time (from/to)	Activity Location/Supervisor and Group Size	Is this activity:			Does the individual have:		Comments Give details
		Age-appropriate?	Meaningful?	Liked?	Choice? Control?	Problems?	
8:15–8:25	calendar review classroom/1:1 with Judy	yes	yes	yes	some	no	Shows lots of interest It is in a quiet corner of classroom with favorite person.
8:25–10:00	reading, math, spelling small-group and independent desk work, with Judy or Tom	yes	yes	generally OK	very little	restless sometimes	Desk work adapted, so works independently Group work—pretty much follows along
10:00–10:20	recess in gym	yes	sometimes	no	could select activity	yes and no	Room is quiet and calm. If left alone, she walks along, trailing fingers on wall, staring at wall or hand. Attempts to involve her: screams, kicks, pulls away
10:20–11:40	in hall, to and from gym large group (2 classes), with Judy + 1 other staff	yes	maybe—the purpose is to get a break, release energy	generally	some	rarely	Same as earlier Noisy, crowded Has trouble holding and carrying bulky things.
11:40–11:50	classroom—academic as before	yes	usually	no	no	yes, always— screams, kicks, resists	
11:50–12:45	Prepare for lunch and recess outside. Gather lunch box and snow clothes to carry to lunchroom	yes	yes	yes and no	no	yes	Likes to eat lunch. Doesn't like to sit near peers. Puts hands over eyes or gets under table.
etc. . . .							

Schedules Need flexibility

The amount of time spent in each activity depends on the learner's age, attention span, and whether the activity is liked, tolerated, or disliked. Three general rules apply:

1. *Time spent on a difficult, stressful, or disliked activity should be brief. The activity must end at or just before the peak of effort and interest.* Subtle, nonverbal signs of fatigue or frustration are signals for the interpreter to end or switch from the disliked activity to a liked activity before inappropriate or ineffective behavior occurs. For example, as the learner shows signs of restlessness, say, "Wow! You have worked hard. You can stop now and do _____" (a liked activity).

To avoid negative or paradoxical effects, it is essential *for a difficult or disliked activity to end before boredom or frustration interrupts attention and effort. If a disliked activity ends after the learner begins to fidget or stops working, the individual will learn to fidget and stop working to end an activity.* This negative reinforcement builds very strong negative behavior.

Figure 12.3 Formula for Sequencing Events in Time To Capitalize on the Reinforcing Qualities of the Activities

Adapted with permission from *Judevine® Training System* (Blackwell, 1998)

Activity 1. Moderately liked activity—a pleasant beginning

Activity 2. Familiar and tolerated activity

Activity 3. Disliked activity

Activity 4. Most liked activity

Activity 5. Familiar or tolerated activity

Activity 6. Familiar or tolerated activity

Activity 7. Another disliked activity

Activity 8. A different highly liked activity

Activity 9. Familiar or tolerated activity

Activity 10. Continue to rotate as above

Final Activity. Pleasant and liked—a positive ending

Definitions

Activities can include functional routines (for example, cooking or dressing), recess, lunch, going home, free time, a leisure activity, work or vocational task, social event, playing a game, or any priority IEP activity.

Liked activities are those that the learner would like to do all the time or that are highly motivating at specific times.

Familiar or tolerated activities are those that the individual is not likely to select during free time but would do willingly if asked or if they were scheduled. These activities may not be totally mastered, but they are familiar and not too difficult. With increasing practice and familiarity, these activities are likely to shift and *become valued and liked reinforcing activities*.

Disliked activities are those the learner resists and tries to avoid. Disliked activities are generally new, difficult, or confusing. A disliked activity needs further assessment to determine which element or elements of the activity are disliked.

2. *The reinforcing, liked activity should last as long as, or a bit longer than, the difficult or disliked activity* that precedes it. To help a learner willingly end a liked activity:

   ■ Prepare the learner with a contingency statement and a timer or other concrete signal. As you set the timer, say, "When the bell rings, it will be time to put the tape player away and do ____" (a familiar tolerated activity).

   ■ The learner must know and trust that the liked activity will be offered again. On the calendar or mini-calendar, indicate when the activity is scheduled again.

   ■ Avoid following a liked activity with a disliked activity.

3. *Decrease time demands when the learner's tolerance is low and the stress level is high*. Recognize and respect the learner's variable tolerance and ability levels. Pushing beyond the learner's tolerance increases resistance, is likely to trigger problems, and decreases the learner's willingness to return to the activity another day.

Schedules Need Variety

Variety increases motivation and flexibility and decreases the likelihood of developing rigid routines. Mothers often report that boredom is a major contributor to restlessness, anxiety, and a variety of repetitive behaviors. Alertness, interest, and effective behavior are increased when change and variety are well organized and structured systematically. Four strategies can guide the inclusion of variety into a schedule:

1. *Change at least one or perhaps several elements of the schedule each day* while the calendar and other basic structures remain the same. Provide a different activity, a different sequence of activities, different materials, different locations, different people, or a different time.

2. *Balance the schedule to include a variety of activities*, some that are inactive and active, fine motor and gross motor, quiet and noisy, as well as those that are liked and disliked. Also include individual, independent, cooperative, and small- or large-group activities.

3. *To avoid resistance, do not repeat the same activity or routine in a single day or a single session unless it would be natural for others to repeat it.* For example, it is normal to eat and wash hands several times a day, but generally it would not be natural to wash the same window twice in one day.

4. *Introduce a new element in the context of a familiar situation* to avoid overwhelming the learner with too much confusing stimulation. For example, a familiar person introduces a new activity in a familiar setting or a new person is introduced into a familiar activity in a familiar setting. An individual calendar provides a familiar situation for introducing variations and new activities.

Step 3. Evaluate and Refine the Schedule

Increasing tolerance leads to increasing practice time, and increasing practice time leads to increasing skills. To ensure progress, the reinforcing qualities of the natural activities must be continually assessed to reflect changing tolerances, skills, and preferences. The reproducible checklist on page 187 will guide the evaluation of a schedule to ensure that it is balanced and organized systematically.

Systematically add new, difficult, and disliked activities and expand the dimensions of activities. For example, if a once-disliked game has now become a reinforcing event, involve different people in playing the game, play the game in different settings, or add a different game in the familiar setting with familiar people. This expansion is essential for generalizing new skills and for increasing flexibility and the number of reinforcing events, people, and settings.

When evaluating a problem that may be resolved by refining the schedule, consider:

1. *An event or a complex, functional routine is composed of many small steps or mini-routines.* Some may be difficult and disliked, others may be only tolerated, while others are easy and liked. Adaptations will be needed if too many elements of a routine are difficult, frustrating, or boring; that is, disliked. For example, visual adaptations may clarify and ease some of the difficult steps of the routine, or a break could be inserted into a routine to relieve frustration or tension. A break could be as simple as "taking five" to get a drink or look out the window for a few minutes before continuing the routine. If a routine is boring, but still an important task, incorporate a self-monitoring system, mini-calendar, or some concrete way to show progress toward completion.

2. *The learner's liked activities may be different from those of his or her peers in integrated settings.* Adaptations may be needed to ensure that reinforcing (liked) activities are sufficiently available.

To illustrate this situation, consider the sample Preference Survey on page 181 and the sample Assessment of Daily Life Activities on page 182, which were completed during the assessment of Becky's problems as described in the following.

Becky was enrolled in a regular third grade class where she participated and worked very well in all the morning activities. At lunchtime, stress was evident, and she screamed and resisted nearly all activities in the afternoon. When the afternoon schedule was analyzed, it was found that every activity was either disliked or barely tolerated. This was very surprising for the teacher, who assumed that all children liked lunch, recess, quiet time when the teacher read aloud to the group, and art and science activities.

It is easy to understand Becky's stress when the requirements of those afternoon activities were analyzed:

- *Lunchtime*: Gather coat, boots, hat, gloves, and lunch box; walk in line to the lunchroom; wait to enter; place belongings on the floor; find a table and eat; wait to be excused; put on outdoor clothes. Nearly every step was painful and disliked. The noise and echoes in the cafeteria also were stressful.

- *Recess*: Outdoor clothing was uncomfortable and restricted movement, the cold wind was painful on Becky's face, and the required play with peers was very confusing and disliked.

- *After recess, quiet/reading time:* Returning to the classroom required another struggle with clothing. Becky didn't understand the language of the story, and sitting quietly with no meaningful activity was difficult for her.

- *Art and science classes*: Changes, movement, and noise from independent activity and unfamiliar directions were confusing.

When Becky's schedule and activities were adapted to match her current needs, she was able to tolerate and participate successfully in most of the afternoon activities. The following adaptations were based on her preferences—quiet spaces, books, puppets, familiar jobs (watering plants, straightening book shelves, washing the sink):

- *Lunch time adaptations*: Leave outside clothing in the classroom; sit with familiar peers at the end of the lunchroom instead of with the class in the middle of the room with conversations all around; ask permission to leave the lunchroom when finished eating; return to the quiet classroom and put on outside clothing. (Assistance will be provided because this task is still difficult.)

- *Recess adaptations*: Before leaving for recess, choose two activities and write them on a cue card for reference on the playground. (Assistance will be provided for difficult cooperative play.) Return to the classroom early when the two activities are complete. Remove outside clothing in the quiet room and then go to the library to straighten books.

- *Quiet/reading time adaptations*: Play quietly at desk with puppets or other liked material selected during calendar review time early in the day.

- *Art and science class adaptations*: Refer to the mini-calendar for the art and science activities. (Intersperse some familiar jobs—watering plants, straightening bookshelves, washing the sink.)

Summary

To prepare for changes and transitions, the learner needs information in a concrete and visual format that can be referenced frequently—a calendar that clarifies what will happen, when it will happen, what will happen next, and when preferred activities will occur. The value of visual references is not unique to autism. Most of us use some kind of calendar, appointment book, or reminder system to help us through busy days. We also schedule our own reinforcers (i.e., coffee breaks or time to read) because we are in charge of our schedule.

A calendar that visually represents an individually designed schedule is a powerful and versatile adaptation for achieving many of the critical goals for those who rarely have total charge of their day. A well-designed and frequently refined calendar system is one of the most efficient and powerful, positive behavioral support systems—one that also supports the acquisition of many critical goals.

Over the course of a day, or week, the schedule includes:

Balance

1. Skill development
- [ ] Developmental skills
- [ ] Academic skills
- [ ] Creative skills
- [ ] Functional skills

2. A balance of:
- [ ] Work
- [ ] Play/leisure (seriousness and silliness)

3. Experiences that are:
- [ ] Learner-directed
- [ ] Interpreter-directed (parent or staff)

4. Activity with others:
- [ ] Partnerships
- [ ] Small-group
- [ ] Large-group

5. Opportunities for:
- [ ] Active involvement
- [ ] Quiet recovery

6. Work and/or leisure requiring:
- [ ] Quiet sitting
- [ ] Movement
- [ ] Strenuous exercise

7. Opportunities to:
- [ ] Be independent
- [ ] Help others
- [ ] Receive help from peers

8. Interactions with others of:
- [ ] Different ages
- [ ] Different interests
- [ ] Different abilities

9. Instruction and practice in:
- [ ] Natural settings
- [ ] Simulated settings

10. Opportunities to pursue:
- [ ] Special interests and aptitudes
- [ ] Special friendships

Structure

- [ ] Is the first activity familiar and pleasant?
- [ ] Is the last activity familiar and liked?
- [ ] Is there at least one familiar/tolerated activity before each disliked activity?
- [ ] Does the number of familiar/tolerated activities in one sequence vary from one to several?

- [ ] Is each disliked activity followed by a highly liked activity?
- [ ] Are new activities added frequently?
- [ ] Does each day's schedule include at least one change?

Organize and Structure Events as Routines

When planning systems to help those with autism spectrum disorders become more flexible and independent, we must look again at their learning strengths and deficits—as well as their likes and dislikes. Those who are unable to modulate their sensory systems to screen out painful and distracting stimuli, and identify and organize the important information required to learn many skills automatically, live in a very frightening world. They tend to avoid new things, make quick associations without understanding the meanings, and develop rigid routines quickly. The problem is, they do learn the things we teach, but we forget to teach them all the steps of the activity needed to be truly independent.

If we want to teach those with ASD to be more relaxed and to function independently without constant verbal prompts, we must a) organize their environment so the important elements are highlighted and meaningful, and b) organize their instruction so every step of a task is clear and meaningfully tied together.

Although the planning processes involved in organizing and structuring environments and instruction seems complex and time consuming, keep in mind that:

1. *It is not necessary to develop complex plans for every single event of the day,* but it is important to plan systematically when:

   ■ Planning instruction;

   ■ Introducing new instruction and new events;

   ■ Explaining changes in familiar routines and events; and

   ■ Evaluating and resolving problem situations.

2. *This planning process becomes more automatic and efficient with experience.* With practice, this process becomes a part of us—a way of thinking and solving problems.

3. *The time spent in planning is offset by the time saved during instruction* and the time saved because there are fewer stress-related problems to solve—it also is helpful to others in the class, so this process actually saves time in the end.

It is often surprising to see the difference in attitude and performance of those with autism when expectations are clearly defined and when the world makes sense. This positive effect increases the feelings of competence and confidence of all who contribute and support the effort.

Organize Events as Routines

An event is anything that occurs in a certain place during a particular interval of time. An event can be any variety of activities—a science class, recess, going to a parade, getting dressed, going to the dentist, working at the local department store, or having a cup of coffee with a friend—anything that a person could be involved with during a day. Each event can be conceptualized as a routine. Every day is filled with a sequence of these routines. For example, a school day is made up of a series of routines:

- Arrival routine;

- Class routines;

- Transition routines;

- Recess routines;

- Lunch routine; and

- End of day routine.

Figure 13.1 Common Components of Routines

The essential components:
1. Initiate
2. Prepare
3. Perform essential steps
4. Terminate
5. Transition to next event

Extension/enrichment components:
6. Solve problems
7. Communicate and socialize
8. Make choices and decisions
9. Self-monitor

Each routine involves a common series of steps or components flowing from the beginning to the end that must be completed to ensure that the goal of the routine is achieved independently (Figure 13.1). Successful participation means that the critical effect or the purpose of the routine was accomplished (Brown, Evans, Weed, & Owen, 1987). Organizing and teaching functional skills in the context of routines capitalizes on the amazing ability of learners with autism to learn routines quickly, and the fact that they are highly motivated to repeat and complete familiar routines. Teaching many individual skills in the context of routines promotes generalization and self-management, while at the same time avoiding the disorientation and stress of multiple changes required during traditional generalization procedures.

The traditional task-analysis planning strategy (which identifies all the essential motor actions necessary for completing a task) is not enough to ensure successful and independent participation. For example, a traditional task analysis for doing laundry would typically include:

1. put dirty clothes in washer;

2. add soap;

3. close washer door;

4. set dials;

5. start washer;

6. when washer stops, open dryer door;

7. open washer door; and

8. transfer wet clothes to dryer . . .

and so on through the process—drying, folding, and putting away.

This type of planning does not ensure that the critical effect is achieved—that of clean, dry clothes folded in the drawer every time. One father highlights this fact as he describes the time his son returned folded, wet clothes to the drawer. The young man had not been taught the complete purpose or the final result of the routine, nor was he taught to monitor the quality of the work or what to do if there were problems, such as a defective heating element in the dryer (Hart, 1989).

To achieve the critical effect of a laundry routine involves completing all the steps, from seeing the laundry basket full of dirty clothes to having clean, *dry* clothes folded and placed back in the appropriate drawers every time. For a party, the routine begins with knowing when it is time to get ready and ends when the party is over and the individual has returned home. A math class routine begins with the walk from the previous class and ends with the walk to the next class.

Most people automatically learn how to participate successfully in the many events of the day. It is never safe to assume that the learner with autism will automatically figure out how to carry out all the steps of a routine that are required for independence. Often, some problem occurs or an error is made that increases frustration or has unfortunate effects. These errors or social blunders are not only demoralizing, they are sometimes dangerous and can lead to an undeserved negative reputation and potential isolation. It is virtually impossible to predict all potential problems when developing a routine, but it is important to predict and prepare the student for as many potential problems as possible.

Gabriel, who was working in a local store, was befriended by two young children who came to the store frequently. One day the two children ran into the store with their mother and rushed to give their friend a big hug, one child hugging each leg. Gabriel stood very still until the children's mother came and rescued him. Tears were running down his face as he said, "I didn't know what to do."

The Process for Organizing Events

The process for organizing any activity or functional routine includes five parts:

1. Define the purpose or critical effect of the routine.

2. Identify the sequence of steps or components needed to achieve the purpose.

3. Identify the natural cues and prompts to initiate and complete each step.

4. Identify and develop adaptations to support independence.

5. Prepare the learner and teach the new routine.

6. Evaluate and refine to solve problems.

These steps can be used quickly and informally to prepare the learner for participation in any new or changing activity but a more detailed and formal plan is required for teaching functional skills in a way to ensure independent participation.

The first three steps of the process are described in this chapter. Chapters 11 and 12 provide strategies for organizing and clarifying the environment to support the routine, and Chapters 14 and 15 provide strategies for developing the visual and verbal support systems to support participation in the routine. Chapter 18 describes the process for teaching the routines.

Form 13.1 (page 195) guides the planning process—a sample of a completed form is shown in Figure 18.5, on page 298.

Figure 13.2 Sample: Routine Planning

This form is partially completed to show the first three steps in developing the support or instructional plan for an activity/routine. This is a transition routine that crosses four settings. It does not end until the learner is engaged in the next major activity. It was developed for an 11-year-old student who had difficulty following bus rules, going directly to his classroom, and starting the day's activities.

Routine Planning
FORM 13.1

Adapted with permission from *Project QUEST Inservice Manual* (Falco et al., 1990)

Student: _____ Date: ___September 25___

Goal/Purpose of Routine: Independently transition from home to school on bus and engage in the first school routine

Settings: Sidewalk in front of house, bus, from bus to front door of school, hallway, classroom

Component	Natural Cues/Prompts	Skills/Sequence of Steps	Adaptations
Initiate	1. Bus stops at house. Door is open.	1. Pick up backpack and move to bus.	
Prepare/Perform	2. At bus step. (Natural prompt: Driver waves checklist) 3. In bus with checklist in hand. 4. On seat. 5. Bus stops at school, door opens, kids get up and walk out door. (Natural prompt: Kid behind pushes to keep moving) 6. Line of kids to front door of school and entering school 7. Inside hall 8. At locker—transition cue (TC) on door	2. Enter and pick up checklist from driver. 3. Scan seats. Select a seat. Sit. 4. Fasten seat belt. Sit quietly. (The bus ride itself is naturally reinforcing.) 5. Pick up backpack and follow kids. 6. Leave checklist with driver. Follow kids through school door. 7. Locate locker. 8. Open locker. Stow coat, etc. Pick up transition cue (TC)	
Terminate	9. TC (transition cue) in hand (TC is an adapted prompt to remember destination.) 10. At calendar 11. TC (transition cue) for first activity in hand	9. Take TC to calendar in classroom. 10. Place TC in appropriate location. Review events on calendar. Pick up TC for first activity. (The calendar review process is naturally reinforcing.) 11. Move to first activity. Place TC in specified location	
Transition	(No additional steps to this transition routine required)	(The first activity should be a familiar and pleasant activity to serve as a natural reinforcer.)	

FORM 13.1 (page 2 of 2)

Student: _____ Date: _____

Component	Natural Cues/Prompts	Skills/Sequence of Steps	Adaptations
Solve Problems	12. Someone in favorite seat 13. Someone teasing 14. Can't find coat/bag to leave bus 15. School door closed 16. Locker won't open 17. Too much noise	12. Find another seat. Sign/gesture, "Can I sit here?" 13. Laugh/sign: "You're funny!" and/or use relaxation/self-talk skills. 14. Search for belongings. Ask for help 15. Open door and walk in. 16. Find appropriate helper. 17. Find ear plugs and insert.	
Communicate/ Socialize	18. Peers or staff greet (on bus/in school) 19. Sitting beside peer on bus 20. Communicate to solve above problems	18. Return greetings, sign "Hi!" or "Good-bye." 19. Share sports magazine 20. Use communication system to solve problems noted in items 12, 13, 14, 16, and 22	
Make Choices	21. Select seat partner 22. Select topic of conversation listed on cue card	21. As in item 12, above 22. Check topic cue card to select	
Self-Monitor	23. Monitor behavior on bus 24. Monitor stress level from bus to first activity in school	23. Refer to checklist 24. Use relaxation routine	

Step 1. Define the Purpose or Critical Effect of the Routine

What is the purpose or function of the event—the meaning, outcome or product? Why is this event important? What is the total critical effect? Where and when will it be used? Identification of the various locations and the variations that may be required at the different sites makes it easier to add those variations early on before rote routines are developed. A clear understanding of the purpose or effect of a routine:

- Provides motivation and clarifies the natural reinforcement for participation and effort.

- Facilitates generalization and ensures that learning will be meaningful rather than rote.

- Provides a base for evaluation to determine whether the total effect is achieved.

Step 2. Identify the Sequence of Steps Required to Achieve the Purpose

Motivation is increased and anxiety decreased when the learner is prepared for and understands the sequence of an activity. This understanding provides a foundation for moving from one step to another and for marking progress to anticipate the end.

1. *Initiate*

   This component answers the questions: When or how do I begin? In Figure 13.2, the initiating action is to pick up the backpack and step onto the bus. Often, the initiating action is to move to the appropriate location.

2. *Prepare*

   What preparation is needed? What materials or supplies are needed? What needs to be done to get ready? One might need to collect a coat, backpack, and lunch before leaving for work or school. In a cooking routine, the preparatory steps involve washing hands and collecting ingredients and tools.

3. *Perform core steps*

   What are the core (essential) steps to achieve the critical effect or outcome? In an academic class, the core steps might include: Listen to teacher, read pages 5–13, write the answers to problems 1–10 on page 12. In a preschool language group activity, the core steps could be: Respond to attendance, sing four songs, listen to the teacher explain the day's schedule, and listen while the teacher reads a book.

4. *Terminate*

   What must be done to terminate the event? Identify those termination tasks, such as cleaning up the kitchen after a meal, paying the bill after selecting purchases, putting away the art supplies, or gathering coat and packages before leaving.

5. *Solve problems*

   What problems are likely to occur within the event? What solutions need to be taught or strengthened?

   Most people have learned from experience how to predict, prevent, or manage small problems—an empty toothpaste tube, something blocking the way, someone sitting in a favorite seat, or a desired food out of reach. Most people know what to do when small accidents occur—something gets spilled or torn, a finger is cut by a sheet of paper, or a tooth begins to ache. Those with autism have few resources for solving a problem in order to move on so planning must target potential problems and specify where to set up natural opportunities to practice these skills.

6. *Communicate and interact*

   What communication and social skills are essential? What others are possible?

   Some routines require communication, cooperation, or other social skills to accomplish the purpose of the event. The goal of some other activities could be achieved without communicating or socializing, but the activity would be more natural or more enjoyable if visiting and sharing were possible. Identify both the communication and social skills required to accomplish the purpose of the event (part of the core skills) and those that would make the event more interesting.

7. *Make choices and decisions*

   What choices or decisions are essential? What others are possible? Are some decisions or choices not possible? Are decisions based on specific, concrete rules, or do they require more subtle judgments?

   Is it possible to choose the activity, to decide when to do the activity, the sequence of doing the task, where to do it, where to sit, whom to work with, which materials to use? How can options be clarified—both the things that can be done and those that are not possible?

   Decisions will be difficult to make if they depend on social judgments, abstract rules, or rules with many exceptions. Adaptations will likely be needed. Decisions based on concrete and unchanging rules are much easier.

   > José worked as a quality control manager in a graphics arts business. It was a job particularly suited to his excellent ability to attend to small visual details. The rule for accepting or rejecting a product was simple and concrete: If there are any paint spots or smears outside the design, reject the product.

8. *Self-monitor*

   Does the quality of the participation or product meet the predetermined standard? Does the speed of participation or work match that of others?

   Most people continually check to see how others are performing to see whether they are keeping up or doing things in a similar way with a similar quality. Most people know if their behavior is out of line and attempt to match their participation to the cultural or setting expectations. The learner with autism is generally unaware of the performance of others unless specifically taught to attend to those subtle cues. The social expectations, as well as the speed and quality expectations, must be identified.

9. *Transition to next event*

   What is the next task? What should occur during transition to the next task?

   To stop one event and move to another, especially when it requires movement to a different location, is one of the most difficult tasks for those with autism. The transition plan must be so clear that success can be achieved without continual verbal direction or undue anxiety.

Step 3. Identify the Natural Cues and Prompts

What is the signal or natural cue for starting the routine? How do others know when to begin this routine? What triggers each action in the routine? What is the natural cue that the event is over? *(What does "finished" look like?)* What prompts are naturally available to everyone in the situation or setting?

- The natural cues and prompts are identified by watching others complete the routine. (What signals do other people use to initiate, prepare, perform, and terminate a routine?) Attention to these natural cues and prompts leads to independence from another person to give directions.

    Note: A basic rule for using cues and prompts is to avoid adding artificial verbal cues and prompts unless they will always be naturally available to everyone in that situation. The addition of artificial verbal cues and prompts lead to dependence on others.

- The natural cue to initiate action may be hearing a bell, seeing the bus arrive, or noticing the laundry basket full of dirty clothes. Sometimes a teacher tells all the students that it is time for a specific event. Perhaps the calendar or appointment book indicates the time. In a routine, the natural cue for one step is frequently the completion of the previous step.

- The cue for terminating a routine could be a timer or the fact that the materials are used up, everything is put together, clean, put away, filled up, or the clock indicates time to end. Achievement of the critical effect or purpose of the routine may indicate being finished (e.g., groceries were purchased, the meal cooked and eaten).

Note the natural cues listed on the Routine Planning sample (see Figure 13.2, page 191).

Summary

A well-planned activity or routine ensures that all the critical elements are addressed so the learner can be as successful and as independent as possible. Planning events as functional routines provides a pattern for preparing the learner for new and changing events, for developing adaptations and support systems, and for evaluating and refining troublesome situations to prevent future problems. In Chapter 18, this process is extended to design adaptations and to plan for teaching and generalizing the routine in the context of the natural environment.

Adapted with permission from *Project QUEST Inservice Manual* (Falco et al., 1990)

Student: _____ Date: _____

Goal/Purpose of Routine: _____

Settings: _____

Component	Natural Cues/Prompts	Skills/Sequence of Steps	Adaptations
Initiate			
Prepare/Perform			
Terminate			
Transition			

Student: _____   Date: _____

Component	Natural Cues/Prompts	Skills/Sequence of Steps	Adaptations
Solve Problems			
Communicate/ Socialize			
Make Choices			
Self-Monitor			

Organize and Structure Visual Support Systems

It is clear that learners with autism spectrum disorders have difficulty taking in, organizing, understanding, and using sensory information from the environment. It is also clear that most of these individuals have visual strengths or can be taught to use information that is visually clear and permanent for frequent reference. Systematic organization of and giving visual structure to events, space, and time provide information that compensates to some degree. However, there is still a need to visually clarify ideas, concepts, sequences, and processes to achieve greater independence.

The success or failure of most instructional or behavioral programs depends to a large extent on the ability to provide information in a way the learner can understand. Learners with ASD generally need more details and information than most other people, but to ensure understanding, it must be carefully organized and presented in a concrete, and permanent visual format rather than only in a transient auditory mode.

There are a few individuals within the autism spectrum that function better with auditory information, but if they are to manage themselves independently as adults, they must also be taught to use some visual systems. For this more auditory group of learners, interpreters must use both speech and visual systems as they provide instruction and support.

The first part of this chapter provides strategies to select the symbols and construct visual systems. The second part introduces a number of visual systems and strategies for clarifying information to highlight meaning, facilitate problem solving, self-management, interactions, and the ability to think and manipulate more abstract ideas. The chapter closes with a discussion of high technology systems—video-modeling and the use of computer instruction that provide both visual and auditory information.

Part 1: Design and Construction of Visual Systems

All successful visual systems must be individualized to match each learner's needs. To ensure that a system will be accepted and used by the individual, the symbols must be meaningful, and the system must be constructed so it will be clear and easy to manipulate and use.

Symbol Selection

Visual information systems are based on symbols to represent real things and ideas. Symbols can be objects, emblems, words, signs, pictures, or conventional marks that represent real things and ideas. Typically, children learn about symbols and begin to use them during the first 2 years of life. They automatically learn that sounds, toys, and photographs can represent real people and things. When these young children begin to imitate and pretend, it is obvious that they understand some fairly abstract symbols. For example, very young children will pick up a toy telephone, a block, or a banana and pretend to talk on a phone. They look at a photo of mother, point to the picture, and smile as they look at mother. A slightly older child sees a stop sign and shouts, "Stop!" while bracing for stopping.

The following progression, listed from the least abstract to the most abstract, is assumed to be the easiest to master for young children with learning differences:

1. Real objects (keys mean ride in the car, cup means drink)

2. Parts of real objects (a piece of chain represents the swing)

3. Miniatures of real objects, such as toys

4. Abstract objects, such as blocks

5. Photographs and magazine pictures

6. Abstract pictures (line drawings)

7. Printed and written words

However, as in other areas of development, those with autism spectrum disorders do not necessarily follow that typical step-by-step progression. Learners with autism are very concrete and routine based, with little understanding of representational thinking. These learners do not automatically learn to use objects to imitate and pretend. For example, one 4-year-old with autism had a toy school bus that was seen as a container—the child turned it upside down and carefully filled it with blocks. Never did he pretend it was a bus to drive about. Yet at the age of 3, he could read some words, read and write numbers, and count to 100—and could also count from 100 back to 1—all without any specific instruction.

When working with learners who have autism, it is difficult to know which symbols are understood or exactly how a symbol is understood by any individual learner. We must remember that accurate and conventional meanings are not automatically associated or attached to objects and experiences.

Typical Problems in Understanding Symbols

Assume that a familiar object such as a medium-sized blue ball is chosen to represent recess time. From the perspective of a very literal learner, confusion could occur for any one or several of the following reasons:

1. The literal interpretation and belief that every object and every rule has a single meaning that will always be true—forever. For example:

   - If a round, blue, bouncy object is a ball, and a ball is to throw, bounce, hit, kick, or catch—how can a football or a golf ball also be a ball?

   - How can a ball or a photograph of a ball relate to a time period, such as recess, where various kinds of ball games might be played and many activities without balls also occur?

   - If a ball is for throwing, bouncing, hitting, kicking, and catching, are those the only things one can do at recess time? A learner who tries to use the symbol literally may resist doing anything other than play ball during recess.

   - If a ball takes on a broader meaning as a symbol for a period of time, it may lose its meaning as a toy for play. How is the learner to know when to play ball and when to simply go to recess?

Consider another situation: If a drawing of a coat is used to represent going outside, it is likely that the learner will insist on wearing a coat whenever it is time to go outside, even in warm weather. This insistence is not related to retardation; neither is it a control issue or stubbornness. The learner is simply trying to follow the rule exactly as taught: "This symbol means put on your coat, then go outside."

2. *The inability to focus on the relevant details and ignore the irrelevant.* Real objects, photographs, magazine pictures, and colorful or comical drawings, all contain myriad details that can distract from the relevant details to make an accurate association. For example, blemishes, labels, color, decoration, faces, or any irrelevant detail can interfere with accurate and precise associations between the event and the symbol and with generalized use of the symbol in various situations.

   - Photographs of people in the setting are confusing to some learners. For example, a photograph of the learner sitting at his desk was confusing to one learner because the chair was always empty when he approached his desk. If a photograph shows the teacher leading a specific class and there is a substitute, the learner will be confused. (From the learner's perspective: "The picture says the teacher must be there. No one else can be in the teacher's place. This isn't right. What do I do now?")

   - A picture cut from a catalog or magazine is likely to have details that will distract the learner from the relevant cues in the picture. For example, a manufacturer's label in a photograph is likely to catch attention before the actual object in the picture.

Colorful picture cards from a commercial language program were used for symbols on Matt's calendar. One day the picture of the sandwich, representing lunchtime, was missing. When his interpreter replaced it with a picture of a sandwich from another set, Matt became upset. He kept saying, "Number 57," and he refused to go to lunch. In assessing the situation, the staff found an exact replica of the original picture and discovered that it had a tiny 57 printed in the top corner. Matt, who was fascinated by numbers, had selected the number as the relevant cue, ignoring the picture even though it was much larger and colorful.

3. *Line drawings, handwriting, and styles of print made by different people cause confusion.* When a symbol is lost and is replaced by one made by a different person, the meaning of the new symbol may need to be retaught. For example, "This is a drawing of a desk and it means time to work. It looks a little different from the old picture, but it means the same thing."

Line drawings that are too specific can cause problems. José learned to get ready for bed by looking at a sequence of drawings that showed him putting on and wearing his favorite blue pajamas with a star on the front. One evening, when those pajamas had been left at his grandmother's house, José refused to put on a different pair. When his mother drew another sequence of pictures that showed him in a different pair of pajamas, he put them on immediately.

Literal understanding of words, the inability to select the relevant details from a visual, and the tendency to learn and to do things literally, exactly as taught, are the major considerations in symbol selection.

Criteria for Symbol Selection

The types of symbols selected for an individual will determine the effectiveness of the system. The gaps, discrepancies, and scattered skills common in autism not only cause confusion for learners but present a dilemma to those who select symbols for their first visual systems.

Select a type of symbol that:

1. *Is used spontaneously and meaningfully for at least a few basic purposes.*

   For example, a child who brings the car keys whenever he wants to go for a ride and who gets a glass to express a desire for a drink is likely to progress quickly with concrete objects as symbols.

2. *Is free of previous* associations that could confuse the meaning or limit generalization to a broader class of activities.

3. *Is generic; that is, free from distracting detail.* For example, one child was shown a photograph of a books spread out on a table to represent reading time. He looked at the picture and said, "Phone." In the background of the picture his sister was playing her cello, with the scroll of the cello beside her ear—he had misinterpreted the picture thinking that the scroll was a telephone.

4. *Is attractive and interesting to the learner.*

5. *Is matched to motor development and ability to manipulate.*

6. *Will be easy to expand or shape to a more abstract level.*

Types of Symbols—Characteristics and Benefits

Concrete object symbols

Concrete object symbols are generally required for very young learners because they have little or no concept that everything has a label or that an object can represent something else. Objects will also be most likely to match the motor skills of the toddler to 3-year-old.

See Activity 4 in Chapter 18 for strategies to move from concrete objects to the use of line drawings and words.

Because they are so literal, concrete, and visual, many learners with autism can progress rather quickly from the use of concrete objects to using line drawings and written words.

Generic black and white drawings

Generic black-and-white line drawings have several unique qualities that make them particularly useful for learners with autism who:

- Have the motor dexterity and control to pick up and carry a card
- Line up toys, books, or papers and notice when they are out of line
- Look at magazines, newspapers, books, or product labels
- Are fascinated by lines or like to draw lines and pictures
- Read or write words
- Show interest in numbers, calendars, and clocks and read or write numbers

Generic black-and-white line drawings generally match the criteria for symbol selection listed previously. They are free of previous associations to confuse the meaning or to limit generalization to a broader class of activities. If designed correctly, they also are free of irrelevant elements and details that interfere with accurate associations, meanings, and generalizations (Groden & LeVasseur, 1995).

Line drawings paired with words

Line drawings paired with words facilitate the movement from objects to words and have several advantages:

■ Many learners are highly motivated by lines and print and by watching someone draw and print. (The learner with autism is not an art critic. Often simple stick figures and outlines are the most meaningful.)

■ They are relatively easy to associate with the intended meaning because these individuals make such literal and quick associations.

For example, print the words Work Time under a simple outline of a desk while saying, "This is a picture of a desk. It means work time." If the drawing is immediately carried to the work area, it will likely be associated with work time after only a few experiences.

■ They are easy to draw to solve an immediate or unexpected problem.

■ They are easy to individualize to match a learner's specific need to highlight the most relevant cues related to a specific problem.

■ They are cheaper and more efficient to incorporate in systems than photographs.

■ They are easy and quick to adapt, add to, or replace when different needs are identified or if the original symbol is soiled, torn, or lost.

Printed or written words

Printed or written words have many of the same advantages as line drawings. As part of the natural language, they are easier for strangers, friends, and mentors to understand. Use of written words in visual systems increases reading comprehension and spelling skills.

Some learners are more motivated by print than by object or photo symbols.

> Matt, 5 years old, was not interested in his communication system or his calendar designed with photographs. His team followed a traditional rule of instruction: If the student makes errors or does not learn the lesson within a reasonable time, drop to a lower level of difficulty. The photos were replaced with miniature objects. When Matt continued to ignore his calendar, his support team sought consultation from a communication specialist who had considerable experience in autism. This assessment showed that Matt was highly interested in line drawings and words and that he could read many words. Much to the surprise of his team, he began to use the systems once printed words and line drawings paired with words were incorporated.

In summary, every symbol, whether it is an object, line drawing, or printed word symbol, must be presented precisely to ensure that the correct associations are made. It is also necessary to be cautious in selecting the specific symbol to represent a specific activity in order to avoid learned errors and a need to reteach a rule as in the earlier discussion of balls.

Construction of Visual Systems

Several design decisions are required before construction begins. The most important decisions relate to the type of symbols, the purpose of the system, how the symbols will be managed, and the amount of detail and information needed.

Once the type of symbols is determined, consider the following criteria and construction strategies as design decisions are made. A visual system must be:

- Quick and easy to construct and use
- Flexible—easy to adapt to match changing needs and situations
- Sturdy to use, reuse, and carry around
- Inexpensive
- Visually clear and concrete, free of unnecessary details or decoration
- Effective and as age-appropriate and nonstigmatizing as possible

The issue of effectiveness is paramount. Although it is important for an adaptation to be age appropriate, if it is not effective, then it has no value.

Construction Strategies

The key to preparing a visual system is to have it ready as quickly as possible and to modify it as soon as a need is identified. When systems are not available immediately, or if they are expensive or require significant time to construct:

- Behavior problems may intensify and needs may change before the system is ready.
- Systems are less likely to be refined as needs change.
- Systems may be protected and preserved and less available to the learner for frequent day-to-day use.

The blocks of time on a calendar system can progress either from left to right or top to bottom.

Several design decisions are required before construction begins. The most important decisions relate to the type of symbols, the purpose of the system, how the symbols will be managed, and the amount of detail and information needed.

Materials for informal, emergency systems

Interpreters always need writing materials close by. In one kindergarten class, all staff members carried pencils and pads of sticky notes in their pockets. One mother made certain to keep a pencil and a pad of paper in the car, her purse, and every room of the house. In emergencies, use whatever is at hand to provide quick information that will clarify a situation—a paper towel, a lunch bag, a scrap of paper from the waste container, or marks in the sand or dirt (as in the illustration on page 176).

Materials for formal or planned systems

A more formal system is planned to achieve longer-term goals that require more thought. Construction of the various parts of a visual system can be burdensome if one person is totally responsible. If the following materials are available during planning sessions, the support-team members can do much of the construction work as the design needs are determined:

- File folders
- Unlined 3" x 5" and/or 4" x 6" file cards in white and a mix of colors
- Felt pens (especially black) and highlighters
- Masking tape, transparent tape, paper clips, stapler, ruler, glue
- Utility or pen knife and scissors
- Hook-and-loop strips and circles
- Poster putty

- Self-adhesive labels of various sizes, shapes, and colors
- Clear, self-adhesive, vinyl for laminating
- Envelopes of various kinds and sizes
- Plastic sandwich bags with locking tops
- A collection of boxes and containers of various sizes (e.g., shoe boxes with lids, plastic dishpans or tubs, margarine or yogurt containers, plastic freezer containers, plastic meat trays, egg cartons)
- Commercially available generic black-and-white drawings and computer programs to develop grids, templates, flow charts, and generic picture symbols (see resources in Appendix B, page 487–488)

Constructing object-symbol systems

Using objects as symbols generally requires a format to represent blocks of time or the sequence of steps. A container is necessary to keep each symbol distinctly separated. A larger container is needed for placing the symbols when the event or the step of the task is completed. Plastic tubs, baskets, or meat trays also can be used to represent time blocks.

See page 317, Activity 4, for description of a strategy for making the transition from this type of object display to the use of line drawings.

- Tape together a series of identical containers—boxes, tubs, or trays that are each large enough to hold a single symbol. Each box represents a block of time. Prepare a larger box for placing the object symbols at the conclusion of each event or time block. Paint over or cover the boxes to mask manufacturers' labels and irrelevant printed details that could distract the learner from the accurate name of the event. (From a learner's perspective, he could be thinking: "Oh, it's Red Wing Shoes® time.") Label the larger box *Finished*, and place it near the display. There could be a smaller container located at the site of each activity where the learner places the object as he arrives.

- Construct a wooden calendar box that has dividers to separate time blocks. Each section has its own hinged lid that can be closed at the end of each event or time block.

- Place objects in clear plastic bags with locking tops and fasten the bags to a cord with clothespins or clips that are easy for the learner to manipulate. The learner can carry the bag (with object) to the activity.

- Fasten objects to a square of tagboard. Hang them in sequence on small hooks or with clips.

Constructing card symbol systems

Line drawings and printed words (or photographs, if required) can be fastened on file cards and laminated. To display a sequence, mount the cards on a display board in some way that makes it easy to move or remove them. Use an adapted classroom card chart, mount a series of envelopes on a bulletin board, or prepare a display board from file folders, etc. Envelopes and display boards are easy and inexpensive to make from file folders.

Making envelopes

- Envelopes can be made from file folders and used as containers for transition cue cards, for placing assigned and completed work sheets, checklists, cue cards, and any number of other purposes. Prepare a supply of various sized envelopes made from file folders and keep them on hand for quick system adaptations.

  Construction: To make small envelopes for holding 3" x 5" cards, cut a file folder in four parts. To hold larger cards, cut the folder in half. Use the whole folder to hold standard 8½" x 11" sheets of paper.

- Backgrounds to display the card symbols in a sequence can be used for calendars, mini-calendars, job folders, and choice or activity option boards. These backgrounds can be adapted to hold any number of symbol cards and any type of card display.

  Construction: To construct a display board for 3" x 5" cards, split a file folder in half. Arrange short sequences of three or four cards on half a file (one strip.) For a longer sequence of six to eight cards, tape two strips together. If 4" x 6" file cards are used, use two folders taped together. Tape or staple an envelope on the top and the bottom to hold transition cues or as containers for symbols at the end of an event. Attach the symbol cards to these backgrounds with hook-and-loop tape (as on Jason's calendar, page 205) or with paper clips (as on Jeff's calendar, on the same page).

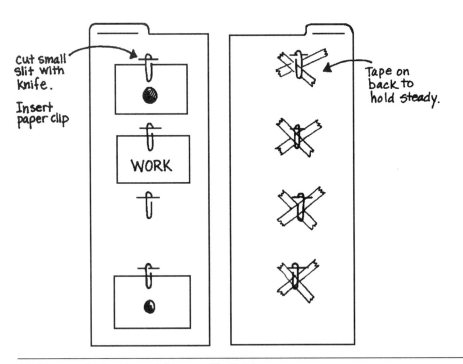

Making a display board from a file folder

Developing Grids or Templates

Develop and use grids and templates for mini-calendars, checklists, and choice or option lists when the format of a system remains the same but the content of the system changes each day. For example, although the activities on Matt's mini-calendar were changed each day, it was important to have a few communication symbols readily available. To save time, a template was made and a supply of these grids was always available. Each morning, Matt's interpreter made simple line drawings to represent the sequence of tasks he was to complete during a specific time period. Matt had several such mini-calendars to fill the day.

■ Picture strip grids—A supply of cartoon-strip formats with two to eight sections makes it quick and easy to prepare checklists and stories when line drawings are required. See examples on pages 214 and 263.

See Appendix B for a listing of computer programs for developing grids, templates, etc.

Evaluate and Refine

The design and construction elements of any visual self-management or information system must be regularly evaluated and refined from the time they are first introduced. Minor refinements are often all that is necessary, but at times it will become obvious that the total system needs revision when:

- The system is rejected after introduction.
    - The system may be too simple or the symbols do not interest the learner, see example of Matt, page 199.
    - The learner has simply memorized the schedule and does not see a need for the calendar— there must be enough variations in the schedule each day to make the calendar useful.
- The learner fixates on some small detail of the system.
- The learner is disorganized or disrupted by the organization of elements.
- It is too burdensome or complicated for the learner to manipulate.
- It is too complicated for the interpreter to adapt each day.

To avoid frustration and to ensure progress to more independent use and increased options, the system must be refined as soon as a problem is identified.

Summary

The design of visual support systems will determine the rate of learning and the level of stress. Those with autism need concrete and literal information *presented in clear, direct, and uncluttered ways* that is always available for review. Concrete objects, generic black-and-white line drawings, and printed or written words must be selected and designed to present a minimum of conflicting stimulation. Because systems must be refined frequently, the construction must be simple and inexpensive.

Part 2: Visual Systems and Strategies

The second part of this chapter describes the considerations for individualizing and using calendar systems, checklists and cue cards, semantic maps, and stories—visual self-management systems to clarify expectations, time, concepts, ideas, and processes. These systems are also used to teach social skills and rules that will enable those with autism spectrum disorders to become more independent.

These visual support strategies will be referred to in all chapters that deal with teaching new skills and solving behavior problems.

The Calendar System

A calendar system consists of a calendar, mini-calendars, and transition cues. A calendar visually represents a systematically and individualized sequence of events in time. The sequence of events is ordered to capitalize on the reinforcing qualities of each activity. An individualized calendar system answers the questions:

- What?
- When?
- Where?
- What's next?

Chapter 12 explains the strategies for organizing events in time to capitalize on liked activities. Chapter 15, page 236, provides guidelines for using contingencies.

These calendar systems are perhaps the most important self-management tools for those with autism, not only because the learner is prepared for coming events, but because the events are ordered so the scheduled reinforcing activities provide motivation, the basis for making contingency statements.

These visual support systems will never be faded, but they will be made more sophisticated as the individual progresses. The ultimate goal of these calendar systems is for learners to independently use lists, appointment books, and standard wall calendars to manage time and life as adults.

Design Decisions

The calendar and its parts serve as natural cues for moving through the events of the day without verbal directions. A learner's first calendar should be quite simple. As the calendar and the calendar symbols take on meaning and the learner's interests and tolerance expand, modifications will be required. The first task is to make design decisions that respect the learner's individual needs. The first decision was to determine and select the appropriate symbols—there are eight other design decisions:

1. The amount of time to display at one time.

   This decision depends on the learner's attention span and experience. Learners with a very short attention span and little or no understanding of sequences and cause/effect (this, then this) need short displays that initially represent three or four short activities in a 5- or 10-minute block of time. As tolerance and understanding increase, the calendar is systematically expanded to represent a half or whole day. Those with a longer attention span who have some understanding of cause/effect and sequence can manage a full day's display from the beginning.

   Weekly calendars to supplement the shorter displays are often introduced when a learner is upset about not going to school on weekends. Standard wall calendars with ample writing space supplement the daily calendar as soon as learners show a need to know when special events will occur in the future.

SUNDAY	MONDAY	TUESDAY	WEDNESDAY	THURSDAY
5 No School Grandma's House	6 School Swimming	7 School Tia to Scouts To Store	8 School McDonald's	9 School

2. The types of symbols.

   Review the discussion of symbol selection (pages 197–201) before making this decision.

3. The format for displaying symbols.

   The format must ensure that the learner knows what to do first, what happens next, and how many more things must be done. Object and card systems can be displayed vertically or horizontally. Some learners find it easier to follow a sequence from left to right, while others more naturally move from the top down. Initially it is important to test out the most natural direction for a specific learner. With experience, most learners become more flexible and follow a list from top to bottom and a wall calendar from left to right and down the page.

4. The system to signify that an event is finished when the symbols are:

   - Concrete objects: As activities are completed, the objects are placed in a box labeled Finished.

   - Line drawings or words on cards: The cards can be turned over or placed in an envelope or box labeled Finished.

   - Line drawings or words on charts, checklists, or grids: Cross out or check off the symbol at the end of each activity.

   - A single activity symbol on a notebook page: Turn over the page when the activity is completed. Secure the page with a clip or rubber band.

5. The amount of detail.

   Some less sophisticated and very literal learners may initially need space on the calendar to represent transitions.

   - Keep the calendar as simple as possible to allow for the greatest flexibility. It is easier to add detail when needed than to remove detail that is confusing. Do not add distracting decorative detail that draws attention from the relevant information.

   - Listing start or stop times—A basic calendar that lists the sequence of blocks that is only labeled to represent the types of activities (music, work, choice, work, lunch) is good for a younger or less sophisticated learner who needs considerable flexibility and whose calendar is located in a specific location. A mini-calendar in each location provides the details to support this more general calendar.

   - Those who can read and tell time, may find it useful to have the beginning and ending times listed if they carry their calendars with them at all times. However, the increased detail reduces flexibility as it is harder to adapt activity length to the learner's varying tolerance level if the specific time is listed.

- Those with compulsive time worries may become anxious if an event does not begin or end at the exact time. The learner can become a clock watcher or become very confused if the specifically stated time passes without the learner's awareness.

- If the learner needs to have the time displayed, avoid this problem by placing symbols around the time (<9:00>) and teaching that "It means about 9:00—maybe a few minutes before, maybe a few minutes after."

6. Design transition cues.

- Making independent transitions is a critical skill. Those with autism can become dependent on others to give them verbal directions. This dependency on verbal cues and directions requires the presence of another person because it is extremely difficult to fade artificial verbal directions. A transition cue is an object or card that triggers the learner to go to a specific place independently without verbal directions. These transition cues also help keep the destination in mind and avoids wandering or getting lost. The symbols from the calendar or mini-calendar are obvious transition cues when carried to the location of an event. In the illustration below, the ball serves as a reminder (a cue) to go to the gym.

- Transition cues to return to the calendar after an activity is finished are also important for those who have difficulty ending an activity and moving on to the next one.

- "Check calendar" could be listed as the last item on the mini-calendar or checklist.

- A specific object or a symbol (a block or a poker chip, or a 3"x 5" card with the learner's name printed on it) can indicate the end of the present activity and return to the calendar. Teach the learner to return the cue to an envelope or box that is labeled and attached to or placed near the calendar.

Jeff was just learning to use a calendar that incorporated labeled line drawings on 3" x 5" cards. Transition cues (see illustrations on page 211) were placed at the end of each mini-calendar so he always knew what to do at the conclusion of the specific time block. His interpreter always carried transition cues to the playground or to other school settings away from the calendar. Initially, Jeff's interpreter met him at the bus each morning and gave him a cue card that directed him to his classroom to hang his coat. Once his coat was hung, the interpreter handed Jeff a cue card with his name on it that directed him to his calendar. Arriving at the calendar, he places the cue card in the pocket labeled Jeff.

A few days after the transition cues were introduced, Jeff was climbing on the playground equipment when it was time to return to class. When his interpreter gave him the transition cue, Jeff looked at it for a moment, and then slowly but independently climbed down and began to walk back to the classroom to his calendar.

7. Design and manage mini-calendars.

A mini-calendar supplements a basic daily calendar and shows the sequence of specific activities scheduled to occur within a small time block such as a class, a therapy session, a trip, a party, or a period of work. The information enables the learner to:

- Prepare for each transition within a time block

- Measure passing time as each activity is completed

- Prepare for a larger transition at the end

A mini-calendar can be a simple, on-the-spot construction to deal with an unexpected situation. It also can be specifically planned and used routinely for periods of time that include several changes or to provide support during a new situation. The last item on a mini-calendar is a transition cue that answers the questions: What do I do next? Where do I go now?

Considerations for the design of these mini-calendars will be the same as for the design of the daily calendar; the symbols will likely be the same, but size and organization will depend on the needs of the setting.

- Actual materials placed in a sequence of boxes or tubs:

    This type is useful for those who are using concrete objects and first learning to work, then play. When all materials are in the Finished box, it is time to play.

- Written as an agenda for group use:

    This type is useful in classes when all students need the reminder to stay focused—circle time in early childhood or preschool classes, Sunday school classes, scout meetings, or therapy sessions. Write the mini-schedule on the chalkboard or a chart pad. To accommodate learners who need pictures, use tiny line drawings (rebus symbols) on 3"x 5" cards in a card chart to represent the critical words or names.

- Constructed from file folders and 3"x 5" cards:

    The sequence of cards, worksheets, or a list can specify activities to do during a specific time block. The interpreter can have the file prepared and in a specific file box to be checked as the learner arrives. This is particularly well suited to those in regular classrooms whose activities are individualized or different from peers (see pages 203–204 for construction details).

- Written on specifically designed grids:

  This is useful for a regular class, a one-to-one work session or individual work session—the learner can cross off each activity as it is completed (see the illustration of Matt's clipboard on page 205).

8. Location and management of the calendar.

- Notebooks, clipboards, or appointment books are either carried by the learner throughout the day or located in an easily accessible place, such as on the learner's desk or work station. The workstation is also a good place to mount a calendar.

Transition cues

Sequence card to teach routine

- Object boxes and display boards are located in non-distracting locations and at a level that enables the learner to see the symbols easily. There are many creative ways to manage a calendar.

- Mount a wall chart format somewhere near or in an area that is out of the main flow of the others but in a location where the learner is comfortable and able to review it whenever he or she feels a need.

- Arrange a transition center for multiple students. For example, one teacher made such a center for three students whose calendars were all different but whose transition times were the same. The transition center was structured around a table that held all three calendars, with chairs for the three students and a single interpreter. The chairs enabled the students to feel centered to focus on their calendars. The interpreter was positioned across the table at the student's eye level to make it easy to glance at each student, identify nonverbal signs of confusion, provide needed assistance, and cue interactions.

Tony and several of his peers needed daily calendars to help them keep track of the events in their third grade class. As the last students arrived in the classroom each morning, Mr. Garcia placed a large sheet of butcher paper on the table in the center of the room. As he began to write out the schedule with a black felt marker, Tony and others gathered around. Some students watched or listened quietly from their desks. Mr. Garcia noted all the changes, explained specific expectations, and answered questions about the day's activities. When finished, he placed the calendar on the bulletin board in front of the room near Tony's desk. It was Tony's job to cross off each event on the calendar as it was completed. In this way, a strategy that was essential for a few students also benefited others.

Expand and Adapt Calendar Systems

Adaptations to Prepare for Planned Changes

Major schedule changes and new expectations do increase stress. This stress can be reduced with thoughtful planning.

José was dependent and possessive of Tom, his interpreter. If Tom was absent or involved with another person, José would become very upset. To resolve this problem, it was decided that Tom would begin sharing his time with other students. Tom used the familiar calendar routine to prepare José for this change. José's calendar was a simple grid with each activity listed on a separate sticky note. The notes for activities that occurred two or three times a week were placed on the edge of the calendar to reuse. Two days before the planned change, Tom placed a note on the edge of the calendar without comment. The note read: *Tom will work with Mary*. On the morning of the change, the note was moved onto the calendar and paired with the note that indicated what José was to do independently. During the regular calendar review session with José, Tom talked about the change. As he told José how he could get help during the period, Tom wrote out the procedure. José checked his calendar several times during the time Tom worked with Mary, but he managed this and future changes without incident.

Adaptations for Unplanned Changes

The calendar also provides a way to minimize the stress from unexpected interruptions and changes that occur each day. The learner has two needs: to know exactly what will happen and when things will return to normal.

Unexpected changes generally involve a cancellation; substitution; or change in time, location, or people. The interpreter immediately takes the learner to the calendar to see how the change affects the expected routine of events. If the calendar is not available when one of these changes occurs, the interpreter uses whatever is at hand to make the information visual (i.e., a scrap of paper from the wastebasket.)

■ Cancellations, substitutions, and changed times are visualized and explained while removing and replacing the calendar symbol or changing its location on the calendar.

■ Changing locations, changing people, and changed behavioral expectations are highlighted on a sticky note and placed on the symbol for the specific activity. Explain the change as the note is placed on the calendar. ("We usually go for a walk after dinner, but tonight Suzy and Tom are coming to visit. We will take a walk tomorrow night. While Suzy and Tom are here, you can read your sports magazine or listen to tapes.")

Adaptations to Increase Independence

Once the learner understands and uses the calendar system fairly independently, it is time to expand the complexity of the calendar system to:

■ Systematically increase the amount of work between reinforcing activities.

■ Add new, disliked activities while varying the tolerated and liked activities (see Chapter 12).

■ Provide more opportunities for self-management.

For example, involve the learner in making choices and decisions about the day. Give them a chance to choose leisure activities or jobs, decide when or where to do an activity, or choose the types of materials or the friends to involve in the activities. Remember that for this process to be successful, the choices or options must be limited—initially, offer no more than two. Have the symbols for the various options displayed for the learner to review before making the choice.

■ Progress to more complex and abstract symbol systems.

- Use more natural formats.

- Expand the goals of the daily calendar review process. For example, change the review format to solve a problem or to practice new communication or social skills. Some higher-functioning learners and those with Asperger's may have contact with an interpreter only once or twice a day, often before and/or after work or school. If a longer review period is scheduled, it may be used to:

  - Review the positive events of the previous day

  - Expand problem-solving and self-management strategies related to real-life concerns

  - Expand conversation and social skills

  - Prepare for the coming day

> When José got off the bus each morning, he wandered randomly about the school and was either very late to class or upset because others had firmly directed him to class. His interpreter decided to preview José's calendar with him at the end of each school day. When José knew what was to happen first the next day (a liked activity), he went directly to class each morning.

Evaluate and Refine Calendar Systems

Evaluation of the calendar system begins when it is introduced. Frequent and thoughtful evaluation is important to ensure that the system is adapted in a manner that matches the learner's expanding skills and increasing independence. Three different possibilities guide the evaluation:

1. *If the learner continues to need considerable assistance*

   Some element or elements of the environment, the schedule, the format of the calendar, or the instructional sequence may be unclear. Note areas of confusion and difficulty. Where have errors occurred? Why? Where are prompts needed? Why? What could be modified or clarified? What may be misunderstood? Why? Sometimes another support-team member can provide a more objective perspective to pinpoint the elements that need revision.

   Review sections related to organization of events in time (Chapter 12) and space (Chapters 12 and 13). Also read Chapters 16 and 17 to pinpoint problems in the instructional sequence. After identifying a possible solution, refine the system quickly.

2. *If the learner is not motivated to use the calendar*

   If the learner was never motivated to use the calendar system, it probably is a problem of symbol selection or design complexity, particularly if the design is visually distracting or disorganized. Review the previous sections and make revisions to clarify the system or the instructional procedures.

3. *If the learner once used the calendar fairly independently* and appeared to be motivated, consider the following reasons for the current lack of motivation or resistance:

   - The design of the calendar, the symbols, or the display may be too simple. Review the discussion of symbol selection (Chapter 14, pages 197–201) and the example of Matt's problem (pages 199 and 201).

   - The scheduled activities are uninteresting or meaningless.

> ▶ Reassess the reinforcing value of activities and the arrangement of the activities to take advantage of liked activities as reinforcers.

> ▶ The activities may have been done too many times over a long period of time; they are too easy or not age-appropriate, and the learner is bored. Review the learner's goals and placement to be sure they are age-appropriate and provide an appropriate level of stimulation.

> ▶ Clarify the meaning and purpose of the activities. Make sure they are important and that there is a reason for doing them.

> ▶ Increase the number of changes and variations in the daily schedule. *When a schedule lacks variety*, the learner memorizes the sequence then has little reason to review the calendar.

- The location of the calendar is inconvenient or interrupts the flow of events. Perhaps a mini-calendar on a small clipboard or pocket card can be carried when a return to the basic calendar would be disruptive.

> ▶ The location of the calendar calls undue or negative attention from peers. This can be a problem for more able learners who want to be like their peers. In this situation, make the calendar more "normal;" for example, place it in the front of a notebook or file folder, or include everyone in the process (see the illustration of Tony, page 212).

> ▶ Verbal prompts have not been faded and the learner is simply moving through a turn-taking routine with the interpreter—a routine that has little or no meaning attached. Review procedures for prompting and fading prompts (pages 252–256). Again, it may take an objective team member to help pinpoint this problem and suggest modifications to increase meaning and independence.

In summary, a functional communication system and a calendar system are the two most important lifelong tools for those with autism who have difficulty communicating; are confused by time and events; and resist changes, transitions, or new experiences. *It is not acceptable to simply stop using the calendar because the learner doesn't like it or doesn't seem to need it.* The schedule, the calendar, or both must be adapted quickly so that the activities are interesting, important, and varied frequently enough so the learner sees value in the calendar. Keep in mind that the ultimate goal for those with autism is to use standard calendars, appointment books, and lists to independently manage their own activities as adults.

The systematic planning process described in Chapters 11 through 15 ensures that critical goals will be addressed. With this structure, each event provides many opportunities for learning those subtle skills and lessons that others learn automatically.

Strategies for teaching learners to use the calendar in the context of functional routines are found in Chapter 18.

Additional Visual Tools—Checklists, Cue Cards, and Maps

Checklists

A checklist is a visual reference that highlights (cues) the steps of a routine, event, or task from initiation to termination and transition to the next routine. A mini-calendar may sometimes use a checklist format. When a checklist is used during initial instruction or when introducing a new activity, it provides a structure to enable the learner to ultimately perform independently without verbal assistance. Creatively designed checklists can provide a format for:

- Clarifying or cuing communication and social strategies

- Marking progress toward completion; keeping the end in sight
- Monitoring productivity, speed, and quality of the performance
- Self-monitoring behavior

Variations and expanded applications

Checklists can be prepared quickly to deal with unexpected problems or developed following assessment and development of a new routine. Checklists can take many forms, serve a variety of purposes, and incorporate any type of symbol.

1. *Typed or written lists* are the most common for those who can read.

- Use a simple checklist to clarify the day's shopping trip.

- When a checklist will be reused in the same form for many days, write on tag-board or a file folder and laminate it. Attach a clothespin or paper clip on the edge, and move it down as each step is completed.

See Story Strategies on pages 221–226.

- Prepare a checklist in story format with a single step on each page.

2. *Picture symbol lists* can take many forms and support routines as diverse as washing windows, preparing a snack, grooming, or having a conversation.

- Pictures on 3"x 5" cards held together on a ring can serve as a checklist. As each step of the sequence is completed, the page is flipped over and secured with a clip or rubber band.

- The picture strip shown here illustrates the steps for participating independently at the swimming pool.

3. *Small objects placed in a specific order on a divided tray* can clarify a sequence of steps and serve as a checklist.

- Objects lined up on a tray—soap, toothbrush, comb, and lotion—show the steps for a grooming routine.
- Materials for completing some assembly or packaging jobs, fastened in the required sequence on a card, tray, or file folder, provide a visual reference (checklist) for completing the job accurately and independently.

When José was 16, he frequently missed school because his mother couldn't get him out of bed and ready for school each morning. He had been denied school bus service in the past because he didn't follow the rules and his mother was unable to transport him. After analyzing José's situation, two checklists were prepared. One highlighted each step of the routine from the time the alarm clock sounded to the time José entered the door of the school bus. The second listed the bus rules translated into very specific behavioral expectations. The driver handed this second checklist to José as he entered the bus. José held the checklist and referred to it during the ride. On arriving at school, he waited until other students had left the bus, then showed the checklist to the driver. The driver quickly rated the quality of his behavior and signed the checklist. Then José took the checklist to his teacher for congratulations.

The checklists were introduced to José with a story that clarified the problem and explained the checklists. José's teacher arrived at his home at 6:30 a.m. on two days to teach him to follow the two checklists. During this period, José's mother learned how to provide support to use the list. The bus driver was shown how to talk to José and how to rate his behavior. José was virtually independent and successful with the checklists after that initial instruction. Figures 14.1 and 14.2 illustrate these checklists and adaptations that support the travel routine on page 217–218.

Figure 14.1 Sample: José's Checklist for Preparing for School

This routine actually begins with a bedtime routine when José showers and selects and lays out his clothing for morning.

1. The alarm clock rings. Turn it off and stretch.
2. Get out of bed.
3. Go to the bathroom.
   Checklist mounted on the mirror directs bathroom tasks.
4. Return to bedroom. Get dressed.
5. Tell Mom, "Good morning."
6. Eat breakfast.
7. Brush teeth.
8. Make bed.

If everything is done before 7:10:
9. Set timer for 10 minutes and listen to tapes.
10. When timer rings, shut off tape player.
11. Put on coat and pick up backpack.
12. At 7:25, tell Mom, "Good-bye."
13. Go outside and stand on the yellow X on the sidewalk.
14. Watch and wait quietly for the bus to stop and the door to open.

Figure 14.2 Sample: José's Checklist for Riding the Bus

This routine begins as José steps into the bus.

When the bus comes and the door is open, pick up backpack and step into the bus.

1. Greet the driver. Take checklist.
2. Locate an empty seat.
3. Sit down on the seat.
4. Fasten seat belt.
5. Hold backpack, take out *Sports Illustrated*.
6. Sit quietly and read magazine.

When the bus stops at school and the door is open:

7. Unfasten seat belt and follow kids to the door.
8. Stop and talk to the driver.

- -

Report for José

José followed the rules.

- He did not yell or scream. He sat quietly.
- He did not run around the bus. He sat quietly.
- He kept his seat belt fastened.

_____

Driver

Cue Cards

The visual information on a cue card is less intrusive and easier for the learner to process than verbal assistance from another person. Because the cue card is visual and concrete, it can be referred to again and again. A simple message can be delivered quickly to help solve a problem. Many learners cannot communicate effectively in stressful situations but can remember to show a card to someone. When stress is high, a simple message on a cue card that clarifies a solution to a problem can prevent a crisis. Shifting attention from direct eye contact to the cue card is calming.

Cue cards provide a visual reference to help the learner:

- Recall a word or phrase
- See the relationship of ideas or variations of meaning
- Recall a new or difficult step or skill to complete a routine or solve a problem
- Recall the meaning of a rule or the various applications of a rule
- Support choice and decision making
- Support transition from one location to another

When people crowded too close to Maria, she became agitated and anxious and sometimes bit or hit them. While standing in line at the theater one day, Maria began to fidget and her face flushed as people began to crowd close. Her mother recognized the subtle signals of agitation and handed Maria a small cue card as she said, "You can tell them to move back." On the card was written, "Please move back." Maria turned and touched the arm of the person behind her and held out the card as she said, "Please." As that person moved back, Maria relaxed and smiled softly.

Situations were set up with other friends and other staff members to give Maria more opportunities to practice using this particular cue card until she could use it spontaneously.

Variations and expanded applications

Cue cards can be used in a variety of ways and in a number of different kinds of situations. Cue cards can be used by those who are nonverbal or those who are quite verbal to use in stressful situations when they have difficulty recalling the words they need.

 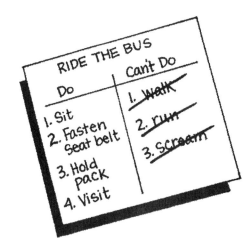

- For messages such as, "Help please," "I need a break quickly," "Please move back," or "Write it down, please."

- A cue card can contain a short list of options to help a learner fit into social situations. For example, a few rules to fit a situation, several options for solving a common problem, or a list of conversation topics are helpful.

- A T-chart format to clearly describe both the Do's and the Don'ts required in a specific situation are invaluable for situations like trips or parties. When learners understand what they are to do and not do, it is more likely that they will be able to function successfully (see the illustration on page 293).

Semantic Maps

Semantic maps—semantic webs or networks, tree charts, flow charts, and so on—provide a format to visualize and understand all the elements or pieces of information that make up a concept, idea, story, sequence, or process. These maps can show the relationship of old information to new information, identify categories, and correct misinterpretations. Two simple maps, using line drawings with words, are shown on page 220.

The use of semantic maps capitalizes on the visual, gestalt mode of processing common in autism. They compensate for the problems associated with literal interpretation and inability to hold together several pieces of information at one time to organize, see relationships and elicit meaning.

Variations and expanded applications

The maps can take innumerable forms to support a variety of needs (Grossen & Carnine, 1992; Pehrsson & Robinson, 1985). Maps can be adapted to use line drawings and printed words. They can be very simple or more complex to show the relationships between many details.

Semantic maps can be used to:

- Improve reading and language comprehension
- Clarify basic concepts or complex concepts outside the learner's experience, as in history or geography
- Illustrate the elements of a decision process
- Visualize events in time past, present, and future
- Plan parties and organize work
- Clarify the various applications of a social rule
- Clarify cause/effect relationships, fact from fiction, opposing views
- Draw conclusions, predict outcomes, or develop a logical argument
- Solve a problem; generate and evaluate alternatives
- Identify family relationships as well as staff roles and responsibilities

Grossen and Carnine (1992) described a procedure for teaching students with poor reading comprehension. They described four types of text-structure maps and strategies to identify the signal words in text to determine which type of map to use: a descriptive or thematic map, a sequential episodic map, a comparative and contrasting map, or a problem-and-solution map.

Story Strategies—Experience Stories and Social Stories

Stories provide a framework for teaching a variety of new skills and for resolving a wide variety of problems. A story can be adapted to match any age or cognitive ability; the strategies are easy for any interpreter to learn. A story provides a permanent visual reference that is easy to review independently in any setting.

- To review and share information about past events.

- They can be used to introduce changes and new routines.

- They can be used to teach social rules as well as academic skills.

- Stories are designed and used to prevent and to solve problems.

There are several types of story strategies. Two specific models are summarized below: Experience stories and social stories.

Experience Stories

These stories are adaptations of the Language Experience Approach (LEA) to reading instruction (Allen & Allen, 1966; Ashton-Warner, 1963). LEA is a highly individualized and integrated language arts program that teaches language, reading comprehension, verbal expression, writing, and spelling in the context of a child's single experience. It is based on a child's expression of his or her own experiences—his or her words written down (symbolized). Modified LEA strategies have been useful for many children with autism spectrum disorders—as the child lives the experience, then hears and sees the words as the interpreter writes them down and, when possible, says the words as the story is read. This multisensory approach engages their memories and emotions, which is so important for comprehension (Greenspan et al., 1998).

Note: It has been this author's experience that for some children, this approach has served as a bridge or scaffold for speaking.

Developing and presenting experience stories

Experience stories can be used in individual or in small group sessions. Initially, interpreters take the lead in developing stories and charts. Depending on the needs of a learner, line drawings or printed words are used. Stories are written about the learner's actual experiences as the learner watches. Correct sentence forms and punctuation are used to prevent learning errors. The interpreter always speaks the words as they are written down. The learner begins to add a few words to complete open-ended sentences and questions. As the learner gains understanding and confidence, new ideas or experiences are contributed spontaneously, either verbally or by taking the pen and drawing or writing them into the story.

Figure 14.3 Samples: Experience Stories

Example 1. A simple, beginning story written at home to share weekend experiences with the teacher

Today is Monday, November 8.

Grandma and Grandpa brought ice cream.

I used the computer.

Example 2. A group story to summarize the day

Greg contributed the underlined words after the teacher had set up the sentence frame. As each child talked, the teacher wrote the child's name so Greg could associate the name to the child. Key words in the story were highlighted with tiny line drawings.

Today is Monday, October 10. The sun is shining.

Kim said, "Tony was sick today and went home."

Greg said, "For lunch today we (Kim, Katy, Caesar, Mary, and Greg) had <u>pizza</u>."

Katy said, "Today was Mary's birthday. She was excited."

Mary said, "Mother brought balloons and cupcakes."

Caesar said, "They were good."

Katy said, "We (all of us) felt sad that Tony missed the party."

Greg said, "In PE, we played with <u>scooter boards</u>."

Example 3. A story about a picture of a boy holding a bat and a girl holding a ball

The children have toys. The bat <u>belongs</u> to Peter. The ball <u>belongs</u> to Jane.

Example 4. A story frame to answer questions about a picture

The picture shows two people washing dishes. The view through a window shows that it is night. The answers are written in complete sentences that culminate in a story about the picture.

Who is in the picture? <u>This is a picture story about a boy and a girl.</u>

Where are the people? <u>They are standing at the sink in the kitchen.</u>

When did this happen? <u>It is dark outside, so it is night time.</u>

What are the people doing? <u>They are washing dishes.</u>

Why are they doing that? <u>The dishes were dirty after eating dinner.</u>

Example 5. A story to summarize a graphing activity in math

There are 19 children in our class.

Everybody eats lunch.

10 children buy school lunches.

4 children bring a lunch box.

5 children go home for lunch.

10 plus 4 plus 5 equals 19.

Variations and expanded applications

Experience stories can supplement or replace a standard reading program for learners who are confused by phonetic or basal reading approaches. Some possible variations and applications are:

- Individual experiences or the experiences of a group can be developed and recorded

- A daily experience story can be developed and used to share information between home and school, and to facilitate conversations and reading at home. For example, near the end of the school day, the learner and an interpreter review the day's experiences and prepare a brief story. The story is copied (on a photocopier or printed or written by the learner). One copy is placed in a notebook for later review at school, and the other is carried home to share with family. The learner is encouraged to read the story to parents and to respond to parents' questions by locating the answer in the story.

  These stories must be brief, positive, and include interesting information. They must not be a summary of the day's behavior, especially if there were problems. (Figure 14.3 includes several experience stories.)

- To stimulate awareness of others and their perspective, write group stories. For example, a series of stories about the group might begin with one that describes each member (color of eyes, color of hair, whether hair is long or short, straight or curly hair, and so on) and requires a partner to get the information and report it for the story. Other stories could be about group members' favorite stories, TV shows, foods, or games. Others could target individual fears or worries. A more advanced story could summarize a common problem or situation that elicits different emotions, opinion, and perspective. The second example in this list is a group story.

- Plan, Do, Review Charts are used to prepare for new events and changing routines, and to review, evaluate, and adapt an activity that will be repeated. An activity or routine is planned and written on a chart. The plan includes the steps of the event as well as some of the environmental cues and behavioral expectations. A chart can be referred to as many times as needed before the activity. Following the event, the chart is reviewed. Some actual experiences may be added, problems may be discussed, and possible solutions can be added for reference before repeating the activity.

- Expand language concepts, learn to interpret pictures, and answer WH questions, using story frames. See the third and fourth examples in this list.

- Clarify math, science, and other academic concepts by summarizing activity-based problems and experiments in the format of an experience story. See the previous example.

- Combine art and writing—as in *Image-Writing Process* (Bingham, 2000; Olshansky, 1998).

In summary, experience stories can be adapted to prevent problems by clarifying information. They will also expand language, communication, and academic skills. Experience stories are written while the learner watches and learns to contribute more and more information.

Social Story Strategies

Social stories as developed by Gray and Garand (1993) are based on the growing understanding of social cognition in autism (Baron-Cohen, 1988; Dawson & Fernald, 1987; Frith, 1989). These short stories describe relevant social and environmental cues, the perspective of others, and a solution or appropriate response to a problem.

If a learner is unable to gain meaningful information about the social environment, the first step for teaching any new social skill or solving a social problem is to provide a careful explanation of the social situation. "Traditional teaching involves interaction between teacher and student, creating a social situation whenever instruction occurs. . . . The use of traditional instruction to teach social behavior presents a student with a compounded challenge: understanding the lesson, and accurately interpreting the social cues used in its presentation . . . Social stories . . . provide . . . direct access to social information" (Gray & Garand 1993, p. 2). Direct access occurs because the learner reviews the story independently; thus, after the first introduction there are no competing social cues to interpret. Improved behavior is often noted within a relatively short period of time.

Developing and presenting social stories

Social stories focus on an individual need or problem. The process for writing the stories is designed to avoid predictable misunderstandings and literal interpretations.

1. Identify the target problem and assess the situation to understand:
   - The learner's perspective and abilities

     Why is the learner doing this? What is misunderstood or interpreted literally? What does the learner believe about the situation?

   - The perspective of others

     How do others understand the situation? What are they doing and why?

   - Relevant environmental cues

     Does the environment contain confusing sensory stimulation? What are the natural cues that are relevant to the situation?

2. *Write the story* in a simple, clear format that is at a level slightly lower than the learner's comprehension level.

   - Write the story from the learner's perspective. For example, address the cause of the ineffective behaviors, fears, sensory intolerances, and misunderstandings.

   - Include at least two or three descriptive sentences to define the situation and the setting.

   - Include the answers to unasked questions (who, why, what, where, when), as appropriate. Descriptions of facial expressions and the perspective and behavior of others add relevant information.

   - Include at least one sentence describing the perspective of others to explain the reasons for their behavior.

   - Include no more than one directive statement to identify an appropriate response—a clear and positive statement (I can, I will. . . .)

   - Use literal and concrete statements. Avoid subjective and relative statements such as *too loud* or *too fast*. Provide concrete cues such as, "The noise will last about as long as it takes you to count to 30."

   - Be objective. Do not judge or assume potential feelings or reactions.

   - Be flexible, to account for the range of variables in the natural setting. For example, do not give specific names to the people in a story because the learner may assume that the story applies only when that specific person is present. Use the words *sometimes* or *usually*, because the words *always* and *never* are often overgeneralized. In fact, unless stated otherwise, a learner with autism will likely assume that a story is true for every setting, forever.

3. Prepare a book. Please note that a nonreader may need a supporting audiotape with the sound of a bell recorded to signal time to turn the page. A story could also be placed on a computer or videotape. A printed story is useful for later review in other settings.

- Place one concept or statement on a page

- Avoid detailed drawings because illustrations are often distracting, misinterpreted, or overgeneralized by those with autism spectrum disorders. Some learners can benefit from the use of simple, black-and-white line drawings that have very little detail.

4. *Introduce the story* as you sit at the child's side.

- Have the learner hold the story and turn the pages while you read. Read the story with the child several times.

- Have the learner read the story to you, then gradually fade yourself out of the process. The goal is for the learner to review the story independently since the new social strategy will be used independently.

- Thereafter, have the learner read the story independently once or twice each day.

- Encourage the learner to share the story with others.

5. *When the story is familiar, cue the child to use the statements or new strategy in the natural situations.* If other interpreters know the story, they can provide cues in various natural situations to help generalize the skills.

6. *Monitor the responses and refine the story as problems are identified.*

7. *Fade the story* by decreasing the number or frequency of reviews, by rewriting and dropping the directive sentence, or by changing the story to target a different situation.

8. *Place the story in a notebook for review* if the problem resurfaces.

Examples of two social stories are in Figure 14.4.

Variations and expanded applications
Stories can be developed and presented in a variety of ways to achieve a number of different goals.

- Curriculum stories can make academic lessons more functional.

- A checklist story has a single step of a routine on each page. Once the routine is familiar, the story can be intentionally sabotaged by omitting a page or placing the pages in the wrong order. These variations provide opportunities for the learner to recognize and correct a problem (an illogical sequence), reorganize a sequence, and discover that a sequence could be performed in different ways.

- Stories can clarify the meaning of a book, TV show, or movie. One young girl who had previously liked apples refused to eat them after seeing the movie, Snow White. A story helped her understand that Snow White is a fantasy, and it is safe to eat apples. Another young man who enjoyed historical documentaries and news reports on TV became confused about the use of the word red. The story on page 257 was developed to clarify the range of meanings.

This summary of procedures for developing and presenting a social story is limited. For a more complete discussion of the strategies, see Gray and Garand, 1993; Gray, 1994; and Gray, 1998.

Although there is, as yet, no empirical data to support the use of social stories, many learners have changed their behavior in a relatively short period after a story was presented. Before initiating a major behavior program to solve a serious problem, it would be logical to first develop a social story that provides the important and relevant details, so the learner understands what is happening, what response would be effective, and why it is important.

Although this strategy seems almost too simple to be effective, one theme that has been repeated throughout this manual is that simple and subtle changes and adaptations often make a significant difference. One higher-functioning young man said, "Now that I know, I can change."

Social stories and experience stories have much in common. The major difference is that social stories specifically emphasize the perspective of others.

Figure 14.4 Samples: Social Stories

Example 1.

This story clearly outlines the social situation, the perspective of others, and the expectations.

The teacher says, "Everybody out!" when swimming time is finished. *(Highlights relevant cue)*

I can hear her say, "Everybody out!" *(Labels sensory perception)*

Most children stop playing in the water. *(Relevant cue)*

I will stop playing in the water. *(Directive)*

Some children may say, "Oh, no! I don't want to stop!" *(Perspective sentence to explain the behavior of others)*

But I will stop playing in the water. *(Directive)*

I will go to the side and climb out. *(Directive)*

The teacher may smile and say, "Good-bye" as she sees the children climbing out. *(Perspective sentence that explains how the teacher may respond)*

I will smile and say, "Good-bye." *(Directive)*

The children go to the dressing room. *(Relevant cue)*

I will go to the dressing room. *(Directive)*

. . . and so on.

Example 2.

This fairly complex story was prepared for a young man who previously had refused to go into the dentist's office, made loud noises, paced about the waiting room, and refused to sit in the chair or open his mouth. After reading the story for two days, he went to the dentist without incident.

My teeth are stained.

They need to be cleaned so I won't get a cavity.

A cavity would hurt.

I will go to the dentist after school on Friday.

The dentist's name is Dr. Jones.

Mother will be at the school with the car to drive to the dentist's office.

The dentist's office is at 1234 Main Street.

Mother and I will walk into the office.

Mother will tell the nurse at the desk, "José is here."

Mother and I will sit down and wait.

I may hear a high, shrill noise. The noise is made by an instrument for cleaning teeth.

Maybe there will be an aquarium to watch while I wait. Maybe not.

I can look at magazines while I wait.

I may look at one magazine, or maybe two or three.

When the nurse calls my name, it is time to see the dentist.

I put the magazine on the chair and follow the nurse.

. . . and so forth to explain the whole procedure.

Computer and Video Strategies

More and more studies are appearing in the literature that support the use of computer and video technology for teaching a wide range of skills to those with autism. Skills addressed include language, social/emotional, academic, self-help and community access. For references about video-modeling, see: Buggey, Toombs, Gardener, and Cervetti, 1999; Charlop and Milstein, 1989; Dowrick, 1999; Haring, Neetz, Peck, and Semel, 1987. For references about computer-based instruction, see Bernard-Opitz, Ross, and Tuttas, 1990; Chen & Bernard-Opitz, 1993; Moore, 1998; Silver and Oakes, 2001; and Tjus, Heimann, and Nelson, 1998, 2001.

Both of these technologies have some similar characteristics that should match the needs of these learners. For example:

- Tapes and computer programs can be developed to highlight relevant sensory information.

- They are free of the confusing array of social stimuli present in person-to-person instruction.

- They eliminate confusion, as directions, information, responses, and consequences are predictable. Correction procedures and prompts may also be available.

- The material can be selected or prepared (as in the case of videos) to match a student's specific needs.

- They can be designed to promote generalization by showing a varied range of photographs or scenes.

- Both computers and videos are highly attractive to most students with autism—in other words, they capture and hold their attention.

- They both save teacher time since practice can be repeated independently as often as necessary.

These technologies are discussed in various places in Chapters 20, 21, and 22. Also see Appendix B, page 487–488.

Summary

Visual supports, references, organizers, and stories are a critical part of any program for those with autism. The two manuals published by Hodgdon in 1995 and 1999 are very helpful. The use of visual systems and strategies are possibly the best tools we have for reducing stress and for teaching new skills. The potential for using computer and video strategies to rehearse and learn new skills is exciting. Several teachers reported that the use of video and computer technology was not only effective but saved considerable teacher and learner time.

Burleigh's Story

—Written by his mother, Mary Anne Seaton

Several things come to mind as I look back at how we have survived these years and how Burleigh has endured them. First, I remember clearly the day (that I first heard that my son had autism). I even remember what I was wearing, the room that we went to, and my first opportunity to see a child who displayed characteristics similar to my child's. I remember how very kind and gentle you both were. But most important, I remember you all saying, "There is no cure; but if you work very hard, you can make a difference for your child." Those words and your caring attitude toward me were the beginning of turning my life around and setting the direction for Burleigh and our family.

Second, having the opportunity to learn how Burleigh's disability affects him clearly changed our lives. Without that information, we would not have survived. It allowed us to come to grips with who Burleigh is and to start accepting him. In addition to learning all I could about autism, I had the opportunity to become involved in the state systems that serve people with disabilities and their families. By my learning about how the systems work and what role they should play in helping people, we were able to get better services for Burleigh.

Third, over the past 8 years, several people have been involved with our family by assisting us at home with Burleigh. They made it possible for Burleigh to continue to live at home. One of those people, however, has had the most impact on our lives. At first, he was a paid assistant to Burleigh in the home and school, and later he became his teacher. But most important, he became Burleigh's friend. One of the things that I am reminded of frequently by parents is that their children with autism don't have friends, and that people who are a part of their lives come in and go out without any closure. Burleigh has been fortunate. His friend continues to take him places—to visit his (own) parents (whom we now call Burleigh's extended family), to walk down by the waterfront, or to just hang out together. They have a special bond. One that Bill (Burleigh's father) and I cannot replace.

Fourth, Burleigh has had some good educational experiences. The most positive experience has been the introduction of "structured teaching" (as defined by TEACCH) into his school program and home life. This process has allowed him to become independent in his activities throughout each day. Now, without someone standing over him and verbally directing him, he can feed the cats, wash and dry the clothes, prepare his lunch, recycle the pop cans, tolerate assistance with hygiene, go grocery shopping, and work in the community in four different jobs. He also takes great pleasure in setting up and putting away his work. But probably the nicest thing about his independence is his sense of pleasure and pride in doing all of these things and understanding what he is doing. This process, called structured teaching, changed Burleigh's life—and mine, too. Things that we could never get Burleigh to do, he will now do without resistance. I get excited each day I see him working. He likes what he is doing.

An update, 8 years later:

What happens to someone who gets to experience predictability in his life for over 10 years, day after day, and be liked by the people who are in your life?

Burleigh is now 28 years old—happy and healthy, and still living at home. His support person, Mike, has been working with him for 10 years. Burleigh volunteers his work time to the public library, and for other state and county programs.

People appreciate him and count on him to do his work. Burleigh also contributes to his family, He helps with grocery shopping daily, washing and drying the clothes, tending to the cats, and recycling. His day is filled with many activities that he can do independently by using his daily schedule and work systems to answer those all-important questions—Where am I going? What work will I be doing? How much work do I do? How will I know when the work is finished? and What comes next? (Note: His work system uses a combination of symbols: objects, photographs, line drawings and written words—he communicates his needs with a Wolf Voca.)

Recently, someone saw Burleigh and Mike downtown and commented on the fact that Burleigh was so in control of his life. Mike was with him, but Burleigh was in charge. He walks with that swagger that shows confidence and control—what a wonderful experience for him and for Mike, too.

Burleigh's life with his family has turned out to be good—he connects with us, and we can joke with him. He continues to be helpful—helping us with our morning and evening routines—making sure everything is put away and in its right place. Occasionally, he has moments when life is not right—and he becomes anxious, but no more than we do. We so understood that being kind and calm with Burleigh proved to be the best way to relate to him. Our opportunity to learn early on about autism and how it affected him allowed us to teach him about his own control—instead of us controlling him. And, because of this, his life is happy and humane.

It is hard for me to remember those painful years when life was so difficult. . . . As I see and work with professionals and the families of children with autism in my job, my advice is that they should not forget to look at the whole family. Agencies are often locked into seeing only the child with the disability. Autism doesn't just impact the child, it affects all parts of daily living for each family member. Early on, Bill and I received counseling, which was very helpful to us—but his two younger brothers did not. While they were growing up, our whole life was centered around Burleigh. So much of Graham and Patterson's childhood was handled on their own—we reared them to be independent—and that they are. While they never gave us any trouble, but now I know that they should have had help with the life they had to experience. Now, as a family, we are working through a lot of what we didn't have a chance to early on—it is good that we do, but it is painful at times. Burleigh's brothers, who are now out on their own, see him on occasion and they have a great relationship with him.

Burleigh continues to help keep us centered. When he gets up each morning, we no longer see a person with autism, we just see this incredible person who has managed to survive in this very complex world of ours.

Advocating for Burleigh has always been at the top of my list. I have learned that families who are successful in making their child's life, have had to devote enormous amounts of time and energy. It truly becomes a full-time job. If families are to be successful advocates, they must learn about the systems, see how they work, and what they can provide. Get to know the people who are responsible for providing services to your child. It is critical to make sure that the information you present is understood—understand that these people also have a learning style—figure out how they best receive information. Write it down—written information is more powerful. Be persistent but courteous; people remember how they were treated more than what was said. Develop a plan that focuses on what you see for your child as an adult and start to work on it. Always see to it that children who can be a part of developing this plan are involved. Never assume that everything will just fall into place. Stay vigilant. Stay in regular contact with people who can help you. And, above all, have a sense of humor, be objective, flexible, and creative.

15 | Organize and Structure Verbal Information

Most learners with autism who can hear have a very good—perhaps excellent—ability to receive or take in and store verbal information. However, auditory processing discrepancies can result in many learning and behavior problems. Because those with autism spectrum disorders do not provide easily understood or consistent feedback to their parents and teachers, they receive less verbal input and fewer opportunities to learn the language and communicate. To reverse this cycle, learners need access to verbal information in a form they can understand. Hearing the language in natural contexts is a prerequisite for understanding and using the language for speaking, reading, and writing. Adaptations, new technologies, and many positive language experiences can result in better understanding and meaningful use of language. It should be noted that there are a few individuals with ASD who do process auditory information better than visual information—they will need a combination of visual and verbal strategies to understand the visual aspects of the world.

The following sections provide basic strategies for talking to those with autism—strategies for organizing and structuring verbal information for more effective learning and behavior.

Basic Guidelines

When to Talk

In general, one talks to a learner with autism at the same times and for the same reasons as one talks with someone who does not have autism. To ensure understanding, it is important to make some specific accommodations in the following situations:

1. During social interactions, to have fun and share experiences
2. When introducing new routines and explaining changes in familiar routines
3. At the beginning and the end of each day, to prepare for and review events
4. When providing feedback to solve problems and defuse stress
5. When providing positive feedback
6. When stress is at a low to moderate level (see Figure 10.1)

When to Stop Talking

Talking is ineffective and can create additional problems under the following conditions:

1. *When stress is at a high level.*

    The addition of extra and potentially confusing auditory stimulation is not useful when stress is high. In fact, it can create or trigger a crisis situation. When stress is high, the learner is generally unable to process verbal information. Although this problem is magnified in autism, it is not unlike the problem of most people who find it difficult to think or act effectively under intense stress.

2. *After the initial introduction of a new routine.*

The learner is likely to become overly dependent on verbal directions and prompts unless the interpreter stops talking and incorporates visual and gestural cues and prompts early in the instructional process.

3. *After asking a question or giving a direction that requires a verbal or motor response.*

The learner needs extra time to process the auditory information and produce a response. Stop talking and wait calmly but expectantly for at least 30 seconds before repeating or rephrasing the question or direction.

Principles for Organizing Verbal Information

There are four guiding principles for organizing and structuring verbal information to increase understanding:

1. *Provide an accurate and precise language model* to prevent confusion and learned errors.

2. *Speak softly and clearly* to respect and accommodate the learner's extreme sensitivity to auditory stimulation.

3. *Provide visual support* to clarify and highlight important words.

4. *Use emphasis to highlight* the words that are important for meaning.

Guidelines for Giving Directions

Guideline 1: Get the Learner's Attention

To get attention in a one-to-one situation:

- The speaker needs to be at the learner's eye level. Touch the learner's arm or shoulder gently but firmly while quietly saying something like, "Tony, look at the (checklist or material) and listen. You need to know ____." Pause to give the learner time to shift attention. Attention may be in the form of brief eye contact or intermittent attention to the designated material. Tapping, touching, or moving the materials also may draw attention. The moment attention is given, begin to deliver the message.

- Attention is not requested simply for compliance but to deliver a legitimate message. The learner is told exactly what to do and why it is important to do it. There is a reason for the request; there is no uncertainty.

  The learner's attention may be brief and intermittent. Experience shows that if the learner stays nearby but looks away, it is likely that the words are heard and intermittent attention will be given to the materials either with direct or peripheral vision.

- A firm but gentle touch on the arm or shoulder often helps the learner to focus. If the learner is extremely sensitive to touch, an occupational therapist can assess the situation and provide suggestions to alleviate the stress and increase tolerance.

To get attention in a group situation:

- The learner must understand the meaning of group directions. For example, words such as *everyone, anybody, class, you folks,* and so on, mean that the speaker is talking to you and all the people in the room or area.

Sometimes the intended audience is implied and not directly stated. Statements such as,

"Lunch time," "Line up," or "Look up here" are unlikely to get the learner's attention without specific instruction. The illustration above shows one strategy for teaching the meaning of these words.

Guideline 2: Speak Calmly and Softly

There is evidence that a learner can attend to, understand, and respond to a calm, soft voice more easily than an excited, loud voice. Some learners respond well to whispered words. In a noisy or dangerous situation, it is natural and appropriate to speak louder and with more emphasis.

Guideline 3: Speak Naturally but Clearly

Speak with normal tone and expression. Do not use baby talk or an unnaturally high voice like that used with infants and toddlers. It is unfair to model a way of speaking that must be relearned later.

Speak at a normal rate. To understand the language of others in the natural environment, one must hear it as used in the normal environment. When introducing a new concept or a critical piece of information:

- ■ Pause briefly to separate the relevant words from ongoing conversations.
- ■ Speak a bit more slowly than usual.
- ■ Pair key words with visual references (words or line drawings).

Express a complete thought to clarify the message.

- ■ *Ineffective:* "Find coat," "Sit down," or "Let's go."

  Learner's perspective: Which coat? Find? Is it lost? Okay, the coat is over there—I found it. Sit down? Okay, but I don't know why I have to sit down here in the middle of the room. Go? Where? When? Why? This is too confusing. I'll just run around the room until I know what to do.

  Effective: "Put on your red coat. Then we can walk to the park."

Speak literally and very specifically.

- ■ *Ineffective:* When directing a learner to identify pictures, an interpreter says, "Give me the cow."

Learner's perspective: I don't see a cow, couldn't lift it if it were here. Guess I'll just sit here until she tells me to do something I can do.

Effective: "Give me the picture of the cow."

■ *Ineffective*: "Put in" or "Put it away."

Learner's perspective: Hmm, in? Put in? What's that mean? It? What's it? There are lots of things here. What do I put away? Where is away, anyway?

Effective: "Pick up the toy trucks and put them in the box."

■ *Ineffective*: "Go and get a towel."

Learner's perspective: Decisions, decisions. Which towel? There are big, little, fat, thin, striped, and flowered towels, red, pink, yellow, and white towels. Hmmm, there are towels in the kitchen and towels in the bathroom, which? Maybe I'll just sit here and rock.

(Note: Most learners need to be taught to attend to more than one attribute or characteristic.)

Effective: "Go to the bathroom and get the big, yellow towel."

Initially you will need to guide the child to the bathroom and help him locate the big yellow towel. Verbally label his actions (i.e., "To the bathroom—big, yellow towel.)

Speak positively. Tell the learner what to do.

■ *Ineffective*: "Don't get out of that chair."

Learner's perspective: Oh dear, I have to stay in this chair always. Or, did he say get out of the chair? Okay, I'll stand up.

Note: Learners often do exactly what they were told not to do. It could be that some do not process the first part of the sentence and hear only the end. If so, they are actually complying to the command as best they can.

Effective: Say, "Sit in the chair," or, better, "Sit in the chair until we finish eating."

■ *Ineffective*: "Don't kick."

Learner's perspective: Don't kick? I can't even kick a ball? Yesterday, Dad told me to kick the ball. What does that have to do with now?

Effective: Say, "You kick balls, not people. Now, keep your feet on the floor."

(Note: The following illustration shows one way to help the learner visualize and understand the meaning of the word.)

■ *Ineffective*: As the learner walked to the library, hitting the walls and doors, the interpreter said, "No! Stop hitting the walls. Keep your hands to yourself. That makes too much noise and bothers others."

Learner's perspective: No? Stop? What does that mean? I know what hands are, but how do I keep my hands to myself? What is the meaning of bothers or too much noise?

Note: The learner still will not know what to do even after processing all those words.

Effective: "Carry these books to the library," or, "Walk quietly to the library with your hands in your pockets."

Use only the words that carry meaning. Leave out words that don't carry information, such as polite forms and sarcasm. Verbalize basic information simply, briefly, and clearly.

■ *Ineffective*: "Would you _____?"; "I would like you to _____"; "It would be great if you would _____"; "Don't you know the dog is hungry?"

Effective: Say, "It is time to feed the dog. He will be hungry."

Guideline 4: Exaggerate Facial Expressions

Model the expression of feelings as emotional situations are explained. Do not discount or ignore feelings even when the learner's expressions do not match the expressions of others in the same situation. Rather, provide a more typical model. For example, if the learner laughs hysterically when a friend is hurt, look sad and say something like, "Mary fell and hurt her knee. She feels bad. I feel sorry because her knee hurts." Use natural facial expressions at other times to avoid distracting attention from the words.

■ *Ineffective*: Look bright and happy when saying, "You're all right. Just get up. It doesn't really hurt."

Effective: Frown, and look sad and concerned while explaining, "Oh, you fell and hurt your knee."

Guideline 5: Support the Words With Visual Cues

Illustrate key words, sequences, and outcomes while speaking. Draw pictures, write words, or point to the learner's visual communication system, if available. Make critical information visual.

■ *Ineffective*: "The book is on the table."

Learner's perspective: Which table? Which book? Am I supposed to do something with the book?

Effective: Gesture toward the table and say, "Your math book is on that table. Put it in the book bag."

■ *Ineffective*: "You can eat at McDonald's on Monday evening."

Learner's perspective: Is this Monday? How many days until Monday?

Effective: Move toward the calendar while saying, "You can eat at McDonald's on Monday evening. Let's write it on the calendar."

Guideline 6: Ask Only Important Questions

Ask questions only when there are real choices and when you do not know the answer.

- ■ *Ineffective*: When the learner is expected to work now, the interpreter says politely, "Are you ready to work?"

  Learner's perspective: Oh, good! I have a choice. I don't really like doing that work, and I still want to watch the leaves blowing in the trees. I'll just stay here.

  Because the demand was never clear, nagging or insistence on compliance is likely to be resisted.

  Effective: "It will be time to work when the bell rings."

  Learner's perspective: Okay, a few more minutes to watch the leaves, then back to the job.

- ■ *Ineffective*: After a field trip to the museum, the teacher says, "What did we just do?"

  Learner's perspective: I just sat down, or, You were there. As long as you already know and it's hard for me to say the words, I'll just sit here until I really need to tell you something.

  Effective: "That was a great trip to the museum. Let's write a story about the things we saw."

  Learner's perspective: Oh, good! Then I can share the story with my Mom.

Guideline 7: Teach the Meaning of Rules and Directions

If a direction is not followed, it is likely that it was not understood. Be prepared to teach and highlight the meaning of directions, both verbally and visually. Then provide assistance to carry out the directions quickly to ensure that the correct response is firmly associated with the directions.

Guidelines for Using Contingencies

A contingency is a contract that specifies and clarifies expectations. It defines the behavior to be performed and the reinforcer to be received. For example, an employee's contract states that for every 20 days of work, the employee will earn $X. The work rules state that after 2 hours of work, the employee will get a 15-minute break. This is not a bribe; it is a contract that motivates the employee to work. If the employer stops paying the wage, the employee loses trust and stops working. Notice that the contract and work rules are stated positively—they specify what is expected and what will be earned.

A contingency is a powerful verbal procedure that provides a structure for addressing a wide range of problems and critical goals. The power of a contingency depends on the wording, the timing, and the payoffs.

Figure 15.1 Contingencies

A contingency is a contract that will:

- Develop trust in the adult who states and honors the contract
- Provide a structure for understanding the language
- Teach sequencing and cause/effect relationships
- Increase motivation to work, to try, and to persist
- Provide the means to predict and prepare for coming events
- Clarify when work will be done
- Prepare for transitions
- Develop natural activity reinforcers
- Increase flexibility
- Decrease behavior problems

Guidelines for successful use:

- State the contingency positively and clearly
- Support the contingency with visual and concrete markers
- Offer a payoff that is valued
- State the contingency before inappropriate behavior occurs
- Payment must be prompt and made as stated
- Contingencies can be renegotiated
- Evaluate and refine—to ensure high rate of success

Guideline 1: State the Contingency Positively and Clearly

State the contingency like Grandma's rule, "Eat your peas, and then you can have dessert"—first the work, then the payoff.

A negative statement made when the interpreter has lost patience includes confusing emotional overtones that are more likely to trigger anxiety and less likely to motivate. A positive statement that reminds the learner of the reinforcer clarifies the situation and is motivating.

■ *Ineffective*: "You can't ride your bike until you are finished."

Learner's perspective: Oh, no! Can't ride my bike? Will I ever ride my bike? What does finished mean? When will I ever be finished? Oh, no!

Effective: "Do two more problems. Then you can ride your bike."

■ *Ineffective*: "You can ride your bike when the clothes are folded."

This kind of statement can lead to confusion or disappointment.

Learner's perspective: Oh, good! I get to ride my bike. Oh, no! I have to fold the clothes. I thought I could ride my bike.

Effective: "When all the clothes in the dryer are folded, you can ride your bike."

Even more effective: "If you fold all the clothes before 5:00 o'clock, you can ride your bike."

This statement is positive and both verbally and visually clear. Stating the time clarifies the situation further so the learner will not be surprised by a sudden and unexpected loss of the reinforcer.

Guideline 2: Support the Contingency With Visual and Concrete Markers

Clarify the amount of work and the payoff. Use visual markers to specify what finished looks like and to show progress toward the payoff. A timer or other signal also can specify that it is time for the payoff.

- *Effective*: Draw a circle around five problems on the worksheet as you say, "Do these five. Then you can look out the window." When the work is completed, set a timer and say, "When the timer rings, it will be time to finish the math paper, then go to lunch."

Note: The timer is objective and concrete. It indicates when it is time to stop looking out the window and return to work. Also note that another contingency was developed to motivate and draw attention to the next reinforcing activity. See the illustration that shows a math worksheet marked to show a clear beginning and ending, as well as the location of a reinforcer to support the contingency.

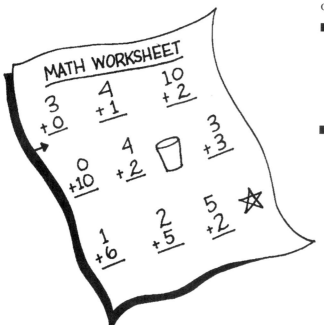

- *Effective*: As Mom takes away all but two pegs, she says, "Put in two more pegs. Then you can run." She helps her child get those two pegs in very quickly. This statement is appropriate for the very young child who is just learning about contingencies.

- *Effective*: Give the learner three chips while saying, "Run around the gym three times. Here are three chips. Drop one chip in this box each time you go around. When the chips are gone, it will be time for lunch."

Guideline 3: Offer a Payoff That is Valued

The power of a contingency depends on the reinforcing quality of the payoff. The Preference Survey (page 99) identifies the individual's liked activities to use as reinforcers. The scheduling formula in Figure 12.3 (page 183) capitalizes on the preferred activities to ensure that naturally reinforcing activities are always available.

Note: Artificial reinforcers, such as candy or toys that are unrelated to the natural activity, are rarely needed when contingencies clarify the work and naturally occurring and preferred activities are scheduled appropriately.

■ *Ineffective*: "If you work fast, you can earn more money."

Learner's perspective: This statement has at least three problems. Money has little meaning to many learners. If the payoff is not valued, it is not likely to motivate. The term "work fast" is unclear; it does not clearly identify the amount of work or the time frame. An "if" statement is a bit like a question and suggests a choice. Use "if" statements only when there are real choices or options.

Effective: "Fold this one basket of towels before the timer rings. Then it will be time to bake cookies."

Learner's perspective: Oh, boy! Baking cookies is fun! Let's get those towels folded!

Effective: While stating the contingency, isolate one tiny bite of each food item on the plate, "First, eat one bite of potatoes and one bite of salad. Then you can play ball."

Learner's perspective: Playing ball is fun. I'll hurry and eat those two bites. That's not much.

Note: The two isolated bites of food clarify "finished." For this learner, the opportunity to play ball is highly valued.

Guideline 4: State the Contingency Before Inappropriate Behavior Occurs

A contingency statement that provides a reinforcer for stopping or ending an inappropriate behavior is a bribe. A bribe teaches the learner to repeat the inappropriate behavior the next time he wants something.

■ *Ineffective*: "When you stop screaming, you can listen to your tapes."

In this situation, screaming will likely be used in the future to communicate, "I want to listen to tapes."

Effective: Ignore the screaming altogether, and say, "You want to stop work. Say, 'Stop.' Then you can listen to your tapes." Quickly provide assistance to communicate stop. In this situation, the appropriate use of the communication system is reinforced and is more likely to be used to solve problems in the future.

Even more effective: At the first signal of boredom or frustration but while the learner is still trying, say, "Only three more _____. Then you can listen to your tapes." Then provide assistance to finish quickly. This type of contingency statement is particularly effective for it not only prevents inappropriate behavior, but increases persistence and attention span.

Guideline 5: Payment Must be Prompt and Made as Stated

When first teaching the learner to understand contingencies, provide assistance to complete the work correctly and quickly, so the payoff is closely associated with the statement of contingency.

Always follow through; remember, a contingency is a contract. The learner must be able to trust the interpreter's words. If the work is completed, the payment must be made.

Note: A good statement sets up the motivation for success and a natural consequence if the learner does not follow through.

Four situations illustrate the complexity of enforcing this rule:

A negatively stated contingency may cause a behavior crisis. If the interpreter makes this mistake, they may not want to follow through.

■ *Ineffective*: In the following illustration, the interpreter has a dilemma. Can the interpreter or the learner stay all night? Can the interpreter follow through to prevent negating trust and the meaning of the words? This statement and most other negative statements set up real power struggles and no-win situations.

Effective: "When you wipe the table, you can go home." With this statement, the interpreter can provide assistance and emotional support to enable the learner to succeed. The learner receives the payoff even though the demands for independence were reduced.

When some natural event gets in the way of the payoff.

■ *Ineffective*: The contingency was, "When you finish mowing the yard, we will go to the ice cream shop." However, guests arrive just as the learner finishes mowing. The payoff is ignored, and the learner is told either that they cannot leave until the company leaves or that the trip is canceled. Any one of these consequences is seen as a broken promise.

Learner's perspective: I worked hard. I did my part. I can't trust them. I wish the company would leave. I'll ask them when they are leaving.

Effective: In the situation above, the interpreter says, "You worked hard and finished the mowing. I am sorry, we can't leave now, but we can go to the ice cream shop tomorrow." The interpreter takes the learner to the calendar and reschedules the trip. "Now you can do _____" (another preferred activity).

Learner's perspective: I can still go to the ice cream shop, and now I can do _____, too! Oh, boy!

Even more effective: In the same situation, say to the guests, "George mowed the lawn, and I promised him a trip to the ice-cream shop. Will you join us?"

When the learner does not do the work, the natural consequence is that the liked activity is not available.

In the previous situation, the contingency did not state a time when the mowing must be completed in order to get the payment. If the learner does not do the work, the interpreter can say, "You have 15 minutes to finish mowing if you want to go to the ice cream shop. I'll set the timer." If the mowing is not complete when the timer goes off, the interpreter says, "I'm sorry, the lawn is not finished, and now it's too late to go to the ice cream shop." The consequence was natural, clear, and fair. If the trip was a valued activity, missing it is enough. Additional punishment, nagging, or criticism sets up a power struggle—another no-win situation. To re-engage the learner in productive activity, provide a new contingency with reduced demands and a slightly less preferred activity.

When a contingency motivates a learner to work faster than expected, an interpreter may be tempted to increase the demand in order to fill the scheduled amount of work time. Increasing the demand is an unfair labor practice and will lead to distrust. The interpreter can do two things:

- Congratulate the learner ("Wow! You did that so fast, you have more time to play"), and

- Congratulate themselves for stating a highly motivating contingency.

Guideline 6: Contingencies, Just Like a Contract, Can Be Renegotiated

The amount of work required at any time must be flexible. More can be required on days when the learner is alert and processing quickly, less on days when the learner is ill or distracted. If tolerance is misjudged and it is obvious that the learner is struggling, becoming restless, but still trying, renegotiate to avoid a crisis or negative experience.

- *Effective*: "You are trying very hard. Let me help you finish so you can _____"; or, "Do only one more, and then _____."

Because the end was associated with trying hard or working hard, those valuable attributes will be strengthened. It is very reinforcing to end or avoid a difficult or painful situation.

Guideline 7: Evaluate and Refine

The benefits of contingencies will be lost if the learner does not do the work but still receives the payoff. If success does not occur at a high rate, analyze the contingency statements, review the contingency rules, and rehearse until a clear and positive contingency can be produced automatically. It may be necessary to ask a support-team member to observe and provide constructive feedback to increase the success rate.

Parallel Talking—Matching Language to Actions

Parallel talking is the process for providing literal, clear, and descriptive language that includes simple but complete sentences related to the people, objects, and actions as they occur every day. The parallel-talking process is much like the reporting of a sportscaster who describes an athletic event so clearly that those at home can visualize the action. This procedure provides another way for those with autism to hear the language in natural contexts that will facilitate language and literacy learning.

This is a strategy used instinctively by parents of typically developing infants and toddlers as they move together through a day. But parents may stop talking to their child with autism because they get so little positive feedback for talking. Some of the considerations for using parallel talking include these:

- Use parallel talking only when the child is calm and alert—DO NOT use this parallel talking strategy when the learner is under stress.

- Take advantage of natural daily routines that directly involve the learner—eating, dressing, riding in the car, buying groceries, and others. When the learner is engaged in some independent activity, pause in passing and provide a brief descriptive comment. Capture additional opportunities for the learner to stay nearby—to see and be involved in the action—when raking leaves, doing laundry, and other activities.

- Label the people, objects, actions, and events as they occur. Identify the purpose or outcome of the action. Include descriptive words—colors, sizes, speeds. When appropriate, label facial expressions and the quality of voices (e.g., "She is frowning, she may be confused," "His voice sounds gruff when. . . . ").

- Make no demands; ask for no responses. Simply give accurate information and highlight critical elements. Questions, requests, and directions change the processing demands and raise anxiety.

- Pause or break the stream of talk before giving a direction or asking a question. This break gives time for the learner to shift attention.

Reflective Listening—Matching Language to Emotions

Reflective listening is used when a person has a problem and anxiety is accelerating—when stress is at a moderate to moderately high level (see Figure 10.1, page 158). This reflective listening strategy:

- Recognizes that a problem exists
- Expresses concern and establishes a mutually respectful relationship
- Identifies and clarifies the problem

Refer to page 158, Figure 10.1. The Profile of Stress. Use the parallel-talking procedure during Stage 4 when the learner is calm and productive. The reflective listening procedure is used during Stage 1 when stress is beginning to escalate

- Provides labels (the language) for the problem, the feelings, and the solution
- Defuses frustration and anxiety
- Sets the stage for solving the problem

This strategy involves the following five steps:

1. *Recognize and identify the subtle, nonverbal cues* (behavioral signals) that indicate the presence of a problem, a need, emotion, or feeling that needs to be communicated. Some of the predictable behavioral signals of a problem are described on pages 159–160.

2. *Quickly scan the environment for cues to interpret the cause* of the problem (see the checklist for identifying the cause of a problem, page 161).

3. *Tentatively verbalize the feeling and the problem* but *do not* highlight or mention the behavior. ("You look hot and thirsty. Do you need a drink?")

   - *A hesitant statement is respectful* and appropriate because an interpreter can never be totally certain of another person's feelings or needs.

   - *However be as precise and descriptive as possible* when labeling feelings and emotions.

   - *Use the range of feeling words to expand* vocabulary (e.g., afraid, bored, disappointed, discouraged, worried, confused, frustrated, lonesome, surprised).

4. *Pause for acknowledgment.* Acknowledgment may be made in a variety of ways; for example, the learner may make fleeting eye contact or become very still and the signs of stress may begin to decrease. If the statement did not accurately express the feeling or need, the stress will continue to escalate. In that case, make another effort to clarify the situation.

5. *Suggest a way for the problem to be resolved and quickly help to solve it.* Because most problems can be solved by asking for help or for clarification, it is appropriate to provide a cue for how to communicate the message. (For example, tell the learner, "You can say, 'Want drink'," as you provide assistance to point to a glass.)

   Note: This reflective listening strategy must be modified to match specific situations. For example, use fewer words for a younger or less sophisticated learner and if the stress level increases.

> Classes had been dismissed early for parent conferences. Jeff paced back and forth in front of the window as he waited for the bus. Every few minutes, he interrupted the teacher to say, "What time will the bus come?" The teacher responded by saying something like, "The bus will be here pretty soon. Just wait quietly." Finally, as Jeff asked the question with increasing agitation, the teacher got down to his eye level and with a soft voice, asked, "Jeff, are you afraid the bus won't come to take you home?" Immediately, Jeff's face and shoulders relaxed as he said, "Yes." The teacher responded, "I talked to the bus driver. She knows that school is out early. She will come to take you home. You can sit in your chair and read these magazines until the bus comes." Jeff sat down at his desk and quietly looked at the magazines.

Summary

Learners with autism need clear and understandable information in order to participate successfully in the community. Interpreters who understand their needs and perspective have a broad range of strategies for providing support. Some of the informational needs can be addressed by evaluating and refining the organization and structure of environments to highlight and clarify relevant cues within the settings and events. Visual systems such as calendars, checklists, cue cards, and stories provide the answers to unasked questions—the who, what, when, where, why, and how questions.

Because people with autism live in a verbal world, they must have a way to understand other people's words in order to learn and function effectively. For this understanding to occur learners need access to the language. *Not only must they hear the spoken language but meaning must be attached to the messages.* To facilitate this process provide the learner with:

- A clear and precise model of the language;
- Visual cues to highlight meaning;
- On-the-spot interpretation; and
- Instruction.

5

Teach New Skills

IN MY MIND

I TRY TO PRETEND I'M
NORMAL AS HUMANLY POSSIBLE
IN MY MIND

I TRY TO GO TO
TEACHING
IN MY MIND

TRY MY BEST
IN MY MIND

GO FOR MY LICENSE
IN MY MIND

GET MARRIED
IN MY MIND

HOPE MY DREAMS CAN
COME TRUE

—David Eastham
  In *UNDERSTAND: Fifty Memowriter Poems*

16 | Critical Instructional Strategies

It is a neurological miracle that most people can organize and integrate massive quantities of information from experiences to learn concepts, rules, and routines without specific instruction. As noted before, it is dangerous to assume that those with autism spectrum disorders will completely understand any concept or rule without at least some specific instruction to clarify it.

See the Summer 2001 issue of the journal, Focus on Autism and Other Developmental Disabilities, 16 (2) a special issue related to the strengths, limitations, and options for using ABA strategies with individuals who have autism spectrum disorders. Articles cover teaching communication, social, and academic skills, as well as interventions to address problem behaviors.

When planning instruction for these literal and gestalt learners, who are easily confused by the language and social rules, it is less risky to be too specific than to assume anything. The field of applied behavior analysis (ABA) has contributed greatly to our knowledge of how to assess, plan, and deliver instruction with the specificity and precision required to ensure that people with the challenges common in autism will not only learn, *but learn the right things.* But because the principles of learning theory are in force at all times, the alternative is also true—if these strategies are not used precisely, these literal learners will learn the wrong lessons. This technology provides a broad range of techniques and strategies that can be specifically selected, adapted, and applied to match each individual's unique needs, whether they have autism or not (Dunlap, Kern, & Worcester, 2001).

The information presented here is a brief summary of those basic ABA strategies and procedures that are essential for providing precise instruction. Parents, teachers, teaching assistants, and coaches must be trained to use these basic procedures—interpreters must become so familiar with these strategies that they can be used automatically and unobtrusively to address any situation. These specific procedures are, in some way, integrated into most all other successful program models for people with autism.

An Analogy for Planning

The process for planning specific and precise instruction is much like the process used by a manufacturer when packaging "The Amazing Machine," a complex and incredibly expensive piece of equipment that must be assembled by the purchaser. Each package contains a great deal of information and details because the manufacturer does not know precisely what the customer will know. The package includes:

1. All the parts
   - The parts that go together are packaged together (a visual chunk) so they are not lost or attached to the wrong component (an association error).
   - Sometimes a few extra tiny wires or screws are included that might be needed in some very specific or unexpected situations (to accommodate potential errors).

2. Visual references
   - A checklist of parts—drawings of each part numbered and labeled

- A list of directions for assembly that clarifies what to do and what not to do
  ▶ Diagrams and a step-by-step assembly sequence for each component
  ▶ The directions for each component, visually chunked and framed
  ▶ Directions for integrating each component to create the whole
  ▶ Cautions and warnings

3. An operator's manual
  ▶ Step-by-step operating instructions
  ▶ Photographs, diagrams, and checklists
  ▶ Warnings, strategies for trouble-shooting and correction procedures
  ▶ Optional uses or applications
  ▶ A telephone number to call for help

The instructional sequence is much like the sequence of events that occurs after the customer decides to buy the "The Amazing Machine." Three things generally occur:

1. *The packaged product is introduced to the customer* (the learner) by the salesperson/trainer (the teacher/interpreter) in a showroom (a familiar setting free of outside-world distractions). The salesperson opens the box; points out the parts, various components, and directions; and explains how the product works (priming or preparing the learner for new instruction).

2. *The salesperson/trainer goes with the customer* and provides assistance and support during assembly and initial operation (instruction in the natural environment).

3. *The salesperson/trainer provides group training to the team* that will use the machine (extra instruction in small groups to develop mentor support for the natural setting).

The manufacturers of "The Amazing Machine" leave little to chance. They want a satisfied customer who can use the machine independently to its fullest capacity.

The following section reviews the principles and strategies for using cues, prompts, and consequences to teach skills fluently so learners can function more independently, to their fullest capacity, and *to prevent the paradoxical affects* outlined in Chapter 9.

The Basic Behavioral Sequence

Behavior happens naturally in a specific sequence:

1. something happens that has an effect on a person;
2. that person responds; and
3. that response affects the situation and results in a consequence.

The effect of the consequence determines whether that person will respond in the same way to the same situation in the future, whether the response will be altered, or whether a new response will be generated. If the consequence is positive or reinforcing in some way, the response is likely to be repeated. If the consequence is negative or punishing in some way, the response is more likely to be altered or a new response will be produced.

This basic behavioral sequence is summarized in Figure 16.1.

Figure 16.1 Basic Behavioral Sequence

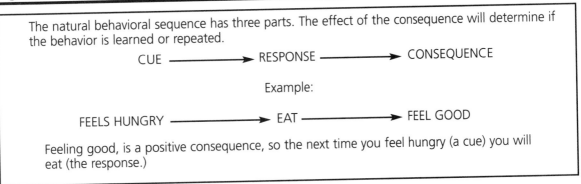

The natural behavioral sequence has three parts. The effect of the consequence will determine if the behavior is learned or repeated.

CUE ⟶ RESPONSE ⟶ CONSEQUENCE

Example:

FEELS HUNGRY ⟶ EAT ⟶ FEEL GOOD

Feeling good, is a positive consequence, so the next time you feel hungry (a cue) you will eat (the response.)

This simple sequence describes only one instance of behavior. But behavior is rarely so simple. Generally there are at least two people involved, and each interaction involves a chain of these sequences, as illustrated in Figure 16.2.

The instructional process changes the issue somewhat, because one person makes a deliberate attempt to build specific skills or alter the behavior of the other. In this situation, it is necessary to ensure that the cue, the correct response, and the reinforcing consequence are closely associated. To make sure this occurs, prompts are added and the consequences are manipulated, as illustrated in Figure 16.3.

Figure 16.2 Development of Behavioral Chains

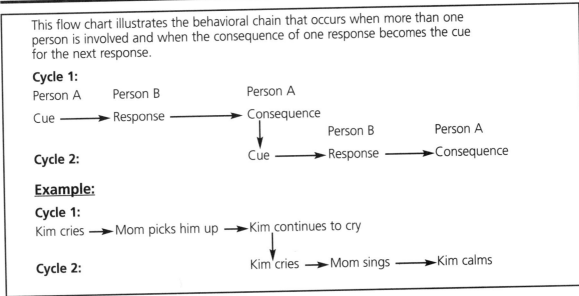

This flow chart illustrates the behavioral chain that occurs when more than one person is involved and when the consequence of one response becomes the cue for the next response.

Cycle 1:

Person A   Person B   Person A

Cue ⟶ Response ⟶ Consequence

          Person B   Person A

Cycle 2:   Cue ⟶ Response ⟶ Consequence

Example:

Cycle 1:

Kim cries ⟶ Mom picks him up ⟶ Kim continues to cry

Cycle 2:   Kim cries ⟶ Mom sings ⟶ Kim calms

Figure 16.3 A Basic Instructional Sequence

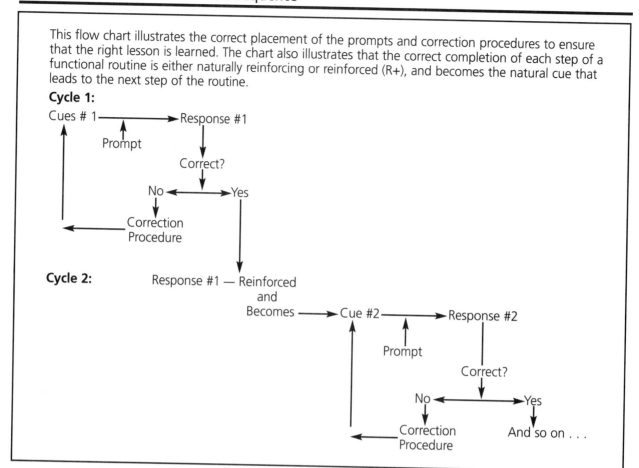

This flow chart illustrates the correct placement of the prompts and correction procedures to ensure that the right lesson is learned. The chart also illustrates that the correct completion of each step of a functional routine is either naturally reinforcing or reinforced (R+), and becomes the natural cue that leads to the next step of the routine.

Cycle 1:

Cues # 1 ———→ Response #1
Prompt
Correct?
No ←——→ Yes
Correction Procedure

Cycle 2:

Response #1 — Reinforced and Becomes ———→ Cue #2 ———→ Response #2
Prompt
Correct?
No ←——→ Yes
Correction Procedure
And so on . . .

Terminology and Guidelines

The clarity of instruction necessary for effective learning depends on the precise use of cues, prompts, responses, and consequences. A common understanding of the terminology and strategies is important for assessing learning and behavior problems and for teaching new skills efficiently.

Cues and Signals

A cue is an event or situation that stimulates or triggers a response. (A cue directs a person to do something.) Other terms are sometimes used with the same meaning, such as antecedent, stimulus, and event. The goal of instruction is to ensure that in the presence of a specific cue a specific behavior will *always* occur.

There are two basic types of cues:

1. Natural cues are signals occurring naturally in the environment that trigger most people to respond in a certain way. For example, the heat from a hot stove is a cue to move away. Feelings and desires can also trigger efforts (serve as cues) to meet those needs.

2. Artificial or adapted cues are developed and added to the natural setting when there is no obvious natural cue. For example, a stop sign is an artificial cue placed at an intersection because too many people disregard the subtle, natural cue—the knowledge of potential danger at every intersection.

Cues can take many different forms:

- Verbal cues

  A spoken direction can be natural (such as, "It's time to go") or artificial in an instructional situation ("Look at me" or "Do this").

- Auditory cues

  A timer, a bell, or the sound of the bus stopping can trigger action.

- Visual cues

  A hand gesture, a frown, walk/wait lights, crumbs on the table, an appointment book, and lists are all natural visual cues used by everyone. Adapted visual cues include transition cues, checklists, tape strips on the floor, etc.

- Tactile/body-state cues

  Feelings of hunger, pain, cold, a pinprick, or sticky fingers may serve as cues for action. Emotions such as fear and worry can also trigger actions.

- Other sensory cues

  The smell of smoke, a bitter taste, and similar physical sensations.

Capitalize on Natural Cues

Traditionally, the instructional process required teachers to manipulate the cues. In Discrete Trial Training (DTT; Lovaas, 1987), adapted or artificial cues are generally used. But if skills are to be generalized, students must learn to respond to the presence of natural cues in many different situations.

A number of incidental teaching procedures depend on the natural cues that are available in the environment or that are based on an individual's feelings and desires. For example, feelings of hunger or the presence of a desired food or toy can serve as natural cues, triggering the child to put forth effort to obtain the item. We, the interpreters, must be alert to these situations and capitalize on them. This is often described as child-directed instruction. But to enlarge and expand on the child's emotion-based actions, the interpreters must set up more and more situations for the child to act upon if we want the child to communicate and act spontaneously.

Incidental Teaching Procedures and Pivotal Response Training (PRT) all capitalize on the presence of natural cues (Koegel & Koegel, 1996; Koegel, Koegel, Harrower, & Carter, 1999). The Floor-time Model is also based on use of natural cues (Greenspan et al., 1998).

Effective Use of Cues

One of the major problems for people with autism spectrum disorders is the inability to scan an environment, screen out the irrelevant information, identify the important relevant cues, and interpret the meaning of those cues. For effective use in an instructional sequence, a cue must be:

1. *Natural or adapted and always available* in the environment when a specific response is required. For example, a full basket of dirty clothes is a natural cue to do laundry.

2. *Clear, so it stands out from the background* and attracts the learner's attention. A lighted sign, signifying that a checkout stand is open and triggers customers to line up.

3. *Highlighted during initial instruction.* A traffic light is a natural environmental cue, but it may not be obvious to the naive learner because it does not stand out from the surrounding wires, signs, buildings, or shrubbery.

Many strategies are provided in Chapters 11–15 for organizing the environment to highlight natural cues and developing visual adaptation to provide support when the natural cues are unavailable or inadequate. See Figure 13.2 for an example of planning natural and adapted cues.

For strategies on how to conduct a functional behavioral assessment and develop a positive behavior support plan, see Chapter 24.

The only common element in all traffic lights is the three lights arranged in the same order. One way to highlight this natural cue is to prepare photographs of three different traffic lights in different locations with different backgrounds. Each photo highlights a different colored light (red, yellow, green). During the initial presentation of the photos, highlight the relevant cues by outlining the traffic signals with a black marking pen. Write a caption for each photo while providing a verbal label ("This is a picture of a traffic light. The red light is on. When the red light is on, it means we stop moving"). After a brief introduction of the picture stories, move to the natural setting and match the pictures to various light posts and continue instruction.

Note: When adapting or highlighting a cue by using photographs, be alert to the fact that certain colors and background detail may distract from the relevant details. If the picture shows the learner in the setting, the literal learner may overgeneralize and believe that it applies only when the same clothing are worn (see Chapter 14 for information about strategies for selecting symbols).

4. *Cues (a stimulus or antecedent) can be manipulated effectively to change behavior (responses).* If behavior is a logical response to the environment in which it occurs (see Chapter 8), to change behavior we must assess the environment and alter or adapt the cues (antecedents) that trigger the behavior. *This is the key principle in the positive proactive behavior intervention approach* (Donnellan, LaVigna, Negri-Shoultz, & Fassbender, 1988; Dunlap et al., 2001; LaVigna & Donnellan, 1986; Meyer & Evans, 1989).

Prompts

A prompt is something added after the cue in order to get a correct response. *It is the added assistance needed to get it right before an error is made.* Prompts are generally required during the initial instruction of a new skill to ensure that the learner makes a clear and accurate association between the cue and the response.

There are two basic types of prompts:

1. *Natural prompts* are those that are always available in situations that require a specific response. For example, when checking out at the store, the total payment due appears on a display (a natural cue); if the customer just stands there without paying, the cashier prompts payment by extending a hand with palm up, while saying, "Cash or credit card?"

2. *Artificial prompts* are added to the setting if there are no natural prompts available or the natural prompts are too subtle. Most artificial prompts need to be faded to enable the learner to become independent. There are many forms of artificial prompts; the form is selected to match the needs of the learner and the nature of the task and setting.

   ■ Physical prompts involve the use of the interpreter's hands or body

     ▶ Blocking prompts—blocking the opportunity to make an error; standing passively in the path to prevent the learner from going in the wrong direction or placing a hand in position to block a throw and smoothly redirect to place the object in the appropriate location.

     ▶ Touch prompts—touching the learner's back, arm, shoulder, or hand as a signal to begin action or to direct the learner toward an appropriate location or material.

     ▶ Full or partial physical assistance requires the teacher, working from behind the student, to move the learner or the learner's hands through the total task or intermittently through parts of the task.

> ▸ Hand-over-hand prompting involves moving the learner's hands through the routine.

- Gestural prompts—pointing, tapping, or placing a hand beside the appropriate material or location to direct or redirect attention to the task, cue cards, checklists, or other adaptations.

- Verbal prompts—restating a verbal cue (verbal directions) or making a statement to redirect, remind, or break down the steps of a task ("Remember, first do _____, then do _____"; "What's next?"; "Stand up, then pick up the _____").

- Within-stimulus prompting—a strategy to highlight the critical element of the cue (e.g., using a blue cleanser in a white sink so it is obvious when all parts of the sink have been washed).

Prompting Problems

Prompting presents many challenges because people with autism learn things exactly as taught. Some prompting strategies will have paradoxical effects:

1. *If a skill is taught as an interactive routine* with the interpreter adding prompts in response to errors, it is likely that the learner will think that errors and prompts are a necessary part of the routine. These long routines are very difficult or impossible to fade.

2. *When prompts are delivered too quickly*, before the learner has time to process a verbal direction and generate an independent response, confusion, frustration and dependency may develop. This procedure can trigger behavior problems and may decrease motivation to try.

3. *When prompts are provided in a sequence* from the least intrusive (gestural or verbal) to the most intrusive (full physical assist), the learner is allowed to make several errors and to experience several correction procedures and prompts. When the correct response is finally produced, the total sequence of errors, prompts, and correction procedures is reinforced. Therefore, this least-to-most strategy establishes a long, cluttered, and interactive routine. Because the complete correct response and the reinforcement are not clearly associated with the original cue, meaning and generalization are not likely to occur—and the learner becomes dependent on the interpreter to continue providing the prompts.

4. *Full physical assistance can lead to resistance, aggression, or efforts to escape.* Overwhelming sensory stimulation, such as close physical proximity or repeated touching, may cause the learner to panic due to his perceived loss of personal control—which can lead to a number of problems. In some learners with autism, full assistance can lead to passivity and dependence. In others it leads to avoidance of the task or interpreter.

5. *If the same prompt is always provided* it will become part of the routine and be difficult to fade.

6. *If prompts are delivered when the learner is not attending to or actively involved* in the process, he or she may become very passive. It is as if he learns: "My job is to just be here and let people move me around—then good things happen (R+)."

7. *The time delay procedure* is often recommended as a way to fade prompts. It calls for the interpreter to gradually and systematically extend the time between the presentation of a cue and the prompt. However, if a familiar and valued reinforcer is delivered after gradually longer periods of waiting,

waiting is reinforced. (Some learners with autism have learned to wait comfortably for 20 to 30 minutes.)

8. *Do not use artificial verbal prompts* because they are very difficult to fade. These gestalt learners insert them into a turn-taking routine: "You say, I do. You say, I do."

Effective Use of Prompts

An effective prompt ensures a correct response and prevents errors during initial instruction (errorless learning). It also ensures that the original cue, the correct response, and the consequence are closely associated. When that association is made, meaningful skills are learned and used independently without someone constantly present to deliver prompts. The following strategies support that goal:

1. *Effective prompts are subtle, delivered quietly, calmly, and without emotion* to avoid highlighting. Calling attention to prompts may inadvertently tie them into the routine.

   ■ Do not prompt in exactly the same way more than once or twice in a row. Vary the type and the placement of prompts to avoid tying a specific prompt into the routine. Anything that happens in exactly the same way more than once may become a routine for the gestalt learner.

   ■ A touch prompt may be placed on the hand, wrist, arm, elbow, or shoulder (see panel B, page 255). A pointing gesture may take the form of a tap on some material, a touch to a specific section of the checklist, or a small, sweeping gesture to direct attention to an array or the location of a material.

   Remember: Cues are highlighted and prompts are varied, subtle, and unobtrusive.

2. *Provide only the amount and type of assistance necessary to ensure a correct response* during initial instruction.

   ■ Allow enough time for the learner to process the cue and generate a response independently but be prepared to prompt quickly to prevent an error. This requires careful observation and free hands (no clipboards).

   ■ If the learner's attention wanders, redirect to the original cue and quickly provide the support needed for the learner to respond accurately.

3. *Identify and capitalize on prompts that need no fading.*

   ■ Direct the learner's attention to the natural prompts that are always available in a specific situation (for example, looking to a seatmate's book to see which page to use, or observing a no smoking sign or a barrier at cliff side).

   ■ Embed prompts into the natural cue. These within-stimulus prompts highlight the relevant parts of the cue and may or may not require fading (for example, in teaching to discriminate between the capital letters *E* and *F*, highlight the third bar of the *E*).

   ■ Use gestures to direct attention to adapted visual references that can remain naturally in the environment (such as a checklist or sequence chart that specifies the steps of a routine, as illustrated in panel C).

   ■ Avoid intrusive verbal or physical prompts that call negative attention to the learner or divert attention from the natural cues. If used at all, they must be faded quickly rather than gradually to prevent the learner from becoming dependent on another person. If the instructional sequence is clear and supported with visual references, intrusive prompts are rarely needed.

4. *Stop talking if the desired outcome of a routine is total independence.* Provide verbal labels for actions and materials during the first one or two sessions (see Initial instruction, Chapter 18); then stop talking. Use touch, gestural, or blocking prompts to redirect the learner to the visual supports that will be natural to the situation. While verbal prompts are often assumed to be the least intrusive and easiest to fade, generally this is not true in autism.

   ■ If the task is ultimately to be performed independently, inform the student of this expectation before beginning instruction. ("I will help you this week. Then you will be able to do it alone. I will stay nearby if you need help" or "This line will help you keep the numbers in order now. In 4 days, you may be able to do the problem without the line.") Story strategies (Chapter 14) and picture sequences can support the message.

5. *Continually evaluate visual attention and active involvement, especially* when using hand-over-hand or other physical prompts. If visual attention shifts from the task or the learner is passive and not putting out effort, quietly and gently hold the learner's hand motionless, as if the world had stopped. When the learner glances back to see why nothing is happening, the world starts again. This type of specificity requires the interpreter to be in a position to see the direction of eye gaze and to maintain a state of awareness necessary to feel the active involvement of the learner's hands.

   ■ A particularly effective way to provide physical assistance or support for handwriting is illustrated in panel A. This hand placement, with your middle and fourth fingers placed under the learner's palm, allows for varied and minimal hand pressure while blocking erratic movements. If the learner's attention leaves the page, this hand placement enables you to gently and unobtrusively lift the hand to stop movements until attention returns to the task.

   Be aware that peripheral vision may be as effective as central vision for some individuals who have autism.

Review Chapter 10 for techniques to continually evaluate and refine the instructional process.

6. *Avoid full physical assistance paired with positive verbal reinforcement.* This strategy often leads to dependence, as learners with autism learn the wrong lesson—"I guess I am to stay limp and let them move me around—because they say I am doing a good job."

   - If the routine or task is modeled while referring to a picture sequence of the task, full assistance is generally not required.

   - Hand-over-hand prompting in combination with positive verbal reinforcement is less effective than simply having the student observe (that is, using a modeling procedure) (Biederman, Fairhall, Raven, & Davey, 1998).

7. *Avoid repeated practice of an unsuccessful instructional sequence.* If an error occurs more than once, clarify and refine the instruction. Make adaptations quickly, as soon as the problem is identified.

With foresight, most of the potential prompting problems can be prevented. An effective prompt provides direction toward a correct response or prevents an action that leads to an incorrect or ineffective response. This ensures that a natural cue, a correct response, and the reinforcing effect of the response are closely associated—*"recorded together on the same tape."*

Responses

A response is a behavior or action that occurs as the result of a cue. In other words, a response is triggered by the effect of the cue. The purpose of instruction is to teach the learner how to solve problems effectively and to accomplish important goals with actions or responses that are within a reasonable range of cultural acceptability.

- A response can be either a reflexive, unintentional reaction to the cue, or an intentional, deliberate action.

- A single behavior can be produced reflexively or deliberately.

- Responses can be either incorrect or correct. A correct response is effective—a problem is solved, an important goal is accomplished, and it is within a reasonable range of cultural acceptability. An incorrect response is ineffective—it does not solve the problem, the problem becomes more complicated, important things are not accomplished, or the response is outside a reasonable range of cultural acceptability.

Response Problems

There are several predictable response problems in autism:

- A tendency to repeat the same action over and over even when the response is followed by a painful or punishing consequence; a limited ability to spontaneously modify an ineffective response or to generate a new, alternative response. For example, the young man who could not get into the school because the door was locked began to bang his head on the door, unable to think of any other solution.

- A limited response repertoire that leaves the learner with only a few reflexive actions to use in response to many different problems (see Figure 8.3).

- Intentional and deliberate responses are often delayed and/or appear labored, out of context, or dysfluent; rote or echoed responses are generally produced quickly and fluently, often without the appropriate meaning attached. Self-generated responses take more time, thought, and energy.

- An appearance of laziness, noncompliance, or lack of obvious effort to try.

This seeming lack of motivation can be related to confusion (lack of instructional clarity or overwhelming sensory stimulation), an inability to initiate a deliberate verbal or motor response, discouragement, or boredom.

Teaching Effective Responses

1. *Systematically organize and structure space, time, and events to visually clarify unanswered questions* (who, what, where, when, why, how) (see Chapters 11–15).

   - Provide visual references when introducing changes or new instruction, events, settings, and people (see Chapters 11–15).

   - Model new routines and tasks before beginning instruction. Those with autism spectrum disorders attend to and learn from watching someone else perform the task (Biederman et al., 1998). Biederman also indicated that video modeling may be more effective than passive-live modeling. Seeing someone else do the task answers the question, "What are we doing here; what does it look like?" Modeling also reduces the need for more intrusive prompts (see strategies for preparing the learner for new instruction, page 302, Chapter 18).

2. *Teach new skills.*

   - Plan instructional sequences systematically to incorporate effective prompts and correction procedures that clarify and strengthen the association of cues, responses, and consequences.

   - Acknowledge and naturally reinforce efforts to initiate, participate, and persist in efforts (see pages 259–264).

   - Capitalize on naturally occurring problems to teach problem-solving skills and expand the repertoire of effective responses (see Chapters 18–22).

3. *Continuously evaluate and refine the instructional sequence* as soon as an instructional problem is identified in order to maintain meaningful and fluent learning, and to avoid repeated errors or dependency (see Chapter 10).

Consequences

A consequence is an event that occurs as a direct result of and immediately following a response; *it is a reaction to the action.* The type and timing of a consequence affects learning and will influence the strength of a response; it also will determine whether a response is likely to recur in the same form or be modified.

There are five types of consequences:

1. Natural consequences
2. Extinction procedures
3. Reinforcement procedures
4. Correction procedures
5. Punishment procedures

Natural Consequences

Natural consequences occur in life as a logical result of actions or behavior. Natural and logical consequences can be either punishing or reinforcing. For example, when turning on the light switch immediately results in the flash of light, pressing the light switch is reinforced and likely to be repeated. When inattention immediately results in a fall, inattention is punished and the need to attend is emphasized. These natural and logical consequences are extremely powerful if they occur very close in time to the response, and if the cause/effect relationship between the behavior and the consequence is obvious and clearly understood.

When natural consequences are not adequate in terms of clarity or timing to strengthen a new behavior or to weaken an ineffective behavior, parents and teachers add or manipulate reinforcers or correction procedures during instruction to achieve the desired results, as shown in Figure 16.3.

Extinction Procedures

An extinction procedure is the opposite of a reinforcer. A behavior that is never reinforced will weaken and become extinct. Extinction procedures are used as part of a positive behavior support plan.

Effective use of extinction

If a behavior is never reinforced, it will weaken and become extinct. Therefore, when (or immediately after) an error has occurred or while an ineffective behavior is occurring—it is ignored in some way. Reprimands and labeling errors reinforce and highlight the error—thus increasing the probability that the error will be repeated. And the learner still does not know what to do. *The rule is: Ignore the error in some way while clarifying what the individual is to do.* See the example of Amy who was sent to bring the red sweater, on pages 265–266, Chapter 16.

1. *If you see that an error is about to be made*, prevent it if at all possible. Block it in some way and provide assistance to shape it to a correct response. Prevention, or errorless teaching techniques, is still the best solution, but it is not always possible.

2. *If a response is incorrect*, quickly assess to determine why the error occurred— *do not talk about the problem, label the problem, or give a reprimand.*

   - Provide a correction procedure and the assistance required to redirect back to and highlight the original cue while saying something like, "Let's try again, I'll help you." Then provide the assistance needed to achieve a correct response; reinforce that correct response quickly even though you have helped. But remember, do not label the error or attend to it in any way.

   (See page 265 for effective use of correction procedures.)

See Chapter 15 and review strategies for using contingency statements, and strategies for using Reflective Listening. Also review the scheduling procedures that provide the reinforcers for contingency statements, Chapter 12.

3. *If a behavior is inappropriate or ineffective, ignore it in some way*—do not make eye contact, provide a reprimand, or talk about it. Then:

   - If the behavior is dangerous, follow the procedures outlined in Chapters 8 and 24 that include strategies for understanding and managing behavior problems.

   - If the behavior is not dangerous, such as screaming, etc., ignore it in some way, for example, turn away and do something else while quickly assessing the problem. When the screaming stops, turn back and continue the task or reflect the individual's problem or feelings and reduce the task—using a contingency statement. For example, "You feel tired and want to quit work, do one more _____, then it will be time to take a break."

     ▶ If the screaming has gone on for a long time, add a quick and startling change. For example, while still ignoring the behavior, when the learner stops to take a breath, quickly and with great exuberance, stand up, gather the materials and as you walk away, say, "Let's work at the table, come along." Add a contingency statement, or

> As the learner stops to take a breath, say, "Good, you are relaxing, when you finish this (indicate a small part of the task), then it will be time to (do a more favored activity—but not the most favorite activity)." See Chapter 15, page 236, for developing effective contingencies.

4. *If the task was done correctly but it was paired with an inappropriate behavior*, ignore the behavior in some way while highlighting the correct response. While the child is behaving inappropriately, do not watch the behavior or look at the learner's face, and do not talk about the behavior. Rather, focus on what the learner is doing correctly and reinforce it while verbally labeling what he is doing correctly.

In the middle of an individual testing situation, Gabriel was unconsciously rubbing his eyebrow and lashes with his left hand. At one point, as he was computing a math problem with his right hand, he rolled his eyelid up. His interpreter shuddered and said with quick emphasis, "Gabriel, don't do that!" Gabriel was startled. He stopped, looked at the interpreter, then slowly smiled and began to roll his eyelid up with happy abandon. He continued to watch the interpreter for a response. Immediately realizing what had happened, *the interpreter calmly and without emotion continued the test, ignoring Gabriel's repeated manipulation of his eyelid*. At one moment when his left hand lay quietly on the table, the interpreter, quietly and with her attention focused on the testing process rested her hand on his. Because she continued the test and reinforced his effort and work, he forgot about the eyelid and continued working.

Critical issues

It is obvious that extinction procedures are based on ignoring errors and problem behaviors. But that is not enough. Ignoring an error does not solve the problem in the long term because an extinction procedure (i.e., ignoring) does not provide information to help the learner be successful. A proactive approach is required:

1. Assess the problem to determine the function of the behavior.

2. Refine and clarify or modify the instruction.

3. Provide assistance and use techniques to avoid errors and problem behaviors in the future.

The learner does not need to know what he did wrong, he needs to know *what to do to get it right*.

Remember: Errorless teaching strategies prevent errors and increase motivation and the rate of learning. Trial-and-error strategies increase the rate of errors and reduce motivation and the rate of learning.

Reinforcement Procedures

Review Chapters 16–18 for errorless strategies.

Reinforcers are added immediately following a correct response if the natural consequence is not adequate to increase the learning rate. To reinforce is to strengthen or to increase. *In the instructional context, a reinforcer increases the rate of learning, increases the strength of new learning, and increases the likelihood that the behavior will recur.* Reinforcement occurs by adding something pleasant or valued or by taking away something painful or disliked.

Any behavior, correct or incorrect (effective or ineffective), that is immediately followed by something of value or ends something painful or disliked will be reinforced and strengthened.

A reinforcer may occur naturally as a direct and logical result of an action or effort, or it may be added or manipulated during instruction to achieve the desired effect.

There are two basic types of reinforcers:

1. *A positive reinforcer* (R+) is something added or gained. The learner gets something of value as a direct result of effort (for example, good feelings as a result of achieving a goal or an opportunity to do something of value).

   Caution: Positive reinforcement strengthens an ineffective and inappropriate behavior as well as effective and appropriate behaviors. For example, if a child screams and is given candy to keep him quiet, screaming will be strengthened and used again the next time the child wants candy.

2. *A negative reinforcer* (R–) is something taken away or removed. The learner avoids a painful situation, or a disliked event was ended as a direct result of effort. For example, the act of turning off lights is reinforced because the irritating buzzing noise ends. Abiding by the speed limit is reinforced because we avoid a speeding ticket.

   Caution: Negative reinforcement strengthens ineffective as well as effective responses or behaviors. For example, if a child expresses displeasure by having a tantrum and the teacher responds by ending the disliked activity, the tantrum will be reinforced and will likely recur in other similar situations.

Both positive and negative reinforcement may occur naturally as a direct result of action or effort, or they may be artificially added or manipulated during instruction.

Reinforcement problems

In general, learners with autism have a limited number of very specific and powerful reinforcers. They:

- Do not automatically learn to value the rewards that motivate most people in this culture.

  For example, most people are automatically motivated to work and conform to get smiles, hugs, good grades; to win a competition; to gain recognition; or to earn money. Those with autism must be taught to value these things. They may never be reinforced by some of these things, such as receiving good grades or winning a competition.

- Become easily bored or satiated by overuse of artificial reinforcers, such as a specific food, toy, or activity.

- Can become upset when a highly reinforcing activity ends or is withheld.

Identify effective reinforcers

1. *An effective reinforcer is:*

   - Naturally available as a direct result of a correct response or the learner's effort to produce a correct response—child is thirsty, wants and asks for drink, gets drink (R+).

   - Easy for an interpreter to deliver quickly as a direct result of a correct response.

   - Not available to the learner without a direct effort to produce a correct response.

2. *To identify the things that are currently reinforcing,* use the Preference Survey (Form 5.8) as a format to elicit information from those who know the learner well.

3. *To identify nontraditional reinforcers* common in autism, consider the following questions:

Review Chapter 12 for strategies to develop reinforcers in the context of the daily schedule.

- What does the learner do when there are no demands, when there is free time? Does the learner look out a window, flick a light switch, straighten the contents of the refrigerator or bookshelf, tear paper, read a specific magazine, click two sticks together? Any of these activities could be used as a reinforcer to develop skills.

- What special interests or sensory experiences are valued?

- What familiar and predictable events are reinforcing for those who live in an unpredictable world? Consider what familiar people, objects, activities, and events provide predictability and comfort: the arrival of the mail, mealtime, a walk after dinner, a specific TV show, looking at a magazine with a friend at a specific time?

- What painful or disliked sensory experiences trigger efforts to escape or avoid— certain noises, foods, activities, locations, people?

- Recognize and use the natural reinforcers identified each time a learner wants something, indicates a problem, or has a need.

Kim pulls his father to the door and indicates a desire to go outside (*this is a spontaneous and intentional communicative action that identifies a natural reinforcer*). His father says, "You want to go outside. I will help you open the door." (*Communication reinforced by acknowledging the message.*) Kim cannot manage the doorknob, so his father provides assistance (*a prompt*) that involves his son's active participation and effort to turn the doorknob.

Active participation, effort, and motor skills are reinforced the minute the door opens. Two critical goals and a functional motor skill were reinforced and strengthened just by capitalizing on this one natural desire; spontaneous requesting, active participation, and opening a door.)

If Kim's father had failed to identify and respond positively to the child's communicative effort (the original cue for the total routine), a natural opportunity and a powerful reinforcer would have been wasted.

Strategies for teaching routines are discussed further in Chapter 18.

- The opportunity to complete a familiar routine is reinforcing. When a familiar routine is interrupted to insert and teach a new skill that would make the routine more efficient or effective, the opportunity to continue and finish the routine provides enough reinforcement to strengthen the new skill (Goetz, Sailor, & Sailor, 1985).

- Systematically expand the number of reinforcing activities and relationships. For example, a daily schedule organized to capitalize on the reinforcing qualities of liked activities provides a context for developing new reinforcers (see Chapter 12).

Deliver reinforcers effectively

1. *The basic rule of reinforcement* is to make certain that a reinforcer (natural or artificial) is delivered immediately after a correct response or effective behavior.

- During initial instruction of a new skill, the reinforcing event must occur immediately as a direct result of every effort or attempt to respond and every more accurate or correct response. The goal is to quickly and firmly associate the reinforcer with the correct response. For a learner with autism, this association can occur very quickly as a result of one-trial learning.

2. *If the learner makes a correct response while engaging in other ineffective behavior*, use an extinction procedure:

   - Ignore the inappropriate behavior in some way as if it wasn't occurring. Do not look at it or the child's face, do not comment about the behavior. But do look at the correct response (usually the hands) while reinforcing the correct answer or positive response. This is the only time you would provide an artificial verbal reinforcer, "You did _____ right." This lets the learner know specifically what was being reinforced. Or,

   - Turn away quickly without a word and attend briefly to your notes, etc., ignoring the child and pretending you didn't see the correct response—try again when the screaming stops.

3. *Avoid pairing an artificial verbal reinforcer with the delivery of a natural reinforcer.* For example, if a child asks for a cookie, give the cookie to reinforce asking. Do not say, "Good job asking for a cookie." Artificial verbal statements such as this distract the child from making the correct association between his spontaneous communication (the cue) that got him the reinforcer (Biederman, Davey, Ryder, & Franchi, 1994).

4. *Ineffective behaviors are developed very quickly when a reinforcer (such as attention) is delivered with emotion or emphasis.* This can easily occur when a behavior is surprising or perhaps shocking. Ignore or unobtrusively and without emotion physically block the ineffective behaviors, and focus reinforcing attention to the co-occurring positive behavior or response (as in the example of Gabriel who was rolling his eyelid, on page 259).

5. *When using an artificial reinforcer to strengthen a new and developing skill*, change the rate of the reinforcement from continuous and quick delivery to a more varied, natural schedule. For example, delay the reinforcer for a few seconds or provide it intermittently at unexpected intervals.

   - This variation occurs naturally in real-life situations as it occasionally takes a bit longer or requires a bit more effort to complete or accomplish a task. In an artificial instructional setting, timing is very important. A continuous rate of R+ will initially increase the rate of responses, but the strength and the quality of the response may begin to decrease as the R+ loses its value because it is so readily available (satiation).

   - The transition from a continuous to an intermittent reinforcement schedule should occur fairly soon, before a rigid and inflexible routine develops. For example, the learner may think that the R+ is a necessary part of the routine and be unable to move to the next step until the R+ is delivered. The intermittent schedule must begin before the learner builds it into his or her routine, before the reinforcer loses its value, and before the learner gets bored and begins to manipulate the situation. Intermittent reinforcement builds very strong behavior—both effective and ineffective behavior.

6. *Artificial verbal reinforcement* provided to strengthen effort and motivation must be unobtrusive so the effort continues without disruption.

José was learning to work independently for longer periods of time. At a moment when he was working, his assistant stopped by his desk and said with enthusiasm, "Wow! You really are working hard!" José looked up, startled, then jumped up and ran around the room.

- Avoid artificial verbal reinforcement of communication and social interactions. These artificial statements interrupt the flow of the interaction and the powerful natural reinforcement inherent in having communication efforts acknowledged.

7. *Negative reinforcement is effective when a learner is tired, frustrated, and/or is having a bad day.* An alert interpreter identifies a point when the learner has done at least some work and is still focused on the task. Then the interpreter says, "You have been working very hard. You can stop now and take a break." Working and attending are reinforced as the hard work ends. Again, timing is critical. Had the interpreter waited to end the task until after the learner lost interest or displayed inappropriate behavior, those inappropriate behaviors would have been positively reinforced.

8. *Do not waste natural reinforcers.* Capitalize on any expression of need or want.

   - If the interpreter ignores these communications or solves the problem without requiring active involvement or effort, a powerful reinforcer is wasted and the learner has fewer opportunities to become more independent and competent.

   - When a need is communicated with an inappropriate behavior, calmly ignore the behavior but acknowledge the need or message. A reflective listening strategy (Chapter 15) provides a model for communicating the message and solving the problem. The active involvement in solving the specific problem is reinforced (as in the example of Kim, page 261).

9. *Capitalize on intense interests to reinforce effort and new learning.* Attempts to ignore, discourage, or eliminate special interests is not only time consuming, but in most cases futile and perhaps unethical.

   - Teach new skills in the context of those special interests. One young boy learned to read, write, and do math while studying washers and dryers in magazines and catalogs. Also, remember how Temple Grandin (Chapter 7) learned to do research and was stimulated to study and earn advanced degrees that led to a successful and satisfying career and friendships with others in her field.

- *Schedule opportunities to engage in special interests* throughout the day as powerful reinforcement for extended periods of hard work.

10. *Capitalize on the reinforcing qualities of stimulating or calming sensory activities.*

   - Analyze the reinforcing sensory properties of the specific behavior and identify more productive activities that have similar qualities. For example, what is reinforcing about clicking the light switch on and off? The clicking noise? The flashing light? Perhaps a computer could be programmed to provide a clicking noise or a flashing light as part of a game or instructional program. One young man who was reinforced by the visual properties of shredding paper now shreds cheese at several local pizza parlors. Another young person now owns a paper-shredding machine and has contracts with several local businesses. There are many possibilities.

   - Follow periods of work with opportunities to release energy. Prepare a specific and somewhat private space where rocking or jumping can occur without disrupting others or attracting undue attention.

     Note: To transition from a reinforcing activity back to work, it is important to highlight a stopping time (perhaps with a timer) and clarify the next activity on the schedule with a contingency statement.

     Jeff, a fifth-grade student with Asperger's syndrome who attended his neighborhood school, spent considerable energy maintaining control while at school. As soon as he returned home each day, he went directly to his bedroom, set the
     timer for 30 minutes, and began to jump up and down and flap his arms. When the timer went off, he stopped, went calmly to the kitchen, opened his backpack, and shared his schoolwork with his mother. Because he knew when, where, and how long he could jump and flap, he was able to control the behavior during the school day; and because he knew when to stop and what to do next, he was able to move on to productive activity.

11. *Use powerful contingency statements, not bribes*, to remind the learner of naturally scheduled events that will reinforce effort (Chapter 15).

Correction Procedures

A correction procedure is added as a consequence of an error or inappropriate response during instruction. The correction procedure provides assistance to give the learner another chance to make an effective or correct response that will trigger a reinforcing event. *A correction procedure facilitates the association of the correct response to the original cue so that learning can progress fluently.* Careful and precise use of prompts and correction procedures are the primary components of errorless learning that is so essential to those with autism.

The difference between a prompt and a correction procedure is subtle, but important:

   - A prompt is added after the initial presentation of the cue to prevent an error and to elicit a correct response quickly.

   - A correction procedure is added after an error and directs attention back to the original cue, then provides assistance to produce a correct response quickly. See Figure 16.3 on page 250 to review the correct placement of prompts and correction procedures.

Remember: When correction procedures are not used or when they are used ineffectively, additional errors can become embedded into a routine. These errors disrupt the fluency of a routine and block or prevent the direct association of the original cue to the correct response and the reinforcing event. When correction procedures are not used carefully and precisely, these gestalt learners will make incorrect associations—they will learn and remember the wrong things.

Effective use of correction procedures

To ensure that learning proceeds fluently and new skills lead to greater independence, a correct response must be directly and firmly associated with the original cue.

1. *Do not highlight an error.* The attention and discussion may reinforce the ineffective response and unnecessarily increase stress. Signs of excitement, exasperation, frustration, or reprimands and nagging will highlight an error. Rather, *ignore the error and with a calm, supportive, and neutral attitude, tell or show the learner what to do.*

2. *Direct attention back to the original cue* and provide support to start again.

   - If an error occurs within the context of a functional routine, stop the action and help the learner return to the last natural cue (or to the checklist, sequence card, or other adapted cue) and proceed fluently through the sequence to the next cue.

   Maria was learning a new routine so she could be more independent in public restrooms. The sequence of steps was represented with pictures on a card. On the third day of instruction, Maria had followed the cue card perfectly until she left the stall. Then she was distracted briefly by the shiny vent on the blow dryer. Just as she started to touch the blow dryer, the interpreter calmly and quietly took her hand and said, "Maria, stop. Try again." Leaving the stall door was the cue to move directly to the sink, so the interpreter guided her back to the stall, pointed to the picture of the sink on the cue card, and stayed nearby as Maria moved fluently to the sink. The opportunity to watch the water and soap bubbles on her hands was a natural reinforcer. Note that if she had been allowed to move about the restroom until the interpreter added a verbal prompt—"Maria, go to the sink to wash your hands"—the water and soap bubbles would have reinforced wandering about. Maria would have learned a different routine—leave the stall, and wander about until the interpreter says, "Go to the sink."

   - If it is not possible to go back and start over, calmly, without commenting about the error, provide assistance to repair the situation quickly and continue the routine. For example, in learning to ride the bus, if the learner forgets to pay the fare, it would be disruptive to return to the street to the original cue. Later, but before the next trip, review the sequence with visual cues and rehearse in a simulated setting. Immediately before the next trip, review the sequence highlighted on the cue card and be prepared to prompt if needed. *Note:* A video modeling procedure could be helpful in situations like this. See page 405.

3. *Do not let the same errors occur repeatedly.* Reorganize and refine the sequence, adapt the visual cues, and remain nearby to prompt and prevent another error.

   Mother asked Amy to bring her red sweater so they could go to the park. When Amy returned with a yellow sweater, Mother said, "No, that's the yellow sweater. I asked for the red sweater. Go back and bring the right sweater."

In analyzing this situation, Mother used too many words in a fairly negative (punishing) way and introduced an extraneous element—yellow. While Amy held and saw a yellow sweater, she heard both colors, yellow and red, associated with it. Would she be able to analyze that complex sequence of words and make the correct associations? What was the original direction? Would she be motivated to repair the situation? Probably not. Very likely, Amy would simply continue to stand where she was or return to the bedroom and move about randomly because she didn't know exactly what to do. Mother used a more effective correction procedure in the following scenario. As she saw the error, Mother reinforced Amy's efforts to comply as she said, "Good! You brought a sweater. I'll help you get the red one." She took the sweater and guided Amy back to her bedroom. With the yellow sweater out of sight, they went to the shelf together. Mother touched the red sweater, pulled it out a bit (to highlight it), and restated the original cue, saying, "This is the red sweater. Bring the red sweater." Mother provided a bit of assistance to speed the process. When Amy had the red sweater in hand, Mother provided a quick reinforcement as she said, "Great! You have the red sweater. Now we can go to the park."

Punishment

As defined in the behavioral sense, punishment weakens behavior and reduces the likelihood that it will recur. For example, if a behavior is immediately followed by a disliked or painful event, it is less likely that the behavior will be repeated. An event acts as a punisher only if the frequency, intensity, or duration of the behavior decreases. For example, the error message on computer games acts as a punishing consequence for most people, but some children with autism are excited (reinforced) by the sound and/or visual display, and they quickly learn to make errors at a faster rate.

Punishers may occur as a direct result, or as a natural and logical consequence, of an action or behavior. In the past, punishers were added and manipulated during instruction in order to change or modify behavior. The type of artificial or added punishers used to eliminate a response or modify a behavior once ranged from taking away privileges or prized possessions, assigning "time-out," or saying, "No, that's not right", to much more aversive procedures. In theory, a behavior that is consistently punished will be weakened and eventually eliminated.

Paradoxical effects of punishment

As with the other types of consequences, paradoxical effects can also result from punishment procedures:

1. *It is confusing* for people with autism to learn to value, stay close to, or establish relationships with people who deliver punishment.

2. *Punishment decreases both positive and negative behavior.* If a positive or effective behavior occurs just before and close in time to a punishing event, it also will be weakened or eliminated. For example, one young man with autism was just sitting down at his desk when, at the same moment, in the back of the room, a light fixture crashed to the floor. The child refused to sit again at his desk.

3. *Punishers provided as a result of an incorrect response do not increase the learning rate;* a punishment provides no information to help the learner make an association between the cue and the correct response. The learner still does not know what to do.

4. *Using punishers during instruction frequently causes the learner to dislike or avoid the teaching situation.*

5. *Punishing events can become valued and can actually increase the rate or intensity of a behavior.* Therefore, to obtain the desired effects, the intensity of the punisher must be increased. For example:

   - A consequence that serves as a punisher for most people may act as a reinforcer for others. For example, a spanking may reinforce and increase the frequency and intensity of a behavior if the learner needs attention and has no other way to get it, is comforted by the predictability of the consequence, or the spanking satisfies a sensory need and the learner is calmed by the physical pressure. Because the behavior still exists or is more intense, it is often seen as a deliberate challenge—so the intensity of spanking is increased.

   - Time-out procedures frequently have paradoxical effects. The time-out environment is quiet and free of demands—a highly reinforcing environment for the learner who is confused and overwhelmed by stimulation. It is not uncommon for a behavior to decrease drastically when time-out is first instituted and then increase in frequency and intensity after the learner discovers that a specific behavior provides access to a quiet, calm area. Teachers are reinforced for using time-out because peace and quiet returns to the classroom. Because both parties are reinforced by time-out, the learner tends to be isolated for ever-increasing amounts of time, deprived of positive interactions and instruction.

   - A punisher that is delivered in a highly consistent manner may become a reinforcer. When life is so unpredictable for people with autism, whatever is predictable becomes valued. Again, both parties are caught in a cycle with increasing frequency and intensity of negative behavior and punishment.

6. *The use of punishment assumes that the learner knows the correct response* or is able to modify or generate and produce a new response by trial and error. Because this assumption is rarely true in autism, the same error is often repeated over and over. The following examples describe situations in which the learner never discovered the right answer but learned the wrong lessons.

As a young child, Kim slapped his head when confused, frustrated, and upset. His behavior plan stipulated that his hands should be restrained for a brief period each time he slapped his head. Although Kim never learned a better way to deal with frustrations, he very soon learned to slap his head, then hold his hands out for his parents or teacher to restrain. As an adult, he continued this unproductive routine whenever upset, even though restraint had not been a part of his program for many years.

Annie, a very active child, cruised about the room, reaching and grabbing things, then dropping them to the floor. This was interpreted as disruptive and inappropriate behavior, and her teachers consistently slapped her hands, held them down, and said loudly, "No! Hands down!" Annie never learned to do any productive things with her hands while at school, but she did learn to keep her hands down. She walked about and sat with her hands at her sides. She didn't pick things up, and she never raised her hands to gesture. Several years later, a new teacher expressed concern about Annie's passivity. To demonstrate, she offered Annie's favorite cookies to all the students in class, saying, "If you want a cookie, raise your hand." Annie started to move her right hand upward, then drew it back as she remembered the rule, "Hands down." Everyone but Annie got a cookie.

7. *Failure, criticism, and the harsh voices associated with punishers and repeated demands cause increasing confusion and anxiety* that frequently lead directly to behavior problems. These situations have the same effect on most people.

> For several years, the consequence of Mike's every mistake was a loud, "No!" followed with a variety of repeated demands and physical assistance. As an adult, Mike screams and claps his hands over his ears whenever he hears the word *no*, even when it is directed to someone else in the room or used in reference to other things.

8. *Punishing errors and negative behavior without identifying the function or message behind the behavior leads to escalating cycles of increasingly intense behavior.* Review the discussion of behavior in Chapter 8 and study the Profile of Stress in Figure 10.1. No amount of punishment will solve learning or behavior problems for the long term because the basic issues or underlying needs are unresolved.

9. *Many severe behavior problems are a result of pain and medical problems.* Previously, these behaviors would have led to punishment—a highly unethical procedure. Refer to Figure 23.1 and the discussion of medical issues in Chapter 23.

10. *Punishing errors decreases the motivation to try and raises anxiety.* The ability and effort to concentrate and to independently produce an effective and meaningful response are diminished. This leads to a cycle of dependency, with the learner dependent on the person who delivers the punishment.

11. Finally, and of critical importance, *those who are punished are seen as less than human by both those who punish and others in the environment who observe the punishment.*

Punishment: A Practical and Ethical Perspective

Some parents and professionals continue to use some forms of punishment because it is generally supported by the culture and because many parents and professionals do not know of other strategies. Most parents and teachers no longer use punishment with their children with autism, but occasionally the behavior is so startling and the adults are so frustrated that they lash out. Punishment that occurs as a natural consequence of actions (e.g., touching a hot stove, the occasional quick, frustrated swat), is very powerful.

Although this occasional reflex reaction still does not teach the child what to do, it probably does no harm. That is, it will do no harm if the situation is then assessed to determine the function of the behavior, to answer the question—Why does this behavior continue to occur? Only when the cause is understood can new and more effective proactive strategies be designed.

But to design, manipulate, and deliver punishers as a regular part of a program is a different matter. *It is unethical* to punish those who cannot analyze a situation to understand the cause-and-effect relationships and generate a more appropriate answer or behavior; those who cannot communicate to express needs, confusion, pain, a need for clarification, or to defend themselves by justifying their actions.

The research on the effects of punishment and the use of positive, proactive approaches supports this position (Carr, Robinson, & Palumbo, 1990; Datlow-Smith, Belcher, & Juhrs, 1994; Donnellan et al., 1988; Durand & Merges, 2001; Groden, Stevenson, & Groden, 1993; Heflin & Alberto, 2001; LaVigna &

Donnellan, 1986; O'Neill, Horner, Albin, Storey, & Sprague, 1990; Schopler & Mesibov, 1994).

Summary

The goal of this book is to provide an understanding of the learning and behavior problems of those with autism, and to provide a process for teaching new skills and preventing or resolving problems in a proactive and positive way that guides the learner to greater independence. The foundation of this positive approach involves carefully planned environments and specific and precisely delivered instruction. The behavioral principles and strategies presented in this chapter provide the foundation, and are critical elements for developing and delivering clear and positive instruction as part of an integrated, positive and proactive approach.

CHAPTER

17

Establish the Foundation for Emotional, Communication, and Cognitive Skills

Establishing the basic foundation for effective emotional, language/communication, and cognitive learning is the most challenging and critical task for those who teach and support individuals with autism spectrum disorders. The pervasiveness and complexity of the communication and social problems encountered in those with autism spectrum disorders can be both surprising and daunting.

That a person can do some things so well and at the same time have such incredible and unexpected gaps and deficits is nothing short of astounding. These discrepancies and variabilities are confusing and often lead to expectations that are either too high or too low. This is especially true in the case of those with Asperger's syndrome—whose intellectual and verbal ability are often quite good, perhaps excellent, but who typically think in such concrete and literal ways that they often do not completely understand the nuances of language or the implications of the language that they use or hear.

Cognitive Development—Defining the Problem

Greenspan et al. (1998) suggests that the significant delay in learning the basic, critical early relationship and thinking skills can be attributed to differences in auditory processing, sensory modulation and processing, and motor planning. For example, most individuals with ASD are either hyper- or hyporeactive to the various types of sensory stimulation present in their world. This means that some of these babies are constantly protecting themselves or shutting out the overwhelming stimulation in their world. Other babies and young children are so underreactive that the stimulation is not registered and they wander about in a self-absorbed fog. In either case, the inability to take in, process, and use information from the environment will severely limit the learning of all skills. It is no wonder that the drive to interact, communicate, think, and solve problems does not develop.

Because the drive to interact and communicate is neither strong nor automatic for people with autism, young learners need many opportunities to practice the interaction habit. Without a strong interaction habit, the learner will not use communication consistently to solve problems, especially in stressful situations. *We must remember that the ability to talk does not guarantee communication.* Learners with autism may be able to speak, point to or label pictures, repeat rules or facts, use signs, write, type, or use a computer; however, spontaneous and meaningful communication will not be generalized to other environments and situations without first understanding that:

- People are interesting, helpful, and somewhat predictable.

- Others do not know what I know or need unless I tell them.

- I must find a communication partner and persist in getting that person's attention.

- Communication pays off!

Models for Establishing the Foundation

Most children with special needs, regardless of their diagnosis, require fairly intense early communication training and support. Two basic instructional models have emerged: the behavioral model based on applied behavior analysis (ABA)—i.e., discrete trial training (DTT)—and a more dynamic developmental social-pragmatic model that involves interactive play. Both models have been used successfully with many but not all children that have been diagnosed with autism. Greenspan et al. (1998) summarized the data from both approaches that suggest that:

■ Those who made the best progress in both models were those who could learn rather quickly to imitate and verbalize.

■ Those who made less progress in either model required a combined or integrated approach, and

■ Even those who had more modest outcomes in the behavioral program made substantial gains in the Floor-time/developmental model.

Greenspan et al. concluded that some children benefit from a combined approach that alternates periods of developmental play with the structured discrete trial teaching sessions.

See Chapter 9 for a discussion of the foundations for learning and teaching strategies, and a discussion of the controversy about the "best" model. Also see Ogletree and Oren (2001) for a historical context of the behavioral model.

Although the search for the "best" approach has led to considerable controversy, it is beginning to moderate, as reported in Chapter 9. Simpson (2001) and others suggest that, "The most appropriate and efficacious programs for children with autism and their families seem to be those that employ a variety of practices, including systematic and ongoing evaluation of interventions and treatment."

Because the behavioral model and strategies were introduced in Chapter 9, and the ABA principles and strategies are reviewed in Chapter 16, this chapter will provide a general overview of the basic components and strategies of the developmental social-pragmatic model.

"The unique features separating this (developmental) intervention model from other models, such as the behavioral approaches (Lovaas, 1987) or the TEACCH program (Schopler, Mesibov, & Hearsey, 1995) is its focus on relationships and affect, developmental level, individual differences and comprehensiveness" (Greenspan et al., 1998, p. 462). Also see a comparison of the behavioral and developmental models in Prizant et al. (2000).

The Developmental, Individual-difference, Relationship-based Model (DIR) model as described by Greenspan et al. (1998) emphasizes following the child's spontaneous initiations in a natural environment—ensuring that the training interactions will be at each child's current developmental level. Strategies are modified to match the child's specific sensory and motor differences. Progress is measured by changes in the type and complexity of thinking abilities, play, communication and social skills to achieve higher developmental levels. Positive results of imitating the child's behavior to increase gaze behavior and other skills have been reported by Field, Sanders, and Nadel (2001); Klinger and Dawson (1992); Lussier, Crimmins, and Alberti (1994); Peloquin (2001); and Tiegerman and Primavera (1984).

The information and strategies in this chapter have been integrated from several sources—the Floor-time approach by Greenspan et al. (1998); the structured play strategies of Klinger and Dawson (1992); and the developmental approaches of others: MacDonald, 1989; Merzer and Chastain, 1982; and Pulice, 1987.

Emotions—the Foundation of Learning

Rote skills are difficult for people with autism to generalize and use because they are taught without an emotional or meaningful context. Greenspan et al. (1998) remind us that a baby's earliest learning occurs as their feelings and emotions are engaged by the touch of a mother's hands, the sound of her voice, and the comfort of her actions. The first years of life are full of action, interactions, and reactions connecting emotions to meaning. For example, "As his brain registers the physical sensation, it simultaneously records the *emotions* those sensations provoke. 'Ow, that's hot!' or 'Yikes, that's cold!' It is this emotional response that secures the learning in his mind" (Greenspan et al., 1998, p. 111). They suggest that to teach these children with autism we must first join them as they are already engaged in self-selected activities. Then we manipulate and expand the interactions to tie their emotional responses to meaningful actions that will express their feelings and intentions. "Without the most basic ability to connect underlying feelings with behavior (or words), the child's sense of purpose, the key ingredient in the developmental progression, is missing" (p. 109).

Fundamental Developmental Skills

These first basic steps or fundamental developmental skills provide the foundation for all learning and functioning, including the development of spontaneous interactive communication, social-emotional, and cognitive learning:

1. *Develop self-regulation and self-calming.* Take an interest in people and attend to and experience the many sights, sounds, and highly stimulating activities and remain calm. Establish a sense of self and make emotional contact with parents/caregivers.

2. *Develop intimacy.* Stay near, watch others, and reach out to parents and others for longer periods of time.

3. *Engage in two-way communication.* Imitate both familiar and new actions, intentionally initiate non-verbal interactions, and take turns giving and taking (objects, smiles, eye contact, etc.)—developing independence and self-assertion.

4. *Share attention and string together longer interactive chains.* Try and persist in trying.

5. *Create and express emotional ideas.* Send verbal or non-verbal signals that stimulate others to new and more creative and pretend actions and to experiment with ideas and words to express feelings, needs, or interests.

6. *Understand cause/effect relationships.* Experience the beginning of logic and problem solving—thinking about and expressing emotions and feelings and understanding the cause of those emotions.

As Greenspan et al. (1998) state, ". . . (as you help your child) master these milestones . . . you will be helping your child develop his emotional, cognitive, motor, speech, and social skills"(p. 71).

Assessment to Determine the Starting Place

Strategies for achieving these basic goals are based on those that are used naturally by parents as they play and care for young, normally developing infants and toddlers. For effective use with children with autism, these intuitive play strategies must become more systematized or structured to keep the stimulation at an optimum level for learning and to accommodate the chronological age, interests, and sensory challenges of the child. Therefore, an assessment must be conducted to determine:

- *Current developmental level*—Which developmental goals has the child mastered? Where should you begin?

- *Sensory and motor strengths and challenges*—How does the child take in and process information? What triggers a strong reaction? What kind of sensory information doesn't seem to register?

Resources for Assessment

- *Asperger Syndrome and Sensory Issues*, by Myles et al. (2000). Includes a number of assessment strategies and tools.

- *The Child with Special Needs*, by Greenspan et al. (1998), Chapters 3 and 5 include observational assessment guides.

- Also see Beckman and Lieber (1994); Lindner (1993); and Wetherby and Prizant (1993).

Structured Play-Based Strategies

Organize and Structure to Plan Instruction

Time Issues

There are differences of opinion about the number of hours required to make significant progress. Twenty minutes a day of imitative play for only 2 weeks made a significant difference in eye contact with mothers (Klinger & Dawson, 1992).

- Fifteen to 20 hours a week of focused and active involvement in one-to-one and other structured activities was found to be a minimum amount for the child to truly benefit. The intervention model was less important than the level of the child's alertness and involvement (from a survey of successful early intervention programs by Dawson & Osterling, 1997).

- Six to ten 20–30 minute sessions a day were optimal for maximum benefit, reported Greenspan et al. (1998). They indicated that one or two sessions a day generally were not enough—at least two sessions at home each day are required for the parents to establish and maintain the emotional attachment with their child.

  If parents become too fatigued, they cannot interact enthusiastically and joyfully with the child. In these situations, several short periods of interactive play at home each day may be more valuable than fewer long sessions. In these situations, parents can:

  - Recruit and train friends and relatives to manage some of the sessions.

  - Develop a cooperative program with the school that involves training therapists and teachers who incorporate the strategies throughout the day.

  - Include intermittent use of the strategies at home during routine activities throughout the day. When the child is drifting passively or stuck in a repetitive activity, parents can join them and expand the activity to be more productive. When dressing, bathing, and during other routine times, they can engage in interactive play with minimal parallel talking so the child learns the language while also interacting and having fun.

Generalization of developing play skills to other settings and people is enhanced when the program is provided by several different people in several environments—but only if everyone involved maintains close contact to share information.

Arrange the Settings

■ At school or clinic: At least initially, the ideal space for structured play is a medium to small, safe area with clear boundaries, free of distractions and clutter to limit choices. In this setting, any choice or action the learner makes can be accepted, used, and reinforced. After a short time, the basic strategies can be incorporated and used in the park, playground, and other settings.

■ At home: Arrange a small play area in the corner of a bedroom or in a small area behind a couch or bookcase. In a larger room, define an area by a small rug, and use the area only when others are occupied elsewhere. The most important consideration is to avoid the distracting stimulation of TV and the activity of others, especially of other children who might want to join the session or to play with the special toys. The setting must be calm enough so both parent and child will not be distracted from each other. Parents must watch intently and respond quickly to the child's often subtle behaviors. Interactive play with peers will occur later, once the child has mastered the critical goal for these early sessions—how to engage emotionally with their caregivers and how the social interaction game works.

Select and Arrange Materials

For initial sessions, select identical sets of small *objects, toys, and materials that are most likely to intrigue and captivate the learner*—and that can be used to draw the child's attention to:

■ The interpreter's actions: Small noise or music makers, sparkling or noisy things to shake, mechanical toys that make noises, small cars or trucks, push-toys that make noise, floppy stuffed animals and dolls, paper sacks, toy telephones, blocks, hammer-and-peg toys, and so on.

■ The interpreter's face: Balloons, scarves, rings to peek through, and so on.

For later sessions, select toys that can be shared and that support or require:

■ Interactions: Blocks, form boards, puzzles, balls, cars, trucks, puppets, and so on.

■ Assistance: Interesting objects in clear containers with tight lids or fasteners, wind-up toys that are interesting but difficult to manipulate, bubbles, and pinwheels that are difficult to blow, and so forth.

■ Opportunities to release energy: Large balls to roll on, small trampoline, etc.

Limit the number of toys at each session to avoid overstimulation and distraction. Although only six or seven different toys or materials are required at any one session, rotate some of the materials every two or three sessions to avoid boredom, broaden experiences, increase flexibility, and keep the child from developing repetitive routines.

Structure the Interactions

The success of structured interactive play is dependent upon the skills and the attitude of the interpreters. See Figure 17.1 for a description of the attitude and role of an effective interpreter.

Figure 17.1 Interpreter's Attitude and Role in Structured
Interactive Play Sessions

1. **Interpreters are alert and observant.** They:
   - Provide an optimal level of stimulation—not too little or not too much
   - Are sensitive to subtle, nonverbal signs of interest, overstimulation, fatigue, or boredom
   - Watch for signs of developing rote routines
   - Watch for subtle, nonverbal behaviors that communicate feelings, preferences, and needs; they acknowledge and accommodate the messages conveyed by these behaviors

2. **Interpreters are flexible.** They have the ability to adapt their interaction styles to match the learner's stimulation needs. They are:
   - Playful, animated
   - Relaxed, calm, and generally quiet (unhurried)
   - Expectant, respectful, interested, and encouraging

3. **Interpreters are responsive and noncontrolling.** They:
   - Set up interesting situations
   - Give the learner control to select activities and levels of interaction
   - Allow the learner to end or change topics (game or action with toy)
   - Respond naturally to reinforce all of the child's efforts to interact
   - Avoid artificial verbal statements (such as, "Good looking") that interrupt the flow of the conversation and interfere with the direct association of the learner's effort to the highly reinforcing natural responses
   - Make no demands; they know that demands for eye contact, compliance, or to play or talk "the right way" decrease spontaneity and willingness to initiate or engage

4. **Interpreters share control.** They:
   - Follow the child's lead, then add variations to share the lead.

5. **Interpreters are dependable, consistent, and clear.** They:
   - Begin and end sessions and interactions in a positive and obvious way
   - Speak for the child, verbalizing the child's intentions and reflecting the child's feelings in clear, concrete language
   - Provide just enough assistance to guide and support expanding effort
   - Arrange the environment so the child can take the lead without concern for safety

6. **Interpreters are systematic.** They:
   - Evaluate and keep records of interactions, noting the types of toys and activities, the nature of the interactions, and any problems
   - Predict potential problems and make modifications to prevent learned errors and nonproductive routines
   - Refine, modify, and add variations in a timely and systematic way to increase and expand motivation and confidence and to maintain progress

They create an environment in which the learner and the interpreter have fun and feel so successful that both want to return for another interaction.

Structure the Beginnings and Ends of Play Sessions

Structure each session to flow from a clear beginning to a clear end. Announce the time for play or represent it on the child's individual calendar. Use a transition cue, a toy, or picture card to help the child transition to the play area. End the session positively *while the child is actively involved*. However, to extend the time in interactions, strive to engage the child in "one more turn" after the child indicates a desire to end the session (MacDonald, 1989):

1. *When it is almost time to end the session*—Set a timer to ring a few minutes before the specified ending time. When the timer rings, say, "It's time to stop playing. Let's put in two more pegs and then put away the toys."

2. *When the child begins to show fatigue* or an interest in leaving the area, say, "You want to stop playing? Let's roll the ball one more time and put away the toys." Then work together to close the container and put the toys on the shelf.

3. *If the child runs off before the session is clearly ended,* gently but firmly return the child to the activity and say, "I see you want to be all done. Put the lid on the bubbles, and then you will be all done." Provide assistance to end the session quickly.

4. *When it is time to leave, prepare the learner for the transition. Say,* "Play time is finished. It's time for _____," while handing the child an object or a picture to show the next event. Have the child take the cue to the designated location.

5. *Clarify the beginning and ending of informal interactions* that occur throughout the day in natural settings. Begin these brief, spontaneous interactions or interruptions by joining the child, who is already involved in an activity. Ease into the play in some subtle way so as not to startle or interrupt. Touch the child's arm, smile, and say, "Hi." Watch a bit before joining into the activity. If the child takes off or turns away, try to turn it into a playful dodging game (e.g., "I see you!" Or, "Ready, set, go!"). End the interaction after the child has acknowledged you and completed one or two interaction cycles but before he or she takes off again. Do not simply walk away—you would not leave a friend without some kind of a statement to give closure (e.g., Get down to his eye level, perhaps hold his two hands as you say, "I must go now, we will play more later," or, "That was fun, see you later").

Core Strategies

Perhaps one of the most important strategies is for the interpreter to provide the level of sensory stimulation that matches the child's need. The child who is overstimulated by the environment needs the interpreter to be interesting but calm. To capture and keep the attention of the child who is underreactive and withdrawn or "drifting off in space," the interpreter must be enthusiastic and exuberant, using exaggerated facial expressions and tone of voice. The interpreter must watch closely and experiment occasionally to alter the interaction style should the child's needs change.

Four strategies form a base that adds familiarity and predictability to the interactions. They enable the child to test and predict the adult's actions and keep the interaction at the child's level of understanding and tolerance. These core strategies are not necessarily used in any particular order or sequence. Rather, the adult moves from one strategy to another in response to small, nonverbal signals of interest, stress, or fatigue. The adult returns to a lower level to relieve stress, and periodically adds variations to advance the level of play and to prevent boredom and unproductive routines.

1. *Imitate or match the child's actions.* Do what the child does in a slightly exaggerated form, so the child is drawn to your actions rather than to the toys or objects.

2. *Sit with your face within the child's natural line of vision* and exaggerate facial expressions while imitating. This calls the child's attention to your facial expression and increases the likelihood of accidental eye contact.

3. *Pause before imitating* to set up an opportunity for taking turns. This gives the child time to think and to vary his actions slightly to test his control over your behavior.

4. *Introduce slight variations* of speed, rhythm, sounds, or actions—with the same or a different object. For example, if the child says, "Ma-ma-ma," you can say, "Ma-ma-mom." This variation provides a model to achieve the next developmental step—incorporating a new topic. These variations increase the child's alertness and set the stage for taking turns and to engage in longer interactions.

Note: Imitating repetitive and stereotypic behaviors is an effective strategy that enables the child to control the level of stimulation and ensures success. There is no evidence that the behaviors are reinforced and strengthened when the core strategies are followed. These core strategies, in fact, decrease repetitive behaviors as the child becomes more involved in a broader array of productive activity and when the optimum level of stimulation is maintained—not too little, not too much. The following vignette is an example of part of an actual session with Caesar, a non-verbal 3-year-old who is very withdrawn and shows few interests.

Caesar and Tom, the speech pathologist, are sitting on the rug with several toys between them. Tom has a duplicate set of toys within easy reach but slightly shielded from Caesar's view.

Tom waits expectantly.

Caesar flaps his hands.
Tom flaps his hands in the same way (matches Caesar's actions).

Caesar continues flapping, unaware of Tom's actions.
Tom continues flapping but begins to exaggerate the action.

Caesar, still seemingly unaware of imitation, stops flapping and begins to rock.
Tom stops flapping and matches Caesar's rocking action.

Caesar continues rocking, then stops and starts to flap his hands.
Tom exaggerates rocking, stops, then exaggerates flapping.

Caesar suddenly looks directly at Tom and stops moving.
Tom stops, and waits expectantly.

Caesar flaps his hands and stops.
Tom delays imitation for 1 or 2 seconds, then flaps for 1 or 2 seconds and stops.

Caesar flaps a bit, then stops and watches.
Tom continues to match Caesar's actions with varied time delay.

Caesar, seemingly very excited, flaps his hands and shakes his entire body.
Tom matches the actions, time, and intensity of the actions.

Caesar stops, waits as if thinking, then hums and rocks, looking away.
Tom waits, then hums and rocks.

Caesar continues looking away, humming and rocking.
Tom continues matching, then suddenly stops and slaps his hands on his knees, leans forward, and waits expectantly (thus adding a new idea to recapture Caesar's interest and avoid routine).

Caesar looks quickly, stops rocking, watches, and waits.
Tom waits briefly, then rocks, stops, slaps his hands to his knees, and leans forward.

Caesar rocks, stops, and slaps his hands to his knees.
Tom matches Caesar's action.

The conversation (interaction) continues, with the interpreter adding small variations—to keep interest and involvement high and avoid rote routines—to add new ideas and expand the topic.

A timer signals the ending of the session. Tom provides assistance as he says, "It's time to stop. Put the toys in the basket. Then play time will be finished. . . . Good! The toys are in the basket. Now it's time to walk back to your class."

Variations for Expanding Interactions

Variations are used in conjunction with the core strategies to maintain the optimum level of stimulation and continued growth. The variations are little surprises—novel actions added to the natural flow of the interaction when the child is engaged and attentive. Some of the variations are set up before the session by arranging materials in certain ways or places.

These variations or new ideas demonstrate the next slightly higher step, a new dimension of the actions on the materials: more complex and longer interactions. The variations also increase flexibility and tolerance for new and novel information. Remember that a variation is added as an option for the child to consider. If that option is ignored or the child shows stress or withdraws, return to the core strategies. Later in this and the next session, reintroduce the same variations several times, making them more familiar to the learner.

1. *Match the learner's actions*, add variations, and wait. Introduce a different action with the same object at the same or slightly higher level of difficulty, or introduce a familiar action with a different object. Then wait. For example, if the child had been shaking a stuffed dog and saying, "Yeh-yeh-yeh," you might briefly shake, then rock the dog while saying, "Yeh-yeh-yeh-ohh!"; or you might pick up and shake a rag doll while saying, "Yeh-yeh-yeh!"

2. *Arrange the materials or activity so the child realizes he needs a communication partner.* This strategy develops *active dependency (Merzer & Chastain, 1982) or interdependence—a realization that a communication partner is important* and that there is a way to send a signal to get what you want or need. For example, place a highly desired object in view but out of reach or stand between the desired object and the child. To obtain the object, the learner must touch or bump you. Interpret this nonintentional touch as a signal to get attention. ("You want me to get you the toy. Here it is.") Show the learner that a touch on the arm will get attention. See the interactions between Ann and Tony, following.

- Once the child has learned to signal his need for help, extend and strengthen the skill by pretending not to hear or see the signal. Then the child must do something to gain your attention and repeat the signal. This is an important, pivotal skill for people with autism who generally do not persist in getting their messages understood.

3. *Introduce interesting objects or activities* that cannot be done alone or that are too hard for the child to do independently. At that moment of realization, guide the child's hand to extend the object (thus teaching a natural gesture), and say, "Want help with the bubbles." While picking up the bubble bottle, say, "I will help you with the bubbles."

Although most children would naturally extend the object to the adult for help, a child with autism is most likely to do one of three things: simply stand there, get frustrated and throw the object, or drop the object and wander off. The adult must be alert to provide assistance at the most optimal point for the child to associate the need for help with a way to express the need. Receiving help quickly reinforces the effort and the action of requesting help.

When you need something, touch my arm.

- The verbal expression of intent must be literal and specific. Help is not the label of the object but an abstract word that applies to a variety of objects and situations. Provide a clear statement of intention that specifies very literally the want or need ("You want *help—with the bubbles*"). This strategy prevents confusion and a *misconception that suddenly the bottle of bubbles is now labeled help*. These verbalizations require no response from the child.

4. *Set up a social or motor routine,* and suggest a way for the child to signal a continuation of the activity. Hold the child on your lap and begin to bounce your legs, then stop. If the child seems to enjoy the routine, continue for a bit and then pause and say, "Stop." Wait briefly for any slight movement. Then say, "Want to bounce," and quickly begin to bounce.

- Add variations so the child must signal differently to specify which action is desired. For example, to continue bouncing, the child must take your hands and give a little bounce; to continue a rocking routine, the child must grasp your hands and lean back.

- To increase alertness and keep the child actively involved, and to prevent a repetitive routine in the situations described previously, move your hands to different locations (high, low, to one side or the other) so the child must search for your hands to send the signal. Otherwise, the child continues the same routine over and over again without involvement or thought, learning nothing.

- Gradually increase the requirement. For example, when the child sends the signal, you acknowledge ("OK, you want to bounce"), tensing your body as if to start. Then pause until the child looks to see why the action did not begin. The moment that eye contact is made, begin the action.

The child will need many experiences to understand that eyes can send messages.

- Acknowledge the request and add another requirement. Indicate whether or not the child's request is forthcoming by responding with exaggerated nonverbal cues. When the child sends the signal, smile broadly, nod your head to indicate yes, and immediately provide the action or object requested.

Tony, 4 years old, did not talk or use gestures to indicate his wishes. The following interactions occurred in his third session with Ann, his interpreter.

Ann sits between Tony and the toys, waiting expectantly.

Tony accidentally bumps into Ann as he tries to reach the bubbles. Ann says, "Tony wants bubbles. I will give you the bubbles." She hands him the bubble bottle, with the lid screwed on tightly.

Tony struggles intently with the lid. Ann guides his hand to extend the bottle toward her, and interprets, "Tony needs help with bubbles." She opens the bottle quickly and waits with the bottle in her hand.

Tony stands on tiptoe, looks into the bottle, and reaches for the wand. Ann says, "Tony, you want to blow the bubbles," and hands him the wand.

Tony looks directly at Ann as he realizes he can't blow the bubbles. Ann says, "You want me to blow bubbles. OK." She takes the wand, fills it with liquid, and waits with the wand in front of her mouth.

Tony looks at her as if to say, "What's holding up the bubbles?" Ann immediately blows the bubbles.

Tony, excited, bounces on his toes as he breaks bubbles. When all are broken, he stands quietly in front of Ann, looking at the bottle. Ann says, "You want more bubbles," dips the wand, and pauses as above.

Tony again looks to see why she stopped. Ann repeats the routine in the same way two more times, and then begins to add variations to keep him actively involved:

- She "accidentally" drops the wand several times in different places at or near her feet. She helps Tony pick up and return the wand to the bottle when he is ready for more. Each time, she pauses with the wand at her mouth until he looks at her.

- She blows the bubbles to land on his hand, then his shoe, as she says, "Bubbles on your hand" or "Bubbles on your foot." She asks, "Where do you want the bubbles?" When Tony twitches his hand, she blows them on his hand. The next time she asks, he moves his foot ever so slightly forward. Each time she says, "The bubbles are on your hand (foot)."

- She blows the bubbles up into the air in different directions, and as Tony dances and breaks the bubbles she says, "Bubbles, bubbles, Pop, Pop, Pop! Tony is popping the bubbles."

Tony looks to the window and starts to move in that direction. Ann takes his hand and says, "You are all done with the bubbles. Let's blow one more time. Then we will be finished." She blows one more bubble with Tony watching, then helps Tony put the lid on the bottle as she says, "We are finished. You can look out the window."

Ann provides a clear ending for the routine: You get it, you do it, and you put it away.

These strategies can also be modified to use with older learners—to help them adjust to new situations, develop trusting relationships, and communicate in more effective ways.

Saul, 17 years old, had just moved to a new school. He had no communication system and became agitated whenever the teacher approached. Lena, the teacher, noticed that he carried several playing cards in his pocket and that he repetitively bent the corners of a card back and forth. This activity seemed to calm him. She decided to join him in this familiar activity.

> Saul is seated at his desk, folding the corners of his cards up and down. Lena with playing cards in hand, sits down quietly at Saul's desk and waits.
>
> Saul continues to fold the cards while staring out the window. Lena begins to fold the corner of one of her cards, matching Saul's actions.
>
> Saul stops and watches Lena briefly, then continues folding his card. Lena pauses for about as long as Saul had, then starts folding again with slightly exaggerated movements. This routine continues for a few minutes.
>
> Saul begins to fold very quickly for about 5 seconds, stops, and watches to see what will happen. Lena waits briefly, then matches Saul's quick actions for about 5 seconds, and stops.
>
> This phase lasts for several turns as Saul varies the activity to test the teacher's responses, folding faster and slower and for differing amounts of time. Finally, after about 10 minutes,
>
> Lena touches Saul's hand briefly as she says, "I must go. This was fun." Then she walks away. Saul watches the teacher closely. When she returns to her desk, Saul walks over and stands quietly beside her.
>
> Lena says, "Hi," acknowledging his presence, and continues to work. After a few minutes, she looks at Saul and quietly says, "I will show you your calendar." She walks to the calendar. Saul follows her and watches quietly as she explains his calendar.

Although their problems were not over, it was a beginning. Each day, Saul's calendar specified a talking time when he and Lena could talk. Each day Lena offered one or two new materials or activities for Saul to choose to expand their conversation. They looked at sports magazines and different kinds of cards, sorted cards, and played modified turn-taking card games. Occasionally, a peer was invited to join them. The communication specialist taught Saul to use a communication system that incorporated line drawings mounted on playing cards. Saul carried a card in his pocket to occupy his hands whenever he had to wait.

Niko was a nonverbal 12-year-old boy with severe autism and cerebral palsy. (He could walk slowly and manipulate some fairly small objects.) He avoided people, demands, and new experiences. His only independent activity was to sift things through his fingers. At recess, he sat on the ground and sifted the dirt. At home, he sifted the dirt in the houseplants, the ashes in the fireplace, or the sugar and rice in the kitchen. His parents were tired.

Niko's support team had determined that he was reinforced by the visual aspects of sifting. The team identified several activities that had the potential for similar visual stimulation: planting seeds, cleaning and raking flower beds, cooking (sifting flour, measuring salt, sorting beans, packaging soup mixes, shredding cheese), measuring soap into the washing machine, and making crafts with colored sand.

A daily calendar and a structured work system were prepared to support the addition of new materials and activities. Staff received extra training to encourage interactive relationships throughout the day. They learned to identify and respond to nonverbal signals, to talk less and use visual supports, to share control by setting up opportunities and waiting, and to join into Niko's own activities. The following sequences illustrate some of the early interactions between Niko and his interpreter, Kate.

Day 1: 10-minute interaction at recess

Niko is sitting in a sandy area of the playground sifting the sand. He is bent over so he can see the sand fall.

Kate joins him quietly, watches for a few minutes and then begins to sift. Occasionally, she labels the activity ("Sifting, sifting, sifting sand"). They progress to taking turns, with a few variations. After about 10 minutes, Kate says simply, "Sifting sand was fun. I have to go."

Day 2: 12-minute interaction at recess

Kate joins Niko as before, saying, "Hi." After re-establishing the turn taking interaction she slowly and tentatively sifts sand into a small pile, then quickly smoothes it out—again making brief comments to label her actions.

Niko watches then smoothes out his pile of sand and waits.

Kate and Niko continue this game for 2-3 turns, then **Kate** uses a small stick to make lines in the sand and places the stick on the ground between them to share.

Niko takes the stick and makes lines in the sand.

When the bell rings, they return to the classroom together. With Niko watching, Kate draws a picture of them sifting sand. She labels the picture, and they put it in a notebook.

Later that day, Kate takes Niko to visit a nearby construction site to see the dump trucks. She shows him a toy dump truck in her shopping bag. She sifts a bit of dirt into the truck to show him how it works. Then they put the truck away and return to class. They draw a picture of a dump truck and put it in the notebook.

Day 3: 12-minute interaction at recess

Kate joins Niko and places the dump truck nearby—she begins to sift sand, matching his actions. After several turns, she pulls the truck close and sifts sand into it. When the truck is full and running over, **Niko** reaches across and dumps it.

Kate laughs and says, "You dumped the truck."

Niko returns to sifting sand.

Kate matches his sifting for a bit, then fills the truck again. When it is almost full, she pushes it to Niko and waits.

Niko watches the truck but continues to sift sand.

Kate sifts sand, taking turns with Niko.

Niko stops, quickly dumps the truck, looks at Kate, and laughs.

Kate laughs and says, "Wow! You dumped the truck."

The interaction continues until the recess bell rings. They walk together back to the classroom where they draw a picture of themselves and the dump truck and put it in the notebook. The interactions progress in other activities in the classroom.

Day 4:

Niko waits for Kate at the door and walks beside her to the playground—a major accomplishment.

Not all days went smoothly. Sometimes Niko was distracted and irritable and not open to new ideas. Kate was patient, calm, and noncontrolling as she continued to introduce different elements and toys to the conversations. The time spent in simple sifting decreased as Niko became more interested in doing a variety of other activities. They enjoyed reviewing the notebook of experiences together. Niko began to point to the pictures and comment as he had seen and heard Kate do in play (approximations of wow, oops, oh, and other exclamations). He began to refer to his daily calendar and to try more new things in the classroom. His parents, pleased by Niko's progress at school, incorporated the structure of a calendar and more interactive opportunities at home.

Expanded Applications

These strategies can be expanded and applied to a broad range of skills and to match the needs of a broad range of learners.

1. *Add new materials, new topics for the interaction.* Select objects with similar sensory elements, and rotate materials and objects frequently.

   ■ Provide structure to make choices and plans. At first, present a choice between items that you have preselected. Later, expand the choice so the learner selects the materials or topics before a session or event begins.

- Block an action or set up a problem to engage the learner in problem solving.

2. Shape and model more complex actions and language.

   - Promote symbolic and pretend play—introduce different ways to play with a toy.

   - Add more complex commentary to label objects, actions, intentions, and feelings. Provide comments that are specific and at the learner's level, with pauses and quiet time between.

   - Shape natural gestures so they are more specific, meaningful, and communicative. For example, as the learner looks and reaches to grab the truck, shape the learner's hand to a point, and say, "Want this truck." Then quickly give him or her the truck.

   - Review past experiences. Draw pictures or write experience stories, and place in notebook for later shared interactions.

   - Introduce new communication systems for expressing preferences, needs, and feelings, and for rejecting or avoiding choices (as described in the Picture Exchange System, Chapter 20).

3. Add new people and different settings.

   - Invite a same-age or slightly older peer to share in interactions, play a game, share in a construction or cooking project or go on a field trip. This peer can serve as a mentor or friend in the regular classroom or in a play group. Wooten and Mesibov (1986) describe reverse mainstreaming strategies. Review the information in Chapter 21 for strategies to introduce play groups to expand interaction and communication skills.

   - Support interactions between peers during recess and exploratory or free-play periods. Capitalize on free-play situations by setting up opportunities for sharing materials interactively and taking turns.

   - Establish social skill groups (Chapter 21) and plan with the learner to both participate and take the lead (see Shuler and Wolfberg [2000] also).

4. *Alternate play and work sessions* to practice making transitions and to learn that: "Sometimes I get to be in charge, but at other times adults are in charge."

During circle time in the kindergarten class, Angelo became restless and began to shake his hands repetitively. His teacher said, "That looks like fun. Let's all shake our hands." Everyone started shaking their hands in the same way. Then the teacher said, "Stop," everyone stopped. In a moment, the teacher said, "Go," and they all started shaking hands again. Angelo grinned. After several rounds of this routine, the teacher said, "Shake, shake, shake, stop!" and firmly stopped her hands on her knees. "Now, stretch, shake your shoulders, and let's sing Old MacDonald." This was a quick and refreshing change of pace for the entire class and a very positive way for Angelo to learn to gain some control over his actions and to get some acceptance. At another time, the teacher asked Angelo and others to take turns leading the group in the hand-shaking activity.

Summary

Adults are responsible for a child's well-being. They must provide limits, boundaries, demands, and instruction so the child is safe and is given opportunities to learn acceptable behavior and self-control. For the most part, this system works well for the child who has a strong social interactive habit. However, the learner with autism withdraws and has no opportunity to become a better communicator when the stimulation is too overpowering; that is, when adults talk too much and dominate the conversations and play with questions and demands.

When adults follow their own agendas and ignore the subtle, nonverbal behaviors that signal feelings, preferences, and needs, learners stop trying. Their early efforts are not expanded into more complex and effective communications.

Learners will spend more time with people when the demands and overwhelming stimulation are reduced, and when their interests, ideas, and efforts are valued. Under these conditions, learners will discover that people are interesting and helpful. However, it will take many, many successful interactions to master those six developmental goals that form the basis for learning the critical cognitive, social, emotional, language and motor skills—the foundation for all future learning.

Interpreters must continuously evaluate and refine their actions, the settings, and the materials to encourage continued progress. Although child-directed play strategies are critical for teaching these foundational skills, there must always be a balance—the child must learn to share control; in some situations the adults make demands and take charge, and in other situations the child will have control. For more complete information for using Floor-time strategies, read *The Child with Special Needs: Encouraging Intellectual and Emotional Growth* (Greenspan et al., 1998). Also refer to Appendix B, for training resources.

Teach Functional Routines

The concept of teaching in the context of routines is introduced in Chapter 13.

Life is made up of a series of activities or events such as getting dressed, traveling, visiting with a friend, or working. Each of these events is actually a routine with a common sequence of steps that flows from beginning to end to achieve a goal. These are functional and practical routines that enable a person to take care of daily needs, arrive at a specific destination, relax and enjoy time with a friend, or earn money. Because people with autism spectrum disorders learn routines quite easily and are reinforced by completing a familiar routine, it is efficient to teach critical goals (page 107) and functional skills in the context of these important natural routines.

The number and variety of the routines that fill a lifetime make it impossible to predict which ones to teach. Even if they could be predicted with any degree of accuracy, there is not enough time to teach them all. Therefore, it is important to select and teach some pivotal processes and concepts that can apply to all routines (Koegel, 1999).

The basic elements for organizing these functional routines that include visually supported work systems were introduced in Chapters 11–16, relating to organization and structure. This chapter begins with strategies for teaching children to use work systems—a pivotal skill that is expanded and applied to teaching all other routines (Mesibov et al., 1994). The second part of this chapter presents strategies for refining the instructional plans and for teaching several functional routines. These strategies are designed to build independent, flexible, and meaningful skills, including communication, social, and problem-solving processes that can be expanded and applied to the broad range of home and community situations now and in the future.

All interpreters, including parents, teachers, and especially the assistants and job coaches, need training in these strategies.

Work Routines and Work Systems

As developed at Division TEACCH (Treatment and Education of Autistic and Related Communication Handicapped Children), University of North Carolina at Chapel Hill. See Appendix B.

Mary Anne Seaton wrote:

> The most positive [educational] experience [for my son] has been the introduction of "structured teaching"* into his school program and home life. This process has allowed him to become independent in his activities throughout each day. Now, without someone standing over him and verbally directing him, he can feed the cats, wash and dry the clothes, prepare his lunch, recycle the pop cans, tolerate assistance with hygiene, go grocery shopping, and work in the community in four different jobs. He also takes great pleasure in setting up and putting away his work. . . . The nicest thing about his independence is his sense of pleasure and pride in doing all of these things and understanding what he is doing. . . . These structured teaching strategies changed his life—and mine too.

Read Mary Anne's story in Chapter 14.

Functional work routines are similar to other routines in that there are common elements and skills that can be applied to every routine regardless of the type of work, from washing windows, feeding the fish, and vacuuming the floor, to vocational jobs, school work, and leisure activities. A work system is composed of all the concepts and visual adaptations needed to support independence.

The initial instructional goal is to teach the processes and concepts for working independently—not to teach specific jobs or tasks. Growth to independence is a flexible three-stage process (see Figure 18.1) that begins at a very early age. These basic work-related concepts and skills are introduced when visual references and small tasks are incorporated into one-to-one play routines. These first work routines capitalize on natural early-childhood manipulative materials and activities. The process for developing work systems and teaching these pivotal skills has been applied to learners of all ages and ability levels. It is especially helpful to those who are dependent on constant verbal cues, resist work, or have not learned to use visual adaptations.

Figure 18.1 Developing Work-Related Concepts and Skills

Adapted from Oregon Regional Autism Services
These three flexible stages will lead to independent performance in natural settings.

Stage 1. Establish basic work-related concepts and skills in 1:1 situations.

- Establish concepts of contingency and cause/effect (work, then play; first this, then this).
- Use visual references (checklists, calendars, etc.).
- Establish a system for working (work from left to right and top to bottom; get task out, do it, put task away) and work-related concepts (begin and end/finish/all done).
- Understand basic rules (stay within a designated area . . .).
- Work and play in various contexts (on the floor, at a table).
- Make transitions (to and from the calendar to a work or play area; from one activity to another; from work to play and return to work).

Stage 2. Expand work-related concepts and skills to more situations.

- Expand skill in using visual references (checklists, cue cards, diagrams, jigs).
- Increase number of work sessions; increase length of tasks and sessions.
- Communicate need for assistance and clarification.
- Expand social skills appropriate to routine.
- Work and play (take breaks) in an increasing number of areas and with others.
- Increase tolerance for supervision, corrections, and interruptions.
- Establish basic self-monitoring strategies and self-control routines.

Stage 3. Transfer work-related skills to the community.

- Use a broader range and more complex visual references (maps, cue cards).
- Expand tolerance for distractions and unfamiliar people and settings.
- Expand flexibility and tolerance for new and changing events and expectations.
- Tolerate corrections and supervision from different people.
- Manage more complex work and cooperative or assembly-line work.
- Extend stamina, routines, sequences, and concepts.
- Improve ability to socialize and to communicate needs with an increasing number of people.
- Increase responsibility (set up own work area, get materials, help others).
- Expand self-monitoring and self-control skills to other settings.

Design the Work System

Work systems are highly individualized to match the learner's interests, preferences, abilities, deficits, and tolerances. Their design involves decisions about:

1. The type of system (how to give the directions and organize the materials).

2. The type of tasks.

3. The variations to expand skills and concepts.

The specificity of the details of a work system are much like those described in the analogy of The Amazing Machine (Chapter 16).

The System

System-design decisions include the types of symbols for giving directions, the organization of the task and task directions, the types of containers for organizing materials, and the organization of work areas. *This organization must be so clear, literal, and logical that after a brief instructional period, the learner can work without verbal or physical assistance.*

The work area and the materials must be uncluttered and organized logically.

Seven questions will guide the planning process, but the final decisions are based on the needs of the specific learner. The quality of a work system can be evaluated by the visual clarity of the answers to those seven questions:

1. *Where am I supposed to be?*

   - The individual calendar provides this information.

   - See Chapter 12 for strategies for clarifying space and boundaries.

2. *What am I supposed to do? In what order?*

   - A mini-calendar or sequence card displays symbols that match tasks organized in baskets, boxes, files, or drawers. Symbols for matching include shapes, colors, numbers, or written words.

3. *Where do I start?*

   - Color codes or an X indicate the starting place to work from left to right or top to bottom.

4. *What do I do, right now, with this?*

   - A checklist, sequenced picture strips, a jig, or a completed sample provides a model for beginning and completing a task.

5. *How much of this must I do? What does* finished *look like?*

   - The material is used up, the finished tasks are gathered in a Finished box, all the symbols on the mini-calendar are turned over or gone, all symbol cards for completed tasks are in an envelope or pocket marked Finished, or all the tasks listed have been crossed off.

6. *What do I do next?*

   - A transition cue placed at the bottom of the mini-calendar or the last item on the checklist indicates the next activity or a return to the calendar to see what is scheduled.

7. *What do I do if there is a problem? If I get upset?*

   - The individual communication system must include a way to request help or to ask for a break.

Selecting Tasks

When teaching independent work skills with a new system, the tasks must be familiar and easy. If a learner does not have the skills to do the task independently, do not include it in an independent work session. During initial phases of instruction, organize all tasks clearly and present all materials so the learner can begin and complete the task without problems. To maintain motivation and feelings of accomplishment, present initial tasks that are:

- Stable—Once together, they do not fall apart.

- Varied—Do not use the same task or materials more than once a day.

- Rotated systematically—Do not repeat a task day after day.

- Balanced—Vary the characteristics and demands of the tasks. For example, do not present all packaging tasks or sorting tasks.

- Logical—Do not require a learner to take apart a product that has just been assembled.

Variations to Expand

Once the system is familiar, the tasks are varied and expanded to teach more complex work concepts and skills. More functional tasks and new routines are incorporated into the system. A wide range of materials may be used to vary and expand the complexity of matching, sorting, sequencing, categorizing, assembly, and packaging tasks. Office, housekeeping, cooking, self-help, and functional academic tasks also may be incorporated into the system.

By changing the focus and the demands, familiar materials and tasks can be used to address critical goals and more advanced work skills:

- Sabotage tasks (initially in small ways) to provide more opportunities to communicate and solve problems.

- Incorporate interruptions to increase tolerance.

- Require the learner to share materials or space with a peer.

- Require the learner to check work quality and correct errors.

- Increase the amount of work to increase attention span and stamina.

- Have the learner set up the materials, using a checklist.

Once the work area, the visual support systems, and the tasks are developed, the basic instructional strategies are implemented. Evaluate continuously to refine the system as problems are identified and the learner's needs change.

A work system developed for a very young child is presented in Figure 18.2.

Figure 18.2 Sample: Work System for a Young Child

These adaptations were made to Matt's interactive play sessions when he was about 3 years old. Matt had learned to enjoy interactions, to share the lead in interactions, and to play with a variety of materials. His productive play was still limited to a small, carpeted area. He had difficulty moving in and out of the play area, and his behavior was disorganized and random when outside that area.

Phase 1. Establish basic work concepts and skills with a work system

Goals

- *Work then play*
- *Follow a mini-calendar*
- *Work from left to right*
- *Concept of finished*

Materials

- *Manipulative tasks that are familiar that can be done independently*
- *Small plastic dishpans or containers*
- *A basket, cart or shelf near the work table*
- *A box large enough to hold at least 3–4 of the containers, clearly labeled FINISHED*

Structure of initial session

Interactive play sessions were structured (as described in Chapter 17). Initially, a 15-minute work session begins and ends with play on the floor. Initially, a 3-year old, will start with only 1 short familiar task that will take a few minutes to complete, (i.e., pegboard with large pegs, shape box, puzzle with three to four pieces). Gradually the amount of work will expand to three to four tasks per period. End the work session while the child is still interested. Refer to scheduling procedures (Chapter 12).

Before the session, place one dishpan on the floor near the play area. After about 5–10 minutes of interactive play and while still on the floor, the interpreter pulls the dishpan over near Matt's left hand and says, "It's time to do some work." She models taking the pegboard and pegs out of the box and places a peg. She hands Matt a peg and said, "It's time to work. The pegs go in the holes." She helps Matt to complete the short task very quickly, and then said, "You are all done. Finished. Put them away." She places the full pegboard into the basket and moves it off to the right as she said, "It's time to play. Work, then play." The interactive play session continues as before until it is time to leave.

Note: The containers, are always arranged to work from left to right

Variations

Each day, something is changed or added to the routine:
- *The talking*–fade the parallel talking strategy (Chapter 15).
- *The Finished box* on the floor to Matt's right, for him to place the completed containers
- *The task*—different but familiar tasks, the length of task, the number of work tasks (from one to three)
- *The number of tasks* per session, used one at a time
- *A new task* every 3 or 4 days
- *A mini-calendar* to preview the tasks and cross off when finished
- *The location of the work area*—moving from the floor to a small nearby table. The interpreter picks up the container and says, "Come, let's work at the table."
- *A timer* to end the play period

(continued)

Figure 18.2 Sample: Work System for a Young Child (*continued*)

Phase 2. Work beside peers, using the work system

Goals

- *Get, do, put away*
- *Follow a visual checklist*
- *Transition between tasks*
- *Take a break and return to work*
- *Tolerate presence of peers*

After an initial instructional period, the group of seven children with a variety of learning problems was supervised by one staff person for a 20-minute period. Matt first entered this group during the second week of school after peers had already learned the routine. The interpreter monitored Matt's stress level carefully and offered breaks before problems occurred. During these breaks, Matt learned to go directly to a mini-trampoline and jump energetically for a few minutes and then independently return to work. As his tolerance increased, he required fewer and fewer breaks.

Materials/Structure

- *Manipulative materials* were stored, one to a dishpan, on low shelves with a work table nearby.
- *Each container was labeled* with colored shapes, and the shelves were marked with the colored shapes to indicate where to return each container.
- *Two pockets were* mounted on the end of the shelves—one was for Matt to place his transition cue, the other pocket held laminated strips. Each strip had a different sequence of four colored shapes. A paper clip was placed on the strip to highlight the first colored shape symbol. These strips, or mini-calendars, structured the sequence of tasks and prevented a child from doing only one task all morning.
- *Plain place mats labeled* with each child's name were placed on a shelf. The word WORK was printed in the center and an X was printed on the left edge.

Procedure

As the 3- and 4-year-old children arrived at preschool each day, their first task after hanging their coats was to work. The work routine had the following structure:

1. *Initiate: Hang up coat.*

   Matt's first task, after hanging up his coat, was to check his calendar and pick up his transition cue (3" x 5" card with drawing of a table).

2. *Prepare*:
   - *Move* to work area.
   - *Place transition cue* in pocket.
   - *Locate and put place* mat on table.
   - *Pick up mini-calendar* (the strip of colored symbols).

3. Perform; conduct essential steps:
   - *Check symbol for first task*. Match to container.
   - *Take container from shelf.*
   - *Place container on the X* on the left side of the place mat.
   - *Remove work* and place on WORK area.
   - *Complete work.*
   - *Return work to container.*
   - *Return container* to appropriate location.
   - *Slide clip down* the laminated strip to the next symbol.
   - *Match next symbol* to container.
   - *Continue* until all tasks are completed—the clip is at the bottom – no more symbols.

(continued)

Figure 18.2. Sample: Work System for a Young Child (*continued*)

4. *Terminate* (Return last container to shelf).

5. *Transition* (Return mini-calendar (strip) to pocket).

6. *Solve problems* (Need help, drop material, someone blocking access, peer sitting too close).

7. Communication/Interaction opportunities (Ask peer or adult for help, ask for break, ask peer to move).

8. *Make choices* (Location at table, opportunity to select basket work for free time).

Variations and adaptations made to accommodate Matt's needs

1. *The mini-schedule and the amount of work* in the containers was controlled so the tasks were very short. Matt's containers were placed relatively close together on the shelf. Length of tasks and the location of containers were gradually extended.

2. *Reflective listening strategies, contingencies, and assistance* to complete tasks quickly kept Matt's stress at an optimum level (Chapter 15).

3. *Brief breaks* to release tension were offered as needed. Breaks were taken in Matt's quiet area, with an opportunity to jump on the mini-trampoline.

Phase 3. Work independently at a work station

This phase was initiated two weeks after Phase 2.

Materials/Structure

- *A small desk in a quiet area of classroom*
- *Shelf over the desk*
- *Materials and mini-calendars* organized as in Phase 2
- *Four containers, placed on the shelf,* containing familiar and easy tasks

Procedures

This routine was initiated when indicated on Matt's individual calendar. The work routine was identical to that listed in the essential steps for Phase 2.

Variations

- *Materials are rotated each day and the sequence of symbols on the strip are changed.*
- *Introduce new toys and manipulative materials periodically in this setting.*
- *Introduce functional classroom jobs* (watering flowers, helping to prepare the snack, feeding the fish). These jobs were illustrated with a sequence of line drawings in a cartoon-strip format. The job strip and the needed materials were placed in a container to be performed as indicated on the job strip.

The Instructional Plan

An instructional plan for teaching a routine includes the following nine steps (see the reproducible Routine Planning Form 13.1, page 195):

1. A description of the purpose of the routine

2. A list of each step of the routine, from the signal to initiate, through termination and transition to the next routine

3. Identification of the *natural cues* for each step and the *natural prompts*, if any

4. The adaptations (visual) to support the learner and lead to independence

5. Identification of the *reinforcers* that occur naturally in the context of the routine and a plan to include others as necessary

6. A plan for incorporating the variations (different settings, people, problems)

7. A plan for introducing the new routine to the student

8. A plan to monitor progress and problems

9. Evaluation and refining

Note: Only the natural prompts are specified in the plan. Added artificial prompts are not specified in advance because they will vary to match the situation or need at the time to prevent an error and ensure fluent movement through the routine.

Design Adaptations to Support Independence

Adaptations are needed when the learner's abilities do not match the demands of the event. The support team may know the learner well enough to predict the steps or components of the routine that will most likely be troublesome. The Checklist for Assessing Environmental Demands (Form 5.3) is helpful to address both the sensory demands of the environment and the processing and skill demands of the activity. Adaptations and support systems, usually visual references, need to be designed for use during initial instruction. Some learners will need a system to provide support through most of a routine, while others may need support in only one or two steps.

Adaptations most often needed to support participation are those that help the learner to:

1. *Clarify the meaning or purpose of the routine*

   Initiating a new event or routine with a clear description of its purpose is a key factor in continuing effort. This information can be provided via a checklist or sequence chart. The illustration below shows a recipe format that simply identifies the purpose of a cooking event—to make and eat scrambled eggs.

2. *Recognize natural cues*

   Line drawings, tape lines, or color coding are three of the many ways cues can be highlighted.

3. *Prepare, complete, and terminate the basic steps of a routine*

   Cue cards and checklists are effective references.

4. *Maintain appropriate behavior or work quality and speed*

   Various visual and/or concrete self-monitoring systems can be devised that the learner can manage independently (including checklists, counters, and timers).

5. *Solve potential problems*

   Cue cards and additions to existing communication systems are often helpful. Generally, situations must be engineered to provide many opportunities to practice identifying and solving problems.

6. *Communicate and interact effectively*

   It is generally necessary to expand and adapt existing communication systems. Cue cards and sequences of line drawings (as in cartoon strips) are also helpful.

7. *Make decisions and choices*

   Preparing a T-chart (see the illustration) is one way to clarify choices and decisions.

8. *Identify the end or completion of a routine*

   The physical arrangement of materials, checklist, or a sequence card can clarify the end of a routine.

9. *Transition to the next event*

   Checklists and maps can provide visual references to manage transitions. Transition cues are especially helpful.

10. *Several problems can be addressed in a single, well-designed calendar,* communication system, or checklist.

Sometimes adaptations can carry over from one routine to another. Adaptations are inserted during the initial instruction of a new routine or task, and may not be needed once the routine is familiar. Other adaptations, such as communication systems, calendars, and cue cards, may always be required. But this is a pretty normal situation—most of us use appointment books, grocery and to-do lists, maps, and any number of visual tools.

See Figure 18.3 for a sample routine to help one young man participate in an art class. See Figure 18.4 for a sample of the art project plan that supported his participation. The illustration below shows a notebook system that integrated several of his visual adaptations. Adaptations were added to complete the transition routine plan introduced illustrated in Figure 13.2 and completed in Figure 18.5.

Figure 18.3 Sample: Routine Planning

This planning form illustrates an art class routine developed for a ninth grade student who could read and communicate verbally. See Chapter 13, page 190 for a description of the routine planning process.

Routine Planning FORM 13.1

Adapted with permission from *Project QUEST Inservice Manual* (Falco et al., 1990)

Student: _____ Date: _____

Goal/Purpose of Routine: Participate effectively in 9th grade art class without constant verbal directions

Settings: Art classroom

Component	Natural Cues/Prompts	Skills/Sequence of Steps	Adaptations
Initiate	1. Schedule indicates time for art class	1. Find classroom.	1. Set up notebook system: • Written schedule on cover; • Map of school with classrooms labeled also on cover; • List of conversation topics inside cover; • Cue card for solving problems inside cover
Prepare/Perform	2. In art class 3. Project folder in hand 4. Folder open 5. Teacher asks for attention 6. Folder open on desk with directions in view	2. Get folder with project directions. 3. Take folder to assigned work area. Open folder. 4. Check folder, assemble and set up supplies. 5. Sit appropriately and follow directions as teacher explains. 6. Follow the sequence of listed steps to complete.	2. Prepare folder that includes daily project directions, materials, and sequence of steps to completion. Folder is always placed in specified location. 3. Assigned seat near stable, capable peer model/mentor. 4. Art supplies, materials, storage area clearly labeled. 5. Special instructional needs: • Review directions with student individually after others begin working. • Specify whether project to be done by end of class or carried over. If carried over, show how to mark stopping place on checklist. • Model any new processes. • Model and check for safe tool use • Clarify pacing (Circle step number, and say, "By 10:20, finish this step").
Terminate	7. Teacher alerts class that bell will soon ring 8. Project completed or stopping place marked on checklist	7. Work quickly to finish project or complete the step. (If not completed, mark stopping place to complete next day.) 8. Follow termination procedure, put materials and project away. Clean area.	
Transition	Final bell rings Folder/materials away	Check area and materials. Is folder put away? Check schedule and map • Move to next class	

FORM 13.1 (page 2 of 2)

Student: _____ Date: _____

Component	Natural Cues/Prompts	Skills/Sequence of Steps	Adaptations
Solve Problems	9. Folder or materials not where supposed to be 10. Materials gone 11. Peer sitting in assigned work space 12. Accident makes a mess	9. Locate teacher, raise hand for attention, specify need. • Check cue list for solving problems. • Watch peers for cue to solution. 10. Ask to borrow materials. Use "Please" and "Thank you." 11. Say, "Can I share this space?"; or scan and locate different area. 12. Clean up or ask for assistance.	9-12. Skills listed on the cue card for solving problems are introduced and rehearsed (role played) in individual and/or small group sessions.
Communicate/ Socialize	13. Visit with or greet peers before/after class 14. Need to borrow or share materials 15. Comment or acknowledge peer's comments about work	13. Use small talk; or, if time, check peer's interest and negotiate topic. 14. As above in item 10. 15. Acknowledge and/or give compliment about work. • As leaving, say, "See you later" or other natural comment to teacher or peer.	13-15. Use of communication cue card is introduced and rehearsed in individual or small group. Skills include: • Small talk • Negotiate topic. ("What do you want to talk about?" or, "I'd like to talk about . . .") • Give and acknowledge compliments. • Share and ask for materials
Make Choices	16. Choice of colors or materials 17. Choice of project (initially, not more than two options)	16-17. Scan and select in timely manner.	16. Options listed on direction sheet; samples to look at 17. Practice making choices in social skills group and in other natural routines.
Self-Monitor	18. Check quality/neatness of work and work area 19. Pace work to complete at specified time	18. Scan area periodically to clean up any mess. 19. Work steadily, following checklist. • Observe peer for pace of work	18-19. Note on Direction sheet (checklist) only if problem occurs.

Figure 18.4 Sample: Visual Adaptation to Support a School Routine

These directions are part of the folder system supporting an art class routine.

Art activity: Silk screen painting—Christmas cards
Quantity: 5 Christmas cards
Materials needed: 5 sheets of paper, screen with frame, roller, ink, drying rack
Directions:

1. Get materials from silk-screen shelf.
   - Choose color of paper.
   - Choose different color of ink.
   - Choose screen pattern with frame.
2. Put materials on your work area:
   - Paper
   - Ink and roller
   - Screen and frame
   - Rack
3. Listen and watch while the teacher demonstrates the project.
4. Insert paper in frame (as the teacher demonstrated).
5. Roll roller in ink and then over screen from left to right.
6. Remove paper from the screen.
   - Put it on the drying rack.
7. Repeat steps 4, 5, and 6 until you have 5 cards finished.
8. Wash roller, screen, and your hands.
9. Put materials back on silk-screen shelf.
10. Get ready for the next class.
    - Talk with friends until it's time to leave.

Identify the Natural Reinforcers

The effort to focus attention, initiate, and participate effectively requires a tremendous amount of energy (Cesaroni & Garber, 1991). Unless the effort leads to a meaningful goal or has a reinforcing effect, the learning rate, motivation, and participation decreases. Each routine must be examined to identify the naturally occurring reinforcing events and to ensure that they occur at a rate to maintain motivation and highlight the critical effect of the effort.

When the natural reinforcement does not occur at a rate to match ability to focus effort or is not powerful enough to maintain effort, the routine will need adaptations. Strategies for maintaining effort include:

■ Inserting short, reinforcing breaks,

■ Use of contingency statements to refocus attention on progress toward a reinforcer, or

■ Providing encouragement and unexpected assistance to reach the goal faster.

Any added reinforcement must be varied (to prevent dependence) *and subtle* (to prevent distracting attention from the natural cues and the fluency of the routine). In general, *avoid using food and artificial verbal reinforcement.* However, providing calm encouragement intermittently during a period of persistent effort, or an enthusiastic but naturally worded compliment at the *conclusion* of a particularly difficult step, can be very important. ("Wow! You worked hard and you got it done" or "Good job! Give me five!")

Figure 18.5 Sample: Routine Planning

This routine was developed for an 11-year-old student who had difficulty following bus rules, going directly to his classroom, and starting the day's activities.

This transition routine does not end until the learner is engaged in the next major activity.

Routine Planning   FORM 13.1

Adapted with permission from *Project QUEST Inservice Manual* (Falco et al., 1990)

Student: _____ Date: _____ September 25 _____

Goal/Purpose of Routine: _Independently transition from home to school on bus and engage in the first school routine_

Settings: _Sidewalk in front of house, bus, from bus to front door of school, hallway, classroom_

Component	Natural Cues/Prompts	Skills/Sequence of Steps	Adaptations
Initiate	1. Bus stops at house. Door is open.	1. Pick up backpack and move to bus.	
Prepare/Perform	2. At bus step. (Natural prompt: Driver waves checklist) 3. In bus with checklist in hand. 4. On seat. 5. Bus stops at school, door opens, kids get up and walk out door. (Natural prompt: Kid behind pushes to keep moving) 6. Line of kids to front door of school and entering school 7. Inside hall 8. At locker—transition cue (TC) on door	2. Enter and pick up checklist from driver. 3. Scan seats. Select a seat. Sit. 4. Fasten seat belt. Sit quietly. (The bus ride itself is naturally reinforcing.) 5. Pick up backpack and follow kids. 6. Leave checklist with driver. Follow kids through school door. 7. Locate locker. 8. Open locker. Stow coat, etc. Pick up transition cue (TC)	2. Prepare checklist that includes: • Bus rules • Behavioral expectations • Steps of relaxation/self-talk routine 2a. Introduce and use as instruction begins 7. Locker highlighted with symbol for favorite professional sports team on door. (Symbol serves as natural reinforcement for getting to locker because student enjoys looking at it.) 8. Envelope fastened inside locker door holds transition cue (TC) to carry to calendar in classroom. (TC = Name written on 3"x5" card.)
Terminate	9. TC (transition cue) in hand (TC is an adapted prompt to remember destination.) 10. At calendar 11. TC (transition cue) for first activity in hand	9. Take TC to calendar in classroom. 10. Place TC in appropriate location. Review events on calendar. Pick up TC for first activity. (The calendar review process is naturally reinforcing.) 11. Move to first activity. Place TC in specified location	9. Envelope beside calendar with name on outside, to hold TC. • Individual calendar prepared - Calendar review process developed 10. Envelope on end of shelf beside first activity for TC. Note: First activity is a familiar and pleasant activity to serve as natural reinforcer. Once the routine is familiar, the opportunity to complete each step is generally reinforcing.
Transition	(No additional steps to this transition routine required)	(The first activity should be a familiar and pleasant activity to serve as a natural reinforcer.)	

FORM 13.1 (page 2 of 2)

Student: _____ Date: _____

Component	Natural Cues/Prompts	Skills/Sequence of Steps	Adaptations
Solve Problems	12. Someone in favorite seat 13. Someone teasing 14. Can't find coat/bag to leave bus 15. School door closed 16. Locker won't open 17. Too much noise	12. Find another seat. Sign/gesture, "Can I sit here?" 13. Laugh/sign: "You're funny!" and/ or use relaxation/self-talk skills. 14. Search for belongings. Ask for help 15. Open door and walk in. 16. Find appropriate helper. 17. Find ear plugs and insert.	12-16. Engineer opportunities to practice solving problems 13. Relaxation and self-talk, taught and expanded in individual and small-group settings 17. Obtain spongy ear plugs; rehearse use in all settings where noise is a problem
Communicate/ Socialize	18. Peers or staff greet (on bus/in school) 19. Sitting beside peer on bus 20. Communicate to solve above problems	18. Return greetings, sign "Hi!" or "Good-bye." 19. Share sports magazine 20. Use communication system to solve problems noted in items 12, 13, 14, 16, and 22	12-22. Communication skills introduced and strengthened in small groups • Backup communication system needed in settings where others do not sign
Make Choices	21. Select seat partner 22. Select topic of conversation listed on cue card	21. As in item 12, above 22. Check topic cue card to select	21. Be sure magazine or comic book is available 22. Prepare cue card to select topic of conversation
Self-Monitor	23. Monitor behavior on bus 24. Monitor stress level from bus to first activity in school	23. Refer to checklist 24. Use relaxation routine	

Plan the Variations

For true independence, instruction must be provided to manage the problems and varied situations that may occur as the routine is carried out in the natural setting. Determine which situations must be arranged to provide opportunities to practice solving problems, making choices, and socializing. If the routine will be used in multiple settings, schedule and set up these opportunities in all or a sample of those settings.

Prepare the Monitoring Plan

Three forms are included to record the data and monitor different aspects of the instruction:

1. *The Routine Data Form 18.1* can be used to monitor the amount and kind of instructional support (i.e., prompts, adapted cues) required to complete a functional routine successfully. Note the space for entering your code to indicate the type of assistance or cues provided (p=point, b=block, v=verbal, etc.)

   This form can be adapted to monitor the variations in the routine by taping short sections of the grid to one edge of the data form. These sections list the steps included in the variation and function as overlays to flip over or under as needed. Thus, all the data related to a routine is held together for easy review.

2. *The Routine Feedback Observation Form 18.2* is an adaptation of the What Happened Flow Log, Form 5.4 page 83. This form provides an opportunity for an observer to record the student's performance during the routine, and to record a description of the student's behavior in response to instructional strategies and environmental conditions. This type of data is useful for problem solving.

3. *The Checklist for Evaluating the Routine Plan—Form 18.3* serves as a cue sheet to ensure that every aspect of the routine is considered—both before and after instruction begins.

During initial instruction, you must have your hands free to model and provide quick prompts and assistance. During the first few days of this period, record the data at the conclusion of the routine, noting problems and the refinements or adaptations made as problems were identified. After 2 or 3 days, plan to collect data at least once a week to monitor progress. Should problems occur or progress is unsteady, enlist an observer to use Form 18.2 to pinpoint possible solutions.

Evaluate and Refine

Evaluation is a continuous and ongoing process. Refinements must be made quickly to maintain success and motivation and avoid embedding prompts and errors into the routine.

As a routine or event is introduced and taught, continue to evaluate. When motivation is low, behavior problems increase, errors are frequent, or the learning rate is slow, look for small clues and patterns that indicate why this is occurring. Consider four possibilities:

1. *Some element of the setting, the schedule, or the event is misunderstood,* unclear, or interfering. For example, a sensory issue, a personal problem, or a worry may distract and interfere with effective participation. Review the Checklist for Assessing Environmental Demands (Form 5.3) to help evaluate aspects of environments and tasks to identify the problem.

2. *The purpose or outcome of the routine is either unclear or not valued.*

3. *The steps of the routine, the natural cues, or the adaptations are unclear* or do not match the learner's need.

4. *The activity is too easy, too boring, or too difficult.* (Recall the discrepancies and variable abilities commonly present in autism.)

The two following examples illustrate the process for evaluating and refining the instruction to achieve positive results.

Kim's job was to stack the chairs following parties and assemblies in the gym. He learned the routine quickly, and he worked steadily so he could be at his next job on time. Soon Kim was doing so well that the supervisor periodically left him to work alone. One day, Kim pushed someone out of a chair as he worked. This apparent act of aggression led to a reprimand. A week or so later, when two people had lingered to visit following the assembly, Kim pushed them out of their seats. After these two unpredictable and seemingly unprovoked acts of aggression, school staff members expressed concern for the safety of others.

Evaluate and Refine:

Pushing people from chairs is potentially dangerous and cannot continue. However, isolation without appropriate intervention leads to a larger problem—a cycle of increasing aggression and isolation. To intervene effectively, it is important to know why the action occurred. Following a functional analysis of the problem, there were two hypotheses: Kim felt rushed to get to his next job on time, and he had no way to deal with the situation when people remained seated in their chairs. The staff action plan to prevent recurrence included the following steps:

1. *Modify and reteach the total routine*—not only how to stack up the empty chairs, but how to solve potential such as people still sitting in their chairs.

2. *Refine Kim's communication system* to include a cue card with a message asking people to move to another area. Teach Kim to use the card for solving related problems (e.g., people standing in the way, one or a group of people remaining in chairs), and teach him how to get their attention politely and to thank them.

3. *Relieve time pressures.* Provide assistance to work out a solution with the supervisor for the times Kim might be delayed.

4. *Teach a self-control routine* for stressful problem situations (see Chapter 22).

Kim was able to keep his job. The school staff members learned that he was not aggressive by nature and that his aggressive actions were motivated by information and skill deficits.

The following vignette illustrates the problems that occurred when:

1. *The job was not adapted to the needs of a learner.*

2. *The learner was not sufficiently prepared.*

3. *Well-meaning staff members were not sufficiently trained to provide effective support.*

On the first day of a new job in a local business, Maria screamed and threw her work materials when she got confused and frustrated. Another employee, a friend who had agreed to be a mentor for Maria, quickly came to provide assistance and give Maria a break to calm down. This happened several times during the first few days of the job. When her mentor could not come immediately, Maria would continue to scream until he arrived. By the end of the first week, the episodes were occurring several times a day and lasting longer. Her mentor felt he had failed, and there was concern that Maria might lose the job. A functional behavior assessment was conducted to identify the cause of the problem and determine how to solve it.

Evaluate and Refine:

1. *It was very hard for Maria to communicate with words.* When she was upset, she would forget to try to communicate and simply scream and throw whatever was in her hands as a *reflex response to frustration and lack of more effective skills.*

2. *Because her friend came quickly each time* and Maria was able to stop a frustrating job to take a break, Maria quickly learned *(she was inadvertently taught)* to scream and throw materials. This happened because three powerful reinforcers were provided each time she screamed and threw materials: quick and predictable access to her friend (positive reinforcement), a break (a favorite activity and a positive reinforcement), and an end to frustrating work (negative reinforcement).

3. *When her mentor was sometimes delayed*, the reinforcement was delivered intermittently or on a varied schedule, which actually strengthened the tendency to scream and taught Maria to scream persistently for a longer period of time.

The Modifications:

A job coach with experience in autism evaluated the situation and developed an intervention plan that included the following adaptations:

1. *The work area, the task sequence, and the materials were reorganized to reduce distractions.* A logical work routine was clarified with visual references. Materials were arranged in a logical and convenient order that clarified the amount of work required before breaks. A simple, easy-to-use visual communication system was developed—a small card with two messages: *I need help* and *I need a break.*

2. *Instruction was provided to teach Maria to use the new systems*, refining the plan as a problem became apparent. The coach varied his position and moved away from Maria's work station periodically, remaining watchful so he could prompt to prevent errors and predictably and quickly respond to her use of the communication card. The reorganized task and her ability to communicate reduced frustration. Seeing the work accomplished and break time coming closer became a major reinforcer.

   On the days when Maria's tolerance was low and she seemed less able to focus or complete the allotted work, her work requirements before break were reduced. Her coach was attentive, and while Maria was still involved with her work, he would say, "You are working so hard, you can take an extra break today." Thus, he negatively reinforced her work effort by ending the frustrating work, and the opportunity to take the break prevented potentially ineffective behavior. She learned to return willingly and work productively because the work itself and the outcome of the work (earning money and seeing the work completed) were now reinforcing. The next step toward independence was to extend Maria's ability to wait and to ask for and accept help from others. Four strategies were incorporated to address these important and realistic goals:

1. *Vary the time between the presentation of the request card and the acknowledgment.* Initially, the variation was short—only a few seconds. Later, the variation was longer, ranging from an immediate response up to a minute or so.

2. *Provide acknowledgment from a distance.* ("Maria, I see you need help. When I finish with Fred, I will help you.") The verbal acknowledgment reinforces the spontaneous request; waiting will be reinforced when the coach arrives at the workstation to provide the assistance.

3. *Provide an alternate, easy task to do while waiting.* Provide instruction and a visual reference to cue and prompt, so Maria learns to shift from one activity to the other. To reinforce shifting tasks, verbally acknowledge Maria's independence. Develop a point system to provide a delayed reinforcer. Teach Maria to self-monitor and give herself points when she shifts independently.

4. *Provide opportunities for Maria to become familiar with potential helpers and develop reinforcing relationships.* For example, the coach can acknowledge her request for assistance: "Maria, I see you need help, but I need to stay with George. Carla can help you now." Carla responds quickly and helps Maria finish the work quickly so she can take her break.

Prepare the Learner

Story procedures are described on Chapter 14. Review Chapter 14 for information to develop visual support systems.

In most cases, a new routine is introduced in a calm and familiar setting when the following information is provided:

- Clarify the purpose and meaning of the routine with visual references—a story, a chart, a checklist. Highlight the value of the outcome or product at the completion of the routine.

- Draw attention to the natural cues and the sequence of actions highlighted by the visual reference (checklists and picture strips). Label objects and materials involved in the routine if appropriate.

- It is important to clarify:

  - When the routine will be initiated (clarify by placing a note on the individual calendar),

  - Where the routine will be performed, and

  - Whether ultimately the routine will be performed independently.

Provide Instruction

The following instructional sequence is designed to:

- Reduce the stress of a new experience
- Ensure that the routine takes on the intended meaning
- Avoid dependency on others to provide verbal cues or directions
- Increase the learning and generalization rate

Initial Instruction

Initial instruction generally occurs in the natural setting. *The goal for this first phase of instruction is to complete the routine fluently without errors so the natural cues are closely associated with the correct responses.* Movement through the following phases should be quite rapid to prevent boredom and to avoid developing rote routines.

Video Modeling Strategies are discussed in Chapter 22.

Phase 1. Model the Routine.

Model the routine once. Provide a running commentary to describe the objects and actions. Make references to the checklist to highlight the natural cues for each step. Review the discussion of parallel talking (Chapter 22). This phase may not be necessary if the learner is already familiar with some parts of the routine. This phase would be omitted in teaching some personal care routines. Video modeling could also be effective.

Phase 2. Conduct the Routine Together.

After modeling the routine once, engage the learner in the flow of the routine. Provide opportunities for active participation—to hold materials and to assist or complete some of the steps. Continue the commentary, highlighting the natural cues and visual references. Provide assistance to prevent errors.

- Naturally reinforce active participation and cooperation.

- Refine the routine or the adaptations if a problem is obvious at this stage.

Phase 3. The Learner Conducts the Routine.

After partially participating in the routine two or three times, say, "Now you know the routine. You can do it alone. I'll help you when you need it. I will stop talking so you can think."

- Stop the commentary and avoid verbal directions and prompts.

- Remain near to provide other subtle prompts (Chapter 13) and to prevent most errors. If an error should occur, use an effective correction procedure (Chapter 13).

- Remind the learner how to ask for help and how to use an adapted communication system, with gestural prompts.

- Vary the aspects of instruction that are not part of the task (that is, the prompts and the position of the instructor) as described in Chapter 13.

- Evaluate and quickly refine the routine, the adaptations, or the organization of the space if problems occur during this stage.

Expand Instruction to Increase Independence

This phase of instruction begins after the routine is quite familiar, but not yet firm. The goal of this phase is to increase flexibility and independence in the variety of situations or settings where the routine will be required: To solve problems, make choices, monitor performance, communicate, and socialize within the context of the routine.

- Set up situations to practice skills needed to manage the range of potential problems, choices, or social opportunities. When the instruction for these new skills is embedded into a familiar routine, the motivation to complete the routine reinforces the effort (Goetz et al., 1985; Haring et al., 1987).

- Move away but stay close enough to cue and assist with the new demands until the learner is able to seek help when needed.

- Errors that occur at this stage provide a context for learning that everyone makes mistakes and mistakes can be corrected.

- Expand the routine and contexts systematically to include different people and the range of settings.

- Evaluate and refine or modify elements of the environment or the systems. Probe to determine whether adaptations or visual references need modifications.

Expanded Applications

Although the same basic planning and instructional steps are involved in teaching most other functional routines, some adaptations are generally necessary to match the requirements of a specific routine, settings, and/or the needs of a specific learner. The following section describes some specific adaptations that may be required for teaching calendar use and specific work routines.

Calendar Routine

Use of an individual calendar involves a mini-routine that serves as a bridge between one completed routine and the next routine. The calendar symbols serve as natural cues for the initiation of the next routine. The calendar routine occurs during the transition component, beginning at the termination of one routine (activity) and ending with the initiation of the next routine. Once the individual schedule and calendar system are developed (as described in Chapters 12–14), the instructional plan is developed.

1. Develop the calendar routine.

2. Design the variations.

3. Develop the visual supports.

4. Organize the daily review procedure.

5. Prepare the learner.

Develop the Calendar Routine

See Figure 18.6, a calendar routine designed for Jeff. This routine was initiated each day when Jeff arrived in the kindergarten classroom. Note how the calendar routine is embedded between each of the daily activities.

Design the Variations

Several variations are considered in planning the calendar routine.

1. *The learner needs to experience the total sequence* of the routine several times rather quickly. Consider the following adaptations for the first day of instruction:

   - Schedule activities that are familiar and easy, to prevent stress associated with instruction of the new routine.

   - Select activities that can occur near the calendar.

   - Keep the activities short.

2. *Identify and plan situations* for making choices, solving problems, and socializing. Develop self-monitoring procedures to incorporate as appropriate.

3. *Plan expansion steps* that transfer calendar skills to other settings (for example, to move from the calendar to other rooms or buildings). Incorporate

Figure 18.6 Sample: Calendar Routine for Jeff

1. **Initiate**
   At the conclusion of the arrival routine when coat is hung up:
   - Pick up transition cue card from pocket mounted over coat hook.

2. **Prepare**
   - Carry card to calendar.
   - Place card in designated pocket.

3. **Perform essential steps**
   - Review calendar with interpreter.
   - Pick up symbol card for the first activity.
   - Carry card (transition cue) to the location of the activity.
   - Place card in designated location.
   - Follow the activity routine through to termination.
   - Pick up transition cue card to return to calendar.
   - Carry card to calendar.
   - Place transition cue in designated location.
   - Pick up symbol card for the second activity.
   - Continue as above throughout the day to the termination of the last activity.
   - Return last transition card to designated area near the calendar.

4. **Terminate**
   - Pick up the symbol indicating time to go home.
   - Carry to designated location near coat.

5. **Transition**
   - Place card in pocket.
   - Put on coat and pick up bag.
   - Leave room.
   - Begin travel routine.

6. **Solve problems**
   - Access to calendar is blocked, container for the symbol is missing, and access to next activity is blocked.

7. **Communicate/Socialize**
   - Ask for assistance or direction.
   - Peer greets and asks, "Where are you going?"

8. **Make choices**
   - Choose route to next activity, select activity for break time.

9. **Self-monitor**
   - Complete the calendar routine fast enough to get to the next activity on time.

checklists and mini-calendars to provide support when the learner is away from the calendar for extended periods.

Develop the Visual Supports

The calendar is an adaptation, a visual reference to clarify events in time. Two other visual references may be needed during the instructional period to clarify the routine and achieve independence at a faster rate:

1. *Transition cues* to support movement to and from the calendar. Determine the type of transition cue and a plan for managing the cues.

2. *A sequence card* to highlight the steps of the routine.

Organize the Daily Review Procedure

For the calendar system to have its intended effect, the learner must know what is scheduled each day. Each morning, review the calendar with the learner, noting changes and expectations for any new activities. Make this a friendly, positive, and interactive experience to begin the day. Initially this daily review takes only a few minutes, depending on the learner's attention span and the amount of time and detail included in the calendar.

Introduce the New Calendar System

Before the initial instruction begins, introduce the calendar and the routine. While pointing to the various parts of the calendar system, say, "This is your calendar. See? Your name is here. These pictures (objects, words) show what you will do each day. Let's see what's on your schedule today. First, _____. Then, _____ and _____. Last, you will _____. Then, see this card? It tell you that it's time to go home on the bus. Okay, let's start at the beginning and see how it works. First, you will do _____" (a liked activity). Continue instruction as described in the basic instructional guidelines (pages 302–303).

Personal Care Routines

Although the basic instructional strategies are effective and will need little adaptation for teaching personal care routines, special attention is needed to prevent dependence on another person to deliver verbal directions and prompts. Two strategies are often helpful:

1. *Prepare and use a checklist to explain the purpose and the routine.* Video modeling, social stories, or illustrations in a comic strip format are useful for rehearsal. Rehearse them a few times before beginning instruction. Specify the date they will begin to do the routine. Refer to and/or rehearse with these visual references during the introductory and the initial instructional periods.

2. *After 1 or 2 days of instruction, stop talking.* Instead, use gestures or touch prompts. Point or gesture to direct attention to the appropriate step on the checklist.

School Routines

Develop functional routines and work systems to support performance in academic classes; manage homework; and participate in assemblies, athletic events, parties, and projects. Organize directions, materials, and work in baskets, folders, or notebook systems.

Summary

If the goal is to have students with autism spectrum disorders as independent as possible in the natural community, we must teach all the skills required for independence. This process for teaching functional skills in the context of natural routines is a highly effective strategy for it ensures that the learner has all the information—all the steps—required for independence. The planning process has many steps and initially takes considerable time to complete. But it saves time in the end, as the rate of learning and the rate of generalization to independence requires much less time. The total planning process also decreases; with a bit of practice, the process becomes automatic.

The basic guidelines for teaching in the context of routines can be adapted and applied to a wide range of routines and learners. Even very young children can learn to use visual references that support functional routines. These visual references and work systems will remain constant and familiar, a context for adding change.

As early routines and skills are established, new activities and increasing demands are constantly added to expand competence. As each new element is added, it creates a measure of stress and uneven behavior much like dropping pebbles, one at a time, into a pool of calm water. Initially the water is agitated and disturbed, but the water soon accommodates itself to the disturbance. The center calms, the radiating waves spread out, and the water is calm once again. If too many pebbles are dropped at one time, the disturbance is greater, the pattern does not develop, and the water remains disturbed for a longer period of time.

Adapted with permission from *Project QUEST Inservice Manual* (Falco et al., 1990)

Student: _____   **Routine:** _____

Setting(s): _____

Natural Cues	Correct Response	Date												
24.														
23.														
22.														
21.														
20.														
19.														
18.														
17.														
16.														
15.														
14.														
13.														
12.														
11.														
10.														
9.														
8.														
7.														
6.														
5.														
4.														
3.														
2.														
1.														
Data Code:	Total Independent:													

Student: _____ **Teacher:** _____ **Date:** _____

Activity/Routine: _____ **Setting:** _____

Start time: _____ **End time:** _____ **Observer:** _____

Time	Routine & Visual Adaptations	What Happened
	1. Initiate	
	2 Prepare	
	3. Core Steps	
	4. Terminate	
	5. Social Interaction	
	6. Opportunities to Communicate	
	7. Make Choices	
	8. Transition	
	Notes	

☐   1.   Is the critical effect or purpose of the routine clearly defined?

☐   2.   Will the learner know when or how to initiate the routine?

☐   3.   Are core steps identified and in the correct sequence?

☐   4.   Are the self-regulatory steps built in?

      ☐   Prepare/get/set up needed materials?

      ☐   Monitor quality?

      ☐   Monitor tempo?

      ☐   Problem solve?

      ☐   Terminate?

      ☐   Transition?

☐   5.   Have enrichment components been identified and embedded?

      ☐   Communication?

      ☐   Make choices?

      ☐   Social interactions?

☐   6.   Are the natural cues for each step of the routine identified?

☐   7.   Are natural prompts identified to support fluent movement through the routine?

☐   8.   Is the natural reinforcement adequate? Will adaptations be needed to maintain motivation:

      ☐   During initial instruction?

      ☐   To maintain independence?

☐   9.   Are adaptations and support systems designed to:

      ☐   Highlight natural cues and prompts?

      ☐   Monitor progress through the routine from beginning to end?

      ☐   Make choices?

      ☐   Communicate?

      ☐   Socialize?

      ☐   Solve problems?

      ☐   Transition from this routine to the next?

☐ 10. Are the variations planned to support generalization?

☐ 11. Other considerations: _____

_____

_____

_____

Kevin's Story—One Mother's Hopes

—Written by Valda Fields, mother of a 13-year-old young man with autism

I hope my son learns the skills that he needs to function at home, at school, in the work place, and in the community.

I wish that school districts had the resources to provide a better functional education, beginning at the middle-school level.

I hope my son learns appropriate social skills to help him at home, at school, in the workplace, and in the community.

I wish that an effective social-skills program existed for individuals with autism.

I hope my son will have an appropriate place to live when he leaves my home.

I wish there were more community-living options available for individuals with developmental disabilities.

I hope my son learns to enjoy community activities with people who are not family members.

I wish that more people would persevere in their relationships with individuals who have autism, so that lasting friendships could result.

I hope my son learns problem-solving skills needed to successfully function at home, at school, at work, and in the community.

I wish I could foresee the problems that he will encounter, so that training could begin now.

I hope my son's program achieves an adequate "mix" of academic and functional skills.

I wish that we could better see the fine line between the two.

I hope that my son's innocence and naiveté don't make him a victim as an adult.

I wish that we could bottle this innocence and naiveté and pass it out generously. If we could, the world would be a much better place in which to live.

Emotional peaks and valleys: Experiencing adolescence with my son who has autism

(An update, 8 years later—Kevin is now 20 years old.)

It's nearly 10:00 PM. I am in my bedroom with the door locked. Kevin is on the other side of the door screaming for me to open it. When I tell him that I need to take a "time-out," he rages and shoves his fist through the door. Now, the words of the developmental disabilities case manager come rushing into my head, "Valda, if it happens again, you need to call the police!" My hands shake as I punch 9-1-1. I tell the dispatcher that my autistic son is out of control and that I do not feel safe.

The minutes seem like hours as I wait for the police to arrive, and I can't help but wonder how we got to this place. Kevin has come much further than I ever dreamed he would. He just graduated from high school where he participated in a Life Skills Program. He now possesses the skills that he needs to tend to an apartment, access the bus system, and hold down a "paid job." So what is the problem? Kevin has known that he has autism since he was in the fifth grade. Until now, he seemed fine with it. In fact, when he was 13 years old, I asked him, "Kevin if you had the choice of having autism or not, what would you choose?" He quickly replied, "Oh Mama, if I didn't have autism then I couldn't make my noises!" The difference is that until now, Kevin did not see his autism as a limitation. Now, he realizes that some friends will be going away to college while he will need to stay here! He begins to talk over and over again about wanting to go away to college, and over and over again I tell him that he can't because he does not have a "regular diploma" and that he needs extra help.

As the days pass, anger builds up inside of Kevin like a pressure cooker that frequently needs to "blow" excess steam.

As I stood in my bedroom waiting for the police to arrive, I realize that my son had begun the process of mourning the fact that he has a disability.

It is now 2002 and a lot has happened since that awful night. Kevin takes medication for depression and another to control his rages. He sees a counselor who is trying to get him to move more quickly through the steps of mourning (he is "stuck" between denial and anger most days, but, true to the inconsistencies of autism, he actually talks calmly about having autism on other days!)

Kevin lives in an apartment with a roommate who does not have a disability. He works part time at a local variety store.

Since his autism will not allow him to see that many other people have challenges to overcome, I believe that it will be a while before Kevin accepts his disability and is ready to move on. When he does, it will be exciting to see how far this truly remarkable human being will go.

Concepts, Rules, and Academic Skills

The impact of the unique learning differences in those with autism spectrum disorders on the development of language concepts, communication and social skills, and the ability to think logically and solve problems cannot be overstated. Jim Sinclair, at age 27, wrote his personal story in which he explains his own learning and thinking problems and abilities—a few of his observations are quoted below.

> "Being autistic does not mean being unable to learn. But it does mean there are differences in how learning happens. . . . [What I think is most] frequently overlooked is that autism involves differences in what is known without learning, . . . gaps between what is expected to be learned, and what is assumed to be already understood. Even when I can point to the gap and ask for information, . . . my questions are usually ignored, treated as jokes, or met with incredulity, suspicion, or hostility. . . . People become impatient when I don't understand things they think I'm "smart enough" to know already or to figure out for myself. . . . Assumptions that I know things which in fact I don't understand often lead directly to conclusions that I can't learn things which in fact I already know. . . . No one guessed how much I understood, because I couldn't say what I knew. And no one guessed the critical thing I didn't know, the one missing connection that so much else depended on: I didn't communicate by talking, not because I was incapable of learning to use language, but because I simply didn't know that was what talking was for. Learning how to talk follows from knowing why to talk—and until I learned that words have meanings, there was no reason to go to the trouble of learning to pronounce them as sounds. . . . I had no idea that this could be a way to exchange meaning with other minds." (Sinclair, 1992, pp. 295–296)

Although Jim describes only his own experience, it is likely that many others with ASD, who are not able to explain their problems, share this experience to some degree. Many parents and teachers have reported that it is often the small missing detail or piece of information that makes the difference between understanding and not understanding. Until there is data to prove that Jim's explanation does not hold true for other learners, the strategies in this chapter are based on the following assumptions:

- One cannot assume that those with autism will automatically learn all the complexities of language meaning by trial and error, from simply hearing it in the context of the natural environment.

- Traditional language-development programs and strategies, while helpful, are not totally adequate because they assume that the child will learn some of the most basic lessons without instruction.

- One never knows which concepts and rules are misunderstood or not fully understood until there is a problem. Learners are either unaware of their erroneous or limited understanding and perspective of an issue, or they cannot ask (or at least they rarely ask) the appropriate questions for clarification. Even if they do ask, often their message is ignored, or perhaps the form of the question is not understood.

Without full and accurate meaning, the language is interpreted and used literally and sometimes erroneously (or eccentrically), based on the individual's own perspective of the world. The gestalt learning style, literal interpretation of information and an inability to see another person's perspective, affects learning and functioning in many unexpected ways. It is obvious that exploratory learning strategies, so effectively used in early childhood programs, are counterproductive when used in programs for those with autism. In fact, these exploratory strategies frequently result in misinterpretations and learned errors.

Two types of strategies are described in the first part of this chapter: informal strategies used as an ongoing part of natural daily life and formal strategies used to systematically teach concepts so they can be used more flexibly in a broader range of situations. These strategies that can be adapted to match each individual's unique needs are as important, perhaps more important, for those who have Asperger's syndrome as for those who are lower functioning.

Informal Strategies

Model Language Use

Learners need to hear and understand the language before they can be expected to communicate with language. They must hear and understand the language to function effectively in the world where others are speaking. The following strategies provide the language model paired with visual references to clarify meaning. For those with auditory processing problems, highlight words and word meanings by making your voice more vibrant—adding vocal emphasis. When language is enhanced, both communication and literacy will be enhanced (Koppenhaver, Coleman, Kalman, & Yoder, 1991). See also Chapter 15 for using parallel talking and reflective listening strategies to match the sound of the words—the language—to every day meaningful feelings and activities.

Labeling Concepts—Four Activities

Spoken and written words are symbols of real things and ideas that allow information to be shared. This is an abstract, complex, and fundamental concept that most young children learn without being taught, but one that must be taught to most learners with autism. Some of the fundamental language concepts that need emphasis are:

1. Everything has a name. You can speak and write the name.

2. Everything can be represented in different ways. ("This is a _____. This is the word for _____. This is a toy ___. This is a picture of _____. This is a drawing of _____.")

3. A word or visual symbol can represent a single thing and relate to something bigger. ("This is a game. These are the parts of the game. This is a drawing of the game. A drawing of a game can mean, 'It's time to play the game.'")

4. Words are powerful. They help you get the things you want.

These basic concepts can be reinforced through the following four activities, which offer multisensory experiences so necessary for most challenged learners.

Activity 1. What's its Name?

Purpose: To teach that everything has a name, and names can be written down

Materials: 3" x 5" cards, black felt marker, tape—sticky notes are easier but less stable

Setting: Natural home or school setting

Procedure: Move about the room with the learner, stopping at various places to name and label furniture, objects, or other features. For example, stop at the door and get down to the learner's eye level. Place your hand on the door and move it about while saying, "This is a door." As the learner watches, quickly print the word *door* on a 3" x 5" card and say, "This is the word door. Help me tape the word on the door." Provide assistance as needed. Depending on attention span, encourage the learner to touch, open, or close the door while describing the actions with the door.

Do not insist that the learner say the word, and do not ask questions. This is neither a test nor an exploratory experience. It is not a time to risk a wrong answer and a misassociation.

Activity 2. See What's New.

Purpose: To teach that everything has a name, parts of things have names, and a thing with many parts can be represented by a single symbol.

Materials: A single new game, toy, food, or material on a table; 3" x 5" card; black felt marker—sticky notes are easier but less stable

Setting: A one-to-one context in a natural setting

Sit with the learner, in a conversational position so it is easy to glance at each other. Have the learner sit facing away from any distracting activity in the room. If the learner still is distracted, move to a more private area.

Procedure: With the new material in view (e.g., a new Candy Land game), use a hand gesture to indicate the whole object—not just a small detail of the object. Say,

"This is a game. It is called Candy Land. See the words here, *Candy Land*." Label the different parts of the game while demonstrating the spinner and the markers on the board. Use parallel talk (page 242) as the learner explores the game. If the learner's attention span is sufficient, play the game. When it is time to leave, print the name of the game on the 3" x 5" card (add a line drawing if needed), and say, "These words are *Candy Land*. When this card is on your calendar, it will mean it is time to play Candy Land." Have the learner carry the game to the shelf and place the card in the box of calendar symbols. Schedule to play the game later in the day or early the next morning.

Introduce only one new material and its symbol at a time. Although conversation is appropriate during the session, *do not test or ask questions that might elicit a wrong response.* This whole process can take only a few minutes.

Variation: Write an experience story about using the material (Chapter 14).

Activity 3. What's That in the Mirror?

Purpose: To teach that:

1. Real people, things, and actions are reflected in mirrors.

2. Drawings and printed words represent real people, things, and events.

3. Drawings and printed words help us remember the things we have done

Materials: Full-length mirror, ball, or other favorite toy; 3" x 5" card; black felt marker; notebook

Setting: A quiet area or separate room with *no distracting images that can be reflected in the mirror*. Sit on the floor facing the learner.

Procedure: Play together with the ball. While playing, draw attention to the reflections in the mirror. Point back and forth between the mirror and the actual situation while saying, "See? That's a reflection of you, Jason. And there's the ball, and there I am. You can see us, Jan and Jason in the mirror, playing with the ball." Initially, clarify the name/pronoun match by firmly patting that person's chest or the object in rhythm with the verbalization of their names.

Play for a few more minutes, pausing periodically to look and gesture to the mirror. Stop the play, and quickly draw and label stick figures and the ball as you say, "See? This is a picture of you, Jason. Here I am—Jan. And here's the ball." Label the picture and draw attention to the words and their referents. Continue to play while periodically drawing attention to the mirror, the drawing, and the actual event. After the session, involve the learner in placing the story in a notebook to talk about later.

Variations: Use the drawing later to introduce the same game. "Look at this picture. There is a picture of you, Jason—and me, Jan, and the ball. Let's play ball." Repeat the activity at different times with different objects. Draw pictures and write brief stories of other experiences in other settings without the mirror. Review the notebook periodically. Send copies of the picture stories home to share with parents. These stories not only teach language but become part of a beginning reading program.

JAN   JASON

"WE ARE ROLLING THE BALL"

Activity 4. Let's Make a Picture.

Purpose: To teach that an object has a name and can tell us what to do, and that a drawing of an object also can tell us what to do

Materials: 3" x 5" card, black felt marker, child-sized scissors, tape

Setting: Sitting at a table in a nondistracting area

Procedure:

Phase 1. With the learner watching, tape a small pair of scissors to a 3" x 5" card and print scissors on the card while saying, "This is a pair of scissors. I am taping the scissors to the card. This is the word, scissors. It's time to cut with scissors." Help the learner carry the card, with scissors attached, to the cutting area and place them on the table. With another pair of scissors, assist the learner to cut. After a few minutes, say, "It's time to stop cutting." Put away the scissors and have the learner carry the card, with scissors still attached, back to place in the box of calendar symbols. Use the same symbol in the schedule during the next few days.

Phase 2. On about the fourth day, trace around the scissors with the felt pen and remove them from the card while saying, "Now we have a picture of scissors. It is time to cut with scissors." Have the learner carry the card and scissors to the cutting area and place them on the table. Assist the learner to cut with those scissors. At the end of cutting time, have the learner leave the scissors in the area and return the card to the storage box.

Variations: Repeat the procedure, using other objects.

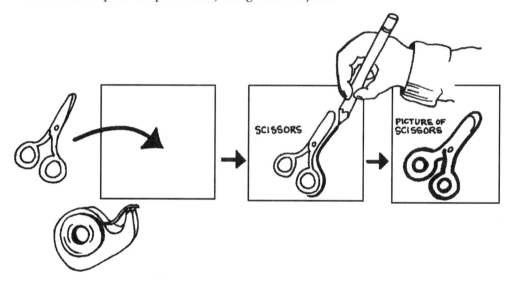

The critical elements of the above strategies are:

1. *The learner must see the object and hear the correct label* at the same time to ensure that they are associated ("recorded on the same tape").

2. *The verbal and printed label of the object or action* must be quickly paired with the action or activity that illustrates its meaning or purpose.

3. *Do not ask questions—this is not a test.* Having to verbalize to answer a question is a totally different kind of task that can prevent the child from making an accurate association between the object and the label. If they give an incorrect answer, they will likely associate the object with an incorrect label.

Formal Strategies for Teaching Concepts

The literalness of thinking and beliefs in autism are such that *unless specified, a concept is assumed to have a single meaning and there's nothing else to add.* For this reason, the instructional sequence for teaching concepts is planned with exquisite detail. This process is based on general case instructional procedures (Albin & Horner, 1988; Horner, Dunlap, & Koegel, 1988). The Concept Planning Guide (Form 19.1) will direct this six-step process. Also see a completed sample of the Concept Planning Guide in Figure 19.1. Again, as with other instruction, when teaching concepts, the initial planning is the most critical part.

In this process, a concept is introduced with an extremely structured process to show the full range of its meanings. Activities are soon added to engage the child in working with the concept.

Plan and Teach for Generalization

Step 1. Identify Concepts for Instruction

Select the concepts for instruction from three sources:

1. *From functional and standardized or criterion-referenced* checklists of basic language concepts.

2. *Concepts that are misunderstood* and trigger problems in daily activities and events.

3. *The abstract concepts and the words that depend on the context for meaning,* that will be required as specific functional and academic skills are taught.

Step 2. Define the Concept

Use the most literal and commonly accepted definitions for concepts (e.g., red is a color, shoes cover feet).

Step 3. Define Related Concepts, Variations, and Contradictions

This is the most critical step in the planning process—to ensure that the meaning is clear and inclusive. Information about related concepts, variations, and contradictions ensures that the instructional examples represent the range of variations. In teaching the concept of red, examples might be selected from each of the variations listed below. (Note: To specify that there are other possibilities, use the terms: . . . and many other things, or . . . there are other ways, etc.)

- Many things can be red, or they can be other colors.

    Crayons, paints, lips, cars, sweaters, balls, flowers, lights, cows, mosquito bites, apples, cars, lights, and *many other things*

- There are variations (or many shades) of red.

    Not pink, *not* orange, *not* brown, *not* purple, *not.* . . .

- Some shades of red have different names.

    Red-orange, scarlet, cerise, cherry red, poppy red, fire engine red, and many other names

- Some things are part red.

    An apple can be red *and other colors;* scissors can have a red handle; fabrics and pictures can have some red and many other colors; other things can be part red, too.

- Big things and little things can be red, part red, or not red.
- The word red is used in many different ways.

    Red face, red hot, red paint, red tape, red light (meaning stop or warning); *and many other ways*
- There is a word that sounds like red, but it is spelled differently and means something else. The word is *read*. I *read* a book. *(This does not mean that you colored a book red.)*

    Note: It is important to identify these variations before beginning instruction, even for a young child. Naturally, they will not all be introduced at one time. To prevent attaching a very literal and rigid meaning to the concept, the child needs to know that a concept can have various other meanings as well.

Figure 19.1 Sample: Concept Planning Guide

The following illustrates the details that must be considered when selecting instructional examples and planning experiences in natural settings. This kind of planning is designed to prevent misperceptions and lead to broader and more flexible understandings necessary for generalization.

Concept Planning Guide

Concept: Red

Define the concept:	Instructional examples		Natural and/or simulated contexts for generalization	Visual references to clarify details and relationships
Red is a color.	Positive examples ("This is a ____")	Negative examples ("This is not a ____")		

Related concepts:
1. Many things are red:
  • Big things and little things
  • Metal, wood, cloth, paper. . .
  • Things that are hard, soft, rough. . .
  • Toys, tools, flowers, food. . .
2. There are variations of red:
  • Bright, light, dark, bluish, orange-red. . .
3. Some variations have different names:
  • Magenta, scarlet, cherry, fire engine. . .
4. Some things are almost red but not red:
  • Orange, pink, fuchsia, brown, purple. . .
5. Some things can be all red.
6. Some things are part red and other colors, too.
7. Sometimes <u>red</u> has different meanings:
  • Red hair, red cows. . .
  • Red faces—flushing that is not really red—might mean a person is embarrassed, sick, upset, hot, or sunburned.
  • Red lights and red signs sometimes mean <u>warning</u> or <u>stop</u>.
  • There are other meanings, too.
	• little red toy truck
	• red apples
	• big red sweater
	• child's red sock
	• new red crayon
	• long red pencil
	• red book
	<u>Later positive examples</u>
	• red and yellow striped apple
	• red-handled screwdriver
	• multicolored fabrics, ribbon, paper. . .
		(Note: Negative examples must be exactly like positive examples except for color.)
		• little yellow truck
		• green apple
		• big orange sweater
		• child's pink sock
		• new fuchsia crayon
			Highlight and talk about red things seen while:
			• Walking or driving down street
			• Doing laundry (matching, sorting)
			• Cooking, eating, buying food
			• Shopping
			• At paint stores and looking at paint samples
			• Looking at magazines and catalogs
			• Mixing paints for art projects
			• Doing preschool sorting or matching tasks
			• When referring to objects when giving directions ("Bring the red towel"; "Eat the red apple")
				• Create semantic maps.
				• Write experience stories.
				• Draw illustrations.
				• Keep a journal or notes during experiences.
				• Keep a concept notebook for saving visual references.

Step 4. Identify Instructional Examples

Because it is not possible or reasonable to present all the variations and contradictions, select examples for initial instruction that represent the range of attributes, meanings, and uses.

Select positive examples and negative examples. For example, a big, red sweater represents the attributes of size, color, and clothing. A negative example, a big, orange sweater that is an exact replica of the other sweater except in the attribute of color, *is not* red. These negative examples provide information to make fine discriminations.

Note that the word *not* is also an abstract word that must be taught. These instructional procedures help to clarify that concept as well.

Other negative examples for the color red might be a small, red, wooden truck and a replica that is brown; a child's red tennis shoe and a replica that is purple, or a new red crayon and a new pink crayon.

Positive examples that represent other variations might include a long, red licorice stick; a short, orange-red string; a small, soft, bluish-red ball; a sheet of red paper; a large, dark-red book; or a bright-red metal bucket.

Note that just these few examples represent the attributes of big/small, soft/hard, long/short, new/old, cloth, leather, plastic, metal, wood, paper, clothing, toys, tools, containers, and foods. They also include colors that are close to red but not red, and different shades of red.

Shortly after the initial instruction, introduce variations. Add a few objects to represent things that are partially red—a red-handled wrench, a yellow and red apple, or a piece of printed fabric that has red in it.

Step 5. Identify Natural Environments for Instruction and Practice

To ensure generalization to a broader range of situations, apply the concept in many different natural situations. Natural experiences for teaching and experiencing red might include:

- Visiting a paint store to see paint chips and color wheels
- Art projects that involve mixing colors
- Observing traffic signals on the street
- Visiting a fabric store, grocery store, auto dealership, toy store
- Sorting laundry, cooking, eating
- Looking at magazines and catalogs
- Performing preschool sorting, attribute, and other tasks
- And many, many more possibilities

Step 6. Plan and Prepare Visual References

Total communication strategies that simultaneously pair signs with speech are useful when teaching some basic language concepts because the shapes and the movement of the signs are highly graphic. Although signs augment and support the instruction, they are transient and leave no permanent reference.

Permanent visual references that show the gestalt of a concept are most always important for those with autism. There are various ways of organizing ideas and details visually to match the specific qualities of the concept or event to the needs of a specific learner.

Blue — color
— feeling

Blew — wind
— bubbles
— out candles

This visual was developed while summarizing a lesson to clarify the homonym blue/blew. The lesson activities involved going outside to feel the wind, coloring with a blue crayon, blowing bubbles, blowing out candles, and making sad faces while talking about feeling blue.

To extend the example of teaching *red*, the objects themselves are visual and appropriate for the initial introduction and instruction. Immediately following the initial instruction, summarize the information with a chart or semantic map that lists each item under the appropriate categories Red and Not Red. Use a *red* and various *not-red* markers to enter the information. Expand this chart as new examples are discovered. Use a color wheel or mark a chart of paint strips to identify the shades of red and colors that are not red.

BALLS

BASKETBALL   GOLF BALL   BEACH BALL
BASEBALL   FOOTBALL   PLAYGROUND BALL   TENNIS BALL

This chart illustrates the gestalt of the word ball— that the word refers to many different types of round and not-round (football) objects used to play games. Later lessons might include a ball of paper, a gumball, and perhaps the concept of ball used in reference to a dance.

Step 7. Provide Initial Instruction

Activity: Sorting to define the concept.

Purpose: To highlight the critical cues that discriminate this word/concept from other words/concepts; to ensure a clear and accurate association of the word/label with the concept; and to prepare the learner to identify and use the concept in natural daily activities.

Materials: Positive and negative examples, and materials to prepare a visual summary—paper, black felt markers.

In teaching some concepts, prepare charts or other visual references before the initial instruction. In the example of teaching the concept of red, prepare two containers large enough to contain the examples. *Cover all extraneous printing or design* and attach a label to one of the containers that indicates Red.

Setting: A one-on-one context where distracting and conflicting stimulation can be controlled.

Procedure: Model a sorting process while verbalizing the label of each example and placing them in the appropriate container. ("This is a *red crayon*" or "This is not red.") Sort and label quickly so the several examples of each concept is closely attached to the label—the child sees it and hears it at the same time so it can all be "recorded on the same tape."

End the first session by making a chart to summarize the basic concept. Use color on this chart only if teaching a color concept. See the discussion of the problems that occur when using colors on pictured symbols, Chapter 14.

Strategies to facilitate discriminations and prevent learned errors:

1. *Verbally attach the label of the attribute* to the label of the objects (red balloon, a red toy car, a picture of the red book on a table). These basic attribute/concept words are descriptive and clarify the item or the action; they are not a new label for the item. The learner must see that the balloon is always a balloon, but this specific balloon is a red balloon; the red car is not a real car, but a toy; in the picture, it is the book that is red, not the table. *This rule is particularly important for those who are exceptionally literal, for they are not likely to learn this basic fact without instruction.*

2. *Avoid confusing the presentation.* Do not label the negative examples other than to say, "This is not _____." The negative examples are simply not examples of the concept being taught. In the example of *red*, the focus is only on red. If the learner makes an error, simply say, "This is not red" and place the item in the correct container.

3. *Do not ask test questions or guessing questions* ("Is this red?" or "What color is this?") during initial instruction. There are at least three reasons for not asking questions during an introduction.

   - This is a receptive language task; the purpose is to present a quantity of accurate information quickly.

   - Asking a question changes the nature of the task to one that requires discrimination, decision making, and production of a verbal response. This causes delay, potential anxiety, and a shifting of focus from the relevant cues.

   - If the learner gives an incorrect answer, the presentation is no longer clean or clear of conflicting information. In teaching concepts, the rule is: no testing, no guessing. After many experiences with a new concept, create situations in natural contexts for the learner to demonstrate understanding (as when Amy was asked to bring the red sweater, Chapter 16).

Step 8. Expand Instruction

Activity. Student sorts objects to clarify the concept.

Materials. Place a number of objects that represent both the positive and negative examples of the concept mixed in a basket. Prepare two containers (as described previously). Vary the sorting materials a bit each day.

Procedure: Model the sorting process as you say something like: "Let's *sort* these things into these cans. This is a red crayon, it goes in this can (point to the word *red* on the can)—this is *not red*, (as you place it in the other can with no label)." After sorting one or two of each, give an object to the child and say, "Now, it's your turn; you sort them. Put the red things in this can (Point to the label on the can) and put the things that are *not red* in this can."

- Use touch, gesture, or blocking prompts to avoid errors.

Step 9. Expand With Variations

- Capitalize on natural situations to highlight examples of the concept in different contexts and settings.

- Organize and integrate the information from natural experiences with stories, logs, or journals.

- Prepare the learner for planned events by starting a story that describes the context for the coming experience (i.e., a trip to the paint store). Keep writing material on hand when in the community, and record experiences for later review. Complete the story at the conclusion of the event while reviewing the notes.

The following story was written to prepare Maria for a trip to the mall to experience the concept red in a variety of natural situations. Tina, the interpreter, used a red felt marker to make line drawings of the red items. The word *red* was always written with the red marker—other words were written in black. When they returned from the trip, they reviewed the story and added additional information:

> Today Maria and Tina will go shopping. They will see many red things and other things that are not red. When the traffic light is red, they will stop and wait. At Shoppers Mall, they will buy red construction paper, red ribbons, and red socks. They will buy a hamburger and put red catsup on it. They will buy a drink. Will the drink be in a red container?

Variations to Correct or Expand the Meaning of a Concept

More experienced learners are likely to have a great deal of information about a concept, but it may be disorganized, distorted, or limited. Provide assistance in organization. First, assess the learner's present understanding of the concept. Then set up opportunities to experience the corrected or expanded meanings or uses. Incorporate visual references. Place concept stories, charts, and semantic maps in notebooks for later reference and for listing additional meanings.

The following story was written to clarify the various meanings of the word red for an older learner with Asperger's syndrome who was confused by the language in TV documentaries, news, and sports shows.

RED

Red is a color.

Not all red colors look the same. Some reds look almost orange. Other reds look a bit purple.

Most red colors are very bright and intense.

Sometimes red is light. Sometimes red is not so bright.

Insect bites, injuries, and sunburn make parts of the skin look red.

Sometimes people use the word red in different ways.

1. The Red Sox is a baseball team from Boston.

2. "Is my face red" is an expression that means to feel embarrassed. When some people are embarrassed, blood rushes to the skin of their faces and makes them feel hot and look flushed (reddish).

3. When people think there are too many government rules, they say, "There is too much red tape."

4. "Red river" and "red tide" refer to pollutants or some kinds of algae that make the water look almost red.

5. People who were members of the Communist political party or who have Communist-like ideas are sometimes called Reds.

6. Some red signs and some red lights mean to stop and wait. Warning signs are sometimes red. Warnings tell us to stop and think and be careful so something bad won't happen.

7. Another word that sounds like red is spelled r-e-a-d. This word is used to say, "I read a book yesterday," or "I just read the thermometer. The temperature was 85 degrees."

8. The word red is used in other ways, too.

Note: When teaching concepts and rules, add the idea that more or different meanings for the concept or rule are likely to be discovered in the future, and that is OK—"That's life."

Teaching Rules

The strategies for planning and teaching concepts can be modified and applied to teach most types of rules, be they social or academic. The following shows how the considerations and the process for teaching rules are applied to social rules because they are subtle, abstract, and have a great number of exceptions.

Some social and behavioral rules are ineffective because they fail to address the reason for the problem and do not specify what the learner should do. Two problems are particularly common in autism: seemingly simple rules are often interpreted literally and followed rigidly, and the rule is memorized without meaning and echoed. Note the potential problems in the following rules:

- Keep your hands to yourself. Keep your hands down. The literal learner will likely have questions and problems. How do you keep your hands to yourself? Where is down? When do you keep your hands to yourself? For how long? Some learners have virtually quit using their hands as they try to follow these rules literally.

- Don't interrupt. What is interrupt? Don't ever interrupt? What if there is an emergency?

- Keep your feet on the floor. How do you walk with your feet on the floor? Does this mean I cannot kick a football?

- You can't hurt people. What is hurt? (Feelings? Is there pain?) Each of these words is abstract. What hurts people? What is it that I do that hurts people? What could I do to solve my problem without hurting people?

To understand and follow social rules requires: (a) the ability to identify relevant and subtle social cues, (b) understand another person's feelings and perspective and the impact of one's behavior on another, (c) understand the meaning of abstract concepts, and (d) modify a response or generate a new response based on changing conditions. These requirements are not learned automatically in autism, so instruction must be carefully planned.

Assess—To Determine the Need

Before planning begins, assess the problem with interviews and observations to identify the relevant cues and the possible reasons for the problem. Could it be a sensory problem? A misunderstanding? A limited understanding of a concept or a skill/concept deficit? There could be at least six reasons why a learner might have a problem standing in line:

1. The individual fears being hurt by the bumping and shoving.

2. The individual is experiencing overwhelming sensory stimulation from the noise, touching, and closeness of others.

3. There is lack of understanding of the concepts line up and stand in line.

4. There seems to be no reason to stay in line.

5. Waiting is hard, and it is unclear how long to stand in line—once for a few seconds or forever.

6. What do you do while standing in line?

In interviews, learners who are more experienced and verbal often can provide important clues to the problem. They also may be involved in developing the solutions and visual references (Gray & Garand, 1993; Lovett, 1985).

The following examples illustrate the importance of a good assessment before teaching a new rule.

The vocational staff members at the sheltered training center were frustrated and nervous about working with Jason. At age 20, he had no functional communication system, would not stay seated at his workstation, would run out of the room, and sometimes urinated in the workroom. When staff members tried to get him back to the workstation or keep him from leaving the room, he would become aggressive. It was decided that he needed to learn the rule, Stay in your chair. Staff members requested a full behavior assessment when the instruction was not effectively solving the problem.

Observations showed that when Jason got out of the chair, staff members physically returned him to the chair, restating the rule. After this cycle was repeated several times, Jason urinated in the chair. During succeeding observations, Jason slugged the staff member who physically restrained him in the chair and then ran into the hall to the restroom to urinate. An interview with his mother revealed that at home he needed to use the bathroom frequently, and he managed his physical needs independently without asking permission. However, while he was at work, there were several reasons why he needed permission and supervision to use the bathroom. Jason was taught to use a communication card that read, "I need a restroom break." Once staff members learned that Jason's behavior problems were logical and that he would use the communication system consistently, they all were more relaxed.

José's family was frustrated that he never followed their directions. His teacher was invited to observe José at home and show the family how to teach him to follow their rules and directions. To everyone's surprise, the observations showed that José followed his mother's directions 100% of the time. For example, when his mother called the family to dinner and told José to sit at the table, he was in his chair before anyone else, stayed about 2 seconds, and then ran off. None of his family saw him sitting at the table. He was always in the right place to do what he was told but if his parents were not present to help him immediately, he was gone. In this situation, teaching rules and directions would have been both frustrating and ineffective. Instead, his family had to learn how to acknowledge his good behavior and engage him quickly while he was following directions.

Develop the Instructional Plan

The planning process is similar to that for teaching concepts and consists of the following steps:

Refer to Chapters 14 and 22 for examples and references about the use of video modeling. Chapter 14 also contains information about various visual supports including story strategies.

1. *Define the problem.*

   What is the reason for the rule? What is the impact of the problem behavior on others, and how does that impact the learner? Does the problem prevent participation in interesting activities and events? Is the behavior unsafe? What could happen if the rule is followed? (Perhaps others would want to be friends, injury and bad consequences might be avoided.) This information provides the meaning, motivation, and natural reinforcement for following the rule.

2. *Define the rule.*

   Develop a rule that clearly and positively states what the learner is to do and clarifies how to do it.

3. *Identify the natural cues* that indicate when and where the rule is applied.

4. *Define some of the alternatives for when the rule does not apply.*

5. *Develop the visual references*—social stories, charts, semantic maps, cue cards, self-monitoring checklists, videos for modeling (Charlop & Milstein, 1989; Green, 2001), or other strategies.

The Instructional Process

Introduce each new rule with its visual references, in a familiar setting. Role play or rehearse as appropriate. Then, provide instruction in the context of natural routines.

Amy's grandmother had become frail and needed care. Amy's mother was responsible for providing the care every afternoon and evening. Nine-year-old Amy, who accompanied her to the elderly woman's home each day, had to entertain herself during this time. During the first week, Amy was noisy and ran about the house, tugging and pulling at her mother to go home. Her mother enlisted the help of Amy's teacher who assessed the situation, and together they developed a plan to teach two rules: *Play quietly,* and *If you need help go to Mom and take her hand.* The new plan included two major components:

1. Organize and structure the space and the events.

   A space near Grandma's room was organized for quiet play, with familiar and liked toys and activities—cutting, drawing, listening to tapes with earphones, rocking in the rocker, jumping on a mini-trampoline, and a beanbag for a rest time. Playtime was structured with a mini-calendar to reflect a schedule varied to rotate quiet work/play and active play (see Chapter 12 for strategies to structure time). The calendar also specified one or two short visits with Grandma. The calendar and arrangement were similar to the ones Amy used at school.

2. Provide visual references.

   A story was written to answer potential questions—why, what, when, where, how, and then what? (See Story Strategies in Chapter 14.) The story included descriptions of the setting (odors, objects, and sounds) and what Mother and Grandma were doing and how they felt. It described the rules, the mini-calendar, and the things Amy could do quietly during her visits with Grandma (rub lotion on her hands, look at a book together). It also specified the things she could not do. The story was illustrated with a series of simple line drawings and an audiotape was prepared.

Mother introduced the story on Friday. As Mother read, Amy followed the line drawings. On Saturday and Sunday, the story was repeated and the audiotape was given to Amy to use with the pictures. On Saturday, Mother also introduced the mini-calendar and showed Amy how to use it.

While Amy was at school on Monday, her mother set up work and play areas at Grandma's house. After school, Amy carried a bag with her things to Grandma's. Amy greeted Grandma, and her mother showed her how to use her schedule and begin. Amy's first activity each day was to listen to the story tape to review the rules. She was soon able to play quietly. Mother was careful to check in frequently to comment on (R+) Amy's responsibility and to admire her work. The activities were varied each day to prevent boredom. While problems occurred occasionally, Amy was generally independent and comfortable within this flexible routine where she understood the rules.

Academic Instruction

The basic guidelines for planning instruction for teaching routines, concepts, and rules also apply to academic instruction as well. But variations are required to match the type and level of skills or the academic subject being taught. If academic instruction is to be useful and generalized, it must be specifically applied to functional contexts during instruction. The functional academic skills listed in Figure 19.2 are a sample of those that must be addressed to increase every learner's independence.

Figure 19.2 Sample: Functional Academic Skills

Math
- Sorting
- Concepts of quantity, space, and size (big/little, long/short, one/many, full/empty, more/less, same/different, equal . . .)
- One-to-one correspondence and counting objects (not rote)
- Identifying numbers and symbols
- Math operations and calculator use to solve real problems
- Money management—budgeting
- Time and time management
- Measurement and functional fractions
- Other

Reading
- Personal data
- Signs/labels
- Lists
- Fill-in-the-blank forms
- Dials, gauges
- Schedules, tables, calendars
- Illustrated advertisements
- Bills, time cards, receipts
- Alphabetizing
- Map skills—community, state, other
- Technical documents
- Phone books, emergency/community resources
- TV guides
- Menus
- Other

Reading for personal management
- Meal planning, recipes
- Sorting junk mail from important mail
- Refrain from responding to credit card applications and offers
- Modified directions for medications
- Survival words
- Directions for household equipment

Recreational reading
- High interest books and magazines
- Reference materials, use of the library
- Directions for games, electronic equipment, computer programs, model kit assembly
- Other

Writing
- Personal data
- Signature
- Forms
- Lists
- Schedules
- Notes and letters
- Other

Because many of these students, especially those with Asperger's syndrome and high-functioning autism, have an aptitude for math, science, music, the visual arts and sometimes poetry (i.e., David Eastham, who wrote the poetry included in this book), these gifts should be encouraged and higher levels of instruction should be offered. Education in the arts and other fields of special interest often serve as a catalyst for more advanced learning, successful careers, friendships and contributions to society. Temple Grandin's successful career is but a single example of this

(Chapters 2 and 7). Also see *Asperger's and Self-Esteem: Insight and Hope Through Famous Role Models* (Ledgen, 2002).

This next section presents some of the general principles for developing and providing academic instruction that are common to all academic areas. With the space limitations of this book, we expand only on instruction to teach the language arts. However, the same strategies and procedures described in this and earlier chapters can also apply to teaching other subjects.

Figure 19.3 A Study Guide for Content Area Classes

The first four sections of this study guide are completed prior to distributing it to the learner with autism (or to all students in the class). You may use a transparency of the guide to introduce the lesson, and again at the end of the class to summarize the concepts and review the homework assignment for all students.

Study Guide

Date _____

1. Today we will study about:

   •

   •

   •

   •

2. New words:

   •

   •

   •

3. We will do these activities:

   •

   •

   •

4. Materials needed:

5. Summary of concepts:

6. Homework assignment:

Figure 19.4 Use of Variations to Increase Learning Rate

Worksheet A—Addition and Carrying

7	9	5	3	6
+7	+3	+7	+8	+6

2	9	3	8	6
+6	+9	+7	+8	+8

5	8	1	7	4
+5	+4	+9	+6	+9

Worksheet B—Addition and Carrying

```
  9        13       304        8      8 + 7 =
 +1       +38      +  7        6
                              +9


  7        82    11 + 9 =     746       77
 +3        19                  86      +44
           47               +  9
          +63
```

General Principles for Planning Academic Instruction

The selection of skills and strategies must accommodate the needs of the learner, rather than hoping the child with autism will be able to accommodate themselves to more traditional strategies. See Grandin (1995) and Twatchman-Cullen (1995) for more insights into planning and delivering academic instruction.

The following basic principles will assist planning:

1. *Organize and present units of instruction to show the gestalt.*

   Introduce units with semantic maps (Chapter 14) or flow charts of the concepts and major points, skills, and activities. Highlight the purpose or importance of the content. Provide visual references and daily study guides. (See Figure 19.3 and refer to Figure 17.4, showing a visual project plan designed to support one young man in an art class.) Darch and Carnine (1986) describe the use of visual references as advanced organizers of content area material. Other techniques and strategies for organizing instruction in content areas are included in articles by Leverett and Diefendorf (1992). Also see Isaacson (1988), Pehrsson and Robinson (1985), and Perhrsson and Denner (1989).

2. *To promote generalization, use variety in practice.* Variations should be added immediately to show the practical applications of a skill or concept.

   The examples used during practice must show the variations that illustrate the range of applications. Incorporate real-life problems and story problems into the practice activities at an early stage.

When a single application or example is practiced repetitively, it will become a rote routine that stands alone and is difficult to expand and generalize. The two math worksheets in Figure 19.4 illustrate this point. If all the instructional examples are the same, (as in Worksheet A), a learner will assume that the rule or process applies only to one type of problem or situation. When a new application is introduced, the learner approaches the problem as if it requires a totally different rule. When variations or applications are introduced and practiced together (as in Worksheet B), the rate of learning to generalization is increased (Albin & Horner, 1988).

3. *Teach thinking skills, organizational skills, and study skills* to support regular education academic programs. See Chapter 23 for strategies for teaching self-management and problem-solving skills. A notebook organizational system is illustrated on page 347. Other resources include:

   ■ *Bright Start: Cognitive Curriculum for Young Children with Autism* (CCYC) (Haywood et al., 1992). The authors directly address the deficits of autism in the areas of thinking, perceiving, and problem solving. In this cognitive approach, the students participate and collaborate in real-life problems and activities as the teacher models, demonstrates, and discusses the mental strategies involved in meaningful learning. This approach is described in *A Cognitive Approach to the Education of Young Children with Autism* (Butera & Haywood, 1992).

   ■ *Advanced Skills for School Success* (Archer & Gleason, 1992–1994; 4 volumes). The four modules for grades 7–12 are: School Behaviors and Organization Skills, Completing Daily Assignments, Learning from Verbal Presentations and Participating in Discussions, and Effective Reading of Textbooks. This series includes many strategies and activities that can be modified to address the needs of learners with autism of various ages and ability levels.

   ■ *Teach Me Language: A Language Manual for Children With Autism, Asperger's Syndrome and Related Developmental Disorders;* and *The Companion Exercise Forms* (Freeman & Dake, 1997). An excellent resource for teaching social language, general knowledge, grammar and syntax, functional knowledge and written expression, and language-based academic concepts such as sequencing, problem solving, time, and money. The manual includes more than 150 reproducible worksheets.

   ■ Computer-based instruction is also a valuable resource for teaching numerous skills—including academic and communication skills. (See the resource list in Appendix B.)

4. *Plan support.*

   ■ Interpreters *(classroom assistants or mentors)* are often required to introduce the goals, clarify abstract concepts and rules, and assist with hands-on activities and practice. An interpreter can teach and support the study and organizational skills required to manage homework and solve problems related to logistics and interpersonal issues as in Figure 19.3.

   ■ Enlist peers as models, mentors, and friends. One young man could not learn the exercise routines for physical education until a peer stood beside him and modeled the movements. Recruit staff or community members who share the learner's special interests to be mentors (Grandin, 1990).

5. Evaluate and refine to identify and resolve problems quickly.

- Monitor skill acquisition in cooperative learning situations. Ensure that the learner understands the meaning and purpose of each task. Many learners find that participation in cooperative groups is interesting, and these groups provide an important context for learning. However, many learners follow along with the group routine without acquiring meaningful academic concepts or skills.

- Individualize and clarify the goals, objectives, and strategies to accommodate the learner's needs. It is often necessary to modify and clarify the amount and type of practice, as well as the testing and grading procedures for learners in integrated settings. This is an especially important issue for those with Asperger's syndrome who hope to move on to college. It may be necessary for them to take a lighter load of classes even though it may require extra time. It is important for parents, staff members, and the learner, as appropriate, to be involved in making these decisions.

- Ensure that needed visual adaptations and supports are available, used, and updated to match changing needs. Especially when teaching math, the learner needs to see and use concrete objects to represent the concepts and processes—they also need to see it written down (Granden, 1995).

- Include a learning disabilities specialist in the child's support team to help evaluate and resolve instructional problems. These specialists have the training and the resources for selecting and individualizing strategies to solve instructional problems.

Perhaps the three most important elements of any instruction are: (a) keep it visual, (b) actively involve the learner in the processes, using hands-on activities and concrete objects, and (c) use charts and maps to help prepare them for new instruction and to organize and summarize the concepts—to show the gestalt.

Teach Reading, Writing, Spelling, and Language

An Integrated Approach

Although many very young children with autism learn to read, seemingly automatically, without instruction, this reading is often rote and without meaning. Traditional developmental and basal reading approaches have been less than successful when used to teach the language arts to many of these children. Therefore, a more wholistic approach that accommodates each child's unique learning strengths, deficits, and interests should be considered.

Koppenhaver and associates (1991) noted that literacy learning begins with language experiences in infancy and early childhood. This is true for those with developmental disabilities as well as for those developing in a more normal way. Many young children with and without autism learn to read at very early ages without formal instruction to match shapes, recite the alphabet, or know the names of the letters. *In fact, those with autism often learn to read words even though they may not be able to speak. However, instruction in a meaningful context is critical for the words to have meaning* (Pehrsson & Robinson 1985). Greenspan et al. (1998) also indicated that children need an emotional and experiential attachment to concepts and words as a prerequisite for understanding.

Selecting the Curriculum

There are a number of issues to consider when selecting teaching models and strategies for learners who are literal, have difficulty identifying critical stimuli while screening out irrelevant information, and who are gestalt learners. We have to remember that those with autism spectrum disorders are gestalt learners (chunks of information are registered quickly) but they are not gestalt thinkers (they cannot break the chunks down to analyze and develop a meaningful unit.)

When strategies do not match this learning style there will be paradoxical effects—they will likely learn the wrong lessons. A few of these issues are illustrated:

1. *Pictures that represent the sounds of the alphabet* require the student to understand what the picture represents, separate the first sound of a word from the rest of the word, and apply it to other words with that letter. We are in trouble from the beginning.

2. *Approaches that require words to be broken apart*, sounded out, and put back together again are confusing and difficult. Some children virtually change the way they speak. One young man learned to break the word apart into the sounds, but did not understand that he was to put the sounds back together to make a whole word—thus he began to speak in sound chunks. For example: "I w-an-t c-oo-k-ee." This is a very difficult problem to repair.

3. *If the sounds are distorted when taught*, as they often are (i.e., b=buh, d=duh), it is difficult to put these back together to make the real sound of the word (i.e., "duh-o-guh").

4. *Approaches that require repetitive drills* are easy for these children to memorize. Some with autism enjoy the repetition of the routine, but they become rigid and cannot use the skill functionally to decode words. Others dislike the meaningless drills and try to avoid them.

5. *If the structure of the words (or letters) are modified to cue the word* (i.e., to include tiny pictures, tumbling down letters), then generalization to other standard reading materials or transferring to standard printing or writing will be difficult.

Before beginning any phonics or decoding instruction, the learner with autism spectrum disorders must understand the fundamental concepts of language: *That everything and everybody has a name, names are words, words can be spoken and they can be written down, and that words have meaning and can communicate ideas.* They also should be able to identify some written and meaningful words before teaching phonics and decoding skills.

Reference is made to two specific reading programs that integrate visual/cognitive and multisensory strategies to teach reading, language, writing, and spelling skills simultaneously, and that have been used effectively with children who have autism:

- *The Open Court Reading* by Adams et al. (2000) is a structured, research-based approach that integrates phonics, reading, and spelling instruction. The phonics program incorporates pictures that represent the actual sound of a letter that prevents distortion of the sounds. For example: The letter H is symbolized by a person running a race, and is called the "tired runner sound, H, H, H" demonstrated as a very breathy sound. They also have a well-developed approach for teaching the sounds of the letter blends and working with word families. The response cards provide a well-organized visual display, the student hears the sound, sees representations of the sounds, and says the sounds.

■ *The Language Experience Approach,* (Allen & Allen, 1966; Ashton-Warner, 1963) as introduced in Chapter 15 capitalizes on actual experiences and integrates reading, writing, spelling, and language instruction. It also provides the structure and content for teaching word-attack and phonological skills. The success of this experiential, multisensory approach has been documented (Bock, 1991; Flowers, 1990; Shepherd, 1983). The LEA approach is highly individualized and can be modified to match the needs of those with Asperger's syndrome as well as for those with limited or no verbal abilities. In fact, Shepherd reported that these LEA strategies were instrumental in teaching his son with autism to read, write, spell, *and speak.*

The context for writing and reading experience stories can vary from one-to-one to small- or large-group settings. Stories can be written and read at the kitchen table, in a restaurant, at the park, in the classroom, or in the speech or play rooms. They can be written on a multitude of materials—note pads or cards, chart pads, chalkboards, on lined and unlined paper in a rainbow of colors and a variety of textures and patterns; and with pencils, pens, chalks, and markers of various colors. A Polaroid camera for instant pictures also may be useful. Also see Bingham (2000) and three manuals by Olshansky: *Image-Making Within The Writing Process: Crafting Collage Stories* (1998), and *Picture Writing: Fostering Literacy Through Art* (1997).

Strategies for Initiating the LEA Program

Initially, the young learners with autism watch as the interpreter (parent or teacher) says the words and writes the story. The basic strategies for this first stage are described in Chapter 14. Also see Chapter 19 for examples of informal activities for teaching language concepts that incorporate the LEA approach. Once the learner understands that written words are meaningful, you can adapt the activities to increase the child's active involvement to contribute to the stories.

Strategies to Increase Active Involvement

Develop a basic routine for story writing that makes the experience comfortable and predictable. As with other routines, vary it to some degree nearly every day to prevent rigidity. At first, set a specific time and place to write stories. Each story might begin with the day and the date written at the top.

In my classes, the 3- to 5-year-old children sat in a circle at the chalkboard to begin and end the school day with an experience story. The opening activity was a story to prepare the children for the events of the day. The story illustrated here was developed in one session to prepare the class for a trip to the beach. The closing activity was a summary of the events of the day. These stories were copied on paper and sent home so the parents could have a meaningful conversation with their child and the child could see, hear, and read the story several times in several settings and with different people (the basis for skill generalization).

In addition to stories to begin and end a day, stories can be written to prepare for and/or review any experience. One of the most important parts of the process is to draw and label small and very basic figures (Rebus) to highlight the meaning of important words (i.e., names of children, materials) as in the figure on page 209. The following strategies will ensure that the child with autism learns the correct language structures and begins to contribute to the story.

Phase 1: Writing the Story

1. *If the teacher is the author,* model correct language, sentence structure, spelling, and punctuation to ensure that the learner with autism does not learn incorrect structures. Write with the child's developmental level in mind—vocabulary, sentence length, etc.

   - Use sentence starters and expectant pauses as cues to contribute. ("For lunch we had ____; Tony pulled the big red ____.") This strategy is particularly effective if a photograph is available to aid recall. If the learner is nonverbal or a response is delayed, make a quick line drawing, label it, and say, "You can show me what we had for lunch. For lunch we had ____." Help the learner point to the picture. Then quickly write the word in the story.

   - Periodically remind the learner that "It's your turn to talk" or "You will be able to talk later." *If the learner is nonverbal, provide response cards, pictures, or words that the child can present.*

   - In group situations, peers can model and provide assistance. For example, peers take turns contributing to the story. If a learner does not respond in turn, ask a peer to help. ("Mary, tell Tony what we had for lunch.")

2. *If the child is the author, writing or dictating,* use a questioning attitude. ("Did I get it right? Is that what happened? What else happened? Let's see, first, we . . . You can fix it—here's the pencil.")

Phase 2: Reading the Story

1. *Model reading while pointing to the word—then expand:*

   - Have the learner point to the words while you read.

   - Periodically pause and wait expectantly to encourage the learner to read the next word or to indicate that the reading should continue. (Do not pause too long or the flow of the story and attention may be lost.)

   - Have the learner locate words in the text to underline or circle—make it a game.

   - Make mistakes and pause for corrections. Once the learner is familiar with the story, make a few mistakes; teach the child a signal to indicate that an error was made ("Stop!"; raise hand; etc.).

2. *If it is a group story,* have the individual students read their own contributions.

   - Select a child to be the leader. They can ask peers to locate and circle specific words. They can take turns leading the rereading, and select the next leader.

Phase 3: Expand Decoding and Language Skills

1. *Develop a word bank.* As learners demonstrate, while reading a story, that they know a word, write it on a 3" x 5" card and place the card *randomly* in a file box. Say the names of the letters while writing the words, and then

quickly say the whole word ("C-a-t, cat" or "*C-a-t spells cat*"). Use these cards for:

- Sorting activities. Sort by first letter or last letter or by blends or digraphs in different positions (bl, br, sh, th . . .). Sort to make lists of word families (cart, mart, part, start . . .). Read the lists aloud to highlight the common sounds. Write the lists so the students can visualize the word families and associate to the rhyming sounds.

- Play games with duplicate sets of word cards—Concentration, Bingo, etc.

- Use the word bank often. Provide frequent experiences to search for a specific word.

- Introduce the alphabet when there are so many words in the bank that it is frustrating to search for a word. Provide alphabetized file dividers and a printed alphabet strip as a visual reference. The concept and value of the alphabet (the letters in a specific sequence) becomes immediately apparent. Model the filing and search processes. Use parallel talking to provide the language for thinking about the task. With the cards in order, continue adding new words to the file and playing games.

2. *Prepare small word strips of the words in the bank.* Make them 1/2" to 1" high and only as long as the word. Make duplicate words, and gradually expand visual discrimination skills by using different types of paper (some with patterned backgrounds) and different ways of forming letters (a, A. . . .). Use these word strips to teach a number of skills:

- Sort words to teach concepts. Initially, select only a few words to use at any one time, but include three or four duplicates of each word. Place a handful of these word strips on the center of the table to sort into a divided tray. This process not only makes it faster to find words; it also expands the concepts of sorting: (a) that upper- and lowercase letters mean the same thing, (b) letters can be made in different ways, and (c) that the word will mean the same thing even if the background is different. These word strips also can be used for fill-in-the-blank activities and for playing Word Bingo and other games.

- Use the word strips to make new sentences and help the students to learn that the position of the word in a sentence changes its meaning. This strategy also provides an opportunity to check for clarity of meaning. (Does the sentence make sense? *The ball wants the girl/The girl wants the ball.*)

- Include punctuation marks on separate strips.

- Play games with the sentences. For example, take turns forming simple but silly directions for the others to follow.

- Prepare sentence-starter strips with spaces left for the learner to fill in the blanks with words from the word-strip bank.

3. *Develop personal dictionaries* that the students can refer to when writing—add new words when they learn to spell a new word or when they ask for help to spell a word.

4. *Write stories and sentences on the computer.* If commercial computer programs are used, make them interactive by having partners work together and take turns contributing parts of the story—perhaps incorporating the pictures as well.

Integration of the Open Court and the Language Experience programs make a powerful language arts program.

Strategies to Develop Writing Skills

Although fine motor skills develop early in some young learners, others have significant problems in this area. There are at least four issues to consider when developing instructional activities for teaching writing skills:

1. *The visual motor integration process involved.* The child must see the letters in the correct order, tell his hand what to do, and make his hand do it. This is a most complex process that can break down at many points.

2. *Difficulties initiating and carrying out the motor actions.* Making the hand start moving fluently, keeping in mind the shape and the order of the letters, continue moving fluently to finish without going too fast (impulsivity) or getting stuck repeating letters or movements (perseveration), add complexity.

3. *Understanding where to start on a paper.*

4. *The motivation to practice.*

Some learners will grab the pencil during the story development process and change a word or add words. Others seem unable to grasp, hold, or manipulate a writing instrument. To address sensory motor and motor problems, consult with an occupational therapist. The idea that they could do the writing themselves is foreign to many learners. The process for transferring words from a model on another piece of paper or the chalkboard also can be a problem.

The following strategies can help resolve some of these problems:

1. *To copy print from a vertical plane to a horizontal plane* over a distance (from chalkboard or chart to paper at a desk):

   - Tape a piece of paper to the chalkboard and label the top and bottom while saying, "This is the top of the paper. This is the bottom of the paper." After writing a brief one-line story, remove the paper and place it on the student's desk for the student to copy. Comment about the location of "the top of the paper" when it is lying flat.

     Note: The learner may believe that it is always necessary to label the top and bottom of the paper unless told otherwise.

   - When writing on the chalkboard, write the letters of each word quite close together (to see the gestalt), and leave a bit of extra space between words. Other strategies to facilitate copying from the board include underlining the sentences, leaving a bit more space between each line, and numbering the lines after writing the story.

   - Keep the chalkboard story compact. If the letters, spaces, and lines are too far apart, it is harder to follow and to see the gestalt of the story.

   - Draw a border around the story or material to be copied to separate it from other material on the board.

   - Try moving the learner's desk closer to the board; but if the desk is too close, it is harder to see the whole story and the learner must twist the head to follow the lines

   - Initially, the story may need to be written at the child's desk for referral during copying.

2. To *initiate and support the writing process:*

- Assure learners that the process will get easier, "Writing the words on paper is hard, but soon it will get easier and I won't need to help you."

- Provide subtle physical support like that described and illustrated in Chapter 16.

- Consult with an occupational therapist for assistance with the visual-motor problems. After a reasonable period of instruction, therapy, and practice, it may be decided to teach the child to use a computer instead of spending an inordinate amount of time on practice that always ends in failure.

3. To identify a starting place:

- Place an X or a dot on the paper, and say, "Start here." Use parallel talk to provide the work system rules ("Top to bottom, left to right"). Note: Say, "The X is here now to help you learn where to start, but soon you won't need it."

4. To *increase motivation:*

- Provide a purpose for the writing. Make a copy of the story to take home to share, write messages to request favorite things from someone in another area or room, or require a signature to check out materials or to check in and out of work or play centers.

5. To *increase motivation to trace the letters:*

- Initially, fasten a piece of tracing paper over the story to make it easier to produce the total story. Doing so will also make it easier to take it home to share with family, place it in a book, or display it on a bulletin board.

- Change the focus—to highlight the best effort rather than the error. Repetitive writing practice is boring and often resisted, but generally necessary. Avoid negative statements. Highlight the positive. For example, circle the best in red as you say, "Wow, that is the best letter." Or, "How many words can you write before the timer goes off?" Or, "How many very good letters can you write on one line or a page?" These activities provide an opportunity for the student to request assistance, to check quality, and to count the number of circled readable letters or words to enter in a graph.

- Perfectionism is often a roadblock for those with autism. They may want their writing or printing to look exactly like the teacher's or just like the book print. Model and teach the concept that some work simply needs to be readable and done quickly, while other work needs to be done carefully to look nice for a special purpose. *Model making and correcting errors with positive self-talk* so the child learns that everyone makes mistakes—it's okay, it can be fixed.

Summary

If the goal is reading, writing, and spelling with meaning, it is taught meaningfully from the beginning. Strategies that expand language meaning and use also expand literacy and comprehension. The opposite also is true. To reinforce concepts and motivation, always have writing material available for quick notes and stories. Keep copies of stories in notebooks. These books can provide a focus for conversations and sharing past experiences and a positive way to practice. Some learners have used the stories as a means of communication—a way to request a desire to repeat an event.

Again, interpreters must remember that seemingly simple concepts that others learn automatically must be specifically highlighted for those with autism. When instruction is organized to include the details and visual references that accommodate these learners' literal perspective and learning style, the learning rate is surprisingly rapid. Small and subtle pieces of information can have a major impact on learning and performance. Teachers in regular classrooms need reassurance that the accommodations described in this chapter will benefit some of their other students as well.

Concept: _____

Define the concept:	Instructional examples		Natural and/or simulated contexts for generalization	Visual references to clarify details and relationships
	Positive examples ("This is a ____")	Negative examples ("This is not a ____")		
Related concepts:				

Expand Communication Skills and Options

Expansion of the ever-fragile interactive communication habit is a major challenge for those with autism spectrum disorders and their teachers. Effective communication is such a complex skill that this expansion rarely occurs automatically. Spontaneous communication will not occur unless there is a clear understanding of the purpose and power of communication and an understanding of how social interactions work (see Chapter 17 for strategies).

As noted previously, the content of language and communication instruction is similar for all children; the problems and the strategies will differ to match each individual's unique combination of skills and deficits. The first part of this chapter begins with a foundation for expanding communication skills. It then addresses some of the problems that disrupt effective communication and behavior—echolalia and repetitive speech. The second part of the chapter summarizes the issues involved in teaching alternative and augmentative communication systems that incorporate formal signs, pictures, written words and the use of technology.

Teaching Spontaneous Communication to Autistic and Developmentally Handicapped Children (Watson, Lord, Schaffer, & Schopler, 1989) describes an expansion process that begins with an assessment of the learner's spontaneous communication skills—the skills used without cues or assistance. It includes many strategies and case examples to illustrate the systematic and highly successful approach developed at Division TEACCH, University of North Carolina at Chapel Hill. Other resources include Quill (2000); and Wetherby and Prizant (2000).

Systematic Expansion

Watson and associates (1989) suggested that communication skills should be expanded systematically across several dimensions to:

- Communicate for a larger number of reasons or purposes (functions); see Figure 20.1

- Communicate with a larger number of people

- Understand and use words more flexibly with a broader range of meanings and accurate word/concept associations (semantic categories)

- Communicate in multiple ways (forms or systems); see Figure 20.2

- Communicate in an increasing number of natural situations and settings (contexts)

New skills are generally introduced in nondistracting situations, but expansion and generalization can only occur in natural contexts where powerful natural cues and reinforcers are available to make the skills meaningful and spontaneous. Communication skills taught and practiced in the context of rote drills tend to be used repetitively without meaning.

Each child's program is individualized and grows from the child's spontaneous efforts, even though those efforts may be tiny. Activities are planned and support is provided to ensure systematic movement in steady but small steps across the dimensions to match gradually changing skills and needs. Interpreters constantly evaluate and refine the environment to set up situations that capitalize naturally on the child's own spontaneous efforts.

Causes and Effects in Communication and Language (Warren & Reichle, 1991) is another excellent resource.

For example, if a child spontaneously takes mother by the wrist and pulls her to the sink to indicate a need for a drink, expansion occurs as the child is taught systematically to indicate other needs by pulling mother to other locations. Next steps involve taking father or teacher by the wrist in other settings or situations

Figure 20.1 Basic Communication Functions

Requests for:
Foods/objects
Action/activity
More, or to continue
Stop, or end action/activity
Bathroom
Assistance
Attention
Affection
Social interaction
Information/clarification
Permission

Response to:
Directions
Yes/no and WH questions

Protest/Reject:
Action/event
Object/food
Removal or denial of object/activity
Changes of routine or environment

Comment:
On self or other person
On objects/people/events (present)
On objects/people/events (not present)

Express:
Pleasure
Pain
Fear
Surprise
Confusion
Frustration/stress
Choices
Other

---

to indicate other needs. Simultaneously, other dimensions are addressed by expanding the child's experiences in natural contexts to learn new concepts (words) and to provide opportunities to communicate different types of messages. In this system, language and communication skills are learned meaningfully, rather than through rote and repetitive drills.

Echolalia

Echolalia—repeating words and sentences produced by others—is a special problem in autism. Echolalia is a natural step in the normal progression of language development. But in autism, learners appear to get stuck or stay in this step for prolonged periods. Prizant (1983) has suggested that the gestalt processing, so common in autism, could be responsible for this ability to memorize "whole" chunks of words—thus not processing and understanding the meaning of each single word. Initially, echolalia was thought to be a repetitive, meaningless, and inappropriate behavior to be extinguished. Now we know that echolalia is actually used as an effort to communicate or interact. However, we must interpret the meaning and the function before we know how to intervene.

For a more comprehensive view of echolalia, see Prizant et al., (2000).

There are several types of echolalia, but we will only discuss the two most common types, immediate and delayed echolalia. Although there are similarities between the two types, assessment and intervention strategies are somewhat different. Both immediate and delayed echolalia show variations in:

- The exactness of the repetition

- The degree of comprehension of the repetition

- The presence or absence of intention

The articulation and intonation of the echoed words in both types of echolalia match that of the original production almost exactly (Prizant, 1988).

Immediate Echolalia

Immediate echolalia occurs just after or very soon after the original words are heard. The echoed words may or may not be used interactively. This type of echolalia serves several different functions. Often it is used to fill a conversational turn, rehearse or process the meaning of the words, or affirm that the message was heard—although perhaps not understood.

Immediate echolalia most commonly follows a question or a demand that the learner does not fully understand but knows that a response is expected. The learner repeats the question—a strategy similar to that used by many people when they need time to think or when they are puzzled by the words and need more information. The difference is in the intensity and the inflexibility of the repetition. Other people can move flexibly from one strategy to another until they fully understand the words and can generate an appropriate response. The learner with autism may have only the one strategy—to echo the chunk of meaningless words over and over. The learner continues until the interpreter either leaves in exasperation or sets up the situation to break the chain, clarify and guide the learner to an appropriate response.

Strategies for Dealing With Immediate Echolalia

1. *Pause following a question or demand* so the learner has time to generate an appropriate response.

2. *Provide visual references to highlight the meaning* of questions and/or an appropriate response—(e.g., cue cards, line drawings of the critical words, stick figures labeled to represent the learner and the interpreter with their words written in bubbles as in a cartoon—see *Comic Strip Conversations*, by Gray, 1994.)

3. *Respond to echoed questions literally* to model an appropriate response, emphasizing the critical words, for example:

   Interpreter: Do you want a cookie?

   Learner: Do you want a cookie?

   Interpreter: *Yes*, I want a cookie, *please*.

   (The interpreter quickly takes a cookie and eats a bite before restating the question.)

   Do *you* want a *cookie*?

   (Note the emphasis on the critical words.)

4. *When the confusion seems to be caused by not understanding the pronouns*, highlight the relationship expressed by the pronoun. For example, while patting your own chest, say, "I, Jan, want a cookie." Then pat the child's chest as you say, "Do you, Tony, want a cookie?" Note that the pronoun and the name are said with emphasis to match the rhythm of the pat. A full hand pat to the child's chest is very concrete and distinct from the kind of touch used to get attention.

5. *Highlight natural or adapted cues and prompts.*

   ■ Quickly write out and give the learner a cue card with the appropriate response ("Yes, I want a cookie" or "Yes, please"). Prepare cue cards for some simple responses and keep them ready to use quickly in other natural situations.

- Say the correct response, as if talking for the learner, while touching the learner's chest ("Yes, I, Tony, want a cookie"). Then hand the learner a cookie.

- Quickly whisper the first part of an appropriate response with exaggerated mouth movements; then pause for the learner to complete the response ("Yes, plea—"). Gradually fade to simply mouthing the beginning sound of the first word.

6. *Teach the meanings of different kinds of questions and directions* and the types of responses that match different types of questions. For example, teach that the answer to a *why* question begins with *because*. Use visual references to illustrate the concepts.

7. *Use sentence frames* to set up situations to practice filling in words to fit the immediate situation. ("I need _____" or "I don't understand _____.")

8. *Set up and practice many different situations* within the context of group instruction so others can model appropriate responses.

9. *Teach rejection responses in natural situations.* ("No, I don't want a cookie" or "No, thank you.")

10. *Avoid teaching rapid and rigid rote responses to questions and directions.* If the responses are taught in natural situations with meaning attached, the learner will be able to apply it flexibly in different situation. Learners with autism must have extra time to process verbal requests or questions and to generate a response to fit the specific situation.

Delayed Echolalia

In delayed echolalia, the words and phrases are echoed days, weeks, or even years after they were originally heard. Often, echoed words were first heard spoken with a great deal of emphasis and emotional content, and now are repeated much like a toddler learns and repeats his parent's swear words at the appropriate emotional times but without understanding the meaning. Some learners may repeat complete conversations, including the words of both partners. For example, during free time one young boy sat alone in the language circle, echoing the complete language lesson—both the teacher's script and the responses of the children.

Delayed echolalia is used for a variety of reasons and to serve several functions, among them: to request, protest, provide information, initiate conversations, and answer questions; and for self-regulation and rehearsal. Higher-functioning learners and those with Asperger's syndrome often intersperse fragments of borrowed phrases into their own creative utterances. In delayed echolalia, no matter how ordinary or how intellectual the words sound, the words themselves are generally repeated without a clear or complete understanding of the conventional meaning.

Delayed echolalia can best be understood in the context of the gestalt learning style common to autism. Words are taken in and stored in unanalyzed chunks that include many bits and pieces of sensory and emotional details from the original situation. A chunk of words is triggered by some common element of the current situation, but the words themselves lack meaning or have a different meaning to the individual with autism than to most other people. In the example of Tony and the cat (Chapter 3), the chunk of words, "The cat jumped off the balcony," was associated with the emotional state of those in the original situation—tension, concern, and excitement—rather than the fact that the cat jumped off the balcony. Thus, that specific chunk of words is triggered whenever Tony is in a situation that includes similar emotional content.

The implications of delayed echolalia are far-reaching.

- People misinterpret the individual's level of ability, assuming that they can understand and function at the same level as they can articulate echoed phrases and concrete information about special interests. When the learners cannot meet those expectations, they are seen as lazy, noncompliant, willful, or spiteful. Family and support staff may become frustrated and angry when they respond from their misperceptions rather than from the learner's perspective.

- Echoed phrases are sometimes misinterpreted as evidence of psychotic behavior, hallucinations, or delusions.

Strategies for Dealing With Delayed Echolalia

1. *Quickly assess to determine if the words are borrowed or echoed.* Generally, but not always, the echoed words are fluent, well articulated, and include the intonation and emphasis used by the original speaker. Original, self-generated utterances are frequently slower, more labored, and generally delivered in a flat, expressionless voice.

   - After giving directions or stating a rule, avoid asking, "Do you understand?" or "Tell me, what did I just say?" Even when the learner repeats a direction or indicates understanding, one cannot assume that the message is truly understood. As one mother explained, "I cannot trust what she says. I can only tell if she understands from what she does. If she truly understands, she does it. If she doesn't understand, she doesn't do it."

   - Do use visual references or ask a more open-ended question. ("What are you going to do?"; "How are you going to do that?"; "Show me what you will do or what you want.") To be certain they understand, make it visual for later reference.

2. *Consider the immediate situation to determine the purpose or meaning* of the borrowed utterance; then use a reflective listening strategy. One girl repeated the Oreo cookie commercial when she wanted a snack—not necessarily a cookie. Her interpreter said, "You feel hungry and want a snack? You can say, 'I'm hungry. I want some pretzels.'" Provide visual references, either in the form of a cue card, a cartoon strip, or a semantic map that illustrates the sentence frame and a variety of available snack foods for filling in the blank.

3. *Check with parents and others who know the individual's history and review records* when assessing the meaning of echoed language. Often, as in the case of the cat jumping off the balcony, there will be a logical reason for some of these echoed phrases. This is especially important for psychologists, counselors, and behavior specialists. Too many individuals with autism spectrum disorders have been misdiagnosed with schizophrenia on the basis of echoed words.

   - Parents need to keep a log of the source and meaning of echoed words and phrases that their child uses in startling or potentially frightening ways. This record should be shared during assessments and evaluations and when transitioning to new programs or living situations. Only when the history of these echoed words or behaviors is documented and understood, can appropriate interventions be developed to change the behavior—to teach new and meaningful ways to communicate those messages.

4. *Ensure that the correct meanings are associated with words and phrases* by reviewing experiences and writing stories as described in Chapter 15, to highlight the important elements.

   In the example of Tony and the cat, when the interpreter discovered where Tony first heard "The cat jumped off the balcony," she reviewed it with Tony while writing an experience story to correct the misinterpretation. The story was illustrated with simple line drawings. She closed the story with the following statements: "Now, when I am surprised or worried, I can say, "Wow! Look what happened!" or "What happened?" or "What do we do now?" or "Wait a minute!""

5. *Do not make assumptions.* The learner with autism frequently does not understand the full meaning of all the words used in echoed statements.

In summary, echoed or borrowed words carry meaning that must be interpreted by others. Do not punish the use of these phrases or try to simply eliminate echolalia. Rather, use social stories or other teaching approaches to help the learner understand the echoed words and learn more effective ways to communicate that will be understood by all in the culture.

Repetitive Questions and Conversations

Questions about time, events, worries, and special interests often continue, seemingly without end. The learner often shows considerable tension and concern as if genuinely worried about something. Sometimes the learner seems to be locked or stuck into this repetitive action and doesn't know how to stop it. On some occasions, the learner will accept only specific answers to the repeated questions. Sometimes, the same questions will be asked of each person in a room, one after the other. If the learner's questions are ignored, the individual may become ever more insistent and upset. Stress can accelerate when the same answers are not provided, when the same answers are provided but they don't answer the question he needed to ask, and especially, when the questions are ignored.

Strategies for Dealing With Repetitive Questions and Conversations

The first step is to determine the function or purpose of the questions or conversations. There are at least four, perhaps more, reasons for repetitive questions and conversations. The learner:

1. *Needs information* but doesn't know how to ask the right questions

2. *Wants a social interaction* but doesn't know how to initiate, extend, or terminate an interaction

3. *Has a genuine concern* about major unsolvable problems

4. *Is locked or stuck into a repetitive action* and doesn't know how to stop it

When Specific Information is Needed, But the Learner Doesn't Know How to Ask the Right Question

1. *Provide a concrete and literal answer with visual references* as appropriate. For example, answers to questions about time are paired with a concrete and visual way to mark the passage of time:

    ■ Mark the occasion on the calendar and count the days.

    ■ Refer to the daily calendar of events and clarify. ("First, _____, then _____.")

    ■ Place three blocks on the table and say, "In 15 minutes it will be time to leave." To show the passage of time, remove a block after each five-minute period.

To calm her son who was concerned that his mother was still talking to a friend when it was time to go to lunch, one mother held up three fingers and said, "I must talk about three more things. Then it will be time for lunch." As she finished talking about each item, she lowered a finger. When all three fingers were down, she ended the conversation and left with her son.

2. *If the same question is repeated several times,* it may be an indication that the learner wants other information but is not able to frame the right question. Stress is likely to build if the interpreter probes with a series of questions. Switch from a face-to-face verbal conversation to a visual conversation on paper. Sit at a table beside the learner, and write down the learner's first question and the answer that you gave. Move the paper closer to the learner, write the repeated question, and change the answer slightly to provide different information; or, ask a slightly different question ("Do you want to know about _____?"). Then put down the pencil.

   ■ Shifting the focus to the paper seems to reduce the stimulation and stress. Altering or broadening the answer with more details seems to help identify the real issue. In some situations, both partners verbalize their answers, but the interpreter still writes it all down. In other situations, both stop talking and they write their own questions and responses. It may take considerable time to arrive at the real need, but the stress level is considerably reduced. One resource teacher used this strategy at school; but instead of staying near the learner while he wrote his response, she moved away until he quit writing, and then she returned to write her response. When the pressures are reduced, many learners can find ways to state their needs more clearly.

3. *Teach the learner to use sentence frames or cue cards* to communicate. ("Let's write this down so I can understand.") The communication notebook shown here was useful to José, who could not recall the words to get information.

4. *When the questions continue after you have made a genuine effort* to provide the needed information, say, "I'm sorry, I don't understand. Let's take a break, and we can try again later." Set a specific time to try again. Only then, offer something to relieve the stress, change the focus, and divert attention—a drink of juice, or time to bounce on a mini-trampoline or rock in the chair.

José's communication notebook

When Repetitive Questions or Conversations are Used to Initiate or Keep a Social Interaction Going

1. *Respond to the question* as you would to initiations of any friend. It is important to attend in some way to all initiations, to show respect and to strengthen the social/communication habit.

   - Stop and discuss the topic for a few minutes. Then say, "Now I would like to talk about _____. We can talk about earthquakes again after dinner" or "I am busy, but I have time to listen to two things about earthquakes." Keep track, holding up one finger and then the next. Then say, "That's two things. We can talk more at 2:00."

2. *Consciously initiate more frequent informal interactions* with the learner. These interactions provide important practice and are a sign of increasing social interest.

3. *Specify some social interaction times* on the daily calendar so the learner can see when the next opportunity will occur.

4. *Structure the scheduled talking and interaction sessions* to expand communication options. Add variations, model new strategies, and provide sensitive feedback. The variations increase skill and flexibility and decrease the amount of time for repetitive questions and conversations. For example, with a person who is very interested and knowledgeable about the weather, try these variations:

   - "We can talk about the weather for five minutes. Then I get to choose the topic." End promptly at the appointed time. If necessary, use a timer.

   - "You can talk about the weather for 4 minutes, but tell me one new thing about the weather. Then it's my turn." Keep a log of new information about weather and another log of other topics.

   - "What do you want to talk about first: the garden, the weather, or the ball game?" When it is understood that there will be opportunities to talk about interests, these individuals are likely to choose other topics.

5. *Teach a process for negotiating conversation topics.* ("I want to talk about _____. What do you want to talk about?")

6. *While the learner watches, prepare a cue card* to clarify conversation rules, topics, and questions. While setting up the cue card in script form, "I will say___, You will say three things about the weather, 1. ___,2.___, 3.___. Then David, you will say, 'What do you want to talk about?'" As the learner talks, have him check off the numbers or write the three statements. Then point to the question David is to ask and wait quietly, or softly cue the learner to read the question so you can suggest a new topic.

Provide honest interest and reassurance. The learner needs self-confidence (I am valuable, my interests are valued, and people like to talk to me). The learner also needs to know that people want to hear new information, like to share talking time, and want to talk about other things, too. The goal is to expand confidence, knowledge, and conversation skills. Visual systems can help the learner manage conversations more satisfactorily.

When the Learner is Genuinely Concerned About Major or Unsolvable Problems.

Stressful and repetitive questions about major problems are most obvious in the highly verbal learners who watch TV or read the news about natural disasters, starving people, wars, crime, and conflicting medical or nutritional research. Even Disney movies can be frightening if the learner does not automatically understand the difference between fantasy and fact. Some learners become upset and ask repeated questions about religious issues after hearing forceful or dramatic sermons.

1. *Assess to determine the learner's existing knowledge of the situation*, the terminology and concepts, and the misperceptions. Then clarify and provide basic information and reassurance. For example, locate the site of a disaster on a map, figure how far away it is, and identify those who are responsible for taking care of the people or the problem (the president, the police, the Red Cross, others). Define fact or fantasy, propaganda, rumor, and theories. Discuss research and the fact that "Nobody knows exactly." Keep the explanation concrete and as literal as possible. Use visual references such as flow charts, lists, and story strategies.

2. *Schedule times to talk about worries.* Develop a routine that allows some time at the end of each session to talk about other things. The schedule should also clarify the activity that will follow these "talking times."

3. *Identify a specific place to talk about worries.* ("We only talk about worries when we sit in these chairs.") Do not schedule the worry time at the dining table or in the bedroom; meal and bed times must not trigger worry.

4. *End the discussions at the stated time with a satisfying or calming phrase* that signals the end of worry talk, provides some reassurance, and reminds the learner of the next activity. Select calming phrases that fit the concern, and use them routinely. ("That's about all we can do"; "It's pretty amazing!"; "Well, the facts are not all in yet"; "That's just make-believe"; "The common cold is not dangerous"; "It's a real tragedy"; "We'll have to leave it to the Red Cross.")

5. *Keep a log of worries* and list the group or person responsible for taking care of each problem. Clarify that big problems take a lot of time to fix. Anxiety may be relieved by participating in food and clothing drives for the homeless or joining in organized walks to raise money for other relief efforts.

6. *If the worry continues*, say, "You can ask two more questions about _____. Then it will be time for _____. You can talk about it again at 8:15." Hold up two fingers or draw two circles to keep track of the two questions. Then move away and make a note on the calendar for the next talking time.

7. *Develop a worry-management routine* that begins with thought stopping and relaxation techniques. When developing the routine, include some of the strategies listed above, such as identifying an appropriate source of information and using positive self-talk. Imagery procedures and cognitive picture rehearsal can lead to greater independence (see Chapter 22).

In summary, to manage repetitive talking, the learner needs information, strategies, options, and respectful assistance. Teach rules, sentence frames, and coping or calming statements. Provide visual references that can be used independently.

Develop and Expand a Primary Communication System

All people need to be able to communicate in every setting. They not only need a consistent and dependable primary communication system but also backup systems. Those who cannot speak need an alternative communication system. Those who can speak need an augmentative system to support or augment their speech when it is difficult to understand or when it is limited or not available for use. For example, extreme stress can make speech difficult to produce consistently; others have difficulty recalling words or initiating speech when stressed. There are still many adolescents and adults with autism spectrum disorders who have no consistent and effective communication system. They manage fairly well in familiar settings with trusted and sensitive interpreters, but they are at a distinct disadvantage when they are alone in new situations. Those without effective and dependable communication systems have more severe anxiety and behavior problems and fewer opportunities and options to participate in society.

Figure 20.2 Forms of Communication

Motoric: Using direct manipulation of another person or object to send a message
  (Pulling mother to the sink to request a drink)

Gestural: Using hand, head, or body actions to convey messages
  (Pointing or nodding to indicate *yes* or *no,* pushing something away to reject, touching a person's arm to ask for attention, and making other gestures)

Object: Using real objects, miniatures, or parts of objects as symbols to convey needs
  (Handing mother a cup to request a drink)

Pictorial: Using photographs or generic line drawings to communicate

Vocal/verbal: Using sounds to communicate
  (Saying, "Ah-ah-ah" to draw attention, producing different sounds for different needs, or using conventional spoken words)

Written: Pointing to printed messages; writing or typing messages

Signed: Using conventional gestures and hand movements developed as a formal communication system for the deaf

Speech is only one of several natural ways to communicate; well over half of communication is nonverbal. Most people use gestures, facial expressions, and body language to convey messages and support their speech. We also use written words and computers to communicate. Many young children with autism are learning to communicate more effectively now that:

- The communication and processing deficits of those with autism are more clearly understood.

- Early diagnosis and appropriate early intervention are available.

- Alternative and augmentative communication (AAC) systems are more commonly available and introduced at an earlier age.

Although it is still not possible to predict the potential achievement of individuals with ASD, it is clear that when those with autism learn to communicate in some way, they tend to be more relaxed, more involved, and more independent.

Because speech is the most efficient form of communication, and because it is understood by most people, speech development continues to be a goal, *but the highest priority and ultimate goal is for every learner to have some way to communicate effectively in every setting and situation.* Those with autism, like most other people, are lifelong learners. With support, they will continue to expand their communication skills and their options throughout life.

Considerations for Making Decisions

When making decisions about AAC systems and planning instruction to expand communication options for those with autism, consider that:

1. *Speech does not ensure communication.* The ability to say words does not ensure that the words can be used to send and receive meaningful messages.

2. *Skill development does not follow the normal or expected sequence.* Probe a broad range of skills in the context of a number of natural and simulated situations to identify the learner's strengths and the gaps. For example, a learner may have low test scores, have no speech, and appear to have very limited potential, but have the ability to read, spell, and write.

3. *That automatic drive to understand and use the communication process is weak.* Even those who are very verbal are not necessarily effective communicators. If those with autism are to learn to communicate effectively, the instructional experiences must be exceptionally clear, meaningful, and positive so the communication habit is continually and naturally reinforced. Whatever type of AAC system is selected, it must be introduced in the context of making spontaneous requests. This ensures that the effort to communicate receives a powerful and natural reinforcer.

4. *Basic skills such as eye contact, motor and verbal imitation, symbol matching, or labeling skills are not a prerequisite* for communication training.

An AAC specialist and an autism specialist are important resources to help the planning team select appropriate communication system(s) and teaching strategies. This requires a comprehensive assessment of the learner's unique learning and sensory processing needs and the demands of his various home, school, and community environments. Before making decisions, review the discussion of symbol selection in Chapter 14. Other considerations are summarized in Beukelman and Mirenda (1992).

Assessment Tools to Identify Needs

An assessment is necessary to determine how and when a system is needed to augment the child's speech or to determine which type of alternative systems would be most effective. Although the language/communication and the AAC specialists will have access to a variety of assessment tools, the following functional assessment tools will also be helpful (see Chapter 5). These functional assessments involve observations, a review of records, and interviews with parents and interpreters:

- An assessment of communication: Form 5.5: Functional Communication Assessment

- An assessment of social skills: Form 5.6: Social Skills Assessment: Informant Interview

- An assessment to identify reinforcers: Form 5.8: The Preference Survey

- An assessment of sensory processing and sensory/motor integration (see Myles et al., 2000, pp. 43–64)

Elements of an Effective System

There are many ways to arrange and display pictures and words for communication purposes. They range from handmade picture, letter, or word boards to extremely high-tech systems with speech output. For discussion of issues to consider in the design, see Beukelman and Mirenda (1992).

High-technology systems can be expensive, so a learner's first system could be handmade to specifically match the individual's abilities to scan and direct attention, enlist a communication partner, understand the picture/word symbols, and physically manipulate the system.

A communication system is effective and will be used when it is:

A simple belt-loop system supported one learner whose interpreter was absent.

1. *Portable, durable, easy to manage, and always available.*

   Systems that require boards, books, clipboards, or computers must be compact, sturdy, and easy to carry. Systems used by small children must be especially sturdy and perhaps waterproof. A system must be large enough for easy use; if it is too large or too complicated, it will get in the way, become a burden, and will be avoided. A system must be easy to transport everywhere and at all times—in a pocket, notebook, purse, fanny pack, or fastened to the belt or around the neck. If the system is not constantly available, it will not be used and the learner will not learn the power of communicating in all settings.

2. *Easy to use and capable of delivering a clear message quickly.*

   A single picture can be labeled with the word or with a sentence to clarify the meaning for an unfamiliar communication partner. Speed is enhanced when the learner needs to touch only one letter, word, or picture to deliver a complete message. *In Silent Words and Forever Friends* (1990), author Margaret Eastham describes the messages that were programmed into a Sharp Memowriter so that her son, David, could send a message by touching only one key. Some of those messages were:

A	=	I WANT TO BE ALONE
H	=	MY HEAD HURTS
J	=	I FEEL JUMPY, EXCITED
X	=	COULD WE GO FOR A WALK?
1	=	I AM SORRY
3	=	I AM FRUSTRATED

3. *Easy to adapt and/or expand.*

   A system must be updated and adapted as the learner's needs and skills change. If the system does not keep pace with the learner's ever-changing needs, it will not be used. Initially, a very young learner may be overwhelmed with more than two or three symbols, while others may be bored and refuse to use a simple display. The ability to manage larger numbers of symbols develops with time and practice.

   - Separate vocabulary boards or books can be prepared to match the needs of a particular setting or situation. These are useful for learners who cannot speak as well as for those who are verbal.

   - Computer programs and commercially prepared picture cards are available to simplify the design and development of a system. See resources in Appendix B.

An ongoing evaluation process is needed to identify problems and modify or refine the system as soon as a need arises.

Assistive or Augmentative Support Systems

As noted earlier, those of us who speak to communicate also use a variety of other systems to augment our communications—in other words, we use gestures, writing, pictures, and sometimes typing to clarify our messages in a variety of situations. Learners with autism spectrum disorders will also need a variety of supports for different situations. They may need gestures to communicate some messages, but in other situations they may need to use a quick sign to say "Help," or a written list to help communicate their choices. Written or printed word dictionaries are useful tools for augmenting speech for very verbal learners who have difficulty recalling words or initiating communication (see the illustration on page 336). The addition of assistive strategies or devices will ensure that some form of communication will always be available.

There are also a number of low, moderate, and high technology strategies and devices that can supplement the primary system. A useful resource is the *Assistive Technology Tools & Strategies: Assessment Manual for Children with Autism Spectrum Disorders* developed by the Wisconsin Assistive Technology Initiative (Pallaske, Reed, & Stokes, July 2000). Also review Chapter 14 for more examples of visual support systems that could be adapted to augment communication.

Alternative Communication Systems

There are three basic types of alternative communication systems:

1. Signing
2. Picture systems
3. Written words

The system selection depends on the learner's spontaneous skills, interests, and sensory and motor abilities. All alternative systems have positive and negative aspects.

1. Signed Communication Systems

Negative aspects: Signed communication requires the presence of a skilled interpreter at all times, it takes a long time to learn a comprehensive sign vocabulary, and motor problems may inhibit learning. A learner needs other augmentative or assistive devices when a sign language interpreter is not available.

Positive aspects: A sign system is portable; signs are relatively easy to shape and prompt; they provide visual, tactile, auditory, and proprioceptive feedback as the signs are shaped and the interpreter simultaneously verbalizes the message. It is relatively easy to teach and expand single signs into sentences; a sign can be held briefly in space to allow for more processing time. Learning to communicate with signs has transferred to spoken communication for some but not all individuals with autism. Most of those who are lower functioning and totally nonverbal may learn a few signs to help them communicate in some essential situations but remain unable to speak.. The use of signs to communicate has also served to reduce self-stimulating or repetitive behaviors (Carr & Durand, 1985).

2. Picture Word Systems

Negative aspects: Picture/word systems are bulky and must be carried about; they have a limited amount of space to display symbols at one time; it is difficult to design pictures to clearly represent a generic label or concept; the process for communicating with pictures is slow; it is difficult to string together the symbols to make sentences.

Positive aspects: Appropriate for those who show interest in pictures, those with motor difficulties, or those who have trouble recalling words. Pictures can be used successfully by the very young and by older learners who function at a concrete level. During early training, it is easy to physically prompt and reinforce picture use; a picture is a concrete image of an object, so it is relatively easy to attach meaning. Pictures are a nontransient and visual system that enable the learner time to scan, process, and select the wanted symbol. Communication partners can understand the meaning of the pictures if they are labeled with the written word; adding printed labels to pictures can facilitate the transition to reading, writing, and spoken words. The Picture Exchange Communication System (PECS; Frost &Bondy, 1994) has been found to be a very effective approach for teaching picture systems and will be discussed later.

3. Written or Typed Word Systems.

There are two basic types of written or typed communication systems:

- Words written or printed by others. Interpreters can prepare the cards or lists of written labels or information for the user to point to and select the message to be communicated.

- Word or messages are written or typed by the communicator.

Negative aspects: Problems with portability—written words requires the presence of writing materials; a typewriter or computer; or the selection of prepared cards, dictionaries or lists, etc. to display. Typing and writing is a slow process for most; it is slower to string together words to make a sentence.

Positive aspects: Written/printed word systems are more interesting and motivating for some learners with autism, even those who are very young or who seem to be quite limited and lower functioning. The ability to read and profit from these systems seems to have little relationship to scores on intelligence tests or "apparent" ability. Typing or writing messages provides unlimited vocabulary options and most people are able to read and understand the messages.

Guidelines for Teaching Alternative Systems

Guidelines for Selecting Vocabulary

Vocabulary for initial picture, word, or sign systems is selected for its reinforcing value to the learner. Initial vocabulary needs to enable learners to access/request their most valued objects, food, drink, or actions. Refer to the results of the Preference Inventory (Chapter 21) and involve the support team members and parents who spend the most time with the individual learner to suggest highly reinforcing foods, objects, or actions. To identify a broader range of potential reinforcers to expand the system, place an assortment of things on a table and see what the learner selects.

Other considerations for selecting initial vocabulary:

- Although the word *bathroom* has significance for mother, teacher, or an older learner, it is not likely to be highly valued by a young child.

- Generic words such as *eat, drink, play,* or *want* represent a broader range of objects, actions, and concepts but they are confusing for the literal learner who associates a single meaning with a single word. Because space is limited on picture/word board systems and it takes a long time to learn a large sign vocabulary, it is sometimes necessary to teach some generic symbols.

- Teach the child that a point = this. Then, for example, the learner can select or shape the symbol for eat, then point to the cookie. The interpreter interprets the message as the symbol: "I want to eat this cookie." Understanding and using the concept of point=this expands the ability to communicate in more settings and situations.

Additional vocabulary depends on age, interests, and the types of problems the learner is likely to encounter each day in various settings. The following messages can be added as the need arises:

- Vocabulary for requesting help, indicating preferences, and for rejecting or protesting (*Help, Yes/No, Stop, All done,* and *Need break*) are high priorities and will reduce many behavior problems.

- The phrase, "I don't know," provides an active alternative response for the learner who does not have the answer.

- Phrases such as: "I don't understand," "Draw a picture," or "Write it down" can relieve stress.

General Guidelines for Instruction

The foundation for expanding communication is developed in those early interactive playtimes with parents and others described in Chapter 17—when the child learns to tolerate and value interactions with people and take turns, and to intentionally initiate and respond to interactions.

The basic instructional guidelines presented in Chapters 16 and 19, and the following instructional guidelines, can be modified and applied to match the individual needs of a specific learner and to teach them to use most AAC systems.

The setting: The initial introduction of a new system or vocabulary can occur in the structured and familiar one-to-one play, work, or therapy setting at home or in school where there are limited distractions. The exact location, session structure, and materials will depend on the vocabulary displayed on the system and the learner's age and ability.

Arrange the area so that you control the materials and choices, which are in view and available to the learner. Initially, present only a single object or action that is most highly reinforcing. With only one option, there is little opportunity for error but a greater probability that the reinforcer will be delivered quickly and a greater likelihood that the correct associations will occur.

Position yourself so you can see where the learner is looking and you can easily guide, support, or shape the learner's hand. Conversations normally occur in a face-to-face position so that natural and spontaneous eye contact can occur easily.

Instructional Considerations

- Teach a new communication system in the context of turn-taking interactions. The power of the system is taught in the context of choice and capitalizes on the learner's natural gesture—reaching to grab. As a young child reaches to touch or grab a highly desired item, the child's hand is shaped to point to a specific picture/word, shaped to form the sign, or assisted to pick up the symbol and place it in the interpreter's hand. The interpreter simultaneously verbalizes the learner's intent and immediately delivers the requested item, thus reinforcing the association of the intention/action, the symbol, and the meaningful consequences.

To ensure that the correct associations are made and to avoid dependence and passivity, in the initial instruction:

- Avoid the use of verbal cues, prompts, and reinforcers (such as "What do you want?" "Do you want the chip?" or "Good pointing!").

Learner's perspective: I sure would like that candy, but my job is to wait till Mom says, "Do you want candy?"

Instead, set up the reinforcing situation and wait expectantly for the learner to express intention by reaching to grab.

■ Do not begin to guide the learner's hand until he or she makes a move that expresses an intention. If assistance is provided too early, it will lead to passivity and the development of a meaningless motor routine.

Learner's perspective: Oh good, when I keep my arm limp so she can move it, I get what I want.

Assistance that is provided as the learner is looking at the object and directing physical effort to reach an object is more likely to result in a spontaneous and meaningful communication habit. Having a request fulfilled immediately after the communication effort strengthens the effort to communicate.

■ If the requested object or action is delivered while the learner is looking away, looking away will be reinforced. *If the learner's attention drifts away before the natural reinforcer can be delivered*, stop all movement and say, "I don't understand. Show me again."

■ An older learner will need to be prepared before initial instruction. For example, the introduction of a new system or a new vocabulary word might include:

   ■ A brief explanation

   ("This is a picture board. You can use it to tell me what you want. This is a picture of _____"; or, "This is a new trampoline. Here is a picture of the trampoline on your board. Touch the picture when you want to jump on the trampoline.") Avoid trial-and-error strategies that can lead to wrong associations.

   ■ A brief demonstration with commentary to model its use and power

   ■ An opportunity to practice using the system with assistance

The following scenario illustrates how the interpreter ensures that Simon is actively involved in the process of learning to spontaneously communicate with a picture board to:

■ Spontaneously initiate the action

■ Actively participate in expressing intention

■ Hear a verbal interpretation of his intent

■ Quickly receive the requested object to reinforce the association between his action and the result

Angie, the interpreter, is sitting across the table from Simon. Several of Simon's favorite small crackers are between them. The picture board (with only the one symbol) also is on the table. Angie's hands are resting on the table ready to provide assistance quickly. After a brief introduction of the board and the materials:

Angie picks up the picture board, holds it close to the crackers, and says, "I want cracker," while pointing to the symbol of the cracker. Immediately she picks up a cracker and eats it. Then she replaces the picture board on the table beside the crackers and waits.

Simon reaches toward the crackers. As he starts to move his hand—

Angie places the picture symbol over the crackers, then simultaneously with one hand she slowly guides and shapes Simon's hand to point. She taps the cracker symbol with her other hand—just as his eyes shift to the picture, she touches his finger to the symbol and says, "Simon wants cracker" and quickly hands him the cracker.

The procedure is repeated with varied gestures and touch prompts. Periodically, Angie takes a turn and models requesting a cracker.

Expand Instruction

Schedule several short, highly structured sessions each day to introduce and integrate new vocabulary into the system. Simultaneously set up or engineer many opportunities to use familiar vocabulary in the context of all natural routines of the day to communicate with more people in more settings. Also remember to take advantage of the child's spontaneous efforts to get something he or she wants—whenever or wherever they occur.

- Ensure that the symbol system is always available—initially, the interpreter will take the responsibility. If the system has been adapted to be easily transported and when the learner understands that the system provides power, he will take more and more of the responsibility.

- Avoid repetitive, rote symbol-labeling activities and testing strategies such as, "Touch jump. . . . Touch help." The ability to label a symbol does not ensure that it will be used communicatively. The system must be used communicatively to express and obtain wishes, needs, and ideas in order to build a strong communication habit. Testing for understanding is best done in natural contexts.

- Introduce new symbols frequently when the learner can use the familiar symbols in other settings and with different people.

Three Augmentative Systems

Picture Exchange Communication System

The Picture Exchange Communication System (PECS; Frost & Bondy, 1994) developed at the Delaware Autistic Program has been used as an initial mode of communication for children as young as 2 years of age. The PECS is used to teach the child to locate a communication partner, present a picture of a desired item, and get the item in exchange for the picture. There are no prerequisite skills for initiating this system. This social communication exchange is based on child-selected reinforcers. The child spontaneously and intentionally initiates the exchange to request a highly desired item. The exchange is completed when the communication partner gives the highly reinforcing item to the child.

Advantages of the PECS are:

- It is taught in the context of the natural environment

- The exchange is obviously intentional and easy to understand

- The child is taught to take the initiative—to seek a partner and deliver the message

- The communication is meaningful and highly reinforcing

This procedure prevents some of the most difficult problems that often occur when teaching children with autism to use picture/word communication systems, as illustrated in the following examples.

> At snack time, Mary gazed out the window as she repetitively tapped the picture of juice. Interpreters were left to wonder whether this was an intentional act or simply a rote routine.
>
> ———————
>
> When Mark wanted his favorite toy, he ran to his communication board and tapped on the picture. When he got no response, he fell to the floor in a major tantrum. He didn't know that he needed a communication partner.

There are six phases of PECS training:

1. *Teach the basic exchange with physical assistance.*

   The child extends the picture and places it in the trainer's hand. No verbal cues, prompts, or reinforcers are used. During initial instruction, physical assistance is provided by a second adult standing behind the child.

2. *Expand spontaneity to locate a partner*, orient, and persist in getting attention.

3. *Discriminate between two or more pictures*, and expand vocabulary to 12 to 20 words.

4. *Build sentence structure with an "I want" picture/word* card to request items present and not present.

   At the end of this phase, the communication system contains 20 to 50 pictures (generally, pictographic line drawings on 3" x 5" or 1" square cards), and the child is communicating with a variety of partners.

5. *Respond to "What do you want?"*

   By the end of this phase, the child spontaneously requests desired items and actions and answers the question, "What do you want?" in all daily activities.

6. *Comment in response to a question, "What do you see?" with an "I see" card.*

By the end of this phase, the communication system contains 30 to 50 pictures and two sentence-starter cards.

Beyond Phase 6, vocabulary, language concepts, and sentence structures are expanded to more people and settings. Children typically progress through Phases 1 and 2 within a matter of days. Phase 3 training can take from several days to several months. Phases 4 and 5 are mastered in a few weeks.

A large percentage of the children who had no form of functional or socially appropriate communication skills acquired speech when started on PECS as preschoolers (Bondy & Frost, 1994).

In a typical case described by Bondy and Frost (1994), a child entered PECS training at age 36 months with no speech and no intentional communication. After 4 months of training, he began to use speech while moving the pictures. Within a few months, his vocabulary grew to more than 100 pictures. After 11 months of training, he used only speech to communicate. Bondy and Frost indicated that the rate of progress varies, but nearly all children who eventually developed speech used the picture exchange system as their only mode of communication for a while.

Note of caution: Green (2001) suggested that if the learner is reinforced for simply picking up a picture (without looking at the details of the picture and knowing what the picture represents) and placing it in the teacher's hand, as in the first level of PECS training, they may have greater difficulty at the next stages when they must discriminate between more than one picture.

Sign Language Systems

Early in the 1970s, nearly every child with autism received sign language training. But as with other strategies and models, it was apparent that a sign language system was not helpful to all children with autism. Some became very confused, while others learned only a few signs as rote motor routines or echoed the signs of others but never generated their own signs. However, signs did permit some children to communicate for the first time, and a few began to speak after first learning several signs—especially when teachers used the total communication strategies (that is, simultaneous use of signs and spoken words.) In some cases signing served as an alternative to repetitive/stereotypic finger and hand movements, an unexpected benefit (Carr & Durand, 1985).

At the age of 7, Maria was unable to speak. She did not use gestures or make any attempts to interact. After learning a few signs, she became more aware of others and learned that communication was a powerful tool. She spontaneously initiated those signs to request specific foods and toys and to request help. One morning, after several weeks of sign language training, she pulled her teacher by the wrist to her new friend who had hurt his finger. Maria signed "Help" and pointed to her friend. She had learned to seek a partner and spontaneously pair a sign and gesture to seek help for another person—an amazing feat!

Matt, whose speech was unreliable, learned many signs. When he needed to say something, he watched his hands as he signed the words; then he spoke the words.

Although signing is not used as frequently now, it continues to be a good option for those with autism who have not been successful with picture systems. If it is decided that a signing system is an appropriate option, the support team must make a major commitment. Training must be systematic over a long period of time, because:

- It takes a long time to learn a functional sign vocabulary.
- Strategies for teaching sign language to a learner with autism are very different from teaching signs to those who are deaf.
- Interpreters must be trained and available in all settings.

Guidelines for Teaching Sign Language

Signed Speech® Language Program for Nonverbal Students (Schaeffer, Raphael, & Kollinzas, 1994) is an important reference to guide the teaching process.

Select the sign system

Several manual sign language systems have been developed for those who are deaf. Some are highly symbolic and based on large or global concepts, while others are based on the English language. A system such as described in *Signing Exact English* (SEE; Gustafson, Pfetzing, & Zawolkow, 1980) is useful for those with autism because it is structured to match the spoken and written language that is seen and heard every day. When matched with the spoken language, this multisensory system avoids confusion for these very literal learners, for it:

- Serves as a bridge to move from signing to speech, reading, and writing.

- Facilitates receptive language development and provides experience to understand the language spoken by others.

- Provides a visual reference to highlight word meanings, articulation, and sentence structure, and to clarify the meaning of prefixes, suffixes, tenses, and other forms.

It is important to select a system such as SEE that has potential for expansion, because it is not possible to predict which young learners will advance to speech, reading, and writing.

Select vocabulary

Review the guidelines for selecting vocabulary presented previously in this chapter. In addition, there are several basic considerations for selecting the first vocabulary words for sign language instruction:

- Select a few highly valued and reinforcing foods or objects.

- The forms of the first few labels/signs should be very different—in terms of shapes, locations, and movements—to avoid any confusion.

  For example, the signs for candy, cracker, and ball are very different. (i.e., the sign for candy is a movement of the index finger on the cheek, the sign for cracker is a chopping movement of the fingers to the opposite elbow, the sign for ball is fingertips together as if holding a ball.)

- Do not teach signs for generic words during the initial stages of instruction, as they are especially confusing for the very literal learner who believes that every label/word refers to a single object. For example, when teaching more remember that this word is used in many varied situations: more food, more time, more space, etc. If the child is asked, "Do you want more?" he is likely to tantrum as he thinks, "No, I want milk." One child learned to sign more whenever he wanted anything.

- Teach that a point = this—the only generic sign that opens the world for the child who knows very few signs for labels. Now he can point to indicate his needs and choices in any environment. What power!

Initial Instruction to Prevent Problems

Step 1: Planning the instruction

Instruction must be designed to make sense from the learner's very literal perspective and the speed of their gestalt processing—these learners are very likely to become echolalic signers or learn to do the wrong things. The instruction must be exceedingly specific with the timing of the various parts of the instruction very precise.

The Signed Speech approach provides a mutisensory experience, in the context of a four-step teaching procedure:

1. *As the teacher first demonstrates* the routine for a new sign, the student sees "the whole thing"—the shape and movement of the sign and its relationship with the object, while simultaneously hearing the teacher verbally label the sign and sees the result, the reinforcer.

2. *A brief pause* is provided for the learner to process and decide to reach for the object.

3. *Without interrupting the flow and energy of the child's spontaneously reaching hand, the teacher shapes the hand to make the sign*—he feels the movement and shape of the sign while he hears the teacher verbalize the label, then quickly receives the requested item.

4. *The child experiences pleasure* as he gets the reinforcing item.

Consider the following basic rules to avoid learned errors while developing the instructional plan:

■ The teacher sits opposite of the child whenever a new sign is introduced. It is important to make spontaneous eye contact easily, ensure that the learner is looking at the material, and be in a position to shape both hands during two-handed signs.

Note: Ensure that the learner's dominant hand is shaped to make the signs. In general, the dominant hand will be the reaching hand but when sitting across the table it is sometimes easy to get confused especially when teaching signs that require both hands.

■ Modify the movement of the sign to match the rhythm of the syllables in the label in order to increase the effect of this multisensory approach.

Also verbalize the sentence frame to emphasize the rhythm of the sign as well as the language and use of the sign. For example, note the following example for teaching point = this:

As Jason begins to reach, start to verbalize the sentence frame as you shape the point—"Jason wants . . . " hesitate until his finger touches the candy, " . . . this . . . candy" and quickly give him the candy. If the goal were to teach the sign for cracker, you would say, "Jason want this *crack-er*," matching your speaking rhythm to the 2 chops of his hand to the opposite elbow.

■ Begin adding variations almost immediately—to maintain flexibility and avoid a fixed rote routine that will be difficult to generalize. For example:

  ■ Vary the physical shaping procedure so the learner doesn't begin to think that you will always be there to provide the same hand-shaping routine.

  ■ Vary the placement of the objects and the location of the session (at a table, on the floor, etc.) but continue to sit opposite the child.

  ■ Take turns asking for and sharing the foods and toys naturally just as would happen in any social situation. Seeing others sign as they label their words/meanings strengthens the communication routine.

■ To avoid learned errors, review the very specific use of cues, prompts, and reinforcers described in Chapter 16. Continually evaluate and refine your use of the instructional techniques.

  ■ Avoid all artificial verbal cues and artificial verbal reinforcers (i.e., "Sign cracker" or "Good signing cracker")—because they distract the learner from the critical natural cues and consequences. The prompts and physical assistance should be so subtle and varied that they do not register or become firmly attached to the routine.

  ■ Avoid teaching signs as a visual/motor imitation task—this leads to meaningless echolalic signing. The student also may learn the wrong things (e.g., he or she may learn a meaningless routine: "The teacher does something, I do the same thing, I get something.").

Strategies to Stimulate and Support Speech

Pairing the signs with the speech during instruction offers a language-rich environment that automatically stimulates speech production. For the very young, speech production is stimulated with interactive vocal and word play. Vocal and word play could be exaggerated during interactive play sessions (Chapter 17).

- Avoid the traditional physical prompting strategies to stimulate sound and speech production because the learner with autism is likely to learn the motor movements of the prompts as part of the speech routine. For example, one child learned to hold his lips together with his fingers as he said, "Mmmm" after the therapist held his lips together during instruction. If prompts are needed, make them as natural as possible. Any prompt that is used in the same way more than once is likely to be learned as a part of a routine.

- If the learner begins to verbalize while signing, accept it as a natural phenomenon. Undue excitement could interrupt the natural and meaningful situation. When speech becomes easier to use than the signs, the learner will automatically and gradually stop signing. Some will continue to use the signs in stressful situations or as a way to support thinking, rehearsal, and self-regulation. Encourage this by asking, "Can you show me what you need?"

In summary, the total communication process for teaching signs and language may overwhelm or confuse some learners with autism. For others, hearing the word, seeing the object, and feeling the movement of the sign simultaneously tends to tie it all together into a meaningful chunk that can lead to a better understanding of the language, increase ability to communicate, and possibly lead to speech. See Schaeffer et al. (1994) for additional strategies and considerations.

Written Communication Systems

Written communication has always been an important option for these highly visual, gestalt learners. The critical prerequisite for using writing as the primary communication tool is to understand communication, its power, and how it works. This foundation is developed during early interactive play sessions. Written systems use familiar symbols that children are exposed to most of their lives—and will continue to use everyday at school. Our task then, is to strengthen and integrate writing skills with communication skills.

Implications for Early Education

To strengthen the communication habit and increase the motivation to communicate with others, the interactive play sessions (see Chapter 17) should continue and be continually expanded to teach higher-level thinking and communication skills. Reading and writing skills should be emphasized and practiced in some way every day. In addition, include the following components as a natural part of a balanced and structured early childhood program regardless of a child's apparent intellectual potential:

1. *Provide many natural opportunities* each day to hear the language and see the language written down. Have the learner watch while visual lists, cue cards, and stories are written. Verbally highlight the letters and words while writing. Label line drawn symbols or purchase picture symbols that are already labeled.

   - Writing and drawing materials should be easily accessible—their use demonstrated and encouraged.

2. *Introduce keyboards, typewriters or computers.* Computers are highly reinforcing to most learners; use them as tools to expand communication. Structure fun and meaningful turn-taking games and exchange messages so learners understand that communication can occur in various ways and can be fun.

Warning: Unstructured random play with a computer is generally not productive, and it has the potential for developing meaningless and repetitive visual/motor routines. The computer's error messages provide highly reinforcing visual and auditory stimulation that has provided the motivation to practice errors.

3. *Provide physical support under the wrist or hand* when a learner is slow to initiate a response (e.g., slow to point to pictures or words while sharing a story book or magazine, slow to select messages on picture communication systems).

- Use a gentle but firm touch to the arm or shoulder to calm and direct attention.

- Hold the learner's hand back to slow down and prevent impulsive movements when typing or writing. This gives the learner time to survey and consider the options and make real choices. Illustration A on page 255 shows one effective way to support the hand.

Although Matt liked to print letters, he made them impulsively, stacking them on top of each other while he looked around the room. His teacher sat to the front on his dominant side so she could support his writing hand and know when he was looking directly at his work. The physical support was provided by placing two fingers under the palm of his writing hand. Each time Matt looked away, the teacher lifted his hand an inch or so from the paper and held it there gently and quietly. When Matt's eyes returned to the paper, the teacher lowered his hand so he could begin to write again.

4. *Review and use* the visual strategies (Chapter 14), the verbal strategies (Chapter 15), the strategies for teaching concepts (Chapter 19), and the strategies for establishing early communication skills (Chapter 17). These strategies will strengthen the learner's understanding of the language, communication and writing skills.

5. *Teach the child to use gestures* and a few basic signs, especially that a point = this.

6. *Teach the child to find and get the attention of a communication partner.* Use social story's or video modeling strategies to teach the child to (a) find someone to listen to him or her and (b) send a message.

7. *Capitalize on all natural opportunities* to communicate and provide the assistance to maintain success—to develop the learner's self-esteem, confidence, and willingness to persist.

Optional Strategy—Facilitated Communication

Facilitated communication (FC) is not a communication system but a way of supporting written communication. FC is a strategy for providing emotional and physical support to help an individual express needs and ideas by spelling on an alphabet board or by writing or typing on a typewriter or computer. The emotional support gives the learner confidence, first to try, and then to persist in efforts to communicate. The physical support to the hand or arm provides resistance that helps learners focus their movements and requires the learner to put forth concentrated and deliberate effort to move toward a specific letter. In effect the facilitation slows and inhibits the extraneous repetitive and impulsive movements.

Because the validity of FC has not been supported by the research, it is now rarely used. It is included in this manual because it has been helpful to some individuals with autism, and because this author agrees with Beukelman and Mirenda (1992), who said, "We believe that people with autism deserve to communicate successfully, even if we are unable to understand exactly how the technique helps them do so" (p. 288).

Facilitated communication should be considered as an alternative for others who are nonverbal and who have not benefited from the more accepted picture, sign, or written word systems.

Historical perspective

The use of emotional and physical support is an accepted procedure used by occupational therapists in their treatment of those with neurological and motor problems. FC was first used with individuals with autism by a physical therapist in Australia (Crossley, 1992). It was logical to try FC with those who have autism for it has been known for some time that they do have neurological and motor problems (Attwood, 1993; Courchesne et al., 1994; and Kanner, 1943). It has also been well documented that hyperlexia—the ability to read and spell at a high level without formal instruction—is fairly common in autism (O'Conner & Hermelin, 1994).

After its introduction in the United States (Biklen, 1990), many thought that this was the "magic treatment." The excitement waned and many stopped using FC because research has provided evidence that facilitators can unduly influence the writing (Twachman-Cullen, 1995).

Facilitated communication—Some effects

Before the FC movement really began in the United States, some families and speech-language pathologists had already discovered that specific physical and emotional support did enable their severely impaired children to express ideas and to communicate by typing on a computer (Schawlow & Schawlow, 1985; Swezy, 1985). Note that David Eastham, whose poetry is included throughout this book, was a nonverbal student with autism and apraxia. He could not speak or write, and communicated by pointing to a word board. In 1982, at age 19, his mother and his speech-language pathologist began using physical support to help him communicate by typing on a Sharp Memowriter (Eastham & Eastham, 1990). Other parents have reported that FC was of value to their child as well (see the following vignettes). These reports cannot be discounted or denied. When a learner writes about information that the facilitator has no way of knowing or little reason to suggest, it is obvious that the learner is writing an original message.

When Angelo arrived at school in an irritable mood, the facilitator asked him what was wrong. He typed: SOMETIMES THE JOY IS GONE. The interpreter was excited about this very poetic statement and shared it with Angelo's mother. Mother chuckled as she explained that he liked to hold a bottle of Joy detergent in front of his eyes and spin around. On this particular morning, the bottle was gone; it had been emptied and placed in the garbage the night before, and Angelo was upset.

Tony was sitting on the couch with a special facilitator, watching and commenting (with facilitation) about a football game on TV. His mother and a friend were across the room visiting quietly. Suddenly, Tony typed, SISSY COLORS. The interpreter was puzzled and said, "Sissy colors? I don't understand." His mother looked up, startled, and said, "Sissy colors? Don't you want a new yellow bedspread?" Tony typed, NO SISSY COLORS. This young man who rarely verbalized and was considered by many to be severely intellectually impaired had heard his mother's discussion about redecorating his bedroom, and he chose to express his opinion. A facilitator would have had little reason to attend to the conversation occurring across the room and even less reason to guide such a comment.

Parents and professionals with many years of experience in autism have developed a healthy skepticism about new "cures" or procedures. They have learned that most, but not all, new ideas have merit and may benefit some individuals with autism, but not every individual. They also know that it is important to explore new ideas with an open mind.

Facilitated communication—One option

Therefore, if an individual with autism has not benefited from the more common picture, signed or written word systems, the planning team may choose to try facilitated communication. Those who have made the most progress with FC are (a) nonverbal or who have limited verbal ability, (b) slow to initiate other responses (especially motor responses), and (c) show interest in TV, magazines, signs, and other printed material. Persons who have made the fewest gains are those who use repetitive or echoed speech. Scores on standardized intelligence tests are not a relevant predictor of potential progress.

Facilitator training

In FC, the facilitator's role is complex and demanding. In addition to providing emotional and physical support, the facilitator also acts as a major decision maker and negotiator of meaning during interactions (Sabin & Donnellan, 1993). With such an important role, *the training to prepare facilitators must be comprehensive to match the actual demands of the task.* Training should include a supervised practicum and follow-up, especially to discuss ethical issues related to decision making. Training competencies are being developed, and more comprehensive training for facilitators is offered at several reputable centers. See the list of resources in Appendix B.

In summary, written communication, with or without FC, is a valid option for many learners with autism. Learners who have never developed a dependable communication system should have the opportunity to try FC as part of a balanced program, regardless of their assumed potential—for facilitation has enabled some learners to become much more interactive. For some, FC has even opened the door to speech. Responsible decision making dictates that options must be kept open, for a child can grow up before all the research questions are answered (Schawlow & Schawlow, 1985).

Summary—Considerations for Interpreters

Expansion of communication options and the ability to understand and use the language to communicate effectively and reliably in every setting is a critical goal for all with autism spectrum disorders. Effective communication provides the foundation for greater independence. Interpreters (e.g., parents, family members, teachers, other school staff), as well as those who provide support in the community (e.g., job coaches, caregivers), will have a major role in expanding the communication habit and communication options for those with autism spectrum disorders. All must make a commitment to learn to use the communication system and to use it with the learner in many different situations. The interpreter's primary roles are to:

- Ensure that the system is always available, in good condition, and used consistently.

- Continue to evaluate and refine the system to match the changing demands of new environments and situations.

- Inform others in new settings about the communication system and encourage communication with other people.

- Model the use of the system to have fun, to play turn-taking games, to share experiences, to augment verbal instructions, and to facilitate interactions with peers.

Everyone needs a dependable system for expressing ideas and needs and to have fun in every setting. Ultimately, accessibility is the key issue, even if it means the individual looks a little different. Just as the person who is visually impaired has a cane and a guide dog, the person with autism has a communication system and an interpreter.

Brad's Story

—Written by his mother, Linda Benson

"Whatever do they have to smile and laugh about?" This was the question asked by my friend, another mother of a child with autism, as we attended our first meeting of Parents with Handicapped Children in 1971. At that point in our grieving lives, little seemed humorous. Indeed, I have a vast litany of horror stories from the early days.

Brad could have horrible nosebleeds. I became quite expert at stopping these. One, however, I couldn't stop. No one knew then he had autism. Of course, this child would not allow the doctor to treat him. A battle began between Brad and all the adults we could gather. The young doctor began swearing at me and screaming that I must be the worst mother he'd ever seen because I couldn't control my child. When the ordeal ended, I came to the lobby to pay my bill and cringed as the people there stared at this terrible mother.

Perhaps this helped build my character. However, I was a pretty nice person before having Brad, so why did I need this? As the years have ticked by, we have come to enjoy this young man, now 24 years old. He has made us laugh, and experiences with him have made us laugh. Imagine that!—actually enjoying having an autistic adult in the home. His innocence has brought on therapeutic belly laughs from his family. We so enjoy his literalness. We enjoy his unique abilities. (When other kids) come into the house, they say, "Hi, Brad. What years was Lassie on the air?" They all want him on their team for Encore and Trivia. When Brad's friend (also with autism) comes over, the other kids try to trick him on sports scores, but they never can. We all like to show off our talents, and those with autism are no different.

Since I have lived with autism for half my life and have been involved with other families, I feel capable of making some observations. It's work, it's time consuming, it's often overwhelming to have a child with autism. However, parents do better if they attend workshops to learn and get inspiration to try new things. I believe it is true that moms who are tough—not abusive, not mean, but tough—do better in the long run. If you know autism, your child, your rights, and the limits of what you will and will not tolerate, you will be further ahead than the mom who withdraws and lets her child run the show. To get where we are today has not been easy. Many mistakes have been made. I was tough on Brad in the early years, for I truly believe my job is to make my son socially acceptable. Being tough paid off. When Brad goes to movies, sporting events, concerts, plays, and out to eat, he acts appropriately.

Early intervention is the key. (Because there was no early intervention when Brad was young), I arranged our schedule by keeping the other kids up late and getting them up early so they would want a nap. Brad, who seemed to need no sleep, and I were then free to work for three hours every afternoon. We acted out prepositions, dramatized words, etc. He learned much from one-on-one experiences.

I remember not going through the years of discontent my friends did. I learned I had better things to do. I remember wondering why they worried about what color to paint the bathroom—not that one shouldn't paint the bathroom occasionally. I began to learn balance. I remember being thrown out of a store. I learned to hold my head up high. I remember kneading bread with a fury. I learned to have useful outlets for my anger. I remember being upset with the school. I learned diplomacy. Brad now works part time in the office at our business. His coworkers enjoy him and even ask him out to lunch. We "buy" other friends for Brad. I learned reality. Parents of garden-type kids often call me when things go wrong with their children. They see me as less judgmental than their other peers. I learned to listen. Our mothers' group took as much delight in bragging about this one being able to walk across the backs of a line of folding chairs; another one knowing all the scores of past ball games; one son being able to recite who produced, directed, and starred in any movie or TV show and the year it was made; one who could build marvelous block towers that defied the laws of gravity; and another who was able to pump the swing as high as it would go while he took off one shoe, scratched his foot, and put the shoe back on. Other mothers had such mundane brags—the honor roll or a hat trick in hockey. Their stories paled in comparison to ours.

Brad still wrings his hands, occasionally loses control, and is obviously disabled. There has been no miraculous cure. He can offer no insights into the world of autism. He never admitted to being autistic until Rain Man was made. Brad saw much of Raymond in himself. It was a status symbol to be like Dustin Hoffman.

He has worked hard to be like other people, and he grows more independent each day. We love our son. It sounds corny, but when things get rough, I always go to my bedroom and read the sign someone sent me: "Bloom where you are planted." I've tried. Hope you do, too.

[*Note*: In telephone conversations, Linda expressed her concern about the move to full integration for all students with autism, especially when it is seen by administrators as a means of saving money. If integration cannot be appropriately supported with staff training, it will be of little benefit and is likely to lead to behavior problems that disrupt the education of other students. Linda also wanted to emphasize that those with autism:

- Need extra time to process the things they hear, because the processing delay is a significant problem.

- Must be kept busy. Boredom and unstructured "down-time" lead to problems.

- Need opportunities to learn factual information about the world. A computer is a great tool for this.

An update, 8 years later:

Is there life after high school? YES. Thankfully those years of work by teachers, family, and friends paid off producing a fairly pleasant autistic adult. (I know, I know, I'm supposed to say a "person experiencing autism," but I've always maintained Brad is autistic. I'm the one experiencing autism.) Presently Brad is 32, a part-time office worker, a regular attendee of the theater and sporting events where he is well known, and a skilled trivia player at the local pub where patrons seek him for their team. Yes, he has a beer or two.

Life with Brad is not always pleasant. There are certain days when I wish I'd stayed a virgin. However, the early drilling of socially acceptable behavior and the constant hauling him to various events has produced a civil person able to be with many different types of people.

There is work still to be done. Why does he walk four paces behind me? Why does he bump people with a grocery cart? Why doesn't he ever give us a compliment or show appreciation? Why not so many things? Oh well. Taking a look at some other parents' problems, I guess we'll just keep working on ours and not feel too sorry for ourselves.

Expand Communication and Social Competence

Many individuals with autism spectrum disorders want to fit in. This is especially true for people with Asperger's syndrome. They want to be socially involved and have various kinds of successful relationships with others. But many of these individuals are baffled by the way others think, talk, and manage social situations—by the way others use words, change topics, and make decisions so quickly. To compound the problem, people with autism commonly hold false perceptions or false beliefs (Figure 21.1) that have a unique impact on their communication and social skills (Baron-Cohen, Leslie, & Frith, 1985, Baron-Cohen et al., 1993).

Figure 21.1 Some False Perceptions That Are Common in Autism

- Every word has a single meaning.
- A rule applies only to a single situation;
  or,
  A rule applies in the same way always and forever.
- Everyone believes the same things I believe.
- If I know something, everyone else knows it, too.
- In a group, the speaker is talking only to me;
  or,
  In a group, the speaker is not talking to me.
- If someone says it, it's true.
- I should do exactly what I'm told, in exactly the way I'm told or taught.
- If I don't know exactly what to do, I should do nothing.

An understanding of these false beliefs, along with a brief review of the specific learning strengths and deficits common in autism (Chapter 2), will provide clues for interpreting the cause of social difficulties and suggest interventions.

We cannot assume that any learner diagnosed with autism fully or accurately understands a particular problem, situation, or expectation—social or otherwise. The fact that gestalt learners take in chunks of information quickly, does not mean that they are gestalt thinkers—for they have difficulty breaking these chunks down, analyzing them, comparing them with other ideas, integrating all the pieces to understand cause/effect relationships, developing broader ideas, and understanding the perspective of others (Winner, 2000). For example, when one young man finally understood why it was important not to interrupt and learned how and when to enter a conversation politely, he stopped interrupting—but he continued to carry on long dissertations about electronic speakers and microphones, unaware of his listener's boredom.

To solve social problems and increase social competence, it is necessary to plan interventions carefully. The first steps are to identify the details that the learner:

- May currently misunderstand or has a limited literal understanding

- May misunderstand during instruction

- May misunderstand in different situations

Systematic analysis and instruction will increase social awareness and competence. But because it is not possible to teach everything, we must decide which skills to teach, which skills might be pivotal and have the greatest impact on a broad range of situations (Koegel & Frea, 1993).

Regardless of how comprehensive instruction may be, some problems will generally remain (i.e., problems with literal thinking, predicting and understanding the perspective of others, making judgments, making considered and safe decisions). Therefore, an interpreter must be available on some regular basis to provide practical assistance, to help the learner make sense of the social world, to assist in solving problems, and sometimes to develop adaptations that provide support in confusing or high-risk situations. The support team, and especially the family, must consider both the risks and the value of increasing independence, and they must ensure that appropriate support is available.

Social problems are manifested differently in each individual, and the instructional and support needs will vary depending on age, verbal ability (or skill with an alternative system), past experiences, level of cognitive development, and the demands of individual environments.

See Figure 21.2 for a sample of the array of complex communication and social skills required for effective participation in different situations. Many of these skills are learned almost automatically by most people, but those with autism need specific information and instruction to manage them.

Communication and social skills are best learned in the context of natural routines—where natural opportunities are available to make choices, solve problems, and use functional communication and social skills (see Chapters 13 and 18 for strategies to develop and teach functional routines). However, the natural activities of the day do not offer enough opportunities either to teach those lessons that others learn without instruction or to practice the complex skills to establish strong social and communication habits.

More opportunities are needed to provide the systematic instruction and additional practice for the more subtle skills such as sharing, cooperating, providing assistance, negotiating, and resolving conflicts. Because these skills cannot be learned in isolation, it is necessary to plan additional contexts. Reverse mainstreaming, a strategy for pairing an expert peer with the learner served in the special classroom, has been a successful first step (Wooten & Mesibov, 1986). For those integrated in regular classrooms, it is necessary to inform the peers about the types of problems that are likely to occur and provide them with strategies to help the learner and to be a friend. In structured small groups, peers can model and provide more natural practice.

Structured play groups provide a natural context for learners younger than 8. For learners who are 9 or older, social-skill groups offer a setting for a more systematic, cognitive approach that can lead to greater independence. After leaving the school structure, young adult learners need social support groups to maintain social contacts and transfer skills to a wide variety of situations (Mesibov, 1986).

Figure 21.2 Skills for Social and Communication Competence

Skills for giving and receiving information

- Locate partner; initiate interaction appropriately.
- Acknowledge and respond to others who want to talk to you.
- Manage conversations:
  —Take/maintain/relinquish turns.
  —Stay on topic, or suggest a new topic.
  —Check for and repair breakdown in understanding.
  —Terminate the conversation politely.
  —Recognize when others want to terminate.
  —Enter an ongoing conversation politely.
- Keep a conversation going:
  —Engage in chit-chat, "hanging out."
  —Identify/negotiate topics.
  —Express messages clearly.
  —Ask for clarification.
  —Give and follow directions.
  —Ask and answer questions to expand the topic.
  —Persuade.
- Delivery:
  —Use appropriate eye contact.
  —Check body language, posture, distance.
  —Check vocal quality, intonation.
  —Check speed.
  —Use courtesy and good manners.
  —Check whether assertive and persistent, or passive, aggressive, or dominating.
- Identify meanings. Are they:
  —Nonliteral (Idioms, sarcasm, jokes, . . .)?
  —Fact, or opinion?
  —Real, or pretend/fantasy?
  —True or false?
- Active listening:
  In individual conversations or small groups:
  —Use eye contact, and give attention to speaker.
  —Identify meaning of nonverbal messages (facial expressions, body language).
  —Identify meaning of verbal messages; generate responses to messages.
  In class:
  —Identify instructions and main points; make notes.
  —Use reflective listening.

Understanding the perspectives of others:

- Who is speaking? Whom does that person see? To whom is that person speaking?
- Who is in the audience? What does the audience see and hear?
- What do other people know? Do they always know what you know?
- What might others feel, think, or believe?
- Who did it? Did it happen to you? To someone else? Did you read about it or see it on TV?

Figure 21.2 Skills for Social and Communication Competence (*continued*)

Skills for peer-group participation:

- Get attention.
- Take turns; share and cooperate.
- Assist, and ask peers for assistance.
- Give compliments; say, "Thank you."
- Watch and imitate peers play and/or communicate.
- Follow group directions.
- Solve conflicts.

Skills for making and keeping friends:

- Identify mutual interests.
- Invite, accept, or reject invitations politely.
- Learn to play a variety of games.
- Plan events for mutual enjoyment.
- Keep in contact (make phone calls, send e-mail or fax messages).
- Offer and provide assistance.
- Provide feedback indicating pleasure and displeasure.
- Cooperate and negotiate.
- Observe social and sexual rules.

Skills for self-management:

- Solve problems.
- Make choices.
- Plan to achieve a goal (social, work, other).
- Make phone calls (at home; from pay phones).
- Seek assistance regarding medical, business, and personal needs.
- Follow workplace and community social rules.
- Obtain and accept assistance.
- Tolerate correction.
- Monitor your own feelings and behavior.
- Manage stress; maintain self-control.

Guidelines for Planning Group Instruction and Practice

Five elements of successful group instruction require thoughtful planning: selection of members, clarification of rules, development of routines, type of leadership, and selection of strategies to promote generalization of new skills.

Membership

An effective instructional group has an even number of members to allow for work, play, or interactions with partners. There can be two or as many as six or eight members, depending on age, abilities, space, and the goals of the learner. Members are selected for their ability to share ideas and model socially acceptable social and communication skills. Although peers who have mild communication or interaction problems can be effective models, those who are streetwise and who model inappropriate behavior present problems for learners who lack social judgment and reasoning ability.

- Membership should reflect a balance of interaction styles and skill levels. It is difficult to have fun if all are withdrawn or inhibited, if all want to dominate, or if all have the same strengths and deficits.

- Peers without autism need preparation to understand how to be helpful without providing unnatural or too much support.

Group Rules

A few simple rules are necessary to facilitate interactions and involvement and to establish and maintain a positive and productive session. For example:

1. If you need help, ask your partner.

2. Everyone gets a chance to talk.

3. When someone else is talking, watch and listen.

Young learners will need support to learn basic group participation skills—to watch and listen to the teacher, to do what the teacher says, and to wait and take turns. They also need to understand the language of group directions and rules.

Group Routine

The considerations for planning a group session are the same as for planning other events and routines. All of the components of a routine must be clarified. See Figure 13.1 for a list of the components and Figure 13.2 for a sample plan.

The primary goals for the first few sessions are to establish a familiar routine and to nurture a working and supportive relationship between the members. The formula for scheduling activities to capitalize on their reinforcing qualities applies to scheduling the daily group activities as well (see Figure 12.3).

- A session begins with discussion of the session schedule (with visual references) and an easy and enjoyable activity or routine to help the members focus on each other.

- The hard work comes in the middle of the session. A central activity or project provides the structure and common focus for the hard work of interacting. The type of activity depends on the age and skills of the group members and the goals for the group.

- The session ends with another easy and enjoyable routine that enables the members to leave calmly but eager to return. For example, summarize the session activities and concepts in a group experience story. A group relaxation and visualization period provides closure and helps members to leave the session relaxed and ready for the next event.

Beginning and ending each session with the same or similar activities develops a comfortable and familiar routine within which the learner can tolerate the hard and demanding interactions. The group experiences must be interesting and fun, and all members must feel successful when they leave.

Group Leadership

The effective group leader is a facilitator and coach (Little, 1989). The facilitator sets up situations, then coaches the action. In setting up the situation, the coach selects the partners for balance (that is, determines the lineup).

In the role as coach, the facilitator:

1. Explains the activity and the rules (the game plan)

2. Uses diagrams and charts

3. Suggests strategies—ways to solve a problem

4. Demonstrates and models

5. Observes and coaches the practice sessions from the sidelines

6. Reviews, provides feedback, and prepares for the next session

In summary, the leader encourages the members to talk, play, and interact with each other. The leader:

- Does not dominate the attention by asking questions to elicit specific responses

- Encourages the members to respond naturally in ways that reinforce a partner ("Tommy said he wanted the yellow truck. Can you hand it to him?" or "Tommy is helping you button your paint shirt. You can say, 'Thank you, Tommy.'")

- Avoids unnatural and intrusive verbal reinforcement (such as, "I like the way you said 'Thank you'"; "Good talking"; "Good playing")

This type of verbal reinforcement interrupts the focus and flow of the activity and the relationship. It also disrupts and clutters the natural reinforcement delivered by the peer as a direct result of efforts to interact, to request, or to suggest.

Strategies for Teaching and Generalization

Develop a plan to share the group goals and new skills with other interpreters so they may support them in other natural contexts. This may be done with a newsletter, a schedule of planned activities, or a group experience story written at the conclusion of each session. Incorporating self-monitoring cards or checklists also contributes to generalization. Parents and other interpreters need to know of any specific or sensitive topics that came up in the sessions.

The following visual and verbal strategies that are effective with older and higher-functioning verbal learners can be adapted for individuals who communicate in different ways:

- Basic verbal strategies: giving directions, using contingencies (Chapter 15)

- Reflective listening (Chapter 15)

- Checklists, cue cards (Chapter 14)

- Semantic mapping (Chapters 14 and 22)

- Problem-solving and cause/effect formats (Chapter 22)

- Social stories (Chapter 14)

- Group planning and rehearsal (Chapter 21)

- Coaching (Chapter 21)

- Modeling with commentary and visual references (Chapter 18)

- Role playing with scripts and feedback (Chapters 21 and 22)

- Videotaping actual or simulated situations for discussion, feedback, and rehearsal (Chapter 21)

- Video modeling (Chapter 22)

- Imagery procedures and cognitive picture rehearsal (Chapter 22)

- Relaxation procedures (Chapter 22)

Most people, including those with autism disorders, do not like to remember, think, or talk about their social failures—this is especially true for those with Asperger's syndrome. Many of these students get angry or may withdraw from or resist discussions or assistance that they perceive to be criticism. It may be more effective, and certainly it is more sensitive and respectful, to focus group discussions, role playing, stories, and other activities around a fictional person who has similar problems.

Some direct-instruction social-skills programs are useful resources; but without modification, the learner with autism is likely to memorize the rules, the scripts, and the responses with little understanding.

Resources for Planning

Books

Coyne, P., Nyberg, C., & Vandenberg, M. L. (1999). *Developing leisure time skills for persons with autism.* Austin, TX: Future Horizons

Fullerton, A. (1994). *Putting feet on my dreams: A program in self-determination.* Portland, OR: Portland State University

Grant, J. O., Lazarus, B. B., & Peyton, H. (1992). The use of dialogue journals with students with exceptionalities. *Teaching Exceptional Children, Summer,* 22–24.

Gray, C. (1994). *Comic strip conversations.* Arlington, TX: Future Horizons

Howlin, P., Baron-Cohen, S., & Hadwin, J. (1999). *Teaching children with autism to mind read: A practical guide.* New York: Wiley and Sons.

Mayo, P., & Waldo, P. (1986). *Scripting: Social communication for adolescents.* (Scripts for role playing.) Eau Claire, WI: Thinking Publications.

Musselwhite, C. R. (1986). *Adaptive play for special needs children.* San Diego: College-Hill Press.

Schmeltzer, K. R., Jordan, K., & Skowron-Gooch, A. (in press). *I'm experiencing technical difficulties: A comprehensive guide to teaching social-cognitive skills to students with Asperger's syndrome.* Salem, OR: Willamette ESD.

Includes a comprehensive listing of the "Critical Curricular Components" for preschool/kindergarten, elementary, and secondary students. Each section is divided into three units: relationships and people, self-advocacy, and leisure. It also includes one or more sample lesson plans for each skill, including typical activities and references to other authors and resources.

Shure, M. B. (1992). *I can problem solve: An interpersonal cognitive problem-solving program for intermediate elementary grades.* Champaign, IL: Research Press.

Also available for preschool, kindergarten, and primary grades.

Vernon, A. (1989). *Thinking, feeling, behaving: An emotional education curriculum for adolescents, grades 1–6 and grades 7–12.* Champaign, IL: Research Press.

Also available for grades 1–6.

Winner, M. G. (2000). *Inside out: What makes a person with social cognitive deficits tick? The I laugh approach.* San Jose, CA: Author.

Especially useful for one-to-one and small groups—includes suggestions for visual clarification and reproducible worksheets.

Wolfberg, P. J. (1999). *Play and imagination in children with autism.* New York: Columbia University Teacher's College Press.

Video Tape and Computer Programs

Walker-Hirsch, L., & Champagne, M. P. (1993). *Circles I. Intimacy & Relationships*. Santa Barbara, CA: James Stanfield.

> The program includes 17 live-action video programs, laminated wall posters, laminated stick-on icons, and a teacher's guide for teaching about social distance and relationship building. (For middle school through adult—Circles II, on avoiding exploitation, is also available.) (www.stanfield.com)

See section on video modeling in (Chapter 22) and computer-based instruction (Chapter 29). Also see Resources in Appendix B.

Integrated Play Groups

The integrated play group model first introduced by Wolfberg and Shuler in 1993 has been shown to be quite effective for young children with autism spectrum disorders—they benefit from seeing their peers engaged as they participate in interactive and imaginative play.

Participation in play with more expert players, especially if those expert players have been prepared or coached to provide support and assistance to the novice player, is particularly helpful (Schuler & Wolfberg, 2000; Wolfberg, 1999, 2000; Zercher, Hunt, Schuler, & Webster, 2001).

Note: These references also provide special considerations and strategies.

A child is prepared to participate with a peer soon after learning to value interactions with an adult in one-to-one play sessions. Other indicators of readiness for a play include:

- Ability to take several turns in an interaction
- Ability to play with a variety of natural materials, and
- Ability to tolerate and engage in short periods of structured play with a single peer.

Goals

Some of the goals for structured play groups are listed in Figure 21.2: Skills for Social and Communication Competence. Sensory and motor skills, symbolic play, and a variety of other developmental goals also can be addressed in play contexts (Musselwhite, 1986).

Organization and Structure

The size of a play group depends on the age and sensory needs of the learner—a 3-year-old child with autism can generally tolerate three other children. As tolerance and skills expand, so can the number of children in the group. An even number of children is needed so everyone can have a partner. Two or three 20–30 minute sessions a week is a minimum amount of time to provide continuity for very young children. Older children can benefit from fewer but longer sessions.

For an optimum level of stimulation so the learner can maintain equilibrium, balance the new with the familiar (i.e., if the peers are unfamiliar, plan a familiar setting, interpreter, materials, and activities). Once the peers are familiar, begin to vary the other elements such as new toys, new activities, etc.

Setting

Provide a relatively small, safe area with limited distractions and well-defined boundaries. A small table with chairs, shelves for materials, and a small rug will define the spaces within the play setting. If the children are to have the freedom to select and direct the play, the setting must be arranged so that essentially anything they choose to do or play will be acceptable and safe. Have materials organized on shelves with labels so children can end the play by putting things in their appropriate places.

Materials and Activities

Materials and activities are those that age-appropriate peers enjoy in the natural setting. But before selecting materials, assess to identify preferences—see Wolfberg (1999) for a Play Preference Inventory. Select the toys and adapt the rules so that sharing, cooperation, and some form of communication is required. For example, for a group of four children, have only two puzzles available so they will have to share. Give each partner half the pieces and require the partners to take turns. Organize a snack time so that one partner holds the jar of peanut butter while the other spreads it on the cracker, and one holds the glass while the other pours.

Strategies

The group rules, routines, and leadership role provide the supportive structure for using a wide variety of strategies. In the role of coach, the interpreter provides suggestions and cues to keep the interactions positive.

Strategies include modeling, parallel talking, and reflective listening Chapters 15, 18, and 22. Visual strategies include the use of a chart or mini-calendar to clarify the session schedule of activities, use of cue cards and gestures during the activities, and stories to summarize the session activities (see the information for using visual strategies in Chapter 14).

Social-Skills Groups

Social-skills groups can be designed to match the needs of children of all levels of ability. They are especially important for those who are higher functioning or who have Asperger's. The social-skills group is an important context for learners between ages 9 and 21 when the more cognitive aspects of thinking, reasoning, and problem solving must be established. This is when they must learn to understand the perspective of others and to learn the skills to set and achieve life goals (Fullerton & Coyne, 1999). The social-skills group provides a safe place to rehearse new ways of interacting and opportunities to develop friendships and mentor relationships.

Goals

The broad range of skills listed in Figure 21.2 can be introduced at a basic level for younger elementary students and expanded to address the needs of the adolescent. Other goals can relate to developing friendships and solving interpersonal problems that can carry over to the playground, and to church, 4-H, scout, and other community groups.

Organization and Structure

Groups generally meet weekly for at least 30 minutes (or one-school period) as a natural part of the regular school program. A limit of six to eight students in each group provides enough time for all to express themselves. The most effective peer models are those who are not perfect—individuals who have some problems but can still provide appropriate models. Without some prior training, high-achieving peers may dominate and inhibit others in the group. Review the guidelines for selecting members on page 372. A beginning and ending routine is often helpful.

Setting

The setting is similar to that for play groups with enough space for larger students to role-play and engage in various projects.

Materials and Activities

Provide butcher paper or chart pads and pens to record ideas and decisions. Other materials will depend on the scheduled activity. A video camera, player, and monitor are useful for recording and reviewing role-play sessions or for observing commercially prepared instructional tapes.

Select activities from a basic social-skills curriculum and resources such as those listed on page 375. Adapt all activities to encourage cooperation, joint efforts, and negotiation.

Strategies for Expanded Applications and Transfer

- Select and vary the activities as naturally occurring school problems dictate so that skills are relevant (parents and teachers are good resources to identify problems).

- Inform parents and other teachers of the learner's objectives and new strategies so they can provide cues and support to use those skills in natural situations.

- Provide cue cards, self-monitoring, and self-reinforcement systems to use in the natural setting. Have the child watch as you prepare the visuals while you explain the meaning of the words and pictures. If he hears it, sees it, and perhaps rehearses it, he is more likely to understand what to do.

- Begin sessions with opportunities to share failures and successes that occurred since the last meeting. Koegel, Frea, and Surratt (1994) describe some systematic ways to teach self-monitoring and self-management skills (also see Chapter 22.)

- Rotate responsibilities for the session as higher-functioning group members become more experienced. With support (and sometimes using rehearsal and cue cards), they can take turns planning and directing the activities, planning and making videotapes of role-played situations, managing the group discussion, and taking responsibility for other tasks.

- Ending a session with a group relaxation exercise is a positive way to prepare for the transition back to the regular school routine.

- Most learners will continue to need an ongoing social-skills group, while peers may need or want to participate only briefly. Changing membership can be a positive experience in that it enables learners to become acquainted with more people. One way to preserve the continuity of the group is to require a commitment for a series of six or eight group meetings. Schedule a new series after a 2- or 3-week break, thus giving peers opportunities to either make a new commitment or drop out. Begin each new series with getting-acquainted activities to establish group cohesiveness and trust.

Social-Support Groups

Support groups are common and productive for those with various kinds of physical or emotional needs after they leave school. Too often, those with autism are isolated without social contacts during the summers and after leaving school. These meetings provide a place where others will understand their unique problems, where they can learn new coping strategies, and where they can have fun. Those with autism also need a place where it is not necessary to always be on guard to control every action and "act normal."

Goals

The primary goals of social-support groups are to develop friendships and to have enjoyable social experiences. A secondary by-product of these sessions is that social skills are strengthened and expanded.

Organization and Structure

Leadership can be shared by parents and professionals from local autism programs or parent groups. Group members can share some responsibilities if support is available. For example, committees can be established for making calls to remind the members of meetings, make arrangements for special events, and plan refreshments for each meeting—for some individuals come to the group because of the food. Committee work can be a valuable means of developing self-esteem, responsibility, and leadership skills.

Membership in the group is open; any adult with autism is welcome to join. Peers without disabilities are recruited to provide support and structure for enjoyable experiences or to be partners in team activities and committees. University students in psychology, social work, or education, who are preparing to work with those who have disabilities, may be excellent peer partners, mentors, and friends. Sinclair (1992) noted that mentors are needed to provide structure so interesting things can happen.

Schedule a series of six to eight meetings or a series that coincides with a school or university term, or meetings can be ongoing. Adult groups generally have evening or weekend meetings, two or three times a month. Meetings can last for 1 or 2 hours to allow time for planning special events, rehearse the skills needed for successful participation in special events, and allow for refreshments and social interactions.

Activities

Regular group meetings should begin with a familiar routine. For example, at a specified time, after everyone is in their chairs, the group leader explains the evening's schedule of activities while writing the schedule on a large chart or chalkboard. Thus everyone can relax and know what to expect.

- Initially, a parent, teacher, or other interpreter will likely need to run the meetings. Later, as the members begin to feel more comfortable with the routine of the meeting, they can take turns or elect another leader from the group.

- Always have a large chart or other writing surface available when plans and decisions are being made to make the information visual.

- Planning for special events, outings, and projects is often the major element of the group meetings. A group might plan to eat at a favorite restaurant, go camping or hiking, attend a sporting event, or participate in a community improvement project or fund drive.

  - Plan a fair or festival for members to display hobbies and collections related to their special interests. This project provides an opportunity to find others with common interests that can be shared outside the group.

  - Hold game nights to learn a variety of games. Both physical and table games can provide a vehicle for interactions in other social settings. Often, game rules need to be adapted to compensate for physical problems or the lack of competitiveness.

- Establish another routine to end the meeting so the members are prepared for leaving—this routine could include a review of the schedule and decisions that have been made or a group sing-a-long—or whatever seems to match the groups needs.

Planning to Capitalize on Group Events

Planning and participating in special events provides many opportunities to practice a wide range of skills while having fun. To capitalize on these opportunities and to ensure that all aspects of an event are considered:

- Plan and review. Establish a familiar group routine for planning special events. A good resource for planning is found in Chapter 13. This process ensures that no detail is forgotten and provides a context for "what-if" problem solving. Both are important issues when planning for those with the range of autism disorders (see also Mesibov, 1986).

- Prepare and rehearse before participation in the event. Review the chart that clearly shows the schedule of the event from beginning to end. They need to review what to take, what to do first, then what to do next, and how to get help if they have a problem.

  - Highlight the important and relevant elements to ensure that everyone has a common experience to share later (i.e., rules of the game, the purpose or important meanings of the event). Without this preparation, the members are likely to have little to share after the event is over, even though they all participated. For example:

    After a trip to the bowling alley, one person may know how many holes are in the ceiling tile, another may know the number of balls of each size and color, one may have been concerned that the bowling shoes were not arranged neatly on the shelf, another may have the snack-shop menu memorized, and still another may have been so overwhelmed that she kept her ears covered and was only aware of the noise of the pins falling over.

- Identify the social expectations of the event. Discuss, rehearse, and role play, or show a video of appropriate manners and rules that will be required to participate successfully.

- Develop individual visual adaptations. A cue card may support one learner at a restaurant, or a card setting forth modifications to the game rules may enable another learner to participate and have fun. Earplugs may provide comfort to those with highly sensitive hearing. See visual strategies in Chapter 14.

- Some members may have more fun if they are assigned specific jobs, such as passing a tray of food, pouring the coffee, managing a guest book, or organizing guests' coats. Many individuals can benefit from cue cards to remind them of things to talk about. Others may feel more secure with something to share that can focus an interaction—some photographs, a magazine, or a small but tricky puzzle. Augmentative communication systems must be available.

- Do it—and have fun.

- Review, share, and modify. Following the event—or at the next meeting—review the event, identify any problems, and discuss solutions. Then decide if people want to do the activity again. If so, modify the plan to avoid earlier problems.

- Do it again.

Individual Support Sessions

The individual instruction or counseling sessions described in this book are not to be confused with traditional psychoanalytic therapies or one-to-one sessions based on clinical behavior modification principles that manipulate the antecedents and consequences. Rather, a more effective approach for those with autism spectrum disorders who are higher functioning and more verbal involves an integration of cognitive and behavioral strategies that actively involve the learner in analyzing and solving real problems and that address the misperceptions (Chapter 21) that confound emotional and relationship problems. Cognitive strategies are practical, and they address issues in a concrete and forthright manner that ensures understanding and increases motivation and self-esteem. See Winner (2000) and Freeman and Dake (1997).

Ideally, these sessions are conducted by a sensitive and skillful interpreter who understands the impact of autism on thinking and behavior. The interpreter might be a teacher, speech-language pathologist, occupational therapist, school counselor, or counselor in private practice.

Goals

In addition to addressing many of the skills listed in Figure 21.2, other complex and sensitive issues can be targeted, such as teaching social/sexual skills and helping an individual manage grief and loss.

1. *Understanding the subtleties of social relationships*

    How do you know whom you can trust? What do you do when someone teases? Tells you to eat garbage? Tells you to take something that is not yours?

    > Sam, age 17, had a number of questions: What is a friend? What is a friend who is a girl? When is a girl a girlfriend? What is a girlfriend? What does a girlfriend expect? What is a date—June 26th or dates you eat? Why do people kiss? (His perspective: "Kissing is not sanitary. If the girl is really nice and likes me, she won't want to kiss me and give me her germs.") Sam decided that he didn't want a girlfriend if it meant she would touch, hug, or kiss him and expect him to touch, hug, and kiss her.

2. *Coping with everyday problems* to make choices, solve problems, and manage stress to maintain self-control

3. *Understanding and dealing with feelings and complex social problems*, such as intense worries or grief and loss related to death and major life changes

    > One young person wondered: What does it feel like to be sad? Where do you feel sad? What makes you feel sad? How does feeling sad look? He told his interpreter, "I knew I should feel sad, but I just watched others feeling sad."

Structure and Strategies

The support team may identify a need for more formal, regularly scheduled individual support to manage confidential emotional and social issues.

More formal individual sessions that address these complex and highly sensitive issues require a certain structure to ensure that learners will achieve their goals. The interpreter or counselor assigned to lead these sessions needs the background and experience to:

■ Establish a rapport and a trusting relationship that supports the learner who is facing these most difficult and sensitive issues. Rapport can often be facilitated by showing an interest in the learner's special skills or hobbies.

■ Establish a familiar routine within the session—a routine that enables the learner to know the basic sequence of activities and to be prepared for the end of the session. When this routine or sequence of the sessions is visual the learner will be able to relax and remain open to think about more abstract concepts.

■ Identify the critical issues, details, and misperceptions—the interpreter must be able to see the problem from the learner's perspective and help the learner see the world from the perspective of others. This requires creative sleuthing and sensitive questioning. It may also require a functional behavioral assessment of the problem situations (page 445). Often, it is the smallest detail that triggers major problems, and it may be the smallest adjustment or bit of information that makes a major difference toward solving a problem.

- Establish a cooperative relationship with parents and teachers in order to:
  - Target and clarify important problems and obtain critical facts about those problems
  - Provide feedback so others can offer consistent support and help the learner transfer new skills and insights to the real world
- Use visual strategies to:
  - Augment verbal information and serve as reference for later use
  - Reduce the effort required to hold the ideas together in order to think about them
  - Organize details and show relationships
  - Solve problems, generate alternatives, and evaluate consequences: "If this, then this."
  - Reduce stress and anxiety to prevent intense emotions
  - Videotapes, fiction books, or non-fiction books about others who have solved similar problems are often useful.
- Allow the learner to use alternative ways to express ideas

Tom, 15 years old, had been expelled from school after getting angry and pushing over a bookcase. The interpreter visited this young man at his home. Tom was relatively open and friendly until the conversation turned to his problem at school. Then he moved to the couch and curled up in a fetal position with his eyes closed. With a yellow tablet and pencil in hand, the interpreter moved calmly to sit on the floor beside the couch. "Is this the way it happened?" she asked, as she sketched a sequence of line drawings to illustrate her explanation of the problem. Tom opened his eyes and watched her draw the pictures as she talked softly to label the pictures. Soon he reached for the pencil to make his own drawing as he said, "No, it was like this." When the pressure of face-to-face discussion was removed, and with an alternative way to express himself, he and the interpreter were able to identify the real problems.

Jeff, 11 years old, was in a regular school program with an interpreter. When in stress, Jeff could express himself better by writing out his thoughts in response to his interpreter's written statements. This script was written during a totally silent, wordless exchange in a counseling session that occurred right after a major tantrum. The punctuation and spelling are his.

Mrs. K: Jeff, here is a rule. Do whatever the teacher says. When the teacher tells you to do something, you need to do it.

Jeff: What if I felt inside that I don't want to do it. But I know what I'm so post to do but it happen sometimes. Mrs. K. Its or right I know you know.

Mrs. K: One of the things you learn to do in school is follow directions, so we'll keep working on you following directions without having a tantrum.

Jeff: Please I know OK. Remember in you r sometimes I could of got out of control and I won't mean to do it. You don't have to get stern no more because every time its my behavior its an accident never on purpose. You can give me a hug sometimes it really happens and its not your dream.

Mrs. K: I know it's an accident Jeff. But when I tell you to do something and I show you how to do it and I make sure you understand, what are you going to do?

Jeff: Remember its just how the way it is. But sometimes Jeff will do it if its that it wont make me feel like I wont do it.

Mrs. K: Jeff, will you follow the teacher's directions?

Jeff: Only if I feel in side Yes it I'll do it.

Mrs. K: Answer yes or no.

Jeff: It just depends If I want to do it or not. It just depend on what its like OK. Sometimes I don't want you doing something I don't want you to do It makes feel like saying NO I don't want to do it OK Its just that you don't know what's going on OK You don't have to get stern because you know why it's just that it depends on how its like OK The only reason why it happens is because you have to know why it happens and guess what you want to be stern. That's the problem. . . .

This type of thinking is typical in autism—an inability to identify the real problem and an inability to simply agree or to make a promise that will end the lecture. To Jeff, a promise meant every time and forever—a promise he could not keep because, "It just depends on what its like . . . its just how the way it is."

Needless to say, this type of session takes a long time, but it is productive. This particular script certainly clarified the fact that other strategies are needed to get this young man to follow the rules.

Dealing With Grief and Loss

People experience a sense of loss about many things—death, lost jobs, friends who move away, personal moves to new communities, houses, or schools, a family illness or divorce. Most people are involved in the process enough to understand when a major change or loss is imminent, and they can prepare themselves. When losses occur, they have many ways to work through their feelings, primarily through remembering and sharing with friends.

Those with autism have little control over their lives and often they don't receive information that would prepare them for these changes or losses. They tend to be left out of the family preparation and grieving process because they appear to be disinterested and devoid of feelings. Their inability to communicate feelings and ask questions contributes to the problem. People move in and out of their lives with little explanation, and they fail to understand why things happen.

For the verbal learner, the first sign of a problem may be when the learner begins to ask repeated questions about the loss. For the learner with limited verbal ability, the first sign may be withdrawal or some form of agitation, resistance, or general "out-of-sorts" behavior. These signs may not occur for many weeks or even months after the loss occurred.

Strategies

These learners need direct and literal preparation for potential changes. During and after the change, the individual needs sensitive, concrete, and literal explanations and opportunities to share memories. Experience stories and social stories provide contexts for preparing for changes and for sharing in the grieving process.

In assessing behavior problems, one important question relates to losses: *Has the individual experienced losses or major changes in the past year—moves, deaths, divorce of parents, sister off to college, or a favorite staff member or support person no longer present?*

> A month after his grandfather died, José began to ask people, "When will Grandpa be back?" He approached his parents, his teacher, the school secretary, even strangers to get information. When he got a different answer from each person, he became more and more upset. It was finally decided that José needed to talk about his grandfather, but that he needed to know whom to approach and when he could approach those people. His calendar was revised to include two 10-minute periods (morning and afternoon) when he would visit the school counselor. The counselor and José's mother coordinated their messages so that both would give him the same information. His mother sent snapshots of the grandfather to school so José could share them with the counselor and place them in an album. As José worked through his grief, other topics of conversation were offered. Gradually, José needed less time to talk about his grandfather.

Although most people assume that those with autism spectrum disorders do not develop loving and close relationships and therefore, they feel no grief at the loss of those relationships, *this is not true*. They need to be included in some way, and whenever possible, they need to be prepared before these changes occur. They need time to say goodbye to a favorite job, coach, dependable teaching assistant, or close family member who is dying. They need to be able to talk or share pictures and experiences to provide comfort. And sometimes they need to develop a way to keep in touch with old friends.

Summary

Communication and social interactions present the most stressful and demanding challenges for those with autism and those who support them. Participation in play groups as young children, social-skills groups as they get older, and social support groups can provide an opportunity to engage in interactions. They can also improve their skills so their communication and interactions can be more successful and satisfying. Many individuals with autism and especially those with Asperger's are gifted in a variety of ways. Improved communication and social skills will help them capitalize on those gifts, to hold more satisfying jobs, and to participate and contribute more fully to their communities.

Individuals with autism feel emotions that they are not able to express in the typical ways. Many want social contacts and interactions with members of both sexes. However, it cannot be assumed that they want those contacts for the typical reasons, or that without instruction they will know how to manage interactions in a way that satisfies both partners. Social/sexual issues are discussed in Chapter 23.

A statement by Jim Sinclair has much to help us understand the nature and the needs of those with autism as we make decisions that will affect their lives:

> "In some ways I am terribly ill-equipped to survive in this world, like an extraterrestrial stranded without an orientation manual. . . . But my personhood is intact. My selfhood is undamaged. I find great value and meaning in my life, and I have no wish to be cured of being myself. . . . Grant me the dignity of meeting me on my own terms. Recognize that we are equally alien to each other, that my ways of being are not merely damaged versions of yours. Question your assumptions. Define your terms. Work with me to build more bridges between us." (Sinclair, 1992, p. 302)

22 | Teach Awareness of Self and Others—Self-Control and Self-Management Strategies

The multiple, interrelated, sensory modulation and information processing factors cause much of the ever-present stress in those with autism spectrum disorders. These neurological differences in processing are also reflected in the so-called "mind-blindness" that prevents those within the autism spectrum from understanding that others have a different worldview. They do not automatically learn to see the perspective of others or to see themselves from the perspective of others. It is this "theory of mind" deficit (Baron-Cohen, 1988) that some see as the core deficit that separates those with autism and Asperger's syndrome from those with other disabilities.

Not only do those with ASD have difficulty understanding their own feelings and the perspective of others, they do not automatically learn the hidden curriculum that is a part of every culture. Every culture has its own set of unspoken rules of conduct and taboos that are never discussed or taught—everyone just knows. These hidden rules are present and often applied in different ways, in school, church, and the community at large. Even more confusingly, the rules are often applied differently depending on the people present or the situation. How could these learners with autism spectrum disorders manage in this situation without losing control? Without learning several very critical and specific skills (Figure 21.1) and the Critical Goals (Figure 6.1, page 107), they will be in an almost constant state of stress and turmoil. Those with Asperger's syndrome are especially vulnerable, as they are most often out working and recreating in the community with little support.

See Chapters 2 and 3 for a review of the affects of autism spectrum disorders on learning. See Chapter 8 to understand the impact of autism on stress and behavior. Review Chapter 10 for strategies to identify and defuse stress; and Chapters 11–15 for strategies to organize and structure events, space, and time. See Figure 6.1, for an expanded list of the Critical Goals.

If those with ASD are to become as independent in the natural community as possible, we must begin at a very early age to teach these skills: to be aware of self and others, to have self-control, and to have self-management skills. During adolescence they also need to learn the skills to solve problems and make choices—to set goals for their life (Fullerton & Coyne, 1999). At least some level of support, and perhaps periodic instruction, will likely be needed throughout life as those hidden cultural rules continue to present themselves in unexpected ways.

This chapter addresses issues of assessment to identify critical needs and provides strategies to teach self-awareness, relaxation skills, self-control routines, problem solving, and strategies for making informed choices.

Figure 22.1 Skills Required for Self-Management and Maintaining Self-Control

- Identify stressful feelings and learn to use relaxation skills.
- Take a break to regain or maintain control.
- Use self-control routine and visual references to maintain control in the natural setting.
- Gain control over repetitive behaviors.
- Solve problems.
- Make informed choices.
- Set goals and make plans.

Strategies for Teaching Self-Awareness and Self-Management Skills

*The term "neuro-normal" was introduced some years ago by a group of adults with higher-functioning autism and Asperger's syndrome when they wanted to differentiate between those with and without autism spectrum disorders.

Many of the strategies and procedures described in this section are commonly used by counselors to help "neuro-normal"* people manage and cope with emotional problems, pain, and the stresses of everyday life. These strategies also are used in therapy to control compulsive behaviors such as smoking, overeating, and panic attacks. Although these self-control procedures would seem to be beyond the abilities of those with autism spectrum disorders, they are, in fact, quite effective with more able verbal learners as well as with those who are seemingly less capable. The degree of independence in using these strategies will vary; some can learn to cue themselves independently, while others will continue to need someone or something (such as a visual system) to provide a signal to initiate and use the strategies.

Planning and Delivering Instruction

Assessment

Many of the tools and procedures for assessing and selecting the high priority needs can be found and reviewed in Chapter 5. If a severe behavior problem has triggered this assessment process, review Chapter 24 and the Functional Behavioral Analysis: Problem Review Worksheet on pages 452–454. All of these processes will involve observations and interviews with all who support and know the learner well.

When assessing those with higher skills, as in Asperger's syndrome, personal interviews are important. In these situations the interview strategies must be very sensitive. Those with Asperger's want to "be normal" so badly that if there is any suggestion that they could have a problem, they may refuse to participate or become very upset.

Select Skills

Target the skills for instruction that will be used to solve current problems and that will be required in many different situations. Select skills (i.e., problem solving, managing stress, making choices) that are essential and require the learner to independently carry out functional daily routines. This policy will ensure that there will be many opportunities to practice and generalize the skills to a number of different situations and settings—to resolve problems faster. In addition, refer to Figure 21.2 and Figure 22.1 for lists of critical skills.

Planning

Planning that is clear and precise is described in Chapter 16. The process for developing and teaching functional routines is discussed and illustrated in Chapters 13 and 18.

- Prepare the learner for instruction. All students, but especially those with Asperger's syndrome, need to have a reason for learning a new skill. They need to know what activities they will do to learn this skill and how long it will take. Why is this skill important? When and where will I use it? How does it fit into what I already know?

Select Strategies—Capitalize on Natural Experiences

See Figure 10.1, Profile of Stress: Basis for Matching Interventions to Needs. Also review the important strategies for using verbal strategies in Chapter 15.

The ability to identify one's own feelings of overwhelming stress, tension, panic, fear, or excitement is a first step toward self-control. Information provided by some adults with autism indicates that they do not automatically learn the concept of feelings—they cannot automatically recognize the feelings of others or their own feelings, nor interpret the causes of those feelings—especially overwhelming panic or excitement (Cesaroni & Garber, 1991; Sinclair, 1992). There are both informal and formal strategies for teaching about feelings and how to identify and control stress.

The following strategies and experiences, when incorporated into the ongoing activities of the day, can increase the ability to identify the learner's own feelings of tension and stress, as well as help them interpret the feelings of others. Refer to the Profile of Stress (Figure 24.3) to determine which strategy to use in a specific situation.

1. *Use parallel talking in natural situations to provide the language to describe facial expressions and body language* that show how others feel and why they feel that way—the cause and the effect. ("When the ball hit Tommy, it scared him and hurt his arm. He is crying.) Insert pauses and use gestures to highlight the critical words. Only use this strategy when the student's stress level is at Stages 1a and 4 (Figure 24.3). Later in the day, capitalize on that situation by developing an experience story or cartoon strip story illustrated with simple line drawings (Chapter 14). "Sometime people cry when they are scared or hurt. Tommy cried when the ball hit him. It hurt his arm. When people cry, their eyes are almost shut. Tears come out of their eyes and run down their faces. Some people make loud noises when they cry, but others make only a little noise. Tommy made loud noises. When Tommy's arm felt better, he stopped crying.") Although the amount of detail depends on the learner's attention span, it is just such detail that those with autism miss.

   Note: There is evidence that when a learner is emotionally involved in an experience, words related to that experience take on greater meaning and are remembered (Greenspan et al., 1998).

2. *Use reflective listening when the behavioral signals of tension and accelerating emotions are identified.* Use this strategy when the student's stress is at Stages 1a and 1b (Figure 24.3). For example, when a learner covers her ears and begins to rock as several people are talking and giving directions, the interpreter tentatively says, "There are too many people talking, and you feel tense and confused" or, when a learner sees peers going to lunch and begins to pace and hyperventilate, the interpreter reflects, "You look worried. Are you afraid you will miss lunch?" This model for associating the label of the emotions to the cause of the problem is a first step for solving problems. If these stories are placed in a notebook, the student can review to rehearse them many times.

3. *Model feelings and emotions by exaggerating facial expressions* while parallel talking about your own goofs and problems ("I really goofed. I feel so frustrated. I forgot to _____.").

4. *Provide practice through role play*, stories, comic strips, art activities, puppet play, and other activities in individual and group contexts. Use of video modeling procedures can also be useful for identifying feelings and problems (Chapter 22). But again, the interpreter must provide clear language to describe these situations and to provide feedback.

Other Resources

These resources provide useful information for assessing problems, for understanding how these individuals think and why they act the way they do, and includes strategies for teaching these critical skills:

Freeman, S., & Dake, L. (1997). *Teach me language: A language manual for children with autism, Asperger's syndrome and related developmental disorders.* Langley, B.C., Canada: SKF Books.

> This manual, along with the Companion Exercise Forms, contains strategies for teaching the language to deal with social/friendship issues, problem solving, giving opinions, and general knowledge/language based concepts: categorizations, brainstorming, reading comprehension, summarizing, math word problems, time and money, and many other important topics.

Fullerton, A., Stratton, J., Coyne, P., & Gray, C. (1996). *Higher functioning young adults with autism: A teacher's guide.* Austin, TX: PRO-ED.

> Also see, Fullerton, A. (1994). *Putting feet on my dreams: A program in self-determination.* Austin, TX: PRO-ED.

Howlin, P., Baron-Cohen, S., & Hadwin, J. (1999). *Teaching children with autism to mind-read: A practical guide.* New York: Wiley and Sons.

> This book includes strategies for both assessment and instruction that include visual supports for teaching five levels of emotional understanding.

Myles, B. S., & Southwick, J. (1999). *Asperger's syndrome and difficult moments: Practical solutions for tantrums, rage, and meltdowns.* Shawnee Mission, KS: Autism Asperger.

> Includes assessment procedures and strategies.

Williams, M., & Shellenberger, S. (1996). *How does your engine run: A leader's guide to the Alert Program for self regulation.* Albuquerque, NM: TherapyWorks, Inc.

> This is a sensory integration program that teaches individuals to be aware of their level of stress and regulate their own sensory systems or ". . . engine speed." See later discussion in this chapter for a more compete description of this resource.

Winner, M. G. (2000). *Inside out: What makes a person with social cognitive deficits tick? The i laugh approach.* San Jose, CA: Author.

> This is an easy-to-read book to understand the specific thinking problems that can prevent understanding of the perspective of others and the big picture of social grammar and syntax, story and letter writing. This book also provides many helpful strategies for addressing academic and other issues.

Video modeling strategies are described in Chapter 22.

Target Self-Monitoring and Self-Control

Relaxation Training—Thought Stopping—Self-Control Routines

The ability to stop your thoughts in a stressful situation and relax in order to decide what to do are basic and critical skills for everyone. Relaxation training for those with autism was first studied and used effectively in the early 1970s (Cautela & Groden, 1978). The strategies discussed in the following section are based on the positive reinforcement principle of learning theory and imagery-based procedures or "covert conditioning" (Cautela & Kearney, 1993). "It is based on the assumption that behaviors such as thinking, feeling, and imagining follow the same laws of learning as do observable behaviors" (Groden & Baron, 1991). "A child imagines performing a desired behavior, then imagines a pleasant event" (Groden & LeVasseur, 1995). Traditional imagery procedures were adapted for teaching those with autism by adding pictures to help them focus their attention and remember the sequence of the self-control strategy—the beginnings of cognitive picture rehearsal (pp. 287–306). At the Groden Center, this training begins with children as young as 3 to 4 years of age.

The following situations observed at the Groden Center in Providence, Rhode Island, illustrate the effects of these relaxation, self-control strategies.

> On returning to their group home after delivering presents to their mothers on Mother's Day, the six adolescent boys with autism were having difficulty settling down. Most of the boys were excited from the afternoon visits, but Jason was upset because his mother had not been home. To complicate matters, Dr. Groden dropped in unexpectedly with a stranger. As the excitement and stress escalated, Dr. Groden suggested that they go into the living room and relax. Immediately, the six young men moved to the living room while staff and guests remained in the dining room. Jason sat in a rocking chair, rocking furiously. Gabriel, one of the more verbal boys, led the group through the relaxation exercise. Some of the boys closed their eyes, and all became quiet and calm. Even Jason stopped rocking. At the conclusion of the session, one of the boys said softly, "Tell us a nice picture," so Gabriel led them through a visual-imagery story about walking on the beach. When the story ended, the boys sat almost motionless for a few moments, then calmly moved away and became involved in various activities.

> ---

> While touring the center with Dr. Groden, we entered a room where Kim was folding towels for gym classes. He was visibly upset, folding and unfolding a towel, rocking energetically back and forth, hyperventilating, and making harsh throat noises. From the door, about 8 feet away from Kim, Dr. Groden held out her hand and softly said, "Stop. What do you need to do?" Kim looked at her, stopped, and took a deep breath. As Kim let out his breath, Dr. Groden said, "Good! You know what to do." She waited quietly for a moment or two as Kim continued to relax himself. Then she moved toward him as she said, "Good! You can relax yourself." She helped him to reorganize and re-engage in his work. When Dr. Groden and I left a few moments later, Kim was working steadily and calmly.

The strategies described in these first three sections must be taught very specifically for maximum benefit—study the references listed at the bottom of this section before initiating instruction.

Progressive Muscle Relaxation

Progressive muscle relaxation (PMR) is a strategy for identifying and relaxing tension in the various muscle groups. The ability to reduce tension is the foundation for self-control and self-management. Unless one can relax enough to focus and think, it is impossible to solve problems or make choices. PMR is used in a variety of ways, for example:

- To reduce general anxiety before and during a stressful situation

- As an incompatible alternative to stereotypic or repetitive motor behavior (e.g., hand flapping cannot occur when the hands are relaxed)

- As an incompatible alternative to aggressive or tantrum behavior (e.g., one cannot scream or kick if the mouth and legs are relaxed)

PMR is useful for anyone who has a high level of stress. Interpreters who learn to use the relaxation strategies can provide a calming model during instruction and in highly stressful or crisis situations. Relaxation skills are combined with imagery-based procedures to establish self-control routines. These routines serve to break the chain of accelerating stress and are useful for maintaining or regaining control.

Strategies for Teaching Progressive Muscle Relaxation

Although PMR is generally introduced and taught in individual sessions, the skills can be initiated in a group. Some learners have difficulty mastering the relaxation responses until a peer sits beside them to model the procedure while the interpreter verbalizes the steps.

■ Initial lessons teach the concepts and the feelings of tighten and relax, first the arms and then the legs. These concepts are not taught as visual-imitation tasks because learners could come to depend on the presence of a visual model. Rather, in teaching the concept of tighten your arm, the interpreter might hold out a pencil. As the learner grasps the pencil, the interpreter pulls it gently, stretching the learner's arm out and up while saying, "Tight." The interpreter stops pulling and lets the learner's arm slowly bend to a relaxing position while saying, "Relax." Reinforcement involves stroking and softly saying, "Good! Your arm is nice and relaxed." (At first, other reinforcers also may be needed.) Once the learner understands how it feels when the arm, neck, or leg is tight and tense, the word tight is no longer used. In real life, the tightness or tension of the muscle is the natural cue to relax.

■ Remember that individuals with autism learn and use skills exactly as taught. If they always lie down on a mat during relaxation training, they will not automatically be able to relax themselves while walking, sitting, or working in various settings. If a pencil is always used or always used in the same way to prompt tightening of the arm muscles, the learner probably will come to believe that tight is somehow related to the pencil rather than to the feeling of tension. Therefore, as in all other instruction, variations are required. Vary the position (sitting, standing, walking, lying down), the location (inside and outdoors), the cues and prompts, the consequences, the instructor, and the number of other people present.

Picture Rehearsal to Teach Self-Control Routines

The goal of this cognitive picture rehearsal strategy is to teach a sequence of skills that will enable individuals to recognize and control their own stress, resolve their own problems, and re-engage themselves in appropriate activity. These routines are introduced and then practiced in imagery as learners visualize themselves calmly solving problems in stressful situations.

Strategies for Developing the Scripts

Stories or scripts used to introduce self-control routines are based on a functional analysis of problem situations (see Chapter 24). These stories identify the conditions in the immediate or distant environments that trigger stress, an appropriate alternative response, and several reinforcers. The stories are developed to match the learners' language and attention abilities. They are highly descriptive to help learners imagine or see themselves in the scenes. Sensory details are included with such statements as, "I hear the sound of the _____"; "I smell the _____"; "I feel the _____." For those who do not like to imagine themselves in a problem situation, the story can be developed to describe someone else with similar characteristics and problems. This procedure, called *covert modeling*, enables the individual to imagine someone else responding with the target behavior and experiencing a rewarding consequence.

The number of scenes in a story is limited. Generally, the routine can be represented in seven scenes:

Scene 1: The problem or trigger for the stress

Prepare several scenes to describe the range of situations in which the stressful problem occurs. Rotate these scenes during instruction to ensure generalization of the new skills to a variety of settings.

Scene 2: The feelings that describe the stress

For example, "My shoulders feel tight, I feel hot, and I start to breathe faster."

Scene 3: Thought stopping

Thought stopping is an imagery procedure that enables a person to gain control of unwanted and unproductive thoughts. It is used frequently in therapy for those with panic disorders and addictive behaviors. As the individual imagines the undesirable behavior (e.g., tension and feelings of panic or fear), he imagines himself shouting, "STOP!" As this quick and sharp statement is imagined, the negative thoughts are disrupted.

Scene 4. The relaxation response

A relaxation response clearly describes what the individual is to do. For example, take a deep breath and relax the neck and shoulders.

Scene 5. A pleasant consequence

A pleasant consequense can reinforce the relaxation response and thought stopping.

Scene 6. Strategies and skills

Strategies and skills can be used to solve or deal with the problem effectively—the new skills to be increased.

This scene redirects attention from the problem and feelings of stress to focus on the solution. The solution might include:

- Self-instruction to initiate positive action ("How shall I start? First, I'll do _____; then I can do _____.")

- A coping statement that relieves the pressure ("If I forget a step, I can go back"; "If I do it wrong, I can fix it"; "If I need help, I can ask _____.")

- An assertive response that acknowledges the problem ("I'll try to do better next time"; "I'll write that down so I'll remember"; "I understand. I can do that now.")

Scene 7: A pleasant scene

A pleasant scene can reinforce the positive direction—the new skills to be increased.

Once the story is developed (see the example of Matt, page 393), the scenes are represented visually for use during instruction. Pictures can be presented in a variety of ways: flashcard-style, laid out on a table from left to right, in storybook form, in a cartoon-strip format with one scene to a frame, or carried in a credit-card folder. In general, "The more abstract the picture, the greater the generalization. Black-and-white line drawings without background can often convey enough information for learning to take place, yet not be so specific that they inhibit generalization" (Groden & LeVasseur, 1995, p. 26).

Rehearsal

Rehearsal begins once the learner has mastered the relaxation strategies and the script and pictures are developed. Picture rehearsal helps the learner to imagine the scene more clearly, thus aiding recall when in a stressful situation. This format is most helpful for those who learn more efficiently with a visual display, who have difficulty attending to a verbal presentation, or who are unable to provide verbal feedback. Self-control routines are introduced individually in a quiet, distraction-free area with the pictures (or the book) laid out on the table. The teacher points to each picture while telling the story, using gestures to point out relevant details. When finished telling the story, they rehearse it again, with the child pointing to each picture as before—but the child repeats the story with prompts from the teacher as necessary. The scripts are rehearsed at least twice a day. When the learner is familiar with the script, it may be taped so the scenes can be rehearsed independently in other settings. Scripts are constantly evaluated and adapted as the situations change. Occasionally, a learner will suggest additional sensory details that make the story more personally vivid.

Matt was having trouble at the library, where one of his jobs was to shelve books. He worked independently on most days but when there was a large stack of books to return, he worried that he would not finish before quitting time. When this panic occurred, he was unable to work steadily or efficiently. He might drop a book several times or begin to hyperventilate or rock repetitively. One day, he was so worried that he pushed a patron who was in his way.

Following an assessment of the situation, Matt was taught a self-control routine containing basic elements that could be varied to apply to different situations.

- I see a big stack of books. I think I'll never get done.

- My shoulders feel tight and tense. I am breathing hard.

- I say, "STOP!" I take a deep breath. I relax my neck and shoulders.

- I say, "That feels good. Now I can deal with this."

- I think about having a tall, cool, glass of soda pop at quitting time.

- If I don't get all the books put back today, I can do them tomorrow.

- If someone is in my way, I can say, "Excuse me," and then wait for the person to move.

- I will sort the books and get started, one book at a time.

- There! That's not so bad. I'm making progress.

- I will stay relaxed. I'll have that glass of soda pop after work.

After being taught the basic routine and the variations, Matt was given an audiotape to listen to *each day before going to work and again at break time* if he felt the need.

References

Study the following references before initiating the relaxation and imagery procedures:

Groden, J., Cautela, J. R., & Groden, G. (1989). *Breaking the barriers I: Relaxation techniques for people with special needs*. Videotape. Champaign, IL: Research Press.

These videotapes, which were developed at the Groden Center, demonstrate instructional procedures and various applications.

Groden, J., Cautela, J. R., & Groden, G. (1991). *Breaking the barriers II: Imagery procedures for people with special needs*. Videotape. Champaign, IL: Research Press.

Groden, J., Cautela, J.R., LeVasseur, P., Groden, G., & Bausman, M. (1991) *Video guide to breaking the barriers II*. Champaign, IL: Research Press.

Groden, J., & LeVasseur, P. (1995). Cognitive picture rehearsal: A visual system to teach self-control. In K. Quill (Ed.), *Teaching children with autism: Methods to enhance learning, communication, and socialization.* Albany, NY: Delmar.

Managing Repetitive Behavior

Repetitive and stereotypic (R/S) behaviors (e.g., rocking, finger flicking, jumping up and down) occur in the presence of problems, stress, and excitement. Repetitive behaviors can also occur automatically when the individuals with autism are not attending to and consciously controlling their behavior (Cesaroni & Garber, 1991; Sinclair, 1992). In general, when other skills increase and more time is spent in interesting and productive activity, the R/S behaviors decrease. Although R/S behaviors are generally reflexive and non-intentional, they sometimes will be used intentionally to avoid or escape demands. This change will occur if the R/S behavior was negatively reinforced by reduced demands (see Chapter 16).

Although there is nothing bad or wrong about the R/S behaviors, they do make the individual stand out and look different or less competent to those who are not familiar with autism. In some situations, an individual will perseverate in the behavior and need someone to break the repetitive cycle. Note: See the discussion of unconventional (repetitive) verbal behavior in Chapter 20.

Strategies

Use the following strategies to avoid making the problem worse and to help the learner gain control:

1. *Develop a balanced schedule that includes:*

   - Frequent opportunities to move about and engage in strenuous exercise (Kern, Koegel, & Dunlap, 1984; Levinson & Reid, 1993; McGimsey & Favell, 1988).

   - A balance of activities that are liked and disliked, familiar and new, active and quiet (see Chapter 12).

   - Frequent opportunities for attention and social interactions.

   - A minimum amount of unscheduled or unstructured time (for example, waiting).

   - Visual support system so learner always knows the expectations.

2. *Ignore the behavior but attend to the message (or function) of the behavior.* End activities at the earliest signs of restlessness, boredom, and fatigue. Use a contingency statement such as, "You need a break? Do one more problem, and then it will be time for a break", or cue the individual to ask for help or for a break. Teach more effective "functionally equivalent" ways to communicate the need for help, breaks, and needs (Carr, 1988).

3. *Teach the learner that the behavior is OK, but there is a time and place to do it*—as in the example of Adam on pages 411–412 who was screaming in the house and was taught to scream in the garage.

4. *Teach the learner a self-control routine to ask for and take a break.* Some individuals who are highly anxious or easily overstimulated need a private space identified in each new setting.

   - Teach the learner to use the thought-stopping/self-control routine, as described previously, and re-engage in the regular activity.

5. *Identify the reinforcing element of the behavior* and provide other more productive or less obvious activities that provide the same type of reinforcement. One young man, who was visually reinforced by the long strings of moving

paper as he shredded the family newspapers, now grates cheese at a pizza parlor. Also see the example of Niko in Chapter 17.

6. *In preschool classes, use group activities to strengthen language concepts* related to self-control. Be sure an interpreter is available to ensure that the student's actions match and are associated with the words. For example:

- Fast/slow: Instruct the children to walk, clap, or jump fast or slow; move to fast and slow drum beats or rhythms.

- Tight/relaxed: Chant, "Get ready, 1-2-3; tighten your fists, 4-5-6; relax, 7-8-9-10; stretch your arms and take a deep breath."

- Stop and go: While walking, running, clapping, jumping, or stomping feet, shout (or whisper) directives at random intervals: "Ready, set, GO! . . . STOP! 1-2-3, GO!" Also see the example of Angelo in chapter 17.

- Use relays, balance-beam activities, and obstacle courses that require alertness and control. These include walking with a beanbag on the head, carrying a ball on a spoon, and stepping over objects on a beam. Balance beams need to be at least 8" to 10" from the floor or higher to motivate the learner to stay alert and in control. Allow for natural consequences of inattention, but have mats and spotters nearby to prevent injury.

Take a Break to Regain or Maintain Control

Most people automatically know when their stress is so high that they must get out of a situation quickly, and they automatically know how to reduce that stress. They think about something else that is pleasant, leave the area, or do any one of a variety of other acceptable options. But those with autism must be taught positive ways to escape overwhelming stress before they lose control. Taking a break to relieve stress is one self-control routine that even very young children can learn to do independently. This break is very different from a time-out after losing control.

The instructional routine

Organize and structure the break area and the instructional sequence just as for teaching any other routine. Because each learner has different needs, assessment must be conducted to determine the specific calming activities or materials required:

1. Prepare a quiet space in a nearby area that is easy to monitor.

2. Prepare or provide a very simple and quick way to communicate the need for a break. Even those who can ordinarily talk need a backup system to use when under stress. One method is to make "break tickets."

3. Prepare a visual representation of the routine—a checklist, story, or series of line drawings.

The general components of a break routine are:

1. *To initiate*

   Recognize the natural cue to initiate a break. Recognizing feelings of overwhelming stress is a self-monitoring task. (Review pages 389–391.)

2. *To prepare*

   Locate a break ticket and give to interpreter.

3. *Perform the essential steps*

   - Touch the interpreter's arm to get attention.
   - Give the break ticket to the interpreter.

- Go to the quiet area.

- Use a relaxation strategy. (This may involve rocking in a rocking chair, jumping on a mini-trampoline, or using PMR and deep breathing.)

- Self-monitor ("Am I relaxed?").

4. *Terminate*

When relaxed, end the break and return to the appropriate area to reengage.

5. *Solve problems—Communicate*

Teach strategies for identifying stress and taking a break when the learner is in a location where the quiet area is not accessible, when an interpreter is not available, when the learner doesn't know what to do to re-engage after break, or when other unexpected complications occur.

Introduce the Routine

Continue to review the Progressive Muscle Relaxation Strategies as you teach all self-control and self-monitoring strategies.

Prepare a visual representation of the routine—the break ticket (if used) and a checklist of the routine. A short video clip or an audiotape might be effective for some learners to use during introduction and rehearsal. Use parallel talk as the quiet area and the routine is introduced. The learner needs to know that this routine will be done independently—therefore, use subtle touch/pointing prompts to follow the checklist and any parallel talking should be faded quickly. When using the video clip or audiotape, the learner can rehearse the routine independently.

Three problems often occur during the instructional process: (a) the learner does not terminate the break when relaxed, (b) the learner leaves the break area before becoming completely relaxed, or (c) the learner repeatedly asks to take a break whether or not stress is present.

1. *If the learner does not terminate the break when relaxed.*

Evaluate the environment and expectations:

- Is the area uncluttered and calm, containing only the material to support relaxation? This is a place to do a specific task—relax—with specific objects or materials. It is not a place to make choices or to play. If a learner needs music to relax, a relaxation tape is in the tape player and other tapes are stored away from the area.

- Are the expectations clear and at the right level? Does the learner know when and how to end the break, what to do next, how to move from the area to the next activity? Is there a visual reference available to clarify the next steps?

- Can the learner identify relaxed feelings?

- Does the learner have difficulty ending one task and beginning another in other situations? Arrange a concrete signal for ending the break. Set a timer (or teach the learner to set a timer) for a reasonable period of time—the time it usually takes the learner to relax.

2. *If the learner leaves the break area before becoming completely relaxed.*

- Use the timer. If the learner is not relaxed when the timer rings, reset the timer and say, "You are still upset. I'll set the timer for another 5 minutes."

- Clarify the concept and feelings of being relaxed. Use visual references, perhaps a comic strip sequence, to highlight the signs of relaxation.

3. *If the learner repeatedly asks to take a break* without the appearance of stress.

   ■ Rejoice! It is a sign that the individual has learned the routine and understands the power of the communication. However, it also is a sign that more work is needed.

   ■ Ensure that the natural setting is interesting, relatively unstressful, and reinforcing—a place where the learner wants to be.

   ■ Structure and visually clarify the number of break options. For example, if assessment of the situation shows that the child is overly stressed on an average of three times in a 2-hour period but has requested as many as seven breaks in that length of time, provide seven break tickets for a 2-hour period. Then systematically vary and reduce the number of tickets. If the learner maintains control and has some tickets left at the end of the specified time period, trade them for a privilege or something pleasant.

Problem-Solving Skills

Because those with autism do not automatically learn to solve problems, they are at a loss to know what to do when the unexpected occurs. The stress and panic that accompanies the inability to manage a situation leads to withdrawal, panic, and severe behavior problems. One of the major self-management skills is to learn a process for solving problems that can be generalized to many different problems.

Strategies

Recognizing that each individual's problems, knowledge, and abilities are different, the instructional plan should address the following issues in some concrete and literal way:

1. *The full meaning of the abstract idea or concept of* problem *may be unclear,* and many things may not be recognized as problems. Teach the concept of *problem*. Provide a clear and literal definition with examples of different types of past problems and some that may be encountered in the future.

2. *The nature and severity of a problem may be unclear.* The learner is as likely to consider all problems as either life threatening or trivial. Use semantic maps, flow charts, or cue cards to teach a process for evaluating the severity of a problem and a process for dealing with the various types of problems.

   ■ For problems that need to be solved quickly, those that are dangerous, or those that stop progress: Incorporate relaxation and a self-control routine to focus attention and behavior on the critical issues.

   ■ For problems that can be solved later, those for which there is time to think and plan: Teach a process for brainstorming to generate new solutions, for evaluating those solutions, and for selecting a solution to try. Once a solution is selected, rehearse it with stories or scripts. Semantic maps are useful in this situation as well. Also see the illustration on the next page.

3. *It may be unclear whether the problem can be solved without assistance or whether help is needed.* Teach a self-control routine that can guide the learner's actions.

   ■ Specify and rehearse strategies for locating a helper, initiating a request for help, and communicating the problem clearly. Expand the learner's communication system to address these needs.

- Provide practice in self-instruction. Model self-instruction strategies in the context of solving real problems, puzzles, or mazes. Provide a self-instruction cue card that clarifies the steps. (What is the problem? How/where do I start? What do I do first?) Include coping statements and self-reinforcement.

4. *Capitalize on visual references.* In addition to semantic maps and flow charts, consider preparing:

   - A problem/solution checklist or chart much like in a technical manual

   - T-charts to visualize the cost/benefit analysis of options

   - Visual references for alternative solutions— use story strategies or comic strips (see pages 221 and 405)

   - Small self-monitoring/self-reinforcing checklists on cards to carry throughout the day. These cards can serve as cues to use the procedures and for recording successful use. The opportunity to record successes is generally a reinforcing event. When checklists are shared with the interpreter, the skills are reviewed and reinforced again.

5. *Plan the instruction, and teach for generalization and flexibility.*

   - Use the same process to solve many different kinds of problems.

   - Incorporate literal description of the setting, highlight the natural cues, and vary the practice in a broad range of natural and simulated situations.

   - A social-group setting offers many opportunities to identify potential problems, generate alternative solutions, and rehearse in a safe and supportive environment. For references for activities and strategies, see

Buser and Reimer (1988); Pehrsson and Denner (1989); and Shure (1992).

- Set up or sabotage some part of a natural routine to create opportunities to practice and receive support and quick feedback in the natural setting.
- Practice in imagery with visual references or use video modeling.

See Figure 22.2, a flow chart that illustrates the numerous components and the complexity of planning involved in teaching independent problem solving. The process begins in early childhood by teaching concepts such as *problem, hurt, safety,* and others; and the process for identifying and solving small problems as they occur. (For example, milk is spilled. The interpreter says, "That's a problem. Let's clean it up.") A similar flow chart can serve as a visual reference to clarify the gestalt of solving problems for adolescents. With a long-term approach, more independence can be achieved in adulthood.

Figure 22.2 Sequence of Concepts and Processes Involved in Solving Problems

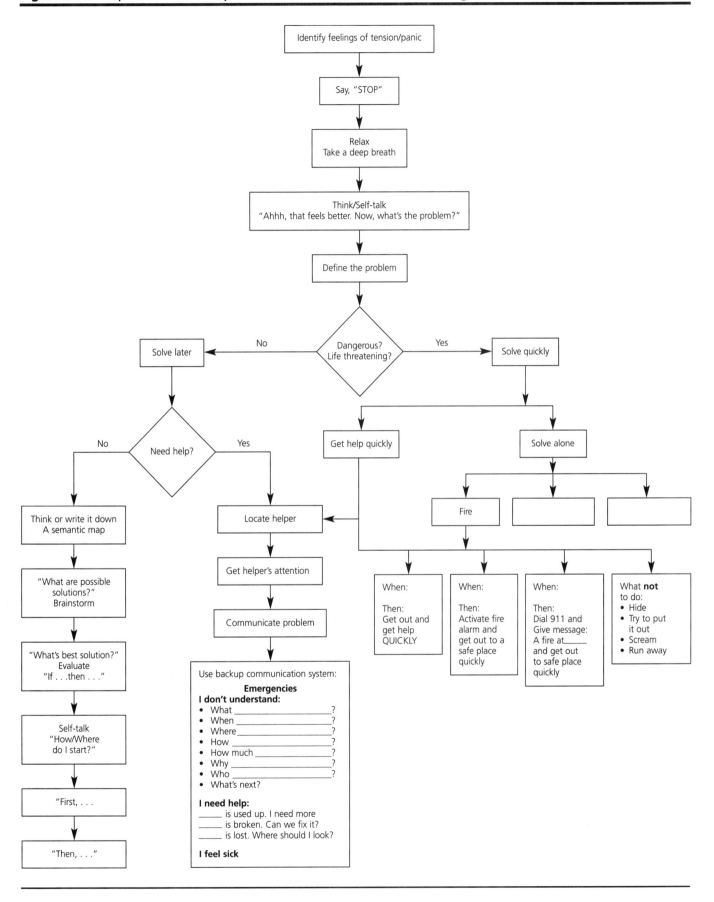

Make Informed Choices

The ability to make informed choices is a complex and high-level skill that has many implications for people with autism, who have a limited number of preferences, resist trying new things, are repetitive, and indicate preferences in unexpected ways that are difficult to interpret. Not only is this a problem area for the younger learners, it is also a problem area for those who are older and higher functioning. In fact, the ability to make informed choices is a critical skill for those with Asperger's syndrome because they move out into the world where the choices have more serious implications. Many behavior problems are related to making choices or indicating choices.

An informed choice implies that *all the options are understood and that the mode of indicating the preference is, first, understood, and second, motorically and communicatively possible.* The following questions highlight some of the problems in autism.

- Can a lack of protest imply informed consent, or merely simple resignation?

- Is habitual or repetitive behavior an active and informed choice? For example, if a person always chooses the object on the right, always chooses vanilla ice cream, or always chooses to rock in the rocking chair when offered several leisure options, can it be assumed that the person fully understands the options?

- If an individual does not do a job, can it be assumed that the person is noncompliant and chooses not to work? Perhaps some part of the task is unclear, the job is not one that is preferred, or the person prefers not to do that work in that way at that time.

- If someone flails about, hits, and refuses to get dressed, has that person chosen to be stubborn and contrary? Perhaps the message is, "I don't like these clothes. I prefer to wear a different outfit" or "I would like to brush my teeth before getting dressed."

- When asked, "Do you agree to the conditions of a behavior contract?" and the individual says, "Yes" and signs the contract, can it be assumed that this is informed consent? Is the individual really saying, "Yes, I choose for you to do these things to me" or "Yes, I agree; these are the best strategies for you to use to get me to do what you want"? Does the person have a way to indicate a desire not to change that behavior? Perhaps the individual signs the contract simply because that was the direction he was given and he always does what he is told.

It cannot be assumed that an informed choice was made in any of these situations. One cannot assume that those with autism understand the language concepts, have enough experience with the options to have a preference, understand the consequences of a specific choice, or have a clear way to indicate either a protest or a different choice. *Rarely is a learner given the opportunity or taught the skill to indicate, "None of these" or "I don't understand."*

Strategies

Skills for making informed choices must be taught. Instruction begins in early childhood by providing two options and an opportunity to choose. Instruction for developing choice-making skills involves the following issues and strategies:

1. *Increase the learner's flexibility and willingness to try new things. Provide experiences from which to develop preferences.*

   ■ Teach the concept of *try* in a contingency format. ("Try a little bite of this, and then if you like it you can have more" or "Try it on, and then you can take it off.")

   ■ Reintroduce new options over several days or weeks. As familiarity increases, tolerance also increases. Then real choices can be made.

2. *Identify the communicative intent* of behaviors and the early signals of preferences and feelings.

3. *Teach more understandable ways to communicate preferences* and to reject, end, or avoid options ("I want/don't want this" or "I like/don't like that"). Use visual supports, such as a cue card that indicates: *Yes—No*; Or, *I want this—I want something else.*

4. *Teach the concepts* choose, finish, now, later, more, *and others* that relate to preferences and making choices.

5. *Provide many opportunities and experiences to choose or select* food, clothing, toys, activities, partners, and working conditions in the context of natural routines.

6. *Generalize choice making skills within the context of the functional and natural routines of the day* (see Chapters 13 and 18).

MAKE CHOICES

We are faced with choices in nearly everything we do each day, whether to choose what to wear, which cereal to eat for breakfast, where we sit in the cafeteria, etc. Those with autism should also be taught to make these small choices, beginning with very limited options, then expanding to the major choices later.

Other Considerations

The support-team members have a responsibility to identify the risks of options and balance those risks with the learner's ability to deal with the consequences.

Do not offer a choice unless there is a real choice.

- At first, offer only options that are both possible and safe. Gradually offer riskier choices as the learner develops competence.

- Avoid overwhelming the learner with too many options. Initially, limit the options to only two or three.

- Avoid overwhelming the learner with too many options when the learner is frustrated or stressed. Decision making is demanding; communicating the decision is even more difficult and likely to accelerate stress to the point of losing control.

- Avoid pressure to make immediate choices. If a decision must be made quickly, provide a concrete means for measuring time, and remain quiet or move away while the learner is considering the options.

- Sometimes a learner may need time to touch, look at, and think about all the options. At other times, the learner may need a way to communicate, "I don't want any of these." Make quick line drawings to represent each option as it is presented. Include a symbol to represent "None of these."

- When the learner is required to make critical choices and decisions that could have long-term implications, use a T-chart and provide assistance to do a cost/benefit analysis.

- Allow for changes of opinion. All people change their minds sometimes. However, when it is necessary to live with a choice, be sympathetic but calm. ("I understand you don't like the licorice ice cream, but we don't have money to buy another flavor just now. You can eat the licorice ice cream, or you can drop it in the garbage. Next time, you can make a different choice. Right now it's time to ____".)

Integrate Self-Management Systems

A learner may have a daily calendar, several mini-calendars, several checklists, cue cards, and stories. To avoid confusing the learner and the interpreter, these systems must be organized. They may be displayed together on a bulletin board or arranged within the individual work area. Pockets or hangers for folders and cue cards also can be placed on a bulletin board. See Chapter 17 for an illustration of an integrated system for a more sophisticated learner who carries a notebook. Stories and semantic maps used for understanding the options and consequences should also be organized in notebooks to review or rehearse later.

Other Self-Control and Self-Management Models and Strategies

The Alert Program for Self-Regulation

How Does Your Engine Run: A Leader's Guide to the Alert Program for Self-Regulation (Williams & Schellenberger, 1996) describes a process to teach children to monitor, maintain, and change their level of alertness to match the demands of a situation or task. This program provides a series of lessons and activities that incorporate sensory integration techniques with cognitive strategies using an analogy of an automobile engine. For example, children are taught that their body runs like a car engine, sometimes it runs on high, sometimes it runs on low, and sometimes it runs just right. The Alert process teaches students with and without autism spectrum disorders to recognize their level of alertness and the situations that make them run on high and those that make them run too slow. The students are also taught strategies that will help them raise or lower their alertness level in order to attend and perform successfully.

SOCCSS

SOCCSS, or Situation, Options, Consequences, Choices, Strategies, Simulation is a process for evaluating a problem situation, and for developing and rehearsing the strategies required to remedy the situation and avoid the same problems in the future. This process was first used in the business community and adapted to support students with social interaction problems. This nonpunitive process involves the student in a one-to-one problem solving session with an interpreter immediately or soon after a problem situation occurs. The student is actively involved to obtain their perspective of the situation as well as the perspective of others—to brainstorm and evaluate options, make choices and develop the plan of action to repair or avoid the problem in the future. Myles and Southwick (1999) adapted a worksheet to use during a session to clarify the information and record the plan. Also see Kaplin and Carter (1995).

Cartooning and Comic Strip Conversations

Gray (1994) expanded the use of story strategies to include comic strip conversations. This strategy helps people with autism spectrum disorders understand what is happening in their world and how they can respond—a way to visualize the meaning of abstract social concepts and rules (see Chapter 14). These picture strips involve very simple stick figures—speech and thought bubbles are added to show what a person is thinking or saying. For example, to illustrate the meaning of the word *interrupt* defined as "when my words bump into words from other people," she drew two stick figures with their speech bubbles overlapping.

Comic strip conversations can be implemented quickly to provide immediate information to clarify a social situation, the range of meanings and information to clarify the hidden curriculum, and the steps to solve a social problem.

Video Modeling

Video modeling is a procedure that enables individuals to see and review a perfect example of themselves or others as they perform a task or skill. There are two ways this procedure is used: (a) self-modeling—watching themselves perform the task perfectly on a carefully edited tape and (b) peer-modeling—watching a competent peer model the task (adult models can also be effective).

We have known for some years that those with autism learn from models, need visual supports, and can benefit from the combination of auditory/visual information.

We also know that those with autism must be alert and focused on the relevant cues in order to learn, but they are confused and unable to ignore the overabundance of irrelevant cues in most settings and are not able to identify those that are relevant. Carefully edited videotapes provide consistent, highly focused information that is attractive and captures their attention. Another major advantage is that video modeling saves time as it increases the learning rate. One 10-year-old boy with Asperger's had difficulty completing his morning routine to get to school on time. The family was stunned when, after his first viewing, his time decreased from more than an hour to 20 minutes. After viewing for 2 weeks, his time remained steady at 30 minutes.

Other advantages include:

- Seeing themselves perform perfectly seems to give a boost to their confidence and willingness to try.

- The tapes can be edited to show the task performed in different settings—thus supporting the generalization of skills.

- Tapes are available to review at any time, in the home or school, so practice can occur many times over several days (i.e., no need to delay practice), between therapy or play group sessions.

Video modeling has been effective for teaching those with autism spectrum disorders of all ages. This strategy has been used to teach speech and language skills (including aspects of intonation and cadence), specific motor skills, self-help skills and routines, shopping, numerous interpersonal/social skills (conversations, making friends, etc.), play skills, academic skills, and a variety of others.

It is amazing that there is not more published information about this strategy, which can be used to teach so many different skills.

Making the Tapes.

Contrary to first impressions, these tapes are easy and relatively quick to make. "These are actually more cost-efficient than live modeling because they require less staff . . . training . . . they can be used with multiple students . . . (and they need less acquisition time). Typically, we have used a standard camcorder (VHS) and then edited the tapes onto a full-sized tape through the TV/VCR. . . . (we are now able to make a tape) . . . in 5 minutes while the students are at PE. . . . We have recently moved to digital videos. We use a digital camera, edit them on the computer with Imovie (Imac) or play them back instantly for the children through the computer. We are . . . (now storing the videos on) . . . CD-ROM so that they can be played back on the computers . . . (at school or at home.)" (From a personal correspondence with L. Haymes, Spectrum Center for Educational and Behavioral Development, Berkeley, CA)

References

Buggey, T., Toombs, K., Gardener, P., & Cervetti, M. (1999). Training responding behaviors in students with autism: Using videotaped self-modeling. *Journal of Positive Behavior Interventions, 4,* 205–214.

Charlop, M. H., & Milstein, J. F. (1989). Teaching autistic children conversational speech using video modeling. *Journal of Applied Behavior Analysis, 22,* 275–285.

Dowrick, P. W. (2000). *Video futures start-up kit.* Anchorage, AK: Center for Human Development.

Dowrick, P.W. (1999). A review of self-modeling and related interventions. *Applied and Preventive Psychology, 8,* 23–39.

Haymes, L. K., & Martin, S. (2002, February). *Video Modeling: A Tool for Skill Building and Improving Performance*. A conference presentation for Annual Western Regional Conference of the California Association for Behavior Analysis, San Francisco, CA.

Summary

Most individuals with autism and Asperger's syndrome can become more independent—aware of the perspective of others and learn to manage stress to maintain self-control. Many can also learn the concepts and skills to manage the hidden social curriculum, solve problems, and make safe choices when:

1. Given appropriate instruction and visual support systems.

2. The environment is stimulating and structured to match needs.

3. An interpreter is available to evaluate and modify the environment or provide assistance when needed.

6

Manage Difficult Problems

UPSETS

GOD I NEED A FEARFUL
FEASIBLE FIT
SAL* SAYS NOT
MOM AGREES
YELLING WOULD HELP
HITTING HEAD WOULD
BRING RELIEF
DAVE REALLY BETTER AFTER
ONLY RELEASE IS TOO
MUCH TROUBLE

—David Eastham
In Silent Words and Forever Friends

*Sal was a former teacher.

23

Managing Specific Problems

Behavior problems are often the first concerns expressed by parents and teachers of those with autism spectrum disorders. Problem behaviors normally begin before the second birthday. This is the stage when toddlers can move about but have not yet figured out how the world works. The problems of typically developing children are similar to those with autism, but the differences in the form and intensity of the behavior and differences in ability to process information from the world requires a more systematic approach when the child has autism. Schopler and Mesibov (1994) offered a useful overview in their book, *Behavioral Issues in Autism.* Also see *Asperger Syndrome and Difficult Moments* (Myles & Southwick, 1999).

One of the major goals of this book is to provide a process for addressing the complex issues related to teaching new skills to prevent problems. The first step in this process is to understand the background of any learning or behavior problem and to identify the perspective, the misperceptions, and the skill deficits that caused the problem. Once the causes of the problem are identified, appropriate strategies become more apparent. The process for intervening to solve or prevent problems is the same as that presented in Chapter 10:

1. Organize and structure the environment to clarify information and eliminate some of the factors that contribute to the problem.

2. Teach new skills, concepts, and rules.

3. Continuously evaluate and refine to address changing needs.

By the time Adam was 3 years old, his parents were extremely frustrated by his screaming. Adam screeched and screamed many times a day, and nothing seemed to make him stop. During the assessment of his problem, it was discovered that Adam screamed when he was confused, sick, or upset because he couldn't have or do something he wanted. He also screamed when excited and when he wanted to play. For the most part, he would stop screaming when his problems were addressed; but when he was excited and when he wanted to play, he was totally out of control and the screaming accelerated. Previous behavior programs were designed to eliminate screaming in all situations because it was such a problem in some situations. Not only were those programs unsuccessful, but Adam's parents hesitated to punish the screaming because he had no other way to communicate his problems.

The strategies for addressing this problem were based on the decision that screaming is not a bad behavior. In fact, it is a positive behavior in the correct place and at the correct time (e.g., when playing outside, when in danger, or when at a sporting event). An intervention program was designed that focused on positive goals to teach Adam:

- When and where to scream

- How to communicate his problems

- How to manage his excitement

- How to initiate social interactions with others

The intervention plan was detailed and contained many elements, including progressive muscle relaxation, a visual calendar so Adam would know when events would occur, and a communication component. The initial strategy was effective, and Adam and his parents enjoyed the results.

The garage was organized to ensure a safe place. When Adam screamed, his mother or father said, "Adam, you can scream in the garage. Let's go to the garage." Once in the garage, parent and child screamed together. After a few minutes of screaming, the parent said, "Okay, STOP!" and a few seconds later signaled, "Okay, SCREAM!" Both began to scream again. After repeating the sequence several times, the parent said, "We can scream one more time. Then it will be time to stop screaming and go inside to play with the _____."

Variations were added after two or three trips to the garage. For example, the parent would change the focus slightly and say:

- "Adam, you want to play. Let's go play."

- "When you want to play, you can touch my arm and say, 'Play.'"

- "You want to play. Do you want to scream or play ball?"

- "I know you want to play, but I'm busy. You can go to the garage and scream alone."

When the focus of the intervention changed in a positive way, Adam's parents were able to relax and have fun with him, knowing that they were teaching him some new skills.

Children with autism spectrum disorders have not only the typical problems of most children, but also more severe problems in several specific situations: maintaining safety, eating and mealtimes, sleeping and bedtimes, toilet training, social/sexual issues, obtaining medical care, encounters with the law, and managing major transitions. Again, the process for addressing these special problems is the same as for any problem.

Safety Issues

Most children with autism are unaware of potentially dangerous situations—a major problem that takes considerable creativity to resolve. They also have some amazing abilities and amazingly profound deficits that can expose them and others to tragedy. Typical problems include:

1. *Many have an amazing ability to open locks and childproof bottles.* Because many of these children are also wanderers, the locks may delay them but not entirely control their wandering. One family's solution is described on page 408.

2. *They may smell, taste, or even eat dangerous things*—cigarette butts, soap, things from the garbage or off the streets, pieces of glass, small tacks. One is never quite sure what they will find to eat, because they are not only

wanderers but climbers. Parents and teachers must be extremely cautious to assure safe storage of any medications, chemicals and garbage. See the discussion of pica on page 409.

3. *Many children will respond unpredictably in emergencies.* Those with hearing sensitivities may try to hide from the noise of sirens and fire alarms. At school, specific staff members must be assigned each day to ensure these children are escorted to safety. Safety drills must be carefully planned and practiced many times in all settings. Some have used video modeling to address these issues. See page 405.

4. *Some children are attracted to windows (banging on or slamming into them), lights, fans, and high places.* Screens or acrylic covers for windows and lights, and again, constant vigilance, is needed.

5. *These children do not automatically know when they hurt or are sick*, that they should tell someone if they hurt, or even know how to get someone's attention to tell them. For example, one mother reported that she discovered that her son had bleeding blisters on his feet only when she was getting him ready for bed. He had given no indication that anything was bothering him.

   ■ A child may bang his ears, head, or face whenever they have an earache, headache, or toothache. In fact, without this information, parents naturally are concerned and give a lot of attention. Thus, the child misinterprets the situation believing that the way to get Mom or Dad's attention is to bang his or her head. This is often the beginning of self-injurious behavior.

One child who wandered away and had no concept of home, who unlocked locks, climbed over gates and ate anything she could pick up off the street, could only be kept safely in one room at a time. This meant that either Mom or Dad had to be with her every minute, day or night. After a great deal of experimenting, they finally solved their problem by having their child's standard bedroom door cut in half. They mounted just the bottom half, with the knob and the lock on the outside of the door. Finally, they mounted an alarm on the outside of the door so that any jolt or movement of the door would set off the alarm. They also had alarms on all outside doors. Interestingly, after making certain that the child had the things needed in her room, and when she could see outside the room with the door closed, she was quite content to stay in the room for longer periods.

Parents must inform the school of any specific safety issues that must be addressed. The school staff must work closely with the parents to monitor health or medical needs as well.

Manage Medical Care

Physical problems and medications are often associated with behavior problems. Some severe behavior problems are triggered by allergies, infections, and a number of other physical conditions (see Figure 23.1).

Assess Providers and Problems

It is important for families to seek and work with physicians and dentists who are either knowledgeable or experienced in providing care for those with autism spectrum disorders, or who are open and willing to seek resources, work closely with

Figure 23.1 Some Behavioral Symptoms and Underlying Medical Conditions

The following problems did not respond to behavior modification but were corrected when underlying medical conditions were treated

Sources: Personal conversations; Marsella and Marsella 1991

- Hitting or banging the head, nose, ears, and sinus area—Related to allergies, ear and sinus infections, migraine headaches; and in one situation, to trigeminal neuralgia, a painful condition affecting the nerves of the face
- Touching teeth to windows and walls, jamming things into the mouth, tantrums while eating and swallowing food without chewing—Related to tooth abscess, cavities, gum injuries
- Breaking things that made noise (vacuum cleaner, toilet, kitchen mixer, stereo . . .)—Related to extreme auditory sensitivities and in one situation impacted and abscessed wisdom teeth
- Tearing and wetting pants, slapping or hitting the lower abdomen—Related to bladder infections, premenstrual discomfort
- Sticking foot in the toilet bowl, reluctance or refusing to walk—Related to overly long toenails, blisters, boils on the ball of the foot
- A myriad of other aggressive, self-injurious, or unusual behaviors—Related to seizure disorders, digestive problems, or drug reactions

families, and consult with support-team members. The willingness to consult with autism specialists is particularly important since there are a number of conditions common in autism that are not commonly dealt with in other populations—for example, those with autism respond idiosyncratically to many prescription drugs. For information about the physical/medical aspects of autism, see Baker and Pangborn, 2001; Gillberg, 1990; Gillberg and Coleman, 1992; Harty, 1990; Handen, 1993; and Tsai, 2000.

Organize and Structure

Once doctors are selected, develop a relationship with them and together develop a plan so care can be more efficient and effective:

1. *Prepare the medical professional and office staff* with information about autism and about the particular patient. Provide medical records, and explain predictable problems and strategies for developing a rapport and reducing anxiety.

   - Ask to attend a regular staff meeting.

   - Show photographs of the new patient—show them that the new patient looks pretty much like other patients.

   - Provide specific information about the individual—about the specific sensory and motor issues and how this particular patient communicates and expresses confusion and anxiety.

   - Enlist staff members' ideas for ways to make medical care easier for the learner. If possible, set up a series of field trips to familiarize the learner with staff personnel, the environment, and the anticipated procedures. Schedule visits at times when the patient load is light and when the learner is not stressed by illness.

   - Provide strategies to help doctors and staff members develop a rapport and communicate effectively with the patient. For example, they should know to:

     ▶ Talk calmly in a low voice.

> ▶ Explain procedures with words, drawings, and other visual references.

> ▶ Provide concrete ways to mark the amount of time to endure a procedure. ("This will be over by the time we count to 20" or "This will hurt only as long as it takes us to sing 'Twinkle, Twinkle, Little Star'."

2. *Keep medical records.* A diagnosis depends as much on past medical history as on an examination (Dalldorf, 1983). Parents need to develop notebooks of medical reports, immunizations, and laboratory tests. Forms for keeping these records can be obtained from most health departments and medical offices.

   - Also keep records of behavioral symptoms that indicated medical problems in the past. Record current symptoms, indicate the conditions that are generally present when those symptoms occur, and write details on how the current episode may be like or different from previous episodes.

   - All interpreters should monitor and record behavior before and after changing medications.

     A trusting relationship between the parents and medical staff can make access to good medical care more efficient.

Jeff had headaches and chronic ear infections. The behavioral symptom of these problems was banging on his forehead and ears. His tolerance for others was very low at these times, and he could lash out at those who talked too loud or came too close. It was difficult for Jeff to tolerate a visit to the doctor during these episodes. His mother and his doctor had worked together on these problems for some time and had developed the following plan:

- When it was obvious that Jeff had a headache, he was routinely given aspirin.

- His mother checked his temperature morning and night. The moment his fever began to climb, she called the doctor, who phoned a prescription to the pharmacy.

3. *Prepare the learner.* In reality, little can be done to change the structure of medical facilities, except to prepare adequately beforehand. If possible, plan and prepare a new routine for going to the doctor or dentist, using the guidelines in Chapter 18, pages 302–304. Before developing the routine, assess the environment to identify sensory elements that need to be addressed. Consult with the nurse to ensure that critical procedures and equipment are correctly labeled and described.

   - Develop a social story (as in Figure 14.4, page 226), or a videotape of the setting for introducing and rehearsing the routine before making the first trips to the office or hospital. Whenever possible, visit the natural settings before illness occurs.

   - Take familiar and favorite materials to use while waiting.

   - Plan for relief from potential sensory discomfort. Earplugs may relieve unusual or painful noises, and eye shields may protect from bright overhead lights.

   - A soft and familiar gown or shirt may be more comfortable than harsh fabric or disposable gowns. A cotton flannel sheet may be less irritating than paper on the examination table.

4. *Structure the trip so it ends with a pleasant activity—not as a reward for good behavior*, but simply as something pleasant to think about and anticipate. If the pleasant activity is contingent on good behavior, the fear that it can be lost may raise stress. If the "reward" is lost in the first moments of the examination, there is no power—or hope—left. Disappointment at the loss of something pleasant can trigger more serious problems.

Teach New Skills

1. *Teach the concepts related to medical or health needs* (i.e., hurt or pain)

2. *Modify the communication system to include terms related to medical care:*

   ■ A way to express pain and to show the location of pain or discomfort. The word hurt paired with pointing can indicate hurt here or hurt this.

   Some young children may not be able to identify the source of pain because of differences in sensory processing.

   ■ Provide a way to signal a need for relief. Most people can tell a dentist to stop a minute for relief, or tell a nurse or doctor when the end of endurance is near. Perhaps a hand signal or a cue card could be used to indicate, "Stop. I need a minute to rest." This communication strategy needs rehearsal before the appointment and with the doctor and nurse prior to the potentially stressful procedure. A measure of control and trust can reduce feelings of panic.

Evaluate and Refine

Interventions, environments, and routines need continuous evaluation to identify possible problems. Address all issues related to developmental changes, new medical staff or procedures, new offices, and new fears and sensitivities.

Eating Problems

There are three basic types of eating problems among children with autism:

1. Refusing to eat or eating very limited amounts or types of foods

2. Problems with chewing, swallowing, gagging, and regurgitating

3. Eating things that are not food (pica)

In some cases, an eating problem may be present at birth. In other situations, the problem may begin from some small incident and expand to life-threatening proportions.

Assess the Problem

Before developing any intervention, keep a record of all foods and nonfoods eaten each day. Include fruit juices, milk, vitamin supplements, and other consumables. Especially note the little between meal bites and snacks. This information, along with a record of weight and growth, will help to determine the extent of any nutritional problem and may indicate possible links to sensory differences. Record answers to these questions:

1. *How did the problem begin?* Has the situation always been a problem or did it begin suddenly, seemingly for no reason? Could it be related to a misperception, an unusual association, or a learned error? For example, did it begin:

   ■ During a bout with the flu or a bad cold? Sometimes the pain of swallowing with a sore throat can be associated with the act of swallowing any food. This might trigger continuing refusals to eat even when the throat is no longer sore.

- After seeing someone else vomit or gag?

- After a coughing or choking episode had received a quick and dramatic response?

- After hearing news reports or a story about the dangers of certain foods, one young man totally quit eating any foods containing fats or cholesterol after hearing a news report of the dangers of high cholesterol.

2. *Could the eating problem be related to physical problems?* Allergies? Cravings related to metabolic or nutritional factors? Dental problems, sores, or injuries in the mouth? Neurological or motor problems related to chewing and swallowing? Indigestion, "nervous stomach," diarrhea, or blockages of some type?

    A medical evaluation is especially important for such problems as regurgitation, weight loss, frequent illnesses, or a drastic change in behavior.

3. *Is the situation a sensory problem* involving the texture, color, odor, or flavor of foods?

4. *Pica—additional assessment questions.* Pica (eating things that are not food) can be related to some of the previous issues as well, especially sensory factors and cravings from metabolic disorders. Pica has also been associated with other factors. To assess problems related to pica, consider the following questions:

    - Did a quick and dramatic response follow attempts to eat objects from the floor? Most toddlers soon stop putting things into their mouths after several corrections; but in children with autism, the attention from corrections may reinforce the activity.

    - Is the situation a discrimination problem or a skill deficit? Does the individual understand the concept of food and nonfood? Does this orderly person know what to do with garbage and things found on the floor and ground?

    - Are nutritious and liked foods available on a schedule that matches the individual's changing needs? For example, during growth spurts, most children require more food, more frequently.

Effective intervention sometimes involves the collaboration of all team members, including an autism specialist, an occupational therapist, a pediatrician, and possibly a nutritionist. Medical problems must receive immediate attention, but medical treatment alone may not totally resolve a particular problem. Whatever the initial cause may have been, the problem may have developed into a strong habit or routine that will require a multifaceted intervention.

Organize and Structure

Organize and structure the environment to match the needs identified during the assessment.

- The location of meals and snacks may need to be changed to one with fewer distractions.
- The eating schedule may need to be changed. Smaller, more frequent meals may be needed.
- Food or snack storage and availability may need to be adapted.
- Trash containers may be needed in all settings.
- Visual and verbal adaptations will be needed to support new instruction and clarify misperceptions.

Teach New Concepts, Rules, and Routines

Incorporate some of the following strategies to teach appropriate eating and mealtime behavior and prevent future problems:

1. *Ignore the behavior.*

    - Do not talk about the problem in the presence of the learner.
    - Do not threaten, bribe, punish, or unnaturally reinforce eating.
    - Avoid using food for reinforcement.
    - Do not force feed unless specifically ordered by a doctor. Force feeding associates the activity of eating with punishment. Treat eating as a natural part of life, without expressing excitement or concern. This does not mean that the problem is ignored; it simply means that we do not give the problem power by highlighting it with excitement and attention.

2. *Teach eating routines and rules.*

    - Schedule several short eating periods—perhaps 5 to 10 minutes every hour or two. Indicate these periods on the individual calendar and follow eating time with pleasant, liked activities. Offering small amounts of food at frequent intervals may also be helpful in treating gagging and regurgitation.
    - Establish rules that can be enforced, such as: We always sit down to eat. We take one bite of everything. We start the meal together. Rules that cannot be enforced backfire and teach the wrong lesson. For example, the rule "Stay at the table till everyone is finished eating" cannot be enforced and results in punishing the whole family. Rules must match the child's attention span and tolerance. Begin at a successful level and gradually expand the child's ability to stay at the table successfully.
    - Vary the eating locations—most of the time meals will be at home at the dining table, but snacks can be eaten at a variety of locations depending on the situation: a child's table, a picnic on a blanket, or a party on the playground. The critical element is that the parent decides where and when eating is done and enforces it. Perhaps one rule is to eat sitting down, so the child does not wander about the house or other locations with food.

        The importance of this type of rule varies from one family to another. Each family must set priorities. It may be more productive to calmly feed the child early, and teach them what to do quietly while the rest of the family eats. This is particularly effective when there are other children in the family who need their share of attention and a calm family mealtime.

- Teach a very basic eating routine to prevent stuffing, gorging, choking, or gagging—problems that make eating a punishing experience. Teach the child to "Take a bite, chew, swallow; take a bite. . . . " or "Pick up your spoon, scoop some food, put it in your mouth, put your spoon down, chew, swallow."

- Consult with an occupational therapist if neurological problems make chewing and swallowing difficult.

3. *Develop a routine for introducing new foods.*

- Systematically offer foods that are new or disliked, tolerated, and favorites. Initially, select new foods that are similar to highly liked foods. Gradually add foods that have slightly different textures, flavors, odors, or colors. This is not a time for the learner to choose which foods to eat first. Rather, offer foods in an order that capitalizes on the reinforcing qualities of the liked foods.

Refer to pages 182–183 and Figure 12.3 for the formula for sequencing events to capitalize on the reinforcing qualities of activities—to develop new reinforcing activities.

- Keep portions small. Offer one or two very small tastes of a new food, then three or four small bites of familiar foods. It is far better to start small and have success than to start big and have failures. If the learner's tolerance is misjudged, reduce demands. For example, isolate one or two tiny bites on the plate and state a contingency. ("One bite, and then _____.") Remember to vary the requirement so a meaningless routine is not developed.

- Review a printed menu or list at the beginning of each mealtime to highlight the foods available. This visual reference will teach food labels, provide a familiar structure for introducing new foods, and make it very clear that both new foods and familiar foods will be offered.

- Systematically make a new food more familiar. Introduce a new food for several days before offering a taste. Select a food with qualities similar to the most liked foods; then use some of the following activities:

  ▶ Involve the learner in buying the food.

  ▶ Show the new food, label it, and talk about it.

  ▶ Prepare a symbol for the food (a line drawing or word), and place it with other symbols of foods that will be added to the menu later.

  ▶ Involve the learner in preparing the food.

  ▶ Model tasting the food. Use exaggerated expressions of pleasure. Offer a taste, but do not insist that it be taken.

  ▶ Use stories with line drawings that show the learner eating a tiny bite of the new food followed by a favorite food.

  ▶ After a few days of these experiences, put the new food on the menu.

  ▶ Schedule food-of-the-week activities. This strategy enables the child to have enough experiences over several days with the new food to develop real familiarity and develop preferences.

Develop these activities as routine and keep them as natural as possible to prevent learned errors. Use stories or cartoon strips to incorporate concepts. ("Mary likes applesauce a lot. I don't like applesauce very well, so I eat only a little bit. Here is a little applesauce. You might like it a lot, so you can ask for more.")

4. *Provide clear and accurate information* about food research and good nutrition.

This is particularly important for the higher functioning learners who watch and talk about TV or read advertisements. Clarify food misperceptions from television, comics, stories, and cartoons, and be sure the learner discriminates between fact and fantasy. End discussions of concerns by saying, "Well, the research is contradictory" or "It's only a pretend story. It didn't really happen."

5. *Give access to nutritious snacks* midway between but not just before meals.

Adolescents in particular need a lot of food. In a few situations, free access to nutritious snacks resolved the problem of eating nonfood items.

6. *Teach new discriminations between foods and nonfoods* to all young children and especially those with pica. Pica is a serious, potentially life-threatening problem. It must be dealt with directly with supervision to prevent the problem, and by teaching appropriate alternative behaviors. Isolating or restricting the learner to a sterile environment can trigger different and often more severe behavior problems.

Review Chapter 19 for strategies to teach those with pica to discriminate between food and not food.

   ▪ Categorize different types of foods according to the major food groups (or foods/not foods). Emphasize that food is stored in cupboards and refrigerators, and litter is placed in the garbage. As soon as a toddler begins to pick up lint or dirt from the floor, teach the child to place it in the garbage.

7. *Use visual references.*

Use stories, imagery, cartoon formats, T-charts, menus, video modeling and other visual references to support these lessons.

Evaluate and Refine

Eating problems can be dealt with only after determining the reasons for the problem. Although each situation is unique, strategies involve some common themes. As with other functional skills, teach new eating skills in the context of natural routines (see Chapters 13 and 18). *Seek medical assistance promptly if a young child begins to lose weight or actually stops eating.*

Sleeping Problems

Families often find themselves caught in rigid nighttime routines that leave them exhausted. Too often, the child sleeps with the parents or a parent sleeps in the child's bed. This situation develops because it is the only way to get any sleep and to ensure the safety of a night-roaming child. These night routines are extremely hard to change and without specific intervention they will be lifelong problems.

Lack of sleep is the parent's problem; those with autism seem to need very little sleep. Two intervention goals are needed: (a) to teach these children to stay safely and quietly in their own rooms at night while others are asleep, and (b) to avoid making problems worse by developing other unproductive routines.

Assess the Problem

Together, parents and other members of the support team can assess and determine the reasons for the problem. Whenever possible, ask the learner, who may be able to provide the critical piece of information.

1. *Why does this learner not sleep or stay in the bedroom at night?*

   - Is it loneliness? fear? restlessness? an inability to stay occupied? hunger?

   - Could it be a need to go to the bathroom at night? This is a particularly complicating factor. If a bathroom problem is not adequately addressed, it can lead to urinating in corners or smearing feces.

   - Is it a sensory problem—the sound of a furnace fan, the outside lights reflecting through moving tree branches or Venetian blinds? Could it be the sound or feel of the child's own heartbeat or breathing in the silence? Is it the feel or odors of bedclothes or the bed?

   - Does the child truly understand what to do in the bedroom at night? Or has the child developed the concept that sleep occurs only in a bed in which others are sleeping?

2. *What safety factors must be addressed in the intervention plan?*

   As noted earlier, those with autism have little sense of danger. When they are in panic or determined, they have an uncanny ability to open locks or climb to the top of cupboards and out windows. Wandering about the house without supervision can lead to other dangerous situations, such as turning on the stove or other appliances; leaving the house; or getting into matches, dangerous chemicals, or hazardous equipment. To prevent these kinds of problems, the child must learn to stay safely and happily in the bedroom.

   - Examine the child's bedroom to identify potentially dangerous situations that must be modified for safety—windows, plug-ins, light fixtures, mirrors, locks, and other elements. The types of necessary modifications will depend on the age, abilities, and interests of the individual.

Organize and Structure

1. *Structure the environment for safety.* The following modifications have helped other parents keep their child safe while they slept:

   - Replace glass windows with acrylic plastic. Place heavy screens or guards on the outside of windows. Install childproof locks on windows.

   - Place alarms and childproof locks on outside doors.

   - Install infrared alarms at the doorway to the child's bedroom and to the kitchen and other areas where there are dangerous materials.

   - Place a lock on the outside of the child's bedroom door. Although this is an uncomfortable decision, it is necessary in some situations. Parents have developed a variety of ways to prevent panic and fear in their children while ensuring their safety. A Dutch door with the bottom half locked and the top open might be enough for some children.

At 4 years of age, Jeff was very active and required only a few hours of sleep each night. As one part of their intervention plan, his parents decided they must lock his bedroom door. When he was in the room alone with the door shut, however, Jeff panicked, screamed, and threw himself at the door. Jeff's father installed a small opening in the original door. The opening was large enough to see out but not to climb through. The parents hung a colorful and interesting picture on the wall opposite the opening to provide a view, and they kept the hall light on all night.

Initially, Jeff's parents taught him to enjoy the room at various times of the day. First, they developed a mini-schedule similar to one he used at school, and they arranged a series of activities for him to do in the room. They played peek games through the opening, first with one parent in the room with him and the other parent on the outside of the door. Sometimes Jeff was outside with one parent and the other parent was inside. After several months, when all the components of the intervention plan were in place, Jeff learned to stay quietly in his room at night.

- Install an electronic monitoring system such as those used to monitor babies.

- Install recessed light fixtures with unbreakable covers. Remove plug-ins or disconnect the power to those in the room. Install protective covers for heaters, heater fans, and thermostats.

- Remove mirrors, glass from picture frames, and other breakable objects or potentially dangerous items.

2. *Structure to address sensory factors.*

   Consult an occupational therapist for help in identifying and resolving sensory problems. The following modifications have helped some learners sleep better and allowed their families to sleep as well:

   - Consider a different type of bed. A water bed, hammock, beanbag chair, or a mummy-type sleeping bag could provide the type of pressure or movement that calms and promotes sleep.

   - Modify sleeping garments, pillows, and bed linens. Sleeping garments need to be soft without harsh nylon labels or seams. Lycra tops and leggings that fit smoothly and tightly may be soothing for some children. Sleeping under heavy blankets or pads may be helpful.

   - Eliminate fan and heater noises if at all possible. To mask other sounds, install some type of safe sound system and play soothing music throughout the night. Tapes of nature sounds or white noise may be helpful.

   - Use battery-operated night lights or soft, indirect lights to mask shadows or wavering lights from outside. Replace Venetian blinds with attractive hardboard window covers inside the windows.

Please note that this list of modifications is a collection of those that have been useful for some families. The assessment process will guide the selection of modifications for each child.

Teach New Skills

Once the environmental and sensory factors are addressed, plan and teach the new skills in the context of a total night-time routine (see Chapters 13, 16 and 19 to review the process and the strategies). *Note:* A plan should include strategies to generalize the new routine (i.e., to allow for trips to Grandma's house or a motel).

1. *Teach a new nighttime routine.*

   Develop the components of a nighttime routine to structure the transition from the family areas to the bedroom. Schedule a bath, story, and other relaxing activities. Offer a few crackers or juice for a snack.

2. *Teach the child to use a nighttime calendar* or mini-schedule similar to one used in other settings. Plan activities that are pleasantly neutral, easy, quiet, and not overly stimulating. Vary the activities or offer limited choices occasionally to prevent boredom. Schedule specific times to lie down and cover up, listen to a relaxation tape, and go to sleep. This structure will provide comfort to these children with autism spectrum disorders.

3. *Establish a system for communicating a need to use the bathroom.* Perhaps the bedtime schedule could include a bathroom break during the night. If a baby monitor is installed—the child could be taught to say, "Potty" or a familiar signal. In this situation, it could be introduced by playing games talking to each other. For example, while Mom and the child are in the parent's room, Dad could be in the child's room calling to them. Then they could switch. A story process or video rehearsal could also help introduce this concept.

4. *Teach a method for determining the passing of time*—how much longer it will be until morning. Provide a watch or clock, and mark the face to show where the hands will be when it is time to get up. Remember, that most of these children do not require much sleep. So a few activities should be available for them when they wake—again, a mini-schedule of activities can be helpful.

Evaluate and Refine

Be alert for any new problems. The routines, schedule, and visual systems must be refined to match changing needs.

Toilet Training

The process for teaching the child to use the bathroom independently can be a daunting and difficult task. The following information provides the basic process and some of the strategies and tips for achieving this major goal.

Most children with ASD can manage this task—those with more significant problems may continue to require some assistance at times. Essentially, toilet training is taught in the context of a functional routine—a routine with the same elements as for teaching all other functional skills.

Preparation

As with other instruction, training cannot begin until an assessment is completed to determine the child's readiness, sensory or motor issues, and past experiences that could affect the child's willingness to use the bathroom—and until a comprehensive plan is developed to teach a complete routine.

If previous attempts at toilet training ended with a struggle, do not begin again until a new plan is totally developed. Do not talk about toilet training or refer to it in any way. Whenever the child's pants are wet or dirty, quickly and quietly change him or help him change himself *without reprimand, comment, or interaction at all. Be neutral!* Also avoid any physical signals of irritation, facial expressions, etc. Again, be neutral.

To avoid confusing the child, both parents and teachers must work together to assess, plan, and begin instruction using the same or a very similar vocabulary, routine and strategies in home and school settings.

Assess Readiness and Current Habits

Collect information to answer the following:

To develop the steps for a clear functional routine, see Chapters 13 and 18. To develop the visual strategies refer to Chapter 14.

1. *Identify current toileting habits.* The first step is to prepare a chart with the days of the week across the top, and the time, in half-hour increments, listed down the side. Use a code such as: D = dry when checked, U = urinated in toilet, UX = accident, B = bowel movement in toilet, BX = accident. Also include comments about special situations, such as ill, traveling, etc. In addition to this information, answer the following question:

   How do you know when the child needs to use the toilet, or has a wet or dirty diaper? How often and how many times a day does he urinate or have a bowel movement? Can you predict when he needs to go? Is the child uncomfortable with wet or dirty pants? What are the earliest behaviors that show the need to go? Does he go off alone or hide to do it? Does he make any effort to tell you that he needs to go, or that he needs his clothing changed?

2. *Assess the restroom or bathroom environment and the child's response to the room.* Is the child sensitive to flickering lights? Fan noises? The noise of the flushing toilet? Distracted by the water and wants to play in the toilet or at the sink? Does the child have balance or motor problems that would make getting on or sitting on the toilet frightening? How does the child react when his pants are off—will he sit on the floor or on chairs with his seat bare?

See Chapter 18 for strategies to prepare (prime) the child for toilet training. Strategies for providing clear and specific instruction are included in Chapters 14 and 15.

3. *Did the child ever use the toilet appropriately? Or willingly?* If previous efforts to toilet train have failed, assess the following issues as well:

   What were the conditions at that time? How long did he use the toilet appropriately? How often did he use it? Did the child ever ask to use the toilet?

   - When did the child first avoid using the toilet? Did something happen at that time to scare or confuse him? For example, did he lose his balance on the toilet seat? Did someone flush the toilet while the child was sitting on it? If a boy, did he stand up to urinate? Did he seem to be uncomfortable with bare legs or sitting on the toilet with his pants down?

   - Was there a medical problem? Was he constipated and appear to have pain? Did the child have diarrhea that could have frightened him? Does the child ever bleed after eliminating? Does he strain hard, cry, or look worried when pants are soiled? Has the child had a bladder infection so urination was painful? Did the child ever have blood in the urine?

Refer to Chapter 16, for use of prompting and correction procedures.

   - Did the child misunderstand something? Or perhaps he learned the wrong lesson in some way? For example, if disciplined for soiling his pants, he may have thought that he was not to defecate at all. Does the child really understand that bowel movements and urine go into the toilet? Has the child watched a brother, sister, or parents use the toilet and heard the noises? Has the child ever been told what is happening when others use the toilet?

A child is probably ready for training when he is dry for at least 1–2 hours, when he shows discomfort with soiled clothing, and/or when he goes off alone to eliminate.

Develop the Toileting Plan

Although the process for developing the routine and teaching the skills for independent use of the toilet are similar to those used to plan and teach other functional skills, there are some decisions to make.

1. *What vocabulary will be used* to avoid confusing the child? For clarity, "pee and poop" are clear but might be embarrassing if shouted out in church.

Some families use the term "do your job" or simply "job," which might not be quite as embarrassing but might be confused with doing other jobs/work. It truly matters not what terms you use as long as they are clear to the child and used consistently by everyone.

2. *Decide how a little boy will be taught to urinate.* If a child shows signs of discriminating between his need to urinate or defecate—clutching the front of his pants or squatting, teach him to stand to urinate. If the child shows no such discrimination, it may be best to simply teach him to sit when going to the toilet. The transition from sitting to standing could be confusing for some of these literal learners who believe that whatever they are taught is what should be done in the same way exactly and forever. The transition will be easier if they have watched Dad or brothers stand. Final thoughts:

   - For the child with severe learning problems, there is really no harm in simply teaching him to sit for both processes.

   - If a young boy is taught to drop his pants to the floor when standing to urinate, he must be taught to keep his pants up as soon as he is old enough to manipulate the zipper on his pants. One father reported seeing an adult with autism standing at a urinal in a public restroom with his pants down around his ankles. This is a sure sign to strangers that he is vulnerable.

   - If the boy's attention shifts while urinating and he sprays the room, place a small piece or wad of toilet tissue in the toilet for him to aim at and try to make it sink. Or use a drop of colored detergent so it will foam. Some have been successful with a Cheerio in the water but this could teach the wrong lesson.

3. *Provide clothing that will be easy and quick to manage.*

4. *Organize the routine so the child will know exactly what to do,* when to do it, where to do it, how to do it, in what order, and then what will happen next—see pages 190–194. This routine will start when the calendar says its *time for toilet* and ends when the hands have been washed and dried and the child checks the calendar to see what happens next. Remember that this is a routine and each toileting time will be represented on the daily calendar.

   - Teach the child how to express a need to go to the bathroom between scheduled times or when away from homes.

   - Plan the strategies for generalizing toilet use to public restrooms and to the homes of friends.

   - The timing is a critical factor. Check the assessment information and set the toileting time 5–10 minutes before he would ordinarily urinate or have a bowel movement. For example, does the child generally eliminate before or after mealtimes, and about how much before or after?

   - How long must the child sit (or stand) in the bathroom before they can leave?

Each child will have different time needs. Begin with 5–10 minutes. If the child gets restless and wants to leave after only a few minutes, try giving him something to help him relax—something to watch (sand running through an hour glass on the counter), hear (a music box or favorite tape), or touch (a smooth stone fastened onto a key chain and attached to the child in some way so it will not drop.)

   - Do not talk to or look at the child while they are trying to eliminate; the child needs to concentrate.

- Scheduling a snack with water or juice just before the toileting time can sometimes speed the process.

5. *Develop the visual systems to support the routine*—a daily calendar to show scheduled times and a mini-calendar to show the sequence of steps. Schedule reinforcing activities immediately following toilet time (see Figure 12.3).

6. *Organize and structure the bathroom environment so the child feels safe and secure.* Make the process as natural as possible—so avoid potty chairs. Do use the standard toilet with an insert for a child. A step stool will make the child feel more secure. If the child is quite unsteady, some type of railing may be needed. If the child is uncomfortable with bare legs, perhaps a small hand towel or soft cloth could be available to drape across their legs. If the fan is too noisy, turn it off.

7. *What if the child soils his clothing?* The critical issue is to avoid reinforcing the problem. For example, a show of disapproval or disappointment provides attention or excitement, and the soiling will be reinforced. Therefore, *ignore the child and the error* while cleaning up. Simply change the child quickly but gently, with no emotion, no eye contact, and no words. If the child likes to be clean, *calmly* say, "Soon you will be able to do it by yourself" or "Soon you will do you BM in the toilet and your pants will stay nice and clean." *Remember, remain neutral.*

8. *Begin the instruction when the teachers and the parents can devote themselves to it.* Do not begin just before a major holiday celebration when there are any major disruptions or changes in the offing. One mother posted a note at the front door that read: *Do Not Disturb—Toilet Training in Process.* For training to be a positive and successful experience for all, the adults must be as consistent, calm, unhurried, and as positive as possible.

Prepare the Learner and Begin the Training

As with any other changes and transitions, those with autism spectrum disorders must be prepared for new information. Toilet training will progress at a much faster rate if several of the following strategies or processes are used:

1. *Introduce the routine with visual systems and strategies*—This preparation period has several steps and can involve several days, and enables the child to clearly understand the language and what they will do before they must try to do it.

   - Two or three days before the child is to participate, introduce the symbol for the new routine with the child's daily calendar to show that toileting is another new activity that will start in a few days. Leave the symbol out beside the calendar so it becomes familiar.

   - Introduce the concept of toilet use. Once the calendar symbol is introduced, show the mini-calendar that highlights each step of the routine. This will serve as a visual checklist. Have the child hang it in the bathroom at his eye level. This mini-calendar serves as a non-verbal prompt.

   - Rehearse the routine 2–3 times a day with social stories to match the mini-calendar—or rehearse with video-modeling strategies.
     - One study reported that a child first initiated toilet use after viewing a video about toileting three times a day for only 3 days. The video was shown just before the scheduled potty times. Within a 2-week period, he initiated three times a day and the number of dry diapers increased almost 50% (Bainbridge & Myles, 1999).

- Having no success after several weeks, one mother developed a social story for her son that explained the total routine. Each step of the routine was illustrated with a basic line drawing and placed in a notebook (one step to a page). The illustration for urinating showed a little boy standing with the urine arcing into the toilet. The illustration of the boy having a bowel movement showed the stool dropping from the boy's seat and into the water. After rehearsing the story and talking about the pictures for several days, the boy began to show progress and had very few accidents after 3 weeks of practice.

- Teaching and practicing the toileting routine. After careful preparation and rehearsal, the actual teaching process is much easier, requiring fewer and less intrusive prompts. From the calendar, the child knew which day the procedure would start. From the mini-calendar and rehearsals he knew what to expect and virtually what to do. Now, the child must engage and match his motor movements to the tasks. See Chapter 16 for teaching and prompting strategies.

  - Remember to stop talking while the learner is trying to eliminate, and do not use any verbal prompt or assistance after the second or third days so the child does not depend on someone to tell them what to do. Vary the prompts periodically so the child does not build them into the routine (see pages 254 and 255).

  - Reinforce progress and successful use. Generally, a natural reinforcer such as flushing the toilet or washing hands for a few minutes is all that is required. This means that if the child does not eliminate, they do not need to (or get to) flush or wash. But trying would be reinforced by following the routine with the next activity on the calendar, which should be a fairly liked activity.

- If the child does not successfully eliminate after a specific period of time, be calm and neutral. Say something like, "You tried, maybe next time you will be able to do it."

Remember that if you want the child to do something independently, stop talking, and vary the prompts. Although some children make remarkable progress after using these special strategies, the progress will be much slower for other children. So, keep trying and stay consistent.

Evaluate and Refine

Evaluate the progress and the process continuously and refine and modify or add any elements that may be required to match the child's changing needs. If the process is moving too slowly or the child is showing resistance, review and reassess to see if something was overlooked during the planning process, or if something has changed or disrupted the familiar family routine. If the plan appears to address the child's needs, check to see if the plan is being followed consistently in all settings.

Periodic regressions are to be expected during normal development—so it is unlikely that the child is merely being stubborn or is too handicapped to learn.

Rather, he is likely confused in some way; either he does not understand the process or he misunderstands some seemingly insignificant part of the process. Review sensory factor, the visuals, and a possible medical condition that may be getting in the way.

Continue teaching the routine while assessing and refining the process. If the training is stopped and then started again later, the child can become very confused. Remember, toilet training can take many months for some children—keep records and rejoice whenever changes are observed.

Additional Resources

Howard, B. J., Mitchell, M., Culley, L., Kline, M., & Hardin, M. (1991). *It's potty time.* Dallas, TX: Learning Through Entertainment.

> This is, a 25 minute long videotape of several children toileting during a birthday party.

Marks, C. (2001). Toilet training . . . is your child ready? *Autism•Asperger's Digest, July/August,* 18–22.

> This is an excellent, quick read article that covers assessment, planning, teaching, trouble shooting along with 75+ Toilet Training Tips.

Wheeler, M. (1998). *Toilet training for individuals with autism & related disorders: A comprehensive guide for parents & teachers.* Arlington, TX: Future Horizons.

> This is an excellent resource with many ideas and suggestions for individualizing and solving problems.

Other resources are listed in Appendix B.

Social and Sexual Issues

See social story strategies in Chapter 14. Refer to the video modeling strategies in Chapter 22.

Social awareness generally increases during adolescence in young people with autism, just as it does in the general population. Many higher-functioning young people and those with Asperger's syndrome are attracted to members of the opposite sex, and they suffer intensely when their awkward attempts to establish relationships are rejected. In general, those with autism want someone to be a friend to go places with, someone who shares and provides comfort, encouragement, and an occasional hug. Some males seem to show little drive for the more physical aspects of a sexual relationship. Attempts to have more serious relationships often end because the person with autism is unable to empathize, reciprocate, or provide emotional support to a partner. Some young learners do "fall in love" and feel sadness and pain when their naive efforts are rebuffed (DesLauriers, 1978). Some who express a desire for marriage and children indicate, on further questioning, that it is because "that's what others do." Until proven otherwise, it can be assumed that those without verbal skills have similar social needs, desires, and problems.

The deficits of autism that are particularly problematic in the area of social and sexual relationships include:

- Difficulty establishing and maintaining friendships
- Difficulty maintaining or regaining self-control
- Poor or no ability to discriminate socially appropriate and inappropriate words and actions, coupled with a general lack of social judgment
- A general lack of empathy and awareness of the perspective and needs of others (Hobson, 1992)
- Difficulty understanding the consequences of a behavior and the effect of that behavior on others
- Difficulty identifying and understanding nonverbal messages, while verbal messages are understood literally or misinterpreted

The implications of these problems are compelling reasons for thoughtful decision making. The world is not tolerant of young people who masturbate on the bus or who appear in public unclothed. Those who interpret a friendly greeting as a romantic invitation are likely to be arrested for harassment or stalking if they make continued attempts to establish a relationship. Naive and compliant young individuals are in danger of exploitation or abuse if their trust is misplaced. A young person with poor self-control, without empathy or sensitivity to the feelings of others, could unintentionally hurt a partner in efforts to achieve self-gratification. Realistically, masturbation may be the only sexual outlet for some, perhaps many, adults with autism (Melone & Lettick, 1983).

Other viewpoints are expressed *in Sex Education and Social Awareness Building for Autistic Children and Youth: Some Viewpoints and Considerations and Responses* by Elgar et al. (1985).

In making program decisions in this sensitive area, the safest course is to involve the total support team, including the parents and the learner when appropriate. Parents know their child's problems from experience in a variety of situations, and they must live with and support the decisions. The professional members of the team can provide balance from their experiences with many other individuals and family situations. As the team considers the criterion of the least dangerous assumption (see pages 105–106) and the family's values, they can make decisions that balance the risks with the individual's needs and abilities.

Considerations and Strategies

Decisions will depend on the individual learner's interests, abilities, living situation, opportunities, support system, and family values. Parents need to be thinking about these issues when their child is young—and be aware of what they are teaching without realizing it.

1. "*Will this behavior or skill still be socially acceptable as an adult?* Because learning is literal and relatively inflexible, attempt to project into the future and decide, if it is appropriate now, will it still be appropriate at age 6? At 12? At 21? At 45?" If it is not, then begin immediately to replace or expand that skill. Teach only those skills that will continue to be appropriate at age 50.

   ■ Tantrums, screaming, and hitting are fairly common ways for 2-year-olds to solve problems, but a 12-year-old or an adult who continues this kind of behavior to problem solve is isolated and restrained.

   ■ Nudity is cute in a 3-year-old, but not in a 12- or 21-year-old.

   ■ A young child who is taught to like hugging and begins to nuzzle up to teachers, volunteers, peers, and acquaintances is seen as sweet and friendly. However, indiscriminate hugging is not appropriate and may be dangerous for an adolescent or adult. Parents and teachers must help the child understand who you can hug and how can you express affection to others who are not part of your close family.

   ■ When teaching toileting skills, plan carefully. Little boys are taught to drop their pants while standing up to urinate. Most boys quickly learn to manage the process like Dad and big brother. As noted earlier, unless taught otherwise, an adult with autism will continue to drop his pants even in public restrooms—a signal to others that he is a naive and vulnerable person.

2. *Teach skills that have immediate and literal relevance* and that deal with the real issues. Be guided by the old story about the child who asked his father, "Where did I come from?" When father finished the story of the birds and bees, the child said, "Oh, I thought we came from Boston."

A young man had invited a new friend, a young woman, to visit him at his group home. When she arrived, he took her into his bedroom and closed the door. The staff raised the question: Should he have a quick sex education course? Later, the team decided to teach him to plan activities for entertaining guests and then evaluate. With help to plan the visits, this young man entertained female guests in the living room, where they watched TV, shared magazines, listened to music, danced, and ate snacks. They did not indicate or suggest that they wanted more private personal time. Lesson: Begin with the simple and concrete solutions, then evaluate and refine if the situation changes.

3. *Some basic concepts and rules are best taught in early childhood*, then expanded and modified over time.

   - Identifying body parts.

     Use correct anatomical terms. This is an important lifelong skill needed to get appropriate medical care and for discussing hygiene and social/sexual instruction.

   - Private and public behavior—the basic rules that guide appropriate behavior

     It is important to teach the exceptions that match the immediate need, and to systematically modify or add to the exceptions as needs change. For example, keep clothing on except when bathing, changing clothing, trying on clothes in the store, swimming, for doctor examinations, etc.

   - Value a variety of social reinforcers

     Teach the learner to value compliments and a high-five salute for additional reinforcers. An arm around the shoulder or a pat on the arm, shoulder, or back can be satisfying, but save hugging for close family members or old family friends. Also teach the concepts for these discriminations.

Sex Education

1. *Identify appropriate skills and instructional resources* from sex-education materials written for those with developmental delays. Adapt the curriculum to match the autism learning style (Dalrymple, Gray, & Ruble, 1991). Also see Appendix B for training resources.

   - Individualize the instruction and deliver it in a natural one-to-one context. This allows the instruction to be modified to fit the learner's specific needs at a specific time and avoids confusion.

   - Use instructional procedures to ensure that the learner makes the correct associations, that he or she understands the correct and relevant information and does not learn unintended lessons. One young man was taught condom use with a banana as a model. Later, he told his instructor that he had had sex. He was asked if he had used a condom, and he replied, "No, I didn't have a banana."

   - Teach private and personal care and hygiene skills in the context of total routines. Incorporate visual adaptations, checklists, cue cards, and other visual references so the learner is less dependent on the presence of others to deliver verbal instructions to manage private personal needs. This policy is as important for toilet training as it is for teaching young women to manage their menstrual needs independently. See resources for teaching private and personal care in Appendix B.

- Use written and taped stories to provide clear and sequential information for understanding the purpose of a new skill or strategy. Include all the relevant details needed for generalizing the skill to different situations. Stories, diagrams, and charts provide opportunities for the learner to review and rehearse the skills privately at home.

2. *Train staff to provide effective instruction and responsible guidance*, and to understand the ethical implications of their actions. Monitor staff members frequently to avoid situations that have the potential for exploitation, confusion, frustration, or disappointment. Hugging, patting, or flirting can arouse sexual feelings that many individuals with autism have little skill in understanding or controlling (Melone & Lettick, 1983).

- To avoid confusion and to protect both staff and client, personal assistance and instruction in private matters should be provided by staff of the same sex. A woman—staff member or client—should not be required to enter a men's restroom nor should a man be required to enter a woman's restroom to provide or receive assistance. Eliminating care by those of the opposite sex is not always possible, but it should be given thoughtful consideration for individuals as young as six or seven years of age. Exceptions to this policy should be made only in extraordinary situations, and should be explained to the learner to avoid misunderstandings.

Additional Resources

Newport, J., & Newport, M. (2002). *Autism-Asperger's & sexuality: Puberty and beyond.* Arlington, TX: Future Horizons.

This book is written by a young couple with Asperger's syndrome.

Masturbation

Masturbation is an issue that needs thoughtful management to prevent serious problems during puberty and adulthood. Whatever management decisions are made, it is important to deal with the situation calmly and in a matter-of-fact way. Emotional expressions of shock, distaste, or "badness" will call undue attention to the behavior and likely will serve as a reinforcer to strengthen and increase the problem. Boredom, lack of physical exertion and strenuous activity, ill-fitting clothing, infections, and inadequate hygiene can intensify the frequency of masturbation.

The basic goal is to teach learners when and where they can masturbate and avoid turning it into a problem. Instruction begins as soon as a young child begins to masturbate outside the bedroom. The child is calmly redirected to the bedroom with the statement, "You can masturbate in the bedroom." It is much easier to teach a young child this important rule than to wait until adolescence when problems may have developed and the consequences of poor judgment are more serious.

Strategies

1. *Organize and structure the learner's time.*

- Provide a balanced schedule of activities so the learner is alert and physically, socially, and intellectually active most of the time (this is simply a good practice that will prevent a number of other problems as well).

Limit the amount of uninterrupted quiet time spent in public areas such as the living room or classroom. Structure these quiet times with interesting and quiet activities that can be done alone. Interrupt quiet times periodically with activities, toys, materials, or social opportunities.

■ Instruct the learner that private places are where private things are done. Specify private places—the bathroom *at home* and the learner's bedroom. Some learners need a reminder that you can do other than private things in those rooms, and that others also use the bathroom. Make sure the learner understands that public restrooms are not private places—other people can come in.

■ Schedule some private, uninterrupted bedroom time. Give this block of time a name—perhaps simply private time. As with any other activity or routine, private time needs a clear beginning and a clear ending. The beginning can be specified on a daily calendar—a mini-calendar could list optional activities. An alarm clock or timer provides an impersonal and concrete way to end this period and make the transition from private to public time.

■ Facilitate the transition from the private period by checking the calendar before it begins to see what happens next. A routine is helpful for some older learners. The routine could begin by managing basic hygiene needs—perhaps with a shower—and continue with an enjoyable activity such as listening to music. ("After your shower, it will be time to play your new CD.")

2. *A caution.*

Be aware that anxiety and frustration are an ongoing part of the autism syndrome. There is little indication that anxiety and frustration will be relieved by sexual gratification alone. Caution is advised if anyone suggests that the learner needs instruction to masturbate more effectively. Confusion and even more frustration are the likely result for those with autism who learn skills exactly as taught. For example, if another person is present to teach the behavior, the learner may assume that another person should always be part of the behavior.

3. *Evaluate and refine to address changing needs or problems.*

■ Include a check for signs of irritation or infection—and the fit of clothing.

■ Review the schedule of activities and the materials. Is the learner bored? Does the learner need more variety, more challenging activities and materials, more strenuous physical activity, or more frequent social interactions?

■ Perhaps one of the rules needs to be modified or clarified, or a new rule may be needed.

More young people with autism are marrying today than ever before. One young couple is working out their own personal relationship—wanting to marry, but unable to live independently, each lives with their own parents. But with the help of their parents, they had a commitment ceremony and are able to spend time together several times each week. With more effective instruction during their school years and with the sensitive support of mentors and interpreters to help clarify the world and fill the gaps, ever more individuals with autism will be able to lead satisfying lives in the future.

Involvement With the Law

Naiveté, overcompliance, impulsivity, and an inability to effectively reason and make social judgments can lead to a variety of problems that involve the law. This is particularly true for those with Asperger's syndrome and higher-functioning autism, who seem so capable but who have broken the law in some way—some have been incarcerated. Some of the problems are a result of victimization—doing things others tell them to do. Other problems involve trespassing and inappropriate approaches to people. In some cases, stereotypic behavior is frightening to those who are uninformed about autism, and this situation can lead to police reports. Child protection agencies also may become involved if there are reports of suspected abuse.

Generally, police officers, social workers, and others who are charged with protecting people have little or no training to understand autism. Strategies for questioning or for gaining the trust and cooperation of those with autism are often contrary to the strategies and procedures for handling others.

Organize and Structure

Get to know the local police and enlist the aid of an officer with some authority as an advocate. Become acquainted with neighbors and local business people. This is easier in small towns than in large cities, but it is particularly important if the learner tends to wander away or hang out with a group of peers. Learners also need to know the local officers so they do not panic when approached by police. *Teach them that police can be trusted to help.*

1. *Set up opportunities to meet police officers* and to develop a rapport with some police officers, neighbors, and local business people. Provide these people with basic information about autism and specific information about this learner so problems can be prevented or resolved more effectively. You may use or adapt information from *Guidelines for Interviewing and Communicating with Individuals Who Have Autism,* the reproducible instructional sheets on pages 435–436.

   Some community police departments have established trading-card programs. Officers carry trading cards, similar to sports trading cards, with photographs of themselves in uniform and brief biographical statements. The cards are distributed personally to local residents, especially to students and senior citizens—students are encouraged to collect cards of the total force. This is a promising practice for making local residents more familiar with community helpers.

2. *Ensure that learners carry personal information for emergencies* and small business cards to indicate that they have autism. Include emergency phone numbers and brief information about a few basic strategies that are calming and will help others communicate with the individual should they become lost or get into trouble. A Med-Alert bracelet or necklace also is useful for this purpose. Some learners could carry personal trading cards with some basic information to hand out when meeting new neighbors or community helpers.

Teach New Skills

Teach critical skills in the context of natural routines. Those with autism must learn to manage themselves in the community, and to use public transportation in order to access goods, services, and leisure activities.

Some of the critical concepts and skills to be more independent and avoid problems with the law include:

- Respect for boundaries and other people's property.

  This involves teaching both concepts and rules. Visual references are essential components—i.e., edges of sidewalks, fences, flower borders, crosswalks; property lines.

- Social skills and appropriate public and private behavior—how, if and when, to approach strangers.

- Communication skills—Learners must know how to provide information in an emergency; and how to ask for help from appropriate people.

- Concepts of rules and laws—what they mean, why they are important, and exactly how to obey a law.

- The concept of punishment for disobeying laws must be taught in very literal ways, as opposed to scary and threatening ways. What is punishing for most people may be an exciting adventure for one with autism.

Evaluate and Refine

Instruction begins in early childhood and continuous evaluations, modifications, and instruction are necessary to match changing needs and skills.

Interviewing Individuals With Autism Spectrum Disorders

When individuals with autism must provide information or interact with strangers, especially in unfamiliar settings, their anxiety is so great that they will not be able to function at optimum levels. Interviews or interactions under these stressful conditions generally are not productive and may result in inaccurate information, no information, or a severe behavior outburst. The guidelines presented on the reproducible form on pages 436–436 will make these interactions less stressful and more productive for the individual with autism and for the professional or paraprofessional involved.

Figure 23.2 Guidelines for Interviewing and Communicating with Individuals Who Have Autism

Autism is a neurological condition that causes sensory and communication problems. Some people with autism can talk, but have difficulty expressing ideas and answering questions. Others cannot talk at all, but can answer questions by pointing to pictures or words. Many can read, and some can write their answers.

These people may be overwhelmed and distracted by noise, lights, crowding, and being rushed. They are easily confused, highly anxious, and often in a state of near-panic. Individuals with autism are typically naive, honest, and compliant. They also are perfectionists. If they do not understand some part of a question or expectation, they likely will not respond at all. If they seem noncompliant, it is likely that they do not totally understand the expectations.

Other problems affect the reliability of information.

- People with autism need a longer time to process the words they hear and to generate a response.
- They understand many words very literally. For example, if told to sit down, they might drop to the floor exactly where they are instead of finding a chair.
- They memorize words quickly and may echo them back. Sometimes they answer questions with "tapes" of things they heard many years ago. Often they do not truly understand the full meaning of the words they echo. Their echoed tapes may or may not fit the present situation and can be misleading. Sometimes these tapes give the impression of being hallucinations or fantasy.
- Time is confusing to those with autism. They may not be able to report an accurate sequence of events. They tend to have excellent memory for details, but the information may be presented in the wrong context or sequence. They may tell of incidents that occurred years ago as if they had happened today.
- Leading questions and questions requiring reasoning or judgment will be very difficult for them to answer.
- Time pressures—being rushed or pushed to move or respond quickly—will increase their stress.

Interview Strategies

The following strategies can reduce stress and make an interview more productive.

1. Prior to the interview, find out:
   - How does this client communicate?
   - What might trigger a problem?
   - What might be calming?
2. Arrange to have a familiar, trusted person in sight. If appropriate, that person could serve as an interpreter. Otherwise, enlist the assistance of someone who knows autism well.
3. Conduct the interview in a calm, distraction-free room. Sit next to the person, rather than across a table or desk. Eye contact and face-to-face contact tends to increase confusion and stress.
4. Talk softly, and remain calm. Use concrete and literal language to ask a question. Leave out unnecessary words. Jokes or sarcasm will likely be confusing and misunderstood.
5. Take the time to establish trust and let the client know what to expect of this meeting. Make a list of the meeting agenda. Involve the client in keeping track of time by crossing off items as completed. Include some brief break periods in the schedule.

(continued)

6. Have writing materials available. Often, the client can think and process information better when the spoken words are illustrated visually.

   - As you talk, write out the key words or make line drawings to illustrate key people, objects, or sequences of events. Print labels on those drawings to compensate for questionable artistic ability.

   - Represent time blocks and sequences of events visually, using a cartoon-strip format with a square for each time block or event. Numbering each square or adding dates may be helpful. Verify the sequence by asking questions.

   - Write out or draw optional answers so the client can respond by pointing. Space the pictures or words far enough apart so it is easy to know which answer is being selected. While drawing, ask, "Is it _____, or _____, or _____? Point to the picture to show me what it is."

   - Prepare a 3"x5" index card with the words:

     YES   NO   I DON'T KNOW (or NONE OF THESE)

     Use this card for answering yes/no questions.

   - If none of the options seem satisfactory, give paper and pencil to the client and say, "Show me the way it was" or, "You fix it the right way."

7. Avoid questions that begin with *"Why?"; "What do you think?"* and *"How."* Be sure that *"when"* and *"where"* questions are very concrete and include the visual options described above.

8. Questions such as, "Did it happen this way?" are likely to receive the automatic response, "Yes." This is the time to have optional answers available ("I don't know" or "None of those"). *Do not ask leading questions.*

9. Provide extra time—perhaps 30 seconds or so—before repeating a question. Try writing out the question and remaining quiet while the person thinks. Give the client the pencil and suggest writing the answer.

10. Relax, and understand that this interview may take a long time or may need to be completed in another session or, perhaps, two.

In summary, people with autism become very confused and may panic when:

- They do not understand exactly what to do
- They are rushed or pressed for a quick answer
- People use harsh voices and keep repeating the same questions
- People talk too loud, too fast, or use too many words
- People get too close, force them to have eye contact, or say, "Look at me"
- People grab and try to restrain them

People with autism are more cooperative and able to give better information when:

- They are relaxed and when expectations are understood
- Questions are concrete and clear
- Spoken words are paired with pictures or written words
- Optional answers are made visual; and "I don't know," "Something else," and other options are included
- They are asked to "Show me _____"
- Anatomically correct dolls are used *without leading questions*

Managing Major Life Transitions

The need to prepare those with autism spectrum disorders for transitions, changes, and new and unexpected events is emphasized throughout this book. It is equally important to prepare new staff members to provide appropriate support in the new situation. This is a particularly sensitive but important issue for those with Asperger's syndrome—for often they do not want other people to think they are any different from other people. The information and strategies presented in this section can be applied to any type of change—a move to a new community, home, or school; changing employment; a stay in the hospital; a move from one classroom to another; or joining scouts, 4-H, church; recreational programs, and other community groups.

Assess and Plan

Use Form 5.1, Determining Home/School Priorities (page 79), to identify the demands of the setting and the sensory factors that may have an impact on the learner's ability to function effectively. Set up meetings with interpreters who know the learner best and the staff members and potential interpreters to develop the transition plan together.

Prepare the Learner for the Transition

1. *Arrange at least one visit to the new setting before the move.* Locate the areas for eating and sleeping, the bathrooms, quiet time; and identify where to go for help. Introduce the critical support staff members and perhaps a peer who might be a mentor/friend.

   - Videotape or photograph this first visit. Review it often before the move.

   - Prepare a floor plan or map of the new area. Label the major spaces.

   - Draw pictures or write stories about the new situation. Compile a list of expectations.

   - Prepare a directory of the new staff members and interpreters. Include their photographs, and describe their jobs and roles. Highlight the primary interpreters.

   - Preview a typical schedule and the rules.

   - Discuss special privileges and opportunities that will be available in the new situation.

   - Reassure the learner that familiar and favorite belongings also will be moved.

2. *Develop a plan for saying good-byes and for keeping in touch* with favorite support people after the move:

   - Prepare a calendar that clarifies the dates of visits or phone calls. Include phone numbers when appropriate so the individual can initiate a call.

   - Videotape the old setting or prepare a photo album for talking about and sharing memories of old friends and experiences. Leaving old friends is a true loss that must be dealt with as other grief experiences. Even in autism, where emotions and feelings are not as obvious or understandable, unresolved grief experiences can result in depression, anxiety, and problem behaviors.

Teach New Skills

Although some transitions happen too quickly to make much preparation, others can be anticipated months in advance. When detailed plans are possible, teach:

- New transportation routes and maps of the area
- Work organizations or systems that match those of the new setting
- The history and resources of a new community
- Background information about a new job
- Strategies for maintaining contact with old friends
- Strategies for dealing with anxiety and accessing resources in the new setting

Prepare New Staff to Provide Appropriate Support

1. *If those in the new setting have no experience with autism,* provide information about the autism thinking style and strategies for interpreters (see Chapters 2, 3, 8 and 10; and the guidelines on pages 435–436). This information will be helpful to support people as they develop rapport and establish relationships.

2. *Arrange to attend a staff meeting to introduce the learner.* If the learner cannot participate in the meeting, show photographs or pictures. If appropriate, have the learner share photographs or information about special interests and skills. Knowledge of special strengths and abilities as well as specific problems provides a balanced perspective for new interpreters.

   - See Form 23.1 for an interview outline. New staff can use this format for obtaining information from parents and previous interpreters, and for organizing information to share with new interpreters.

   - See Form 23.2 for a quick-reference outline that can be used by new or substitute staff members to summarize basic and critical information. Keep this form in a confidential but easily accessed location.

3. *Arrange for new support persons to visit the old setting to observe:*

   - How the learner operates in a familiar environment
   - The types of adaptations and visual systems that are used
   - How others relate and provide support to the learner

One mother prepared a booklet to introduce her son to the staff at his new preschool. The booklet, titled I Am Robby, featured his photograph and a number of sections that were written as if he were speaking. New staff found this very helpful. It could be modified to match the characteristics of the older child as well:

My family and my life until now. I am Robby. I'm almost four years old . . .

(This section also included a brief description of Robby's family, typical activities and previous school programs and support services.)

How I communicate. At home and at school . . .

(This section included photographs of his communication systems and two or three schedules.)

This is how I tell you what I want or need. If I'm thirsty . . .

This section included a series of line drawings showing familiar signs for basic needs.

These are my favorite activities:

These are my favorite foods:

Sleep. I like to go to sleep . . .

Discipline. Please don't . . .

I like to do my work system. This section included types of work and drawings to illustrate the structure.

These are the ways I learn best:

These are things I just can't abide!

These are things I can tolerate:

Ways to calm me:

When typical major life transitions are addressed in a systematic way, learners can make these changes with more confidence. With more confidence, they project increased competence. People who project competence are accepted and integrated into new groups and have more options for interesting lives.

Summary

While problems cannot be avoided, effective solutions can be developed through efforts to understand the impact of autism on the learner, understand the background of the problem, and understand the basic strategies. Interpreters who maintain sensitive, evaluative attitudes will be able to adapt and refine to prevent most severe problems while increasing the individual's independence.

Use this form to obtain important information from parents or previous staff. Expand and clarify answers with examples.

Student's name_____**Date** _____

Interviewer _____**Phone** _____

Interviewee _____**Phone** _____

☐ Parent   ☐ Guardian   ☐ Other_____

1. Communication Abilities

Does the student have a special communication system? Describe. _____

_____

How does the student communicate wants and needs?

- Food _____

- Activity _____

- Break _____

- Assistance _____

- Feelings _____

- Need for bathroom_____

- Other _____

_____

Does the student misinterpret things other people say? Interpret things literally? Describe.

_____

List the student's pet phrases with specific meaning. _____

_____

How does stress affect the student's ability to communicate? _____

_____

What behavioral symptoms does this student show when stressed and anxious? List early warning signals.

_____

2. Problems

What problems can be expected? Describe.

- Sensory problems or sensitivities that trigger anxiety or efforts to escape?_____

_____

- Compulsive behaviors? _____

(continued)

- Problems with change and the unexpected? _____
- What activities, foods, events, or strategies are especially disliked?_____
- List triggers that accelerate stress or potential crises._____

What situations are particularly upsetting? _____

_____

When the student is under stress, what is calming? _____

_____

What is the best way to give information or direction? _____

_____

Has the student ever required physical restraint or movement? If so, please give details about:

_____

Situations and environments_____

_____

Emergencies _____

How long did it take for the student to relax? _____

3. Establishing rapport and cooperation

What are the student's special interests and abilities? _____

What are special food and activity preferences? _____

Please give details of strategies that have been especially helpful. _____

Does the student use an individual calendar or work system? If so, describe. _____

What things are particularly comforting that should always be available? (These are the things that the individual should never have to work for or fear that they will be taken away.)

_____

_____

4. Other specific concerns and suggestions

_____

_____

_____

_____

Summary of Basic and Critical Information for New or Substitute Staff Members

Keep this form in a prominent but confidential location. Review periodically to keep information current.

Name _____

Date _____ Birth date _____ Age _____

Teacher _____

Parent _____ Phone _____

Communication	Preferred Activities/Foods	Sensitivities/Dislikes/Triggers
Primary system _____	Highly preferred/interesting (Include repetitive, stereo-typic, or compulsive interests)	
Alternative system _____	_____	
How does the student let you know:	_____	
• Wants/Needs _____	_____	
• Object/Activity _____		
• Assistance _____	ALWAYS keep available _____	Warning signals and emergency procedures (medical and behavioral)
• Need for break/Stop _____	_____	
• Feelings _____	_____	
_____	_____	
• When confused/frustrated _____	Specific help needed (bathroom, eating, other)	
• Sick _____	_____	
• Need for bathroom _____	_____	
How can you provide information? (Check all that apply)	_____	Notes _____
☐ Visual references ☐ Signs ☐ Writing		
☐ Pictures ☐ Objects ☐ Gestures		
Describe _____		

Assess and Plan Interventions for Severe Behavior Problems

The processes and strategies developed in the preceding chapters comprise functional, proactive approaches for preventing severe behavior problems. These strategies are summarized in Figure 24.1.

All of these strategies are non-intrusive and non-aversive (Carr et al., 1990). They do not include the addition of painful or punishing consequences for behavior that occurs as a result of boredom, confusion, stress, medical problems, or lack of skill—and an inability to express feelings and needs. Experience and a growing body of research support this positive educational approach as a practical way to reduce the frequency and the intensity of problem behaviors while increasing competence and independence. "We must go beyond the use of single interventions and develop comprehensive, multi-component plans of support that are responsive to the unique demands of each person and setting and are guided continually by functional assessment data" (Lucyshyn, Olson, & Horner, 1995, p. 28).

In general, the only times an aversive procedure such as restraint might be considered is to prevent life-threatening self-injury (eye gouging, severe head banging, severe biting) or to prevent injury to another person. Even then, restraint would be used only as an emergency procedure, to be followed immediately by a comprehensive functional behavioral assessment of the problem and the implementation of positive, behavioral support strategies to prevent recurrence.

Just as in the population as a whole, those with autism will occasionally lose control. Learners with ASD will continue to face challenges, including medical or physical problems, that reduce tolerance and intensify stress simply because of difficulties or discrepancies in their ability to:

- Understand the culture
- Understand and use the language
- Predict future events from past experiences
- Tolerate sensory stimuli
- Generate solutions to problems

Interpreters must know how to react to the learner's rapidly accelerating stress to prevent a crisis and possible injury. The information in this chapter extends the decision-making and management process described in Chapter 10 by including assessment and intervention strategies for the most severe behavior problems. The procedures described in this section are based on the foundation for understanding the effects of autism on stress-related behavior problems presented in Chapter 8. A case study to illustrate the functional behavioral assessment and intervention planning process concludes this chapter. With this information, teachers and other support personnel can assess the situation and resolve many of the problems themselves.

There are times, however, when families and other interpreters are too close to the situation to be objective—too emotionally involved or worn out from past efforts. Then it is important to call an outside consultant to provide a fresh, more objective perspective. This is particularly true if the behavior is life threatening or dangerous to others. It is also important to engage an outside consultant if the problem has persisted and the individual is in danger of being moved to a more restrictive setting.

Any consultant, psychologist, autism specialist, or behavior consultant involved in conducting a comprehensive functional behavior assessment of serious behavior problems must have a current understanding of the impact of autism on communication and behavior. The consultant also should have experience with positive, non-aversive strategies for developing an effective and productive intervention or positive behavioral support plan for those with autism spectrum disorders.

Figure 24.1 Proactive and Reactive Strategies

A positive behavioral support plan is a multicomponent intervention plan that includes both proactive and reactive strategies designed to meet the needs of each individual's unique needs.

Proactive Strategies To prevent problems		Reactive Strategies In response to problems
Organize and Structure Provide support to match need	**Teach New Skills** To prevent recurring problems	Interpreter available and trained to: • *Predict and prevent problems*
• *Space* 　—Clarified visually 　—Free of overwhelming 　　sensory elements 　—Materials clearly labeled 　　and located 　—Uncluttered and safe • *Activities* 　—Organized as routines 　—Meaningful 　—Varied/balanced 　—Clarified visually 　—At an appropriate level to 　　prevent boredom or failure • *Time* 　—Schedule balanced 　—Flexible 　—Clarified visually • *Sensory conditions* 　—Noise/light/crowding 　—Movement/temperature	• *Communication skills* • *Social skills* • *Relaxation/self-control* • *Self-management/self-monitoring* • *Functional routines and skills* • *Skills to manage change* • *Skills to accept new situations* • *Skills to use visual references* • *Instructional Strategies:* 　—Cues, prompts, correction 　　procedures, and reinforcement 　　based on learning style • *Teach when and where a 　behavior is appropriate*	—Identify behavioral signs 　　of problems 　—Interpret cause and 　　acknowledge need 　—Use reflective listening 　—Provide assistance to prevent 　　or resolve problems quickly • *Manage crises with safe, 　supportive, and nonaversive 　strategies* 　—Model calm, quiet, reassuring 　　behavior 　—Give space; stay an arm's 　　length away 　—Minimize talking and 　　auditory stimulation 　—Reduce demands 　—Calmly, clearly, simply, tell 　　learner what to do 　—Support any sign of 　　relaxation and control 　—Avoid demands for eye 　　contact or explanations
Evaluate and refine in a timely manner, to address ever-changing needs		

Figure 24.1 Proactive and Reactive Strategies (*continued*)

A positive behavioral support plan is a multicomponent intervention plan that includes both proactive and reactive strategies designed to meet the needs of each individual's unique needs.

Proactive Strategies To prevent problems		Reactive Strategies In response to problems

Organize and Structure
Provide support to match need
	Teach New Skills
	To prevent recurring problems
		Interpreter available and trained to:
		• *Manage crises with safe, supportive, and nonaversive strategies*
		—Avoid restraint procedures:
		  • Unless there is imminent and critical danger to self or others
		  • Unless trained in nonaversive procedures
		  • Unless help is available

• *Information/expectations* —Complete and visually clear —Use contingencies • *Support system* —Interpreter(s) always available —Mentors and friends to model —Visual calendars and work systems available and used • *Success/failure rate* —High success rate • *Changes and new experiences* —Systematic preparation —Clarified visually —Adequate support		
Evaluate and refine in a timely manner, to address ever-changing needs		

The Functional Behavioral Assessment

Assessment Goals

A functional assessment or analysis of a severe behavior problem identifies the relationship of the behavior to environmental conditions and the needs of the learner. Potentially dangerous behaviors increase when the individual has problems without the skills or resources to solve them. Thus, in assessing problem behaviors, the goal is to:

1. *Identify and understand the background* of the problems

   ■ When, where, and why does the behavior occur?

   ■ Why does this person respond to problems in this specific way?

   ■ Why does the individual want to escape or avoid this situation?

   ■ Why does the behavior seem like noncompliance? Why aren't instructions followed?

   ■ What might the learner say in this situation, if he could?

   ■ Why must this person get attention in this way?

Saul, a large adolescent boy with severe autism who was unable to speak, was in serious trouble. He was about to be placed in an institution because he was so aggressive. Several teachers and teaching assistants had bruises from being hit. So far, there were no major injuries, but the program administrator was rightfully concerned. An ex-police officer was hired as an assistant to make sure that nobody was hurt, and a consultant was called in to assess the situation.

During the assessment, it was reported that Saul would hit when upset, and sometimes he hit without warning and for no apparent reason. One situation occurred during an observation as Saul and his assistant were walking down the street. Saul seemed to be relaxed, but suddenly he hit his assistant hard in the chest with a backhand movement. Later, while discussing the situation, one hypothesis was put forward: Could it be possible that Saul was trying to initiate a social interaction or make a comment? It had been observed that his assistant never talked to him except to give directions. A trial intervention was instituted that included teaching Saul two basic communication strategies: to get attention by touching his assistant's arm and to point to interesting things. The assistant was trained to attend to any of Saul's efforts to initiate an interaction, to quickly block and shape a potential hit into a touch, and to parallel talk. ("If you want to tell me something, you can touch my arm.") Saul also was given strategies for initiating other conversations about things they saw. These strategies eliminated the backhanded hitting and provided strong justification for teaching appropriate communication skills to relieve stress in other situations.

2. *Identify the components of an effective and positive behavior support plan.* What needs to be modified or taught that will help the individual deal with problems more efficiently and effectively?

   ■ What specific skills does this person need to learn to prevent or solve problems independently?

   ■ What will interpreters need to do differently to prevent or decrease the frequency and intensity of the problem or to manage the problem more effectively?

   ■ What environmental conditions need modifications to reduce stress and clarify information?

Assessment Process

The functional assessment of a severe behavior problem depends on three major activities:

1. *A detailed record review*

2. *Interviews with those most knowledgeable about the situation* and those who know the learner's history. In many cases, an interview with the learner also can provide information to pinpoint the exact cause of the problem.

3. *Observations of the learner in various situations* where the problem does and does not occur

To achieve the assessment goals, consider the following elements and questions:

■ Space

   Are there sensory elements that may overwhelm and reduce tolerance or trigger problems (e.g., noise, light, crowding, disorganization, clutter, odors)?

- Activities

  Are activities meaningful? Balanced between easy/liked, difficult/disliked, active/inactive? Varied to prevent boredom? Are they age-appropriate? Is the length of work periods flexible to match the learner's ever-changing tolerance level? Is there a calendar to clarify the schedule of activities?

- Success rate and expectations

  Is there too much failure, too little challenge, or too little support? Are expectations clear? Does the learner always know what to do?

- Peers

  Do peers tease, undermine, or set up problems? Do they model inappropriate behavior, or are they good models, relating positively? How could they be used to support effective behavior?

- Staff members

  Do staff members identify and deal effectively with early signals of problems? Do they use calm voices and have good rapport with the learner? Are interactions positive or negative?

- Social interactions

  Do interpreters and friends periodically initiate friendly interactions that have no demands or require specific correct responses? Are social opportunities scheduled regularly? What does the learner have to do to get a social interaction? Are interactions generally positive or negative? Does the learner have enough quiet time alone?

- Physical factors

  Could allergies, infections, medications, dental or medical problems be a contributing factor?

- Worries and compulsions

  Is the learner concerned or worried about conditions in the world (e.g., famines, wars, environmental disasters), community, or the home? One young man was so concerned about his father's drug problem that he was unable to maintain focus on the demands of school.

Assessment Tools

There are many different forms and formats for conducting a functional analysis of severe behavior problems (Autism and Asperger Syndrome Resource Center, 1997; Groden et al., 1993; Meyer & Evans, 1989; O'Neill et al., 1990). The following tools and procedures are specifically designed to elicit the detailed information required for understanding the relationship of the problem behavior to environmental conditions.

To Track the Behavior—To See How It Looks
- Incident Report (Form 24.3)
- Brief Incident Report (Form 24.3)

These forms are used to track incidents of severe behavior. They are designed to serve two functions:

1. *To satisfy the legal requirement* for an incident report following a behavioral outburst with potential liability
2. *To assess the environmental conditions that triggered* the problem and to identify the communicative intent of the behavior

When one of these forms is completed in detail following an incident, it provides the data for understanding the situation from the perspective of the individual with autism.

When completing the incident reports, include very clear, concrete and specific information and give examples:

- What was happening just before the problem occurred?

   What was the learner doing? Were there demands, questions, corrections? What were others doing? What were the sensory conditions (e.g., noise, crowding, rushing)? Was the activity structured or unstructured, liked/easy or disliked/difficult? Was the activity just beginning or had it been going on for some time? Were there any warnings—agitation, making noises, changes in breathing pattern, or others?

- What was happening during the incident?

   What did the learner do, with what, and to whom? How was the situation handled? Were additional support people called? This statement clearly but briefly describes the actual behaviors so someone who was not there could understand exactly what occurred. (Words such as noncompliant, attention-getting, angry, and deliberately are *not* helpful.)

- What happened immediately after the incident?

   What did the learner do—smile, scream, run? Was the learner exhausted after the incident? Did the learner sleep? If so, for how long? What did interpreters and peers do? Indicate the intensity of the reactions. Were there consequences? Describe any property damage, injury, or treatment.

- Why do you think the behavior occurred?

   From the learner's perspective, what might have been confusing or misunderstood, or what might have triggered the problem? Was the learner trying to initiate a social interaction or trying to request, protest, or reject something? Describe what you might have done or said if you had been in the learner's position.

To Understand the Background of the Problem—The Environmental Conditions That Trigger or Maintain the Problem

Refer to Chapter 5 for a description of the following tools and reproducible forms.

- Functional Behavioral Analysis: Problem Review Worksheet (Form 24.1)

   This worksheet is designed to obtain a history of the behavior and determine which of the many factors known to be associated with severe behavior problems might be implicated in this specific situation. The interview format has been used to help staff think through the problem to identify possible reasons and potential solutions and to identify the need for further evaluation.

- Checklist for Assessing Environmental Demands (Form 5.3)

   This checklist provides a systematic process for understanding the sensory and instructional demands of the environment that affect tolerance and stress levels or that could trigger severe behavior problems.

- What Happened Flow Log (Form 5.4)

   This form is adapted from a procedure developed at the Judevine Center. It provides a format for recording the frequency and duration of behaviors within the natural context. At the same time, it allows for recording unidentified skills and strengths and the sensory factors that influence behavior.

Also see Chapter 12 for strategies to capitalize on preferences to design a daily schedule that reduces stress-related behavior problems.

■ Preference Survey (Form 5.8)

Many behavior problems occur when a learner must engage in long sequences of activities that are nonpreferred, difficult, or stressful. Therefore, it is necessary to understand not only the preferred or reinforcing activities but to understand which are disliked or only tolerated. Information elicited from this form is used to evaluate the data obtained from the Assessment of Daily Life Activities (Form 6.7). For completed samples of the Preference Survey, see page 181, and the Case Study, on page 480.

■ Assessment of Daily Life Activities (Form 5.9)

This form provides a format for analyzing the reinforcing or punishing qualities of the daily schedule and highlights the elements of activities that may trigger a problem.

To Understand the Message Behind the Behavior

■ Functional Communication Assessment: Informant Interview (Form 5.5).

Assessment of functional communication is one of the most important tools for understanding behavior problems—the behaviors that signal emotions, needs, and ideas. Not only is this tool helpful for assessing the communicative behavior of those who are not verbal, but it is invaluable for assessing the breakdown of communication resulting from stress in those who are verbal and higher-functioning. This form is discussed more completely on page 76. Figure 24.2 includes a completed sample of the summary sheet.

To Understand Physical Conditions Associated With Behavior Problems

■ Signs of physical problems, cyclic behavior, and sudden changes of behavior (including problems related to sleeping, eating, or self-abuse) will be highlighted in the incidence reports, observations, and interview reports. A physical exam may be required to rule out or address any contributing medical factors.

Summarize the Data

A functional behavioral assessment yields an abundance of detailed information to be organized and interpreted from the perspective of the individual with autism. The Functional Analysis Summary (Form 24.4) is an effective tool for organizing the data to show the relationships of the environmental conditions, the triggers, behavior signals, and the communicative function of the behavior. After seeing the data in this visual format, interpreters can quickly grasp the problem and begin to generate logical strategies and modifications for the intervention plan. For a completed sample of this form, see the Case Study in Appendix A.

In summary, there are many different ways to structure a functional behavioral assessment. The procedures described above elicit the detailed information that is so important for developing intervention plans to prevent future problems and manage those that may occur. Once the assessment information is summarized and presented to the team, it will be possible to develop an effective and positive behavior support plan. Turn to page 460 for the intervention planning process.

Chapter 24 continues with information on intervention on page 460.

Figure 24.2 Completed Example of Form 5.5

Functional Communication Assessment: Summary
Adapted with permission from *Project QUEST Inservice Manual* (Falco et al. 1990)

Child:_____

Date: _____

Code:　/ = Uses sometimes
　　　　+ = Uses consistently
　　　　(Use a different color ink for each informant or setting.)

	A. FEELINGS							B. REQUESTING								
Forms of Language and Communication	1. Likes	2. Dislikes	3. Feels good ★★★	4. Pain ★	5. Hungry ✗	6. Discomfort ★	7. Afraid	8. Attention	9. More	10. Continue ✗	11. Stop	12. Start ✗	13. Help	14. Eat/Drink ✗	15. Object	16. To Do Action ★★
Speech: a. One word																
b. Two or three words																
c. Complex utterance																
Sign: d. One word																
e. Two or three words																
f. Complex utterance																
Combined forms: Speech g. One word　No, More, Hug	I	I		I				I	I			I				
h. Two or three words　Don't like		I				I										I
i. Complex utterance																
Echolalia: j. Immediate: Exact																
k. Immediate: Mitigated																
l. Delayed																
Nonverbal behavior: m. Gesture/Pointing																
n. Manipulation of other																
o. Vocalizations																
p. Cries				I		I	I									
q. Gaze								I								
r. Gaze shift		I														
s. Proximity: Moves closer	I							I								
t. Proximity: Moves away																
u. Facial expression			I					I								
v. Head nod																
w. Bodily contact　Hugs			I													
x. Action (**grab**, reach, give, other)　*throws pushes away*		I		I				I	I			I				
y. Self-injurious behavior　slaps head					I							I		I		
z. Aggressive behavior　Hits - punches		I													I	I
aa. Tantrum behavior												I				
bb. Other:　Does or gets w/o communicating or ignores	I			I						I		I			I	

Notes:

★　Sometimes says "sick or "hurt" at random times

★　"Pants wet" sometimes = discomfort, sometimes not

✗　Does not communicate

★★　May say "Outside" When he wants to do other things—then tantrums.

★★★　Inconsistent response

▲　With Prompt

Figure 24.2 Completed Example of Form 5.5 (*continued*)

						C. PROTESTING					D. RESP.			ACKNOW.				F. COMMENT					G. NON-COM.			
17. Bathroom ★★★	18. Affection X ★★★	19. Choose object ★★★	20. Choose action ★★★	21. Choose without seeing	22. Clarity	23. Information X	24. Activity	25. Object/Food	26. Not allowed	27. Taken object	28. Change X	29. Directions ★★★	30. WH questions X	31. Yes/No questions ★★★	32. Greeting ★★★	33. Response to greeting ★★★	34. Polite words ◄	35. Take turns ★★★	36. On self X	37. On others X	38. Object/Action X	39. Not present X	40. Past/Future X	41. Say labels X	42. Direct self X	43. Unrelated X
I							I	I		I																
							I																			
															I	I										
		I													I	I										
															I	I										
I																										
	I																	I								
																		I								

Functional Behavioral Analysis: Problem Review Worksheet (Interview Format)

Adapted with permission from Oregon Regional Autism Services

Student: _____

Informant: _____

Interviewer: _____

Date: _____

1. Description of the Social/Behavior Problem	Data/Description	Need More Information
What actions are involved in the behavior? What are the warning signs or behaviors that lead up to the behavior of concern? How long is the behavioral episode? How intense is it? How often does it occur? How long has the behavior been a problem? What is the intervention history? Other:		

2. Student Characteristics	Description	Need More Information
Are there any physiological symptoms closely associated with the behavior? (Does student show signs of allergies, headaches, seizures, fever, other conditions?) Is student on medication? What related elements seem to go along with this behavior (such as signs of pain, discomfort, changes in mood)? Does student have an effective communication system? Does student have a way to say, "My head aches"; "I'm tired"; "I'm scared"; "That surprised me"; "I don't like that"; "I like _____"; "I want _____"? What are student's learning strengths and weaknesses? What are student's likes and dislikes? What activities are very hard for this student? What activities are very easy for this student? What is student's response time? Is there a processing delay? What are student's personality traits (active/inactive, introvert/extro-vert, fearful/trusting, flexible/rigid, anxious and tense, etc.)? Other:		

(continued)

	Description/Comments	Possible Factor Y/N/?
3. Antecedents—The context—instructional or environmental conditions that precede (set off or trigger) the behavior of concern		
A. Environmental setting:		
Where does the behavior occur?		
Where doesn't the behavior occur?		
What are the environmental conditions in the setting where it occurs? (Too hot or cold, crowded, cluttered, noises, lighting, other factors)		
Have there been changes in the environment just prior to or simultaneous with the behavior?		
Does the student have a way to say, "I'm hot", "He's too close to me", "It's too noisy", etc.?		
B. Time factors:		
Does the behavior occur in a cyclical pattern? (Good day, bad day)		
Time of day when it occurs?		
How long has the student been engaged in the task?		
Does the student know the schedule and what is to happen next?		
Does the student know or have a way to ask about how long until time to stop or take a break?		
Is the student prepared for endings and beginnings? ("It's almost time to clean up. Then it will be time for _____.")		
C. Others in the environment:		
Number of adults (staff/student ratio):		
Do adults talk to the student and give information?		
Are the behavioral expectations, directions, and consequences clear?		
Do adults recognize and acknowledge the student's nonverbal and verbal attempts to communicate?		
Do they talk about the student's problems where the student can hear?		
What is the nature of their interactions? (positive, reinforcing, negative, challenging, consistent, etc.)		
Number of students in the environment?		
Are peers good models?		
Do other peers tease or intimidate student?		
Are peers close to, bumping, or touching student?		
Does student have a way to greet others? Express humor? Seek attention and interaction? Protect self? Say, "Bug off", "I like you"?		
Does the problem behavior often occur in the presence of any particular adult or student? Describe.		

(continued)

3. Antecedents (continued)	Description/Comments	Possible Factor Y/N/?
D. Task/Activity factors:		
Does the behavior usually occur while student is engaged in any specific task or activity?		
Is the task too hard? Is student making many errors?		
Is the correction procedure clear?		
Are the consequences for making errors punishing?		
Is the task too easy?		
Does the task have meaning for the student?		
Has the student done the task or used the same materials for too long in the same way? (Is the student bored?)		
Is there a clear task or activity?		
Is it a liked or disliked activity?		
How long has the student been engaged in the task (or in free time)?		
What was the preceding task? Was it a liked or disliked activity?		
Were there sudden changes in the activity?		
What activity was scheduled to follow? Was it a liked or disliked activity?		
Does the behavior occur during transition periods?		
Are there clear directions during transitions?		
Does the student have a way to say, "I need help; "I don't understand"; "I need a break"; "This is too hard"; "But I've done this a million times"?		
Does the student have any choices or options for activities?		
4. Consequences—What did people do immediately after the behavior of concern?		
What occurs immediately after the behavior of concern:		
• Teacher interaction/attention		
• Peer attention		
• Excitement and turmoil in room		
• Acquisition of wants (food, objects, activities)		
• Removal of instructional or activity demands		
• People move away		
• Isolation/time alone		
• Sensory stimulation		
• Other		
Are the consequences intermittent?		
Does the student appear to be more upset as a result of the consequence?		
Does the student appear to enjoy the consequence?		

Adapted with permission from Oregon Regional Autism Services

Note: The information in this report is confidential. It will satisfy liability concerns and will provide data for developing effective and ethical intervention plans. Use specific descriptions of the behavior—do not use terms such as *deliberately, inappropriate, avoiding,* etc.

Student: _____ **Date:** _____

School: _____ **Teacher:** _____

1. **Activity:** _____

    Location: _____ Date/Day of week: _____

    Time incident began: _____ Ended: _____

    Staff members present when incident occurred:

    Name: _____ Address: _____

    Name: _____ Address: _____

    Others (nonstaff members) present when incident occurred:

    Name: _____ Address: _____

    Name: _____ Address: _____

2. **Describe what was happening just before the behavior occurred.**
    Describe the environment—noise, crowding, and other conditions.

    What was the student supposed to be doing?

    What was the student doing?

    What were others doing?

    (continued)

3.　**Describe in detail what the student did and what happened during the incident.**

Was anyone called to assist?　☐ No　☐ Yes　If yes:

Name: _____ Address: _____

Was anyone injured?　☐ No　☐ Yes　If yes:

Name: _____ Address: _____

Describe:

_____

4.　**Describe what happened to the student immediately after the incident. Include any consequences.**

If student was injured, describe injury and any treatment (what and by whom).

_____

5.　**Additional information for team evaluation and planning**
(To be completed by the staff person most directly involved in the incident)

Why do you think the incident occurred—why the person behaved in this way? (From the perspective of the student, could something have been misunderstood or confusing? If so, describe.)
What recommendations do you have for preventing a recurrence or for managing the problem if it occurs again?

Additional comments (Use extra sheets if necessary)

_____

6.　**Reported by:**

Name: _____

Address: _____ Phone: _____

Adapted with permission from Oregon Regional Autism Services

Student: _____ **Date:** _____ **Time began:** _____ **Ended:** __

What happened?

What happened just before?

What happened right after?

Student's point of view?

Reported by: _____ Phone: _____

Address: _____

Functional Analysis Summary

Adapted with permission from Oregon Regional Autism Services

Student: _____   Date: _____

Environmental Events that Affect Tolerance (Allergies, weather, worries, sensory conditions)	Antecedents or Triggers	Escalating Chains of Behavior (From earliest signals of stress to most intense behavior)	Communicative Function (The problem from the learner's perspective)

Notes:

Intervention Planning Worksheet

Adapted with permission from Oregon Regional Autism Services

Student: _____   **Date:** _____

Stage 1. Escalation	Stage 2. Crisis level	Stage 3. De-escalation	Stage 4. Equilibrium
Intervention goal: Defuse stress, return to equilibrium	**Intervention goal:** Prevent escalation, keep people safe, support deescalation	**Intervention goal:** Support self-control, reengage	**Intervention goal:** Evaluate/refine, organize/structure and teach skills
Behavior signals:	**Behavior signals:**	**Behavior signals:**	**Behavior signals:**
			Strategies:
			Evaluate and refine:
Strategies:	**Strategies:**	**Strategies:**	**Organize and structure:**
			Skills to teach, strengthen, or generalize:
Avoid:	**Avoid:**	**Avoid:**	**Avoid:**
			Plan staff/family training and support:

Intervention Planning—A Positive, Proactive Support Plan

When the information gleaned from the functional behavior assessment is summarized, it will naturally lead to a positive plan for supporting effective learning and behavior. The Intervention Planning Worksheet (Form 24.5) is based on the Profile of Stress Figures 24.3 that provides a key for matching intervention efforts to the learner's fluctuating needs. For a completed sample of the Intervention Planning Worksheet, see the Case Study on page 482 of Appendix A.

Before completing the Intervention Planning Worksheet, review Chapters 8 and 10 that carefully describe the effects of autism on stress and behavior, and the processes and strategies for reducing stress to prevent problem behaviors.

This planning worksheet illustrates that the learner's behavior and the interpreter's goal and strategies are different at each of the four stages. For example, the goal at Stage 1 is to identify and solve problems to defuse anxiety and move directly to Stage 3, thus avoiding a crisis. Stage 2 is not a teachable moment; it is the time to implement the crisis management plan. At this level of stress, the learner is unable to think and hear clearly or to use good communication skills. Stage 3 is a vulnerable period when stress could easily re-escalate. The most productive period is during Stage 4, when the demands of the environment match the competence and tolerances of the learner.

The things that happen during this stage of equilibrium will influence the frequency, duration, and intensity of future problems. The interpreter's role at Stage 4 is to teach new skills, expand flexibility, and continually evaluate to identify problems and refine elements of the environment to maintain equilibrium.

Consider the strategies listed below that will match the learner's needs at each stage of stress as the intervention planning form is completed.

Stage 1—Guidelines for Defusing Stress

These strategies can be incorporated into the support plan when the learner's stress level is accelerating (at Stage 1). A more complete range of strategies can be found on pages 149–153. Remember, that the planning goal for Stage 1 intervention is to defuse stress and prevent a crisis.

1. *Listen to what the learner says.* It may provide a clue to the need or problem.

2. *Use reflective listening strategies.* Acknowledge the feelings and the cause of the problem if it can be identified. Clarify the situation in some simple way, and calmly show support. ("We can work it out"; "I'll help you to _____"; "Let's write it down.")

Review Reflective Listening in Chapter 15.

3. *Help the learner resolve the problem or tell the learner something specific to do.* If the problem could not be resolved in time, cue the learner to take a break, and/or use his individualized relaxation routine. Or tell the person to do something very simple, but natural, that is incompatible with hitting or kicking. ("Put your hands in your pockets," or "Sit down," or "Hold this pillow.") If the person does this simple thing, give reinforcement for listening and responding.

   Do not say, "Don't hit" or "Stop yelling." In many cases, these statements are said in a harsh voice, which is another trigger for increased anxiety. The learner does not know what else to do at that moment. Tell the learner what to do.

4. *Reinforce the learner's every effort to self-control.* The primary goals are to calm down and to regain control. Verbally reinforce calming down and self-control. If the learner puts his hands in his pockets as requested, say, "Good! You can control yourself." When a learner who had been screaming stops for breath, say, "Good! You took a deep breath. You can calm yourself. Let's

take another deep breath," as you model deep breathing. Use a calm, even, quiet voice, and time the reinforcement to the calming—not the out-of-control behavior.

5. *Introduce a surprise.* In some rare moments just before a crisis when it seems the learner may be caught in a perseverative cycle of behavior, it may help to do something dramatic to startle or break that cycle.

One young man was rocking back and forth, waving his arms about in a threatening manner and shouting, "Don't hit! Don't hit!" over and over again. When the recommended strategies failed to break this repetitive cycle, his teacher suddenly turned away and said cheerfully, "I'm leaving." She said to the other students, "Let's go to recess quickly." They all got up and left the room. (They were in a safe place, and supervision was available: An assistant was working quietly in one corner of the room.) Later, the assistant reported that the learner looked a little stunned, then moved quietly to sit at his desk with his head down on his arms. When the class returned, he was relaxed and ready to join in the normal activities.

Figure 24.3 Profile of Stress: Cue Sheet for Developing the Crises Management Plan

To identify the points or stages of the emotional sequence when specific kinds of interventions are not only critical but most effective

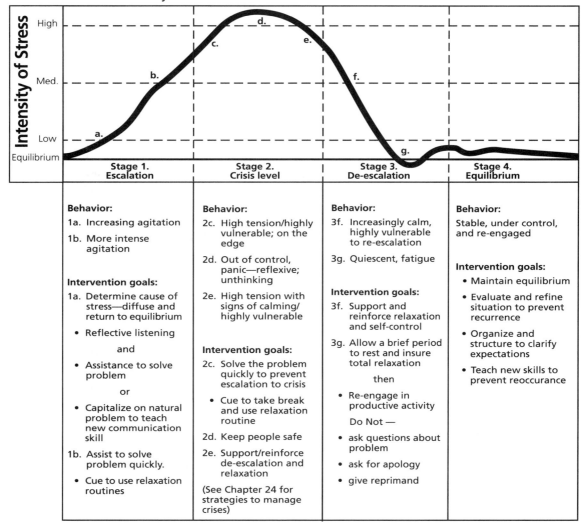

Stage 1. Escalation

Behavior:

1a. Increasing agitation

1b. More intense agitation

Intervention goals:

1a. Determine cause of stress—diffuse and return to equilibrium

• Reflective listening

and

• Assistance to solve problem

or

• Capitalize on natural problem to teach new communication skill

1b. Assist to solve problem quickly.

• Cue to use relaxation routines

Stage 2. Crisis level

Behavior:

2c. High tension/highly vulnerable; on the edge

2d. Out of control, panic—reflexive; unthinking

2e. High tension with signs of calming/ highly vulnerable

Intervention goals:

2c. Solve the problem quickly to prevent escalation to crisis

• Cue to take break and use relaxation routine

2d. Keep people safe

2e. Support/reinforce de-escalation and relaxation

(See Chapter 24 for strategies to manage crises)

Stage 3. De-escalation

Behavior:

3f. Increasingly calm, highly vulnerable to re-escalation

3g. Quiescent, fatigue

Intervention goals:

3f. Support and reinforce relaxation and self-control

3g. Allow a brief period to rest and insure total relaxation

then

• Re-engage in productive activity

Do Not —

• ask questions about problem

• ask for apology

• give reprimand

Stage 4. Equilibrium

Behavior:

Stable, under control, and re-engaged

Intervention goals:

• Maintain equilibrium

• Evaluate and refine situation to prevent recurrence

• Organize and structure to clarify expectations

• Teach new skills to prevent reoccurance

Stage 2—Guidelines for Developing the Crisis Management Plan

The strategies and principles listed in this section are general guidelines for managing an emergency situation. If a learner has shown the potential to become seriously out of control in a way that could cause injury to self or others, interpreters must be trained in safe and effective non-aversive physical management strategies. A specific crisis management plan can only be developed after a comprehensive functional behavioral assessment is completed.

The total support team, including the parents and a program administrator or case manager, develops the crisis plan to implement when the learner is in a Stage 2 level of stress. The team may need additional information from consultants. An occupational therapist could assess sensory problems and make recommendations for strategies that might be calming. An autism specialist could focus attention on the effects of the autism learning style (misperceptions and lack of skills) in different situations. The school counselor, a resource teacher, behavior specialist, or psychologist also could provide insights and balance.

The crisis plan will include:

1. *The behavioral signals that precede and follow a loss of control*

   The sequence of signals exhibited during stress stages 1, 2, and 3 are identified during the functional assessment.

2. *A plan to prevent injury in all settings, to maintain a safe environment and keep others safe*

   - Team members review these plans in a trouble-shooting "What if _____?" format to ensure that all situations are covered. General guidelines include:

   - A description of what to do at stages 1 and 3 to defuse anxiety, prevent crisis, and permit the learner to regain self-control

   - A description of the things to do at Stage 2 to prevent injury and help the learner regain control

   - A description of the things to avoid doing at all stages that have the potential for triggering a crisis

3. *A training plan for interpreters and others in the environment*

   - Interpreters, including parents and primary caregivers, need training and opportunities to practice with feedback.

     Siblings, students, roommates, co-workers, and others in the environment need training to keep themselves safe. Schedule crisis drills and training sessions. Tell siblings and peers that the learner sometimes gets confused and anxious, and when that happens they can help by being very quiet and not watching. Train them to carry out the crisis drill quickly when they are given a signal.

4. *A record keeping and monitoring plan to review progress*, identify potential problems, and modify elements of the plan to match the learner's changing need

5. *A staff and parent support plan*

Remember: A crisis plan is a situational plan, not a teaching plan.

Guidelines for Managing a Crisis

Generally, the danger of a crisis increases as anxiety and panic increase. Therefore, the goals of any crisis management plan are, first, to defuse anxiety and panic; and second, to keep people safe.

Strategies for defusing anxiety and panic

It is important to understand that anxiety and panic increase when:

1. *Others panic and show anger, fear, or excitement*

   Model calm, quiet, reassuring behavior. Relax your shoulders, your face, your eyes, and take a deep breath. Keep your arms and hands relaxed and in view but ready to use if needed to block or deflect a thrown object or a hit.

2. *Personal space is invaded*

   Step back with one foot and stay at least an arm's length away. Do not move in closer. This supportive stance honors personal space, reduces the overwhelming feeling of being blocked into a corner, and offers an escape route. This position also offers the interpreter protection from a hit or a kick. Be alert but move slowly and in a relaxed manner. Break the direct face-to-face gaze and use peripheral vision to monitor.

3. *People talk too much or too loud*

   Minimize talking, keep your voice calm, and use an even rhythm. Match the volume of your voice to the distance (that is, talk softly if close to the learner, raise your voice if you are at a distance). Identify a single interpreter to manage the crisis and do the talking. Others in the room will attend to other matters unless signaled to assist. *Those assisting do not talk.*

4. *Pushed to give eye contact or to verbalize*

   Reduce demands during periods of elevated stress. Do not say, "Look at me;" eye contact may only confuse the learner. Do not force a choice or say, "Tell me what is wrong;" talking is stressful even under calm conditions. Insistence on a verbal response is likely to trigger increased anxiety and complicate the situation. Repeated demands are strongly associated with an increase in severe behavior problems.

5. *Threatened with the loss of a powerful reinforcer*

   Clearly, calmly, simply, tell the learner what to do. Provide visual supports. Threats are unproductive; they simply give additional reason for stress. A threat does not clarify the situation or provide clear instruction. The learner still has no solution, only more problems.

6. *Physically restrained or engaged in a physical struggle—cautions:*

   Do not attempt physical restraint or engage in a physical struggle unless there is imminent physical danger to the learner or to others. *Without proper training, do not attempt to restrain a person alone unless the person is considerably smaller. Caution: A smaller learner, although easier to restrain, is also easier to injure.*

   - If restraining a small young child, do it from the back to avoid panic from the overwhelming stimulation of physical closeness. Try to get the child in a sitting position in front of you, so you both are sitting down. (Once you start, it may be a long time before the child can be released.) Hold the child firmly and securely enough so you will not be hurt and so it cannot become a struggle, but gently enough so the child will not be hurt. Some young children are soothed by gentle rocking motions or soft singing. As the child relaxes, periodically say something soothing like, "Good. You are relaxing" or "It will be okay, I will help you."

The child is ready to be released when you can feel the child's total relaxation. Release will reinforce the relaxed attitude.

If released before totally relaxed, the child's tension and stress are likely to accelerate and require another struggle and further restraint. When the child has been totally relaxed for 5 or so minutes, state a contingency to set a direction for re-engagement. Do not ask, "Are you ready to get up?" or "Are you relaxed?" The response generally will be, "Yes."

- If restraining an older or larger learner—do not restrain if you are alone. If there is potential for injury to self or others, send for backup assistance—the principal or a neighbor who can come quickly. Once the emergency is over, plan ahead. If restraint was ever needed, convene the team members to develop or modify restraint procedures to ensure that help is quickly available. If an appropriate proactive program is in place, these situations should not recur.

Staff members and parents need hands-on training from certified trainers in non-aversive, physical management procedures. Contact state or local developmental disabilities offices for references. Procedures may need some modifications to accommodate the autism learning style.

Remember—Proper restraint is not a punishing consequence; it is a safety measure to use in an emergency. Do it quietly, calmly, with a matter-of-fact, supportive attitude, and an appropriate emergency plan.

Stage 3—Guidelines for Re-engagement

The time following a major crisis is a highly vulnerable period. Generally the learner is exhausted and vulnerable, so a new crisis could be triggered easily. The following strategies can be incorporated into the support plan to facilitate movement through the Stage 3 level of stress and a return to the normal routine that occurs during the stage of equilibrium.

1. *Independence comes from learning to calm oneself independently.* The interpreter sets the stage and remains calm, quiet, and supportive.

   Move away and keep busy with writing or some quiet activity while monitoring the situation with peripheral vision. This strategy gives the learner space to relax without the stress of being watched intently. It also provides time for you to relax and make notes for reporting the incident.

2. *Do not nag, ask questions, make demands, or ask for apologies.* Avoid any effort to have the child respond to questions about the problem or what they should have done. This is not a time to teach cause/effect or problem solving. In fact, any of those strategies may lead to re-escalation. Address these issues at a different time.

3. *Do not attempt to re-engage* until the learner is totally relaxed.

4. *Structure the transition* back to natural activity once the learner is relaxed.

   - Use cue cards or other visual references.

   - Set the timer and say, "In 5 minutes, we will check your schedule to see what is next"

   - State a simple and easy contingency: In a quiet and calm voice, say, "I'll help you finish your job, and then you can have a break" or "First get a drink, and then check your calendar."

Review Chapter 10 for a more comprehensive description of the strategies for defusing stress and maintaining equilibrium.

5. *Avoid a return to a difficult or disliked task.* Provide support until the learner has completed one or two familiar, short and relatively easy tasks successfully.

Most crises can be defused with these strategies. The key is to model a calm and quiet demeanor, and acknowledge the feelings and the problems. Avoid overreacting; overreactions often accelerate the problem.

In general, behavioral crises are not premeditated or manipulated to punish you directly. The learner is confused and anxious *and doesn't know what else to do to solve the problem or to relieve anxiety. However, a learner whose needs continue to be disregarded may learn that severe aggression or self-injury is the only way to get relief from demands and overwhelming stress.*

Stage 4—Evaluate and Refine

With the information from the incident report forms, reorganize and restructure the environment and the support so the child can maintain that optimum level of stress (see page 137). This is also the time for teaching new skills so the learner has the ability to manage similar situations in the future. Stage 4 is the most productive time, for the learner is alert, calm, and able to focus on instruction and work.

Keep Records

Most school and community programs have liability insurance that requires reports of any serious behavioral outbursts that had potential for injury. Also, the support team needs not only the basic descriptions of these incidents but objective and subjective information to use in modifying an intervention plan to prevent recurring problems. Use Form 24.2 when the incident caused (or might have caused) an injury. Use Form 24.3 when there was no physical struggle. Directions for completing the incident forms are on page 447. Staff will need training and time to include the appropriate information in the incident forms.

Interpreter Support Plan

High-anxiety situations are always exhausting and emotionally draining for everyone involved. Although most of the attention and concern is focused on the vulnerable person, the learner, the interpreter who defuses or manages the crisis also needs support.

■ At home, alone

Each parent must develop a routine to follow after any highly stressful period. The routine includes plans for:

- A safe, comfortable place to settle the child with things to keep occupied for a short period of time. It is helpful for parents and teachers to work together to develop a plan that has common elements in both the home and the school setting (e.g., a visual calendar or checklist, relaxation routines).

- Engage in a low-key, relaxing activity—a coffee break in front of the TV, a call to a supportive friend, screaming into a pillow, a shower, or a structured relaxation or visualization routine.

■ In school, vocational, or group-home setting

The interpreter who is actively involved in the incident needs a break—a brief time alone or an opportunity to debrief and talk about the situation to a member of the learner's support team. This break might include time to complete the incident report while the details are still fresh.

Caution: This highly personal and confidential information must be handled discreetly. Do not share the dramatic details with others over coffee in the staff room. Although it is reinforcing for others to sympathize and comment about the interpreter's courage, patience, and skill displayed while handling this situation, it does nothing for the learner's reputation. Sharing the information indiscriminately is not only unethical, but it will make it more difficult to recruit mentors and advocates if staff members have heard only fearful stories.

Summary

Severe behavior problems are a symptom of an environment that does not match the needs, the skills, or the tolerance levels of a learner. When the problem is understood from the context of autism, it is possible to both predict and clarify information to prevent most problems. It is impossible to prevent all problems; but with this understanding and these strategies it is possible to effectively prevent most severe behavior problems.

The case study in Appendix A summarizes not only this chapter but also the processes and strategies presented throughout this book.

In Conclusion—Understanding the Challenges and the Gifts

This has been a long book, but there are many things to consider when teaching and supporting those with autism spectrum disorders, for each individual has such a unique combination of abilities and deficits. The processes and strategies are presented to show how they can be adapted and implemented to match the unique needs of each individual—from those who are most severely affected to those who are much higher functioning—including those with Asperger's syndrome. For Leekam, et al. (2000) said, "Higher-functioning children and adults have special educational, occupational and leisure needs that differ from those with more severe disabilities, even though the basic principles of an autism-specific approach remain the same."

Although those with autism spectrum disorders present major challenges, they also provide major rewards for anyone who takes the opportunity to *understand* their unique perspective. "Individuals with autism also have gifts—that occur as a result of their strong visual abilities, attention to minute details, unique and unusual interests, and amazing memory. Other common traits, such as honesty, naivete, gentleness, compliance, and perfectionism, are exceedingly refreshing and unexpected. . . . The ability to focus intensely on the unexpected and the literal, the concrete understanding of the language and the environment, leads to 'enchanting logic'" (Seaton, as cited in Janzen, 1999, p. 151.). Some of those who have made major contributions to society have had an autism spectrum disorder (Ledgen, 2002). Others have said that if we cure autism we may no longer have geniuses.

The ability to *understand* and deal effectively with the challenges of autism forces us to be creative and flexible. Those who live with and support the person with autism will never stop learning!

Our interventions will be successful only if we *understand* the world, or the situation, from the perspective of the individual with autism. We must thank David Eastham, other adults with autism spectrum disorders, and their parents who have so eloquently described their own experiences and given us insight into the nature of autism, their struggles, their fears, and their dreams.

UNDERSTAND

I WANT PEOPLE TO UNDERSTAND
I KNOW ITS HARD TO DO
I THINK THEY CAN IF THEY TRY
UNDERSTAND WON'T YOU?

UNDERSTANDING IS SO HARD
I LONG TO SEE IT REAL
I JUST HOPE, REALLY HOPE,
ITS NOT A LOST IDEAL

—David Eastham,
In UNDERSTAND: Fifty Memowriter Poems

Appendices

Tony—A Case Study
Summary Report
Functional Assessment, Consultation, and Training

Student: Tony

Date: April 15

Functional Assessment of Problem Behavior

1. Interview Tony's support team (parents, foster parents, vocational staff, and local autism consultant) to:

    - Establish baseline and identify concerns (Form 25.1)

    - Identify preferences (See attached Preference Survey, page 480)

    - Identify elements of Tony's environments that contribute to problems (Form 6.7)

    - Identify Tony's current functional communication abilities (Form 5.5)

2. Direct observation:

    - At home and vocational site

    - During 1:1 testing: Selected subtests of the Adolescent/Adult Psychoeducational Profile (AAPEP)

3. Review incident reports

4. Provide 6 hours of consultation and training to the support team:

    - Explain the impact of autism on communication and behavior

    - Provide strategies for identifying stress and attempts to communicate

    - Provide strategies for identifying and interpreting the cause of problems

    - Match interventions to stress level, teaching use of visual references

    - Provide strategies for reviewing and fine-tuning the intervention plan

Background

Tony is a tall, slender, 20-year-old male with severe autism who is in transition from school to a vocational site. In addition to severe communication and social problems, he has coordination and other motor problems and migraine headaches. He continues to have back pain from surgery to repair a curvature of the spine.

Although Tony has been considered to be severely retarded, there is evidence that he can read with meaning (at least to some degree). He rarely initiates interactions with others or persists in getting the attention of a communication partner. On occasion, however, he has been heard to make meaningful comments in a very soft voice, to no one in particular. Most of the time, his messages are not heard and thus are not acknowledged. Occasionally he uses a Wolf (an electronic communication system), but in general he has no consistent system for communicating in various settings.

Tony was referred for a functional assessment and assistance because he is in danger of losing his vocational placement due to behavior and safety concerns. Tony lives with a foster family and visits frequently with his parents; all were involved in the assessment and training.

The following concerns were identified by the support team.

Behaviors of concern

- Self-abuse: Slapping face and head, biting hand, throwing himself on floor
- Aggression: Hitting others, hitting or striking at objects
- Emotional responses: Laughing or giggling unrelated to situation, crying, extreme mood shifts, and rapid acceleration of problem behavior

Transition concerns

- People: Responses to his current foster mother's absences and visits from parents and former foster family
- Safety: Fire drills (in home and vocational site), staff injury from hitting
- Changes: Activity schedules, routines, travel to and from home and work site

Communication concerns

- How to communicate effectively with Tony
- How to develop a system for Tony to communicate with others

Assessment Summary

I. Learning Style—Strengths and Deficits

General activities and abilities

- Tony sorts by size, shape, color, food, animals, and other basic categories.
- He can follow a familiar routine in a familiar place with a familiar person. He can perform a few routines (such as assembly tasks) independently. Tony continues to need assistance with many personal care routines.
- He has difficulty following familiar routines with a new person, even when the setting is familiar.
- He has difficulty with unexpected schedule changes.
- Tony follows visual directions when given one or two clear demonstrations.

Disorganization/Distractions

- Tony is confused by clutter in the immediate physical environment.
- He is confused when materials needed for a task are disorganized or cluttered.
- He is overwhelmed when several people talk at once, even when those conversations are soft, a distance away, and unrelated to him.
- Tony has a tendency to "hyperscan" the environment. He is constantly watching and alert to where people are and what they are doing.

- He is easily distracted by unexpected movement of people within the environment.

Programming note: Tony worked and responded best when he could see the entire area about him. When he could look up briefly to watch the surrounding movements, he was able to return to the task in front of him without prompts or reminders. When people moved or activities changed outside his visual range, he became anxious, resisted tasks, and began to slap his face and bite his hand. When placed with his back to the activity, he turned around when he heard or saw movement from the corner of his eye, and then was unable to reorient to the task behind him. Arrange his work space so he can see what people are doing.

Cause/Effect

When Tony did not understand what was expected or what was going to happen (when to begin or end a task and what would happen next), he became agitated and anxious. Verbal information was not enough to clarify and reduce his anxiety.

- Visual references paired with verbal explanations reduced his anxiety, and transitions were easier.

Tony quickly learned new task routines when:

- The materials were clearly organized to work from left to right
- A simple visual model (reference) clarified the sequence of steps, and the end of the task and the finished product were clearly indicated by a "Finished" box or container.

When the sequence of the task was clear, Tony quickly learned to anticipate the activity and persisted in attempts to complete the task and correct errors.

Programming note: Tony is a perfectionist. When the task was clear, he recognized and corrected his own mistakes. However, when verbal demands, prompts, or reinforcement were provided in this process, he slapped his face, rocked, made loud noises, and bit his wrist. This behavior escalated with each verbal request or warning. *Prompt with quiet gestures; use line drawings and photographs with written labels or short phrases.*

Understanding the language and communication of others:

- Tony displayed a significant processing delay (the time needed to process information he heard and to generate a response).
- He was more confused by lengthy or complex verbal directions when anything (person, task, materials, schedule, or location) was unfamiliar and he was expected to generate a verbal or motor response.
- When Tony was anxious or confused, repeated verbal demands or prompts given by even one familiar person caused escalating behavior problems. Escalation was more rapid when two or more people tried to help by giving more verbal directions or diversions.

    Programming Note:

- He was able to understand and follow clear, one- or two-step familiar commands or directions within familiar situations.
- Pointing without talking was helpful to direct or refocus his attention.
- He was able to follow clear visual instructions and models (line drawings, pictures, demonstrations).

II. Summary of Functional Communication

Expression of wants and needs

- Tony scans the environment for a familiar person or preferred item. If he can locate the item, he simply gets it without interacting with another person.

- If the item cannot be located, he takes the wrist of a nearby adult and attempts to guide that person toward the item.

- If something is not where he expects it to be, he gets upset, begins to rock, slap his face, and bite his wrist.

Expression of protest or refusal (activity, object/food; something not allowed, taken away, or changed)

- Tony softly verbalizes, "No." Often, this is not heard by others and is rarely repeated.

- He may walk away from the person or activity.

- He may push away an object.

- If a staff member insists on compliance, speaks loudly, or rushes him, he hits himself, bites his hand, or hits and tries to push the person away.

Request for attention or affection:

- Tony approaches the preferred person, "nuzzles" the person's cheek or hair, and whispers softly. He may sit next to the preferred person and lean into the person's shoulder or side.

Expression of dislike/confusion:

- Tony vocalizes and slaps the side of his face. If the person near him pauses, waits, and clarifies quietly with a gesture or visual cue, often Tony will stop after two or more slaps. However, if the person says, "No slapping" and repeats the demand or tries to hurry him to compliance, the behavior escalates.

Expression of extreme confusion:

- Tony slaps his face, vocalizes loudly, talks to himself (often using echoed phrases), paces, and may remove his glasses. At these times, if approached too rapidly or given verbal corrections or verbal demands to stop, he may strike out or drop to the floor.

Expression of pain or fear:

- He says, "Ow," "Uh-oh," screams, yells, or cries. When in pain (with backache or headache), he winces and presses his sinuses or back, or lies down.

- When afraid, he becomes tense, stares, yells loudly, and may stomp his feet.

- When startled, he may quickly hit the person nearest him (a reflexive response.

III. Summary of Conditions that Affect Behavior

See attached Functional Analysis Summary (page 481).

Tony's problem behaviors occur in a fairly predictable pattern or chain that begins with an appropriate verbalization, then escalates rapidly if the situation is not clarified or his need is not addressed.

Environmental events that reduce tolerance

- Physical problems: Headaches, backaches
- Sensory problems: Noise, too many people talking, too much movement, disorganization, and clutter
- Changes and transitions: Routines, places, people, schedules, expectations
- Lack of clarity: Missing information that causes confusion

Situations that trigger problem behavior (antecedents)

- Demands:
  - When unexpected
  - To change from a highly preferred to a disliked activity/task
  - From a new person, whether the task is familiar or unfamiliar
  - Rapid, repeated demands or corrections from a familiar or unfamiliar person
  - Repeated demands and verbal assistance from more than one person at the same time
  - To return to or do more of an activity that he thought was finished
- Changes and transitions when tolerance is low
- Being rushed
- Being stopped in the middle of a routine, especially when required to start it over
- Physical restraint, especially if two or more people keep talking
- Being told, "No hitting" or, "It's not okay to hit"
- Time out (unless taken quietly by a familiar person before stress intensifies)

Escalating chain of behavior, and staff role at each stage

Stages correspond with those illustrated on the Profile of Stress; see attached Intervention Planning Worksheet (page 482).

Stage 1a
Tony's signals

- Verbalizes softly: "Uh-oh," "No," "Knock it off"
- Pauses or stops moving
- Flushes
- Touches head or face where he slaps
- Places hands together, then stretches arms over his head

Staff/interpreter role: Identify the signal, clarify the problem, and help Tony solve the problem

Stage 1b–2c
Tony's signals

- Verbalizes in louder voice: "Oh-oh-oh"; echoes, "Knock it off, Tony"; or, "Don't hit me"
- Holds head
- Hits or slaps head or face two or three times, then pauses
- Puts hand to mouth as if to bite
- Cries, screams

Staff/interpreter role: Model calm; reduce stimulation and demands; cue or assist to a safe, quiet space

Stage 2d
Tony's signals

- Bites hand
- Hits nearby person
- Butts head into other person or wall
- Lies on floor, hitting head on floor
- Pulls off clothes (only rarely)

Staff/interpreter role: Keep people safe, model calm, quietly reinforce efforts to become calm

IV. Critical Goals and Strategies

Autism is a neurological disorder that affects how a person makes sense of and responds to information—the things they hear, see, smell, taste, and feel. The following critical goals are lifelong concerns for all with autism. Focusing on these goals will help family and staff members develop the support systems required to reduce Tony's anxiety and confusion and enable him to function more effectively at home, work, and in the community. As these strategies are implemented, behavior problems will decrease.

Goal 1: To increase flexibility and tolerance for change; to develop willingness to try new things

1. Inflexibility, rigidity, and fear are a result of too little information. A person must have all the information possible in order to predict a particular situation and be able to plan ahead. Because Tony understands some of what he hears, people tend to think that he understands everything they say. This is not true. He needs information about events in a visual format so he can see "the whole thing." Then he can refer to the visual aid and know what, when, and where things will occur. Tony needs:

   - Daily, weekly, and monthly calendars, and brief mini-calendars to clarify expectations for specific activities and changes

   - Cue cards and checklists with line drawings and printed words. Use these visual aids while quietly giving him verbal information—the answers to questions he cannot ask (who, what, when, where, why, how, how much, how long, what's next).

2. Plan Tony's routines and schedules so that small changes occur systematically and regularly. He can learn to tolerate these changes because they will be supported by visual information. The systems for giving information will remain familiar; therefore, he will learn that change is okay.

   - Develop Tony's daily schedule of activities to capitalize on the reinforcing qualities of preferred activities. See the attached Preference Survey (page 480).

   (Note: There was not enough training time to show how to implement this strategy. We suggest that additional training be scheduled.)

Goal 2: To be independent of constant verbal and physical directions and prompts

1. Provide visual references, as discussed previously, to clarify the expectations and to cue the steps of an activity or routine. Introduce new information with these visual references. Demonstrate new skills. Prompt by pointing to the appropriate location on the visual reference or the materials. *Avoid verbal prompts and repeated verbal directions. Avoid hand-over-hand and full physical assistance.*

2. Organize the environment so it is logical and uncluttered. Arrange Tony's work space so he can scan the entire room without turning away from his work.

   - Label material and storage areas. Show Tony where things are and how to return things to their appropriate spaces.
   - Organize his work space so he can work systematically from left to right.
   - Clarify the beginnings and ends of tasks, activities, and events.

As Tony learns to make sense of his environment and he is given enough information, he will be able to function more independently.

Goal 3: To communicate intentionally and effectively

We recommend that a speech-language pathologist and/or communication specialist be engaged to provide training and support for staff members and family as they implement these recommendations. A more comprehensive assessment of Tony's language and communication needs also may be required.

1. The Wolf communication device is familiar, and Tony uses it periodically when it is present. Expand the system with new vocabulary and make it available to him at all times. He will need more instruction to use the system more independently. Those who support Tony will need specific training in how to communicate with him by using the Wolf.

2. Tony must learn how to find a communication partner and persist in getting that person's attention before he delivers a message.

3. Tony needs backup communication systems for times when he wants to talk about something that hasn't been programmed into the Wolf, when the Wolf is unavailable, or when he is too stressed to remember how to communicate. Teach him to use "break cards" and signals of distress that mean "Help me quickly."

4. Provide sports magazines and photo albums of Tony's favorite people, activities, and places so he can visit and share with friends at work or at home. He needs to know when he will have opportunities to socialize and visit with friends. Specify these times on his daily schedule.

5. Because Tony can read with meaning (at least to some degree), facilitated communication is an option that needs to be explored.

Goal 4: Learn relaxation and self-control strategies

Your local autism specialist has access to the following resources for accomplishing this most important goal:

Cautela, J.R., & Groden, J. (1978) *Relaxation: A comprehensive manual for adults, children, and children with special needs.* Champaign, IL: Research Press.

Groden, J., Cautela J.R., & Groden, G. (1989). *Breaking the barriers I: Relaxation techniques for people with special needs.* Videotape. Champaign, IL: Research Press.

Groden, J., Cautela J.R., and Groden, G. (1991). *Breaking the barriers II:Imagery procedures for people with special needs.* Videotape. Champaign, IL: Research Press.

V. Other Recommendations

1. Share information with all staff members. Duplicate the attached Functional Analysis Summary and the Intervention Planning Worksheet (pages 481–482). Share them with all members of Tony's support team. Use these forms as guides for matching interventions with specific needs, to prevent the frequency, intensity, and duration of behavioral crises.

   Train all staff members in safe, nonaversive, physical management procedures and sequences for carrying out the crisis management plan.

2. Identify one person to be in charge. Tony must always know who is in charge—the person who is available to clarify information and provide comfort and support. To avoid inflexible dependence on a single person, systematically change the one in charge. Each morning, Tony needs to meet the one in charge. If that person is changed during the day, inform Tony immediately. Perhaps the one in charge could wear a distinctive name tag or pin so Tony could quickly scan the area and locate support. *If a second person is needed to assist during a crisis, that person should not talk or give distracting information.*

3. Plan the visits with Tony's former foster family. Determine whether Tony wants and needs the visits or if only his former family wants the visit. If the visits are for Tony, they should be carefully scheduled and planned. Some of the following strategies also can make visits with his natural family more successful.

   – Plan for the visits to occur at his current foster home or a familiar nearby location.

   – Arrange for Tony's current foster mother to be present to follow through with familiar support.

   – Schedule relatively brief visits—perhaps no more than 30 minutes.

   – Prepare Tony before the visit. Write the event on his daily schedule.

- Provide a mini-calendar so Tony will know what he will do during the visit—perhaps share photo albums, go for a walk, go to a restaurant for a snack, or do other familiar, low-key activities. *He also needs to know what he will do after they leave.*

If the visits are primarily for the comfort of Tony's former foster parents, perhaps they could meet more frequently alone with Tony's natural mother, instead of with Tony, to share memories and catch up on his current life.

4. Support Tony's team. Tony's autism will not be cured. His stability will depend on the sensitivity and skill of those who support him. While the above strategies and skills will decrease problems and increase Tony's abilities, at times Tony will be overwhelmed with too much stimulation, confusion, and changes. New problems will arise. *His team needs to be very well trained, and they will need to meet frequently to solve problems and coordinate information and strategies.* They also need to meet frequently to support one another. It is helpful if the team members can consult periodically with a specialist in autism who has broad experience with others like Tony. Such a consultant brings perspective and new ideas and can help the team members to assess, clarify, and solve problems before they reach critical levels. We suggest that Mark continue to work with Tony's team.

In summary, Tony is a great person and we have enjoyed this opportunity to get to know him. The members of his team are to be commended for their commitment. If there are any questions about this report, feel free to contact us.

Autism Consultants: _____ Date: _____

Figure A.1 Preference Survey (Form 5.8)

Adapted with permission from *Judevine® Training System* (Blackwell, 1998)

Student: ___Tony___   Date: ___April 15___

LIKES What people, objects, or activities are liked a lot or selected during free time?	TOLERATES What is done when asked, but never done if not asked?	DISLIKES What people, objects, or activities are resisted, avoided or rejected?
People • Parents and foster parents • Peers: Nick and Dawn • Vocational trainers, especially Bonnie	**People** • New people at a distance • New or nonpreferred people on his own terms	**People** • People "getting in his face" • New people moving in too soon or too close

Activities
 	
• Playing chase games
• Walking and eating at the mall
• Going for walks
• Listening to music
• Watching others
• Watching all sports, especially football
• Attending sports events with family, friend
• Looking at photo albums
• Looking at sports magazines
• Eating (lunch breaks; all meals)
• Watching TV
  Game shows
  Cartoons
  Star Trek
  Sports shows
	Activities
	
	• Brushing teeth
	• Washing hair
	• Putting things away
	• Assistance with dressing
	• Familiar work (once, but not repeated later)
		Activities
		
		• Mother leaving after visit
		• Losing control of himself
		• Too many requests or demands
		• Waiting
		• Events that last longer than expected; lunch delayed
		• New jobs, activities, routines
		
		Transitions
		
		• Bus between work and home
		• Between work/lunch/work
		• Ending interactions with favorite people before he is ready

Sensory • Touching soft blankets • Touching women's hair • Baths/showers	**Sensory** • Walking on bumpy ground	**Sensory** • Loud sounds, loud voices • Overlapping conversations • Wool next to his skin
Foods • Pizza • Grilled-cheese sandwiches • Hamburgers • Pancakes • Finger foods • Popcorn • Spaghetti	**Foods** • Sweets	**Foods**
Other	Other	Other

Figure A.2 Functional Analysis Summary (Form 24.4)

Adapted with permission from Oregon Regional Autism Services

Student: Tony   **Date:** April 15

Environmental Events that Affect Tolerance (Allergies, weather, worries, sensory conditions)	Antecedents or Triggers	Escalating Chains of Behavior (From earliest signals of stress to most intense behavior)	Communicative Function (The problem from the learner's perspective)
Tolerance decreased by:	• Demands:	*Stage 1a:*	• I am confused.
• Migraine headaches	—When unexpected	• Soft verbalizations: "Uh-oh," "No," "Knock it off"	• Don't rush me.
• Back pain from surgery	—Made in a loud voice	• Pauses/stops moving/watches	• Be quiet, I can't think.
• Fatigue	—To change from preferred to disliked activity	• Flushes	• Where did it go? I can't find it.
• Working too long in one place	—From an unfamiliar person	• Touches head or face where he slaps	• My (head, back) hurt.
• Working too long at a single task	—Rapid, repeated demands or corrections	• Hands together, then stretches arms over his head	• I need a break.
• Boredom	—Repeated demands from more than one person at the same time	*Stage 1b - 2c:*	• I don't want to (or, I want to stop).
• Too many people talking at once	—To return to or do more of a task that he thought was finished	• Louder verbalizations: "Oh-oh-oh"; echoes, "Knock it off, Tony," "Don't hit me"	
• Movement and noise of transitions	• An unexpected change	• Holds his head	
• Background noises that are out of view	• Being startled or afraid	• Hits or slaps his head two or three times, then pauses	
• Changes—new routines, places, people, or expectations	• Being rushed	• Puts hand to mouth as if to bite	
• Disorganization and clutter of space and materials	• Being stopped in the middle of a routine, then required to start over	• Cries or screams	
	• Physical restraint by two or more people (especially if all are talking)	*Stage 2d:*	
	• When told, "No hitting," or "it's not okay to hit"	• Bites hand	
	• Time out (unless taken quietly by a familiar person before stress intensifies)	• Hits nearby person	
		• Butts head into other person or wall	
		• Lies on floor, hitting head on floor	
		• Pulls off clothes (only rarely)	

Notes:
• Tony worked best when he could see what others in the area were doing.
• He has significant information-processing delay.
• He is a perfectionist. If expectations were clear, he recognized and corrected his own mistakes. If prompted verbally during this process, he slapped his face and bit his hand (escalated with each prompt or reprimand).
• Tony responded well to quiet gestural or pointing prompts and line drawings or photos with written labels or short phrases.

Figure A.3 Intervention Planning Worksheet (Form 24.5)

Adapted with permission from Oregon Regional Autism Services

Student: Tony   **Date:** April 15

Stage 1. Escalation	Stage 2. Crisis level	Stage 3. De-escalation	Stage 4. Equilibrium
Intervention goal: Defuse stress, return to equilibrium	**Intervention goal:** Prevent escalation, keep people safe, support deescalation	**Intervention goal:** Support self-control, reengage	**Intervention goal:** Evaluate/refine, organize/structure and teach skills

Behavior signals:
• Noises/Words: Squeals, "Uh-uh-uh," "Knock it off"
• Pauses/Stops moving
• Touches head where he slaps
• Stretches arms over head
• Flushes
• Rapid breathing/hyperventilation
• Puts hand to mouth as if to bite
 	
Strategies:
Talk softly; acknowledge feelings/problem.
If "stuck" or looking confused:
• Say, "Are you stuck?"; "Do you need help?"; "Let me show you"; "Start here"; then model or point to visual references.
• Or: Cue to check schedule.
• Or: Quickly draw and talk simply to clarify.
If faced with change or unexpected event:
• Say, "That surprised (or worries) you," and pause; then visually clarify.
• Or: Refer to calendar and modify to clarify.
If bored, tired, sick:
• Say, "You look _____. (bored, tired, sick).
  Do you need a break?"
• Clarify contingency ("Do this much, then break") with a quick drawing.
If Tony wants something he can't have:
• Say, "I know you want _____, but that belongs to _____"
• Or: "You can have/do it on _____"; then mark the calendar.
• Or: "I'm sorry. I know you want to go to the Cotton Bowl, but _____"; then offer diversion.
If overloaded with too much noise/confusion:
• Say, "It's too noisy. Do you need a break?"; then provide a break.
If you do not understand the problem:
• Say, "Can you show me in your book?"
• Or: "I'm sorry, I don't understand"; then offer diversion.
If acceleration continues:
• Cue to go to safe area before he loses control.
 	
Avoid:
• **Do not** ignore or try to divert until attempt is made to understand and solve the problem.
• **Do not** demand, push, or rush Tony beyond his tolerance level.
	Behavior signals:
	• "Oh-oh-oh" as he slaps head
	• Echoes, "Knock it off, Tony" or "Don't hit me"
	• Holds head
	• Hits head two or three times, then pauses
	• Bites hand
	• Cries/screams
	• Hits nearby person
	• Butts head into wall or other person
	• Lies on floor, hitting head on floor
	• Pulls off clothes (only rarely)
	Note: These behaviors will intensify if stress and pressure continue.
	
	Strategies:
	Model calm, and:
	• Stop talking; or use a few calm, quiet words to tell Tony what to do:
	• "Put your hands in your pockets."
	• "Relax, take a deep breath."
	Model calm, slow, deep breathing.
	Move back to avoid crowding him, turn slightly sideways, keep your hands relaxed.
	If he is not in a safe place:
	• Cue others to move away.
	  —or,
	• With one other, well-trained person, physically assist him to a safe place. Do this in a calm and nonthreatening manner. If at all possible, say, "We will help you to a safe place before starting to move him."
	If he stops screaming to take a deep breath:
	• Softly say, "Good! You took a deep breath. You can calm yourself."
	
	Avoid:
	• Do not make demands.
	• Do not push, rush, confuse, or crowd him with two or three people giving directions.
	• Do not say, "It's not okay to _____" or, "Stop hitting (or, biting)." Instead, give positive directions. Tell him what to do.
	
	Remember:
	This is not a teaching time or a time to threaten or bribe. It is a time:
	• To keep people safe
	• To reduce demands, be calm and supportive, and talk only a little
		Behavior signals:
		Calming, watchful
		
		Strategies:
		Calmly and periodically, reinforce Tony's efforts to regain control and relax. Give him hope.
		• "We'll solve the problem"; "You will learn to _____."
		Give cue or contingency so he will know how to resume normal activity.
		• "First a drink, then do _____, then it will be time for a break"; "When the timer rings, we will check your schedule."
		• As you talk, prepare a cue card to highlight these sequences.
		If returning to a task that triggered the problem:
		• Reduce the demands or ensure that the end of the task is visually clear.
		• Provide assistance to help Tony focus and make progress.
		Watch carefully for signs of increasing stress.
		• Use contingency and help end job quickly to take break before he loses control.
		
		Avoid:
		• Do not rush him to return to the task before he is totally relaxed.
		• Do not lecture, blame, or push for an apology.
		• Do not punish. Punishment will not help him know what to do the next time he has a problem.
		
		Also to do:
		While he is relaxing:
		• Write a flow log of his calming behavior. (Use "What Happened?" Flow Chart, form 6.2.).
		• Make notes; later, record the incident.
		• Relax yourself.
			Behavior signals:
			Stable, calm
			
			Strategies:
			Evaluate and refine:
			• The crisis management plan
			• The schedule:
			  Activities appropriate? Balanced? Flexible to match fluctuating tolerance?
			• Visual systems (communication, work systems, calendar)
			• Staff support plan
			
			Organize and structure:
			• The work area with visuals:
			  —To clarify the space, boundaries, and materials
			  —To reduce clutter
			  —To answer what, when, where, how, how long, and what's next
			  —To arrange so the entire room is in view
			• A quiet break area
			
			Skills to teach, strengthen, or generalize:
			• Communication skills to locate helper and persist in getting attention
			• System to express:
			  —"I don't understand"
			  —"Don't rush me"
			  —"It's too noisy; I can't think"
			  —"Where did it go? I can't find it"
			  —"My head (back) hurts"
			  —"I need a break"
			  —"I don't want to"
			  —"I want to stop"
			• To recognize stressful feelings; then ask for and take a break
			  —Relaxation and self-control strategies
			• To use visual work systems
			
			Remember: Problem behaviors are a symptom of: misunderstandings, lack of ability to communicate needs, boredom, lack of skills, too much noise or crowding, head or back pain, or panic reactions.
			They are not intentional or deliberate efforts to hurt or humiliate.

B Resources

Organizations

The Autism Society of America (ASA)
7910 Woodmont Avenue, Suite 300
Bethesda, MD 20814-3067
Phone: (301) 657-0881—(800) 3-AUTISM
Online: www.autism-society.org

> With both parent and professional members, ASA was organized in 1965 to promote information and public awareness about autism. The organization operates through a network of more than 190 state and local chapters in 48 states. ASA maintains an active advocacy and lobbying effort, sponsors an annual national conference, and publishes *The Advocate* six times a year. This newsletter provides current information about medical and educational research, political advocacy issues, and stories about families and individuals coping with autism.

> **State or local ASA chapters.** These local parent/professional groups are important sources of family support and information about regional resources. Local groups play a critical advocacy role to ensure appropriate services in a community. They may sponsor workshops, conferences, lending libraries, or newsletters. Check the phone book and newspapers, or call a local information and referral service.

> The Autism Network for Hearing and Vision Impaired Person is also sponsored by the ASA.

The Autism National Committee (AUTCOM)
734 Ardmore Ave.
P.O. Box 6175
North Plymouth, MA 02362-6175
Online: www.autcom.org

> AUTCOM was founded in 1990 to advance and protect the civil rights of people with autism/PDD and related disorders of communication and behavior. The organization publishes a quarterly newsletter, *The Communicator*.

Cure Autism Now (CAN)
5225 Wilshire Blvd, Suite 226
Los Angeles, CA 90036
Phone: (213)549-0500
Online: http://canfoundation.org

> CAN is an organization founded by parents dedicated to mobilize the scientific and medical communities to action and to fund medical research with direct clinical applications to the treatments of autism.

Autism Training Centers

There are numerous private and public centers across the country that offer effective training to parents and professionals as well as services to those with autism and their families. The following centers are listed here because their philosophy of autism and autism services is consistent with that proposed in this book. I visited each of these programs and was impressed with the quality of their professional and parent training programs and the skill and sensitivity shown to their clients with autism.

The Groden Center
86 Mt. Hope Avenue
Providence, RI 02906
Online: www.grodencenter.org
Phone: (401) 274-6310
Contact: June Groden, Director

> This private, nonprofit center pioneered the work in relaxation and self-control training for those with autism. The center provides an on-site program as well as support to individuals who are integrated into local school and community living and supported employment programs. The Groden Center offers workshops and training in relaxation and self-control procedures to parents and professionals in other states and countries.

The Judevine Center for Autism
9455 Rott Road
St. Louis, MO 63127
Phone: (314) 849-4440
Online: www.judevine.org
Contact: Lois Blackwell, Director

> Judevine is a private, nonprofit center for applied research and treatment offering a multitude of services to children and adults with autism and their families in home, local school, and community settings across the state. Specialized training for parents is offered both on-site and in-home. Diagnostic classrooms are used as practicum sites for professional training. The Judevine provides assessment, consultation, and specialized training to those from other states and countries.

Division TEACCH
University of North Carolina at Chapel Hill
CB # 7180
Chapel Hill, NC 27599-7180
Phone: (919) 966-2173
Online: www.teacch.com
Contact: Gary Mesibov, Director

> The TEACCH Program (The Division for the Treatment and Education of Autistic and Related Communication Handicapped Children), established in 1972, is the first statewide, comprehensive, community-based program dedicated to improving the understanding of and services to those with autism and related disabilities. As a part of the university, it provides many different training programs for students at every level. In addition to the local services provided by nine regional centers in North Carolina, the TEACCH Program offers assessment, consultation, and training to parents and professionals from other states and countries.

Autism Resource Centers

Autism Research Institute (ARI)
4182 Adams Avenue
San Diego, CA 92116
Phone: (619) 281-7165
Online: www.autismresearchinstitute.com
Contact: Bernard Rimland, Ph.D., Director

> The Autism Research Institute, is a valuable resource for treatment information. It maintains one of the largest data banks on individuals with autism and evaluates various forms of treatment. It publishes a quarterly newsletter, *The Autism Research*

Review International, and for several years has sponsored the Defeat Autism Now! (DAN) Conferences—from this conference of physicians and others, it has developed *The DAN Protocol,* an excellent diagnostic and treatment reference for physicians and parents.

Autism Resource Network
904 Mainstreet, Suite 100
Hopkins, MN 55343
Phone: (952) 988-0088
Contact: Cherri Saltzman, Director

This is a non-profit Minnesota corporation established by a parent, Cherri Saltzman. She has developed an autism bookstore and distributes an excellent catalog that includes books written about autism by professionals and those with autism. It also includes children's books about autism, and teaching materials. They also prepare an informative newsletter—with information presented for quick reading.

The Indiana Resource Center for Autism at Indiana University
Indiana Institute for Disability and Community
2853 East 10th Street
Bloomington, IN 47408
Phone: (812) 855-6508
Online: www.iidc.indiana.edu
Contact: Cathy Pratt, Ph.D., Director

This center offers training and short papers on specific issues, pamphlets, manuals, and videotapes. For a catalog of publications, write to the above address.

Interdisciplinary Council on Developmental and Learning
Disorders (ICDL)
4938 Hampden Lane, Suite 800
Bethesda, MD. 20814
Phone (301) 656-2667
Online: www.icdl.com

ICDL is developing a national training and certification program to increase the numbers of trained clinicians who can provide Developmental, Individual Difference, Relationship Based (DIR) training across the country. It also sends quarterly newsletters with articles about new research findings and clinical insights from Dr. Greenspan, and includes upcoming conferences and training for using the DIR approach.

The Autism Services Center
P.O. Box 507
Huntington, WV 25710-0507
Phone: (304) 525-8014
Online: www.autismservices.com
Contact: Ruth Sullivan, Director

This is a licensed behavioral health center and an information and referral center that includes the National Autism Hotline.

The Center for Neurodevelopmental Studies
5430 W. Glenn Drive
Glendale, AZ 85301
Phone: (623) 915-0345
Contact: Kay Marie King, Director

This center distributes information about and offers training in sensory integrative therapy and provides therapy services to children with autism and related disorders.

National Information Center for Children and Youth with Disabilities (NICHCY)
Phone: (800) 695-0285 (Voice/TT)

An information clearinghouse, NICHCY provides free information on disabilities and disability-related issues, publishes the *NICHY News Digest* (free subscription within the United States). The organization provides personal responses to questions, referrals to other organizations, and information searches; and maintains databases and a library.

The Geneva Centre
250 Davisville Ave., Suite 200
Toronto, Ontario, Canada M4S 1H2
Phone: (416) 322-7877
Online: www.autism.net.

This resource center sells a wide range of printed material and videotapes related to autism and related disorders. The center maintains a computerized resource library of current information. Write for the *Catalogue of Autism Resources*.

Facilitated Communication Institute
Syracuse University
370 Huntington Hall
Syracuse, NY 13244
Phone: (315) 443-1870

This center distributes information about facilitated communication, conducts research, and offers workshops to train communication facilitators.

MAAP Services, Inc.
P.O. Box 524
Crown Point, IN 46307-0524
Phone: (219) 662-1311
Online: www.maapservices.org
Contact: Susan Moreno

MAAP Services, Inc., gathers and disseminates information about those with autism who are "more advanced," and distributes a newsletter for sharing information about higher-functioning individuals on the spectrum. See the web site for references, articles, and excerpts from the newsletter.

Note: *See The Autism Treatment Guide, 2nd edition* (Gerlach, 2000) for a more in-depth list of treatments and resources.

Autism Publications

The Advocate
Autism Society of America
7910 Woodmont Avenue, Suite 300
Bethesda, MD 20814
Online: www.autism-society.org

Newsletter published six times a year.

See the fourth edition, 2001 (Volume 34, No. 4) of *The Advocate*, published by the Autism Society of America. It is a special edition that discusses dietary issues and treatments as natural alternatives.

Autism—The International Journal of Research and Practice
SAGE Publications Ltd. and the National Autism Society of UK
PO Box 5096
Thousand Oaks, CA 91359
Email: nas@nas.org.uk
Online: www.oneworld.org/autism_uk

Published bimonthly.

Autism Research Review International
Autism Research Institute
4182 Adams Avenue
San Diego, CA 92116

Published quarterly.

Journal of Autism and Developmental Disorders
Plenum Publishing
233 Spring Street
New York, NY 10013

Published quarterly.

Focus on Autism and Other Developmental Disabilities
PRO-ED, Inc.
8700 Shoal Creek Blvd.
Austin, TX 78758

Published bimonthly.

Autism•Asperger's Digest
Future Horizons Inc.
721 W. Abram St.
Arlington, TX 76013

Published bimonthly.

The Communicator
Autism National Committee
P.O. Box 6175
North Plymouth, MA 02362-6175
Online: www.autcom.org

Newsletter published quarterly.

Our Voice
Autism Network International (ANI)
P.O. Box 448
Syracuse, NY 13210-0448
Contact: Jim Sinclair

Our Voice is the newsletter of the Autism Network International (ANI), an independent organization and newsletter run entirely by and for individuals with autism/PDD.

Catalogs for Books and Teaching Materials

Autism Resource Network, Inc.
For a catalog, phone: (952) 988-0088

> This catalog includes numerous books on autism for parents, professionals, and children. It also includes PECS materials, BoardMaker, Picture This . . . photo guides and CDs, *Picture Communication Symbols—Book 1* (Mayer-Johnson) for making visual supports, and teacher/parent training videos.

Future Horizons Inc.
For a catalog, phone: 1-800-489-0727
Online: www.futurehorizons-autism.com.

Autism Society of North Carolina Bookstore
For a catalog, phone: (919) 743-0204
Online: www.autismsociety-nc.ort/bookstore.html

James Stanfield Publishing
For catalog, phone: 800-421-6534
Online: www.stanfield.com

> This company offers a catalog of educational programs to develop social competence—features complete programs including video modeling, slide shows, teachers guides with scripts, charts, etc. designed specifically for those with special challenges. The programs address transition/work skills, daily living/social skills, relationship/sexuality skill, and conflict resolution skills. Two programs in particular, Circles and Life Horizons, teach about relationship/sexuality issues in a clear but sensitive way that is easy to individualize.

The Attainment Company—IEP Resources
Online: www.attainmentcompany.com

> This company provides resources for people with developmental and other disabilities including software, videos, and materials for hands-on training—language, math, reading, social skills, etc.—many effective with autism.

FastForward
Online: www.scientificlearning.com

> FastForward is computer-based training for language and reading.

Laureate Learning Systems
www.llsys.com

> Laureate offers computer software for teaching many different skills to those with severe to mild developmental problems—many useful for autism. Software includes activities of daily living, vocabulary, sentence structure, categories, following directions, etc.

Lindamood-Bell
Online: www.lindamoodbell.com.

> Their auditory comprehension programs such as "Visualize-Verbalize" has been successful with this population.

Locutour Media
Online: www.learningfundamentals.com

> Locutour Media offers cognitive rehabilitation CD-ROM technology and other computer software for developing speech/language skills. Train Time, was developed specifically for children with autism.

Mayer-Johnson Company

Mayer-Johnson offers BoardMaker, Picture Communication Symbols, and Writing with Symbols 2000—resources for making picture symbols for communication systems and calendar systems.

Glossary

Adaptations. Modifications or alterations of the curriculum, support systems, environments, or teaching strategies to match individual needs (strengths and deficits). The adaptations ensure that the student can participate actively and as independently as possible.

Assessment. The process of determining skills and deficits for educational planning. It is also used to indicate a thorough review of environments, programs, and strategies to ensure they match the learner's needs.

Behavior. Any observable activity in response to internal or external stimuli.

Behavioral signals. See, **signals.**

Calendar. A visual representation of scheduled activities. In this book, a distinction between a schedule and a calendar is made to emphasize the importance of the planning process involved in ordering the events in time to achieve goals and the importance of the calendar for communicating that sequence of events to the learner. See Chapter 12. A mini-calendar supplements a basic daily calendar and shows the sequence of steps or specific activities scheduled to occur within a small block of time. See also, **scheduling.**

Calendar system. The combination and integration of all the elements that make up an effective calendar—one that will have an optimum effect. For example, it includes the systematic ordering of activities, the physical design of the calendar, transition cues to move from one location to another, etc. See Chapters 13–15.

Central nervous system (CNS). The structure that consists of the brain, spinal cord, and related systems that controls all aspects of learning, thinking, and movement.

Chunk. A substantial amount of something. In this context, it refers to the gestalt processing style that results in one-trial learning—when all the information present in the environment at one time is recorded together without analysis in chunks. These chunks include both relevant and irrelevant material.

Clutter. A disordered heap; litter. In this context, the word refers to irrelevant or unrelated environmental events or details that compete with the relevant information so that critical associations cannot be made. Sounds of crackling paper, people breathing, or a truck starting up; the odors of nearby people; the touch of a prompt; or the feel of a scratchy shirt label on the neck may overpower or clutter the important details of a demonstration or verbal direction.

Cognitive. Pertains to the mental processes of thinking, knowing, and reasoning.

Cognitive picture rehearsal. An application of imagery procedures. It incorporates a visual display to help a person visualize the scenes associated with a problem situation.

Cognitive processes. The neurological processes involved in knowing, thinking, reasoning, and solving problems.

Communication. An interactive process that conveys information and ideas from one person to another. Communication is a social skill that has the potential for influencing others and gaining some control over one's environment.

Consequence. Something that occurs as a direct result of action or effort. Consequences can be pleasant and reinforcing or unpleasant and punishing. Some consequences occur naturally. (When you touch a hot stove, you get burned.)

Contingency. A contract that specifies and clarifies expectations. It defines the expected behavior (work or effort) and the reinforcement (payoff). Contingencies are generally stated in an if/then or when/then format.

Conventional signals. Words, gestures, signs, or behaviors that are understood by everyone in the same cultural group. Whether the signal is verbal or nonverbal, most people in that group could easily interpret it. Nonconventional signals are signals not commonly used or understood in the culture. For example, flicking fingers, flapping arms, or biting wrists can be used to signal a variety of problems, but they do not carry a commonly understood meaning.

Covert conditioning. An imagery procedure. In this context, it is based on the work of J. Cautela and assumes that thinking, feeling, and imagining follow the same principles of learning as observable behaviors. Covert positive reinforcement occurs when a person imagines the target behavior that results in a positive consequence. The imagined positive consequence strengthens the behavior or increases the likelihood of it recurring. Covert modeling is the act of imagining another person performing the target behavior and visualizing that it resulted in a positive consequence. See strategies for teaching self-control routines in Chapter 22.

Covert modeling. See, covert conditioning.

Covert positive reinforcement. See, covert conditioning.

Criterion. A standard for judging mastery or level of accuracy. For example, mastery is assumed if a skill occurs with a specified degree of accuracy or within a specified amount of time.

Critical skills. Skills that most people learn automatically, that those with autism do not learn without very specific instruction.

Delayed echolalia. See, echolalia.

Developmental goals. Goals relating to the sequence of normal development of language, cognitive, social, motor, and academic skills. The progression to the next step depends on mastering a lower step; for example, discrimination of shapes and sounds leads to recognition of letters, letter names, letter sounds, and then to reading. Those with autism skip many steps of the developmental sequences.

Echolalia. The repetition of speech produced by others. The echoed words or phrases can include the same words and exact inflections as originally heard, or they may be slightly modified. Immediate echolalia refers to words echoed immediately or a very brief time after they were first heard. Delayed echolalia refers to echoed "tapes" that are repeated at a much later time—days or even years later.

Evaluation. A process for determining the significance of symptoms, as in a diagnostic study of a physical or mental condition. In this context, the term refers to the process for determining the presence of autism; the evaluation will determine how or if a child's symptoms are like, or not like, those of others with autism

Forms of communication. The means or method of communication—gestures, pictures, signs, spoken or written words, and other methods.

Functional. Useful, practical.

Functional analysis of behavior. See, **functional assessment.**

Functional assessment. A process for documenting an individual's actual ability to function in the natural environment. A functional analysis of behavior is the procedure for identifying the relationship between aspects of the environment and behavior. These functional procedures provide information for understanding the reasons for problems, for setting practical (functional) goals, and for identifying support needs.

Functional goals. Goals that lead directly to increased independence in the real world, such as cooking, doing laundry, or managing a bank account or leisure time.

Functional routines. The set or sequence of steps or procedures directed to achievement of a practical purpose (e.g., a routine for washing dishes or for going to a movie).

Functions of communication. The purpose or reasons to communicate (e.g., to request, protest, comment).

Generalize, generalization. The ability to learn a skill or a rule in one situation and be able to use or apply it flexibly to other similar but different situations. The term overgeneralize refers to the tendency of those with autism to use a skill in all settings just as it was taught, without modifications that reflect the differences in a situation.

Gestalt, wholistic. Terms used to describe the distinctive processing mode common in autism. Information is taken in (recorded) and stored quickly in whole units or "chunks," without analysis for meaning. These "chunks" are stored directly in the long-term memory system.

Glitch. A defect, error, or malfunction, as in a machine. A brief or sudden interruption or surge in electric power.

Hyperlexia. An ability to learn to read at advanced levels without instruction.

Imagery-based procedures. Procedures that promote learning by thinking, imagining, or visualizing one's self or a model performing a behavior that results in a pleasant consequence. See also, visual imagery.

Immediate echolalia. See, echolalia.

Instructional sequence. A systematic teaching plan that specifies the materials, settings, variations, adaptations, and teaching strategies to ensure effective learning.

Integrated model. The consolidation of theories, models, and strategies and the selection of those that will address the unique needs of each child.

Integrated systems. The organization or consolidation of all the visual information systems to clarify meaning and avoid confusion.

Intentional communication. Behavior that is done with a purpose and the knowledge of potential effect. Unintentional communication is reflexive behavior, done automatically without the knowledge of potential effect.

Interpreter. One who can explain or provide the meaning; a person who can clarify the meaning of events, words, and experiences. In the context of autism, the interpreter must also take on the role of guide who provides assistance to reach a destination or goal, who shows and comments upon, supplies advice or counsel, highlights important details, attracts the eye, and provides quick reference.

Joint attention. When an infant and caregiver coordinate their attention about an object of mutual interest. This involves shifting their attention from each other to an object and back. Joint attention is sometimes called referential looking.

Language. A set of symbols with meanings and rules for use that are commonly understood and used by all in a cultural group for the purpose of communication.

Learner. This term is used in this book to refer to those with autism spectrum disorders of any age, sex, and ability level.

Learning style. A distinctive manner or way of taking in and processing information in order to learn, think, remember, and function in the world.

Learning theory. The study of how learning occurs; the resulting ideas and principles that explain how learning happens.

Mini-calendar. See, calendar.

Natural cue. An object or event that is always present or always occurs as part of the natural environment, that stimulates or triggers a response or action (e.g., a full laundry basket is a signal that it is time to do the laundry, the sound of the cash register ringing up the total is a signal to pay).

Natural prompt. Something that calls attention to a missed cue or that assures a correct response (e.g., if payment is not made at the expected time, the checker holds out a hand and says, "That will be $10"; If a person in line does not move up, the person behind says, "Hey, move along.")

Neuro-normal. A very informal term that refers to those without the neurological problems common in autism. This term was first used by high-functioning young adults as they described the differences in the way they understood the world.

Nonconventional signals. See, conventional signals.

Overgeneralize. See, generalize.

Perseveration. The redundant repetition of a word, thought, or action without the ability to stop or move on. For example, when a person steps through the door, then rocks back and forth, seemingly unable to follow through with the other foot; or, when one erases a mistake until the paper is worn through.

Perspective. A point of view based on location, experiences, prior knowledge, beliefs, etc.

Pica. Eating things that are not food.

Pragmatics. The practical aspects of using language to communicate in a natural context. It includes the rules about eye contact between speaker and listener, how close to stand, taking turns, selecting topics of conversation, and other requirements to ensure that satisfactory communication occurs. Many of these rules have a cultural base.

Problem. Any situation or event that one does not understand, that causes uncertainty and requires a solution.

Progressive muscle relaxation. A type of therapy procedure for reducing stress. A person is taught to identify feelings and location of tension and to consciously relax the muscle groups that are tense. For example, the feelings of tension in the neck and shoulders cues the person to consciously relax the neck and shoulder muscles.

Proprioceptive. Stimuli from the nerve receptors located in the muscles, tendons, and inner ear that provide a sense of the position of one's body in space.

Punishment. An unpleasant event that occurs as a direct consequence of a behavior, which decreases the strength of the behavior or the likelihood that it will be repeated.

Rebus. A symbol, line drawing, or representation that illustrates or suggests the meaning of a word or phrase.

Referential looking. See, joint attention.

Reflexive. Actions that occur quickly, automatically, and without thought as an immediate response to some type of stimulation or emotion (e.g., the fight-or-flight responses that occur as a result of panic, surprise, or pain).

Reinforcement. A pleasant event that occurs immediately as a direct result of an action that increases the strength of the action or the likelihood that the action will be repeated.

Representations. Symbols that take on the meaning of a real object or idea. For example, signs and words are symbols that represent real things. An understanding of symbols enables a person to use words (symbols) in thinking.

Response cost. A type of punishing procedure that involves the loss of something valued (a reinforcer) as a direct result of an action (behavior), thus decreasing the likelihood that the behavior will reoccur. Response cost involves the giving up of something already in possession; it is not simply that reinforcement is withheld. For example, a child who draws on the wall must give up crayons; a person who is caught speeding must give up money.

Response. An action or behavior that is triggered by a preceding cue or stimulus (object, action, or event).

Savant. A person who exhibits unusual gifts and abilities in a few areas (or a single area) that contrast sharply with abilities in other areas.

Schedule. See, scheduling.

Scheduling. A planning process that organizes a sequence of events to achieve a goal. A *schedule* is the product of that planning process—a plan or an arrangement of events to accomplish goals. A *calendar* is the visual representation of that schedule.

Semantic categories. The type of meaning a word has when used to communicate an idea or concept. An example of the category *object wanted* is, "Want ball." An example of the category *action* is, "I jumped."

Semantic maps. Diagrams or flow charts that show the meaningful relationships between elements of concepts, processes, or events.

Sensory channels or systems. The neurological pathways for receiving information from the environment (for example, eyes: visual channel; ears: auditory channel; nose: olfactory channel).

Signals. Objects or events that trigger or cue a response or action; for example, traffic lights. Behavioral signals are actions that indicate an emotional state (e.g., flushing and hyperventilation may be a signal of increasing stress). See also, **conventional signals.**

Social cognition. The thinking, understanding, and reasoning skills involved in or required for social interactions; knowing about others and their perspectives.

Social stimuli. The sensory stimulation provided by people and interactions. The amount and the type of stimulation presented by people is highly unpredictable. The stimulation includes expressive and changing facial features (especially the eyes and mouth), loud and often high-pitched talking, odors, unexpected movements, and touches.

Standardized tests. Assessment tools that measure one individual's performance against the performance of many other individuals who have taken the test under the same precise conditions. Standardized tests involve highly specific directions and generally provide age/grade-level or intelligence (IQ) scores.

Support systems. The adaptations and assistance required to ensure increasing independence. One learner's support system may include a daily calendar, transition cues, a one-on-one interpreter for some classes, and a consulting occupational therapist.

Syndrome. A condition characterized by a cluster of co-occurring symptoms that has a specific effect on a group of individuals; for example, fetal alcohol syndrome, Down syndrome, and autism.

Synergistic effects. The concept that the total effect produced by the interaction or integration of multiple elements is greater than the sum of the effect of each element alone. For example, it is the interacting or synergistic effects of all the learning style elements that complicates the picture in autism. The combination of extreme strengths and the extreme deficits causes paradoxical effects.

Theory of mind. Terminology used to describe the concept of thinking about thinking; thinking about what we know and think, and what others know and think.

Transition cue. An object that serves as a reminder of the targeted destination. For example, the car keys held in the hand trigger or cue moving to the car; a 3"x5" card with a drawing of the gym serves as a reminder to continue moving to the gym.

Unintentional communication. See, **intentional communication.**

Visual adaptations; visual support systems. Written schedules, lists, charts, picture sequences, and other visuals that convey meaningful information in a permanent format for later reference. Visual adaptations enable the person with autism to function more independently without constant verbal directions. These visual adaptations serve the same purpose for those with autism as a hearing aid and sign language serve for the person who is deaf. A person who is blind gets information from reading Braille or from an interpreter.

Visual imagery. An instructional strategy that involves the ability to imagine scenes, feelings, and actions. A traditional counseling strategy.

Wholistic. See, **gestalt.**

Work system. The visual organization of directions, materials, and environments to clarify expectations. This clear visual organization promotes independence from another person to provide verbal cues and prompts.

References

Adams, M. J., Bereiter, C., Brown, A., Campione, J., Carruthers, I., Case, R., Hirshberg, J., McKeough, A., Pressley, M., Roit, M., Scardamalia, M., & Treadway, G. H. Jr., (2000). *SRA open court reading, level K and level 1*. Columbus, OH: SRA McGraw-Hill Companies.

Akerley, M. S. (1984). Developmental changes in families with autistic children: A parent's perspective. In E. Schopler & G. M. Mesibov (Eds.), *The effects of autism on the family* (pp. 85–98). New York: Plenum Press.

Albin, R. W., & Horner, R. H. (1988). Generalization with precision. In R. H. Horner, G. Dunlap, & R. L. Koegel (Eds.), *Generalization and maintenance: Lifestyle changes in applied settings* (pp. 99–120). Baltimore: Paul H. Brookes.

Allen, R. V., & Allen, C. (1966). *Language experiences in reading*. Chicago: Encyclopedia Britannica Press.

American Psychiatric Association. (1994). *Diagnostic and statistical manual of mental disorders* (4th ed.). Washington, DC: Author.

Archer, A., & Gleason, M. (1992–94). *Advanced skills for school success, 4 modules 1–4 for grades 7–12*. North Billerica, MA: Curriculum Associates.

Ashton-Warner, S. (1963). *Teacher*. New York: Simon and Schuster.

Attwood, A. J. (1993). Movement disorders and autism: A rationale for the use of facilitated communication and an alternative model for training staff and students. In *1993 International Conference Proceedings: Autism. A world of options*. International Conference on Autism, Toronto. Arlington, TX: Future Education.

Attwood, T. (1998). *Asperger's syndrome: A guide for parents and professionals*. London: Jessica Kingsley.

Autism and Asperger Syndrome Resource Center. (1997). *Assessing the setting demands in the classroom*. Kansas City, KS. (www. KUMC.edu/AARC)

Autism Society of America. (2001). Natural alternatives: Focus on vitamins, minerals and diet. *Advocate, 34*(4), 20–29.

Ayres, J. A. (1983). *Sensory integration and the child*. Los Angeles: Western Psychological Services.

Bainbridge, N., & Myles, B. S. (1999). The use of priming to introduce toilet training to a child with autism. *Focus on Autism and Other Developmental Disabilities, 14*(2), 106–109.

Baron-Cohen, S. (1988). Social and pragmatic deficits in autism: Cognitive or affective? *Journal of Autism and Developmental Disorders, 18*, 379–402.

Baron-Cohen, S., Leslie, A. M., & Frith, U. (1985). Does the autistic child have a "theory of mind?" *Cognition, 21*, 27–46.

Baron-Cohen, S., Saunders, K., & Chakrabarti, S. (1999). Does autism cluster geographically? A research note. *Autism: The International Journal of Research and Practice, 3*(1), 39–43.

Baron-Cohen, S., Tager-Flusberg, H., & Cohen, D. J. (1993). *Understanding other minds: Perspective from autism*. Oxford: Oxford University Press.

Beckman, P. J., & Lieber, J. (1994). The social strategy rating scale: An approach to evaluating social competence. *Journal of Early Intervention, 18*(1), 1–11.

Bernard-Opitz, V., Ross, K., & Tuttas, M. L. (1990). Computer assisted instruction for Autistic children. *Annals of the Academy of Medicine, 19*(5), 611–616.

Beukelman, D. R., & Mirenda, P. (1992). *Augmentative and alternative communication: Management of severe communication disorders in children and adults*. Baltimore: Paul H. Brookes.

Biederman, G., Davey, V., Ryder, C., and Franchi, D. (1994). The negative effects of positive reinforcement in teaching children with developmental delay. *Exceptional Children, 60*(5), 458–465.

Biederman, G. B., Fairhall, J. L., Raven, K. A., & Davey, V. A. (1998). Verbal prompting, hand-over-hand instruction, and passive observation in teaching children with developmental disabilities. *Exceptional Children, 64*(4), 503–511.

Biklen, D. (1990). Communication unbound: Autism and praxis. *Harvard Educational Review, 60*(3), 219–314.

Bingham, J. (2000). Image-making within the writing process: Combining art, writing & autism. *Autism/Asperger's Digest, March-April*, 33–36.

Blackwell, L. (1998). *Judevine® Training System: Competency-based training for parents and professionals*. St. Louis: Judevine Center for Autism.

Blanche, E., Botticelli, T., & Hallway, M. (1995). *Combining neurodevelopmental treatment and sensory integration principles*. Tucson, AZ: Therapy Skill Builders.

Board of Education of the Hendrick Hudson Central School District vs. Rowley. 458 U.S. 176 (1982).

Bock, M. A. (1991). A modified language experience approach for children with autism. *Focus on Autistic Behavior, 6*(5), 1–15.

Bondy, A. S., and Frost, L. A. (1994). The picture exchange system. *Focus on Autistic Behavior, 9*(3), 1–19.

Bristol, M. M., & Schopler, E. (1983). Stress and coping in families of autistic adolescents. In E. Schopler & G. B. Mesibov (Eds.), *Autism in adolescents and adults*, (pp. 251–276). New York: Plenum Press.

Brown, F., & Bambara, L. (1999). Special series on interventions for young children with autism. *Journal of the Association for Persons with Severe handicaps, 24*, 131–132.

Brown, F., Evans, I., Weed, K., & Owen, V. (1987). Delineating functional competencies: A component model. *Journal of the Association for Persons with Severe Handicaps, 12*(2), 117–124.

Bryson, S. E., Landry, R., & Smith, I. M. (1994). A case study of literacy and socioemotional development in a mute autistic female. *Journal of Autism and Developmental Disabilities, 24*(2), 225–231.

Buggey, T., Toombs, K., Gardener, P., & Cervetti, M. (1999). Training responding behaviors in students with autism: Using videotaped self-modeling. *Journal of Positive Behavior Interventions, 4*, 205–214.

Buser, K. P., & Reimer, D. (1988). Developing cognitive strategies through problem solving. *Teaching Exceptional Children, Winter*, 22–25.

Butera, G., & Haywood, H. C. (1992). A cognitive approach to the education of young children with autism. *Focus on Autistic Behavior, 6*(6), 1–14.

Carr, E. G., (1988). Functional equivalence as a mechanism of response generalization. In R. H. Horner, G. Dunlap, & R. L. Koegel (Eds.), *Generalization and maintenance: Life-style changes in applied settings*, (pp. 211–241). Baltimore: Paul H. Brookes.

Carr, E. G., Robinson, S., & Palumbo, L. W. (1990). The wrong issue: Aversive versus nonaversive treatment—The right issue: Functional versus nonfunctional treatment. In A Repp & R. Singh (Eds.), *Aversive and nonaversive treatment: The great debate in developmental disabilities*, (pp. 361–379). DeKalb, IL: Sycamore Press.

Carr, E., & Durand, V. (1985). Reducing behavior problems through functional communication training. *Journal of Applied Behavior Analysis, 18*, 111–126.

Cass, H. (1998). Visual impairment and autism: Current questions and future research. *Autism: The International Journal of Research and Practice, 2*(2), 117–138.

Cautela, J.R. & Kearney, A. J (1993). *The Covert Conditioning Casebook*. Pacific Grove, CA: Brooks/Cole.

Cautela, J. R., & Groden, J. (1978). *Relaxation: A comprehensive manual for adults, children, and children with special needs*. Champaign, IL: Research Press.

Cesaroni, L., & Garber, M. (1991). Exploring the experience of autism through firsthand accounts. *Journal of Autism and Developmental Disorders, 21*(3), 303–313.

Charlop, M. H., & Milstein, J. F. (1989). Teaching autistic children conversational speech using video modeling. *Journal of Applied Behavior Analysis, 22*, 275–285.

Chen, S. H. A., & Bernard-Opitz, V. (1993). Comparison of personal and computer assisted instruction for children with autism. *Mental Retardation, 31*(6), 368–376.

Coling, M. C. (1991). *Developing integrated programs: A transdisciplinary approach for early intervention*. Tucson, AZ: Therapy Skill Builders.

Courchesne, E., Akshoomoff, N. A., Egaas, B., Lincoln, A. J., Saitoh, O., Schreibman, L., Townsend, J., & Yeung-Courchesne, R. (1994). Role of cerebellar and parietal dysfunction in the social and cognitive deficits in patients with infantile autism. In Autism Society of America (Eds.) *Autism Society of America Conference Proceedings, 1994, Nevada* (pp. 19–21). Arlington, TX: Future Education.

Coyne, P., Nyberg, C., & Vandenburg, M. L. (1999). *Developing leisure time skills for persons with autism*. Austin, TX: Future Horizons.

Crossley, R. (1992). Getting the words out: Case studies in facilitated communication training. *Topics in Language Disorders, 12*(4), 46–59.

Dalldorf, J. S. (1997). Medical aspects of developmental disabilities in children birth to three. *Physical and occupational therapy in pediatrics, 17*(4), 85.

Dalldorf, J. S. (1983). Medical needs of the autistic adolescent. In In E. Schopler & G.B. Mesibov (Eds.), *Autism in Adolescents and Adults*. NY: Plenum Press.

Dalrymple, N., Gray, S., & Ruble, L. (1991). *Sex education: Issues for the person with autism* (Rev. ed.). Bloomington, IN: Indiana Resource Center for Autism, Indiana Institute on Disability and Community.

Darch, C., & Carnine, D. (1986). Teaching content area material to learning disabled students. *Exceptional Children, 53*(3), 240–245.

Datlow-Smith, M. (1990). *Autism and life in the community: Successful interventions for behavioral challenges*. Baltimore: Paul H. Brookes.

Datlow-Smith, M., Belcher, R. G., & Juhrs, P. D. (1994). *A guide to successful employment for individuals with autism*. Baltimore: Paul H. Brookes.

Dawson, G., & Fernald, M. (1987). Perspective-taking ability and its relationship to the social behavior of autistic children. *Journal of Autism and Developmental Disorders, 17*, 487–498.

Dawson, G., & Osterling, J. (1997). Early intervention in autism: Effectiveness and common elements of current approaches. In M. J. Guralnick (Ed.), *The effectiveness of early intervention: Second generation research*, (pp. 307–326). Baltimore: Paul H. Brookes.

Delprato, D. J. (2001). Comparisons of discrete-trial and normalized behavioral language intervention for young children with autism. *Journal of Autism and Developmental Disorders, 31*(3), 315–325.

DeMyer, M. K., & Goldberg, P. (1983). Family needs of the autistic adolescent. In E. Schopler & G. B. Mesibov (Eds.), *Autism in adolescents and adults,* (pp. 225–250). New York: Plenum Press.

DesLauriers, A. M. (1978). The cognitive-affective dilemma in early infantile autism: The case of Clarence. *Journal of Autism and Developmental Disorders, 8*, 219–228.

Dewey, M. (1991). Living with Asperger's syndrome. In U. Frith (Ed.), *Autism and Asperger syndrome,* (pp. 184–206). Cambridge, UK: Cambridge University Press.

Dewey, M. (1992). Autistic eccentricity. In E. Schopler & G. B. Mesibov (Eds.), *High-functioning individuals with autism,* (pp. 281–288). New York: Plenum Press.

Dewey, M., & Everard, M. (1974). The near-normal autistic adolescent. *Journal of Autism and Developmental Disorders, 4*, 348–356.

Donnellan, A. M. (1984). The criterion of the least dangerous assumption. *Behavioral Disorders, 9*(2), 141–150.

Donnellan, A. M., LaVigna, G. W., Negri-Shoultz, N., & Fassbender, L. L. (1988). *Progress without punishment: Effective approaches for learners with behavior problems.* New York: Teachers College Press.

Dowrick, P. W. (1999). A review of self-modeling and related interventions. *Applied and Preventive Psychology, 8*, 23–39.

Dowrick, P. W. (2000). *VideoFutures Start-Up Kit.* Anchorage, AK: Center for Human Development, a University Affiliated Program of the University of Alaska.

Duke, M. P., Nowicki, S., & Martin, E. A. (1996). *Teaching your child the language of social success.* Atlanta, GA: Peachtree.

Dunlap, G., & Kern, L. (1997). Behavior analysis and its relevance to special education. In J. L. Paul, M. Churton, H. Roselli-Kostoryz, W. Morse, K. Marfo, C. Lavely, & D. Thomas (Eds.), *Foundations of special education: Basic knowledge informing research and practice in special education.* Pacific Grove, CA: Brooks/Cole.

Dunlap, G., Kern, L., & Worcester, J. (2001). ABA and academic instruction. *Focus on Autism and Other Developmental Disabilities, 16*(2), 129–136.

Dunn, W. (1999). *Sensory profile.* San Antonio, TX: The Psychological Corporation.Durand, V. M., & Merges, E. (2001). Functional communication training: A contemporary behavior analytic intervention for problem behaviors. *Focus on Autism and Other Developmental Disabilities, 16*(2), 110–229.

Eastham, D. W. (1985). UNDERSTAND: *Fifty memo-writer poems.* Ottawa, Ontario, Canada: Oliver-Pate.

Eastham, M. W., & Eastham, D. (1990). *Silent words and forever friends.* Ottawa, Ontario, Canada: Oliver-Pate.

Edelson, S. M., Arin, D., Bauman, M., Lukas, S. E., Rudy, J. H., Sholar, M., & Rimland, B. (1999). Auditory Integration Training: A double-blind study of behavioral and electrophysiological effects in people with autism. *Focus on Autism and Other Developmental Disabilities, 14*(2), 73–81.

Ehlers, S., & Gillberg, C. (1993). The epidemiology of Asperger syndrome. *Journal of Child Psychology and Psychiatry, 34*, 1207–1250.

Eisenmajer, R., Prior, M., Leekam, S., Wing, L., Gould, J., Welham, M., & Ong, B. (1996). Comparison of clinical symptoms in autism and Asperger's disorder. *Journal of the American Academy of Child and Adolescent Psychiatry, 35*, 1523–1531.

Elgar, S. D., Knoll, B., Toriskey, D., Toriskey, C., Money, J., Lettick, A. L., Cardamone, J. A., & Mesibov, G. B. (1985). Sex education and sexual awareness building for autistic children and youth: Some viewpoints and considerations and response. *Journal of Autism and Developmental Disabilities, 15*(2), 214–227.

Everard, M. P. (1976). *Mildly autistic young people and their problems.* Paper presented at the International Symposium on Autism, St. Gallen, Switzerland.

Faherty, C. (2000). Asperger's: *What does it mean to me? A workbook explaining self awareness and life lessons to the child or youth with high-functioning autism or Aspergers.* Arlington, TX: Future Horizons.

Falco, R., Janzen, J., Arick, J., Wilgus, K., & DeBoer, M. (1990). *Project QUEST inservice manual: Functional assessment of student needs and functional instruction for communication, social interactions, self-management, and choice.* Portland, OR: Department of Special and Counselor Education, Portland State University.

Feinberg, E., & Vacca, J. (2000). The drama and trauma of creating policies on autism: Critical issues to consider in the new millennium. *Focus on Autism and Other Developmental Disabilities, 15*(3), 130–137.

Field, T., Sanders, C., & Nadel, J. (2001). Children with autism display more social behaviors after repeated imitation sessions. *Autism: The International Journal of Research and Practice, 5*(3), 317–323.

Flowers, T. (1990). From my classroom: Teaching reading for information. *The Advocate, 22*(1), 10.

Ford, A. (1987). Sex education for individuals with autism: Structuring information and opportunities. In D. J. Cohen, A. M. Donnellan, & R. Paul (Eds.), *Handbook of autism and pervasive developmental disorders* (pp. 430–439). New York: John Wiley & Sons.

Frankel, R. M., Leary, M. & Kilman, B. (1987). Building social skills through pragmatic analysis: Assessment and treatment implications for children with autism. In D. J. Cohen, A. M. Donnellan, & R. Paul (Eds.), *Handbook of autism and pervasive developmental disorders* (pp. 333–359). New York: John Wiley & Sons.

Freeman, S., & Dake, L. (1997). *Teach me language: A language manual for children with autism, Asperger's syndrome and related developmental disorders.* Langley, British Columbia, Canada: SKF Books.

Frith, U. (1989). *Autism: Explaining the enigma.* Oxford, UK: Blackwell.

Frith, U. (1991). *Autism and Asperger syndrome.* Cambridge, UK: Press Syndicate of the University of Cambridge.

Frost, L. A., & Bondy, A. S. (1994). PECS: *The picture exchange communication system—Training manual.* Cherry Hill, NJ: Pyramid Educational Consultants.

Fullerton, A. (1994). *Putting feet on my dreams: A program in self-determination.* Portland, OR: Portland State University.

Fullerton, A., & Coyne, P. (1999). Developing skills and concepts for self-determination in young adults with autism. *Focus on Autism and Other Developmental Disabilities, 14*(1), 42–52.

Fullerton, A., Stratton, J., Coyne, P., & Gray, C. (1996). *Higher functioning adolescents and young adults with autism: A teacher' guide.* Austin, TX: PRO-ED.

Garnett, M. S., & Attwood, T. (1995). *The Australian Scale for Asperger's Syndrome.* Paper presented at the 1995 Australian National autism Conference, Brisbane, Australia. In T. Attwood (Ed.), *Asperger's Syndrome: A guide for parents and professionals.* London: Jessica Kingsley Publishers. Available from Online Asperger's Syndrome Information and Support (OASIS) — http: // w w w.udel.edu/bkirby /asperger/. For permission to reprint, contact (bkirby @udel.edu).

Gense, M. H., & Gense, D. J. (1994). Identifying Autism in children with blindness and visual impairments. RE:view, 26(2), 55–62.

Gerlach, E. (1998). Beatlejuice therapy and other treatments for autism. *The net: Newsletter of the AUTISM Society of Oregon, January, 7.*

Gerlach, E. (1999). *Just this side of normal.* Arlington, TX: Future Horizons.

Gerlach, E. K. (2000). *Autism treatment guide* (2nd ed.). Arlington, TX: Future Horizons.

Gillberg, C. (1986). Onset at age 14 of a typical autistic syndrome: A case report of a girl with herpes simplex encephalitis. *Journal of Autism and Developmental Disorders, 16,* 369–375.

Gillberg, C. (1990). *Diagnosis and treatment of autism.* New York: Plenum Press.

Gillberg, C., & Coleman, M. (1992). Biology of the autistic syndromes (2nd ed.). London: MacKeith Press.

Gillberg, C., Gillberg, C., Rastam, M., & Wentz, E. (2001). The Asperger syndrome (and high-functioning autism) diagnostic interview (ASDI): A preliminary study of a new structured clinical interview. Autism: *The International Journal of Research and Practice, 5*(1), 57–66.

Gilliam, J. E. (1995a). *Gilliam Autism Rating Scale (GARS).* Austin, TX: PRO-ED.

Gilliam, J. E. (1995b). *Gilliam Asperger's Disorder Scale (GADS).* Austin, TX: PRO-ED.

Girolametto, L., Pearce, P. S., & Weitzman, E. (1996). The effects of focused stimulation for promoting vocabulary in young children with delays: A pilot study. *Journal of Children's Communication Development, 17*(2), 39–46.

Goetz, L., Sailor, G., & Sailor, W. (1985). Using a behavior chain interruption strategy to teach communication skills to students with severe disabilities. *Journal of the Association for Persons with Severe Handicaps (JASH), 10*(1), 21–30.

Grandin, T. (1990). Needs of high-functioning teenagers and adults with autism: Tips from a recovered autistic. *Focus on Autistic Behavior, 5*(1), 1–15.

Grandin, T. (1992). An insider's view of autism. In E. Schopler & G. B. Mesibov (Eds.), *High-functioning individuals with autism* (pp. 105–126). New York: Plenum Press.

Grandin, T. (1995b). *Thinking in pictures: And other reports from my life with autism.* New York: Doubleday.

Grandin, T. (1995a). The learning style of people with autism: An autobiography. In K. Quill (Ed.), *Teaching children with Autism: Strategies to enhance communication and socialization* (pp. 33–51). Albany, NY: Delmar.

Grandin, T., & Scariano, M. (1986). *Emergence labelled autistic.* Novato, CA: Arena Press.

Grant, J. O., Lazarus, B. B., & Peyton, H. (1992). The use of dialogue journals with students with exceptionalities. *Teaching Exceptional Children, Summer,* 22–24.

Gray, C. A. (1994). *Comic strip conversations.* Arlington, TX: Future Horizons.

Gray, C. A. (1995). Teaching children with autism to "read" social situations. In K. Quill (Ed.), *Teaching children with autism: Strategies to enhance communication and socialization* (pp. 220–242). Albany, NY: Delmar Publishers Inc.

Gray, C. A., & Garand, J. D. (1993). Social stories: Improving responses of students with autism with accurate social information. *Focus on Autistic Behavior, 8*(1), 1–10.

Gray, C. A. (1998). Social stories and comic strip conversations with students with *Asperger Syndrome and high functioning autism.* In E. Schopler, G. B. Mesibov, & L. Kunce (Eds.), Asperger's syndrome or High Functioning Autism (pp. 167–198). New York: Plenum Press.

Green, G. (2001). Behavior analytic instruction for learners with Autism: Advances in stimulus control technology. *Focus on Autism and Other Developmental Disabilities, 16*(2), 72–85.

Greenspan, S. I., Wieder, S., & Simons, R. (1998). *The child with special needs: Encouraging intellectual and emotional growth.* Reading, MA: Addison-Wesley.

Groden, G., & Baron, M. G. (1991). *Autism: Strategies for change.* New York and London: Gardner.

Groden, J., Cautela, J. R., & Groden, G. (1989). *Breaking the barriers I: Relaxation techniques for people with special needs* [Videotape]. Champaign, IL: Research Press.

Groden, J., Cautela, J. R., & Groden, G. (1991). *Breaking the barriers II: Imagery procedures for people with special needs.* Videotape. Champaign: IL: Research Press.

Groden, J., Cautela, J. R., LeVasseur, P., Groden, G.., & Bausman, M. (1991). *Video guide to breaking the barriers II* [Videotape]. Champaign, IL: Research Press.

Groden, J., Cautela, J. R., Prince, S., & Berryman, J. (1994). The impact of stress and anxiety on individuals with autism and developmental disabilities. In E. Schopler & G. B. Mesibov (Eds.), *Behavioral Issues in Autism* (pp. 177–194). New York: Plenum Press.

Groden, J., Diller, A., Bausman, M., Velicer, W., Norman, G., & Cautela, J. (2001). The development of a stress survey schedule for persons with autism and other developmental disabilities. *Journal of Autism and Developmental Disorders, 31*(2), 20–217.

Groden, J., & LeVasseur, P. (1995). Cognitive picture rehearsal: A visual system to teach self-control. In K. Quill (Ed.), *Teaching children with autism: Methods to enhance learning, communication, and socialization* (pp. 287–306). Albany, NY: Delmar Publishing Company.

Groden, G., Stevenson, S., & Groden, J. (1993). *Understanding challenging behavior: A step-by-step behavior analysis guide.* Providence, RI: Manisses Communications Group.

Grossen, B., & Carnine, D. (1992). Translating research on text structure into classroom practice. *Teaching Exceptional Children, Summer,* 48–53.

Gustafson, G., Pfetzing, D., & Zawolkow, E. (1980). *Signing exact English.* (4th ed.). Los Alamitos, CA: Modern Signs Press.

Gutstein, S. (2001) *Autism/Aspergers: Solving the relationship puzzle.* Arlington, TX: Future Horizons.

Handen, B. L. (1993). Pharmacotherapy in mental retardation and autism. *School Psychology Review, 22*(2), 162–183.

Hardy, P. M. (1985, July). *Anxiety and panic disorder in autism.* Paper presented at the Annual Meeting and Conference of the National Society of Autistic Children, Los Angeles, CA.

Haring, T., Neetz, J., Peck, C., & Semel, M. (1987). Effects of four modified incidental teaching procedures to create opportunities for communication. *Journal of the Association for Persons with Severe Handicaps, 12*(3), 218–226.

Haring, T. G., Kennedy, C. H., Adams, M. J., & Pitts-Conway, V. (1987). Teaching generalization of purchasing skills across community settings to autistic youth using videotape modeling. *Journal of Applied Behavior Analysis, 20,* 89–96.

Hart, C. (1989). *Without reason: A family copes with two generations of autism.* New York: Signet.

Harty, J. R. (1990) Pharmacotherapy in infantile autism. *Focus on Autistic Behavior. 5*(2), 1–10.

Haymes, L. K., & Martin, S. (2002, February) *Video modeling: A tool for skill building and improving performance.* A conference presentation for the Annual Western Regional Conference of the California Association for Behavior Analysis, San Francisco, CA.

Haywood, H. C., Brooks, P., & Burns, S. (1992). *Bright start: Cognitive curriculum for young children.* Watertown, MA: Charlesbridge.

Heflin, L. J., & Alberto, P. A. (2001). Establishing a Behavioral Context for Learning for Students with Autism. *Focus on Autism and other Developmental Disabilities, 16*(2), 93–101.

Hill, D., & Leary, M. (1993). *Movement disturbance: A clue to hidden competencies in persons diagnosed with autism and other developmental disabilities.* Madison, WI: DRI Press.

Hobson, R. P. (1992). Social perception in high-level autism. In E. Schopler & G. B. Mesibov, *High-functioning individuals with autism* (pp. 157–184). New York: Plenum Press.

Hodgdon, L. A. (1995). *Visual strategies for improving communication—Volume 1: Practical supports for school and home.* Troy, MI: QuirkRoberts.

Hodgdon, L. A. (1999). *Solving behavior problems in Autism: Improving communication with visual strategies.* Troy, MI: QuirkRoberts.

Horner, R. H. (1994). Facilitated communication: Keeping it practical. *Journal of the Association for Persons with Severe Handicaps, 19*(3), 185–186.

Horner, R. H., Dunlap, G., & Koegel, R. L. (1988). *Generalization and maintenance: Life-style changes in applied settings.* Baltimore: Paul H. Brookes.

Horner, R. H., & MacDonald, R. S. (1982). A comparison of single instance and general case instruction in teaching a generalized vocational skill. *Journal of the Association for the Severely Handicapped, 7*(3), 7–20.

Howard, B. J., Mitchell, M., Culley, L., Kline, M., & Hardin, M. (1991). *It's potty time.* Dallas, TX: Learning Through Entertainment.

Howlin, P., Baron-Cohen, S., & Hadwin, J. (1999). *Teaching children with Autism to mind read: A practical guide.* New York and London: Wiley and Sons.

Isaacson, S. (Ed.). (1988). Special focus: Teaching written expression. *Teaching Exceptional Children, Winter,* 32–39.

Note: This special focus section includes short descriptions of: The directed reading and writing procedure (DRAW), by J. P. Cox and E. Wood; The self-instructional strategy training procedure (SIST), by K. R. Harris and S. Graham; Computers and Writing Instruction (SCAN procedure), by C. A. MacArthur.

Janert, S. (2000). *Reaching the young autistic child: Reclaiming non-autistic potential through communicative strategies and games.* London: Free Association Books.

Janzen, J. E. (1999). *Autism: Facts and strategies for parents.* San Antonio, TX: Therapy Skill Builders.

Jordan, R., & Powell, S. (1997). Les enfants autistes: Les comprendre, les integrer a l'ecole. Paris: Masson. [Book review]. *Autism: The International Journal of Research and Practice, 2*(3), 318–320.

Kanner, L. (1943). Autistic disturbances of affective content. *Nervous Child, 2,* 217–250.

Kanner, L. (1973). *Childhood psychosis: initial studies and new insights.* New York: Winston/Wiley.

Kaplin, J. S., & Carter, J. (1995). *Beyond behavior modification: a cognitive behavioral approach to management in the school.* (3rd ed.). Austin, TX: PRO-ED.

Kasari, C., Sigman, M. D., Mundy, P., & Yirmiya, N. (1990). Affective sharing in the context of joint attention. *Journal of Autism and Developmental Disorders, 20,* 87–100.

Kern L., Koegel, R. L., & Dunlap, G. (1984). The influence of vigorous versus mild exercise on autistic stereotyped behavior. *Journal of Autism and Developmental Disabilities, 14*(1), 57–67.

King, L. J. (1991). Sensory integration: An effective approach to therapy and education. *Autism Research Review International, 5*(2), 3–6.

Kinney, J., & Fisher, D. (2001). *Co-teaching students with autism in the regular education classroom.* Verona: WI: The Attainment Co.

Klinger, L. G., & Dawson, G. (1992). Facilitating early social and communicative development in children with autism. In S. F. Warren & J. Reichle (Eds.), *Volume 1: Causes and effects in communication and language intervention* (pp. 157–186). Baltimore: Paul H. Brookes.

Koegel, R. L., & Frea, W. D. (1993). Treatment of social behavior in autism through the modification of pivotal social skills. *Journal of Applied Behavior Analysis, 26*(3), 369–377.

Koegel, R. L., Frea, W. D., & Surratt, A. V. (1994). Self-management of problematic social behavior. In E. Schopler & G. B. Mesibov (Eds.), *Behavioral issues in autism* (pp. 545–565). New York: Plenum Press.

Koegel, R. L., & Koegel, L. K. (Eds.). (1996). *Teaching children with autism: Strategies for initiating positive interactions and improving learner opportunities.* Baltimore: Paul H. Brookes.

Koegel, L. K., Koegel, R. L., Harrower, J. K., & Carter, C. M. (1999). Pivotal response intervention: Overview of approach. *Journal of the Association for Persons with Severe Handicaps, 24,* 174–185.

Koegel, R. L., O'Dell, M. C., & Koegel, L. K. (1987). A natural language paradigm for teaching non-verbal autistic children. *Journal of Autism and Developmental Disorders, 17,* 187–199.

Koppenhaver, D. A., Coleman, P. P., Kalman, S. L., & Yoder, D. E. (1991). The implications of emergent literacy research for children with developmental disabilities. *American Journal of Speech-Language Pathology, 1*(1), 38–44.

Krug, A., Arick, J. R., & Almond, P. (1993). *Autism behavior checklist.* (ABC) Austin, TX: PRO-ED.

Krug, A., Arick, J. R., & Almond, P. (1993) *The autism screening instrument for educational planning–2 (ASIEP–2).* Austin, TX: PRO-ED.

LaVigna, G. W., & Donnellan, A. M. (1986). *Alternatives to punishment: Solving behavior problems with non-aversive strategies.* New York: Irvington Publishers.

Layton, T. L., & Watson, L. R. (1995). Communication enhancement. In K. Quill (Ed.), *Teaching children with autism: Strategies to enhance communication* (pp. 73–104). Albany, NY: Delmar.

Ledgin, N. (2002). *Asperger's and self-esteem: Insight and hope through famous role models.* Arlington, TX: Future Horizons.

Leekam, S., Libby, S., Wing, L., Gould, J., & Gillberg, C. (2000). Comparison of ICD–10 and Gillberg's criteria for Asperger syndrome. *Autism: The International Journal of Research and Practice, 4*(1), 11–28.

Leverett, R. G., & Diefendorf, A. O. (1992). Students with language deficiencies: Suggestions for frustrated teachers. *Teaching Exceptional Children, Summer,* 30–35.

Levinson, L., & Reid, G. (1993). The effects of exercise intensity on the stereotypic behaviors of individuals with autism. *Adapted Physical Activity Quarterly, 10,* 255–268.

Levy, S. 1988. *Identifying high functioning children with autism.* Bloomington, IN: Indiana Resource Center for Autism, Institute for the Study of Developmental Disabilities, Indiana University.

Lindner, T. W. (1993). *Transdisciplinary play-based assessment: A functional approach to working with young children* (Revised). Baltimore: Paul H. Brookes.

Little, J. (1989, March). *Being an effective coach for communication.* Paper presented at the Annual Autism Conference, Eugene, Oregon.

Lord, C. (1991, June). *Followup of two-year-olds referred for possible autism.* Paper presented to the biannual meeting of the Society for Research and Child Development, Seattle.

Lord, C., Rutter, M., Dilavore, P. C., & Risi, S. (1999). *Autism diagnostic observation schedule (ADOS–G).* Los Angeles: Western Psychological Services.

Lovaas, O. I. (1987). Behavioral treatment and normal educational and intellectual functioning in young autistic children. *Journal of Consulting and Clinical Psychology, 55,* 3–9.

Lovett, H. (1985). *Cognitive counseling and persons with special needs.* New York: Praeger.

Lucyshyn, J., Olson, D., & Horner, R. (1995). Building an ecology of support: A case study of one young woman with severe problem behaviors living in the community. *Journal of the Association for Persons with Severe Handicaps, 20*(1), 16–30.

Lussier, B. J., Crimmins, D. B., & Alberti, D. (1994). Effect of three adult interaction styles on infant engagement. *Journal of Early Intervention, 18*(1), 12–24.

MacDonald, J. D. (1989). *Becoming partners with children: From play to conversation.* San Antonio, TX: Special Press.

Marks, C. (2001). Toilet training . . . Is your child ready? *Autism•Asperger's Digest, July/August,* 18–22.

Marsella, A., & Marsella, B. (1991). The medical side of behavior. *The Advocate: Newsletter of the Autism Society of America, Spring,* 15.

Martin, R. (2000). *Getting your child with autism what they are entitled to under federal law.* Morgantown, WV: Mathews Media.

Martin, R. (2001). *Summer break: 5 years of lost time? Extended school year services for children with autism.* Morgantown, WV: Mathews Media.

Mayes, S. D. & Calhoun, S.L (1999). Symptoms of autism in young children and correspondence with the DSM. *Infants and Young Children, 12,* 90–97.

Mayes, S. D., & Calhoun, S. L. (2001). Non-significance of early speech delay in children with autism and normal intelligence and implications for DSM–IV Asperger's disorder. *Autism: International Journal of Research and Practice, 5*(1), 81–94.

Mayo, P., & Waldo, P. (1986). Scripting: *Social communication for adolescents. Scripts for role playing.* Eau Claire, WI: Thinking Publications.

McGimsey, J. F., & Favell, J. E. (1988). The effects of increased physical exercise on disruptive behavior in retarded persons. *Journal of Autism and Developmental Disabilities, 18*(2), 167–179.

Melone, M. B., & Lettick, A. (1983). Sex education at Benhaven. In E. Schopler & G. Mesibov (Eds.), *Autism in adolescents and adults* (pp. 169–186). New York: Plenum Press.

Merzer, S., & Chastain, L. (1982). Social skills: Assessment and interventions. In C. Smith, J. Grimes, & J. Freilinger (Eds.), *Iowa monograph: Autism—programmatic considerations* (pp. 106–131). Des Moines: State of Iowa Department of Public Instruction.

Mesibov, G. B. (1986). A cognitive program for teaching social behaviors to verbal autistic adolescents and adults. In E. Schopler & G. B. Mesibov (Eds.), *Social behavior in autism* (pp. 265–283). New York: Plenum Press.

Mesibov, G. B. (1992). Treatment issues with high-functioning adolescents and adults with autism. In E. Schopler & G. B. Mesibov (Eds.), *High-functioning individuals with autism* (pp. 143–156). New York: Plenum Press.

Mesibov, G. B., Schopler, E., & Hearsey, K. A. (1994). Structured teaching. In E. Schopler & G. B. Mesibov (Eds.), *Behavioral issues in autism* (pp. 195–210). New York: Plenum Press.

Mesibov, G., Schopler, E., Schaffer, B., & Landrus, R. (1988). *Adolescent and adult psychoeducational profile* (AAPEP). Austin, TX: PRO-ED.

Meyer, L. M., & Evans, I. M. (1989). *Non-aversive intervention for behavior problems: A manual for community and residential settings.* Baltimore: Paul H. Brookes.

Minshew, N. J. (1992). Neurological localization in autism. In E. Schopler & G. B. Mesibov (Eds.), *High-functioning individuals with autism* (pp. 65–89). New York: Plenum Press.

Minshew, N. J., (2001) Editorial Preface. *Journal of Autism and Developmental Disorders, 31*(1), 1–3.

Moore, D. (1998). Computers and people with autism/Asperger syndrome. *Communication: The magazine of The National Autistic Society, Summer,* 20–21.

Moreno, S. (1991). *High-functioning individuals with autism: Advice and information for parents and others who care.* Crown Point, IN: MAAP Services.

Moreno, S. (1992). A parent's view of more able people with autism. In E. Schopler & G. B. Mesibov (Eds.), *High-functioning individuals with autism* (pp. 91–104). New York: Plenum Press.

Mukhopadhyay, T. R. (2000) Beyond the silence: *My life, the world and autism (with foreword by Lorna Wing).* London; San Diego, CA: The National Autistic Society.

Musselwhite, C. R. (1986). *Adaptive play for special needs children.* San Diego: College-Hill Press.

Myhr, G. (1998). Autism and other pervasive development disorders: Exploring the dimensional view. *Canadian Journal of Psychiatry, 43,* 589–595.

Myles, B. S., Brock, S., & Simpson, R. (2001). *Asperger Syndrome Diagnostic Scale (ASDS).* Austin, TX: PRO-ED.

Myles, B. S., Cook, K. T., Miller, N. E., Rinner, L., & Robbins, L. A. (2000). *Asperger syndrome and sensory issues: Practical solutions for making sense of the world.* Shawnee Mission, KS: Autism Asperger.

Myles, B. S., & Southwick, J. (1999). *Asperger syndrome and difficult moments: Practical solutions for tantrums, rage, and meltdowns.* Shawnee Mission, KS: Autism Asperger.

Newport, J. (2001). *Your life isn't a label.* Arlington, TX: Future Horizons.

Newport, J., & Newport, M. (2002). *Autism-Asperger's & sexuality: Puberty and beyond.* Arlington, TX: Future Horizons.

O'Conner, N., & Hermelin, B. (1994). Two autistic savant readers. *Journal of Autism and Developmental Disabilities, 24*(4), 501–515.

O'Neill, R. E., Horner, R. H., Albin, R. W., Storey, K., & Sprague, J. R. (1990). *Functional analysis of problem behavior: A practical assessment guide.* Sycamore, IL: Sycamore Press.

Ogletree, B. T., & Oren, T. (2001). Application of ABA principles to general communication instruction. *Focus on Autism and Other Developmental Disorders, 16*(2), 102–109.

Olshansky, B. (1997). *Picture writing: Fostering literacy through art.* Durham, NH: Laboratory for Interactive Learning, University of New Hampshire.

Olshansky, B. (1998). *Image-making within the writing process: Crafting collage stories.* Durham, NH: Laboratory for Interactive Learning, University of New Hampshire.

Ousley, O. Y., & Mesibov, G. B. (1991). Sexual attitudes and knowledge of high-functioning adolescents and adults with autism. *Journal of Autism and Developmental Disabilities, 21*(4), 471–481.

Pallaske, M. W., Reed, P., & Stokes, S. (2000). *Assistive technology tools & strategies assessment manual for children with autism spectrum disorders.* Oshkosh, WI: Wisconsin Assistive Technology Initiative. Polk Library, 800 Algoma Blvd., Oshkosh, WI. (800-991-5576 or www.wati.org)

Pangborn, J. B., & Baker, S. M. (2001). *Biomedical assessment options for children with autism and related problems: A consensus report of the DEFEAT AUTISM NOW! (DAN).* San Diego, CA: Autism Research Institute.

Pehrsson, R. S., & Denner, P. R. (1989). *Semantic organizers: A study strategy for special needs learners.* Rockville, MD: Aspen.

Pehrsson, R. S., & Robinson, H. A. (1985). *The semantic organizer approach to writing and reading instruction.* Rockville, MD: Aspen.

Peloquin, L. J. (2001). Connecting with your child through DIR: The developmental, individual difference, relationship-based approach. *Autism•Asperger's Digest, September-October,* 8–11.

Peschel, E. (1994). Autism and PDD (autism spectrum disorders) in the context of other neurobiological disorders: Recent findings from the neuroscience revolution. *In Autism Society of America Conference Proceedings 7–9.* Arlington, TX: Future Education.

Premack, D., & Collier, G. (1962). Analysis of nonreinforcement variables affecting response probability. *Psychological Monographs: General and Applied, 76,* 5. Washington, DC: American Psychological Association.

Prizant, B. M. (1983). Language acquisition and communicative behavior in autism: Toward an understanding of the "whole" of it. *Journal of Speech and Hearing Disorders, 48,* 296–307.

Prizant, B. M. (1988). Communication problems in the autistic client. In N. J. Lass, L. V. McReynolds, J. L. Northern, & D. E. Yoder (Eds.), *Handbook of speech-language pathology and audiology*, (pp. 1014–1039). Philadelphia: B. C. Becker.

Prizant, B. M., & Rydell, P. J. (1993). Assessment and intervention considerations for unconventional verbal behavior. In J. Reichle & D. Wacker (Eds.), *Communicative approaches to the management of challenging behavior*. Baltimore, MD: Paul Brookes.

Prizant, B. M., Wetherby, A. M., & Rydell, P. J. (2000). Communication intervention issues for young children with autism spectrum disorders. In A. M. Wetherby & B. M. Prizant, (Eds.), *Autism spectrum disorders: A transactional approach*. (pp. 193–224). Baltimore, MD: Paul Brooks.

Pruitting, C., & Kirchner, D. (1987). A clinical appraisal of the pragmatic aspects of language. *Journal of Speech and Hearing Disorders, 52*(5), 105–119.

Pulice, P. (1987). *Autism and attachment: An attachment-based intervention guide for children with autism and other pervasive developmental disorders*. Minneapolis: Minneapolis Children's Medical Center.

Quill, K. A., (1995) Enhancing children's social-communicative interactions. In K. A. Quill (Ed.), *Teaching children with autism: Strategies to enhance communication and socialization* (pp. 163–192). Arlington, NY: Delmar.

Quill, K. A. (Ed.). (1995). *Teaching children with autism: Strategies to enhance communication and socialization*. Arlington, NY: Delmar.

Quill, K. A. (2000). *Do-watch-listen-say: Social and communication intervention for children with autism*. Baltimore, MD: Paul Brookes.

Raaz, N. (1982). Working with parents of students with autism. In C. Smith, J. Grimes, & J. Freilinger (Eds.), *Autism—Programmatic considerations: A monograph of the Iowa State Department of Public Instruction* (pp. 238–258). Des Moines: Iowa State Department of Public Instruction.

Rimland, B. (1991). *ARI recommendations on treatments for autistic and other mentally and neurologically handicapped children*. ARI Publication 49. San Diego: Autism Research Institute.

Rimland, B., (1994). Recovery from autism is possible. *Autism Research Review International, 8*, 2–3.

Rimland, B. (1999). The ABA controversy. *Autism Research Review International, 13*(3), 3.

Rimland, B., & Edelson, S. (1994). The effects of auditory integration training on autism. *American Journal of Speech-Language Pathologists, 5*(5), 16–24.

Rosenhall, U., Nordin, V., Sandstrom, M., Ahlsen, G., & Gillberg, C. (1999). Autism and hearing loss. *Journal of Autism and Developmental Disorders, 29*(5), 349–357.

Rutter, M. (2000). Genetic studies of autism: From the 1970s to the millennium. *Journal of Abnormal Child Psychology, 28*, 3–14.

Rydell, P. J., & Prizant, B. M. (1995). Assessment and intervention strategies for children who use echolalia. In K. Quill (Ed.), *Teaching Children with Autism* (pp. 105–132). Albany, NY: Delmar.

Sabin, L.A., & Donnellan, A. M. (1993). An ethnographic study of the process of Facilitated Communication. *Journal of the Association for Persons with Severe Handicaps. 18*(3) 200–211.

Schaeffer, B., Raphael, A., & Kollinzas, G. (1994). *Signed Speech® language program for nonverbal students*. Seattle: Educational Achievement Systems.

Schawlow, A. T., & Schawlow, A. L. (1985). Our autistic son. In M. Brady & P. Gunter (Eds.), *Integrating severely and moderately handicapped learners: Strategies that work*. Springfield, IL: Charles Thomas.

Schmeltzer, K. R., Jordan, K., & Skowron-Gooch, A. (in press, 2002). *"I'm Experiencing Technical Difficulties": A comprehensive guide to teaching social-cognitive skills to students with Asperger's syndrome*. Salem, OR: Willamette ESD.

Schopler, E., & Mesibov, G. B. (1992). *High-functioning individuals with autism*. New York: Plenum Press.

Schopler, E., & Mesibov, G. B. (1994). *Behavioral issues in autism*. New York: Plenum Press.

Schopler, E., Mesibov, G., & Hearsey, K. (Eds.). (1995). Structured teaching in the TEACCH system. In *Learning and cognition in autism*. New York: Plenum Press.

Schopler, E., Mesibov, G. B., & Kunce, L. J. (Eds.). (1998). *Asperger syndrome or high-functioning autism?* New York: Plenum Press.

Schopler, G., Reichler, R. J., Bashford, A., Lansing, M., & Marcus, L. M. (1990). *Psychoeducational profile—Revised (PEP–R)*. Austin, TX: PRO-ED.

Schopler, E., Reichler, R. J., & Renner, B. R. (1988). *The childhood autism rating scale (CARS)*. Los Angeles, CA: Western Psychological Services.

Schuler A. L., & Wolfberg, P. J. (2000). Promoting peer play and socialization: The art of scaffolding. In A. Wetherby & B. M. Prizant (Eds.), *Transactional foundations of language intervention* (pp. 251–277). Baltimore, MD: Brooks.

Schwartz, L. (1990). *What would you do?* Santa Barbara, CA: The Learning Works.

Shea, V., & Mesibov, G. B. (1985). Brief report: The relationship of learning disabilities and higher-level autism. *Journal of Autism and Developmental Disorders, 15*(4), 425–435.

Shepherd, T. R. (1983, July). *Using experience language (LEA variation) to teach an autistic-like child with visual disorder to read (and write and talk).* Paper presented at the Conference of the Great Lakes Regional International Reading Association. Available through: U.S. Department of Education, National Institute of Education, Educational Resources Information Center (ERIC).

Shevin, M., & Klein, N. K. (1984). The importance of choice-making skills for students with severe disabilities. *Journal of the Association for Persons with Severe Handicaps, 9*(3), 159–166.

Shure, M. B. (1992). *I can problem solve: An interpersonal cognitive problem-solving program for preschool, kindergarten/primary, and intermediate elementary grades.* Champaign, IL: Research Press.

Silver, M. (2000). *The emotion trainer.* A multimedia computer program in 5 sections. Source: www.emotiontrainer.co.uk or send a SASE to : Dr. Miriam Silver, St. James university Hospital, Beckett St., Leeds LS9 7TF, UK (email: miriam@webmancer.feeserv.co.uk)

Silver, M., & Oakes, P. (2001). Evaluation of a new computer intervention to teach people with autism or Asperger syndrome to recognize and predict emotions in others. *Autism:The International Journal of Research and Practice, 5*(3), 299–316.

Simpson, R. L. (2001). ABA and students with autism spectrum disorders: Issues and considerations for effective practice. *Focus on Autism and Other Developmental Disorders, 16*(2), 68–71.

Sinclair, J. (1992). Bridging the gaps: An inside-out view of autism (Or, Do you know what I don't know?) In E. Schopler & G. B. Mesibov (Eds.), *High-functioning individuals with autism* (pp. 294–301). New York: Plenum Press.

Skinner, B. F. (1953). *The behavior of organisms: An experimental analysis.* New York: Macmillan.

Smith, T. (2001) Discrete trial training in the treatment of autism. *Focus on Autism and Other Developmental Disabilities, 16*(2), 86–92.

Stehli, A. (1991). *The sound of a miracle.* New York: Doubleday.

Swezey, S. (1985, November/December). Never too late. *The Advocate: The Newsletter of the Autism Society of America,* 8.

Tiegerman, E., & Primavera, L. H. (1984). Imitating the autistic child: Facilitating communicative gaze behavior. *Journal of Autism and Developmental Disorders, 14*(1), 27–38.

Tjus, T., Heimann, M., & Nelson, K. E. (1998). Gains in literacy through the use of a specially developed multimedia computer strategy. *Autism: The International Journal of Research and Practice, 2*(2), 139–156.

Tjus, T., Heimann, M., & Nelson, K. E. (2001). Interaction patterns between children and their teachers when using a specific multimedia and communication strategy: Observations from children with autism and mixed intellectual disabilities. *Autism: The International Journal of Research and Practice, 5*(2), 175–188.

Tsai, L. (2000). Children with autism spectrum disorders: Medicine today and in the new millennium. *Focus on Autism and Other Developmental Disabilities, 15*(3), 138–145.

Turnbull, A. P., & Turnbull, H. R. (1990). *Families, professionals, and exceptionality: A special partnership.* Second edition. Columbus: Merrill.

Twachman-Cullen, D. (1995). Methods to enhance communication in verbal children. In K. Quill (Ed.), *Teaching children with autism: Strategies to enhance communication and socialization* (pp. 133–162). Albany, NY: Delmar.

Twatchman-Cullen, D. (1997). *A passion to believe: Autism and Facilitated Communication phenomenon.* Boulder, CO: West View Press.

Twachman-Cullen, D. (2001). Combining speech and occupational therapy. *Autism•Asperger's Digest, 13,* 13.

Van Bourgondien, M. E., & Mesibov, G. B. (1987). Humor in high-functioning autistic adults. *Journal of Autism and Developmental Disorders, 17*(3), 417–424.

Vernon, A. (1989). *Thinking, feeling, behaving: An emotional education curriculum for adolescents, grades 1–6 and grades 7–12.* Champaign, IL: Research Press.

Vicker, B. (1988). *The high-functioning person with autism also has a communication problem.* Bloomington, IN: Indiana Resource Center for Autism, Institute for the Study of Developmental Disabilities, Indiana University.

Walker-Hirsch, L., & Champagne, M. P. (1988). *Circles 2: Stop abuse.* Santa Barbara, CA: James Stanfield.

Walker-Hirsch, L., & Champagne, M. P. (1993). *Circles I. Intimacy & relationships.* Santa Barbara, CA: James Stanfield.

Warren, S. F., & Reichle, J. (Eds.). (1991). *Causes and effects in communication and language.* Baltimore: Paul H. Brookes.

Watson, L. R., Lord, C., Schaffer, B., & Schopler, E. (1989). *Teaching spontaneous communication to autistic and developmentally handicapped children*. New York: Irvington.

Webster's New Collegiate Dictionary. (1977). Springfield, MA: G. & C. Merriam.

Wetherby, A. M., & Prizant, B. M. (1993). Profiling communication and symbolic abilities in young children. *Journal of Childhood Communication Disorders, 15*(1), 23–32.

Wetherby, A. M., & Prizant, B.M (Eds.) (2000) *Language issues in Autism and pervasive developmental disorders: A transactional developmental perspective*. Baltimore, MD: Paul H. Brookes.

Wetherby, A. M., & Prizant, B. M. (2001). *Communication and symbolic behavior scales (CSBS) developmental profile: Infant/toddler checklist*. Baltimore: Paul Brooks.

Wheeler, M. (1998). *Toilet training for individuals with autism & related disorders: A comprehensive guide for parents and teachers*. Arlington, TX: Future Horizons.

Williams, D., (1992). *Nobody nowhere: The extraordinary autobiography of an autistic*. New York: Avon Books.

Williams, D. (1994). *Somebody somewhere: Breaking free from the world of Autism*. New York: Times Books.

Williams, K. (1995). Understanding the student with Asperger syndrome: Guidelines for teachers. *Focus on Autistic Behavior, 10*(2), 9–16.

Williams, M. S., & Shellenberger, S. (1996). *How does your engine run: A leader's guide to the Alert Program for self-regulation*. Albuquerque, NM: TherapyWorks, Inc.

Wing, L. (1980). Foreword. In C. Webster, M. Konstantareas, J. Oxman, & J. Mack (Eds.), *Autism: New directions in research and education*. Elmsford, NY: Pergamon Press.

Wing, L. (1991). The relationship between Asperger's syndrome and Kanner's autism. In U. Frith (Ed.), *Autism and Asperger syndrome* (pp. 93–121). Cambridge, UK: Cambridge University Press.

Wing, L. (1992). Manifestations of social problems in high-functioning autistic people. In S. Schopler & G. B. Mesibov (Eds.), *High-functioning individuals with autism* (pp. 129–142). New York: Plenum Press.

Wing, L. (1997). The history of ideas on autism: Legends, myths, and reality. *Autism: The International Journal of Research and Practice, 1*(1), 13–23.

Wing, L. (1998). The history of Asperger Syndrome, in E. Schopler, G. B. Mesibov & L. J. Kunce (Eds.), *Asperger syndrome or high-functioning autism?* (pp. 11–28). New York: Plenum.

Wing, L., & Attwood, A. (1987). Syndromes of autism and atypical development. In D. Cohen, A. Donnellan, & R. Paul (Eds.), *The handbook of autism and pervasive developmental disorders* (pp. 3–19). Silver Spring, MD: V. H. Winston & Sons.

Wing, L. & Gould, J. (1979). Severe impairments of social interaction and associated abnormalities in child: epidemiology and classification. *Journal of Autism and Childhood Schizophrenia, 9*, 11–29.

Winner, M. G. (2000). *Inside out: What makes a person with social cognitive deficits tick? The I laugh approach*. San Jose, CA: Self-published (4871 Trent Drive, San Jose, CA 95124).

Wolery, M., Bailey, D. B., & Sugai, G. M. (1988). *Effective teaching strategies: Principles and procedures with exceptional students*. Boston: Allyn & Bacon.

Wolfberg, P. J. (1999). *Play and imagination in children with autism*. New York: Columbia University Teacher's College Press.

Wolfberg, P. J. (2000). Making make-believe: Enhancing communication & social skills through integrated play groups. *Autism•Asperger's Digest, May-June*, 12–17.

Wolfberg, P. J., & Schuler, A. L. (1993). Integrated play groups: A model for promoting the social and cognitive dimensions of play. *Journal of Autism and Developmental Disorders, 23*(3), 1–23.

Wolfberg, P. J., & Schuler, A. L. (1999). Fostering peer interaction, imaginative play and spontaneous language in children with autism. *Child Language Teaching and Therapy Journal, 15*(1), 41–52.

Wolf-Schein, E. G., (March 1998) Considerations in assessment of children with severe disabilities, including deaf-blindness and autism. In *International Journal of Disability, Development and Education. 45* (1) 35–55.

Wooten, M., & Mesibov, G. B. (1986). Social skills training for elementary school autistic children with normal peers. In E. Schopler & G. B. Mesibov (Eds.), *Social behavior in autism* (pp. 305–319). New York: Plenum Press.

Wright, P. W. D., & Wright, P. D. (2001). Advocating for your child:Getting started. *Autism•Asperger's Digest, September-October*, 28–29.

Yirmiya, N., Sigman, M. D., Kasari, C., & Mundy, P. (1992). Empathy and cognition in high-functioning children with autism. *Child Development, 63*, 150–160.

Zercher, C., Hunt, P., Schuler, A., & Webster, J. (2001). Increasing joint attention, play and language through peer supported play. *Autism—The International Journal of Research and Practice, 5*(4), 374–398.

Index